EXPERIENCE MUSIC

Third Edition

EXPERIENCE MUSIC

Katherine Charlton
Mt. San Antonio College

Connect
Learn
Succeed™

Boston   Burr Ridge, IL   Dubuque, IA   Madison, WI   New York   San Francisco   St. Louis
Bangkok   Bogota   Caracas   Kuala Lumpur   Lisbon   London   Madrid   Mexico City
Milan   Montreal   New Delhi   Santiago   Seoul   Singapore   Sydney   Taipei   Toronto

This book is printed on acid-free paper.

Printed in the United States of America

3 4 5 6 7 8 9 0 DOW/DOW 10 9 8 7 6 5 4 3

ISBN: 978-0-07-802513-6
MHID: 0-07-802513-3

Publisher: *Christopher Freitag*
Marketing Manager: *Stacy Ruel*
Developmental Editor: *Sarah Remington*
Production Editor: *Holly Paulsen*
Manuscript Editor: *Janet Tilden*
Design Manager: *Andrei Pasternak*
Text Designer: *Amanda Kavanagh*
Cover Designer: *Lisa Buckley*
Photo Research Coordinator: *Nora Agbayani*
Photo Researcher: *Judy Mason*
Buyer: *Louis Swaim*
Composition: *10/12 Minion Regular by Thompson Type*
Printing: *45# New Era Thin, RR Donnelley*

Vice President, Editorial: *Michael Ryan*
Editorial Director: *William Glass*
Director of Development: *Lisa Pinto*

Cover: © zoechan/iStockPhoto

www.mhhe.com

To my husband, Jeff Calkins, who likes music with tunes he can hum.

Brief Contents

Note: The chapter on Rock Music is available for free download at www.mhhe/charltonexperience3e.

Contents

Note: The chapter on Rock Music is available for free download
at www.mhhe.com/charltonexperience3e.

List of Boxes

musicurious

hearing the difference

Experience music **actively.**
Connect to music **personally.**

Imagine a class where students...

 are actively and personally engaged with music.

 listen to, rather than just hear, music.

 connect to the concepts and elements of music and learn how to identify them in a variety of different pieces.

Now imagine that same class—those same students—so confident that they are able to participate effectively in class, work efficiently through the exercises outside of class, and perform better in the course.

With *Experience Music*'s new digital solution, *Connect Music*, students can connect to a better experience. *Connect Music* is the most successful digital platform in music: a truly integrated teaching and learning program that provides both one-click access to the program's music selections and interactive exercises that focus on the listening process.

Katherine Charlton has drawn on her extensive experience in the classroom to create a listening experience that motivates and engages students. *Connect Music* ensures that students can come to class confident and prepared, as they develop the active listening skills they need for success in the course and a lifetime of more meaningful musical experiences.

Experience music **actively.**

Learning to appreciate music is a skill. *Experience Music* helps students develop that skill with a variety of features and resources.

Connect Music provides a path to student success, making students active participants in their own listening experience.

The program's music selections stream in two ways: in a simple player or in online Listening Outlines. In the latter, students not only listen to the piece, but have instant access to background about the piece, lyrics, and a visual representation of the structure of the piece.

Instructors can assess the development of students' listening skills—online and at any time—so that they don't have to wait for a midterm for an update on their progress.

A wide array of online listening experiences, including comparison exercises, First Hearing and Finale activities, and audio click/drags, are available. Learning objectives link to chapter sections and in turn to print and online activities, so that students can immediately assess their mastery of the material.

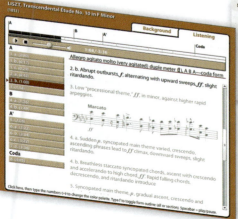

♪ A **First Hearing** opens each chapter and guides students through their first encounter with a piece with specific questions intended to encourage closer listening.

♪ The **Featured Listening** is a step-by-step listening guide that returns students to the work first heard in the First Hearing and trains them to discern the meaningful elements, theme, and instrumentation of the selection.

♪ Each chapter ends with a **Finale**. The students use knowledge acquired in the chapter to respond to more advanced questions about the piece encountered in the First Hearing and Featured Listening. Having studied the piece in the chapter, the students will see how much more they are now able to hear in the same piece of music.

♪ **Listening Guides** in each chapter and found within *Connect Music* walk students through key works discussed in the book step-by-step. This guided listening experience trains the listener's ear by pointing out meaningful elements, themes, and instrumentation of key works.

Historical coverage in just the right places gives students the context they need to understand how people lived in each era and how music has always been part of peoples' lives.

♪ **Preludes** open each part and provide historical, social, and cultural background on various periods of music.

Composer Boxes provide biographical information on key composers along with a list of their important works.

Connect to music **personally.**

Katherine Charlton strives to spark student engagement with music that will serve them throughout their lives. She makes the development of active listening skills a meaningful endeavor that students can extend to their daily lives.

MusiCurious

THE KING OF INSTRUMENTS

What instrument is called the King of Instruments and why?
The organ was given that title by Mozart. The earliest organs were invented during the third century BCE. By the baroque period, the organ had developed to the point that it could fill a church or concert hall with the most majestic of sounds. Yet it could also play gentle and soft music. Depending on the pipes connected to it, the organ's range of high to low notes could be greater than that of an orchestra, making it the most versatile of all single instruments—in other words, "the king."

What are the pipes for?
The sound comes through the pipes, and the player uses the keyboard, or set of keyboards called the *console*, to select the pipes that will sound. In addition to the console, the organist uses a full display of buttons and knobs, called stops, to assign the pipes for each keyboard to play. Large organs have many sets of pipes. The biggest can be as long as thirty-two (or more) feet for very low notes, and the smallest are pencil-sized ones that sound very high. The pipes can be made of many different materials such as wood or metal and can be sounded by air blowing directly through them or through reeds connected to the pipes. The use of stops to choose the pipes allows the player more control of the sound than is available to a player of any other musical instrument.

So, can pipe organs ever be moved?
Hardly ever. Pipe organs have to be built specifically for the church or concert hall in which they are to be used. The sets of pipes on some organs take up quite a bit of space and can be spread out around the church or hall, or they can be in a set together facing the congregation or audience. During the medieval and Renaissance periods there were small organs with a single set of pipes that could be moved around, but those were not the instruments referred to as the "king."

♪ NEW! **MusiCurious** provides answers to a variety of student questions about musical experiences, such as what it is like to be a composer, when to clap at an opera performance, how one performs an aleatoric work.

♪ NEW! **Further Listening** suggestions at the ends of chapters enhance the listening experiences of interested students.

Further Listening

Frédéric Chopin, Ballade no. 1 in G Minor. This beautiful solo piano work is based on three contrasting themes, each of which returns one or two times after being first presented. The first theme is waltzlike, the second tender and lyrical, and the third faster with the insertion of triplets to free the steadiness of the beat. The overall effect is free-flowing and a perfect example of the romantic spirit.

Franz Liszt, *Les jeux d'eaux à la Villa d'Este* (The fountains at Villa d'Este). Liszt loved to visit the beautiful Villa d'Este in Tivoli, near Rome, Italy. The fountains in the villa's Re- naissance garden have over a hundred jets and water spraying into pools and running in troughs. The sound of the fountains inspired this work.

Robert Schumann, *Carnaval*. This set of twenty character pieces for solo piano represents Schumann and his friends at a carnaval celebration (a feast before Lent). "Eusebius" is Schumann in a dreamy introspective state and "Florestan" shows him to be playful and impetuous. "Chiarina" is his future wife Clara, and "Chopin" is the composer/pianist Frédéric Chopin.

Hearing the Difference

MOZART'S SYMPHONY NO. 40, FIRST MOVEMENT, AND ZWILICH'S SYMPHONY NO. 1, FIRST MOVEMENT

Both of these works are first movements from symphonies. (see Listening Guides on page 121 and page 319). Mozart's symphony is from the classical period and is based on the sonata form, which has often been used as the basis of first movements. Zwilich's symphony is from the late twentieth century and is structured much differently from traditional symphony form. Answer the following questions as you listen from one work to the other:

- Which work keeps a constant tempo throughout, and which contains sections with different tempos?
- Which work has more of a sense of symmetrical balance with themes presented at the beginning and

repeated again at the end, and which work is held together by a gradually developing motive without a repeat of the beginning at the end?

- Can you relate the general thinking of the era to which each work belongs with the type of structure it has? You might want to look back at the Preludes to remind yourself about the characteristics of these eras.
- How do the instruments in the orchestra compare? What instruments do you hear in Zwilich's symphony that are not present in Mozart's?
- Which work maintains a duple meter, and which one is duple with some interpolations of triple meter?

♪ At the end of each group of chapters that covers a period, a review table calls out key characteristics of that period of music and helps students reexamine the content of those chapters.

♪ **Hearing the Difference** emerged directly from the author's teaching experience and gives students more practice with identifying particular works. Students concentrate on particular characteristics of two similar recordings. The format of the features allows students to practice this skill on their own or as part of a classroom activity. The level of listening skill builds throughout the book, and students hone their ability to discern different styles.

CHARACTERISTICS OF RENAISSANCE MUSIC

Texture	Mostly polyphonic
Tonality	Church modes
Rhythm	Measured
Singing style	Four-part singing common, some virtuoso singing; late madrigal and chanson used word painting
Large vocal works	Polyphonic Mass
Small vocal works	Motet, madrigal, chanson, lied
Musical instruments	Whole and mixed consorts, solo instrumental works
Instrumental music	Ricercari, fantasias, dances

The complete content of Katherine Charlton's *Experience Music* is available to instructors and students in traditional print format as well as online with integrated and time-saving tools.

Three audio CDs are packaged with each copy of the text. The CDs contain all of the works discussed in the Featured Listening and selected works discussed in the Listening Guides. Another set of three CDs is available for optional purchase at an instructor's discretion.

Blackboard and McGraw-Hill Higher Education have teamed up! Now, all McGraw-Hill content (text, tools, and homework) can be accessed directly from within your Blackboard course—all with a single sign-on. McGraw-Hill's content is seamlessly woven within your Blackboard course. Connect assignments within Blackboard automatically (and instantly) feed grades directly to your Blackboard grade center. No more keeping track of two grade books! Even if your institution is not currently using Blackboard, McGraw-Hill has a solution for you. Ask your sales representative for details.

Tegrity Campus is a service that makes class time available all the time by capturing audio and computer screen shots from your lectures in a searchable format for students to review when they study and complete assignments. With classroom resources available all the time, students can study more efficiently and learn more successfully.

CourseSmart, the largest provider of eTextbooks, offers students the option of receiving *Experience Music* as an eBook. At CourseSmart your students can take advantage of significant savings off the cost of a print textbook, reduce their impact on the environment, and gain access to powerful web tools for learning. CourseSmart eTextbooks can be viewed online or downloaded to a computer. Visit www.CourseSmart.com to learn more.

McGraw-Hill Create allows you to create a customized print book or eBook tailored to your course and syllabus. You can search through thousands of McGraw-Hill texts, rearrange chapters, combine material from other content sources, and include your own content or teaching notes. Create even allows you to personalize your book's appearance by selecting the cover and adding your name, school, and course information. To register and to get more information, go to http://create.mcgraw-hill.com.

Chapter-by-chapter changes

Chapters 4–39 Further Listening

The Fundamentals of Music
Chapter 3   All new photos of instruments.

The Culture of Medieval Europe
Chapter 4   MusiCurious: Medieval Nuns' Daily Lives

The Renaissance: The Rebirth of Humanism
Chapter 5   MusiCurious: Home Entertainment During the Renaissance

The Triumph of Baroque Style
Chapter 6   MusiCurious: How Opera Makes Singers into International Stars; new Listening Guide and recording: Claudio Monteverdi, "Tu se' morta" ("You Are Dead") from Act Two of *Orfeo*

Chapter 8   MusiCurious: Oratorio or Opera? Know the Difference; new Listening Guides and recordings: George Frideric Handel, *Messiah*

Chapter 9   MusiCurious: The King of Instruments; new Listening Guide and recording: Elisabeth-Claude Jacquet de la Guerre, "Aria" ("Air"), sixth movement, from Sonata in D Minor for Violin and Basso Continuo

Chapter 10   MusiCurious: How Baroque Performers "Decorate" Music; MusiCurious: Attending a Concert

The Classical Era: Reason and Revolution
Chapter 11   MusiCurious: Why Composers Write "Boring" Slow Movements; MusiCurious: What Does the Conductor Do?

Chapter 13   MusiCurious: Chamber Music Concerts

Chapter 14   MusiCurious: Classical and Romantic Opera (The Castrato Bows Out)

Music of the Romantic Era
Chapter 16   MusiCurious: How Does a Composer Write a Piece of Music?; new Listening Guide and recording: Clara Wieck Schumann, "Leibst du um Schönheit" ("If You Love for Beauty's Sake")

Chapter 17   New Listening Guide and recording: Franz Liszt, Transcendental Étude No. 10 in F Minor

Chapter 18   MusiCurious: Does the Listener Need to Know the Program in Program Music?

Chapter 20   MusiCurious: *Romeo and Juliet:* The Alternate Endings

Chapter 23   Composer box: Gustav Mahler

Chapter 24   MusiCurious: Attending an Opera

Chapter 25   MusiCurious: Opera Productions

The Early Twentieth Century
Chapter 27   MusiCurious: Music for Ballet

Chapter 29   MusiCurious: How Can Art Be Great If It Is Ugly?

American Innovations in the Arts
Chapter 30   New Listening Guide and recording: Stephen Foster, "Jeanie with the Light Brown Hair"

Chapter 31   MusiCurious: Improvisation; new Listening Guide and recording: Scott Joplin, "Maple Leaf Rag"

Chapter 32   MusiCurious: Attending a Jazz Concert

Chapter 35   MusiCurious: Musicals and Operas: Similar, but Different

New Ideas and Styles from Twentieth-Century Internationalism
Chapter 37   New First Hearing, Featured Listening, Finale, and recording: "Srepegan (slendro nim)" by Wayang kulit and dance repertoire

Chapter 38   MusiCurious: Performing in an Aleatoric Work; Hearing the Difference: Wayang kulit gamelan ensemble's "Srepegan (slendro nim)" and Cage's Sonata V

A Chat with Katherine Charlton

How did *Experience Music* evolve?

More than anything else, students have shaped this book. I like to encourage my students to ask questions and talk to me about what they hear in the music I play for them. Happily, I have been teaching an honors section of music appreciation for some years. That class has only twenty students who take many of the same classes in our honors program and know one another. For those reasons, my honors students tend to be more open with questions and more eager to take part in discussions than the students I have had in larger classes. Most of the pedagogical features in *Experience Music* came from my work with them. Other decisions I made about the content of the book, including the exclusion of music notation, and the placement of world musics before music in the late twentieth century, were also based on the reactions and interests of my students.

How do you decide what to cover?

I tried, and I think I succeeded, to keep the coverage of the material that is necessary for a general music appreciation course as concise and clear as possible. I know that I put more listening activities in the book than any instructor has time to use in a single semester or quarter, but this gives instructors flexibility to choose what activities to cover. I sometimes use one "Hearing the Difference" exercise with one class, and another with another class, just to give myself some variety.

What's new in this edition?

I had fun writing a new feature called "MusiCurious" that answers questions that I find students wonder about and might ask in class. Again, that idea came from discussions with my own students. I also added "Further Listening" selections to the end of each chapter so that if students like the music in a particular chapter, they can now more easily find other music they can enjoy. And, of course, I'm very excited about *Connect Music*. *Experience Music* always connected students to the music, but Connect does it in an even more powerful way. I can't wait to use it in my own classes.

Any final comments?

I hope very much that students who use this book will come away from their music appreciation classes with the listening skills and an appreciation of music that will last their entire lives.

— Katherine Charlton

About the Author

Katherine Charlton teaches at Mt. San Antonio College in Walnut, California. During a sabbatical in 1990, she taught music history at the American Institute for Foreign Study at the University of London. She holds degrees in classical guitar performance and music history and she has performed on medieval gittern, Renaissance lute, and baroque guitar with her late first husband, Andrew Charlton, who was well known in the field of early music. The two toured and performed in Southern France and Tuscany with the early-music group Li Troubador, led by Gloria Ramsey. In addition to performing early music, she has played percussion in the California University at Fullerton Wind Ensemble and toured Japan with the group. Charlton developed a class in the history of rock music and wrote the best-selling text on that subject, *Rock Music Styles: A History,* currently in its sixth edition and published by McGraw-Hill. In 2007–2008 she took a sabbatical leave to do a project on women in music to help her colleagues include more women in their courses.

Acknowledgements

I acknowledge with gratitude the many reviewers who took the time to read and critique the manuscript.

Lyle Archibald, Salt Lake Community College
Jeri-Mae G. Astolfi, Henderson State University
Candace Bailey, North Carolina Central University
Kevin Bartram, Mary Washington College
Isabelle Belance, Harold Washington University
Michael Billingsley, Camden County College
Mary Dave Blackman, East Tennessee State University
Andra C. Bohnet, University of South Alabama
Dana Brown, Kent State University
Rebecca Butler, Albright College
Jefferson Campbell, University of Minnesota, Duluth
Gregory Carroll, University of North Carolina, Greensboro
Henrietta Carter, Golden West College
Christopher Chaffee, Wright State University
Jonathan Chenoweth, University of Northern Iowa
Richard Cole, Virginia Polytechnic Institute
Laura Dankner, Southeastern Louisiana University
Seth Davis, Kingwood College and Alamo CCD
Marc Dickman, University of Northern Florida
Hollie Duvall, Westmoreland County Community College
Kevin Eakes, Trident Technical College
David H. Evans, Henderson State University
Richard Allen Fiske, Shasta College
Sheila Forrester, Santa Fe Community College
Cliff Ganus, Harding University
Ron Garber, Butler Community College
Richard Greene, Georgia College & State University
Jesse Guessford, George Mason University
Nancy Gunn, University of Southern Maine
David Haas, University of Georgia
Shana Hammett, East Carolina University
Kelly Dean Hansen, University of Colorado, Boulder
Edward Hart, College of Charleston
Kristin Hauser, Tennessee Technological University
Michael Hillstrom, Heartland Community College
David Johansen, Southeastern Louisiana University
Gregory Jones, Truman State University
Robert Jones, Palm Beach State College
Laura J. Keith, Claflin University
Dorothy Keyser, University of North Dakota
Sandra Kipp, California State University–Northridge and Moorpark College
Robert Knop, California State University–San Bernardino
Orly Krasner, City College/CUNY

Nancy C. Lefter, The Citadel, The Military College of SC
Milton A. Lites, Pulaski Technical College
Aaron Liu-Rosenbaum, The City College of New York
William Malone, Pikes Peak Community College
Grant Manhart, Northern State University
Alan Mason, Barry University
Brian Mason, Morehead State University
Cynthia McGregor, Southwestern College
Barry McVinney, Pulaski Technical College
Shelly Meggison, University of Alabama
Nevalyn Moore, Campbellsville University
Charlotte Mueller, Lee College
Mikylah Myers McTeer, Fort Lewis College
Tom Noonan, Front Range Community College
Patricia Nuss, Middle Georgia College
Debra O'Dell, North Idaho College
Jay O'Leary, Wayne State College
Jill O'Neill, Winthrop University
Stephanie Berg Oram, Red Rocks Community College
Natalka Pavlovsky, Gloucester County College
Richard J. Perkins, Anoka-Ramsey Community College
Pamela J. Perry, Central Connecticut State University
Clark Potter, University of Nebraska–Lincoln
Alan Rawson, Minnesota State University–Moorhead
Stephanie Robinson, San Diego City College
Anthony Scelba, Kean University
David Schiller, University of Georgia
John Schreckengost, Valparaiso University
William Shepherd, University of Northern Iowa
Matt Shevitz, Harold Washington College
Stephen Simmons, Midlands Technical College
Mark L. Singer, Morgan State University
Walter Skiba, Calumet College of St. Joseph
Floyd Slotterback, Northern Michigan University
Frederick Key Smith, Santa Fe Community College
Ross E. Smith, Centenary College of Louisiana
Wayne C. Smith, Spokane Falls Community College
Ron Stinson, Johnson County Community College
Virginia Stitt, Southern Utah University
Karla J. Stroman, North Hennepin Community College
Sarah Nell Summers, Temple College
James Syler, University of Texas at San Antonio
Tawana C. Teague, Northeast State University
Randy Tinnin, University of North Florida
Andrew Tomasello, Baruch College
John F. Vallentine, University of Northern Iowa
Beverly Vaughn, The Richard Stockton College of New Jersey

Chris White, Loyola University, Chicago
Cathryn Wilkinson, College of Du Page
Marvin Williams, Kingsborough Community College
Dieter Wulfhorst, California State University–Fresno
Katrina Zook, University of Wyoming

I want to express my particular gratitude to these professors whose valuable suggestions were incorporated into the text:

James McGowan, Laurentian University, Sudbury, Ontario, Canada
Patrice Ross, Columbus State Community College
Dale A. Scott, Oklahoma State University

I have many people to thank for their help in the writing of *Experience Music*. First, of course, is my co-author on the first two editions, Robert Hickok. My dedication is to my husband, Jeffrey Calkins, for many reasons. He has done a lot of proofreading, but he has also spent many an evening coming home from his job as a research attorney at the California State Court of Appeal to end up cooking dinner and calling me away from my computer when it was ready. Now that the book is finished, I will have to learn how to cook all over again. In addition to being a brilliant attorney, Jeff is a political scientist who was very helpful in making suggestions to improve the Preludes in the book.

Colleagues who helped me with their suggestions and proofreading include Gary Toops and Kevin Wiley. Gary is an organist who has recently retired from teaching music appreciation at my college and was very helpful in suggesting additions that enriched the book. He also provided wonderful insights when I wrote the "MusiCurious" box about playing the organ. Kevin is an accompanist and librarian in my department. Other colleagues who advised and encouraged me in various ways include Scott Zeidel, Dr. Margaret Meier, Dr. Robert Bowen, Jason Chevalier, Kevin Mayse, Dr. David Cahueque, and Greg Stier. One of my former teachers, Dr. Robert Stewart, was also very encouraging. I learned more about contemporary music from him than from any other source, and I constantly find myself quoting him when I teach the subject. Dr. Larry Timm, author of *The Soul of Cinema: An Appreciation of Film Music,* is an old friend of mine and was very helpful in making suggestions to improve the chapter on music in film.

I'm grateful to McGraw-Hill sales representative Lorraine Zielinski, who suggested to the company that I would be right for this project. I would like to thank Tom Laskey of the Custom Marketing Group at Sony BMG Music Entertainment for his work in researching the recordings used and in producing the CDs that accompany the book. I appreciate the work of the many McGraw-Hill editorial, media, marketing, and production staff members and freelancers who were involved in this book. In addition to those who are listed on the copyright page, I would like to specifically acknowledge the work of Carol Einhorn, Chris Freitag, Susan Gouijnstook, Marley Magaziner, Sarah Remington, Lisa Pinto, and Holly Paulsen.

As I indicated earlier, the most important people who guided my choices and attitudes about this book were the many students I have had over the years. I hope that the students who use this book enjoy it, learn from it, and feel encouraged to ask questions in class. After all, we teachers and writers work for them.

—Katherine Charlton Calkins

Prelude

The Fundamentals of Music

By the time you have finished reading this text, you will have listened to a wide range of works, including symphonies, chamber music, opera, and jazz. Despite their apparent differences, these works are all made from the same component parts: sound, rhythm, melody, and harmony. Before you can begin a serious study of music, you need to understand its most basic elements, and you need to understand how those elements combine to form individual pieces. In addition, for a full appreciation of music, it is helpful to be familiar with the orchestra and various musical instruments. The following chapters will give you the fundamental vocabulary necessary to study music of all kinds.

The London Philharmonic Orchestra in concert

A classical singer is accompanied by a pianist.

Elements of Music: Sound, Rhythm, Melody, and Harmony

Music is built from elements that we describe using a particular vocabulary. After you have studied that vocabulary, you will be in a much better position to discuss a piece of music with a friend, write a report that describes music you have listened to, and understand what someone else has written about music. For example, a review that criticizes a conductor for not using enough dynamic contrasts or says that an opera singer had problems maintaining good tone quality in certain pitch ranges will make more sense to you when you know what dynamics, tone quality, and pitch ranges are. Without knowing those terms, you might still understand that the reviewer did not like everything about the performance, but the musical vocabulary communicates more than that simple fact.

Sound

Music is an art based on the organization of sounds in time. A sound, any sound, is the result of vibrations in the air set in motion by the activation of a sounding body—the slamming of a door, the ringing of a bell, or the playing of a musical instrument. In the case of a *musical* sound, the vibrations are so definite and steady that they produce what is called a *tone* (also referred to as a **note**), the highness or lowness of which is called the **pitch.**

The precise pitch is determined by the *frequency,* as measured in cycles per second, of its vibration—the *faster* the frequency, the *higher* the pitch, and, conversely, the *slower* the frequency, the *lower* the pitch. When music is written down, the higher pitches are represented by notes that are higher (toward the top of the page) on the **staff:** the set of five horizontal lines on or between which the notes are placed. That staff helps us measure how much higher or lower one note is in comparison with another. Each line and each space represents a different pitch:

The higher the position of the note on the staff, the higher the pitch of the tone:

Higher

Lower

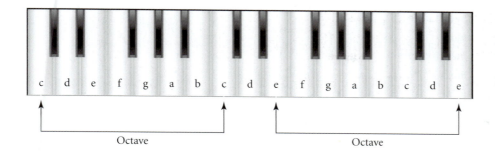

FIGURE 1.1
Piano keyboard with one octave from C to C and another octave from E to E marked

The following is an example of the contour (or high and low shape) of pitches (without the staff) for the beginning of "The Star-Spangled Banner."

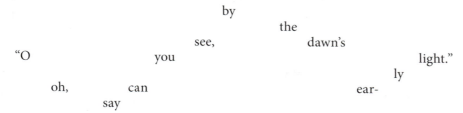

The distance between two pitches is called an **interval.** The smallest interval that occurs when two identical pitches are played one after the other is called a **unison.** Another interval, called an **octave,** is that between notes of the same name—for example, one C and the next C above it (Figure 1.1). They will sound similar to one another because the higher pitch is produced by exactly double the number of vibrations that it takes to produce the lower pitch. For example, the words *say* and *see* in "The Star-Spangled Banner" are separated by an octave. Between the two notes that mark an octave, there are eleven other notes and many intervals possible among them.

As you look at the piano keyboard, you will notice that the black keys are grouped in patterns of twos and threes. Each note looks different from any other, depending on where it fits within those groupings. Any note on the white key just to the left of a set of two black keys, for example, will be the note C. If you play one C and then the next higher or lower C, you have played an octave. If you play the notes on the white keys from one C to the next, you are playing a C **major scale,** sometimes referred to as the *do-re-mi* scale because those syllables are used to identify the notes as follows: C = *do,* D = *re,* E = *mi,* F = *fa,* G = *sol,* A = *la,* B 5 *ti.* If you were to continue on and play the notes up to the next higher C, you would be playing what is called a two-octave scale. The two-octave scale has a greater **pitch range** than the single-octave scale. The distance between the lowest and the highest notes an instrument or a voice can produce is referred to as the instrument's or voice's *pitch range.*

Another important aspect of musical sound is **dynamics,** or levels of loudness and softness. Sometimes musicians use a variety of dynamic levels when playing a single piece of music. If the musician wants to emphasize one note over the others, he or she can **accent** it by playing it louder. *Piano,* which means soft, and *forte,* which means loud, are Italian terms used by musicians to indicate dynamic levels. Extremes of those dynamic levels are written by adding the suffix "*issimo.*" In other words, *piano* is soft and *pianissimo* is softer yet. *Forte* is loud and *fortissimo* is even louder. *Mezzo* means medium, so *mezzo piano* is medium soft and *mezzo forte* is medium loud. Sometimes letters are used as an abbreviation of the full dynamic terms. To abbreviate the *issimo* terms, simply double the letters (*pianissimo* is notated as *pp,* and *fortissimo* as *ff*). "Mezzo" is represented by an *m,* so *mp* is medium soft and *mf* medium loud. These dynamic levels are listed below, from the softest to the loudest:

pianissimo	*pp*
piano	*p*
mezzo piano	*mp*
mezzo forte	*mf*
forte	*f*
fortissimo	*ff*

Other terms are used to indicate a gradual change in dynamic levels. **Decrescendo,** or **diminuendo,** indicates that the music is getting softer, which can often give the effect of a calming of tension; and **crescendo** indicates that it is getting louder, which can express exuberance.

Different instruments and voices each have their own distinct kind of sound. A melody played on the flute sounds different from the same melody played on the clarinet because the sound quality of the clarinet is clearly different from that of the flute. The distinctive sound quality of an instrument is called *tone color,* or **timbre** (pronounced *tam-bur*).

Rhythm

Rhythm is the ordered flow of music through time. The regular, recurrent pulsation in most music is called the **beat.** Perhaps the beating of our own heart is the most basic beat we feel. In some music the beat is pounded out by a drum or other instrument and is consequently so clear that you may find yourself clapping along. That steady beat helps us measure musical time, but the word *rhythm* refers to much more than that. Rhythm includes the way music flows between the beats. Although the presence of a steady beat is common, in some music the beat is not clear at all, perhaps because the composer wished to evoke a smooth or even floating effect. We can see such an effect in nature if we watch waves washing up on a beach. The waves do not pound away at any steady sort of beat, but the effect they create is indeed very rhythmic. It is rhythmic because of the sense of flowing motion they create. In other words, *beat* refers to the steady pulse you might hear in music, whereas *rhythm* covers much more about musical time. A beat can be part of rhythm, but musical rhythm can exist without a beat.

Sometimes individual notes are played on each beat, but notes can also be held for more than or less than a whole beat. In the first phrase of "America," observe the notes that are longer than one beat—the note for the word *'tis,* for example. Also notice that the longer notes are followed by notes that are held for less than one beat, such as the note on *of.* The word *liberty* has three notes of varying lengths, and *sing* is held for a full three beats.

	"My country	'tis	of thee, sweet land	of	li-	berty.	Of	thee	I	sing."
Beats:	/ /	/	/ /	/ /	/ /	/ /	/	/ /	/	/ /

Against this background of regularly occurring beats or pulsations, notes of varying lengths make some beats sound more prominent—or "heavier"—than others. That does not necessarily mean that those notes should be played louder; they usually stand out because of the patterns of long and short notes. In the case of "America," the first of every three beats is given more weight. The following example groups the beats into patterns of three.

	"My country	'tis	of thee, sweet land of	li-	berty.	Of	thee	I	sing."
Meter:	**1** 2 3	**1** 2 3	**1** 2 3	**1** 2 3	**1** 2 3	**1**	2	3	

This organization of beats into regular groups is called **meter,** and the units themselves are called **measures.** Different types of meters are defined by the number of beats in the measure. The example we heard in "America" is called **triple meter,** because it consists of three beats per measure. The first beat of each group, the one that carries more weight, is called the **downbeat.** On the CDs that came with your book, the recording of "When I Am Laid in Earth" from Purcell's opera *Dido and Aeneas* is in triple meter. Listen to it and see if you can hear the meter.

When music has two beats in each measure, which means an accent on every other beat, we say it is in **duple meter.** "Mary Had a Little Lamb" is in duple meter.

"Mar-y had a little lamb, little lamb, little lamb, Mar-y had a little lamb, Its fleece was white as snow."
Meter: 1 2 1 2 1 2 1 2 1 2 1 2 1 2 1 2

On the CDs that came with your book, the recording of the first movement of Mozart's Symphony no. 40 is in duple meter. Listen to it and see if you can hear the meter.

Music played to a four-beat measure is in **quadruple meter,** which can sound a lot like music in duple meter because the groups of four beats are usually also two groups of two beats. There is, however, a difference: in duple meter, every other beat is a downbeat, but this is not the case in quadruple meter. The four beats of quadruple meter begin with a strong downbeat followed by a weaker second beat. The third beat is stronger than the second or fourth beats but not as strong as the downbeat. The following example of quadruple meter also has a short note before the downbeat. That short note is called an **upbeat.**

"Mine eyes have seen the glory of the coming of the Lord. He has . . ."
Meter: **1** 2 **3** 4 **1** 2 **3** 4

On the CDs that came with your book, the recording of "Comfort Ye" from Handel's *Messiah* is in quadruple meter. Listen to it and see if you can hear the meter.

Another common meter, called **sextuple,** has six beats in each measure. The six beats are usually divided into two sections of three beats each. The accents fall on beats one and four (**1** 2 3 **4** 5 6). The following example, "Silent Night," is in sextuple meter:

"Si- lent Night, Ho- ly Night! All is calm, all is bright"
Meter: 1 2 3 4 5 6 1 2 3 4 5 6 1 2 3 4 5 6 1 2 3 4 5 6

On the CDs that came with your book, the recording of "America" from Leonard Bernstein's *West Side Story* is in sextuple meter. It is also accented to sound like triple meter at times, however, making it an interesting combination of meters. Listen to it with meter in mind, and you will hear that "I want to be in A-" is sextuple and then the rest of the word, "-merica" sounds triple. Actually, what Bernstein has done is accent the sextuple meter **1** 2 3 **4** 5 6 for "I want to be in A-" and then accent it **1** 2 **3** 4 **5** 6 on "-merica."

Other meters, such as **quintuple,** with five beats per measure, and **septuple,** with seven, are not nearly as common as those we have discussed, though composers of the twentieth century and beyond, particularly jazz and art-rock musicians, have used them with some frequency. In many cases in which those unusual meters are used, the musicians are trying to give an effect that noticeably counters the meters we are accustomed to hearing. If you have ever heard the song "Money" by the rock band Pink Floyd, for example, the lyrics are about money-grubbing people who care only for themselves. The song's meter is septuple, making it seem a bit odd and difficult to dance or tap your foot to. The music, in other words, is just as uncomfortable as the subject of the song and therefore supports the lyrics very effectively. If you listen to the recording, the repeating bass line, which outlines the seven beats, should help you follow the meter.

Earlier in this chapter, we touched on the term *accent.* Ways of accenting a note include playing it louder, longer, or higher or lower than its surrounding notes. Accents cause notes to stick out and grab our attention. Sometimes composers accent notes that are played between, rather than directly on, the steady beat. This effect is called **syncopation.** The beginning of Stephen Foster's song "Camptown Races" is syncopated: both times "dah" is sung, it comes before the beat, though the listener most likely expects to hear it on the beat. You could sing the song with the "dahs" exactly on the second beats, but the effect would lack the energy added by the syncopation. The lyrics and beats follow:

	"Camptown ladies		sing this	song,	doo dah,		doo dah"	
Beats:	1	2	1	2	1	2	1	2

All aspects of rhythm are very much affected by the **tempo,** or pace, of the music. The tempo is the rate or speed of the beat. If the beat is quick, the tempo is *fast;* if the beat is long, the tempo is *slow.* Indications concerning tempo are usually given in Italian and most often appear at the beginning of the piece, though they may also appear in other sections, particularly if the tempo changes abruptly:

very slow:	*largo* (broad)
	grave (grave, solemn)
slow:	*lento*
	adagio (leisurely; literally, at ease)
moderate:	*andante* (at a walking pace)
	moderato
fast:	*allegretto*
	allegro (faster than allegretto; literally, cheerful)
very fast:	*vivace* (vivacious)
	presto (very quick)
	prestissimo (as fast as possible)

These basic terms are often accompanied by the following modifiers: *molto* (very), *meno* (less), *poco* (a little), and *ma non troppo* (not too much). For example, *allegro molto* is very fast; *poco adagio* is somewhat slow; and *allegro non troppo* is fast but not too fast. *Accelerando* (getting faster) and *ritardando* (becoming slower) indicate gradual changes in tempo. To reestablish the original tempo, the term *a tempo* is used.

Tempo can be altered in other ways. The term **rubato** indicates freedom to move ahead and fall behind the tempo, and the symbol ⌢ (**fermata**) tells the performer to hold the note longer than its normal time value—momentarily suspending the meter and tempo. As was the case with dynamic indications, tempo indications are approximate and relative, leaving a great deal of discretion to the performer.

Melody

Whereas rhythm measures the flow of music in time, **melody** fits into a given rhythm by adding a series of pitches that we might enjoy humming along with. We often will remember the melody—whether it is sung with words or played instrumentally—better than any other aspect of the music.

We can define a melody as a series of notes that add up to a recognizable whole. Melody gives music a sense of physical movement as it progresses forward in time. Different melodies follow different patterns of movement. Those that move from one note to another in a major scale (*do* to *re* in the *do-re-mi* scale, for example) move by steps. When the notes of a melody skip notes (or steps) of the scale (from *do* to *mi* or some other note in the scale), they are moving by leaps.

Melody also comprises the way in which notes connect with one another. If the notes seem to flow naturally and smoothly from one to the next, we say the melody is played or sung **legato.** If the notes sound "choppy"—that is, short and detached from each other—we say the melody is played or sung **staccato.** We will hear many examples of each of these effects as we explore the musical examples in this book.

Melodies are often made up of shorter sections called **phrases.** When a phrase or a melody ends with a sense of finality, that resting point is called a **cadence.** In the song "Row, Row, Row Your Boat," for example, the two phrases are equal in length, with the second phrase sounding like a completion of the first. The phrases are identified by letters of the alphabet—"a" for the first phrase and "b" for the second. When you sing the song, notice that the end of the "a" phrase does not sound complete, but rather sets us up to expect the "b" phrase. That type of seemingly incomplete ending is called an *incomplete cadence.* The entire melody ends with a complete cadence.

> phrase "a"   "Row, row, row your boat gently down the stream,
>
> phrase "b"   Merrily, merrily, merrily, merrily, life is but a dream."

Sing the melody to "Row, Row, Row Your Boat" again and notice that there is a sense of energy on the first "merrily." This energy is created by the fact that that note is the highest note in the melody. Such a melodic high point is called the *climax.*

When a melody is made up of two very similar phrases, we do not use the letter "b" for the second phrase. Instead, we identify it as a varied version of the first phrase by calling it "a′." Such is the case with the song "Mary Had a Little Lamb."

> phrase "a"   "Mary had a little lamb, little lamb, little lamb,
>
> phrase "a′"   Mary had a little lamb; its fleece was white as snow."

Of course, many melodies are much more complicated than the two we have cited. Some melodies are made up of phrases of unequal lengths. Sometimes, too, we find melodic patterns repeated at different pitch levels. This is called a **sequence.** The song "America" uses a sequence. The words "Land where my fathers died" and "Land of the Pilgrim's pride" are sung to the same melodic pattern, but the second phrase is sung at a lower pitch than the first.

The melody is an extremely important part of any piece of music. In a long composition, some melodies assume greater importance than others. A melody that serves as the starting point for an extended work is called a **theme.** In the course of a musical composition, important themes may be stated and restated in many different forms.

Harmony

If melody is the horizontal aspect of music, **harmony** is the vertical. That is, instead of sounds in succession, harmony involves notes sounding at the same time. Most Western music depends on harmony to help enhance its expressiveness.

We have defined *interval* as the distance between two notes in a melody, but we can also use it to refer to the distance between notes that are sounded together to make harmony. Thus, harmony is a composite sound made up of two or more notes of different pitches that are played or sung simultaneously. The smallest harmonic unit is one consisting of two notes, but we usually have three or more notes played or sung together to create harmony. Those groups of notes make up what we call **chords** (pronounced "cords"). A series of chords is called a **chord progression.**

An important quality of a given harmony is its degree of consonance or dissonance. A combination of notes that is considered stable and without tension is called a **consonance.** A combination of notes that is considered unstable and tense, so much so that they sometimes sound as if they are fighting with one another, is called a **dissonance.** Dissonance adds variety and a sense of forward motion to music. Dissonance usually occurs as a transient tension in a harmonic progression. *Resolution* usually refers to a dissonant chord moving to a consonant chord. The movement from dissonance to consonance can give a sense of dramatic or psychological resolution, like seeing the villain get what is coming to him or her in a movie.

The general character of most pieces is consonant, even though they may feature some dissonance. Joseph Haydn's String Quartet, op. 33, no. 3, is a good example.

Listen to its fourth movement on the CDs that accompany your book and notice that the music sounds as though the notes all fit together into a pleasing harmonic unit. Other works are predominantly dissonant, such as John Cage's Sonata V from *Sonatas and Interludes for Prepared Piano*. When you listen to Cage's work, you will hear many groups of notes that clash against one another, creating much tension. As we move through music history from century to century, we find that the relationship of consonance and dissonance begins to change, with a gradual increase in the importance or prevalence of dissonance as we approach the twentieth century.

The simplest chord is the **triad.** It is made up of three notes that are usually spaced one note apart—*do, mi,* and *sol* in the *do-re-mi* (major) scale, for example. The first note of any scale—in this case, *do*—is called the **tonic** note. The triad built on the notes beginning with *do* is, therefore, called the *tonic chord.* Tonic chords sound very stable and are traditionally played at the end of a musical composition in order to supply a sense of conclusion to the harmonic progression.

Chords can be broken up so that their notes are played one at a time instead of all together. This is called an **arpeggio.** Arpeggios can be used to accompany melodies or they can create a melody themselves. The melody to the words "Oh say can you see" from "The Star-Spangled Banner" is composed out of an arpeggio because all of the notes come from a single—in this case, tonic—chord.

Summary

Music is made up of many different, and simultaneously present, elements. When we listen to a melody, we are also listening to the rhythm on which that melody is based. That rhythm can be a steady beat, and it may or may not fall into a particular meter (pattern of accented notes). The melody itself is composed of a series of pitches that might fall in a very narrow range of notes (close to one another), or the melody might jump around from very high to very low notes. Either way, listening for both melody and rhythm adds to the enjoyment of music.

Tempo is an important part of rhythm. Many longer pieces of music are made up of several sections of contrasting tempos. One section might be fast and lively, while the next section might be slow and smooth sounding. Another fast section might follow to add contrast and balance.

A single piece of music might vary in dynamic levels. A melody might create a sense of tension by beginning softly and then gradually reaching a crescendo. Dynamic contrasts add to the expressiveness of music in much the same way that a dynamic speaker might shout part of the time and speak slowly, softly, and directly at other times.

Harmony is the vertical aspect of music—the notes that are played together to accompany the melody. Harmonies can be consonant (sounding as though they fit well together and create a sense of relaxation), or they can be dissonant (sounding as though the notes are all fighting one another). Most music includes both consonances and dissonances.

New Concepts

accent, 5

adagio, 8

allegretto, 8

allegro, 8

andante, 8

arpeggio, 10

beat, 6

cadence, 10

chord, 9

chord progression, 9

consonance, 9

crescendo, 6

decrescendo, 6

diminuendo, 6

dissonance, 9

downbeat, 7

duple meter, 7

dynamics, 5

fermata (⌢), 8

forte (f), 5

fortissimo (ff), 5

grave, 8

harmony, 9

interval, 5

largo, 8

legato, 8

lento, 8

major scale, 5

measures, 6

melody, 8

meter, 6

mezzo forte (mf), 5

mezzo piano (mp), 5

moderato, 8

note, 4

octave, 5

phrase, 10

pianissimo (pp), 5

piano (p), 5

pitch, 4

pitch range, 5

prestissimo, 8

presto, 8

quadruple meter, 7

quintuple meter, 7

rhythm, 6

rubato, 8

septuple meter, 7

sequence, 9

sextuple meter, 7

staccato, 8

staff, 4

syncopation, 7

tempo, 8

theme, 9

timbre, 6

tonic, 10

triad, 10

triple meter, 7

unison, 5

upbeat, 7

vivace, 8

Elements that Structure Music: Key, Texture, and Form

> Music gives soul to the universe.
> —PLATO [CA. 427–348 BCE]

2

We have seen that combinations of individual types of sounds produce the basic elements of music: sound, rhythm, melody, and harmony. In this chapter we explore the ways in which these elements combine to give structure to complete pieces of music. Our discussion of sound described pitches that came together to form scales, which are the basis of many melodies. We now expand the idea of the scale into an overall sense of a key, or tonal, center for an entire musical composition. When we discussed melody, we dealt with single melodies. Now, we discuss music that has more than one melody at one time, creating a denser texture. Our discussion of melody also showed how melodies are often made up of phrases that repeat or contrast with one another. When we view a complete composition, we see how melodies are sometimes repeated and contrasted to give the music a sense of structure that we call *form*.

Key

One of the fundamental characteristics of Western music is its reliance on **tonality** as an organizing element. *Tonal music* is characterized by the presence of the *tonic,* the central note around which a specific musical composition is organized, and of a chord built on that note, called the *tonic chord* (discussed in Chapter 1). The tonic chord acts as the musical center of gravity, a kind of home base in that when it is played it can give a sense of completion to the music. If the tonic note is C, we say that the melody is in the **key** of C. In other words, *key* refers to the central note, scale, and chord. Another word for key is *tonality.*

Melodies are usually based on the notes in a particular scale. The notes from one C to the next C on the white keys of the piano make up the C **major scale.** The C major scale has a particular sound because of the placement of the black keys between the white ones on the keyboard (see Figure 1.1). When two adjacent white keys have a black key between them, they are a whole step apart. When two adjacent white keys have no black key between them, they are a half step apart. The distance between any note and the next possible note, black or white, is also a half step. A whole step is made up of two half steps, represented by the black key between the two white ones that are a whole step apart. The major scale (*do-re-mi* scale), then, is made up of the following pattern of whole and half step intervals: w - w - h - w - w - w - h (Figure 2.1).

Another common type of scale is the **minor scale,** which resembles the major scale but has a number of lowered notes. When a note is lowered, it is played on the black key to the left of the white one, lowering its pitch by one half step. The notation of a flat sign (♭) indicates the notes that are lowered. This lowering of some notes gives a minor melody a different sort of psychological effect from a major melody. The lowered notes can sound a bit sadder than the ones in a major scale, although that is certainly not always the case.

To this point, we have been basing our scales on the C tonic, but other notes can be tonic notes too. If we start a major scale on the note D and use it as the basis of our music, we say that the music is in the key of D major. Conversely, if we base our music on a minor scale that begins on the note D, our music will be in the key of D minor. Compositions can be found in major or minor keys based on every tonic note we have.

When we notate music in different keys, we use the flat sign (♭) to lower a note a half step (move it down to the next possible note, usually the next black key to the left) and the sharp sign (♯) to raise it a half step (move it up to the next possible note, usually the next black key to the right). If our entire composition is going to need certain notes to be flatted or sharped all the way through, we indicate that at the beginning of each line of music instead of putting the signs in front of each note. This indication is called a **key signature.** When we play a D-major scale, for example, we have to raise (sharp) all of the F and C notes for the scale to sound major (like the *do-re-mi* scale). Because the key signature is printed at the beginning of every line of music, the player knows to sharp all of the necessary notes (F and C in this case) as he or she plays the music. If the composer wants to cancel one of the sharps or flats, a natural sign (♮) is placed before the note.

A scale that includes all notes (on both black and white keys played in order on the piano) is called a **chromatic scale.** This scale is not the basis of a particular key because all of the notes are just one half step apart, and no single note sounds like home base. In fact, a chromatic scale does not have to start or end on any particular note. Because a chromatic scale includes all notes, including many that are dissonant with one another, composers can use it to create dissonance and tension not present in a standard major or minor scale. Composers often use that dissonance for special, dramatic effects.

Sometimes, for variety, longer pieces of music change from one tonal center, or key, to another during the flow of the music. The shift from one key to another within the same composition is called **modulation.** No matter how many times a piece of music modulates, it usually ends by going back to the tonic key with which it began, making use of the sense of home base the tonic creates. In other words, a piece in the key of D major will begin and end with D as its tonic, even though many other keys might have been played in the middle of the piece.

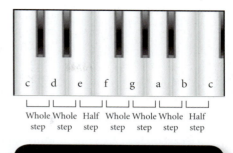

FIGURE 2.1

Texture

Like cloth, music is woven of horizontal and vertical strands. We think of melody as moving horizontally, because one note follows the next along the flow of time. We describe harmony as vertical because it is based on sounds that occur simultaneously and in combination with one another. **Texture** describes the way the vertical and horizontal strands of melody are interwoven. In this sense, texture combines both melody and harmony. In addition to strands of melody, the term *texture* can refer to how many different layers of sound are heard at the same time. Three basic musical textures are commonly found in Western music: **monophony, polyphony,** and **homophony.**

The simplest musical texture is monophony, which literally means "one sound," although in music it means one melodic line with no accompaniment. (You can hit two rocks together and create one sound, but that would not create monophonic texture.) If you sing or hum by yourself, you are creating monophonic music. Music is also monophonic if a single melodic line is performed by more than one instrument or voice at the same time. In that case, we say that the instruments or voices are playing or singing in unison. We have used the term *unison* before to describe the interval when two identical pitches are played one after the other. Here, the two pitches are played or sung together. Even if men and women sing the same melody at the same time, with the women singing an octave higher than the men, the texture is monophonic.

On the CDs that accompany your book, the recording of the "Dies irae" ("Day of Wrath") chant is an example of monophonic texture. Listen to it and notice that it is sung as a single-line melody with no accompaniment.

When two or more melodies of equal interest are performed at the same time, the texture is polyphonic ("many sounds"). In discussing texture, we often call a single line of music a *voice* because it is a melody that one person could sing. Independence and equality of voices are the defining characteristics of polyphony. Independence refers to a voice's ability to compete with other melodic strands for the attention of the listener.

In polyphonic music we need to listen carefully to the relationship between or among the independent, simultaneous melodies. Our attention will shift from one melodic line to another, depending on which is most prominent at any given moment. The melodic lines thus enhance and enrich each other, contributing to the expressiveness of the overall sound. The technique of combining several melodic lines into a meaningful whole is called **counterpoint.** The term *contrapuntal texture* is sometimes used in place of the term *polyphonic texture* because notes (points) of each melody tend to move in different directions, countering one another.

Sometimes in polyphonic music we hear one melodic idea presented by one singing voice or instrument and then hear it restated immediately by another voice or instrument. This is called **imitation** or *imitative polyphony* because the second voice sounds like an imitation of the first. Several voices can enter the music one after the other, each imitating the first melody.

If you listen to the beginning of "Ave Maria" by Josquin des Prez on the book's CDs, you will hear an example of the type of gentle beauty and sense of unity of purpose that imitative polyphony can create.

Imitative polyphony, in which all of the voices play the same melody all the way through with no variation, is called a **round** or a **canon.** A round is an example of what we could call *strict imitation*. In performance, a first voice begins alone, and when it gets to a particular part of the melody, a second voice starts at the beginning. Similarly, other voices enter one at a time, each singing the same melody from the beginning. Once the earlier voices finish the melody and drop out, the last voice finishes alone, giving a round a very simple beginning and ending with much imitative polyphony in between. The songs "Row, Row, Row Your Boat" and "Three Blind Mice" are both examples of rounds.

The CDs that came with your book include a recording of William Billings's "When Jesus Wept," which is a round. Listen to it and make note of the imitation as new voices enter. Notice that when more than one voice sings, the texture is polyphonic.

In homophonic ("same sound") music, a *single* melodic line predominates, while the other voices or instruments provide an accompanying harmony. The listener's attention is focused on the melody; the harmonic accompaniment is heard as a kind of musical background. Harmonic accompaniment to the melody can take various forms—from the simple strumming of chords on a guitar to a full orchestra playing music that supports, but does not get in the way of, the melody.

The recording of Amy Beach's "Ah, Love, but a Day" on the book's CDs is an example of homophonic texture. Listen to it and notice that the primary single melody is sung with piano accompaniment.

Another type of homophonic texture occurs when several melodies are played together in the same rhythm. That rhythm may include the presence of a steady beat or meter, or it may flow gently without a beat but with all of the melodies staying together. Because all of the voices follow the same rhythm patterns, the lower melodies do not stand out as separate from the highest melody, which usually dominates the listener's attention. This type of texture occurs when several people sing a hymn tune or praise song in church. It is sometimes called *homorhythmic texture* because of the similar rhythms in all of the parts.

Actually, much music employs both polyphonic and homophonic textures. Frequently, a piece of music alternates between or among textures. An essentially homophonic section, for example, may be followed by a polyphonic one. What is important here is that you understand what the textures are in their clearest examples and then listen for them in the more complex music you will encounter later.

On the CDs that accompany your book, John Farmer's "Fair Phyllis" uses a combination of textures. Listen to it and note that the phrase "Fair Phyllis I saw sitting all alone" is monophonic. The song then turns polyphonic until the last phrase, "Oh, then they fell a-kissing," which is homophonic, with all voices singing in the same rhythm.

Form

The organization of musical ideas (which are usually melodies but can be some other combination of sounds) in time is called **form.** Sustaining the listener's interest in music depends on the presence of two essential factors: unity and variety. Unity is usually achieved through **repetition** of musical ideas, and variety through the introduction of new, often **contrasting,** musical ideas. Repetition of musical ideas provides an overall sense of unity by engraving an important melody or other musical idea, such as a distinctive rhythm pattern, in the mind of the listener. An important and returning melody in a musical composition is called a *theme.* When a theme is played at the beginning of a piece of music and returns at the end, it gives the music a feeling of balance and symmetry.

In addition to repetition and contrast, **variation** is often an important element in the form of a piece of music. Composers vary themes in any number of ways, but all variation retains some features of the original musical idea. For example, you might hear a piece of music that begins with a melody and simple accompaniment followed by a variation of the melody, or theme. In the variation you will probably still be able to pick out the notes of the melody, but you might hear some of those notes changed, or you might hear them with a different kind of accompaniment. Some very interesting pieces of music are based on a theme and a series of varied versions of that theme. The form of this type of piece is called **theme and variations.**

There are many different organizational forms, but two of the most common are the three-part form, called **ternary form,** and the two-part form, called **binary form.** The three parts of ternary form include a beginning section, a contrasting middle section, and then a repeat of the beginning. Binary form has only two parts. Letters are often used to describe these forms. For example, ternary form is usually shown by the letters ABA. The first A represents the section of music at the beginning; the B represents a contrasting section. The repeat of the letter A indicates that the beginning music returns or is repeated. The second A section does not have to be as long as the first, but it must include the same theme or themes to be considered a return of A. Sometimes the second A has the same themes as the first, but there are some changes in the way they are presented: for example, they might be played on different instruments. When that is the case, we diagram the form as ABA'. The A' stands for "A with some changes." The B section includes different themes from those in A.

Binary form consists of a beginning section followed by a contrasting second section. The two sections can be of equal or unequal length and may or may not be repeated. The simplest example of binary form is diagrammed as AB. Notice that this is different from ternary form because the A section, or beginning music, does not come back at the end of the piece. With repetitions, binary forms can include AABB or AAB or ABB.

Summary

The melody, rhythm, and/or harmony in music discussed in the previous chapter are held together by an overall structure. Much music we hear today is tonal, which means that the melodies and harmonies fall into a particular key, or tonal center. Long or short sections of the music sometimes change to a new key, although the key of the beginning of a piece of music usually returns at the end to create a sense of balance and finality for the overall composition.

The relationship between the horizontal (melody) and vertical (harmony) aspects of music comes together through texture. A composition's texture is created by a layering of sound. A single melody played or sung alone creates a monophonic texture. Two or more melodies played at the same time, each sounding independent of the other(s), creates polyphonic texture. One melody played with an accompanying harmony is homophonic in texture. Many pieces of music change from one texture to another, and listening for those changes adds to our appreciation of the music.

Most compositions have sections that repeat music that was heard before. It is also common to hear music that contrasts or creates a variation on music heard earlier. We determine the form of music by listening for repetition, contrast, and variation. Some forms are easier to hear and recognize than others, but once you learn to listen for repetition, contrast, and variation, you will begin to recognize the composition's larger structure.

New Concepts

binary form, 15

canon, 14

chromatic scale, 13

contrast, 15

counterpoint, 14

form, 15

homophony, 13

imitation, 14

key, 12

key signature, 13

major scale, 12

minor scale, 12

modulation, 13

monophony, 13

polyphony, 13

repetition, 15

round, 14

ternary form, 15

texture, 13

theme and variations, 15

tonality, 12

variation, 15

Musical Instruments and Ensembles

The great variety of musical instruments available to the composer or performer today offers a tremendous range of qualities of sound. Instruments are usually categorized into what we refer to as *families*. The standard families are voices, strings, woodwinds, brasses, percussion, keyboard, and electronic. In this chapter we discuss the most commonly used instruments in each of these families. We concentrate on modern instruments; however, most modern instruments have early predecessors, and a few of those predecessors are mentioned in this chapter. We use the year 1750 to mark the break between the use of old and modern instruments because it roughly dates the time period in which some of the older instruments dropped out of favor, the piano came into common use, and the orchestra as we know it today began to develop.

Voices and Vocal Ensembles

Because it is part of the human body, the voice is in many respects our most fundamental musical instrument. The expressive qualities of the voice are greatly enhanced by its ability to combine music and words. Individual voices vary in pitch range, but

A concert choir performs in Los Angeles

3

male and female voice types are generally divided into high, middle, and low registers. Arranged from highest to lowest pitch register, the basic vocal categories are

Female (or boys with unchanged voices)	**soprano**
	mezzo soprano
	alto (also called *contralto*)
Male	**tenor**
	baritone
	bass

These vocal types are often written by the first letter of the name: for example, a mixed **choir** that includes both women and men is often called an *SATB choir* because the four voices are soprano, alto, tenor, and bass. A women's choir is often referred to as an *SSA choir* because it includes first and second sopranos and altos. If the music is composed for two sections of sopranos and two of altos, it is called an *SSAA choir*. A men's ensemble is often referred to as *TTBB* for first and second tenors and two basses. We discuss different types of solo singing styles in later chapters.

Stringed Instruments

Stringed instruments can be played by plucking, striking, or bowing the strings. The earliest stringed instruments were plucked or struck, but the sound of a plucked or struck string decays (softens and fades) very quickly. The invention of the bow allowed the instruments to sustain their sound and play smooth and connected melodies. Strings can be made of gut (animal intestines that are dried and twisted), silk, plastic, nylon, metal, or metal wound around nylon centers. Each type of material produces its own distinctive tone quality. Some materials lend themselves to plucking or striking, and others to bowing. Silk, plastic, and nylon are so smooth that they do not catch the hairs of the bow very well and therefore are more commonly found on plucked or struck stringed instruments. Gut and metal-wound strings tend to be used for bowed instruments.

Plucked Stringed Instruments

Prior to 1750, the most popular plucked stringed instruments included the *lute* (a halved-pear or bowl-shaped body with a fingerboard), *psaltery* (a flat wooden box with strings across it that were either plucked or struck with hammers, much like the *hammered dulcimer* still in use today), and the *harp* (strings stretched across a triangular frame). All of these instruments were small enough to be held in the lap of an individual player, and they all sounded at a very soft dynamic level. They were used to accompany solo singers, to play in small instrumental ensembles, or to take part in mixed **consorts** (groups of different types of instruments playing together).

Today, the most common plucked stringed instruments are the guitar and the harp. They can be played both as solo instruments and in ensembles.

Guitar—the acoustic guitar has a figure 8-shaped hollow body and a fingerboard. Electric guitars can have hollow or solid bodies in various shapes.

Harp—strings are stretched across a triangular frame with a hollow side to resonate the sound. Harps are often used as part of an orchestra.

The harp

Bowed Stringed Instruments

Three families of bowed stringed instruments were in common use before 1750: the *viol* family (with fat bodies, flat backs, and fingerboards), the *rebec* family (bowl-shaped body with a fingerboard), and the *violin* family (thinner body with a shaped back and a fingerboard). The word *family* is used for each of these types of instruments because they were made in many sizes. The same names we use for voices are used to describe the pitch range of the instruments: soprano, alto, tenor, and bass. A viol consort (group of instruments of the same type, in this case, viols) might include a soprano viol, an alto viol, a tenor viol, and a bass viol.

Of these three historical bowed stringed families, the violin family is most commonly used today. From highest to lowest in pitch range, the bowed stringed instruments include the following:

Violin—the neck is held with the left hand, and the tail rests beneath the player's chin.

Viola—held in the same way as the violin, but it is larger and produces a lower and somewhat more somber tone quality.

Cello—much larger and deeper sounding than the violin or viola, played upright with the body held between the player's knees.

Double bass—also called a *string bass,* the largest and lowest-pitched member of the family. Because of its size, the player sits on a stool or stands upright.

These instruments are called *bowed* because their strings are normally played by drawing a bow (a stick with horsehair, which has tiny barbs that catch the string being bowed, attached at both ends) across the string or strings. They can also be plucked by the player's finger, a technique called **pizzicato.** For special effects, they can even be played by striking the strings with the bow, but that is rather rare.

A variety of musical effects can be achieved by using different bowing techniques:

legato—smooth and connected up-and-down strokes of the bow

staccato—short and detached strokes of the bow

tremolo—fast, repeated notes played by very rapid strokes of the bow

The tone quality of each instrument can be made richer or warmer by the use of **vibrato:** rapid vibration of the left hand while pressing the string against the fingerboard. A subdued, velvety tone is

The double bass

The violin

The cello

produced by the use of a **mute,** a device clamped onto the bridge (across which the strings are stretched) to soften the sound.

Woodwinds

Woodwind instruments produce sound when air is blown through the tubelike body of the instrument. The length of the vibrating air column is controlled by opening or closing small holes along the side of the instrument with fingers or pads activated by a key mechanism. In closing or opening the *finger holes,* the player lengthens or shortens the air column, thereby lowering or raising the pitch of the notes produced.

Woodwind instruments in common use before 1750 had few, if any, keys. They included the *transverse flute* (side blown), the *recorder* (a whistle-type instrument blown from the mouthpiece at the end), and instruments such as the *crumhorn, shawm,* and *bagpipes,* often called "the buzzys" because they had double reeds that buzzed against each other, creating a slightly nasal tone quality. Bagpipes also have an air bag and a pipe that plays a continuous note while the other pipes play melodies. That continuous note is called a **drone.** You might think of bagpipes as purely Scottish, but they were in common use all over Europe during the Medieval and Renaissance periods.

The following woodwind instruments are used in modern orchestras:

Piccolo—a small, high-pitched flute.

Flute—side blown and made out of metal, although early flutes were made from wood.

Oboe—played with a double reed of two pieces of thin cane that vibrate against the player's lips.

Clarinet—end blown with a single reed on the mouthpiece.

English horn—a lower-pitched version of the oboe.

Bassoon—also a double-reed instrument, but bigger and lower pitched than the oboe or English horn.

Bass clarinet—a larger and lower-pitched clarinet.

Contrabassoon—a larger and lower-pitched bassoon.

The **saxophone** was invented in the mid-nineteenth century by Adolphe Sax (1814–1894) of Brussels. Although it is made of metal and does not look like a woodwind instrument, a single-reed mouthpiece places it in the woodwind family.

The flute

The clarinet

The bassoon

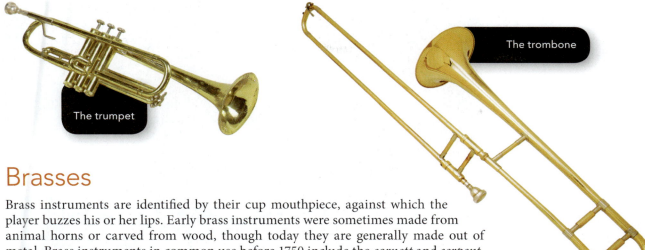

The trumpet

The trombone

Brasses

Brass instruments are identified by their cup mouthpiece, against which the player buzzes his or her lips. Early brass instruments were sometimes made from animal horns or carved from wood, though today they are generally made out of metal. Brass instruments in common use before 1750 include the *cornett* and *serpent,* both of which were carved out of wood and covered with black leather. Metal brass instruments of early times included the *trumpet, slide trumpet,* and the *sacbut.* The valves (a set of keys that open or close parts of the instrument's tubing, allowing for easy changes from note to note) we see on many brass instruments today were not invented until 1815. Players of early brass instruments changed notes by adjusting the tension of their lips against the mouthpiece, although they could also cover and open finger holes to help adjust pitches. Players of the slide trumpet and the sacbut changed notes by moving a slide that effectively shortened or lengthened the instrument, thereby raising or lowering the pitch of the note being played.

Brass instruments in common use today include the following (from highest to lowest pitched):

Trumpet—the modern trumpet uses valves to move from note to note.

French horn—the modern horn also uses valves to change notes.

Trombone—a slide is used to change notes by adjusting the length of tubing.

Tuba—a very large and low-pitched instrument that uses valves to change notes.

Other brass instruments, such as the *cornet* (similar to the trumpet) and the *euphonium* (of the tuba family) are used in both concert and marching bands. Both the trumpet and trombone are popular jazz instruments.

Percussion Instruments

Whereas the stringed, woodwind, and brass instruments we have discussed have become standard members of the modern symphony orchestra, percussion instruments—those that produce sounds when struck, shaken, or scraped—vary greatly from ensemble to ensemble and from composition to composition. Essentially, percussion instruments fall into two categories: those that produce *definite* pitch or pitches and those that produce a sound without a definite pitch.

Percussion instruments in common use before 1750 included *bells, cymbals* (two metal discs that are hit against each other), *triangles, nakers* (two drums tied around the player's waist and hit with sticks), the *tabor* (a single drum), and *timpani* (large kettle-shaped drums). Of those, the bells, cymbals, and triangles were made of metal. Bells often came in sets of different sizes and produced definite pitches, which meant that they could be used to play melodies. Cymbals and triangles had no definite pitch. Nakers, the tabor, and timpani were drums with animal skins stretched and tightened across them. Nakers and the tabor were not tuned to any particular pitch, although they could produce high or low tones depending on their size. A small naker would

The percussion section of a youth orchestra

sound higher than a larger one. Timpani had screws around the edges that allowed the player to tighten or loosen the drum head in order to raise or lower its pitch, making it one of the few early drums that produced a definite pitch.

The most common percussion instruments found in a modern orchestra belong to two categories: those of definite pitch and those of indefinite pitch.

Definite Pitch

Timpani—also known as *kettledrums.* Usually found in sets of two to five drums of varying sizes. Modern timpani are tuned by pedals that are easier to adjust than were screws.

Glockenspiel—two rows of steel bars, each producing a definite pitch. A crisp bell-like sound is produced by striking the bars with mallets (sticks with padded tips).

Celesta—a glockenspiel with a keyboard that makes it look something like a small upright piano.

Xylophone—made of tuned wooden bars that produce a hollow sound when struck by mallets.

Marimba—a xylophone with resonators under each bar of the instrument.

Chimes—a set of tuned metal tubes suspended vertically in a frame. They are played with one or two mallets, and their sound resembles that of church bells.

The *vibraphone* has metal bars arranged similarly to the keyboard of a piano and an electrical mechanism that produces the instrument's characteristic vibrato (fluctuation of pitch) effect. Vibraphones are popular in jazz but are not common orchestral instruments.

Indefinite Pitch

Percussion instruments of indefinite pitch include just about anything that can be struck, scraped, or manipulated in some other fashion to produce a sound. Those used most commonly today include the following:

Bass drum—a large, deep-sounding drum with two heads.

Side (or **snare**) **drum**—a drum that has two heads. The top head is hit with sticks; the bottom head is rigged with metal wires that vibrate against it when the top head is struck.

Tambourine—a circular wooden frame, usually with a single head, and metal discs that jingle when the instrument is shaken or struck.

Triangle—a triangle made of a bent metal rod, struck with a metal beater.

Cymbals—metal discs that ring when they are hit against one another.

Gong—also called a *tam-tam,* usually a large suspended metal disc that is struck with a padded mallet.

Tom-toms—cylindrical drums with two heads but no snares. Tom-toms are made in many sizes and are played with sticks, mallets, and brushes for different effects.

Bongos—a pair of attached small drums, each with one head, played with the hands.

Congas—a tall drum with a single head played with the hands.

Percussionists in modern orchestras also have a host of handheld instruments such as the *cowbell,* the *ratchet, sleigh bells,* the *whip* (two pieces of wood that sound like a whip when hit against each other), *castanets,* and many others. Some of these instruments have sounds that relate to familiar images, such as sleigh bells for music depicting a winter scene or castanets to create a Spanish character.

Keyboard Instruments

Keyboard instruments are played with the hands and can produce many notes at one time. They function well as both solo and accompaniment instruments because they can play both melodies and chords. Several types of keyboard instruments were in use before 1750. One type had strings that were plucked, struck, or even bowed when the player pushed the keys, and another had pipes through which wind blew when the player opened them by pushing the keys. Those whose strings were plucked belonged to the *clavier* family, including

The harpsichord

The piano

the *harpsichord* and the *virginal*. The *clavichord* was a small, soft-sounding keyboard instrument that had metal tangents to strike the strings. The *hurdy-gurdy*'s strings were bowed by a wooden wheel that the player cranked with one hand while playing a keyboard with the other. It also had drone strings that played without the keyboard, giving it an almost bagpipe-like sound.

Keyboard instruments with pipes fall into the general category of *organs*. Organs had bellows to push air through the pipes in much the same way that wind players blew into their flutes, oboes, or other instruments to produce sound. Organs varied greatly in size. Little portative (portable) organs had short keyboards that the player played with one hand while pumping the bellows with the other. The large organs we find in churches often have many sets of pipes and consequently make a great variety of sounds available to the player. Some organ pipes even have double reeds, giving them a buzzy tone quality.

The most common keyboard instruments in use today are the piano and the organ:

Piano—a keyboard instrument developed during the mid-eighteenth century. Hammers hit the strings when the keyboard is played. The hammer mechanism allows the player to vary the dynamic level of the music. It was originally called a *fortepiano* or a *pianoforte*; both terms refer to the dynamic levels of *piano* (soft) and *forte* (loud).

Organ—originally wind instruments played with a keyboard, though today they often produce their sound electronically.

Electronic Instruments

One of the most powerful and far-reaching forces in music during the twentieth century was the application of electronics to the performance, reproduction, and creation of sound. Electronic instruments fall into two general categories: (1) instruments that produce acoustic sounds that are modified electronically and (2) instruments that generate sounds using electronics. Some acoustic instruments that are often electronically modified include guitars, keyboards, and woodwinds.

Electronics are used both to modify the tone quality of the instruments and to make them louder. The tone can be altered by pushing the sound through an amplifier that adds qualities such as vibrato or fuzztone to the sound. The wah-wah pedal, used to give music an undulating dynamic, became popular during the 1960s.

There were obviously no electronic instruments before 1750; however, the first electronic instrument was invented much earlier than you might think. In 1860, Hermann Ludwig Ferdinand von Helmholtz (1821–1894), a German physicist, invented the Helmholtz Resonator, which used electromagnetically vibrating metal resonating spheres to produce complex sounds. The Helmholtz Resonator was followed by other inventions, including a tone wheel in which a disc rotating through a magnetic field created a tone. The tone wheel principally influenced the development of the Hammond organ in the 1950s.

A vacuum tube capable of amplifying radio signals was invented in 1906. This not only made radio broadcasting possible but also was used in early televisions and computers. Vacuum tubes are still sometimes used to transmit extremely high frequencies, and some audiophiles still prefer the sound of amplifiers with vacuum tubes to solid-state circuitry. The transistor, which can be used for amplifying as well as generating sounds, was invented in 1947. Small transistor radios became widely popular in the early 1960s. Transistors allowed for the invention of several types of music **synthesizers.** A synthesizer can imitate natural acoustic sounds, or it can design new sounds. Some early synthesizers were played by keyboards and others by touch-sensitive contact pads. The earliest synthesizers could produce only one note at a time, so it took the mixing of several recordings to produce music with full chords or multiple melodies.

Much electronic music is recorded—rather than played live—because composers like to experiment with various sounds and then mix the ones they want to create the final composition. In recent years, composers have used computers to create just about any sound or effect they desire. Those sounds can imitate the tone qualities of natural acoustic instruments, or they can create completely new combinations of sounds.

Instruments in Non-Western Cultures

When we discuss instruments used in non-Western cultures, we generally categorize them differently from those used in Western cultures. For example, instead of dividing the two groups of woodwind and brass, we put all non-Western wind instruments into one category. We also do not separate percussion instruments into pitched and nonpitched groups. The following categories are generally used in discussions of non-Western instruments:

Chordophones—all stringed instruments, including those that are plucked, struck, or bowed.

Aerophones—wind instruments of all kinds.

Idiophones—solid instruments that are hit, struck together, shaken, scraped, rubbed, or have a hard extension (such as a piece of metal attached to the instrument) that is plucked to produce their sounds.

Membranophones—drums that produce their sounds by the vibration of a membrane that is stretched across all or part of the instrument.

The music of non-Western cultures is a study in itself. In this book, we discuss non-Western music as it influenced Western music of the twentieth century, when music and instruments from several non-Western cultures became an important source of new ideas for Western composers.

Instrumental Ensembles

Chamber Ensembles

Chamber music is a general term for small groups of instruments in which each musician plays his or her own part. Chamber groups are small enough for the players to hear one another, so they do not need a conductor to keep them together. There are many different names for chamber groups; some names give a clear indication of the instruments in the group, and others do not. A *string quartet,* for example, is a group of four players of bowed stringed instruments, but a *piano trio* is not necessarily composed of three pianos, although it might be. Usually a piano trio is made up of one violin, one cello, and one piano. A much more complete discussion about chamber music is presented in Chapter 13, in which we listen to a movement from a string quartet by the classical composer Joseph Haydn.

The Orchestra

An **orchestra** is a group of instruments from different families. The orchestra began to develop during the seventeenth century, when several bowed stringed instruments played together with whatever woodwind and/or brass instruments the composer chose to include. These early orchestras usually made use of a keyboard instrument such as a harpsichord or an organ.

In the middle of the eighteenth century, the orchestra became more standardized. The strings remained dominant, but the woodwind and brass instruments took on an

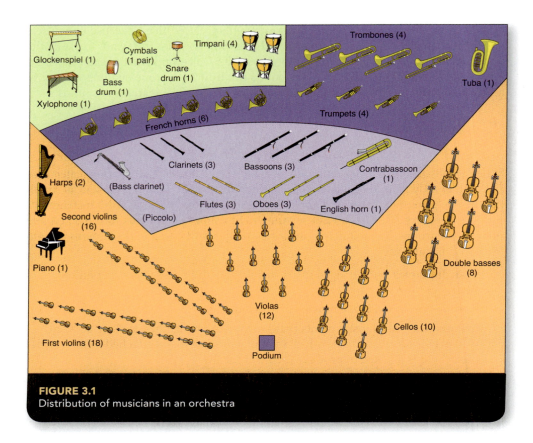

FIGURE 3.1
Distribution of musicians in an orchestra

increasingly important role. Timpani were also added, often to play in support of the majestic-sounding brass instruments.

In the early nineteenth century, many inventions helped to expand the range of woodwind and brass instruments and make them easier to play in tune. By the second half of the nineteenth century, the orchestra had grown extensively in both size and makeup and included many more percussion instruments than it had in past centuries. Today's symphony orchestra consists of a nucleus of as many as one hundred players, with additions and subtractions made to suit the requirements of individual pieces. The players are distributed according to the plan in Figure 3.1.

The Wind Ensemble

Wind ensembles (also called *concert bands* or *symphonic bands*) are made up primarily of woodwind, brass, and percussion instruments. The only bowed string instrument used in most wind ensembles is the double bass. Although a great body of music has been composed expressly for wind ensembles, much orchestral music has also been arranged to be played by wind ensembles. It can be quite interesting to hear the same piece played by an orchestra and then by a wind ensemble.

The Conductor

Large ensembles such as orchestras, wind ensembles, and choruses require the leadership of a **conductor.** Standing in front of the musicians, usually on a podium, the conductor directs the ensemble and is responsible for all aspects of the performance. The craft of conducting is a complex one, and conducting techniques and styles are highly individual and vary widely. In general, the conductor's right hand indicates the tempo and basic metrical structure of the music. With the left hand, the conductor cues the entrances of instruments, guides the shadings or dynamics, and indicates other nuances involving the expressive character of the music.

Summary

In this chapter we have discussed the types of instruments we will be hearing in the musical discussions to follow. Instruments are categorized by families or types according to the ways in which they produce their sound. Common families include stringed instruments (both plucked and bowed), woodwinds, brasses, percussion (both pitched and unpitched), keyboard, and electronic. Voices are categorized by their vocal ranges, from high voices to low. These ranges include soprano, mezzo soprano, alto, tenor, baritone, and bass.

A great number of combinations and groupings are common with both instrumental and vocal music. Chamber ensembles include trios, quartets, and a number of other small groups, with usually one voice or instrument assigned to a part. Larger groupings, such as the orchestra, wind ensemble, or chorus, often have several voices or instruments performing a single part.

New Concepts

aerophones, 25

alto, 18

baritone, 18

bass, 18

bass clarinet, 20

bass drum, 23

bassoon, 20

bongos, 23

celesta, 22

cello, 19

chamber music, 25

chimes, 22

choir, 18

chordophones, 25

clarinet, 20

conductor, 26

congas, 23

consort, 18

contrabassoon, 20

cymbals, 23

double bass, 19

drone, 20

English horn, 20

flute, 20

French horn, 21

glockenspiel, 22

gong, 23

guitar, 18

harp, 18

idiophones, 25

legato, 19

marimba, 22

membranophones, 25

mezzo soprano, 18

mute, 20

oboe, 20

orchestra, 25

organ, 24

piano, 24

piccolo, 20

pizzicato, 19

saxophone, 20

side (snare) drum, 23

soprano, 18

staccato, 19

synthesizer, 24

tambourine, 23

tenor, 18

timpani, 22

tom-toms, 23

tremolo, 19

triangle, 23

trombone, 21

trumpet, 21

tuba, 21

vibrato, 19

viola, 19

violin, 19

wind ensemble, 26

xylophone, 22

Prelude

The Culture of Medieval Europe

The Medieval Period (476–1450)

The medieval period (the Middle Ages) in music history lasted about one thousand years and served as a bridge between the ancient and modern worlds in Europe. One of the ancient cultures that had a great deal of influence on the modern world was that of classical Greece (fifth century BCE). The Greeks idealized the human body in their artworks, as seen in the statue of *Poseidon*. They also stimulated independent thought through philosophical writings and plays and encouraged citizens to develop athletic skills through participation in the Olympic games. Rome conquered Greece in 146 BCE and made much of Greek culture part of its own, as you can see in the Roman copy of a Greek sculpture of *The Apollo Belvedere*.

After the fall of the Roman Empire in 476 CE, the Christian church gained power. Throughout the medieval period, Europeans followed church doctrine that encouraged them to concentrate on living for the afterlife instead of celebrating their lives and experiences on earth. *Madonna Enthroned* by Cimabue illustrates this new focus. This cultural shift came full circle with the invention of the printing press with movable type in 1450, which made books less expensive and spread literacy and independent thought to more Europeans. A new attitude about life resembling that of the ancient Greeks resulted, ending the medieval period and ushering in the modern world.

The fifth century might seem terribly late to begin a study of the history of music when one considers how many songs and musical instruments are mentioned in the Old Testament of the Bible and other writings from ancient times. Certainly, many artworks from ancient Greece are full of portrayals of people singing, playing, and dancing to music. The Greeks studied music as a science, and some, such as Plato, thought that music controlled people's moods. The reason our detailed study of music is skipping all of this ancient history and beginning with the medieval period is that we cannot read the limited types of music notation from those periods and, therefore, do not know for certain what the music sounded like. The notation we can read developed around the twelfth century, and that is the music with which we will begin our study.

Medieval Culture

Once Christianity was accepted by Roman leaders, it began to spread across the massive expanse of land that was to become Europe. Church monasteries, particularly before the development of towns in the twelfth century, were the principal patrons of art and architecture. They were the vehicles for the preservation of literacy and of great literary works. In the monasteries, music became inextricably tied to important written works. Music in the form of liturgical chants was used in the recitation of religious texts, and monks composed new music for feast days. Books of these texts were copied by hand. Music notation was developed in order to preserve the traditional chants and distribute

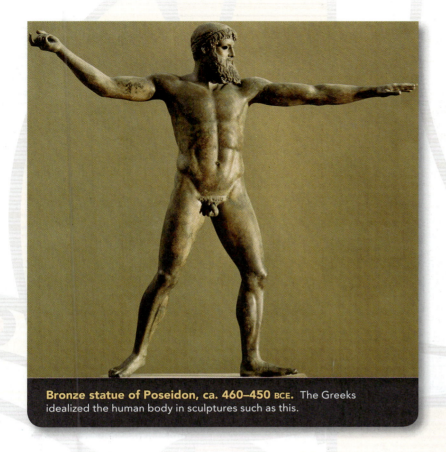

Bronze statue of Poseidon, ca. 460–450 BCE. The Greeks idealized the human body in sculptures such as this.

The Apollo Belvedere. This Roman copy of a Greek sculpture idealized the human form.

them to new monasteries in distant places. See a page of medieval chant notation from the Squarcialupi Codex on page 32.

Between the seventh and twelfth centuries, Europe turned into a mosaic of self-sufficient farms and manors that were controlled by secular lords or by the church. Most people worked on land under the protection of the lord or church, and the goods they produced were shared by the other workers and the protectors. Mobility was difficult, and people would generally live their lives never traveling beyond the area in which they were born.

By the eleventh and twelfth centuries, interregional trade became more common. Villages developed into towns and cities, and major universities were established at Paris and Bologna. Bishops, using cities as administrative centers for a wealthy and powerful church, built great cathedrals that in the later medieval period replaced monasteries as the focal buildings of Europe.

Artists generally considered that their abilities or achievements were a gift from God, and most did not sign their works for that reason. In many cases we have names of composers only because church records indicate the name of the person who was employed to write music around the time a piece was composed. Artists, including composers, created their works out of devotion to God, not to draw attention to themselves. This intention is clear in the art of the period. Look again at the painting of *Madonna Enthroned*. Notice the stiff portrayal of Mary and the rigid, even adult, look of the Christ child. As was often the case, religious figures are shown with large, unrealistic gold halos around their heads—more symbolic than natural looking.

Few people outside of the church had learned to read because hand-copied books of text, and music as well, were both difficult and expensive to obtain. Music was sung from large, shared books of chant notation and sung by members of the clergy. The congregations did not take part in the singing.

Once most people settled in towns and cities, they could practice trades and exchange goods with one another, making them more independent than people had been in the early part of the period. Men

Madonna Enthroned by Cimabue (1240–1302). The stiff formality of this painting makes it more symbolic than realistic.

were generally in charge of families, and most community and church leaders were male. Marriages were arranged by parents. The oldest male child in a family would often grow up to inherit what his parents owned, and other children would have to begin their own careers or dedicate their lives to the church. Women were trained to do jobs such as spinning, weaving, dyeing, and sewing. They also spent many hours preparing and preserving food. Women were not necessarily limited to such duties, however. They were able to own and run businesses, manage estates, and, if they could afford it, be educated. Although only men performed in plays or musical presentations in public, many men and women wrote poetry and songs to play and sing for their own or their friends' or families' enjoyment in their homes.

Some women chose, or their fathers chose for them, lives dedicated to the church and joined convents. The musical activities of women were somewhat restricted because of biblical verses that commanded that women be silent in church. (The sources for that view can be found in 1 Corinthians 14:34–35 and 1 Timothy 2:11–12.) Accordingly, the big city cathedrals were off-limits to women as far as music making was concerned. Convents were bound by different rules, however, and women were both composers and active participants in musical services.

In our study of the medieval period, we will listen to examples of both secular and sacred music.

Sumer is icumen in,
Lhude sing cuccu!
(Modern English: "Summer
is coming in, loudly sings
the Cuckoo!")

—ANONYMOUS SONG TEXT (CA. 1250)

Medieval Music

))) **First Hearing**

CONNECT   **CD 1: Track 1**

Listen to the recording of "Viderunt omnes" ("All Have Seen"), beginning section, by Léonin and take notes on what you hear. Even if you are working with other students in a paired or group listening session, keep your own notes. Give some attention to the following:

- Can you tap your foot to a steady beat in the music, or does the music seem not to have a regular beat? Is there any sense of meter at all? If so, what is the meter? Does it change near the end of the composition? How does the rhythmic flow change?

- How many melodies can you hear being sung at the same time? Does the number change near the end?

- In the first section, you should hear one melody moving faster than the other. Which moves faster—the high one or the low one? How would you describe the movement of the faster melody?

- Does the piece have a general mood that might give you a hint about the situation in which it was performed? What might that situation be?

- Can you determine the language of the text?

Keep your notes from this First Hearing to compare with your impressions about the piece after you study the information in this chapter.

4

Medieval Sacred Music

As the early Christian church grew, music played a major role in its ceremonies, and the body of music developed to accompany religious rites expanded enormously. At first, this music was not written down but was passed on by oral tradition to the monks, priests, and nuns of succeeding generations.

Pope Gregory I, who ruled as pope from 590 to 604, is generally credited for having ordered the simplification and cataloging of music assigned to specific celebrations in the church calendar. Many experts in medieval music today believe that it was really Pope Gregory II, who ruled from 715 to 731, who deserves this credit. Regardless of which pope really made the order, this decree resulted in the development of a standardized system of musical notation and the preservation of one of the greatest bodies of musical literature in the history of Western civilization. We call this music **Gregorian chant.**

A page of medieval chant with decorations from the Squarcialupi Codex, Italy, fourteenth century CE

Gregorian Chant

The chants, also known as *plainsong* or *plainchant,* are monophonic in texture (single-line melodies). Their texts are in Latin, and many are derived from the Bible, particularly the Book of Psalms.

The rhythm of the chants is unmeasured (non-metric, no regular pattern of beats or accents), and the tempos are flexible. The melodic material is based on a system of scales now referred to as *church modes.* They are similar to the major and minor scales used today, but their half steps fall in different places so that they do not express as strong a tonic (tonal center) as do today's scales. If one plays only on the white keys of the piano, the major scale goes from C to C and the natural minor scale from A to A. Other modes used in the Middle Ages can be played by going from D to D, from E to E, from F to F, and so on.

The chant melodies achieve their aesthetic beauty with the most modest means. They have an undulating, wavelike quality and a simplicity that is wholly in keeping with their religious intent as a functional part of worship. Generally, chant melodies follow the implied inflections of the text, with its stressed and unstressed syllables.

"Salve, Regina" is a chant that was sung as part of vespers (evening worship). The first line of both the medieval notation of the chant and a modern transcription are included here, along with a recording of that part of the chant. It is not necessary to be able to read the music as a performer would; simply follow the text and watch the notes go higher or lower as you hear them in the recording. The medieval notation is different in many ways from the modern notation, but you might be able to see how the two examples follow the same melody. The point is that, by this time in the medieval period, music notation had developed enough that we can be fairly certain about how the music sounded.

As mentioned in the Prelude, the composers of most Gregorian chants, such as the one we will now hear, are unknown. Such composers wrote to glorify God and considered their authorship unimportant.

CONNECT CD 4: Track 1

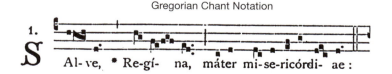

Gregorian Chant Notation

1.
S Al-ve, * Re-gí- na, máter mi-se-ricórdi- ae:

Gregorian and modern notation

Modern Transcription

Ant.
1.

Sal - ve, *Re-gi - na, — ma-ter mi-se-ri-cor-di - ae:

CD 4: Track 2

"Dies irae" ("Day of Wrath"), beginning section ANONYMOUS

Date: Medieval period, date not certain

Genre: Gregorian chant

Texture: Monophonic

Voices: A small group of men sing the chant in our recording. The chant could also have been sung by all boys or men and boys together or alternating with one another. Notice the pure vowel sounds ("ah," "eh," "ee," "aw," "oo") that are emphasized in the Latin language.

Language: Latin

Meter: Nonmetric

Duration: 1:12

Context: The beginning of this particular chant melody has traditionally represented death and is often quoted in compositions for or about the dead.

	Timing	Latin text	English translation
2	0:00	Dies irae, dies illa,	The day of wrath, that day
		solvet saeclum in favilla,	which will reduce the world to ashes,
		teste David cum Sibylla.	as foretold by David and the Sibyl.
	0:16	Quantus tremor est futurus,	What terror there will be,
		quando iudes est venturus,	when the Lord will come,
		cuncta stricte discussurus.	to judge all strictly.
	0:34	Tuba, mirum spargens sonum	The trumpet, scattering a wondrous sound
		per sepulcra reionum,	among the graves of all the regions,
		coget omnes ante thronum.	will assemble all before the Throne.
	0:53	Mors stupebit et natura,	Death and nature will be stupefied,
		cum resurget creatura,	when again all creation will rise,
		judicanti responsura.	to answer to the judge.
	1:12		The recording fades out.

Hildegard of Bingen

As discussed in the Prelude, the medieval church followed biblical instructions and required women to be silent in the cathedrals. In convents, however, where there were only women, they were often involved in musical activities. One of the best known of the female composers of sacred music in the medieval period was **Hildegard of Bingen** (1098–1179).

Hildegard was the tenth child born of noble parents in a small village near Rheinhessen, Germany. When she was 8 years old, she was given to the Church to be raised and educated. She became a Benedictine nun at 15, and the nuns elected her abbess of the convent when she was 38. After eleven years in that position, Hildegard moved herself and her nuns to a new convent in Bingen, Germany. From that place she became known as Hildegard of Bingen.

Throughout her life she claimed to have received visions that gave her insights from God. She began to write about her beliefs and completed the work *Scivias (Know the Ways of God)* in 1151. The book included some of the songs she had composed. It was well received by many who were able to get copies, and it gave Hildegard an opportunity to be known by and to correspond with several powerful people of her time, including the pope, King Henry II of England, and Henry's wife, Eleanor of Aquitaine. Hildegard later wrote other major works, such as *Causae et Curae (Causes and Cures),* in which she reported various medical practices and remedies used by people of her time. A cure for baldness in her book involved making a paste of ash from burned wheat and bear's fat and putting it on the bald spot. A cure for headache was a drink of sage and vinegar.

Hildegard's best-known musical works are a collection of sacred songs, *Symphonia (Symphony of the Harmony of Heavenly Revelations)* and the musical play *Ordo virtutum (Play of Virtues).* The *Play of Virtues* is the earliest complete morality play we have from the medieval period, and it must have been a fascinating production to see with Hildegard's nuns singing the roles of the virtues (Charity, Humility, Chastity, Fear of God, and so on), the soul who needs direction, and the devil who tempts the soul (a spoken role).

Hildegard's music is different in many ways from the preexisting Gregorian chant repertoire. Her melodies tend to be freer and less controlled in range from high to low notes. They are still, however, monophonic and are written with unmeasured rhythms. In modern performances of her music, instrumentalists often add accompaniments to her songs.

On her death at age 81, Hildegard's followers considered her a saint and applied to the pope for her canonization. No official documents were ever filed, but she is still thought of by many in modern Germany as Saint Hildegard. "MusiCurious: Medieval Nuns' Daily Lives" describes what Hildegard's life might have been like.

HILDEGARD OF BINGEN
(1098–1179)

- Born near Rheinhessen, Germany; died at age 81 in Bingen, Germany.

- Founder and abbess of her convent in Bingen.

- Author of *Scivias (Know the Ways of God), Causae et Curae (Causes and Cures), Ordo virtutum (Play of Virtues),* and composer of many sacred songs.

 **Listening Guide**

 CONNECT CD 4: Track 3

"O pastor animarum" ("Shepherd of Souls") HILDEGARD OF BINGEN

Date: ca. 1150

Genre: Sacred song

Texture: Monophonic

Voices: One female singer

Language: Latin

Meter: Nonmetric

Duration: 1:17

Context: This would have been sung by a nun in Hildegard's convent. The wide leaps in the melody are typical of Hildegard's style. In Gregorian and other medieval chants and songs, it was more common for notes to flow from one to another nearby on the mode or scale.

	Latin text	English translation	Musical events

3	O pastor animarum, et
	   o prima vox
	perquam omnes create
	   sumus,
	nunc tibi, tibi placeat,
	ut digneris nos liberare
	de miseries et languoribus
	   nostris.
		Shepherd of souls, and first
		   voice
		through which we were all
		   created,
		may it now please you
		to deign to free us
		from our miseries and
		   feebleness.
			Melody uses wide
			leaps, and the rhythmic
			flow is quite free and
			fitting to the text.

MusiCurious

MEDIEVAL NUNS' DAILY LIVES

What was it like to be a nun in medieval times?

It was not fun. Nuns' days were long. Church services began as early as two o'clock in the morning. Services were followed by work and other religious duties until the final church service at sundown. Nuns usually received only one meal a day. Some nuns worked in convent fields planting, caring for, and harvesting fruit, vegetables, grains, and herbs for food and medicines. Other nuns, usually ones who were from wealthy families who had given the convent valuable donations, were able to avoid that hard physical work and, instead, spend time studying and writing.

Were the nuns locked in the convent, or could they freely go out into the world?

Basically, locked. Nuns were closed off from the rest of the world. Church law did not allow nuns to travel outside the convent, but a few nuns such as Hildegard of Bingen got around that restriction. At least once, she traveled to some nearby cities to preach. For the most part convents were places for the nuns to live, be educated, and worship God. The books that were available were treasured because books had to be hand-copied. Many nuns learned to read and write even though the general public was mostly illiterate. Other than written communication, the nuns generally had little contact with other people.

Could anyone from outside the convent visit the nuns?

No. Male priests would visit the convents to preside during celebrations of the Mass, and people who were sick or hungry were sometimes let in to be cared for. Otherwise, the nuns were self-sufficient. In addition to gardening, they made their clothing, decorated church tapestries, and copied books. Like their male counterparts in monasteries, the nuns took vows of poverty, chastity, and obedience.

What could nuns do to entertain themselves?

Not much. Women were not allowed to sing in the cathedrals that were open to the public, but convents had their own churches in which nuns sang during the services. There were no congregations of believers to hear the nuns singing. The nuns sang directly to God. Hildegard's *Ordo virtutum (Play of Virtues)* was probably performed as part of a celebration, perhaps even the opening of a new convent, and might also have been performed before or after a Mass. A visiting priest would have spoken the role of the devil in the play while the nuns sang their parts.

Why did girls become nuns?

For various reasons. Some girls who entered chose to devote their lives to God, but many were children given to convents by their parents as Hildegard of Bingen was. Even a woman who had been widowed and who did not want to live the rest of her life alone could enter a convent and become a nun.

Throughout the medieval period and into modern times, convents have been an important part of the church and an option for women wanting to devote their lives to the service of God.

The Mass

The **Mass** is the most solemn service of the medieval Christian church. It is the commemoration and symbolic reenactment of the Last Supper of Christ. The **liturgy** of the Mass, the prescribed ceremony, is divided into two parts: the **Ordinary** (using those texts that do not change from day to day) and the **Proper** (using those texts that vary according to the religious nature of the specific day in the church year). The Mass service combines and sometimes alternates items from the Ordinary and the Proper. An outline of a full Mass follows.

The Order for Performance of the Mass

As you read the sections of the Mass, from top to bottom, notice that the texts of the Ordinary, the ones for which composers wrote new music, are interspersed among the sections of the Proper. In a concert performance of a Mass, it is only the Ordinary that is performed.

Ordinary (same texts at each service)	**Proper** (texts that changed according to the calendar)
	Introit (Processional)
Kyrie (Lord have mercy on us)	
Gloria (Glory to God . . .)	
	Collect (Prayer)
	Epistle (from New Testament)
	Gradual (from biblical Psalms)
	Alleluia/Tract (expression of joy or penitence, depending on the season)
	Sequence (a hymn, or religious song)
	Gospel (from New Testament)
Credo (I/we believe in one God . . .)	
	Offertory (bread and wine offered to God and offerings collected)
Sanctus (Holy, Holy, Holy . . .)	
Agnus Dei (Lamb of God . . .)	
	Communion (service of the bread and wine)
	Ite missa est (congregation is dismissed)

Composers who wrote music for the Mass generally wrote music to be sung to the texts from the Ordinary, because that would allow their music to be performed whenever the Mass was celebrated, regardless of the time of year. The titles of the texts from the Ordinary that came to be favored for musical settings were the Kyrie, Gloria, Credo, Sanctus, and Agnus Dei; you can make out these words as you listen to many Gregorian chants. Works based on those texts formed the first large composition to be made up of several sections, or movements. They have been a source of inspiration for many famous composers, including Bach, Mozart, Beethoven, and Stravinsky. Today, these works are more often performed in concert halls than in church services because they have become major parts of classical repertoire.

Polyphony and Measured Rhythm

Music remained monophonic and unmeasured until the tenth century, when two or more voice parts began appearing in combination. This new method of composition went through a number of stages over a long period of time. The development of polyphonic music from the twelfth to the fourteenth centuries was centered in northern France and was dominated by the Notre Dame school under the leadership first of **Léonin** (fl. ca. [flourished about] 1163–1190) and then his successor, **Pérotin** (fl. ca. 1190–1225). The earliest polyphonic (a texture with more than one melody line) works were called *organa* (singular, **organum**). This period and style is called the *Ars antiqua* (Old Art—ca. 1170–1310).

The rhythm of early organa was unmeasured, as it was just two melodies moving at the same time. Eventually, the voice parts assumed rhythmic independence. Léonin approached this by taking a preexisting chant as a low part and slowing it down into very-long-held notes. He then composed a faster-moving melody to be sung above that slow chant, so that his music was really two melodies being sung at the same time but not moving to the same rhythm pattern. For this new music, a new type of notation was developed in which the relative time values of notes in the melody were indicated with precision (measured)—a technique called *mensural notation*. Pérotin further complicated Léonin's compositions. He added two or three newly composed melodies above a slow-moving chant melody. An example of this early type of organum follows. It is assumed that Léonin composed the work we will listen to next because he was the composer in residence in Paris where the manuscript was found. Like composers of earlier sacred music, Léonin did not sign his work.

))) **Featured Listening**    **CD 1: Track 1**

"Viderunt omnes" ("All Have Seen"), beginning section LÉONIN

Date: Late twelfth century

Genre: Organum/plainchant

Texture: Two-part polyphony, then monophonic chant

Voices: Two melodies and then one, with each melody (or voice) sung by a small group of men

Language: Latin

Meter: Slight feel of triple meter in the section of two-part organum, then nonmetric chant

Duration: 2:09

Context: This work would have been performed first in the Notre Dame Cathedral in Paris on Christmas Day. The sense of triple meter would have represented the religious importance of the Trinity (Father, Son, and Holy Ghost).

	Timing	Latin text	English translation	Musical events
1	0:00	Viderunt omnes	All have seen	The high voice enters first and is joined by the much slower-moving lower one.
	1:17	fines terre Salutare dei nostril jubilate Deo omnis terra.	of the earth have seen the salvation of our God, all earth.	The text moves much faster in this section of plainchant. The rhythm is freer than it was in the first section.

The independence of simultaneous melodies that moved in different directions *melodically* and at different times *rhythmically* resulted in what became known as polyphony. Thus two major developments in Western music took place: (1) the change from monophony to polyphony and (2) the change from unmeasured, relatively free rhythm to **measured rhythm,** in which precise time values were related to each other. Polyphony and measured rhythm were fully developed in the polyphonic setting of the Mass and the motet. We discuss the motet form later in this chapter.

Guillaume de Machaut

One of the most important composers of the fourteenth century was **Guillaume de Machaut** ("Ma-show," ca. 1300–1377). His name means "William of Machaut." Machaut is a town in northern France, just northeast of Rheims. Most of the extant records about Machaut's life are connected with his education and work in Rheims, a city with a beautiful and important cathedral where much music was sung. Machaut took holy orders but never became a priest. By the end of his life he had advanced to the position of canon, a clergyman who practices the rules of the church but who has not taken the full vows of a priest and who lives outside a monastery.

Machaut was one of the most literary men of his time and was employed as a scribe and private secretary by several aristocrats. He also became friends and shared some of his musical compositions with the king of France, Charles V. Although we are studying Machaut's importance as a composer, he was perhaps better known in his time as a poet who wrote many poems about his work with these important men.

In addition to large quantities of secular music and motets, Machaut wrote the earliest polyphonic setting of the entire Ordinary of the Mass, *Messe de Nostre Dame (Mass of Our Lady).* Before Machaut, different composers wrote each section of a Mass, creating an inconsistent overall style. Machaut's Mass was beautifully constructed and represented the most advanced compositional techniques of his time, including four voices with more ornamentation and contrary motion than had been common in earlier three-voiced works. After you have studied the "Agnus Dei" from the Ordinary of that Mass, turn to "Hearing the Difference: 'Dies irae' and Machaut's 'Agnus Dei'." Machaut was buried in the cathedral at Rheims, where his music has often been performed.

Machaut's compositions represent the style called *Ars nova* (New Art—ca. 1310–1377), in which rhythms are more independent of the text; the expressiveness of melodies can be heard as leading into the new style of the early Renaissance. Those independent rhythms can be heard in Machaut's "Agnus Dei."

CD 4: Tracks 4–6

"Agnus Dei" ("Lamb of God") from *Messe de Nostre Dame (Mass of Our Lady)* GUILLAUME DE MACHAUT

Date: ca. 1364

Genre: Movement from Mass Ordinary

Texture: Polyphonic

Voices: Four

Meter: Triple

Duration: 3:25

Context: This would have been performed in cathedrals as part of the Mass service.

	Latin text	English translation	Musical events
4	Agnus Dei, qui tollis peccata mundi: Miserere nobis.	Lamb of God, who takest away the sins of the world: Have mercy upon us.	A section with more rhythmic motion in the upper two parts
5	Agnus Dei, qui tollis peccata mundi: Miserere nobis.	Lamb of God, who takest away the sins of the world: Have mercy upon us.	B section with new music, also most motion in upper parts
6	Agnus Dei, qui tollis peccata mundi: Dona nobis pacem.	Lamb of God, who takest away the sins of the world: Grant us peace.	Repeat of the music for the A section, but with new text at the end

Medieval Secular Music

In addition to the music of the church, the medieval period witnessed the growth of a rich tradition of **secular,** or nonreligious, music. Gregorian chants used Latin, but secular texts came to be written in the **vernacular,** or everyday, language of the country of origin. Like today's popular music, these texts often concerned the subject of love. Some texts were humorous, and some were quite bawdy; others treated political subjects or told stories of vagabonds.

The most important early secular vocal music was created and performed by poet-musicians, called **trouvères** in northern France, **troubadours** in southern France, and **minnesingers** in Germany. These poet-musicians were generally members of the nobility, even kings, who would not have performed in public but instead would have sung

 **Hearing the Difference**

"DIES IRAE" AND MACHAUT'S "AGNUS DEI"

Although we have heard both of these works before (see Listening Guides on page 33 and page 38), now we will compare them to understand the changes later composers such as Machaut made in their compositions for the Church. Answer the following questions as you listen from one work to the other:

- Does one have a more regular beat and sense of meter than the other?

- Obviously, Machaut's "Agnus Dei" has more melodies being sung at the same time than the chant does, but do those overlapping melodies help or hurt the understanding of the text? (You might need to look back at the Latin text in the Listening Guides to determine that.)

- Does the flow of the music follow the text in both examples, or does one work seem to fit the text into a predetermined beat pattern?

- Which work has repeated sections? Do those sections help give the music a sense of balance (beginning and ending sounding similar)? Does that add to your enjoyment in listening to the composition?

- Do both works seem to fit the sense of seriousness that one would expect of music performed in a church service in a medieval cathedral?

German poet-composer and minnesinger Frauenlob (ca. 1255–1318) with musicians. The instruments shown, from left to right, are a drum, a flute, a shawm (oboe), viols (viola and violin), a psaltery, and a bagpipe.

their songs to their families and friends in their own homes or at royal courts. Sometimes they would give their songs to lower-class musicians to perform in public. Those traveling street performers were called **minstrels** or **jongleurs.** Frauenlob, a German poet-composer, was a minnesinger.

The number of musical and poetic works created by these poet-musicians is enormous. The melodies of their songs, like the melodies of chant, were monophonic and simple in design. The songs mainly paired one note of music with one syllable of text, with occasional ornamental **melismas** (several notes sung to one syllable of text). In the case of the trouvères and troubadours, the form of their pieces was rather free, often including a **refrain**—a recurring line of words and its distinctive melody. Many of the songs were **strophic** in form, with each verse of text being sung to the same melody.

Improvised Accompaniment to Monophonic Songs

The song manuscripts written by medieval poet-musicians are all in monophonic notation. On the other hand, drawings, paintings, and other artistic portrayals of the time show people singing and playing instruments. Some modern performers of medieval music take the manuscripts as they are and sing the music monophonically without accompaniment. Many other modern-day performers assume that instruments originally accompanied the songs, as portrayed in medieval artworks, and add instruments to their performances. No one can be certain exactly what the instruments should play, but we do know from written descriptions of music of the time that instrumentalists did a lot of improvisation around existing melodies. Drones were popular on instruments such as the bagpipe and the hurdy-gurdy, so instruments playing dronelike long-held notes might be acceptable as accompaniments. A Listening Guide to a troubadour song with improvised accompaniment follows.

Listening Guide

CONNECT
CD 4: Track 7

"Tant m'abelis" ("So Much I Love") BERENGUIER DE PALOU

Date: Early twelfth century

Genre: Troubadour song

Form: All verses sung to same melody, but exact notes of melody vary according to text

Texture: Original song monophonic, but instruments that accompany the singer in our recording make it homophonic

Voices and Instruments: One female voice singing a text written by and for a man to sing accompanied by a harp, an oud (lute-like plucked string instrument with a fingerboard), two fiddles (early violins), a recorder, and large, deep sounding drums

Language: Medieval southern French (Langue D'oc)

Meter: Duple, but the voice sometimes sings to the rhythmic patterns of the text, not following the duple meter played by the instruments

Duration: 4:52

Context: This song is one of many troubadour songs that fit the tradition known as "courtly love," which expresses adoration from afar. The music to songs such as this one was copied and given or sold to other troubadours or even to lower-class singers such as *jongleurs* to perform, so this performance by a woman is well within that tradition. The instrumental parts have been improvised for this recording and were not part of the song that exists in medieval music notation.

Timing	Medieval southern French text	Modern English translation	Musical events
			Introduction by harp joined by oud
7 0:00	Tant m'abelis jois et amours et chans, ert alegrier deports e cortezia, que l'mon non a ricor ni manentia don mielhs d'aisso'm tengues per benanans.	So much I love joy and love and song, mirth, sport and courtesy, that in the world there is no wealth nor riches that could make me feel happier.	
0:50	Doncs, sai ieu ben que mi-dons ten las claus de totz los bes qu'ieu aten ni esper, e ren d'aiso sens lieys non puesc aver.	Therefore, I know well that my lady holds the keys of all the good that I expect and hope for, and none of this can I have without her.	Large drum enters.
1:18			Instruments joined by recorder and two fiddles for extended instrumental section; those melody instruments stop playing when the voice returns
1:48	Sa gran valors e sos humils semblans, son gen parlar e sa bella paria, m'an fait ancse voler senhoria plus que d'autra qu'lieu vis pueys ni dabans: e si'l sieu cors amoros e suatus e s amerce no'm denha retener, ja d'als amors no'm pot far mon plazer.	Her great courage and her modest look, her gentle speech and her fair company, have made me always love her dominion more than any other's I have seen before or since: and if her loving and tender heart deigns not to keep me under her mercy, Love cannot please me with anything else.	
2:18	Tan tai volgut sos bes e sos enans,	So have I wanted her good and her renown,	

(continued)

Timing	Medieval southern French text	Modern English translation	Musical events
	e dezirat lieys e sa campanhia	and so have I desired her and her company	
	que ja no cre, si lonhar m'en volia	that I believe, if she wanted me to leave her;	
	que ja partir s'en pogues mos talans;	I would never be able to part from her;	
	e s'ieu n'ai did honor, ni be ni laus,	and if I declare her honor, her good and her fame,	
	no m'en fas ges per mas-songier tener,	I could not be held to be a liar,	
	qu'ab sa valor sap ben proar mon ver.	since her worth proves my honesty.	
2:48			Recorder and fiddles join in again for an extended instrumental section.
3:16	Belha domna, corteza, benestans,	Fair lady, courteous, kind,	
	ab segur sen, ses blasme ses folhia,	of sure judgment, without blemish or folly,	
	so tot no'us vey tan soven cum volria,	although I do not see you as often as I would,	
	mos pessamens aleuja mos afans	my fancy lightens my desire	
	en que'm delieyt, e'm sojorn e'm repaus,	in which is my delight, my ease and my repose,	
	e quan no'us puesc extiers dels huelhs vezer,	and when my eyes cannot see you,	
	vey vos ades en pessan, jor e ser.	I see you in my thought, day and night.	
3:46	Sabetz per que no'm vir ni no'm balans	Do you know why I do not turn aside or hesitate	
	de vos amar, ma beha, dous'amia?	in loving you, my fair, gentle friend?	
	Quar ja no'm cal doptar, si ieu'us avia	Because if I had you, I should not fear	
	que meslessetz falsia ni enjans;	that you put forward any falsehood or deceit;	
	per qu'lieu am mais, quar sol ablirar n'aus,	for I prefer, although I only presume it,	
	que vos puscatz a mos ops eschazer	that you could some day be mine	
	qu'autra bizar, embassar ni tener.	than kiss, embrace or hold another woman.	
4:15			Recorder and fiddles join for an instrumental section.
4:31	Doncs si'eu ja'm vey dins vostres bratz enclaus	So if I ever am held in your arms	
	si qu'ambedu nos semblen d'un voler,	so that both of us are of one mind,	
	meravil me on poiria'l joy caber.	I wonder how I could contain my joy.	

Instruments not only accompanied songs but also played an important role in the accompaniment of dances. Many types of instruments were employed, including the harp, the vielle (a precursor of the modern violin), the psaltery (a kind of zither played by striking or plucking its strings), lutes, horns, drums, trumpets, a variety of wind instruments and bells, and portable organs. Medieval and Renaissance dance music is discussed in Chapter 5.

The Motet

Much as the organa had added an independent line of music to the chant, the **motet** added a second set of words (the name *motet* comes from the French word *mot*, meaning "word"). Originally a form of religious music, the motet grew out of the two-part organa in the thirteenth century. As the motet form evolved, the upper voice began to sing in the vernacular. The subject matter was usually secular. Gradually, composers added a third and even a fourth voice part. Most medieval motets were, therefore, a combination of the sacred and secular. With the original chant in Latin on the lower (or lowest) part and the secular text(s) in French above that, many of the motets were *polylingual*, or sung in multiple languages. When they had two or three parts added above the chant, those parts each had separate texts and separate rhythms, making the music *polytextual*. With two or three independent melodies being sung at the same time, motets were also polyphonic in texture.

By the fourteenth century, the motet had increased in length and had become more elaborate in its melodic and rhythmic structure. But even with the increased number of melodic lines and texts, the range of voices remained narrow, and the chant was almost always retained in some form in the lowest voice part. By the fifteenth century, the motet had evolved full circle. Once again it became primarily a religious form, using one text for all voices. The text was almost always taken from the Bible. The motets of the Renaissance developed from the late medieval motets.

Summary

Western music grew out of the religious music of the medieval period. The liturgy of the Mass is divided into the Ordinary and the Proper. The Kyrie, Gloria, Credo, Sanctus, and Agnus Dei became the parts of the Ordinary most favored for musical settings. Chants, closely allied with the Roman Catholic liturgy, were codified and compiled during the time of Pope Gregory (I or II), and a system of music notation was developed to preserve them. In the following centuries the simple, monophonic form of these chants evolved into the more complex, polyphonic forms of organa, polyphonic settings of the Mass, and the motet. The motet of the medieval period generally included secular verses in the vernacular, along with chant melodies with Latin texts.

Secular music was also developing at this time. Early vocal music was performed by trouvères in northern France, troubadours in southern France, and minnesingers in Germany. Their songs were sung in the vernacular and were sometimes quite bawdy. The songs of these poet-musicians were monophonic, but instruments were probably used to accompany them.

New People and Concepts

Gregorian chant, 31
Guillaume de Machaut, 38
Hildegard of Bingen, 33
jongleurs, 40
Léonin, 37
liturgy, 36
Mass, 36
measured rhythm, 38

melisma, 40
minnesingers, 39
minstrels, 40
motet, 43
Ordinary, 36
organum, 37
Pérotin, 37
Proper, 36

refrain, 40
secular, 39
strophic, 40
troubadours, 39
trouvères, 39
vernacular, 39

Finale

CD 1: Track 1

Listen again to the recording of "Viderunt omnes" ("All Have Seen"), beginning section, by Léonin and compare your impressions now with your notes from your First Hearing. Consider the following questions:

- The beginning section of the two-part organum with a sense of triple meter would have sounded very modern to the first people who heard this work and were used to nonmetric plainchant. What religious beliefs were supported by the triple meter?

- Past traditions return when the nonmetric flow of the chant begins. What religious beliefs were supported by the return to the old chant style?

- Is it easier to follow the text in the section of two-part organum or in the monophonic plainchant section? Might church leaders have disliked having the sound of the music overtake the understanding of the text? Why would they care about the text if the same texts were performed very often and were very familiar to the singers and the listeners?

- Given that the work would have been performed in a large cathedral of stone and stained glass, might the echo effect have enhanced the sound? Might the pure vowel sounds of the Latin language help one understand the text in that situation?

- If you were going to describe this music to a friend, what would you say?

Further Listening

Medieval Sacred Music

Other Gregorian chants and songs by Hildegard of Bingen.

Guillaume de Machaut, *Messe de Nostre Dame (Mass of Our Lady)*. Only the "Agnus Dei" of this Mass was covered in this chapter, but the entire mass is worth hearing. It is one of the earliest and best-known polyphonic settings of the Ordinary of the Mass.

Medieval Secular Music

Other troubadour, trouvère, and minnesinger songs from the medieval period are listed on the Internet, but be aware that sometimes a term like "troubadour" is used to describe modern country singers. Look for songs identified as being from the medieval period.

Medieval dance music, particularly those called *estampie*, *saltarello*, and *ductia*.

Medieval motets, particularly ones by Philippe de Vitry and Guillaume de Machaut. Some performances have only the top melody sung and the lower parts performed on instruments, which makes them sound like accompanied solo songs. The original medieval motets had all parts sung, as was described on page 43.

CHARACTERISTICS OF MEDIEVAL MUSIC

Texture	Chants and songs were monophonic; later Masses and motets employed polyphony
Tonality	Church modes
Rhythm	Chants employed unmeasured rhythm; later sacred music and secular music employed measured rhythm
Singing style	Sacred music: solemn, expressive, small voice range
	Secular music: often more rhythmic than sacred music
Large vocal works	Polyphonic Mass settings
Small vocal works	Chant, organum, motet
Musical instruments	Instruments accompanied songs and dances
Instrumental music	Dances and other secular compositions

Prelude

Although medieval Europe idealized meditative withdrawal from worldly concerns, the Renaissance (1450–1600) stressed activity and worldly excellence. *Renaissance* is the French word for "rebirth," and what was reborn in 1450 was the kind of pride in being a fully realized human being that had been common in ancient Greece. With the invention of the printing press and, in turn, the spread of literacy, education in all fields expanded. Reason began to replace faith as the intellectual norm. In the new climate, portraiture and the ideal nude—kinds of art that had vanished since the fall of Rome—again became the fashion. Look carefully at the statue of *David* by Michelangelo and notice the sense of pride in the human body and spirit it portrays. Similarly, Renaissance portrayals of the Madonna and child, such as Raphael's *Madonna del Granduca* (page 48), show the Christ child to be much more human and vulnerable than had the medieval ones.

Renaissance Culture

Interest in exploration of the world outside of Europe increased during the Renaissance, and that exploration opened up many new cultures, attitudes, and goods to Europeans. After Columbus discovered the New World, such items as coffee, tobacco, and chocolate became part of Europeans' experience. Other explorers ventured to Asia and Africa, in addition to continuing to explore the American continents. In Britain and on the continent of Europe, mail service began during the Renaissance, allowing communication over great distances.

Literacy and a well-rounded education became so important that we sometimes use the term *Renaissance man* to credit a person who is well educated and talented in many fields. The most famous historical example of such a person during the Renaissance is Leonardo da Vinci (1452–1519), who was a painter, sculptor, architect, engineer, scientist, poet, and musician.

In a different shift away from the dominance of the Roman Church, Martin Luther (1483–1546) and his followers in Germany split from the Church over claims of corruption and disagreements about doctrine. Luther ignited a firestorm of conflict in which Protestants saw themselves as individually responsible for their spiritual destinies, not subject to papal authority. John Calvin and several other religious leaders followed Luther in forming new Protestant religions that still exist today. Having lost the allegiance of so many, the Roman Catholic Church made reforms in some areas of its practices. One primary reform required composers to simplify sacred music so that the liturgical text would be better understood.

The lives of average people during the Renaissance were much like those in the late medieval period, except that increased trade and business allowed men to elevate their status and power in ways that women could not. Women lost much of the independence they had exercised during the medieval period and were seen primarily as assistants to their husbands, working alongside them to earn a living. Most women could not attain the Renaissance ideal of multiple skills because education was not as available to women. The daughters of aristocratic families learned Latin and Greek, which allowed them to read religious literature and classic texts. Some of these educated women became writers, but female artists and composers were rare.

The more worldly outlook of the Renaissance influenced the music of the period. No longer required to reflect the meditative simplicity of medieval styles, composers could develop the old religious chants into longer, more complex, multivoiced works. New secular vocal and instrumental dance music also emerged.

The printing press with movable type allowed easier reproduction of music, and printed music became more widely available. With the ability to purchase music by a variety of composers, the average educated person with no talent for composition could learn to read, sing, and play music in the company of family members and friends. Performers could make a good living by providing music

David, by Michelangelo (1475–1564). This is one of many Renaissance sculptures that display the sense of pride in the human body that we see in Greek and Roman sculptures such as *Poseidon* and *The Apollo Belvedere* (page 29).

Madonna del Granduca, by Raphael (1483–1520). Like Raphael and other Renaissance painters did in their art, Josquin des Prez depicted an idealized Virgin Mary in his music.

or dance instruction to members of wealthy families. They were also often hired to entertain at more formal parties.

The medieval focus on living primarily to glorify God and to reach the afterlife did not allow for the kinds of societal advancements that began in the Renaissance. In general, the Renaissance is considered the beginning of the modern world, because Renaissance attitudes of humanism, respect for the individual and for independent thought, and interest in learning about the world through scientific investigation led directly to the development of the sciences, arts, and philosophical concepts we have today. The Renaissance's more humanistic outlook influenced European art for the next several hundred years.

> The better the voice is, the meeter it is to honor and serve God therewith: and the voice of Man is chiefly to be employed to that end. Since singing is so good a thing, I wish all men would learn to sing.
>
> —COMPOSER WILLIAM BYRD [1543–1623]

Renaissance Music

))) First Hearing

CONNECT CD 1: Tracks 2–3

Listen to the recording of "Ave Maria" by Josquin des Prez and take notes on what you hear. Even if you are working with other students in a paired or group listening session, keep your own notes. Give some attention to the following:

- How many voice parts do you hear? They enter one at a time at the beginning, so that will help you separate them as you listen.

- Are there any instruments accompanying the voices, or is the work performed a cappella?

- Most of the work is in duple meter, but there is a section that suddenly changes to triple before the duple meter returns. Listen closely for the change to triple meter and see if you also notice both the meter change and a change of speed.

- Is the texture polyphonic, homophonic, or some of each? Which texture do you hear at the very end?

- Can you tell the language of the text? Can you guess what kind of composition it is?

Keep your notes from this First Hearing to compare with your impressions about the piece after you study the information in this chapter.

5

Renaissance Sacred Music

The Renaissance in literature and the visual arts began in the 1300s and was centered in Italy. The Renaissance in music began around 1450 in what is today northern France, Holland, and Belgium. The style that developed in these countries spread to all parts of Europe.

The composers of this northern style, sometimes referred to as *Franco-Flemish,* most often wrote music in four voices. For many of their Masses and motets, they continued to use chant melodies as one of the voices, but for the first time they did not keep the chant in the bass. They composed new bass lines and placed the chant in another voice above it. They sometimes even abandoned chant melodies altogether, creating completely new compositions. Occasionally, Renaissance composers used a secular tune as one of the voices in their religious compositions, something that composers of the medieval period would have thought inappropriate. This music is performed **a cappella,** or without instrumental accompaniment.

The polyphonic style of these Franco-Flemish composers emphasized the true independence of each of the four voices in their works. **Imitation** was common. At the beginning of "Ave Maria," you will hear imitation when a melodic fragment is stated in one voice and is then repeated, or imitated, by another voice a measure later. Each voice comes in one at a time, imitating the melody that was sung first. The imitation does not continue throughout the composition, but it creates an effective beginning that composers often used in the Renaissance.

Josquin des Prez

The composer of "Ave Maria," **Josquin des Prez** ("Joss-can de-pray," ca. 1450–1521), was one of the most influential composers of the Renaissance; his style was copied by many other composers. It is not known exactly where Josquin was born, but it is generally assumed to be in what is today northern France or Belgium. The year of his birth is sometimes given as 1450, but that date is uncertain.

Josquin was a member of the choir at the court of Duke Galeazzo Maria Sforza in Milan in 1474. When the duke was assassinated in 1476, Josquin went to Rome, where he got a job singing at the chapel of Cardinal Ascanio Sforza. While in Rome, Josquin also spent some time singing in the papal choir. In 1501 Josquin went to France and spent two years singing at the court of Louis XII. He moved on to the Italian court at Ferrara but left there after only one year to avoid an outbreak of the plague. That was a smart move on his part, because his successor died from the plague. Josquin spent his last years singing at a cathedral in Condé, France.

Throughout his life Josquin composed music and taught students while making his primary living as a singer. He was well aware of his talents and often demanded higher pay than was common for his colleagues. He did not put dates on his compositions, and his name was so well known in his own time that some other composers put his name on their works to sell them. All of this causes some confusion in the collection and evaluation of his work. Josquin left many motets, many Masses, and a considerable amount of secular music. He was also a gifted teacher, and many of his pupils became outstanding figures in the next generation of composers.

As we discussed in Chapter 4, medieval motets had a sacred Latin chant as the lowest voice with secular texts in the vernacular (everyday language) above them. In some cases, there were two or three melodies with secular texts (different texts on each part) above the sacred text. The texture was polyphonic, and a listener would have a very difficult time understanding any of the texts, particularly the sacred one. By the Renaissance, motets dropped the secular influences and became sacred, with one Latin text for all voices. Josquin's "Ave Maria" is a good example of a Renaissance motet.

JOSQUIN DES PREZ
(ca. 1450–1521)

- Born in what is today northern France or Belgium; died at approximately age 71 in Condé, France.

- Best remembered for his Masses, chansons, and motets.

In the motet discussed in the Featured Listening selection, notice the changes from polyphonic to homophonic (in which all voices are sung to the same rhythm) textures and notice when each is used. Sometimes the homophonic texture calls attention to the text because it is easier to understand the words, if one knows Latin. Homophonic texture is used at the beginning of the section in triple meter, helping to stress the new meter. Because of the importance of the Holy Trinity (Father, Son, and Holy Ghost) in Christianity, triple meter is sometimes used to signify purity. Is there anything particularly significant about the text in the triple-meter section that the new meter might have been intended to stress? Notice that the three beats of the triple-meter bars are fit into the same amount of time as the two beats of the rest of the motet, which is in duple meter. When Renaissance music changes from duple to triple meter, it is typical to have the notes in the triple section speed up to keep a constant pulse for each bar. Also, note the vocal part entries at the beginning of "Ave Maria." Notice that the sopranos begin, followed by the altos, the tenors, and then the basses:

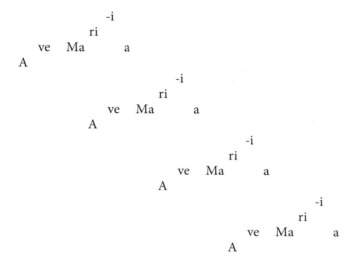

The "rebirth" of classical knowledge and humanistic thought of the Renaissance as well as the love of sacred subjects can clearly be heard in the following motet.

Featured Listening

CONNECT   CD 1: Tracks 2–3

"Ave Maria" ("Hail, Mary") JOSQUIN DES PREZ

Date: 1470s

Genre: Motet

Texture: Polyphonic and homophonic

Voices: Four

Meter: Duple, with one section in triple meter

Duration: 4:37

Context: This motet would have been sung in a cathedral or a monastery, but not as part of the Mass service.

	Timing	Latin text	English translation	Musical events
2	0:00	Ave Maria, gratia plena, Dominus tecum, Virgo serena.	Hail, Mary, full of grace, the Lord be with you, fair Virgin.	Polyphonic texture with much imitation

(continued)

Timing	Latin text	English translation	Musical events
0:45	Ave cujus conceptio, solemni plena gaudio, coelestia, terrestria, nova replet laetitia.	Hail to you whose conception, full of solemn joy, fills heavenly and earthly beings with new gladness.	Homophonic texture Polyphonic texture
1:22	Ave cujus nativitas nostra fuit solemnitas, ut lucifer lux oriens verum solem praeveniens.	Hail to you whose nativity was our solemn feast, indeed was the morning star rising preceding the true sun.	Polyphonic with voices paired Imitative polyphony
1:59	Ave pìa humilitas sine viro foecunditas cujus annunciatio nostra fuit salvatio.	Hail, holy humility, fruitful without man, whose annunciation was our salvation.	Homophonic with paired voices More polyphonic with paired voices
☐3☐ 0:00	Ave vera virginitas, immaculata castitas, cujus purificatio nostra fuit purgatio.	Hail, true virginity, undefiled chastity, whose purification was our cleansing.	Triple meter stressed by a homophonic beginning, then somewhat polyphonic
0:37	Ave praeclara omnibus angelicis virtutibus, cujus fuit assumptio nostra glorificatio.	Hail, to you, admirable in all angelic virtues, whose assumption was our glorification.	Return to duple meter Polyphonic texture
1:32	O Mater Dei, memento mei. Amen.	O, Mother of God, remember me. Amen.	Homophonic texture

Giovanni Pierluigi da Palestrina

One of the most distinguished of Josquin's successors was **Giovanni Pierluigi da Palestrina** (1525–1594), who spent the greater part of his life as choirmaster of St. Peter's in Rome. Palestrina's great contribution was to return church music to the simplicity and purity of earlier times. Although his motets are masterpieces of composition, his Masses constitute his most important work.

Palestrina lived and worked during the **Counter-Reformation,** the reaction by the Catholic Church to the spread of **Protestantism.** Central to this reaction was the **Council of Trent,** which met from 1545 to 1563 to formulate and execute the means by which church reform could be accomplished. The Council investigated every aspect of religious discipline, including Church music. It was the opinion of the Council that sacred music had become corrupted by complex polyphonic devices that obscured the text and diverted attention from the act of worship. To remedy this situation, the Council called for a return to a simpler vocal style, one that would preserve the sanctity of the text and discourage displays of virtuosity by singers. In addition to this, the Council objected to the use of loud instruments such as sacbuts (early trombones) in indoor church services and banned all secular melodies from the composition of Masses. They also decided to continue to perform services in Latin instead of changing to the vernacular, as the Protestant churches had done.

Legend has it that in order to prevent the Council from abolishing the polyphonic style entirely, Palestrina composed a Mass of such beauty and simplicity that he was able to dissuade the cardinals from taking this drastic step. Palestrina composed many other Masses that are equally beautiful, and we do not know exactly how close the Council was to abandoning polyphony, but the story is that this particular Mass, *Pope Marcellus Mass* (1567), saved polyphony for the Roman Catholic Church. The

Kyrie from that Mass is the only section of the traditional Mass that is written not in Latin but in Greek.

Palestrina understood the Counter-Reformation leaders' demands for respect for the Mass texts while still composing rich and beautiful polyphonic music, as can be heard in the Kyrie to the *Pope Marcellus Mass.* Pope Marcellus II died after only three weeks as pope in 1555. Palestrina, remembering the pope's insistence on the text being clearly understood when the Mass was celebrated, named the Mass after him.

Listening Guide

CONNECT   CD 4: Track 8

"Kyrie" ("Lord") from *Missa Papae Marcelli (Pope Marcellus Mass)* GIOVANNI PIERLUIGI DA PALESTRINA

Date: 1562–1563

Genre: Mass movement

Texture: Polyphonic

Voices: Six a cappella voices (soprano, alto, two tenors, and two basses)

Language: Greek

Meter: Duple, but with little accent on the beats; flows much like medieval chant

Duration: 4:23

Context: This is the first section of the Ordinary of the Mass that would have been performed in St. Peter's Cathedral at the Vatican in Rome. The voices imitate one another, but they blend so gently that the imitation does not cause them to sound separate from one another. All voices come together rhythmically at the close of each section.

Timing	Greek text	English translation	Musical events
8 0:00	Kyrie eleison.	Lord, have mercy upon us.	Tenors begin and are soon followed by sopranos and then other voices.
1:22	Christe eleison.	Christ, have mercy upon us.	All voices begin and end together, but gently imitate one another in between.
2:56	Kyrie eleison.	Lord, have mercy upon us.	Sopranos begin and are joined by richly blended other voices; the duple meter is more obvious in this section than it had been in the others.

See "Hearing the Difference: Josquin's 'Ave Maria' and Palestrina's 'Kyrie'" to understand how the music to each enhances the text.

Renaissance Secular Music

In addition to being a time of great piety, the sixteenth century was also a period of bawdy earthiness, irreverent humor, and celebration of sensual love. The same composers who created works for the greater glory of God also wrote compositions of this character. In Italy and England, the principal form of secular vocal music was the **madrigal;** in France, it was the *chanson;* in Germany, the *lied.*

Hearing the Difference

JOSQUIN'S "AVE MARIA" AND PALESTRINA'S "KYRIE"

Both of these works (see Featured Listening on page 51 and Listening Guide on page 53) sound similar in a number of ways. They are both sacred polyphonic vocal works for a cappella voices, but they both also have some sections where the voices join together in homophonic texture. As you listen to the works again, try to concentrate on the differences because that will help you appreciate how the music to each one enhances the text. Answer the following questions, as you listen from one recording to the other:

- Which work sounds fuller and richer? What might contribute to that fuller sound?
- Both works are in duple meter, but which one stresses the meter more and which one sounds more like smooth-flowing chant?
- As discussed earlier, Josquin's "Ave Maria" has a section in triple meter. Does the meter or the feel of the beat within the meter change in Palestrina's "Kyrie," or does it maintain a constant mood and rhythmic flow?
- When you listen carefully to the text, what one word begins most sections of "Ave Maria" and is not heard at all in "Kyrie"? Listening for that word is a good way to determine which of these works you are hearing.

The Madrigal in Italy

The Renaissance madrigal is a poem set to music. It had its beginnings in the fourteenth century among the aristocrats of the small Italian courts. The texts, written in the vernacular, were often twelve-line poems or fourteen-line sonnets whose subjects were sentimental or erotic. The early madrigal was written in a predominantly homophonic style. It was usually in three, but sometimes four, parts, and its expressive qualities were subdued and restrained. The madrigal of the mid-sixteenth century was written usually for five and sometimes for four or six voices. Its texture was more polyphonic than that of the early madrigal, and a greater attempt was made to capture in the music the expressive possibilities of the words.

The final flowering of the madrigal took place during the closing decades of the sixteenth century. The late madrigal was an elaborate composition, invariably not strophic, with a mixture of homophonic and polyphonic textures. It used chromaticism (the inclusion of notes that create tension through the use of dissonance) for bold effects, often to express sadness. The compositions also used coloristic and dramatic effects. One of the most interesting elements of the madrigal style was **word painting,** which meant that the melody was written to represent the literal meaning of the text being sung. For example, on the word *heaven,* the melody would ascend, or on the word *water,* it would rise and fall in a wavelike motion. On the word *death,* the music might become chromatic, creating dissonance and tension.

Many Italian composers wrote madrigals, not the least of whom was Claudio Monteverdi (1567–1643), who published eight books of madrigals. Monteverdi was an active composer of the late Renaissance who changed his style to that of the next period, the baroque, in approximately 1600. His early madrigal books are wonderful examples of the madrigal of the Italian Renaissance, and his late ones represent the new style. We will study Monteverdi as an early opera composer in Chapter 6. Other major Italian madrigal composers include Adrian Willaert, Carlo Gesualdo, and Luca

 **MusiCurious**

HOME ENTERTAINMENT DURING THE RENAISSANCE

Since most of the kinds of entertainment we enjoy today were not available during the Renaissance, what did people do to entertain themselves?

They made their own music. People could enjoy music in church services or even taverns, and plays were available to the general public during the Renaissance. Wealthy families would often hire musicians to come to their homes and perform for them and their guests. Many people, however, also regularly sang and played music in their homes for their own enjoyment.

The invention of movable type made printed music readily available to those who could afford to purchase it. In fact, a standard part of a good education was the requirement to learn to **sight sing** from music notation or to play an instrument. In England, books of madrigals were often handed out to people after dinner with the expectation that everyone would join in singing the madrigals. The madrigal composer Thomas Morley told of this practice in his *Plaine and Easie Introduction to Practicall Musicke*, first published in 1597: "But supper being ended and music books (according to the custom) being brought to the table, the mistress of the house presented me with a part earnestly requesting me to sing; but when, after many excuses, I protested unfeignedly that I could not, everyone began to won-

der; yea, some whispered to others demanding how I was brought up." The story might well be one that Morley made up in order to encourage more people to buy and sing his music, but the practice of group singing after dinner was very common in wealthy, noble, and royal households, including those of King Henry VIII and his daughter, Queen Elizabeth I.

Today, re-creations of the Renaissance practice of singing around the dinner table have become increasingly popular, usually around Christmastime. Early music societies, churches, or schools sometimes put on "madrigal dinners," in which a madrigal group dressed in Renaissance costumes sits at the "royal" table in the front of the dining room, and the guests are served dinner while being entertained by the singing. In more elaborate dinners of this type, the entertainment will also include actors, jugglers, dancers, or other types of performers. Attending the dinners can be lots of fun for the guests who, today, are not generally required to participate in the singing. Many of the places that put on such meals do so for fund-raising purposes and advertise through local newspaper ads or even on the Internet. To find one on the Internet, you can type "madrigal dinner" and your city and state, and treat yourself to an evening in the Renaissance.

Marenzio. "MusiCurious: Home Entertainment During the Renaissance" discusses the use of this form of music in personal life.

There were many fewer women composers during the Renaissance than men, but one deserves mention here. Maddalena Casulana was one of the first women composers to consider herself a professional musician. She was an active singer, lutenist (lute player), and music teacher who composed and published three volumes of madrigals in addition to other, individual, works. Her books were so popular that the first was reprinted twice. The dedication in her first book says, "to show the world . . . the futile error of men who believe themselves patrons of the high gifts of intellect, which according to them cannot also be held in the same way by women." She must have been quite a feminist for her time.

The Madrigal in England

Around the middle of the sixteenth century, the Italian madrigal was brought to England. There it flourished under a variety of names in addition to madrigal: *song, sonnet, canzonet,* and *ayre*. William Byrd (1543–1623) and his student Thomas Morley were the first English composers to cultivate the genre. Morley wrote simplified versions of the madrigal, known as *balletts*. Adapted from the Italian *balletti*, they were usually characterized by a "fa-la-la" refrain of the type that appears in the English carol "Deck the Halls." Enlivened by accents and a regular beat, the music was largely homophonic.

The madrigal "Fair Phyllis" was composed by **John Farmer.** Not a lot is known about Farmer's life. His birthplace and year are not known for certain, but around 1595 he was employed as an organist and choral director of Holy Trinity (now Christ Church) Cathedral in Dublin, Ireland. He was in London by 1600 and is assumed to have spent the rest of his life there. He is best known for his four-part settings of biblical texts from the Psalms and also for his four-part madrigals. The humanistic value given to everyday life that was popular during the Renaissance can be heard in the next work we will listen to, which is typical of many madrigals and other secular vocal works of the period.

CD 4: Track 9

"Fair Phyllis" JOHN FARMER

Date: 1599

Genre: English madrigal

Texture: Mostly polyphonic with a homophonic ending

Voices: Four

Meter: Duple

Duration: 1:20

Context: This might well have been sung in an aristocratic English home, after dinner, with the singers still sitting around the table, reading music from madrigal books.

Text	**Examples of word painting**
9 Fair Phyllis I saw sitting all alone,	Sopranos sing this line alone.
Feeding her flock near to the mountainside.	More voices join as Phyllis is joined by her flock.
The shepherds knew not whither she was gone,	Polyphonic texture as if singers were looking for her.
But after her lover Amyntas hied.	
Up and down he wandered whilst she was missing;	"Up" is sung to higher notes than is "down."
When he found her, O then they fell a-kissing.	Homophonic texture as the two lovers kiss.

The Chanson in France

In the sixteenth century, the *chanson* (the French word for "song") was to France what the madrigal was to Italy and England. Chansons modified the motet style with strong accented rhythms, frequent repetitions, and short phrases ending simultaneously in all parts. They were usually sung by three, four, or five voices, and sections of simple imitation alternated with sections that were essentially homophonic. Word painting occurred frequently in the early chansons, as it had in madrigals.

The Lied in Germany

In Germany, the counterpart to the French chanson was the *lied* (plural, *lieder*), also meaning "song." The lied dates from the middle of the fifteenth century, when both monophonic melodies and three-part settings appeared. The early lieder, which were heavily influenced by the Netherlands' polyphonic style, later provided the Lutheran Church with many melodies for **chorale** tunes (sacred songs).

In the sixteenth century, Germany looked to Italy and France for musicians to staff its courts and municipalities. As a result, lieder composers began to write in a style more typical of the chanson and madrigal, with various melodies set in imitative counterpoint.

Lute Songs

In Chapter 4 on medieval music we heard a troubadour song. Solo songs continued to be popular in later periods, but by the Renaissance composers usually wrote parts for specific instruments instead of leaving accompaniments to be improvised by whatever instrumentalists might be available. **Lute songs,** also called *ayres* in England, were composed for a lute accompanying a solo voice. A Listening Guide to a lute song by English composer and lutenist (lute player) **John Dowland** (1563–1626) follows.

Song accompanied by the lute was a popular form of entertainment during the Renaissance.

 **Listening Guide**

 CD 4: Track 10

CONNECT

"Flow My Tears"   JOHN DOWLAND

Date: Late sixteenth century

Genre: Lute song

Form: Strophic (all verses sung to the same, or close to the same, melody)

Texture: Homophonic

Voices and Instruments: Tenor voice and lute

Meter: Duple

Duration: 3:41

Context: This is a secular composition that might have been performed by an individual both singing and playing, or by two people, one singing and the other playing the lute. It was probably performed in an aristocratic home, but it could also have been performed by professional musicians in public, perhaps before a play or other type of entertainment.

English text	Musical events
10 Flow, my tears, fall from your springs. Exiled forever, let me mourn; Where night's blackbird her sad infamy sings, there let me live forlorn.	Voice and lute enter together with the lute softly accompanying the voice and adding a little flourish at the end of the verse.

(continued)

English text	Musical events
Down vain lights shine you no more.	Second verse is sung to the same melody as the first.
No nights are dark enough for those	
that in despair their last fortunes deplore,	
light doth but shame disclose.	
Never may my woes be relieved,	Third verse follows the same melody as the first two.
since pity is fled,	
and tears, and sighs, and groans my weary days,	
my weary days of all joys have deprived.	
From the highest spire of contentment,	Fourth verse follows the same melody as the first three.
my fortune is thrown,	
and fear, and grief, and pain for my deserts,	
for my deserts are my hopes since hope is gone.	
Hark you shadows that in darkness dwell.	Melody changes for this final verse, which is repeated.
Learn to contemn light.	
Happy, happy they that in hell	
feel not the world's despite.	

Renaissance Instrumental Music

Although most of the music of the Renaissance was written for voices, the role of instrumental music should not be underestimated. Instruments were used in church, at many festive and social occasions, as part of theatrical productions, and in private homes.

The earliest music played on instruments was sacred or secular vocal music. During the Renaissance, some music was written specifically for instruments. Most of it was dance music, because dancing was an important part of Renaissance social life. A fairly large collection of this music has been preserved, but apparently much of it was improvised on well-known tunes or harmonic bass patterns, as jazz is today.

The most popular instrument of the 1400s and 1500s was the lute, a plucked string instrument with a bowl-shaped body and fingerboard. The earliest lute music consisted of **transcriptions** (arrangements of compositions for a medium other than those for which they were originally written) of vocal pieces and dance music, but in the sixteenth century, composers began to write original pieces for the lute. These *ricercari,* or *fantasias,* were elaborate polyphonic pieces that demonstrated the virtuosity of the performer, who was often also the composer. Beginning in the early sixteenth century, volumes of solo music for the lute were published in Italy, France, Germany, England, and Spain.

Keyboard instruments, especially the clavichord, harpsichord, and organ, were also popular during the Renaissance. Keyboard music evolved through the same phases as lute music, from vocal music to dance music and then to original compositions that, in some cases, were quite complex.

Small chamber music ensembles, called *consorts,* were favored among those who performed music in their homes. When the consort was made up of all instruments of the same family, it was called a whole consort. Whole consorts could be made up of viols (bowed stringed instruments) or woodwind instruments, such as recorders. Sometimes consorts would include a mixture of instruments of different types. They were called mixed consorts. Music for brass and reed instruments was popular for outdoor occasions, for festive church ceremonies, and for dancing. Often, the exact instruments that should play the music were not specified by the composer, so it was played using whatever instruments were available.

We will listen to three dances composed by **Michael Praetorius** (1572–1621), a German composer of the late Renaissance. Although Praetorius began his musical career as a church organist and organ consultant, he moved on to become a court

A lutenist accompanying dancers, illustration in a Book of Hours, Tours, France, 1530–1535

musician for a duke in Wolfenbüttel, near Braunschweig, Germany. In addition to working at the duke's court, he also composed for and conducted a variety of musical ensembles in other parts of Germany. His works include many settings of Lutheran chorales, including some large-scale polychoral works. These ballets were published in a set of 312 dances called *Terpsichore* (1612). Although this set of dances was composed when the next style period in music history—the baroque—was beginning in Italy, the collection of dances is very Renaissance in style.

 **Listening Guide**

 **CD 4: Tracks 11–14**

CONNECT

Three Dances from *Terpsichore* MICHAEL PRAETORIUS

Date: 1612

Genre: Dance music

Texture: Polyphonic

Voices and Instruments: Four melodic instrumental lines plus percussion

Meter: Duple

Duration: 3:16

Context: These dances might have been performed by the family and guests at an aristocratic home or a court with professional musicians playing the music.

	Dance	Instrumentation
11	Ballet des Baccanales	**SATB** (soprano, alto, tenor, bass) recorders, lute, and tambourine
12	Ballet des Feus	SATB brass instruments and drum
13	Ballet des Matelotz	SATB bowed string instruments with low brass and drum
14	Ballet des Matelotz	**Tutti** (all instruments in the ensemble)

A set of dances like the one we just heard would have been played and danced to at a royal court such as the one at which Praetorius was employed. Renaissance musicians generally **embellished** (added to or changed notes of the melody) the music when they repeated any section, allowing the composition to be extended without sounding too repetitious to the dancers.

Summary

Sacred music of the Renaissance was primarily vocal, polyphonic with occasional homophonic sections of pieces, and performed a cappella. Motets and movements of the Mass Ordinary were the primary types of compositions performed in the churches. With the exception of the Kyrie, which was in Greek, the language of the Roman Catholic Church and of sacred works written for it continued to be Latin. Protestant churches broke away from that tradition and used the vernacular.

Secular music became popular for performance in noble, royal, or other wealthy and educated people's homes during the Renaissance. Secular music was sung in the ver-nacular so that the fun and sometimes quite bawdy texts could be appreciated by the singers and the audience. Common secular forms were the madrigal in Italy and England, the chanson in France, and the lied in Germany.

Instrumental music of the Renaissance evolved from vocal music to dance music and then to more complex original compositions. The most popular Renaissance instrument was the lute, with keyboard music and chamber consorts also coming into use. Dancing was an important social activity, providing musicians with steady employment at the homes and palaces of the wealthy.

New People and Concepts

a cappella, 49
chorale, 57
Council of Trent, 52
Counter-Reformation, 52
embellishment, 60
Giovanni Pierluigi da Palestrina, 52
imitation, 50

John Dowland, 57
John Farmer, 56
Josquin des Prez, 50
lute song, 57
madrigal, 53
Michael Praetorius, 58
Protestantism, 52

SATB, 59
sight sing, 55
transcription, 58
tutti, 59
word painting, 54

Finale

CD 1: Tracks 2–3

Listen again to the recording of "Ave Maria" by Josquin des Prez and compare your impressions now with your notes from your First Hearing. Consider the following questions:

- How many voice parts are there, and in what order do they enter at the beginning?

- What happens to the speed of the beat when the meter changes from duple to triple? Might that change have been made to draw attention to the text at that verse? Why might Josquin have wanted to do that? (You might need to refer to the Featured Listening on pages 51–52 to check the text at that section.)

- You have heard both polyphonic and homophonic textures through the work, but the ending is clearly homophonic. What is the text at the very end? Might that texture have been used to signify unity of thought on the final words? (Again, you might need to check the text in the Featured Listening.)

- The work is performed a cappella, as was usually the case for Renaissance motets; however, this same music, composed of clear, distinct melodies, could be played by instruments without voices at all—at least, no one could stop instrumentalists from trying that if they liked the sound of the music. How would the sound be different from the voices if it was played by all bowed stringed instruments, louder woodwind or brass instruments, or a combination of strings and winds? What if a group of musicians and singers decided to have some melodies played on instruments and others sung? Which instruments might sound best with voices, and which might not work very well?

- If you were going to describe this music to a friend, what would you say?

Further Listening

Renaissance Sacred Music

Josquin des Prez, *Missa Pange Lingua.* This Mass was composed around 1514, and was probably Josquin's last Mass. One of the great masterpieces of the Renaissance, it was based on the plainsong hymn, "Pange Lingua gloriosi."

Giovanni Pierluigi da Palestrina, *Missa Papae Marcelli (Pope Marcellus Mass).* Only the Kyrie was covered in this chapter, but the entire mass is beautiful.

Renaissance Secular Music

Maddalena Casulana, "Morir no può il mio cuore" ("My heart cannot die"). A beautiful Italian madrigal about unrequited love.

Thomas Morley, "April Is in My Mistress' Face" and "Now Is the Month of Maying." Two of Morley's most famous madrigals that are typical of the English madrigal style.

Clement Jannequin, "Chant des oiseaux" ("Song of the Birds"). A French chanson that includes singers imitating the sounds of birds such as the cuckoo.

Renaissance dance music. A great variety of recordings are available and the instruments used for the dances vary greatly. Because the music was often written to be playable on any number of instruments, you might find the same pieces played by completely different instruments, depending on the composition of the group that made the recording.

CHARACTERISTICS OF RENAISSANCE MUSIC

Texture	Mostly polyphonic
Tonality	Church modes
Rhythm	Measured
Singing style	Four-part singing common, some virtuoso singing; late madrigal and chanson used word painting
Large vocal works	Polyphonic Mass
Small vocal works	Motet, madrigal, chanson, lied
Musical instruments	Whole and mixed consorts, solo instrumental works
Instrumental music	Ricercari, fantasias, dances

Prelude | The Triumph of Baroque Style

The early baroque period is best reflected in Italian art and shows the recovery of the Roman Catholic Church after the Protestant challenge of the sixteenth century. As part of the Counter-Reformation, the Catholic Church had reexamined its rituals and established the Jesuit order as an international force for teaching, missionary work, reconversion, and protection of the faith. By the seventeenth century, those efforts had paid dividends: most of Europe remained bound to Catholicism and Rome.

After 1600, the arts were used by the Italians to celebrate the power and glory of the Church. New churches and palaces were decorated with rich gilding and other ornamentation. Rome became an unparalleled cultural center where artists from many different countries came to admire the classical ruins and modern wonders of the city. Pilgrims and noblemen visited Rome and returned home with marvelous tales of "the first city of the world." The new Roman style rapidly spread to the rest of Europe and became international.

Style changes were generally reflected in all of the arts. The rich gilding and other ornamentation that decorated churches and palaces had its counterpart in paintings and sculpture with very active and dramatic scenes and figures. Baroque music often has a fairly constant sense of motion and much melodic decoration, with the addition of ornaments such as trills (two notes played back and forth very quickly). Stark contrasts between light and dark in paintings are common in much baroque art. In music, we will also hear dramatic contrasts between dynamic levels, in which one musical phrase will be played loudly, followed by another that is much softer, almost like an echo of the first.

We can see these striking contrasts between light and shadow, as well as vigorous action and realism, in Caravaggio's (1573–1610) painting *The Conversion of St. Paul* (1600–1601). The biblical story shown is that of Saul of Tarsus, who had persecuted Christians but who was instantly converted to Christianity on the road to Damascus by a vision of Jesus that temporarily blinded him. The painting captures the very moment of the blinding and conversion, which is typical of the type of action seen in much baroque art.

Of course, there are many other artists whose works display similar activity and contrast. The sculptor Gianlorenzo Bernini's (1598–1680) *David Slaying Goliath* (1623) serves as a good example of baroque style when compared with Michelangelo's depiction of the same biblical personality (see page 47). David was the young future king of Israel (ca. 1000–960 BCE) who used a slingshot to slay a Philistine giant named Goliath who had challenged the Jews. Bernini's *David* is seen in the actual act of throwing the stone, whereas Michelangelo's sculpture shows a more sedate, relaxed pose. Neither sculpture is more religious nor more representative of the story than the other. They just focus on different times in the story, reflecting the popular style of the period.

David Slaying Goliath, by Bernini (1598–1680). This sculpture shows the kind of activity often portrayed in baroque art.

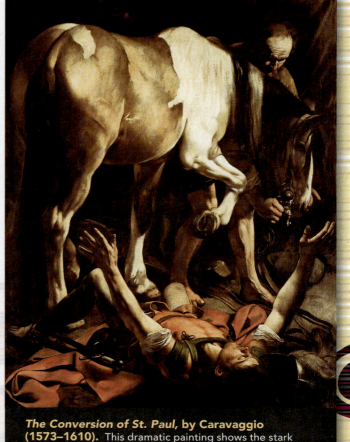

The Conversion of St. Paul, by Caravaggio (1573–1610). This dramatic painting shows the stark contrasts between dark and light that are common in much baroque art.

Baroque Culture

Music continued to play an important role in the life of the churches, as it had in the Renaissance. Sounds, perhaps more than the visual arts, could move, elevate, and involve a congregation and thus intensify the spiritual experience. Whereas Protestants were skeptical of visual displays and the veneration of images, they warmed to the use of music in church services. In the seventeenth century, major Protestant churches began to form orchestras and choirs, to have large organs built for their churches, and to hire organists, soloists, and music masters. The greatest baroque church musician was Johann Sebastian Bach, who spent a major part of his career at Leipzig, leaving a vast treasure of sacred music, vocal and instrumental, at the time of his death in 1750.

The concentration of baroque art and architecture was not exclusively religious. In France monumental art was used to enhance the position of Louis XIV and his court. The efforts of architects, stonemasons, sculptors, painters, furniture makers, and gardeners were carefully coordinated to remake the royal palace at Versailles in the latter half of the seventeenth century. By 1700, a visitor to Paris would have been overwhelmed by French monuments to the power of the Crown. During the eighteenth century, Paris replaced Rome as the leader in European culture and design.

The grandness of baroque style reflected the tastes of the Church and the ruling class. Most people were, of course, farmers who never even saw the great cities of Rome or Paris. In the cities, though, many workers and artisans constructed and decorated the great monuments of the period. The average worker labored about sixteen hours a day, six days a week, and families looked much like the one depicted in the painting *Peasant Family* by Louis Le Nain. Entertainment for the lower classes included visits to alehouses, where musicians, storytellers,

Peasant Family, by Louis Le Nain (1603–1648). Most peasants worked many hours just to live and had no way of appreciating the grandness of baroque style.

and gambling were available. Some common spectator sports such as cockfighting were violent and bloody. Stealing, swindling, and murder were common and were punished by whipping, branding, having a body part cut off, or death.

There was not a very large middle class, but there were well-to-do nobles and merchants who had much better lives than the poor workers. They enjoyed hunting, gambling, and various types of ball and board games, as did the aristocracy. Educated people learned to play musical instruments or sing, and enjoyed performing with or for friends in their homes. Public entertainments such as plays, balls, and masques (skits based on allegorical stories performed with elaborate staging and costumes) were popular. Opera, eventually, was added to the list of entertainment options available to those who could afford to attend. By the baroque period, the New World products of coffee, chocolate, and tobacco were easily

available and enjoyed by the noble and royal classes, although they were still unavailable to the average person.

Marriages were still arranged by parents, and there was little chance of ending a marriage. Even separations were next to impossible because the running of a home absolutely required people in both roles of husband and wife. Yet romantic affairs were common and accepted among the upper classes.

As was the case for the music we studied from the medieval and Renaissance periods, the music from the baroque era that is available for us to study was composed for and played by or for the upper and royal classes. The types of songs and dances that were enjoyed in the alehouses or other types of street entertainments were not usually recorded in music notation, and we can only guess what they sounded like. We begin our study of baroque music with opera, one of the grandest of the arts and one that was born at the beginning of the baroque period.

> An opera begins long before the curtain goes up and ends long after it has come down. It starts in my imagination, it becomes my life, and it stays part of my life long after I've left the opera house.
>
> —OPERA SINGER MARIA CALLAS
> [1923–1977]

Baroque Opera

Listen to the recording of "Thy Hand, Belinda" and "When I Am Laid in Earth" by Purcell and take notes on what you hear. Even if you are working with other students in a paired or group listening session, keep your own notes. Give some attention to the following:

- These two songs are performed one after another toward the end of an opera. Their vocal styles are quite different from each other. Which one has a freer rhythm and which one follows a more regular beat?

- In opera singing styles, some singing is more speech-like (recitative) and other singing is more song-like (aria). Which of these songs seems to be recitative and which one sounds more like an aria?

- Considering both the texts and the general sound of the music, what is the mood created by each song? Are the moods similar, or do they contrast with each other?

- "When I Am Laid in Earth" is introduced by a solo bass line that continues to repeat throughout the song. Is there anything about the sound of that bass line (tempo, direction, and so on) that fits the meaning of the text of that song?

- "When I Am Laid in Earth" has repeated sections. What words repeat? Does the music repeat when the words do? Does the music at the beginning come back at the end or not?

Keep your notes from this First Hearing to compare with your impressions about the piece after you study the information in this chapter.

6

The Birth of Opera

A whole new relationship between words and music began in Florence, Italy, around 1600. A group of scholars and musicians calling themselves the *camerata* (Italian for "a society of friends") sought to recapture the spirit of Greek drama by writing melodies for the actors to sing as they played dramatic roles. Greek scholars today are certain that the actors of ancient Greece did not sing their roles, but it is a wonderful accident of history that the camerata thought that they might have, because their sung dramas developed into the grand art of **opera.** Because the words of the plays

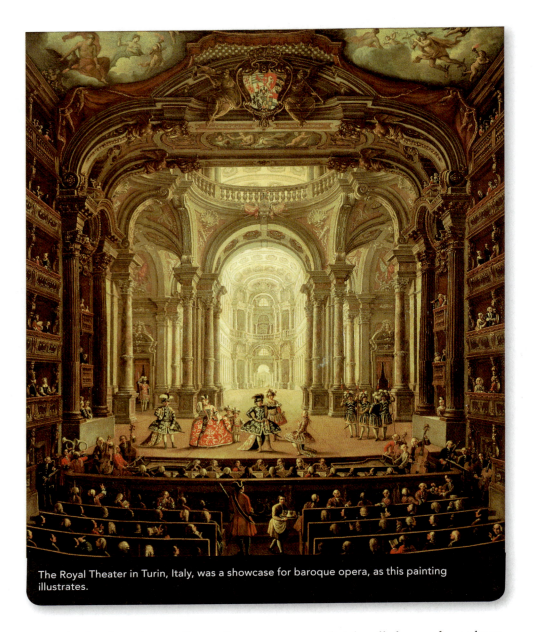

The Royal Theater in Turin, Italy, was a showcase for baroque opera, as this painting illustrates.

had to be clearly understood by audiences, a new vocal style called *monody* was born. In monody, a solo singer provided the predominant sound. The rhythmic flow of the singer's melody followed the accented patterns the text would have had if it were spoken. The singer was accompanied by harmonies played by a combination of instruments called **basso continuo,** or simply **continuo.** Monodic texture is homophonic because it includes only a single prevailing melody with accompaniment.

Basso continuo literally means "continuous bass," but it was really more than that. The composer wrote a bass line with a kind of musical shorthand, called *figured bass,* under some of the notes. The notes of the bass line, along with the shorthand, told a player of a chordal instrument such as a lute, a harpsichord, or an organ what chords to play and improvise on to provide a simple accompaniment to the vocal line. The bass line was also played by a melodic bass instrument such as a cello or bassoon.

Although the basso continuo originated to accompany singer-actors in early baroque operas, it came to be applied to virtually all music throughout the period, both vocal and instrumental. So prevalent was the continuo practice that the baroque period was later nicknamed the *continuo period.*

Baroque Vocal Styles

Recitative is a kind of combination of singing and speech that served as dialogue in baroque operas and other related works. Like monody, its musical rhythm was flexible and dictated by the natural inflection of the words. The tempo was slowed down or speeded up according to the singer's interpretation of the text. When it was accompanied by basso continuo instruments alone, it was called *secco recitative* ("dry singing"). In some more dramatic situations, recitative singing could be accompanied by continuo, along with other instruments, even a small orchestra, in which case it was called *accompanied recitative.* In either case, recitative was intended to be clear to allow audiences to understand the text.

A more lyrical style of singing in early operas was that of the **arioso,** which was a more melodic and expressive type of recitative. The **aria** was an expansion of arioso-styled singing. Very early baroque operas were all or mostly recitative, but once the aria developed, it became the focal point of vocal expressiveness. Arias were usually composed to be able to stand apart from the story of the operas as complete songs. They were often symmetrically balanced in a three-part form, ABA. The first section is represented by the letter A, the B represents a contrasting section, and the return of A indicates that the singer ends the aria by repeating the first section. An aria in this form is called a *da capo aria* because the words *da capo,* which mean "the head" in Italian, are written into the music to tell the singer to repeat the beginning (head) section of music. Singers usually embellished the repeated A section in order to display their vocal skills.

When the story of an opera included a group of people, such as citizens of the town in which the action was taking place, the opera included a **chorus,** or group of singers. Composers tended to handle texts for choruses differently from those for solo singers because it was more difficult for audiences to understand the words when they were sung by several singers together. For that reason, operatic choral singing is much more homophonic in texture than is typical for much Renaissance group vocal music. Operatic choral texts also had more repetition of important sections of words than was common in earlier music. Again, the primary goal was to be understood by the audience. "MusiCurious: How Opera Makes Singers into International Stars" discusses some of the types of performers who sang in operas.

The earliest surviving opera was written by a member of the camerata named Jacopo Peri (1561–1633), whose *Eurydice* dates from the year 1600. Based on the Greek legend of Orpheus and Eurydice, it consists almost entirely of secco recitative. In accordance with the principles of the camerata, Peri wrote in the foreword to his opera that its style was intended to "imitate speech in song." The development of the arioso and aria made operatic singing more expressive than secco recitative and contributed to the expanding popularity of opera.

The first woman known to have composed an opera, Francesca Caccini, might have performed in Peri's *Eurydice,* as did her father, Giulio Caccini. In addition to being a talented singer, Francesca played the harpsichord and the lute and became a court composer for the Medici family in seventeenth-century Florence. The opera for which she is best known is *La Liberazione di Ruggiero* (1625). The Medici family had her compose the opera to be performed for the visiting Prince Wladislaw Zygmunt of Poland. The prince enjoyed its performance so much that he took a copy of it back to Poland with him and had it translated into Polish and performed there. It is famous for being the first opera to be performed outside of Italy.

Claudio Monteverdi

The first master of operatic composition was the Italian **Claudio Monteverdi** (1567–1643). Monteverdi's life spanned the change of style from the Renaissance into the baroque. His early madrigals are wonderful examples of music in the Italian Renaissance.

MusiCurious

HOW OPERA MAKES SINGERS INTO INTERNATIONAL STARS

Were women finally able to sing in public during the baroque period?

Yes. In most of Europe the earlier restriction against women performing in public was dropped by the seventeenth century. In fact, many female singers became quite famous, including composer Francesca Caccini (1587–ca. 1640). Caccini's father was a composer, and her mother and sister also sang in operas produced for public audiences.

There were a few places, particularly in the Italian papal states, where it was still not considered respectable for a woman to perform in public situations. In those places, female roles were sung by high-voiced male singers known as *castrati*.

Who were castrati?

Castrati is plural. A **castrato** was a man who had been castrated before puberty. When the castrato grew up,

Farinelli (Carlo Broschi) was the most famous castrato.

his voice did not change to a lower pitch, and yet it did mature. The castrato voice was, therefore, high, clear, and strong. The castrato voice was commonly heard in churches even back in the Renaissance, because women were not allowed to sing, and the castrato's strength was needed to balance with the male singers on the lower musical parts. When opera began, castrati were used for heroic male roles as well as female roles in the few places where women were not allowed on stage. For example, Julius Caesar, who was certainly not a castrato in real life, was played by a castrato in Handel's opera of the same name.

If castrati sang heroic male roles in baroque operas, did that mean that they were rich and famous?

In some cases, yes. The most famous castrato was Carlo Broschi (1705–1782), known as **Farinelli.** A film *Farinelli* was made in 1994 about his life. The film director kept Farinelli's speaking voice that of a "normal-sounding" man, when the real Farinelli would have had a high voice when speaking as well as when singing. Farinelli's singing voice in the movie was created by electronically combining the voices of a **coloratura** (high female soprano) and a **counter tenor** (high male tenor). The film dramatized Farinelli's operatic career from his beginnings in Italy through his stardom in England. The English did not approve of the Italian practice of castration, but they were willing to hire and enjoy the singing of some of the best of the Italian castrati who traveled to England.

What happens when baroque operas are performed today?

Good question. Obviously, there are no castrati today. The roles they would have sung in the baroque period are usually sung today by women or by counter tenors. Sometimes directors attempt to rewrite the music so that a normal-voiced tenor or baritone can sing it. A major problem with that solution is that when the singer taking the lowered castrato part has to sing with another singer, the other singer's part must also be changed. The result is a sound that is not really true to what the composer intended.

Despite the problems involved in producing a modern performance of a baroque opera, some opera companies occasionally attempt them. George Frideric Handel, whom we will study as the composer of the **oratorio** *Messiah,* composed wonderful operas while he was in London, and some of those are still performed on a regular basis.

His operas, however, represent the new style of the baroque. Monteverdi's treatment of the legend of Orpheus and Eurydice, *Orfeo*, marks the beginning of opera as a major art form. First performed in Mantua in 1607, *Orfeo* had elaborate costuming, staging, and lighting, an instrumental ensemble of forty players, and a chorus of singers and dancers.

In the Greek legend of Orpheus and Eurydice (Orfeo and Euridice, in Italian), a messenger approaches Orpheus to give him the sad news that his wife, Eurydice, died from a snakebite while avoiding the advances of another man. Devastated by the news, Orpheus made his way into the underworld to find Eurydice and bring her back to life. His beautiful playing of a lyre convinced the king of the underworld to allow Eurydice to follow Orpheus back to the upper world if he would trust that she was following him and not look back at her until they were out. Orpheus made the mistake of looking back, and as a result Eurydice returned to the world of the dead. After he was back in the upper world, Orpheus refused to have anything to do with other women. He must have been quite attractive, because the women were so upset because he ignored them that they actually tore his body to pieces. His body parts were buried at the foot of Mount Olympus, and his head was thrown into the sea, where it floated to Lesbos and became an oracle (fortune-teller).

The **libretto** (text) for Monteverdi's *Orfeo* changed the Greek legend to be more suitable for the Christian beliefs of his time. The opera began with Orfeo and Euridice singing of their love for each other. Later, Orfeo received a messenger, who told him that Euridice died from a snakebite while out picking flowers. Orfeo had to have God's help to be able to enter the world of the dead, where he was finally able to get permission to bring his wife back to life. The condition of not looking back at her was given, and, as in the Greek version of the story, he did just that and lost her as a result. To create a happy ending, Monteverdi's *Orfeo* then called on his divine father, Apollo, who allowed Orfeo to ascend into heaven, where he could see Euridice in the stars for eternity.

Many librettists have changed opera plots to fit the tastes of their audiences. In a later version of *Orfeo* by Christoph Willibald Gluck (1714–1787), Orfeo was completely forgiven for looking back, and Euridice returned to a happy life with her husband.

An excerpt from Monteverdi's *Orfeo* follows. This is a section from Act Two in which Orfeo receives the news of Euridice's death and vows to go into the underworld to get her back.

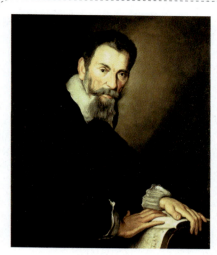

CLAUDIO MONTEVERDI
(1567–1643)

- Born in Cremona, Italy; died at age 76 in Venice, Italy.

- Music master at St. Mark's Cathedral in Venice.

- Best known for six books of madrigals and the operas *L'Orfeo (Orfeo)* and *L'incoronazione di Poppea (The Coronation of Poppea)*.

CD 4: Track 15
CONNECT

"Tu se' morta" ("You Are Dead") from Act Two of *Orfeo* CLAUDIO MONTEVERDI

Date: 1607

Genre: Opera recitative

Texture: Homophonic

Voices and Instruments: Tenor voice with continuo that includes a small organ and a bass lute

Meter: Nonmetric recitative

Duration: 2:53

(continued)

Context: In this recitative, Orfeo states that he is going to the underworld to either bring his beloved wife back to life or remain with her in death. This sets up the action for the rest of the opera.

	Timing	Italian text	English translation	Musical events
15	0:00	Tu se' morta, mia vita, ed io respiro? Tu se' da me partita per mai più non torrare, ed io rimango?	You are dead, my life, and do I breathe? You are gone from me never to return, and do I remain?	Short introduction and continued accompaniment with long-held chords on organ and arpeggiated chords on the bass lute; rhythm of the voice is quite free and emotional
	1:02	No, che se i versi alcuna cosa ponno, N'andrò sicuro a' più profondi abissi, E, intenerito il cor del re de l'ombre,	No, for if my verses can do anything, I will go surely to the deepest abysses, and, having softened the heart of the King of Shades,	
	1:38	Meco trarrotti a riveder le stelle: O, se ciò negherammi empio destino, Rimarrò teco, in compagnia di morte.	I will bring her back to see again the stars: Oh, if wicked destiny refuses me this, I will stay with you in the company of death.	
	2:17	Addio, terra, addio cielo e sole, addio.	Farewell earth, farewell heaven and sun, farewell.	

HENRY PURCELL
(1659–1695)

- Birthplace in England unknown; died at age 36 in London, England.
- Known for both sacred and secular works including the opera *Dido and Aeneas* and music for the dramatic work *The Fairy Queen*.

As was the case with *Orfeo*, baroque operas were generally based on Greek legends or, in some cases, Roman history. It was thought that opera was such a grand art form that it should not be wasted on stories of contemporary lifestyles or events. The earliest operas were performed for gatherings of aristocrats, but the appeal of music and drama together was so great that by 1637 public opera houses were built, and operas became a popular form of entertainment for the middle class, as well as aristocrats.

Opera Outside of Italy

During the baroque period, the popularity of opera spread throughout Europe. Because of the need for audiences to understand the text, operas were often composed in the vernacular, although there are many examples of operas being composed and performed in Italian outside of Italy. The English composer **Henry Purcell** (1659–1695) based his opera *Dido and Aeneas* on a Roman legend adapted from the first and fourth books of Virgil's epic poem, *Aeneid* (19 BCE).

The plot of the opera was based fairly closely on the original story, which likely would have been familiar to educated people of Purcell's time. The story of the opera opened at the royal palace of Carthage, where the widowed queen, Dido, expressed her love for the Trojan hero, Aeneas, who has been shipwrecked on her shore. Aeneas returned her love but could not stay in Carthage with Dido because he was destined to sail on to Italy, where he was to become the founder of the great city of Rome.

A fire had been built on the shore to help Aeneas and his sailors see their way out of the harbor. As he left, Dido stood by the fire and sang her funeral song, "When I Am Laid in Earth," after which she threw herself into the flames or fell back into Belinda's arms, depending on the production. The opera ended with the singing of a chorus of cupids who came down from the sky to spread roses on Dido's body.

Featured Listening

CONNECT   CD 1: Track 4

"Thy Hand, Belinda" and "When I Am Laid in Earth," from Act Three of *Dido and Aeneas*   HENRY PURCELL

Date: 1689

Genre: Recitative and aria from an opera

Texture: Homophonic

Form: Recitative free form; aria binary form (AABB)

Voices and Instruments: Soprano voice, theorbo (lute-like plucked string instrument), first violins, second violins, viola, and bass violin

Language: English

Meter: "Thy Hand, Belinda," quadruple meter, but sung with much rhythmic freedom; "When I Am Laid in Earth," triple meter

Duration: 4:28

Context: This recitative and aria are sung by Dido just before her death. In Virgil's epic poem on which the story for this opera is based, Dido stabs herself at what would be the end of this aria. In Purcell's opera, she either falls into a fire or merely drops into Belinda's arms and dies. The way in which the **ground bass** (continuously repeating low melody) introduces the aria, by descending slowly and then repeating throughout the aria, adds to the seriousness of the mood.

Timing	Text	Musical events
	RECITATIVE	
4 0:00	Thy hand, Belinda; darkness shades me. On thy bosom let me rest. More I would, But Death invades me; Death is now a welcome guest.	Voice is accompanied by a theorbo playing arpeggiated chords and a bass violin
	ARIA	
0:47		A ground bass line played on theorbo with Dido's aria beginning on the last tenth note; the bass line then continues to repeat through the aria
1:02	When I am laid, am laid in earth, may my wrongs create no trouble, no trouble in thy breast.	A section: violins and viola play long-held chords over the repeating bass line
		A section repeats
2:16	Remember me, remember me, but ah! Forget my fate. Remember me, but ah! Forget my fate.	B section: strings and repeating bass line continues
		B section repeats
	(Dido dies.)	

DOWLAND'S "FLOW MY TEARS" AND PURCELL'S "WHEN I AM LAID IN EARTH"

These works (see Listening Guide on page 57 and Featured Listening on page 71) both demonstrate differences in their time periods. The settings in which they would have been performed differ. Dowland's song would have been sung in a home, although it could have been used as outdoor entertainment as well. Purcell's aria was performed as part of an opera. Answer the following questions as you listen from one work to the other:

- What are the texts of each song or aria about? How serious and potentially long-lasting are the emotions expressed in each?

- Does the accompaniment to the voices appropriately support the seriousness of the texts in either or both compositions? What do the instruments do that supports, or does not support, the meaning of the texts in each work?

- Both compositions have repeated melodies. Where does the melody repeat in each? How many different melodic sections does each work have for the voice?

- Are there important melodies in the instrumental accompaniment for either work? Does either work, or both, have melodic accompaniment?

Dido and Aeneas was Purcell's only real opera, although he composed other theater music, as well as works for chamber ensembles and organ and many anthems for the Church of England. He was close to the English court and composed funeral music after the death of Queen Mary (1694). He served as the principal organist at the Chapel Royal and also at Westminster Abbey in London.

"Hearing the Difference: Dowland's 'Flow My Tears' and Purcell's 'When I Am Laid in Earth'" demonstrates some changes in solo songs and their accompaniment from the Renaissance to the baroque period.

During the latter part of the baroque period, Italian opera spread throughout Europe, reaching its heights in the Italian operas of Handel in England. The Italian style had less influence in France, where the composer Jean-Baptiste Lully (1632–1687), ironically an Italian, headed the group that created and supported French opera. In his operatic style, Lully concerned himself with the text and composed arias that were much like recitative. He added musical interest with choruses, dances, and instrumental pieces when he could fit them into the story.

Summary

The baroque era began in Italy around the year 1600. Fundamental style changes were brought about by a reaction against Renaissance vocal polyphony and a desire to make music serve and reflect the mood and meaning of the words. This attitude resulted in the monodic style, in which a single voice is accompanied by a group of instruments called basso continuo.

Many new vocal forms developed during the baroque period, notably the speechlike recitative and the lyrical arioso. The da capo aria is an expansion of the arioso and is characterized by an ABA form. The opera is an elaborately staged dramatic form based on secular themes. The first great opera was *Orfeo,* written by the Italian Claudio Monteverdi.

The popularity of opera spread all over Europe. Some of the greatest operas of the baroque era are those that Handel (whose oratorio, *Messiah,* we will study) composed in the Italian style while he was in England. In France, Jean-Baptiste Lully developed a style of opera that included more dance and simpler arias than had the Italian operas.

New People and Concepts

aria, 67	coloratura, 68	libretto, 69
arioso, 67	continuo, 66	opera, 65
basso continuo, 66	counter tenor, 68	oratorio, 68
castrato, 68	Farinelli, 68	recitative, 67
chorus, 67	ground bass, 71	
Claudio Monteverdi, 67	Henry Purcell, 70	

 **Finale**    **CD 1: Track 4**

CONNECT

Listen again to the recording of Purcell's "Thy Hand, Belinda" and "When I Am Laid in Earth" and compare your impression now with your notes from your First Hearing. Consider the following questions:

- What are these songs about, and how does each song use rhythm and tempo to best express the meaning of its text?
- How does the sound of the music and singing in "Thy Hand, Belinda" set the mood for the aria "When I Am Laid in Earth" and the death that follows it?
- What instruments accompany each song, and how are those instruments used to support the seriousness of the texts in each?
- What effect does the bass line have in "When I Am Laid in Earth," and what is it about the line that enhances the meaning of the text? If the bass violinist had not shown up for the performance, would the song have been just as effective without that part?
- What is the musical form of "When I Am Laid in Earth"?
- If you were going to describe this music to a friend, what would you say?

Further Listening

The 1994 movie *Farinelli.* The story is based on the life and career of the very famous castrato opera singer Carlo Broschi, whose stage name was Farinelli. The movie displays some of the grandeur of baroque opera and the stardom of some of the singers.

Claudio Monteverdi, *Orfeo.* Several performances of the entire opera are available on DVD. CDs are available too, but operas are theater in addition to music and are best seen as well as heard.

Henry Purcell, *Dido and Aeneas.* The final recitative and aria are discussed in this chapter, but seeing the entire story of love and abandonment is worth the time and cost.

George Frideric Handel, *Giulio Cesare in Egitto (Julius Caesar in Egypt).* This is one of many operas that the German composer Handel wrote in the Italian style and language for his English audience. Happily, the DVDs have subtitles in English. Note the title "Julius Caesar in Egypt." This is taken from earlier in Caesar's life than the story of Shakespeare's play *Julius Caesar,* in which Caesar dies.

Cantata

> Beautiful music is the art of the prophets that can calm the agitations of the soul; it is one of the most magnificent and delightful presents God has given us.
>
> —MARTIN LUTHER [1483–1546]

  **))) First Hearing** CONNECT **CD 1: Track 5**

Listen to the recording of "Wachet auf" ("Sleepers Awake"), seventh movement, by Bach and take notes on what you hear. Even if you are working with other students in a paired or group listening session, keep your own notes. Give some attention to the following:

- Have you ever heard music like this before? If so, where and in what situation? Is there anything about the mood or general sound that might tell you the situation in which this work would be performed?

- What voices do you hear? Are both men and women singing, or just one or the other?

- Can you hear instruments with the voices? What instruments do you hear?

- How would you describe the texture of this composition?

- Do you hear any repeated melodies or sections?

- Can you understand the text? What might the language be?

- Keep your notes from this First Hearing to compare with your impressions about the piece after you study the information in this chapter.

7

A **cantata** is a dramatic work for solo voices, sometimes a small chorus, and either basso continuo or a small orchestra. The same types of vocal styles we heard in opera were used in cantatas, including recitative to provide clear dialogue, arioso, and aria. Baroque cantatas were quite different from operas, however, in that they were short—usually not more than twenty minutes long—and they were not performed with scenery, costuming, or stage action. Like operas, they needed to be understood by their audiences and were generally composed in the vernacular. Secular cantatas were performed in palaces or wealthy people's homes, as well as in town halls for gatherings of prominent citizens. Sacred cantatas were performed in churches, often as part of a service that could be as long as three hours, the cantata being only a short episode somewhere in the middle. Because they were not staged, cantatas were much less expensive to produce than operas, and they were very popular during the baroque period.

The Secular Cantata

The secular cantata was a popular form of musical entertainment in baroque Italy. Prominent composers such as Giacomo Carissimi (ca. 1605–1674) and Antonio Cesti (ca. 1623–1669) wrote numerous cantatas for performance at social gatherings in

the homes of wealthy aristocrats. The earliest secular cantatas had several contrasting **movements** but were comparatively short and consisted of recitatives, ariosos, and arias.

One of the most prolific composers of secular cantatas was Barbara Strozzi (1619–ca. 1664). Between 1644 and 1664, Strozzi published eight volumes of vocal works containing a total of about one hundred pieces, most of which were individual arias and secular cantatas for soprano and basso continuo. The texts of many of her cantatas centered on stories about unrequited love, a favorite theme among seventeenth-century composers. In all probability, Strozzi performed these pieces for the *Accademic degli Unisoni,* a Venetian fellowship of poets, philosophers, and historians who met in the home of her father.

Bach, discussed in detail later in this chapter, was well known for his sacred cantatas, but he also composed some wonderfully entertaining secular ones. One fun example is his "Schweigt stille, plaudert nicht," also known as the "Coffee Cantata." This cantata was composed in 1734 for performance in a coffeehouse that was regularly visited by musicians and music students, including two of Bach's sons. It consisted of ten movements for three soloists: a soprano, a tenor, and a bass. The tenor sang the role of narrator, the bass the role of the father, and the soprano the role of a coffee-addicted young daughter. In the story, the father tried to get his daughter to stop drinking so much coffee by threatening to not allow her to marry until she gave up the habit. She promised, but while the father was out finding an appropriate husband, the daughter spread the word all over town that she would consider no husband who would not allow her to drink coffee whenever she wanted. The "Coffee Cantata" is only a little over twenty-five minutes long, and it was probably not performed with staging, but it was about the closest Bach ever came to composing in the secular dramatic form of opera.

The Chorale

Of the founders of the different Protestant religions that broke away from the Roman Catholic Church during the Renaissance, both Martin Luther (1483–1546) and John Calvin (1509–1564) shared the belief that it was important for their churches to have music that the congregations could sing together. They wanted the music sung in church to be simple and in the vernacular language so that everyone in the congregation could be part of the musical performance and understand what they were singing. They based their songs on melodies from Gregorian chants, secular tunes, and newly composed songs. These *chorales* or *hymns* were single melodies sung in monophonic texture at first. Simple parts were eventually added below the main melodies to give the music a fuller sound. Luther himself composed many such chorale melodies.

By the baroque period, more than one hundred years after the Renaissance, many of Luther's chorale melodies were well known by the members of German Lutheran churches. Bach enhanced the music by resetting the chorale tunes into more complex compositions. Many of Bach's chorales not only functioned as the basis for congregational singing but also provided a rich body of materials from which larger and more complex vocal and instrumental musical structures such as sacred cantatas could be built.

The Sacred Cantata

Like opera, the cantata went through considerable transformation from early to late baroque, reaching its height in Germany in the works of Dietrich Buxtehude (ca. 1637–1707) and Bach. By Bach's time, the sacred cantata often included the standard baroque elements of recitative, aria, chorus, and instrumental ensemble. Cantatas generally included several movements that featured a variety of solo singers, and they usually concluded with a four-part setting of a chorale melody.

Sacred cantata texts related to specific feast days of the church year, and for church musicians such as Bach, the writing of cantatas was a routine professional obligation. Between 1704 and 1740, Bach composed cantatas on a regular basis for the churches he served. He is believed to have written more than 300, although only 195 have been preserved.

We will listen to the fourth and seventh movements from Bach's "Wachet auf" ("Sleepers Awake"), Cantata no. 140.

Listening Guide

CONNECT   CD 4: Track 16

"Wachet auf" ("Sleepers Awake"), Cantata no. 140, fourth movement JOHANN SEBASTIAN BACH

Date: 1731

Genre: Tenor chorale from a church cantata

Texture: Polyphonic

Voices and Instruments: Tenor voices with first violins, second violins, and violas in unison (playing the same notes together) and continuo, harpsichord, organ, and bassoon

Language: German

Meter: Quadruple

Duration: 4:13

Context: This is the fourth out of seven movements in the cantata. The complete cantata was composed to be performed as part of a Lutheran church service. The first, fourth, and seventh movements are all based on a hymn with text by a sixteenth-century German poet, Philipp Nicolai.

	Timing	German text	English translation	Musical events
16	0:00			Strings and continuo play ritornello (a melody that will keep returning). Instruments continue to accompany the voices.
	0:43	Zion hört die Wächter singen, das Herz tut ihr vor Freuden springen, sie wachet und steht eilend auf.	Zion hears the watchmen sing, her heart springs with joy, she wakes and immediately rises.	
	1:52	Ihr Freund kommt von Himmel prächtig, von Gnaden stark, von Wahrheit mächtig, ihr Licht wird hell, ihr Stern geht auf.	From heaven comes her splendid friend, great with grace and powerful with truth, her light is bright, her star ascends.	Ritornello returns.
	2:47	Nun komm, du werte Kron, Herr Jesu, Gottes Sohn. Hosianna!	Now come, you worthy crown, Lord Jesus, the Son of God. Hosanna!	Ritornello returns.
	3:28	Wir folgen all'zum Freudensaal und halten mit das Abendmahl.	We will all follow to the hall and share the Lord's supper.	Ritornello in minor key
				Ritornello returns in major key.

 **Featured Listening**

CONNECT   CD 1: Track 5

"Wachet auf" ("Sleepers Awake"), Cantata no. 140, seventh movement JOHANN SEBASTIAN BACH

Date: 1731

Genre: Chorale from a church cantata

Form: AAB (verse, verse repeats, new melody for last verse)

Texture: Homophonic, also called homorhythmic texture because all parts follow the same rhythms at the same time

Voices and Instruments: Full SATB (soprano, alto, tenor, bass) choir, one French horn, two oboes, oboe da caccia (tenor oboe, or English horn), violino piccolo (small, high violin), violins, and violas with organ and bassoon continuo

Language: German, except last three words ("in dulci jubilo") in Latin

Meter: Duple

Duration: 1:30

Context: This is the final movement of the cantata, in which Bach had the hymn on which the cantata was based sung in simple four-part harmony. It is likely that the congregation would join the singing for this final movement.

(continued)

	Timing	German text	English translation	Form	Musical events
5	0:00	Gloria sei dir gesungen mit Menschen und eng- lishchen Zungen, mit Harfen und Cymbeln schon.	Glory be sung to you with tongues of men and angels, with harps and cymbals.	A	Full choir singing in the same rhythm as the orchestra, organ, and basso continuo
	0:24	Von zwölf Perlen sind die Pforten an deiner Stadt; wir sind Konsorten der Engel hoch um deinen Thron.	Of twelve pearls are the gates of the city; we attend the angel high above your throne.	A	
	0:48	Kein Aug' hat je gespürt, kein Ohr hat je gebört solche Freude. Des sind wir froh, io, io, ewig in dulci jubilo.	No eye has ever seen, no ear has ever heard such joy. Therefore we are joyful, io, io, eternally in sweet jubilation.	B	New melody, homorhythmic texture continues

Johann Sebastian Bach

JOHANN SEBASTIAN BACH
(1685–1750)

- Born in Eisenach, Germany; died at age 65 in Leipzig, Germany.
- Prolific composer best known for such secular works as six Brandenburg Concertos, *The Well-Tempered Clavier,* and the *Art of the Fugue,* and major sacred works including the *St. Matthew Passion, The Magnificat,* and hundreds of cantatas.

Johann Sebastian Bach (1685–1750) was one of the most prolific composers of the baroque period. He came from a family of musicians that reached back four generations before him and that was carried forward by three of his sons. His father, Johann Ambrosius, was a musician in service to the town council of Eisenach in eastern Germany. Bach's father was an excellent violinist and taught him to play stringed instruments.

Orphaned when he was only 10, Bach was sent to live with his eldest brother, Johann Christoph, an organist at the nearby town of Ohrdruf. He remained there five years, taking organ and harpsichord lessons from his brother, earning some money as a soprano, and studying at the town's famed grammar school. He did so well at the school that he was offered a scholarship to St. Michael's, a secondary school in Lüneburg, a city in northern Germany.

In 1703 Bach obtained his first musical position, as a violinist in the small chamber orchestra of the ducal court of Weimar, but when a post as church organist became available in Arnstadt in August of 1703, he accepted the position. Dissatisfied with working conditions in Arnstadt and the poor state of the church choir, Bach left in 1707 to become organist at the church of St. Blasius in the Free Imperial City of Mühlhausen. In that same year he married a cousin, Maria Barbara Bach.

Soon entangled in disagreements over the type of music that the congregation wanted to hear as opposed to what Bach wanted to write, Bach left Mühlhausen in 1708 to become court organist, and later concertmaster, in the ducal chapel of Weimar. His nine years in Weimar constituted his first major creative period. There he composed a number of cantatas and some of his greatest organ works.

Because of his evident talents as a composer, performer, and conductor, Bach expected to be offered the top position of *Kapellmeister* (chapelmaster) at Weimar when it became available in 1716. However, he was passed over in favor of another composer. The following year he accepted the position of court conductor to the small principality of Anhalt-Cöthen.

Bach enjoyed a growing reputation as an organist and composer of church cantatas, and he made annual performing tours to important centers such as Kassell, Leipzig, and Dresden. His duties at Cöthen were marred by the death of his wife in 1720. Bach soon remarried, however, and his new wife, Anna Magdalena, proved to be a hard-working, cheerful companion who raised Bach's four children by Maria Barbara along with her own. Anna gave birth to thirteen children in all, six of whom survived.

In 1723 Bach was offered the position of kantor (director of music) at St. Thomas Church in Leipzig, one of the most important musical posts in Protestant Germany. However, it was not a completely auspicious beginning for Bach, as the city council turned to him only after it had been turned down by two other composers. His duties included composing cantatas for St. Nicholas Church, as well as for St. Thomas Church, supervising the musical programs in all the municipal churches, and teaching Latin in the St. Thomas choir school.

Despite the irksome nature of some of his duties and his uneasy relationship with the Leipzig town council, Bach remained in Leipzig for the rest of his life. He personally supervised the musical education of his most gifted sons, Wilhelm Friedemann, Carl Philipp Emanuel, and Johann Christian, and saw them embark on promising musical careers. Though, like Handel, he went blind in old age, his creative powers remained undimmed. His last composition, dictated to a son-in-law a few days before his death, was a chorale prelude, "Before Thy Throne, My God, I Stand."

Summary

Cantatas were multiple-movement dramatic works for one or several solo singers accompanied by basso continuo or by a small orchestra. They were different from operas in that they were not staged with costumed singers or action, and they were usually not longer than twenty minutes. Secular cantatas were performed in the palaces or homes of the wealthy classes, as well as in more public places, such as town halls or coffeehouses. Sacred cantatas were usually performed in churches, at times as part of a three-hour or longer service.

New People and Concepts

cantata, 74   Johann Sebastian Bach, 78   movement, 75

Finale

CD 1: Track 5

Listen again to the recording of "Wachet auf" ("Sleepers Awake"), seventh movement, by Bach and compare your impressions now with your notes from your First Hearing. Consider the following questions:

- What type of work is this, and where was it intended to be performed?
- What voices do you hear? Are there both men and women singing, or just one or the other?
- What instruments do you hear with the voices?
- What is the texture of this composition?
- What is the form of this composition?
- What is the language being sung, and what is the text about?
- If you were going to describe this music to a friend, what would you say?

Further Listening

J. S. Bach, "Schweigt stille, plaudert nicht" ("Coffee Cantata"). This wonderful little cantata is about a coffee-addicted daughter and her father who thinks she drinks too much coffee.

J. S. Bach, "Wachet auf" ("Sleepers Awake"). Only movements four and seven of this cantata were in this chapter, and it would be good to hear the entire cantata. Like movements four and seven, movement one is based on the Lutheran hymn "Wachet auf" by Philipp Nicolei. Movements two and five are short recitatives, and movements three and six are duets in ternary form.

> I should be sorry, my Lord,
> if I had only succeeded in
> entertaining them; I wished
> to make them better.
>
> —COMPOSER GEORGE FRIDERIC
> HANDEL [1685 1799]

Oratorio

Listen to the recording of "Ev'ry Valley" by Handel and take notes on what you hear. Even if you are working with other students in a paired or group listening session, keep your own notes. Give some attention to the following:

- This aria is sung in English, so you should be able to understand the text, although you might have to hear it more than once to understand it all. What is the text about? What emotion, if any, does the text convey?

- What does the word *exalted* mean? When you hear that word, what kind of melody is it sung to? Is the melody slow? Low and sad? High and intense? Fast-moving and energetic? Is there another way to describe the melody on repetitions of that particular word?

- What voice type sings the text, and what instruments accompany the voice?

- Where do you think this piece was intended to be performed? In an aristocratic home? A church? A concert hall? A tavern or some other place?

- Can you guess at the texture and meter of this aria?

Keep your notes from this First Hearing to compare with your impressions about this piece after you study the information in this chapter.

8

Oratorio

An *oratorio,* as mentioned in Chapter 6, is a dramatic work for chorus, solo voices, and orchestra. Unlike opera, it does not include scenery, costuming, or stage action. It is similar to the cantata in many ways except that it is longer and is performed on a much larger scale. The oratorio developed as part of the Roman Catholic Church's efforts for reform after the Protestant Reformation. In order to reach out to as many community members as possible, the Congregation of the Oratory built buildings close to churches that were used for talks, lectures, and musical performances through which religious subjects could be taught outside of the liturgical services offered by the church. Because they were intended to teach, the earliest oratorios were often based on Bible stories and had a singing narrator to explain what was happening before and between the other musical sections. The stories were then enhanced by a series of arias, recitatives, choral movements, and instrumental sections. Some churches in Rome had oratorios with Latin texts, but most were in Italian so that the citizens could easily understand them. When oratorios were composed in other countries, the text was in

ORATORIO OR OPERA? KNOW THE DIFFERENCE

How is an oratorio different from an opera?
Both are based on stories, but they are performed much differently. Generally speaking, operas are plays in which the parts are sung. Thus, opera singers wear costumes. They act. They use sets. Oratorios are concerts performed without costumes, staging, or scenery. Operas are like movies. They *are* the story. Oratorios are concerts that *tell* the story.

If the singers in an oratorio are still part of a story, why don't they act their parts?
Because they have more than one part. In oratorios, each singer can represent several characters at different times. An opera singer would represent just one character. The solo singers in an oratorio usually sit in front of a choir and orchestra and stand only when it is their turn to sing. There are usually four soloists—two women and two men.

Are the stories told in operas and in oratorios similar?
No. Oratorios tell stories from the Bible in order to help listeners learn and appreciate the beauty of those stories. Operas can be based on religious stories, but in the baroque period they were usually based on classical stories, such as Greek plays, myths, or Roman histories.

Do both operas and oratorios use choirs?
Not really. Operas sometimes have a chorus if it fits the story. The chorus could be a group of singers who represent people who are acting as part of a celebration at a palace or the townspeople in a less formal setting. Like the soloists, members of an opera chorus are costumed and act their roles. Oratorios feature large choruses in many major movements of the works. The "Hallelujah" chorus from Handel's *Messiah* is just one of many examples. Oratorio chorus members usually wear choir robes or matching dresses and tuxedos because they do not represent individual people in the story.

Do both use orchestras?
Yes. In both cases the orchestras are often very large and play an important role in setting the mood at the beginning of the performance by playing an *overture*, sometimes called a *sinfonia*, to introduce the performance, and they continue to be important in accompanying the vocals. Oratorios differ, however, in that they were usually performed in churches and used the church organ as part of the orchestra. Operas were performed in secular settings that did not have large organs, although small, portable ones could be brought in for special effects.

Who keeps all of the singers and instrumentalists together?
Both operas and oratorios are led by a conductor. During the baroque period, that conductor sometimes also played the harpsichord. In a large setting, the singers and members of the orchestra cannot see or hear one another, so the conductor's role is essential.

We also studied the cantata. Is it anything like either an opera or an oratorio?
Think of cantatas as mini-oratorios. They are performed on a much smaller scale and are much shorter than either operas or oratorios. In fact, cantatas usually do not exceed twenty minutes. Oratorios, by contrast, can last over two hours, and operas can last as long as three hours.

the vernacular of that country for the same reason. "MusiCurious: Oratorio or Opera? Know the Difference" gives you a brief look at this type of performance.

Oratorios take as long as two hours or more to perform. In Italy, they were particularly popular during Lent, when theatrical performances such as operas were banned. The oratorio rose to its height in England in the monumental works of George Frideric Handel.

George Frideric Handel

George Frideric Handel (1685–1759) was born in Halle, Germany, a trading center some eighty miles southwest of Berlin, the son of a prosperous barber-surgeon attached to the court of the Duke of Saxony. His father had in mind a legal career for the boy but did allow him to begin music study at age 8 with the organist of the town's principal Lutheran church. Aside from learning to play the organ, harpsichord, violin, and oboe, young Handel also studied composition, writing church cantatas and numerous small-scale instrumental works.

Out of respect for his father's wish, Handel enrolled at the University of Halle in 1702. At the end of his first year, however, he withdrew from the university and went to Hamburg to pursue his interest in music. Musical activity in Hamburg, as in most cosmopolitan cities of the time, centered on the opera house, where Italian opera thrived. Soon after Handel arrived in Hamburg in 1703, he obtained a position as violinist in the theater orchestra and industriously set about learning the craft of opera composition. His first opera, *Almira* (1704), reflected the curious mixture of native German and imported Italian musical styles then prevalent in Hamburg; the recitatives were set in German, the arias in Italian. The work was a popular success, and three other operas soon followed. In 1706, feeling that he had learned all that Hamburg had to offer, Handel decided to go to Italy.

His three-year stay in Italy was amazingly successful. Traveling back and forth between Florence, Venice, Rome, and Naples, he met many of Italy's greatest composers and was the frequent guest of cardinals, princes, and ambassadors. Much of his popularity stemmed from the success of his operas *Rodrigo* (1708) and *Agrippina* (1709).

Through one of the friends he made in Italy, Handel obtained the position of musical director to the Electoral Court of Hanover, Germany. He had just taken up his duties in 1710, however, when he asked permission from Elector Georg Ludwig to visit London. Italian opera was then in great vogue with the English aristocracy, and the success of his opera *Rinaldo* (1711) led Handel to ask permission for another leave of absence the following year. By promising to return to Hanover "within a reasonable time," Handel stretched out his second London visit indefinitely.

Because European kings and queens had to be of royal blood and because England's Queen Anne died with no English heir, Handel's former employer from Hanover, Elector Georg Ludwig, ascended to the British throne as King George I. How Handel settled the embarrassing problem of his long-neglected contract with the Electoral Court is unknown. But the annual pension Queen Anne gave him was continued and even increased by George I, and within several years he was in high favor at the royal court.

Handel became an English citizen in 1726. He continued to compose successful operas, including some for the Royal Academy of Music, organized by British nobility under the sponsorship of the king. During the academy's eight-year existence (1720–1728), Handel's career as an opera composer reached its highest point. One of his most important operas from that period was *Giulio Cesare in Egitto (Julius Caesar in Egypt,* 1724*)*.

The popularity of Handel's operatic style received a blow, however, in 1728, when John Gay's *The Beggar's Opera,* which had spoken dialogue instead of recitative, short catchy songs instead of arias, and a story about dishonest businessmen and thieves, pleased large audiences in new ways. A parody of Italian style, *The Beggar's Opera* was widely imitated, and a new form of light, popular musical entertainment was created and sung in English.

Though Handel continued to compose Italian operas, such as *Xerxes* (1738), for more than a decade after the appearance of *The Beggar's Opera,* he turned increasingly to the oratorio. His first English oratorio, *Haman and Mordecai* (later revised and renamed *Esther*), was composed in 1720. Others followed during the 1730s, but it was not until 1739, with the completion of *Israel in Egypt* and *Saul,* that he seemed to sense the full musical and dramatic possibilities of this form. Neither of these works was an immediate success, but others that followed were. In 1741, Handel was invited to conduct several oratorios in Dublin, Ireland, during Holy Week, when operatic theaters

GEORGE FRIDERIC HANDEL
(1685–1759)

- Born in Halle, Germany; died at age 74 in London, England.

- Traveled from Germany to study opera composition in Italy, returned to Hanover, Germany, and then settled in England.

- Prolific composer whose works include several major Italian-style operas such as *Giulio Cesare in Egitto (Julius Caesar in Egypt)* and *Xerxes,* English oratorios such as *Messiah,* and instrumental works such as *Water Music.*

were closed. He decided that a new oratorio based on the birth, death, and significance of Jesus Christ would make for a successful ending to the series. Proceeds from the performance were to be given to charity. He composed that oratorio, *Messiah,* in just over three weeks, earning a large sum for charity and even more esteem for himself.

In his last years, Handel was universally recognized as England's greatest composer. His popularity with all segments of English society steadily grew, and the royal patronage of George I was followed by that of George II. Despite declining health and the eventual loss of his eyesight, Handel continued to maintain a heavy schedule of oratorio performances, which he conducted himself from the keyboard. While attending a performance of *Messiah* on March 30, 1759, he suddenly grew faint and had to be taken home. He died two weeks later and was buried with state honors in London's Westminster Abbey. His will revealed that he had accumulated a substantial private fortune, which was dispersed—along with his music manuscripts—among friends.

Today the fame of Handel rests largely on his oratorios (particularly *Messiah*), some of his operas, and a variety of instrumental works. The bulk of Handel's oratorios are dramatic, with singers taking the roles of specific characters. *Messiah* is a nondramatic oratorio in which the chorus dominates, narrating and describing the events. The solo voices do not represent specific characters as they would in a dramatic oratorio. Instead, they complement and act as a foil for the chorus.

Messiah

Messiah is based on the life of Jesus. Although we might expect that the text for this oratorio would come from the Gospels of the New Testament, in which the life of Jesus is recorded, Handel chose to take the bulk of the libretto from prophetic passages in the Old Testament. The opening texts we will hear are from Isaiah 40:1–5.

Messiah was composed in only twenty-four days. It was a success in Handel's lifetime and has become one of the most loved and popular pieces of music in the history of Western civilization. At its first London performance in 1743, King George II was so moved by the opening of the "Hallelujah" chorus that he stood during its performance, a precedent that most audiences follow still.

Legend has it that King George II set a precedent when he rose to his feet during the "Hallelujah" chorus at this early performance of *Messiah*.

Altogether, *Messiah* represents about two and a half hours of music for four solo voices (a soprano, an alto, a tenor, and a bass), a four-part chorus, and an orchestra. The oratorio is structured in three parts and comprises fifty-three movements. The movements include arias, recitatives, choruses, and orchestral sections. Part I deals with the prophecy of the coming of the Messiah and his birth; Part II, the sacrifice of Jesus and the salvation of humanity through his suffering and death; Part III, redemption through Christianity. An **overture,** sometimes called a *sinfonia,* introduces the work.

The overture to *Messiah* is structured according to what is generally called the *French overture.* Needless to say, this form was first popular in France, but it worked so well as a dramatic introduction for large-scale works of all kinds that it was used by many baroque composers. The idea behind the French overture is simple. It has two sections that contrast in style. The first section uses stately rhythms based on a pattern of long notes followed by short notes, one after the other. The flow of long-short-long-short-long-short note values creates a rather crisp, even majestic, effect. Musicians use the term *dotted rhythms* to describe this rhythmic pattern. The dotted first section of a French overture is followed by a faster section that has one melody after another following in imitation. Some French overtures end with a return to the dotted style of the beginning. Handel used the French overture style to introduce many of his operas, as well as this oratorio.

In this and many other dramatic works, the overture sets the mood for the story. The following Listening Guides include a recitative, an aria, and a chorus from *Messiah*.

Listening Guide

CD 4: Track 17

"Comfort Ye" from *Messiah* GEORGE FRIDERIC HANDEL

Date: 1741

Genre: Accompanied recitative

Texture: Homophonic

Voices and Instruments: Solo tenor voice with two violins, viola, and continuo played by organ and cello

Language: English

Meter: Quadruple

Duration: 3:03

Context: This is the first solo in *Messiah*, sung immediately after the Overture played by the orchestra. It begins the Christmas section of the oratorio.

Text (note: the singer repeats several phrases of text)	**Musical events**
17 Comfort ye, comfort ye my people, saith your God. Speak ye comfortably to Jerusalem, and cry unto her, that her warfare, her warfare is accomplish'd, that her iniquity is pardon'd. The voice of him that crieth in the wilderness: Prepare ye the way of the Lord, make straight in the desert a highway for our God.	The orchestra introduces the recitative and often maintains a rhythmically steady accompaniment. Sometimes the musicians become silent to allow the singer to be heard alone.

Featured Listening

CD 1: Track 6

"Ev'ry Valley" from *Messiah* GEORGE FRIDERIC HANDEL

Date: 1741

Genre: Aria

Texture: Homophonic

(continued)

Voices and Instruments: Solo tenor voice with two violins, viola, and continuo played by organ, harpsichord, and cello

Language: English

Meter: Quadruple

Duration: 3:25

Context: This aria follows the recitative "Comfort Ye," in the beginning section of *Messiah*. The vocal melody often displays the text using word painting.

Text	Word painting
6 Ev'ry valley, ev'ry valley shall be exalted, shall be exalted, shall be exalted, shall be exalted,	The word "exalted" is stretched out over several bars of exuberant and highly decorated melody.
and ev'ry mountain and hill made low,	"Mountain" is begun on a high note and finished on a low note, just as the shape of a mountain.
	The melody on "hill" has a little rise and fall.
	The word "low" is sung to a low note.
the crooked straight,	"Crooked" is sung to two notes that go back and forth as if they were crooked, and "straight" is held on a long note as if it were straight.
and the rough places plain, the crooked straight, the crooked straight, and the rough places plain, and the rough places plain.	"Plain" is on a long note.
Ev'ry valley, ev'ry valley shall be exalted,	"Valley" starts on a high note and ends on a low one.
	"Exalted" is again stretched out over an exuberant melody.
ev'ry valley, ev'ry valley shall be exalted, and ev'ry mountain and hill made low, the crooked straight, the crooked straight,	"Crooked" has notes that jump around; "straight" is long-held.
the crooked straight, and the rough places plain, and the rough places plain, and the rough places plain, the crooked straight, and the rough places plain.	

Listening Guide

CONNECT   CD 4: Track 18

"Hallelujah" from *Messiah* GEORGE FRIDERIC HANDEL

Date: 1741

Genre: Choral work

Texture: Polyphonic and homophonic

Voices and Instruments: SATB chorus (sopranos, altos, tenors, and basses), also called a *mixed* chorus; two oboes, two trumpets, first violins, second violins, violas, cellos, basses, timpani, organ, and harpsichord

Language: English

Meter: Quadruple

Duration: 3:33

Context: The "Hallelujah" chorus is placed late in *Messiah,* after the Easter section and before the shorter Redemption section. When only the Christmas section of *Messiah* is performed, this chorus is usually moved to the end of that section to serve as a finale.

Text	Features and textures
	Instrumental introduction
Hallelujah!	Homophonic texture
for the Lord God omnipotent reigneth;	Monophonic
Hallelujah!	Homophonic and finally polyphonic
The kingdom of this world is become the Kingdom of our Lord and of His Christ;	Homophonic
and He shall reign for ever and ever,	Monophonic, then polyphonic with imitation
King of Kings, and Lord of Lords, for ever and ever, Hallelujah,	Homophonic with interruptions of "for ever and ever" and "Hallelujah"
Hallelujah!	Homophonic

Messiah is often performed today, but the entire work may be too long for some types of seasonal concerts. The length is often cut down for those performances. At Christmastime, many churches or schools perform only Part I, about the birth of Christ, and then end by skipping to the famous "Hallelujah" chorus from Part II. At Easter, one can hear many performances of the Overture, followed by Parts II and III of *Messiah* without any of Part I. Either way, the famous "Hallelujah" chorus is part of the performance, and most audience members still stand up through it as did King George II in 1743. "Hearing the Difference: Bach's 'Wachet auf,' Cantata no. 140, seventh movement, and Handel's 'Hallelujah' Chorus" examines two religious works sung by a full chorus and with an orchestra.

The Passion

A **Passion** was a musical setting of the story of the suffering and crucifixion of Jesus Christ as told in the Bible by the Gospels. Passions were usually identified by the particular gospel writer whose text was used. The Passion was often performed during Holy Week (leading up to Easter), especially on Good Friday, when the crucifixion was remembered. The early settings of the Passion text—for instance, those of the great German master of the early baroque, Heinrich Schütz (1585–1672)—employed only the biblical text with an introductory and concluding chorus. By Bach's time, musical settings of the Passion had expanded to include nonbiblical texts in the form of commentary about the events described in the Gospel.

In Bach's monumental (over two and a half hours) *Passion According to St. Matthew,* the Gospel account of the betrayal, arrest, trial, and crucifixion of Christ was told by soloists in recitative, secco for all characters except for Christ, who was accompanied by a string quartet. The chorus assumed various roles, such as the crowd and the disciples. The nonbiblical contemplations were interspersed between sections of the Gospel story in the form of da capo arias sung by soloists and numerous chorales in which the congregation joined the choir and orchestra.

BACH'S "WACHET AUF," CANTATA NO. 140, SEVENTH MOVEMENT, AND HANDEL'S "HALLELUJAH" CHORUS

Both of these works are religious and are sung by a full SATB chorus with orchestra (see Featured Listening on page 77 and Listening Guide on page 86). As you listen to them again, concentrate on finding differences between them. Consider the following:

- Which work is the more homophonic (that is, homorhythmic with all voices singing together in the same rhythms) in texture? Which one also has sections that are monophonic (one melody line) and polyphonic (more than one separate line)?

- Which work is more exuberant and which is more solid and stately? Why might they differ in these ways? To answer this, consider that "Wachet auf" ends a cantata and "Hallelujah" ends the Easter

section of an oratorio about Jesus. Where was each intended to be performed and for what audiences? Is each work composed to be appropriate to its purpose?

- The languages of these two compositions are different. What is the language of each? Can you understand the text to the one that is in English, or does the music get in the way of hearing the words being sung?

- Can you determine the meter of each work?

- Does either work contain a word or words that repeat fairly often, indicating a stress on that word or words? What is repeated, and why is it stressed through repetition?

Summary

An oratorio is a large-scale dramatic work for chorus, solo voices, and orchestra, performed without scenery, costuming, or stage action. Most oratorios are based on biblical texts and were intended to both instruct and entertain audiences. George Frideric Handel, a German composer who studied opera composition in Italy and then spent most of his life in England, composed some of the most popular of all oratorios. The most often performed is *Messiah*, based on the birth and death of Jesus and on the redemption offered by his sacrifices. *Messiah*

features soprano, alto, tenor, and bass soloists, as well as a large choir and orchestra. It is still performed often during the Christmas and Easter seasons.

The Passion was a musical setting of the story of the suffering and crucifixion of Jesus as told in the Bible by the Gospels. Early in the baroque period, Passions were short and performed as part of church services during the week before Easter. By the late baroque, however, they became monumental compositions to be performed independently of a religious service.

New People and Concepts

George Frideric Handel, 82   overture, 84   Passion, 87

 **Finale**

 CONNECT   CD 1: Track 6

Listen again to the recording of "Ev'ry Valley" by Handel and compare your impressions now with your notes from your First Hearing. Consider the following questions:

- What is the aria "Ev'ry Valley" about, and how does it fit into the theme of *Messiah*?
- What is expressed by the music when the word "exalted" is sung? What about other words that are painted by the melody, such as "crooked" being made "straight," and "rough" places being made "plain"? How do those fit the meaning of the text? What do they say about the religious theme of the aria?
- What voice type sings the text, and what instruments accompany the voice?
- What are the texture and meter of this aria?
- If you were going to describe this music to a friend, what would you say?

Further Listening

George Frideric Handel, *Messiah.* Many performances of the entire work are available on CD and DVD.

Giaccomo Carissimi, *Jepthe.* This oratorio is based on a story from the Book of Judges in the Old Testament of the Bible in which Jepthe has promised God that he will sacrifice the first person who greets him if he is victorious in battle, and that person turns out to be his beloved daughter. The oratorio ends with his daughter singing before she dies, followed by a moving chorus.

J. S. Bach, *Passion According to St. Matthew.* A Passion from the Biblical Gospel of St. Matthew that tells of the betrayal, arrest, trial, and crucifixion of Jesus.

Baroque Solo and Chamber Music

> The aim and final end of all music should be none other than the Glory of God and the refreshment of the soul.
> —COMPOSER JOHANN SEBASTIAN BACH (1685–1750)

First Hearing

CONNECT · CD 1: Track 7

Listen to the recording of "The Little Fugue in G Minor" by Bach and take notes on what you hear. Even if you are working with other students in a paired or group listening session, keep your own notes. Give some attention to the following:

- This composition begins with a single melody. What enters next and soon after that? Do you hear any similarities to the beginning of Josquin's "Ave Maria" that we heard from the Renaissance period? How is this beginning similar and how is it different?

- How many instrumental melodies enter at the beginning and then continue to play throughout the work? In what relative order do the melodies enter? High first, lowest second, another order? What is the texture created by the various melodies?

- Listen for places where the melody that introduced the piece is played again. When it is played again, is it always in a high part or low part, or does it come back at different pitch levels? What pitch level is used for the last statement of that melody?

- What is most noticeable about the sound of the instrument(s) that play(s) this work? Does it or do they sound more like a harpsichord or more like a group of wind instruments?

- Can you count the beat and determine the meter? What do you think the meter is?

Keep your notes from this First Hearing to compare with your impressions about the piece after you study the information in this chapter.

9

The baroque era was not just a period of magnificent achievement in vocal composition; it also saw the gradual development of a significant body of instrumental music. The baroque was the age of the great violin makers, among them the members of the Stradivari family. Improvements were made in the construction of virtually every wind and brass instrument, and the organ and the harpsichord became the basic keyboard instruments. By the end of the baroque era, instrumental music had gradually equaled or surpassed vocal music in importance.

Keyboard Music

A large body of music for keyboard instruments—the organ and harpsichord—was written during the baroque period. We will see the piano take over in importance in later periods, but it was just being invented in the late baroque. These keyboard pieces

Harpsichords, like the one being played in this depiction, were well-suited for much of the music from the baroque period.

appeared with various titles—toccata, fantasia, prelude—all of which were fairly free in structure.

The term *toccata* derived from the Italian verb *toccare* ("to touch") and implies a piece full of scale passages, rapid runs and trills, and massive chords. The *fantasia* was a piece characterized by displays of virtuosity that made it seem to the listener that the music was spontaneously flowing from the player at the moment it was being played. The *prelude* was also generally free in form and improvisatory in style. It customarily introduced another piece or group of pieces. The toccata, fantasia, and prelude were often used as an introduction to a fugue, one of the great intellectual musical structures of the baroque era.

Fugue

A **fugue** is based on the polyphonic development of a melody called the **subject.** Fugues are composed for a certain number of *voice parts*. These voice parts are not necessarily sung by singers, although they may be. They are melodies that are often played by individual musical instruments or by a single instrument such as a keyboard or lute that can play several notes and melodies at the same time. It is essential that each voice maintain its musical independence from the other voices. The precise manner in which the subject is developed among these voice parts varies from piece to piece. However, the initial section of virtually every fugue follows a plan that is more or less standard. This section is called the **exposition.**

The exposition begins with a single voice stating the subject. As the subject ends, the second voice enters in imitation, stating the subject while the first voice continues with a contrasting melody called the **countersubject.** The countersubject *counters,* or is played along with, the imitation of the subject. This process of imitative entrances of each voice in turn continues until all voices have stated the fugue subject, at which point the exposition has been accomplished. Without pause, the piece continues with a number of sections that function either as new statements of the fugue subject or some variation of it, or as transitions between statements of the subject. The transition sections are called **episodes.** Although the exposition is part of virtually every fugue, what follows the exposition is quite free and varies greatly from fugue to fugue.

Outline of the Exposition of "The Little Fugue in G Minor"

Notice that the terms *soprano, alto, tenor,* and *bass* are used for instrumental high to low ranges just as they are used for voices.

Subject in soprano, countersubject, free play ⟶

Subject in alto, countersubject, free play ⟶

Subject in tenor, countersubject, free play →

Subject in bass, free play →

The primary musical interest of the fugue lies in remembering the subject when you first hear it and then recognizing it when it is played or sung again throughout the course of the composition. Sometimes, the subject is presented in slower or faster versions than it had been at the beginning, but that does not happen in the fugue we will be listening to. This fugue was composed by the unchallenged master of the baroque fugue, Johann Sebastian Bach. We heard an aria from a cantata by Bach in Chapter 7. Bach composed works in every form of musical composition prevalent in the baroque period with the exception of opera.

))) Featured Listening

 CD 1: Track 7
CONNECT

"The Little Fugue in G Minor" JOHANN SEBASTIAN BACH

Date: 1709

Genre: Organ fugue

Form: Fugue

Texture: Polyphonic

Instruments: Solo organ

Meter: Quadruple

Duration: 4:03

Special feature: Notice that the subject is played through in its entirety before it is imitated in other voices. That is different from the imitation at the beginning of most Renaissance vocal works, such as Josquin's "Ave Maria" in Chapter 5, in which each voice enters before the beginning melody is completed.

Context: This fugue is called "the little" because Bach composed another, longer, fugue in G minor. The title helps to distinguish which fugue is meant. Bach composed the little one when he was the court organist at the duke's palace and chapel of Weimar. It was most likely written and first played for the duke and his family and guests.

	Timing	What to listen for
7	0:00	The first playing of the subject in the highest (soprano) voice
	0:18	The imitation of the subject in the next lower (alto) voice, while the soprano voice continues by playing the countersubject
	0:41	The imitation of the subject in the next lower (tenor) voice, while the soprano and alto voices continue playing

Timing	What to listen for
0:58	The imitation of the subject in the lowest (bass, played on the pedals) voice, while the soprano and tenor voices continue to play
	Episode (transition during which the subject is not played)
1:25	The tenor voice begins the subject and the soprano picks it up and finishes it
	Episode
1:52	The alto voice plays the subject
	Episode
2:20	The bass voice plays the subject
	Episode
2:54	The soprano plays the subject
	Episode
3:40	The bass makes the final statement of the subject

In addition to being fun to listen to, this little fugue illustrates a major stylistic feature of much baroque instrumental music in that it features an uninterrupted, steady flow of music from the first note to the last chord. Quite unlike later styles, in which sections of music are separated by pauses, the polyphonic instrumental style of the baroque is characterized by continuous motion and progression from beginning to end. We mentioned this feature in the prelude to the baroque period, in which we pointed out the general sense of activity seen in much baroque art. Music remained constantly active, just as the art did.

Baroque organ literature included many works intended for performance in conjunction with religious ceremonies, and many of these pieces were based on chorale melodies. For instance, as an introduction to the service, the organist would play a work based on the particular chorale tune appropriate for the specific day in the church year, and that piece would be called a *chorale prelude*. Many of Bach's chorale preludes introduced the same chorale melody that was used later in the same service as the basis of a cantata. "MusiCurious: The King of Instruments" explains how organists achieve rich and varied sounds on this instrument.

Suite

Another type of composition popular among baroque composers was the **suite.** Unlike the fugue, a piece of music that can stand by itself or be paired with some type of introductory piece such as a prelude or toccata, suites are multimovement works. Most suites comprised a series of movements, each based on a particular dance rhythm and style. A typical suite included the German *allemande,* the French *courante,* and the *sarabande* (originally a rather erotic dance from Spain but changed to a slow, courtly dance by the French and Germans), and the French *bourrée,* and ended with the English or Irish *gigue* (jig). Many suites also included the French *gavotte* and, at times, nondance movements such as an introductory prelude. Baroque suites were not intended for dancing, as were the pairs or sets of dances of the Renaissance, but the collection of dances in most suites provided interesting contrasts in meter, tempo, and texture.

Suites were composed for almost any solo instrument or group of instruments, including orchestras. Bach's orchestral suites and Handel's *Water Music* remain popular today. The next Listening Guide discusses a Bach bourrée, "Cello Suite no. 3 in C Major."

THE KING OF INSTRUMENTS

What instrument is called the King of Instruments and why?

The organ was given that title by Mozart. The earliest organs were invented during the third century BCE. By the baroque period, the organ had developed to the point that it could fill a church or concert hall with the most majestic of sounds. Yet it could also play gentle and soft music. Depending on the pipes connected to it, the organ's range of high to low notes could be greater than that of an orchestra, making it the most versatile of all single instruments—in other words, "the king."

What are the pipes for?

The sound comes through the pipes, and the player uses the keyboard, or set of keyboards called the *console,* to select the pipes that will sound. In addition to the console, the organist uses a full display of buttons and knobs, called *stops,* to assign the pipes for each keyboard to play. Large organs have many sets of pipes. The biggest can be as long as thirty-two (or more) feet for very low notes, and the smallest are pencil-sized ones that sound very high. The pipes can be made of many different materials such as wood or metal and can be sounded by air blowing directly through them or through reeds connected to the pipes. The use of stops to choose the pipes allows the player more control of the sound than is available to a player of any other musical instrument.

Organs like this one from the baroque period often have elaborate, magnificent sets of pipes.

So, can pipe organs ever be moved?

Hardly ever. Pipe organs have to be built specifically for the church or concert hall in which they are to be used. The sets of pipes on some organs take up quite a bit of space and can be spread out around the church or hall, or they can be in a set together facing the congregation or audience. During the medieval and Renaissance periods there were small organs with a single set of pipes that could be moved around, but those were not the instruments referred to as the "king."

Why do organists also play with their feet?

Because many organs have a full keyboard of pedals that are played with the feet. This *pedal board* is most often used to play bass notes, such as the lowest lines we heard in Bach's fugue, but it is also possible to play higher melodies and even chords on the pedals.

Is it only the size of the pipes that control the loudness of the sound?

No. Dynamic levels on some organs are changed by use of a *swell box* with shutters. The swell box opens to let out as much sound as possible, or closes to soften the sound. The swell box is controlled by pedals above the pedal board that look like the accelerator pedal on a car or bus.

"Bourrée I" from Cello Suite no. 3 in C Major, BWV 1009

JOHANN SEBASTIAN BACH

Date: ca. 1720

Genre: Solo cello music

Form: Binary (AABB)

Texture: Monophonic, but there are times when the melody jumps from high to low and back to high again, suggesting that one's ear could connect the high sounds together and the low sounds together to imagine the sound of two melodies

Instruments: Solo cello

Meter: Quadruple with two fast pickup notes on beat four at the beginning

Duration: 1:19

Context: This bourrée is the fifth of six movements from the third of six suites that Bach composed for a cellist at the court of Prince Leopold at Anhalt-Cöthen in Germany. It was probably performed for the prince and his guests as general entertainment.

	Timing	What to listen for
19	0:00	The A section of the form
	0:12	Repeat of the A section
	0:24	The B section of the form
	0:51	Repeat of the B section

Baroque Sonata

In the beginning of the baroque period, the term **sonata** was applied to instrumental pieces that varied greatly in structure, character, and the number and type of instruments. Usually it was a multimovement work, but the number of movements varied from piece to piece.

Gradually there developed a distinction between the sonata written to be played in a church, the *sonata da chiesa,* and that intended to be played in a chamber or room in a home or palace, the *sonata da camera.* The *sonata da camera* became essentially a dance suite, and the *sonata da chiesa* a four-movement work in which the movements alternated in tempo: slow-fast-slow-fast.

Toward the latter part of the baroque period, three types of sonatas were predominant: the sonata for unaccompanied instrument; the *solo sonata,* for a solo instrument (usually the violin) and continuo; and the *trio sonata,* usually employing two violins for the upper voices with a cello and keyboard instrument for the continuo. Corelli, Vivaldi, Handel, and Bach all made important contributions to the sonata literature.

ELISABETH-CLAUDE JACQUET DE LA GUERRE
(1665–1729)

- Born in Paris, France; died at age 64 in Paris.
- Composed music for one ballet, one opera, several cantatas, and a few songs as well as harpsichord music and both trio and solo sonatas.

Elisabeth-Claude Jacquet de la Guerre

Elisabeth-Claude Jacquet de la Guerre (1665–1729) was a very talented female composer of the baroque. Elisabeth's father, Claude Jacquet, was a musician who taught his daughter from an early age to play music. A child prodigy, she was performing on the harpsichord as young as age 5. The family lived in Paris and when King Louis XIV heard her play, he not only praised her performance, but he hired her to entertain himself, his mistress, and their guests on a regular basis. He also supported her musical education and attended many of her concerts. She, in return, dedicated many of her compositions to him.

Elisabeth married another musician, Marin de la Guerre, in 1684. The couple had one son, who was only 10 years old when he died. Living through the loss of her son in the early 1700s and then her father and her husband in 1702 and 1704 respectively, she managed to continue her career. She performed at public recitals and composed extensively until the end of her life. Her works include songs, cantatas, operas, and sonatas for chamber groups. Her publications sold well, and she was also a successful performer as both a harpsichordist and singer. The following Listening Guide features a movement from one of her violin sonatas. (*Note:* The title "Aria" is usually used for a work that is sung, but here it refers to the singable melody of the instrumental work.)

CD 4: Track 20

"Aria" ("Air"), sixth movement, from Sonata in D Minor for Violin and Basso Continuo ELISABETH-CLAUDE JACQUET DE LA GUERRE

Date: ca. 1695

Genre: Baroque sonata

Form: Rondeau with a repeating theme that changes pitch levels and shifts from minor to major and back to minor with extended sections of variations

Texture: Homophonic

Instruments: Solo violin and continuo played by a harpsichord and a viola de gamba

Meter: Triple with a single beat pickup note at the beginning of each section

Duration: 3:49

Context: The composer wrote this work as part of a collection of six sonatas that were performed for King Louis XIV while he was taking his luncheon. It was reported that the king spoke with her after the performance and praised her work as being most beautiful and original. The sonatas were published in 1707 in Paris and dedicated to the king.

Timing	What to listen for
0:00	Theme in D minor
0:12	Theme repeats
0:24	Theme in F major
0:36	Theme in D minor further embellished
0:49	Theme in G minor
1:02	Theme in D minor
1:14	Theme in D major played by viola dagamba
1:27	Variation on theme from major to minor, viola da gamba plays a high duet with the violin
1:43	Theme in D major, with theorbo
1:55	Variation on theme from major to minor, viola da gamba plays a high duet with the violin
2:04	Variation continues
2:15	Theme in D minor
2:26	Theme in D minor, extended
2:45	Theme as short coda

[20]

Summary

The baroque era saw the rise of instrumental music due in part to the development and improvement of existing instruments.

The harpsichord and the organ were the chief keyboard instruments of the baroque period. Single-movement works written for these instruments include the fantasia, the prelude, and the toccata. The fugue, in which a melodic subject is presented and developed in a variety of ways, is one of the most significant forms of the baroque period. Fugues often appeared in keyboard, instrumental, and vocal works. Chorale tunes were an important part of literature written for the organ. The suite is an example of the multimovement keyboard form that became popular for other solo instruments and ensembles.

The baroque sonata is a multimovement work for one or more instruments. Later developments include sonatas for unaccompanied instruments, solo instruments with accompaniment, and two or more instruments with accompaniment.

New People and Concepts

countersubject (of a fugue), 91

Elisabeth-Claude Jacquet
  de la Guerre 96

episode, 92

exposition, 91

fugue, 91

sonata, 95

subject (of a fugue), 91

suite, 93

Finale   CD 1: Track 7

CONNECT

Listen again to the recording of "The Little Fugue in G Minor" by Bach and compare your impression now with your notes from your First Hearing. Consider the following questions:

- Describe similarities and differences between the exposition section (beginning) of this fugue and the beginning section of Josquin's "Ave Maria."

- How many instrumental melodies enter at the beginning and then continue to play throughout the work? What is the texture created by the various melodies?

- Listen for places where the melody that introduced the piece is played again. When it is played again, is it always in a high part or low part, or does it come back at different pitch levels?

- What kind of instrument plays this fugue, and how does it make its sound?

- What is the meter of the fugue?

- If you were going to describe this music to a friend, what would you say?

Further Listening

J. S. Bach, Toccata and Fugue in D Minor, BWV 565. This is one of Bach's most famous organ works, which was also transcribed for orchestra and used in Disney's film *Fantasia* (1940). Disney used it again in the 1954 movie *20,000 Leagues Under the Sea.*

J. S. Bach, Cello Suite no. 3 in C Major, BWV 1009. The bourrée from this suite was in this chapter, but the entire suite is a pleasure to hear because of the interesting contrasts among the dances. The movements are Prelude, Allemande, Courante, Sarabande, Bourrée, and Gigue.

The suite has also been transcribed for classical guitar, and recordings of that version are also easily available.

Elisabeth-Claude Jacquet de la Guerre, Sonata in D Minor for Violin and Basso Continuo. The sixth movement of this seven-movement sonata was discussed in this chapter. The entire sonata is a pleasure to listen to, again, because of the contrasts among the movements. The sonata includes the movements Grave, Vivace e Presto, Adagio, Allegro, Adagio, Allegro, Aria, and Allegro.

All in all, Vivaldi composed about 450 concertos of one sort or another. People who find his music too repetitious are inclined to say that he wrote the same concerto 450 times. This is hardly fair: he wrote two concertos, 225 times each.

—MUSIC JOURNALIST DAVID W. BARBER

[B. 1958]

The Baroque Orchestra

CONNECT   CD 1: Tracks 8–12

))) First Hearing

Listen to the recording of "La Primavera" ("Spring"), first movement, from *Le Quattro Stagione (The Four Seasons),* by Vivaldi and take notes on what you hear. Even if you are working with other students in a paired or group listening session, keep your own notes. Give some attention to the following:

● The general theme of this work is hinted at by the title "Spring," from *The Four Seasons.* Are there any musical sounds that you can imagine as being associated with springtime? If so, what is it that the orchestra plays that might remind you of spring?

● List the instruments you hear playing. What instrument do you hear that is not a bowed string instrument?

● Does any single instrument seem to be featured more than the rest? When and how does that happen? Is it louder, or is it playing by itself at any point?

● Do you hear any section of the music more than one time? When do you hear the section the first time, and how many other times do you hear it?

● Can you determine the meter of this work?

Keep your notes from this First Hearing to compare with your impressions about the piece after you study the information in this chapter.

10

The Orchestra

The first orchestras were used to accompany singers in baroque operas, cantatas, and oratorios. The rich orchestral sound was so pleasing that it did not take long for royalty and other wealthy families to hire musicians, along with a composer-conductor, to come to their palaces or estates and provide instrumental music for themselves and their guests. Many of these court orchestras at first were made up of only bowed stringed instruments, though woodwinds and others were gradually added.

King George II of England, for whom Handel composed, enjoyed the variety of sounds provided by an orchestra. Handel's *Water Music* is called that because it was composed to be performed for the king and his guests on a barge on the Thames River, which runs through London. *Water Music* is made up of dances that can be formed into three suites, although the exact order of performance for the king is not known. The following is a minuet from *Water Music.* Its use of French horns, oboes, and bassoon, along with strings, gave the music an unusually full, orchestral sound for the period.

Musicians in costume perform baroque music.

 Listening Guide

 CONNECT   CD 4: Track 21

"Minuet" from Water Music GEORGE FRIDERIC HANDEL

Date: 1717

Genre: Orchestral suite

Form: Minuet and trio (ternary, ABA form)

Texture: Homophonic

Instruments: Two horns, two oboes, one bassoon, first violins, second violins, violas, cellos, basses, and harpsichord; the trio cuts down to just strings and continuo

Meter: Triple

Duration: 2:21

Context: The first performances of this work on the king's barge could not include harpsichord because there was not enough room for it. Because the harpsichord is usually part of a baroque orchestra, it is appropriate to add it to modern performances such as this one. Notice the contrast in dynamic levels between the minuet and the trio. The return of the minuet at the end gives the dance a nice sense of balance.

	Timing	What to listen for
	Minuet	
21	0:00	Orchestra
	Trio	
	0:38	Strings and continuo
	Minuet	
	1:37	Orchestra

 **MusiCurious**

HOW BAROQUE PERFORMERS "DECORATE" MUSIC

Baroque music seems to be very active, even in slow movements. Why is that?

Constant activity was part of baroque style, in art and architecture as well as music. Composers often wrote long-held notes, expecting that musicians would improvise even more notes to maintain creative energy. The term for that is *embellishment*. Players would also add little stylized decorations called *ornaments* as part of their embellishment of melodies. Those ornaments could be as simple as two fast notes going back and forth (called a *trill*) or more complex musical decorations.

If musicians embellished fugue subjects, wouldn't that make them harder to recognize when they come back?

Yes, and for that reason baroque music that is as strictly organized as a fugue is usually played the way it was written. Also, some solos were deliberately written to be played so fast that embellishment would be difficult. Embellishment is not expected in such cases.

Then when *do* musicians embellish and add ornaments?

Usually in slow movements and repetitions of music they played earlier. Binary form was commonly used for dances, sonatas, and other single movements during the baroque period. Because a movement in binary form has two sections, each of which is repeated (AABB), players generally embellished the repeats with extra fast notes, runs, or ornaments.

Wouldn't embellishment make players or singers of the same music sound different from one another?

Yes. The practice of embellishment was one way in which individual musicians who were not necessarily composers themselves had an opportunity to display their talents and attract listeners to their performances. Part of the pleasure of hearing baroque music played well is in noticing when players or singers change the music as it repeats.

The pitting of soft sounds against loud ones fit the interest in contrasts central to the arts of the baroque period. **Concertos** developed out of this interest. The term *concerto* comes from the Latin word *concertare*, which means to fight or contend. In music, that idea was applied to the joining together of dissimilarly sized groups, or a solo instrument with an orchestra, to "oppose" each other to provide an interesting and harmonious, but contrasting, sound. The two types of concertos we discuss are the **concerto grosso,** in which a small solo group opposes the orchestra, and the **solo concerto,** in which the relatively soft sound of an individual solo instrument opposes that of an orchestra.

The two concerto movements we will listen to are in what is known as **ritornello** form. *Ritornello* is Italian for "return" or "repetition." As we will hear in our examples, short sections of orchestral music return during the movements. This form is easy to listen to because the constant return of the usually energetic introductory orchestral melody provides the listener with a sense of unity for the entire movement. "Musi-Curious: How Baroque Performers 'Decorate' Music" illustrates how musicians inserted their personalities into their performances.

Concerto Grosso

The concerto grosso is a multimovement work in which a small group of solo instruments, called the *concertino,* and the full orchestra, called the *ripieno* (Italian for "full"), are contrasted. The basic structure and number of movements of the concerto grosso varied, with the three-movement structure (fast-slow-fast) the most commonly used outline.

Bach, whom we discussed earlier as a cantata composer, spent time providing music for court orchestras, particularly when he was employed at Cöthen. The instrumentation for his orchestras varied according to what players he had available and what sort of event the music was to be part of. Some of his orchestral works were composed for fairly large ensembles that included several violins, a viola, two or three oboes, one bassoon, two or three trumpets, two timpani, and harpsichord with cello and double bass as continuo instruments.

Bach completed six works dedicated to Christian Ludwig, the Margrave (a hereditary title given to some German princes) of Brandenburg, in 1721. Although Bach referred to these pieces as "concertos for several instruments," they have come to be known as the Brandenburg Concertos. Three of them (nos. 2, 4, and 5) follow the tradition of contrasting concertino and ripieno groups. By his choice of instruments for the concertino, Bach created a contrast in timbre *within* the solo group, as well as *between* the solo group and the ripieno. In the fifth Brandenburg, for example, the three members of the concertino—the violin, the flute, and the harpsichord—all have quite different tone qualities.

A harpsichord is shaped something like a small grand piano and, like the piano, has metal strings that run parallel to the long side of the body of the instrument. What makes it different from the piano is that its strings are plucked instead of being hit with hammers. That plucking action gives the harpsichord a crisp tone quality that worked well in baroque orchestras because it could cut through the sound of the other instruments and be heard clearly. The plucking also sounds at the same dynamic level, no matter how hard or lightly the keys are played. Some harpsichords have two manuals (keyboards) that each pluck a different set of strings. The player can *couple* the keyboards so that playing on one will cause both keyboards to work and sound both sets of strings together. That makes the sound of the instrument much louder than it would be if either keyboard were played by itself. It is also possible to play using a *lute stop,* which deadens the strings to make them sound more like a lute. Many sizes and types of harpsichord or related instruments were used throughout the baroque period.

CD 4: Tracks 22–24

Brandenburg Concerto no. 5, first movement JOHANN SEBASTIAN BACH

Date: 1721

Genre: Concerto grosso

Tempo: Allegro

Form: Ritornello (the ritornello theme, or part of it, returns throughout with contrasting sections between)

Instruments: Concertino: flute, violin, and harpsichord; Ripieno: string orchestra with continuo

Meter: Quadruple

Duration: 10:00

Context: The date on the music is 1721, but some musicologists believe that this concerto was first composed and performed in 1719 to show off a new harpsichord at the Cöthen court where Bach was employed. Bach was a fine harpsichordist, and he might well have played in the first performance of this concerto since the harpsichord part indeed requires a **virtuoso** (exceedingly talented) musician to play it.

	Timing	What to listen for
22	0:00	*Ritornello theme (ripieno),* complete statement of vigorous melody that surges upward, setting rhythmic drive in motion
	0:20	*Contrasting section (concertino),* fragments from ritornello theme; imitation between flute and violin, with harpsichord an independent third part in constant motion
	0:45	*Ritornello theme,* partial statement from beginning of theme
	0:50	*Contrasting section,* continued imitation between flute and violin
	1:10	*Ritornello theme,* partial statement, begins where last ritornello left off.
	1:16	*Contrasting section,* harpsichord enters; flute and violin echo in single notes, then develop other fragments.
	1:37	*Ritornello theme,* partial statement, taken from where the last ritornello left off
	1:43	*Contrasting section,* interplay between violin and flute; fast notes, virtuosic display draw attention to harpsichord
	2:24	*Ritornello theme,* partial statement from middle of theme
	2:30	*Contrasting section,* figures tossed back and forth between flute and violin; new melodic fragment introduced and developed; extended length; final trills lead to:
	4:12	*Ritornello theme,* partial statement from beginning of theme
	4:16	*Contrasting section,* continued imitation between violin and flute
23	0:00	*Ritornello theme,* full statement of theme
	0:11	*Contrasting section,* continued imitation between flute and violin moving smoothly into:
	0:39	*Ritornello theme,* continued imitation between flute and violin moving smoothly into:
24	0:00	*Contrasting section,* the longest contrasting section; virtuosic display draws attention to harpsichord; flute and violin drop out, leaving harpsichord, with trills and passage work, leading to the return of:
	3:44	*Ritornello theme,* complete statement of the theme.

Solo Concerto

The concerto grosso and another type of concerto called the ripieno concerto, in which the ripieno group plays without a solo instrument or instrumental group, were popular throughout the baroque period. Eventually, though, the desire for more contrast led to the development of the solo concerto.

Antonio Vivaldi

One of the most prolific composers of baroque solo concertos was the Italian composer **Antonio Vivaldi** (1678–1741).

Vivaldi was the son of a violinist who played as part of the instrumental ensemble at St. Mark's Cathedral in Venice. His father taught him to play the violin, but when he was young he was more interested in becoming a priest. For whatever reason, possibly his ill health, Vivaldi turned his attention from religion to music. He obtained a job as a violin teacher and composer at a girls' orphanage. Because he had red hair, which was not all that common in Italy, and was also a priest, he became known as the Red Priest.

Orphanages not only took care of girls who had no parents, but they also taught the girls a trade so that they could one day support themselves. The orchestra at the

ANTONIO VIVALDI
(1678–1741)

- Born in Venice, Italy; died at age 63 in Vienna, Austria.
- Best known for over five hundred concertos, many sonatas, and large-scale vocal works including operas and cantatas.

orphanage in which Vivaldi taught became famous enough that it was hired to perform at courts and general city functions, entertaining any number of important visitors. By such performances, the girls earned some of their support, and Vivaldi earned a great deal of recognition. He composed concertos, particularly solo concertos, to display the talents of girls who played particularly well.

Of all Vivaldi's concertos, the group called *Le Quattro Stagione (The Four Seasons)* is perhaps the most interesting because of the extramusical basis of its inspiration. Vivaldi was one of the first to try to depict through music the feelings and sounds of the changing seasons. These four violin concertos are an early example of baroque descriptive or **program music,** and the music for the solo violin, which calls for virtuoso playing, demonstrates Vivaldi's skill at writing for the instrument. In spite of their descriptive intent, all of the concertos follow the three-movement formal outline—fast, slow, fast.

Each of the four concertos bears the title of one of the seasons—spring, summer, fall, and winter—and each is preceded by a sonnet, which may or may not have been written by Vivaldi, describing that particular season. For instance, the first movement of the concerto entitled "La Primavera" ("Spring") has the following introduction:

> Spring has come, and the birds greet it with happy songs, and at the same time the streams run softly murmuring to the breathing of the gentle breezes.
>
> Then the sky being cloaked in black, thunder and lightning come and have their say; after the storm has quieted, the little birds turn again to their harmonious song.

The poem depicted in the second and third movements continues to portray aspects of the spring season:

> Second movement: "Here in a pleasant flowery meadow, the leaves sweetly rustle, the goatherd sleeps, his faithful dog at his side."
>
> Third movement: "Nymphs and shepherds dance to the festive sound of the pastoral musette under the bright sky that they love."

Listening Guides to all three movements follow. "MusiCurious: Attending a Concert" describes what it is like to hear this music.

  **))) Featured Listening**   **CD 1: Tracks 8–12**

CONNECT

"La Primavera" ("Spring"), first movement, from *Le Quattro Stagione (The Four Seasons)* ANTONIO VIVALDI

Date: 1725

Genre: Solo concerto

Tempo: Allegro (fast)

Form: Ritornello

Instruments: Concertino: solo violin (joined occasionally by two more solo violins); Ripieno: string orchestra with continuo and archlute (a lute with extra bass strings)

Meter: Quadruple

Duration: 3:14

Context: Among Vivaldi's duties as music teacher at an orphanage for girls was the composition of two solo concertos each week for the girls to perform at Sunday concerts given at the orphanage. This concerto was probably first performed at one of those concerts. Notice that the music is composed to sound like birds singing, streams murmuring, and thunder and lightning from a storm in order to fit the poem.

	Timing	What to listen for
8	0:00	*Ritornello,* orchestra, first phrase of optimistic spring theme stated forte; echoed piano
	0:13	Second phrase of spring theme, stated forte; echoed piano
9	0:00	*Contrasting section,* three solo violins, high pitch, trills, suggest bird calls
		Ritornello, orchestra, second phrase of spring theme, forte
10	0:00	*Contrasting section,* orchestra, smoothly flowing, soft note pairs suggest streams and breezes
	0:21	*Ritornello,* orchestra, second phrase of spring theme
11	0:00	*Contrasting section,* forte tremolo (fast, repeated notes) in orchestra for thunder, scales rushing upward for lightning; solo violin added with new lightning theme, tremolo continues in orchestra
	0:23	*Ritornello,* orchestra, second phrase of spring theme
12	0:00	*Contrasting section,* three solo violins suggest bird calls; sustained note in bass
	0:19	Orchestra, forte, ritornello-related theme
	0:31	Solo violin with continuo, passage work
	0:45	*Ritornello,* orchestra states second phrase of spring theme forte; echoed softly to conclude

Listening Guide

 CD 4: Track 25

"La Primavera" ("Spring"), second movement, from *Le Quattro Stagione (The Four Seasons)* ANTONIO VIVALDI

Date: 1725

Genre: Solo concerto

Tempo: Largo e pianissimo sempre (slow and soft throughout)

Form: A long, extended melody with some sections beginning like the opening of the melody, but then continuing on with variations and embellishments of that melody

Instruments: Solo violin, first violins, second violins, and violas

Meter: Triple

Duration: 2:17

Context: This slow movement serves as a contrast to the first and third fast movements played by the soloist with orchestra and continuo. It omits the low strings and continuo, keeping it higher and lighter sounding than the other, faster, movements. The poem on which this concerto is based refers to a faithful dog at the side of the sleeping goatherd. The viola's repetition of a short note followed by a long one is intended to depict the barking of the dog. The rustling of the leaves is depicted by the smooth rocking motion of the orchestral violins.

(continued)

	Timing	What to listen for
25	0:00	Violins imitate the rustling leaves; the viola enters playing a long note followed by a short note imitating the dog.
	0:04	Solo violin begins its long, extended melody.
	0:23	The solo violin begins a melody much like the opening one, with embellishments and a long extension.
	1:03	The solo violin again imitates the opening melody but again extends it with embellishments.

 **MusiCurious**

ATTENDING A CONCERT

How should I dress up to attend a classical concert?

That depends. Dress varies with the time of day and individual taste. Generally, people dress up more for a concert on Friday or Saturday evening than for an afternoon concert. On week nights, many people have come directly from work and might be wearing office attire. You will see the most formal dress at opening night at an opera that will be performed several times, since opening night is when reviewers from the newspapers are there and parties might be held after the performance. Basically, if you just look neat and clean, perhaps wearing something you might wear to a religious service or to a nice restaurant, you will fit in just fine. There is absolutely no need for a young man to wear a suit or a woman to have a pricey dress. Most of the time, audience attire varies greatly.

How much will the tickets cost?

Ticket prices can be high for the seats closest to the stage or those that are placed where the sound is best in the auditorium. Operas tend to cost more than other concerts because of the great expense of the costumes, scenery, and solo singers in addition to a fairly large orchestra. Whatever the regular ticket cost, students should know that many concert halls will discount tickets greatly for those who arrive to buy a ticket an hour or two before the concert. The people in charge of putting on the concert want to fill all of the seats, and they offer such discounts in hopes that students might enjoy the concert and continue to attend concerts even at full price.

When I get to my seat, what will be expected of me?

Before you get there, you will probably be given a program. Try to look at it before the music begins. If you

see a multimovement work on the program, such as Vivaldi's "La Primavera" ("Spring") from *Le Quattro Stagione (The Four Seasons)*, you will see the titles of each of the three movements indented under the main title as follows:

Violin Concerto "La Primavera" ("Spring")
from *Le Quattro Stagione (The Four Seasons)*
by Antonio Vivaldi

Allegro

Largo e pianissimo sempre

Danza pastorale: allegro

Those three movements were composed to go together and to contrast with one another, the first and last movements being fast and the middle movement slow. Most members of the audience will want to hear all three movements without clapping, talking, or other disturbances between the movements, so it is important that you stay quiet until the entire work is finished. When in doubt, it is a good idea to stay quiet until everyone around you applauds.

Should I clap at any other time?

Yes. Concert goers clap when the concertmaster (first violinist in the orchestra) comes out on stage, when the conductor comes out, and when the soloist (violinist, in the case of Vivaldi's work) comes out. You will also applaud those same people at the end of their entire performance. If members of the audience really enjoy the concert, they might stand up while they clap at the end. That sometimes encourages the performers to play or sing an extra short piece that is not on the program. That added piece or pieces is called an *encore*.

 CD 4: Track 26

"La Primavera" ("Spring"), third movement, from *Le Quattro Stagione* (*The Four Seasons*) ANTONIO VIVALDI

Date: 1725

Genre: Solo concerto

Tempo: Danza pastorale: allegro (pastoral dance: fast)

Form: Ritornello

Instruments: Solo violin, string orchestra, archlute, and continuo with harpsichord

Meter: Quadruple

Duration: 3:34

Context: The poem on which this piece is based mentions the dancing of nymphs and shepherds, and the light repetition of the ritornello theme imitates that. The musette mentioned in the poem was a type of bagpipe that was popular during the baroque period. The sound of the long-held note, or drone, in the lower strings imitates the sound of the musette.

	Timing	What to listen for
26	0:00	*Ritornello* played by the orchestra
	0:27	Solo violin with continuo
	0:47	*Ritornello*, orchestra
	1:14	Solo violin with another violin, harpsichord, and then later bass that eventually drop out
	2:05	*Ritornello*, orchestra
	2:37	Solo violin with cellos and basses, no continuo
	3:02	*Ritornello*, orchestra

Summary

The orchestra began in the baroque period. Baroque orchestras varied in size and instrumentation, and several types of works were composed for them. The concerto grosso is a multimovement work that pits a small group, the concertino, against the full ensemble, the ripieno. A solo concerto differs from the concerto grosso in that the concertino is reduced to a single instrument. The three-movement pattern of the concerto (fast-slow-fast) and the use of the ritornello form in the first movement were common.

New People and Concepts

Antonio Vivaldi, 103

concerto, 101

concerto grosso, 101

program music, 104

ritornello, 101

solo concerto, 101

virtuoso, 102

Finale

CD 1: Tracks
8–12

Listen again to the recording of "La Primavera" ("Spring"), first movement, from *Le Quattro Stagione (The Four Seasons),* by Vivaldi and compare your impression now with your notes from your First Hearing. Consider the following questions:

- What instruments are used to imitate a birdsong, a murmuring stream, and thunder and lightning? Do they sound anything like those sounds of nature, in your opinion? Do you think flutes imitating a bird's song, instead of violins, would be more believable?

- The presence of the harpsichord is common in baroque orchestras, but it was not used in orchestras of later periods. Do you think it provides a pleasant contrast to the bowed strings, or do you think that it is unnecessary?

- Do you hear the contrast between the solo violin and the violins of the orchestra? When does the solo violin stand out the most? In the beginning, the middle, or the end of the movement?

- The fact that the orchestral *ritornello* returns is what gives this form its name. Do you hear the *ritornello* as a sound that gives the movement a sense of continuity, or does the *ritornello* just get in the way of the springtime sound effects?

- What is the meter of the movement?

- If you were going to describe this music to a friend, what would you say?

Further Listening

George Frideric Handel, *Water Music.* This entire work is really three suites, only one dance from which we heard in this chapter. The instrumentation Handel used was effective for the outdoor setting for which the work was composed . . . to be played on a barge on the Thames River as the king and his guests traveled. The movement we heard included two horns, two oboes, and bassoon in addition to strings and continuo. Other movements add flute and trumpet, both of which can be heard well outdoors.

J. S. Bach, Orchestra Suite no. 3 in D Major. This well-loved suite includes the very beautiful second movement, "Air on a G String."

J. S. Bach, Brandenburg Concertos. We heard the first movement from the fifth concerto from this set of six concertos that Bach gave to the margrave (military governor) of Brandenburg when he visited the court of Anhalt-Cöthen where Bach was employed. The instruments in the concertino (solo) groups vary from one concerto to the next, and all six are masterworks that should be heard and appreciated.

Antonio Vivaldi, *Le Quattro Stagione (The Four Seasons).* Only the first of the four seasons was covered in this chapter. The other seasons, "Summer," "Autumn," and "Winter," are just as enjoyable to listen to. They are also based on poems depicting the seasons, as we heard in "Spring." The poems were presumably written by Vivaldi himself.

CHARACTERISTICS OF BAROQUE MUSIC

Texture	Homophonic, polyphonic
Tonality	Major-minor system with dissonance used for special effects
Rhythm	Measured
Singing style	Monody, recitative, aria, arioso, large-scale choral works
Large vocal works	Opera, oratorio, Passion, Mass
Small vocal works	Cantata
Musical instruments	Harpsichord, organ, lute, orchestras made up of bowed strings with some woodwinds and/or brass instruments with basso continuo
Solo instrumental music	Fantasia, prelude, toccata, fugue, suite
Group instrumental music	Sonata da chiesa, sonata da camera, concerto grosso, solo concerto
Other features	Activity, contrasts, and much improvised embellishment to decorate the musical lines

Prelude

The classical era in the arts lasted from about 1750 to about 1800. This fifty-year period was highlighted by the American Revolution (1775–1783) and the French Revolution (1789–1799), both of which shocked conventional attitudes about monarchies and the citizens they ruled. Intellectuals of the age perceived themselves as living in an age of enlightenment and reason. They believed in human control over a rational universe that had been created by a God who was more of a great watchmaker than a father or judge. Denis Diderot (1713–1784) and other French philosophers compiled the first encyclopedia. It was a set of twenty-four books that assembled all of the knowledge the writers were aware of from the past to the present. Intellectuals of the late eighteenth century glorified the power of the individual to control and order the world, a viewpoint that nurtured both economic growth and the notion that governments should reflect the will and interests of the people. That attitude is reflected in both the American and French revolutions.

The Rococo Style

A popular artistic style of pre-revolutionary France, known as the *rococo*, lasted well into the classical period. The name of the style came from the French word *rocaille*, which means "a shell, or shell work." The rococo style emphasized elegance, delicacy, softness, and playfulness but retained much of the ornamentation of the baroque. The tastes of the period can be seen in the work of painters such as Jean-Honoré Fragonard (page 112), as well as in the interiors of aristocratic French palaces, which were decorated with beautiful gold-and-white carved woods, crystal chandeliers, and gilt ceilings.

Two of the most important rococo composers were Francois Couperin (1668–1733) and Jean-Philippe Rameau (1683–1764). Their music has many of the characteristics of the baroque, including the use of basso continuo in chamber or orchestral works. It tends to be even more highly decorated with ornaments and embellishments than was common in most baroque music, however. The extreme amount of ornamentation fits with the gilded interiors just mentioned.

A word associated with French rococo dress is *macaroni*. It meant the ultimate in French fashion at the time. Think of the pancake makeup, long brocaded coats, and pompadour wigs that you often see in movies showing the period, such as the 1984 Academy Award–winning movie *Amadeus*. In its day, though, "macaroni" was the height of style. British soldiers fighting Americans in the Revolutionary War made fun of their adversaries by casting them as country bumpkins in the song "Yankee Doodle." Yankees were so unsophisticated that they thought that merely sticking a feather in their caps would qualify as "macaroni." Clearly, it took more than a mere feather to project the French style.

The Birth of Classicism

The style that foreshadowed the classical period in Germany and Austria was known in

An eighteenth-century French interior

its day as *Empfindsamkeit,* or *sensitive style.* It sharply contrasted with the rococo music of France by using simpler melodies and less ornamentation. Carl Philipp Emanuel Bach (1714–1788), son of Johann Sebastian Bach, was one of its primary composers.

This German-Austrian sensitive style eventually became known as *neoclassicism* or *classicism* because it derived its primary inspiration from the clean lines and balanced forms of art and architecture of ancient Greece and Rome. Just as rococo music corresponded with the ornate interiors of French palaces, the classical style had its parallel in many buildings all over Europe and even in America. The Georgian style of architecture—named for the Georges who were the kings of England in the 1700s—had columns that seemed to be copied from Greek temples. That influence was also exemplified in the lives of wealthy Americans, particularly in the South, who were devoted to Greek art and literature. Compare the photo of the Parthenon, built in 448–432 BCE in Athens, Greece, with that of the rotunda of the University of Virginia at Charlottesville (page 115).

An artistic example of classicism can be seen in the works of Jacques-Louis David (1748–1825), a painter whose style avoided the "capricious ornament" of the rococo. Instead, in such works as *The Death of Socrates* (page 112), he created solemn scenes of noble sacrifice and great historical moments in a clear, balanced, linear style. Again, an interest in ancient Greece is reflected here. Socrates (ca. 470–399 BCE) was a Greek philosopher who was convicted of not believing in the gods of Athens and of corrupting his students. He was forced to commit suicide by drinking hemlock. In the picture, he is surrounded by his students, who grieve for him.

***The Bathers,* by Jean-Honoré Fragonard (1732–1806).** Paintings such as this one display the elegance, delicacy, softness, and playfulness of the French rococo style.

***The Death of Socrates,* by Jacques-Louis David (1748–1825).** This painting of the Greek philosopher Socrates about to drink the hemlock is a good example of the kind of clear and balanced artistic style that was popular during the classical period in Europe.

The two composers most commonly associated with the style are two Austrians, Wolfgang Amadeus Mozart (1756–1791) and Franz Joseph Haydn (1732–1809). Both depended on commissions for most of their careers—Mozart as a concertmaster to the Archbishop of Salzburg and then later as a composer and music teacher in Vienna, and Haydn as a music director for a series of four Hungarian princes in the Esterhazy family.

The French Revolution

The rococo era in France would come to an abrupt end with the French Revolution. In July of 1789, a mob of angry French citizens stormed the Bastille, which was the state prison in Paris. This was the first of a series of attacks on the government that escalated into the French Revolution. An assembly of these revolutionaries wrote *A Declaration of the Rights of Man,* as well as a new constitution that limited the control of the monarchy. They presented it to their king, Louis XVI (1754–1793), who claimed to accept it but then fled the country.

The French Revolution was a particularly bloody affair. The king was brought back to Paris as a prisoner, tried for treason, and beheaded by a guillotine in a public ceremony in 1793. Later in the same year his wife, Marie Antoinette (1755–1793), and many other members of the aristocracy were also beheaded. The revolution led to the French revolutionary army engaging in a series of battles with the armies of France's more monarchical neighbors. From these contests emerged a new French hero and leader—Napoleon Bonaparte (1769–1821). By 1799, Napoleon had enough power to take over the French government. During the next fifteen years he came to control almost all of Europe.

One of the effects of the French Revolution was the discrediting of the ideals of rationality and order that had dominated the 1700s. Those ideals had, in the minds of many people, led to the bloodshed of the French Revolution and the rise of Napoleon's despotism. Clothing became much simpler, corresponding to the orderly simplicity of the music of Mozart and Haydn. Beau Brummel, an English style setter, omitted the needless ornamentation and frills that had dominated the rococo style in fashion in the 1800s and adopted cuts that still influence clothing today.

Looking Ahead

The classical style would linger a little longer, and its transition to the next major era, the romantic, as well as that era's rejection of classicism, can be seen in the works of the German composer Ludwig van Beethoven (1770–1827). Beethoven initially felt a great amount of admiration for Napoleon Bonaparte, who was only one year his senior. He paid tribute to Napoleon by originally naming his third symphony "Bonaparte." That respect and admiration was crushed, however, in 1804, when Napoleon took the position of emperor of the French. When Beethoven heard that news, he tore up the title page of his yet-unpublished symphony and renamed it the

Napoleon Bonaparte, the French military hero.

Eroica, "heroic symphony." Beethoven would even go so far as to write a piece celebrating "Wellington's Victory" over Napoleon at Waterloo.

Beethoven serves as our best example of the transition from the classical period to the romantic period, as can be heard by listening to his works. Many of his earlier works do not sound too much different from those of Mozart. His later works would exhibit the great emotional flourishes and periods of quiet and crescendo that we associate with the romantic era, as is discussed in Prelude: Music of the Romantic Era.

The Classical Symphony

> Mozart is just God's way of making the rest of us feel insignificant.
>
> —MUSIC JOURNALIST DAVID W. BARBER
> (B. 1958)

))) First Hearing

 CONNECT   CD 1: Track 19

Listen to the recording of Symphony no. 94 in G Major, second movement, by Haydn and take notes on what you hear. Even if you are working with other students in a paired or group listening session, keep your own notes. Give some attention to the following:

- Listen carefully to the opening of this work and then make a note each time you hear music that sounds anything like the opening again. Is it just repeated over and over, or does it change when you hear it the other times?

- Notice the dynamic (loudness and softness) levels of the music. Is there a time when dynamics are used for a special effect? Where and how?

- What instruments do you hear? Do you hear the harpsichord, which was so often part of the orchestra in the baroque period?

- Can you determine the tempo? This is the second movement of a symphony; what is the likely tempo of the movement before it?

- What is the meter?

Keep your notes from this First Hearing to compare with your impressions about the piece after you study the information in this chapter.

11

The term *classical* is applied to music in several different ways. In one sense, we speak of a "classic" as any work of lasting value. "Classical" sometimes designates so-called serious or concert music, as opposed to popular music. In such an instance, the term is applied without regard to historical or stylistic factors, so that composers of different style periods—Bach, Beethoven, and Tchaikovsky, for example—may all be considered classical composers. In a narrower and more accurate sense, the term is applied to European music from about 1750 to about 1800, particularly the works of Haydn, Mozart, and, to an extent, Beethoven and Schubert. Beethoven and Schubert were transitional in that their compositions were based in classicism but also contained elements of the coming romantic period.

As we discussed in Chapter 6, the style of the baroque period began as a reaction against the vocal polyphony of the late Renaissance. Gradually, the homophonic style of early baroque music was transformed into a new kind of polyphony based on the major-minor harmonic system.

Similarly, the style of the classical era was the result of a reaction to the instrumental polyphony of the late baroque period, particularly in the music of Johann Se-

The Parthenon in Athens (left, 448–432 BCE) and the rotunda at the University of Virginia (right, 1819–1826) are both examples of classical architecture.

bastian Bach. Actually, J. S. Bach's music was considered old fashioned by the end of his life, and it was not often played or commonly respected until the mid-nineteenth century, when composers such as Felix Mendelssohn rediscovered him.

The new "classical" style was essentially homophonic rather than polyphonic; it was based on the idea of successive contrasting melodies rather than the contrapuntal expansion of one melody. In general, classical music tends to be structured in clear sections with clear divisions, even occasional pauses. Baroque music tends to flow without pauses and stopping points from the beginning to the end of individual pieces or movements.

Although the basso continuo was gradually abandoned in the classical era, composers continued to use the major-minor tonal system. That type of tonality, homophonic texture, and contrasting melodies are all common in the sonata style of the classical period.

The Form of Classical Multimovement Works

The meaning of *sonata* varies from age to age in music history. Originally, it meant something to be played, as opposed to a cantata, which was to be sung. The term had various applications throughout the baroque period. We studied several types of sonatas in Chapter 9. In the classical era, *sonata* took on a specific and important meaning.

The classical sonata is a multimovement work in one of two schemes, either of which has three or four movements: the forms listed for each individual movement indicate the basic structure the music most often follows. We discuss the details of each form later in this chapter and in the following chapters. The names are given here just to make the outlines complete.

Three-Movement Plan

First movement	*Second movement*	*Third movement*
Fast tempo	Slow tempo	Fast tempo
Sonata form	Sonata, theme and variations, or other form	Rondo, sonata, or other form

Four-Movement Plan

First movement	*Second movement*	*Third movement*	*Fourth movement*
Fast tempo	Slow tempo	Medium tempo	Fast tempo
Sonata form	Sonata, theme and variations, or other form	Minuet and trio or scherzo and trio form	Rondo, sonata, or other form

Single-Movement Sonata Form

In both plans, the first movement is invariably cast in what has become known as the single-movement **sonata form.** Sonata form is based on the overall plan of the statement of two contrasting melodies, or **themes,** the manipulation of those themes, and the restatement of those themes. This general plan is realized in three specific sections of the movement: (1) the exposition, (2) the **development,** and (3) the **recapitulation.**

Single-Movement Sonata Form

Optional Introduction

Exposition of theme 1, theme 2

Development

Recapitulation of theme 1, theme 2

Coda

Exposition

The exposition introduces themes, usually two, that form the basis of the entire movement. In Mozart's works particularly, the first theme is usually fairly energetic, and the second theme contrasts with it by being more lyrical. These themes are connected by a *bridge.* The first theme establishes the tonality for the movement; the second theme is always in a different key. The bridge serves the function of modulating from the key of the first theme to the new key of the second theme. Usually there is a clear and definite cadence, pause, or both separating the bridge and the second theme. Frequently, a short section called a *codetta* is employed after the second theme to bring the exposition to a close. In almost all cases the exposition is repeated to help the listener remember the themes and recognize them when they reappear later in the movement.

Development

The development concentrates on the themes that were presented in the exposition and manipulates them in a variety of ways. The themes may be fragmented into small melodic or rhythmic **motives** (short themes or parts of themes). These motives can be expanded, or the themes or parts of them might be repeated at different pitch levels. Changes in timbre, rhythm, and dynamics are among the many devices that may be employed. No two development sections are the same; however, what is common to all of them is the process of **modulation,** or the frequent changing of tonal centers.

Recapitulation

The recapitulation is a restatement of the whole exposition, with one important change—the second theme appears at the pitch level of the home key (the tonal center of the overall movement) rather than in a contrasting key, as it did in the exposition. The reaffirmation of the tonic key and the return of the themes of the exposition create a sense of unity and balance for this formal structure. In some pieces, the **coda** ("tail") is added as an extended conclusion of the movement.

Occasionally a movement in sonata form is preceded by a slow introduction. The introduction, however, is not part of the form and is not usually included in the repetition of the exposition or in the recapitulation.

Single-movement sonata form is outlined below:

Exposition	Development	Recapitulation
Theme 1 (tonic)	Transformation of themes from the exposition	Theme 1 (tonic)
Bridge (modulates to new key)		Bridge (extended)
	Rapid modulations	Theme 2 (tonic)
Theme 2 (new key)		Coda
Codetta to cadence		Final cadence
Exposition repeated		

Theme and Variations Form

Another popular form that was often used for second movements of multimovement works and also for independent compositions is the **theme and variations** form. As the name suggests, a movement or piece in this form begins with the presentation of a theme, or main melody. That statement is then followed by a series of varied versions of the same theme. Letters are not usually used to describe the theme and variations form, but if they were, the form would be A1A2A3A4A5 and so on, perhaps ending with a coda.

Minuet and Trio Form

Another form, or structure for an individual movement, is the **minuet and trio.** This form is most often used for the third movement of a four-movement work. Styled after the minuet dance, it is written in triple meter. The minuet and trio follows a ternary form as outlined below:

A	B	A
Minuet	Trio	Minuet

The term *trio* for the middle section is a carryover from the 1600s, when the second of two alternating dances was often scored for three instruments. In the classical sonata, the trio is rarely a three-voice piece but does contrast with the minuet in a variety of ways.

Beethoven experimented with the minuet and trio a great deal and eventually adopted, in place of the minuet, a much faster type of piece known as a **scherzo** and trio. As we shall see, the scherzo and trio became a movement of great power and drama in his works. "MusiCurious: Why Composers Write 'Boring' Slow Movements" gives you some insight into these pieces.

The Classical Orchestra

In the baroque era, instrumental music became an independent idiom, and a vast literature for instrumental ensembles was produced. But the baroque orchestra, aside from the usual complement of strings, had no fixed makeup.

In the classical era, the composition of the orchestra became standardized to a great extent, largely due to the work of **Johann Stamitz** (1717–1757), a violinist, composer, and conductor of the orchestra at the German city of Mannheim. Under his direction, the Mannheim orchestra developed into the most celebrated musical ensemble in Europe. The excellence of its playing was praised by the leading composers of the day.

 **MusiCurious**

WHY COMPOSERS WRITE "BORING" SLOW MOVEMENTS

Well, why *do* composers write slow movements?

Slow movements are composed for several reasons. As we discussed earlier, baroque musicians used slow movements as opportunities to improvise embellishments and add their own creative touches to their performances. Slow movements also provide a welcome contrast when placed before, after, or in between faster movements. If you remember the three movements of Vivaldi's "Spring" concerto from *The Four Seasons*, you'll remember the middle movement was slow. In that case, the lower strings and continuo were also omitted from that slow movement to give it more contrast from the movements before and after it.

So are the slow movements only there for contrast?

Not really. They are, or can be, enjoyable in their own right. There are certainly many full pieces of music that are slow and quite beautiful. We will hear the slow second movement from Haydn's "Surprise" Symphony in this chapter. Notice how its beauty is apparent in how the opening melody was repeated in varied ways.

When we get to Beethoven and hear the first movement of his "Moonlight Sonata" for solo piano, we will find that Beethoven decided to break away from the standard of starting and ending the three-movement sonata at a fast tempo and, instead, began the sonata with a slow movement. Few listeners would find that movement "boring." In fact, many people think of it as the entire sonata and forget that the next two movements are faster.

Yes, those pieces are nice, but I still generally prefer faster music.

That's fine; not everybody likes everything. It is true that slow music might not grab your interest in quite the same way that faster music does, but hearing music based on more than one tempo in a longer work such as a sonata, symphony, or concerto adds to its appeal.

By baroque standards, the Mannheim orchestra was of large dimensions. In 1756 it consisted of twenty violins divided into two sections (first violins and second violins), four violas, four cellos, and four basses. The wind section included four horns in addition to pairs of flutes, oboes, clarinets, and bassoons. Trumpets and timpani were also used, usually together. The German poet and musician D. F. D. Schubert (1739–1791) recorded his impressions of the orchestra in his *Essay on Musical Esthetics:*

> No orchestra in the world ever equaled the Mannheimers' execution. Its forte is like thunder, its crescendo like a mighty waterfall, its diminuendo a gentle river disappearing into the distance, its piano is a breath of spring. The wind instruments could not be used to better advantage; they lift and carry, they reinforce and give life to the storm for violins.

"MusiCurious: What Does the Conductor Do?" discusses the importance of the conductor to the sound of the orchestra.

Although we will concentrate on Mozart in this chapter and on Haydn in Chapter 13, "Classical Chamber Music," it was Franz Joseph Haydn who did so much to develop both the classical **symphony** and the string quartet forms that he is often called the Father of the Symphony and the Father of the String Quartet. As we discuss in greater detail later, Haydn was responsible for producing music for a series of princes who wanted new symphonies and string quartets, often in order to entertain their guests or to play for their own enjoyment. As he composed one work after

 **MusiCurious**

WHAT DOES THE CONDUCTOR DO?

I see the conductor in front of the performers waving his or her hands or a stick. Why is that necessary?

One of the primary reasons for that is to keep the musicians together. The hands or stick, called a *baton*, are usually waved in particular patterns that follow the meter of the piece. The speed at which the conductor makes those movements establishes the tempo (speed of the beat) at which the entire orchestra plays.

Can't the musicians read their music, hear one another, and stay together on their own?

It depends on how many musicians are in the group. Small orchestras of the baroque and classical periods were sometimes led by the harpsichordist or the first violinist. In those cases, the orchestras were small enough that the musicians could stay together on their own with only occasional nods from the conductor who was also playing with them. Larger orchestras of the later classical period and beyond, however, had too many musicians for that. A musician sitting on the side or the back of an orchestra of sixty to a hundred musicians, for example, cannot hear anyone other than the musicians nearby. The conductor's motions are essential for keeping everyone playing together and at the same tempo, as well as slowing the group down or speeding up in unison as is sometimes required by the music.

I see conductors keeping the beat, but they also make lots of other pronounced gestures with their hands and bodies. Why is that?

The conductor needs to balance the dynamics so that some instruments do not stand out by playing louder or get covered up by playing softer than they should. The conductor uses hand motions to communicate that. Also, sometimes individual musicians do not play through long sections of the music, and it is important that the conductor let the players know exactly when to come in. The players have the music and it tells them how long to wait before playing, but over a long rest they could easily get lost and come in at the wrong time were it not for the help of the conductor. The conductor is also responsible for the **phrasing** (the degree to which lines are played smoothly or detached), the **articulation** (the way a musician starts and stops the tone quality of each note), and other details of musical interpretation for the group. Each conductor communicates those kinds of instructions to the orchestra in his or her own way. Watching different conductors and comparing them with one another can be quite interesting.

The conductor brings the various parts of the orchestra together to create one cohesive sound. Here Gustavo Dudamel conducts the Simon Bolivar Youth Orchestra at Carnegie Hall.

Does the conductor follow the same kind of musical notation that the individual musicians do?

The conductor's sheet music is much bigger. The conductor has all of the music that the individual musicians do, but it is written in what we call a *score*, which means that all of the parts are lined up vertically so that the conductor can see what everyone is playing at the same time. Individual musicians only need to see their own parts. Sometimes conductors have the music memorized and are able to conduct without their score, but they use it in rehearsal and often refer to it in performance as well.

At the end of a piece, I see the conductor asking several other people to bow to the audience during the applause. Why?

To share the credit and applause with others in the group. The conductor usually acknowledges the first violinist (the concertmaster or concertmistress), who has been responsible for the bowing of the string parts and for overseeing the tuning of the orchestra. He or she will also acknowledge any musicians who played solo parts and allow the audience to give them special applause. However, it is the conductor who takes most of the credit for the quality of sound the orchestra produces.

another, Haydn devised ways of getting a fuller and fuller sound out of the orchestra or quartet, something that was well liked by his listeners and copied by other composers, including Mozart.

Wolfgang Amadeus Mozart

The first major composer of the classical period we will study is **Wolfgang Amadeus Mozart** ("Ama-day-use Moats-art," 1756–1791). Mozart was born in Salzburg, Austria, and began his musical career as one of the most celebrated child prodigies in eighteenth-century Europe. His father, Leopold, a highly respected composer and violinist, recognized his son's extraordinary talent and carefully supervised his musical education. Mozart began harpsichord lessons when he was 4 and wrote his first compositions when he was 5. When he was 6, he and his older sister, Maria Anna ("Nannerl"), were taken by their father on a concert tour of Munich and Vienna.

Up to age 15 Mozart was almost constantly on tour, playing prepared works and improvising. Although the harpsichord and later the piano remained Mozart's principal instruments, he also mastered the violin and the organ. In addition to keyboard pieces, he wrote church works, symphonies, string quartets, and operas. In 1769, on a long trip to Italy, Mozart was commissioned to compose his first major opera, *Mitridate,* which was performed in Milan in 1770. His success in Italy, as triumphant as Handel's had been some sixty years earlier, brought him a number of commissions for operas.

His father, Leopold, court composer and vice chapelmaster to the Archbishop of Salzburg, obtained a position for his son as concertmaster in the archbishop's orchestra. But the new Archbishop of Salzburg, installed in 1772, failed to appreciate Mozart's genius. Relations between the haughty churchman and the high-spirited young composer steadily deteriorated until, in 1781, despite his father's objections, Mozart quit his position and settled in Vienna.

The first years in Vienna were fairly prosperous. Mozart was in great demand as a teacher; he gave numerous concerts and his German *singspiel*—a German comic opera with spoken dialogue—*Die Entführung aus dem Serail (The Abduction from the Seraglio,* 1782) was a success. He married Constanze Weber, a woman he had met several years earlier on a concert tour. Overall, the marriage was a happy one, but Constanze was a careless housekeeper, and Mozart was a poor manager of finances. He never achieved a permanent post at the court. Public taste changed, and his teaching began to fall off. Except for occasional successes—his opera *Le Nozze di Figaro (The Marriage of Figaro,* 1786) and the singspiel *Die Zauberflöte (The Magic Flute,* 1791)— the last ten years of his life were spent, for the most part, in poverty.

In 1788 Mozart gave up public performances, relying on a meager income from teaching and loans from various friends to sustain himself and his family. He was Catholic but also a member of the Freemasons, a secret society that believed in brotherhood and helping one another. He gave credit to the aid he received from his Mason friends by including many Masonic symbols and practices in his last opera, *Die Zauberflöte (The Magic Flute).* In spite of his troubles, he continued to compose, but his health began to decline. When he died in 1791 at the age of 35, he was buried in an unmarked grave in a part of the cemetery reserved for the poor.

Unlike the meticulous Haydn, who kept a chronological list of all his compositions, Mozart never bothered to organize his musical papers in any consistent fashion. In the nineteenth century, Ludwig von Köchel compiled a roughly chronological listing of Mozart's music (numbering up to 626 pieces). This catalogue, along with substantial revisions and additions by later musicologists, remains in use today, the number of each work being preceded by "Koch" or the initial "K" for the man who did the organization.

WOLFGANG AMADEUS MOZART
(1756–1791)

- Born in Salzburg, Austria; died at age 35 in Vienna, Austria.

- A major, prolific composer known for forty-one symphonies, many operas including *Le Nozze di Figaro (The Marriage of Figaro),* concertos, chamber works, and a *Requiem Mass.*

Mozart was able to carry around finished compositions in his head, once re- marking that "the committing to paper is done quickly enough. For everything is already finished, and it rarely differs on paper from what it was in my imagination." His instrumental music includes forty-one symphonies, twelve violin concertos, over twenty-five piano concertos, some fourteen concertos for other instruments, twenty- six string quartets, seventeen piano sonatas, over forty violin sonatas, and numerous other chamber music works. All of this is in addition to a large amount of vocal music, which we discuss in Chapter 14.

We discussed the classical sonata earlier. Symphonies are often constructed in a similar way. Some early symphonies followed the three-movement plan, but most symphonies of the classical period have four movements. Of the four standard move- ments in Mozart's Symphony no. 40, we will hear the first and third movements. The first is in sonata form, and the third is in minuet and trio form.

In accordance with the four-movement sonata plan, the second movement con- trasts with the first. It is slower in tempo (andante, a walking pace), different in meter (sextuple), and in a contrasting key. As an example of a second movement, we will listen to a movement from a symphony by Haydn. A discussion of the third movement follows as an example of minuet and trio form. "Hearing the Difference: Vivaldi's 'La Primavera,' first movement, and Mozart's Symphony no. 40 in G Minor, first move- ment" will help you compare these works.

CD 1: Tracks 13–18

Symphony no. 40 in G Minor, first movement   WOLFGANG AMADEUS MOZART

Date: 1788

Genre: Classical symphony

Tempo: Allegro

Form: Sonata

Texture: Homophonic

Instruments: Orchestra consisting of one flute, two oboes, two clarinets, two bassoons, two horns, and strings

Meter: Duple

Duration: 8:12

Context: Mozart composed the original version of this symphony in 1788 intending to take it to England for its opening performance. That trip never happened, and sometime after that the composer added two clarinets to the composition that he had not originally included in the orchestra. It is not known whether Mozart ever actually conducted a performance of the symphony, but it is one of his most famous and often performed symphonies to this day.

	Timing		What to listen for
Exposition			
13	0:00	Theme 1	Violins play bouncing theme 1; agitated accompaniment in violas
	0:24	Bridge	Theme 1 restated; orchestra plays forte (loud), rushing strings, emphatic close
14	0:00	Theme 2	Violins play floating theme 2, answered by woodwinds
	0:24		Strings take over, crescendo, build twice to high point; soft descending scale

(continued)

Timing		What to listen for
0:37		Rhythmic motive from first theme traded among woodwind instruments and strings alternating soft and loud
0:55	Closing (The exposition is repeated.)	Rushing downward string scales, emphatic closing chords

Development

15	0:00		Piano, theme 1 in violins, new harmonies
	0:14		Sudden forte, theme 1 traded between low strings and violins
	0:42		Soft, static version of phrase traded between violins and woodwinds
	0:53		Woodwind answer reduced to three-note motive
	0:59		Sudden forte, three-note motive traded between violins and low strings
	1:08		No strings, flute and clarinets trade three-note motive descending into:

Recapitulation

16	0:00	Theme 1	Violins; woodwinds answer; loud chords
	0:24		Violins begin theme again
	0:35	Bridge	Forte, upward-leaping motive in violins, then low strings back and forth
	0:41		Rushing string scales, emphatic close
17	0:00	Theme 2	Flowing theme 2 in violins; woodwind answer
	0:24		Strings take over, crescendo, build twice to high point; soft descending scale
	0:42		Rhythmic motive from theme 1 traded among woodwind instruments and strings alternating soft and loud
18	0:00	Coda	Rushing string scales, build to woodwind chord
	0:12		Violins begin theme 1, answered by violins, violas, woodwinds; sudden forte, emphatic closing chords

 **Featured Listening**    CD 1: Track 19

CONNECT

"Surprise," Symphony no. 94 in G Major, second movement FRANZ JOSEPH HAYDN

Date: 1791

Genre: Classical symphony

Tempo: Andante

Form: Theme and variations

Texture: Homophonic

Instruments: Two flutes, two oboes, two bassoons, two horns, two trumpets, first violins, second violins, violas, cellos, basses, timpani

Meter: Duple

Duration: 6:21

Context: Haydn composed this symphony on a visit to London, and it was first performed there in 1792. The second movement is famous for its "surprise" loud chord, which was aimed at listeners who tend to get bored by slow movements.

Timing		What to listen for
19 0:00		Statement of the theme in violins, played staccato (in short, detached notes)
1:07		Variation 1, violins add high melody above the theme
2:14		Variation 2 in minor, violins play theme in major
3:23		Variation 3, oboe plays theme in faster note values, then theme returns with flute and oboe above
4:29		Variation 4, woodwinds, brasses, and timpani play theme, then strings play theme with new rhythm
5:54		Oboe and orchestra play theme.

 CD 4: Tracks 27–29

Symphony no. 40 in G Minor, third movement WOLFGANG AMADEUS MOZART

Date: 1788

Genre: Classical symphony

Tempo: Allegretto

Form: Minuet and trio

Texture: Homophonic

Instruments: Orchestra consisting of one flute, two oboes, two clarinets, two bassoons, two horns, and strings

Duration: 4:56

Context: We studied the first movement of this symphony above. As became standard for classical multimovement works, this third movement is in minuet and trio form. Earlier, we heard a minuet and trio from the baroque period from Handel's *Water Music.*

Timing		What to listen for
27 0:00	Minuet (A)	First phrase played by orchestra, forte; first phrase repeated
0:38		Second phrase, more dissonant; moves directly into repeat of first phrase, varied
1:16		Repeat of second phrase and varied first phrase
28 0:00	Trio (B)	Relaxed, lyrical phrase in strings, woodwinds, then strings; lyrical phrase repeated
0:51		Lower strings begin, answered by woodwinds; woodwinds complete the phrase; horns join strings in varied return of lyrical phrase; phrase completed by horns with woodwinds, then strings
1:26		Strings and woodwinds repeat second phrase; horns with strings, then woodwinds, repeat varied return of first phrase
29 0:00	Minuet (A)	First phrase, forte
0:18		Second phrase and return of first phrase repeated; soft ending in woodwinds

VIVALDI'S "LA PRIMAVERA," FIRST MOVEMENT, AND MOZART'S SYMPHONY NO. 40 IN G MINOR, FIRST MOVEMENT

We heard Vivaldi's "La Primavera," first movement, from the baroque era, and we heard the first movement of Mozart's Symphony no. 40 in G Minor, from the start of the classical period (see Featured Listening on page 104 and Listening Guide on page 121). Answer the following questions as you listen from one work to the other:

- These two works represent two different style periods in music history. Vivaldi's "La Primavera" was composed in the baroque period and Mozart's Symphony no. 40 in the classical period. They are both typical of first movements of multimovement works of their times, but one major difference between them is their form. Which is organized and balanced by an opening theme that keeps returning? Which has two themes that return at the end but also are developed in the middle? That development section marks a new style that will continue to be used for such movements.

- Vivaldi composed "La Primavera" to imitate sounds of springtime as they were outlined in a poem about spring. Is there anything about Mozart's symphony that imitates nonstandard musical sounds, such as birds or water? Is there any story being told in that symphony? If not, it is called **absolute music** because it has no program or story.

- How does the instrumentation differ between these two works? Which has a full orchestra with woodwinds and brass instruments, and which has a string orchestra without those winds? Which includes the harpsichord?

- Which work features a solo instrument? What is that instrument, and how is it featured?

- What is the tempo and meter of each?

Summary

The classical period in music history lasted from about 1750 to about 1800. German and Austrian composers such as Haydn, Mozart, and Beethoven organized their compositions according to the same sense of balance and symmetry common in artwork of the classical civilizations of ancient Greece and Rome. Such organization included three- or four-movement works with each movement following a balanced formal structure.

One of the most popular ways of structuring a movement, often the first movement, was the sonata form. It featured an exposition that "exposed" two themes on which the rest of the movement would be based. That was repeated to allow the listeners to hear the themes enough times to remember them. The next section was the development, during which the composer varied the themes or parts of them. The idea of balance was created by the next section of the form, the recapitulation, in which the themes return to remind the listener where the movement began. A coda sometimes brings the movement to a conclusion.

Other single-movement forms studied in this chapter are theme and variations and minuet and trio. In both of those forms, too, themes from the beginning repeat at the end, even if the repeat is in a varied form.

One of the most prolific and brilliant composers of the classical period was Wolfgang Amadeus Mozart. He was a child prodigy, trained by his composer father, who composed music in every genre (type of work) of the classical era.

New People and Concepts

absolute music, 124

articulation, 119

coda, 116

development, 116

Johann Stamitz, 117

minuet and trio, 117

modulation, 116

motive, 116

phrasing, 119

recapitulation, 116

scherzo, 117

sonata form, 116

symphony, 118

theme, 116

theme and variations, 117

Wolfgang Amadeus Mozart, 120

))) **Finale**   CONNECT **CD 1: Track 19**

Listen again to the recording of Symphony no. 94 in G Major, second movement, by Haydn and compare your impression now with your notes from your First Hearing. Consider the following questions:

- In what ways does the orchestra create variations of the opening theme?
- Why is the symphony from which this movement is taken called the "Surprise" symphony? Do you hear any surprises in this movement? What is surprising?
- What is the instrumentation of the symphony?
- What is the tempo?
- What is the meter?
- If you were going to describe this music to a friend, what would you say?

Further Listening

Johann Stamitz, Symphony in A major ("Mannheim No. 2). As is true of many early symphonies, this symphony has three movements and is a good example of the classical three-movement plan for orchestra. The movements are Allegro, Andante, and Presto, following the "fast-slow-fast" plan introduced in the baroque period and continued into the classical period.

Wolfgang Amadeus Mozart, *Eine Kleine Nachtmusik (A Little Night Music)*. This is a short, lovely example of the classical four-movement plan for strings. It also serves as a good example of some of the classical forms in this chapter. The first movement is in single movement sonata form, the second in rondo form, the third in minuet and trio form, and the fourth in sonata-rondo (a combination of sonata and rondo) form.

Wolfgang Amadeus Mozart, Symphony no. 40 in G Minor. The first and third movements were covered in this chapter, but the entire symphony is best heard as a complete work because of the contrast as one movement follows the other, as Mozart composed them. The movements are Allegro, Andante, Minuet and trio, and Allegro assai, a good example of the classical four-movement plan discussed in this chapter.

Franz Joseph Haydn, "Surprise," Symphony no. 94 in G Major. One of the symphonies Haydn composed while he was in London. The symphony is sometimes referred to as the symphony "with the kettledrum stroke," referring to the loud chord in the second movement. It is another good example of the classical four-movement plan commonly used for symphonies.

The Classical Concerto

12

))) First Hearing

CD 1: Tracks 20–28

Listen to the recording of Piano Concerto no. 23 in A Major, first movement, by Mozart and take notes on what you hear. Even if you are working with other students in a paired or group listening session, keep your own notes. Give some attention to the following:

- This work is called a piano concerto, but you hear no piano at all for the first two minutes. What do you hear? What instruments play during that time? Do you hear one theme (main melody), or do you hear an opening theme followed by a new theme?

- Once the piano begins to play, does it play music that contrasts with what you heard earlier, or does it repeat any melodies you have already heard?

- Do any of the themes you heard at the beginning of the movement repeat again toward the end? What instruments play it (or them)?

- Do you hear any sections where only the piano is playing? If so, when does that happen?

- What instrument or instruments do you hear at the very end of the movement?

Keep your notes from this First Hearing to compare with your impressions about the piece after you study the information in this chapter.

During the baroque era, the term *concerto* referred to both the concerto grosso (Bach's Brandenburg Concerto no. 5) and the concerto for solo instrument and orchestra (Vivaldi's *The Four Seasons*). In the classical era, composers continued to develop the solo concerto, while the concerto grosso fell into disuse. The violin and piano were the favored solo instruments, but solo concertos were also written for other instruments, such as the cello, trumpet, bassoon, horn, and clarinet. Typically, the classical

French pianist Hélène Grimaud performs Brahms's Piano Concerto No. 1, with the Australian Youth Orchestra at Royal Albert Hall in London.

concerto follows the three-movement sonata plan outlined in Chapter 11 and consists of a fast-slow-fast movement sequence *without* a minuet and trio.

The contrast between the solo instrument and the orchestra was an essential element in the concerto, and the formal structure of each movement was planned to give the soloist an opportunity to be featured along with or apart from the orchestra at several important places. As we discussed in Chapter 11, the conductor is the person who, among other things, is in charge of the dynamic levels of the orchestra, which sometimes means quieting them down to allow the soloist to be heard.

Concerto Soloists

Large concert halls such as those we have today did not exist in the eighteenth century, and yet members of the growing middle class wanted to hear music. Public concerts were usually held in theaters or in halls that had been constructed for other uses. Most of the halls held no more than a few hundred listeners seated in chairs. Admission was fairly expensive and was limited to subscribers, so the audiences were fairly certain to be knowledgeable about music and interested in what they were going to hear. On the other hand, they were much larger and less exclusive audiences than were common in palaces. Performers whose incomes depended on their being popular enough to be invited to perform again had plenty of incentive to please their listeners. Concerto soloists were no exception.

Many composers were also concerto soloists and so wrote music to showcase their musicianship and technical ability. Much of the rest of the time, composers wrote concertos for their students or for musicians who could afford to commission (pay for) works. Johann Joachim Quantz (1697–1773), for example, composed about three hundred concertos for flute and orchestra, which both he and his patron, Frederick the Great, King of Prussia (1712–1786), performed. Frederick the Great would not have performed in public houses, but he enjoyed playing in his own chambers. Quantz performed the works both in the king's chambers and for the public.

Generally, when performing a concerto, the soloist sits or stands to the left of the conductor, in front of the orchestra. When the music features the soloist, attention is drawn to him or her. Many concertos include a special time for the soloist to showcase his or her skills in what is called a **cadenza.** Cadenzas are often placed somewhere toward the end of fast movements. Right before a cadenza, the orchestra usually sustains a chord and then stops playing completely, allowing the soloist to take over. Classical cadenzas were usually improvised by the soloist, and even the length was not dictated by the composer. Soloists were free to play using whatever techniques they thought would please the audience, though they usually related their playing to the themes of the preceding movement. When they felt their solo drawing to a close, they used the playing of a **trill** (two notes played back and forth very fast) to indicate to the conductor that it was time to bring the orchestra back in.

Today, musicians who play classical music are seldom taught to improvise, and famous soloists have composed suggested cadenzas that are published and often used by other players. If you attend a concert or buy a CD of a classical concerto performance, you will often see the words "cadenza by . . . ," giving credit to the person who composed it. By the next period in music history, the romantic period, it became more common for composers to write out the cadenzas because they wanted more control of what was played under their names. Mozart, always ahead of his time, frequently composed suggested cadenzas. This is the case for the concerto we will listen to, Mozart's Piano Concerto no. 23 in A Major.

Double-Exposition Sonata Form

First movements of classical concertos were based on the single-movement sonata form discussed in Chapter 11. The form was handled somewhat differently, however, when it was used in concertos. Where the standard sonata form repeated the exposition so that the listeners would be able to remember the themes, the concerto exposition was not repeated. Instead, concerto composers wrote the themes out two or more times so that both the soloist and the orchestra had an opportunity to play them. Because the themes were written out at least twice, this version of the sonata form is called *double-exposition sonata form.*

As in all movements in sonata form, a development section followed the exposition. In the development the composer had much freedom to switch from the orchestra to the soloist and back whenever he or she desired.

The recapitulation followed, again presenting the main themes to allow the listeners to hear them return much the way they were played in the exposition. The cadenza was usually placed somewhere toward the end of the recapitulation (although it could be elsewhere, even at the end of the development). Wherever the cadenza occurred, the full orchestra was brought back to end the movement.

"Hearing the Difference: Bach's Brandenburg Concerto no. 5, first movement, and Mozart's Piano Concerto no. 23, first movement" compares the first movements of two concertos from different musical periods.

 **Featured Listening**  CONNECT   CD 1: Tracks 20–28

Piano Concerto no. 23 in A Major, first movement, K. 488 WOLFGANG AMADEUS MOZART

Date: 1786

Genre: Classical concerto

Tempo: Allegro

Form: Double-exposition sonata

Texture: Homophonic

Instruments: Solo piano, flute, two clarinets, two bassoons, two French horns, and strings

Meter: Quadruple

Duration: 11:33

Context: This concerto was composed and first performed in 1786, the same year as Mozart's opera *Le Nozze di Figaro (The Marriage of Figaro)*, which we will study in Chapter 14. Mozart might have played the piano part himself in the first performance. The cadenza was composed by Mozart.

	Timing		What to listen for
	First Exposition		
20	0:00	Theme 1	Strings play the theme; winds repeat the opening; strings and then winds return.
	0:33	Bridge	Full orchestra plays bridge theme; violins play fast phrase.
21	0:00	Theme 2	Violins play theme 2 softly.
	0:16		Theme repeated by violins and bassoon, flute enters at repeat
	0:31		Full orchestra; high woodwinds; pause
	Second Exposition		
22	0:00	Theme 1	Piano solo accompanied by strings; piano varies the theme on repeat
	0:30	Bridge	Orchestra plays bridge theme.
	0:50		Piano, accompanied by strings and staccato (short, detached) winds
23	0:00	Theme 2	Piano plays second theme; violins and flute repeat it.
	0:30		Piano and orchestra
	1:15		Full orchestra; pause
	Development		
24	0:00		Strings and piano introduce new theme.
	0:26		Clarinet, then piano with strings
	0:33		Flute, then piano with strings
	0:41		Woodwinds, piano, then strings
	1:30		Solo piano, orchestra leading to:
	Recapitulation		
25	0:00	Theme 1	Theme 1 played by strings, then woodwinds
	0:16		Piano with woodwinds
	0:30	Bridge	Orchestra plays bridge theme.
	0:39		Piano with strings; staccato violins and woodwinds
26	0:00	Theme 2	Solo piano plays theme 2; winds repeat, piano joins.
	0:31		Piano with orchestra
	1:04		Solo piano plays theme from development; woodwinds repeat theme.
	1:49		Orchestra plays bridge and development themes, then holds chord and pauses.
	Cadenza		
27	0:00		Piano solo, ends with long trill
	Coda		
28	0:00		Full orchestra, cadence (final-sounding ending)
	0:14		Woodwinds; orchestra; flutes and violins trill

 **Hearing the Difference**

BACH'S BRANDENBURG CONCERTO NO. 5, FIRST MOVEMENT, AND MOZART'S PIANO CONCERTO NO. 23, FIRST MOVEMENT

These first movements from two concertos are from two different style periods—the baroque and the classical (see Listening Guide on page 102 and Featured Listening on page 128). They both represent common types of concertos composed during those periods. Answer the following questions as you listen from one work to the other:

- The featured keyboard instruments in these concertos are different from each other. How would you describe the sound of each, and how do they compare?

- What is different about the soloists in these two concertos besides the differences between the harpsichord and the piano?

- Mozart's concerto movement is in double-exposition sonata form. How is that different from the ritornello form of Bach's concerto? Which has a development section? Where does that happen?

- The sense of balance created by themes from the beginning being repeated at the end of a movement was important in the classical period. Is there also a sense of that kind of balance in Bach's concerto? What kind of theme from the beginning repeats at the end?

- Do you hear instruments in Mozart's orchestra that are not in Bach's? What instruments are different?

Summary

Classical concertos were usually solo concertos for violin, piano, or other instruments with orchestra. They most often followed the three-movement sonata plan, with fast-slow-fast tempos for the movements. The primary element of a concerto is the soloist contrasting with the orchestra, with each having an opportunity to be featured.

The primary opportunity for the soloist to showcase his or her talents came in the cadenza, a solo section toward the end of most fast concerto movements. Though composers sometimes wrote them out, cadenzas were most often improvised by the players. Today, soloists can improvise cadenzas or use cadenzas that were written and published by composers or other soloists. Improvised cadenzas end with a trill to let the conductor know that it is time to bring back the orchestra.

First movements in concertos follow the double-exposition sonata form. "Double exposition" indicates that the themes are written out for both the orchestra and the soloist and are not repeated as they would be in a standard symphonic sonata form. After the double exposition, the concerto form has development and recapitulation sections similar to those in the standard sonata form, although these sections allow time for the concerto soloist to be featured along with the orchestra.

New Concepts

cadenza, 128   trill, 128

Finale

CONNECT   **CD 1: Tracks 20–28**

Listen again to the recording of Piano Concerto no. 23 in A Major, first movement, by Mozart and compare your impression now with your notes from your First Hearing. Consider the following questions:

- What instruments begin the movement, and what do they play that is important later in the work?
- When the piano enters, what does it play that you have heard before?
- What happens in the recapitulation?
- What happens in the cadenza?
- If you were going to describe this music to a friend, what would you say?

Further Listening

Wolfgang Amadeus Mozart, Piano Concerto no. 23 in A Major. We heard the first of three movements in this chapter, but the entire concerto should be listened to as a complete work. The concerto was completed about the time Mozart wrote the music for his opera *Le Nozze di Figaro (The Marriage of Figaro),* which we will hear in Chapter 14, Classical Vocal Music.

Joseph Haydn, Trumpet Concerto in E flat Major. This concerto was composed for Haydn's friend Anton Weidinger, who had a new form of the trumpet that used keys to allow him to play melodies that natural trumpets could not play. The instrument was quite special in its time, yet it is much easier to play the concerto using modern trumpets with valves.

Wolfgang Amadeus Mozart, Oboe Concerto in C Major, K. 314 or Flute Concerto No. 2 in D Major, K. 314. These are the same concerto that was originally composed for oboe and orchestra, and then later rewritten for flute and orchestra. Both are very popular concertos for those instruments.

Classical Chamber Music

> Haydn had neither the flashy individuality of Mozart nor the brooding, romantic passion of Beethoven. He was more of a middle-management type.
>
> —MUSIC JOURNALIST DAVID W. BARBER
> (B. 1958)

))) First Hearing

CD 1: Tracks 29–36

Listen to the recording of String Quartet op. 33, no. 3, fourth movement, by Haydn and take notes on what you hear. Even if you are working with other students in a paired or group listening session, keep your own notes. Give some attention to the following:

● Since this work is called a "string quartet," you can guess that it is played by four stringed instruments. What specific instruments do you hear?

● Do you hear any theme or themes from the beginning return later? How many themes return? How often do they return?

● This piece is subtitled "The Bird." Do you hear any sounds that might have been intended to imitate the sound of a bird? When do you hear those sounds?

● Do you hear the bird sounds all the way through the movement, or are there contrasting sections between them?

● Can you guess what the tempo might be? Can you guess the meter?

Keep your notes from this First Hearing to compare with your impressions about the piece after you study the information in this chapter.

13

Chamber Sonatas

Despite the popularity of the orchestra, music for smaller ensembles continued to thrive as wealthy patrons commissioned works to be performed in their palaces for private audiences. We call music for small ensembles **chamber music.** Most chamber music is composed for two to nine instrumentalists. The pieces are often titled according to the number of players, as follows: *duet* (2), *trio* (3), *quartet* (4), *quintet* (5), *sextet* (6), *septet* (7), *octet* (8), and *nonet* (9). Sometimes the names of the works make it obvious what instruments are needed to play them. For example, a guitar duet is a work for two guitars. In other cases, the titles are not so telling. A **piano trio** is written for violin, cello, and piano; a **piano quartet** is written for violin, viola, cello, and piano; and a **piano quintet** is for string quartet and piano. Sometimes chamber works are given titles such as *sonata* followed by the names of the instruments needed to play them.

Normally, chamber music is performed with one player on each part, but occasionally string players double or triple up on the parts to create a chamber orchestra. Mozart's "Eine kleine nachtmusik" ("A Little Night Music"), for example, was composed for a string quintet (five players), but it is often performed by a string orchestra. Such a change does not require any revision to the music; the sound is just much fuller.

One of the great beauties of chamber music is its intimacy. No conductor is needed because the musicians can communicate among themselves about such things as when to start or what tempo to use. A mere nod or two from one of the players is enough to tell the group to begin. Chamber music is often referred to as the music of friends because of the close proximity of the players and the fact that each player can be heard clearly within the group sound.

The multimovement sonata structure that we encountered was also used in chamber music for a wide variety of instrumental combinations. The **string quartet,** consisting of a first and second violin, a viola, and a cello, became in the classical era the most important chamber music medium. Its popularity continued well into the twentieth century in the works of Béla Bartók, Paul Hindemith, and others. "MusiCurious: Chamber Music Concerts" discusses this type of music in detail.

Franz Joseph Haydn

Franz Joseph Haydn ("Hi-den," 1732–1809) was the first great master of string quartet composition. Haydn was born in Rohrau, a small Austrian village located near the Hungarian border southeast of Vienna. His parents, both of peasant stock, seem to have encouraged their son's musical ability and entrusted his earliest musical training to a relative, Johann Franck, a schoolteacher and choirmaster in the nearby town of Hainburg. At age 6, Haydn was already singing in Franck's church choir and had begun playing the **clavier** (a generic name for a keyboard instrument) and violin.

In 1740, the composer and choirmaster at St. Stephen's Cathedral in Vienna stopped in Hainburg to recruit singers for his choir. Impressed with the 8-year-old's voice, he arranged to take the young boy back with him to Vienna.

For the next nine years, Haydn was employed as a Catholic choirboy. He received a smattering of elementary education at St. Stephen's choir school and continued with violin and voice lessons, but his training in composition and theory was so erratic that he was largely self-taught. In 1749, when his voice began to mature, Haydn was dismissed and had to find work outside the church.

The following years were difficult. At first Haydn made his living teaching clavier by day and playing in street bands and serenading parties by night. His reputation as a teacher and vocal accompanist, however, gradually spread, and he started serious composition. In 1759, he was appointed *Kapellmeister* (conductor) and chamber composer to a Bohemian nobleman, Count Morzin. He composed his first symphonies for the count's small orchestra.

The year 1761 proved to be good for Haydn. He was hired as assistant music director to Prince Paul Anton Esterházy, head of one of the most powerful and wealthy Hungarian noble families. Haydn's contract stipulated that he was to compose whatever music was required of him (which would become the property of his patron), keep the musical instruments in good repair, train singers, and supervise the conduct of all of the musicians.

Despite the rigid and burdensome requirements of his contract, Haydn enjoyed his work and was to say later, "My prince was pleased with all my work, I was commended, and as conductor of an orchestra I could make experiments, observe what

FRANZ JOSEPH HAYDN
(1732–1809)

- Born in Rohrau, Lower Austria; died at age 77 in Vienna, Austria.

- Major, prolific composer best known for at least 104 symphonies, much chamber music including string quartets and piano trios, Masses and other major choral works, concertos, operas, cantatas, oratorios, and many other works popular during the classical period.

- One of Beethoven's teachers.

CHAMBER MUSIC CONCERTS

How is playing chamber music different from playing in an orchestra?

The main difference is that each musician has more independence in chamber music. String players, for example, can choose their own way of bowing and phrasing their parts. In an orchestra, the concert master or mistress tells the players how to bow their parts. That is because when the bow is moved down it tends to sound a bit heavier than when it moves up. A whole group of violins sound most unified if they all bow together. Wind players often play their own distinct parts in an orchestra, but they still have to follow the conductor and use the articulation and phrasing the conductor wants. By contrast, chamber musicians listen to one another more and phrase as they see fit for the music. Of course, since chamber music groups usually have no more than nine players, they can hear one another. That would be impossible with a large orchestra.

Even knowing that chamber musicians can hear one another, they still must need to plan out how fast to play and other things about how the music should sound.

Oh, yes. The real work in chamber music happens during rehearsal sessions. A chamber group will often use their first rehearsal to simply read through the music they will perform, playing the music to give the musicians an idea about what the composer intended and how they will eventually interpret it. Depending on how comfortable each player feels with his or her part and what ideas come up in discussions about the music, further rehearsals will be planned as necessary. Players responsible for particularly difficult sections will take their music home to practice their part so they will be ready for the next rehearsal. Difficult or awkward sections of the music will often be practiced many times until the entire group is comfortable.

How do they know when to start without a conductor to tell them?

Planning. Because the musicians will have agreed on the exact tempo they will use, it usually takes only a single nod from one member to have them all start together. That same player might nod in tempo at other times to help the group gradually slow down, speed up, or make other changes to the tempo together. Of course, chamber music sometimes begins with a single musician playing solo, which makes it easy for the others to join in where appropriate.

Why do chamber musicians tune their instruments on stage in front of the audience? Can't they do that earlier and walk out on stage ready to play?

No. The stage is its own environment. The musicians have tuned before going on stage, but stage lights can be very hot and that heat affects an instrument's pitch. Also, if there is a keyboard instrument as part of the group, it is not available backstage and the other musicians need to make sure that their instruments are in tune with it. The tuning you hear just before the group plays is only final checking and adjusting to be sure that the music will go well despite the conditions on stage.

Does the audience clap at a chamber concert at about the same times as might be expected in an orchestral concert?

Yes, the timing of the applause is much the same. The audience usually applauds when the musicians walk out on stage. The musicians then take their seats, check their tuning, look to the person who will nod for them to begin, and then play the music. As with other classical concerts, the program will have the tempos or titles of individual movements in multimovement works indented under the general titles of the pieces, and the audience avoids clapping or making other sounds between the movements. The musicians will stand and bow at the end of each major work they perform.

Haydn is depicted here directing a string quartet rehearsal.

Esterházy Palace in Fertod, Hungary, was where Haydn composed and debuted much of his work.

strengthened and what weakened an effect and thereupon improve, substitute, omit, and try new things; I was cut off from the world, there was no one around to mislead and harass me, and so I was forced to become original."

Haydn remained in the employ of the Esterházy family for almost thirty years, serving first Prince Paul Anton and then his brother, Prince Nikolaus. Despite his isolation at their country estate, his fame gradually spread throughout Europe. He was able to work on commissions from other individuals and from publishers all over the continent.

Prince Nikolaus loved music and invited many important guests to his palace to hear Haydn's compositions, which included symphonies; chamber works of all kinds, particularly string quartets; and operas. The prince played a cello-like bowed string instrument called the baryton and enjoyed playing with Haydn and other musicians in the privacy of his quarters. Haydn also provided the music for those sessions.

Haydn's music has a wonderful sense of humor and, although he was a hired servant, he had a good relationship with the prince. Both his humor and his ability to communicate with the prince are evidenced in his Symphony no. 45, *The Farewell* (1772). It was composed after a long summer during which Prince Nikolaus had entertained hundreds of guests and had required much music for their entertainment. It was the time of year for the musicians, who did not live at the summer palace full-time, to go back to their primary residences and be with their families. Not able to directly tell the prince that the musicians needed leave, Haydn composed Symphony no. 45 to communicate the message for him. During the last movement, one or two of the musicians at a time stopped playing, snuffed out their candles, and left the room. Only two violinists, the concertmaster and Haydn, were left to finish the symphony. The prince was confused at first, but then got the point and allowed them to go home for their winter break.

When Prince Nikolaus died in 1790, Haydn was retained as nominal *Kapellmeister* for the Esterházy family, but he was now independent. Moving to Vienna, he resumed his friendship with Mozart, whose talent he had admired since their first meeting in 1781. Haydn also gave lessons to a young, rising composer named Ludwig van Beethoven. He made two successful trips to London (1791–1792, 1794–1795), where he conducted a number of his own symphonies, written on commission for the well-known impresario Johann Salomon. After his second London visit, he ceased writing symphonies, turning instead to the composition of Masses and oratorios. After 1800, his health began to fail, and he lived in secluded retirement. He died in 1809 at the age of 77.

Haydn's **opus** (work number within the collected works of a particular composer) 33 is a set of six string quartets. The set is sometimes called the Russian Quartets, because the audience for their **première** performance included the Russian Grand Duke Paul (later Tsar Paul I) and his wife, who were visiting Vienna. Number 3 is nicknamed "The Bird" because of the birdlike trills and ornaments in the first, second, and fourth movements. We will listen for bird sounds in the fourth movement.

 **))) Featured Listening**  **CD 1: Tracks 29–36**

CONNECT

String Quartet op. 33, no. 3 ("The Bird"),
fourth movement FRANZ JOSEPH HAYDN

Date: 1781

Genre: String quartet

Tempo: Presto (very fast)

Form: Sonata rondo (AB-development-AB-development-A)

Texture: Homophonic with some polyphony in the first development section and a monophonic repeated note in the second development

Instruments: Two violins, one viola, one cello

Meter: Duple

Duration: 2:41

Context: This work was first performed in Vienna by a professional string quartet made up of musicians with whom Haydn had worked. Present at the performance were the Austrian imperial family and the future Russian Tsar Paul I and his wife. The quartet is called "The Bird" because birdcalls are imitated in some melodies.

	Timing	Form	Instrumentation
29	0:00	A	Bouncy theme, staccato, repeated
	0:12		Repeated-note birdcalls, motive from bouncy theme accompanies; repeated, clear stop
30	0:00	B	More flowing theme, repeated; goes directly into:
Development			
31	0:00		Opening motive of bouncy theme and repeated-note fragment developed in rapid-fire polyphony; four-note motive tossed back and forth, reduced to two-note motive; sudden pause
32	0:00	A	Bouncy theme
	0:11		Repeated-note theme, goes directly into:
33	0:00	B	Flowing theme, goes directly into:
Development			
34	0:00		Long notes in first violin, bouncy theme motive accompaniment; flowing theme motive repeated, reduced to repeated monophonic note, transition back to:
35	0:00	A	Bouncy theme
	0:10		Repeated-note theme, clear stop at end
36	0:00	Coda	Two-note motive and bouncy motive tossed back and forth, moves quickly to pause; moves further to apparent emphatic closing; piano (soft), bouncy motive and repeated-note motive to actual quiet close

Rondo Form

This movement by Haydn introduces a form we have not heard before, the **rondo.** A rondo is an extended alternating form in which the first theme, A, returns several times with contrasting music (represented by letters B and C) between the A's. Using letters to identify the order in which the themes appear, the most common rondo is ABACA or ABACABA. The rondo we will listen to differs slightly from the norm in that it has two sections of development, in which the themes are tossed around and reduced to two notes. Because development sections are usually part of the single-movement sonata form, this form combines the two and is called a **sonata rondo.**

A Sonata for Flute and Guitar

Sonatas were composed for many different combinations of instruments in addition to string quartets; the guitar was a particularly popular instrument because it was soft and gave an intimate sound for small performance situations. An important composer of chamber music with guitar was the Italian **Mauro Giuliani** (1781–1828). He played the violin and the cello in addition to the guitar and composed music for solo guitar and guitar with many other small ensembles. His largest works were three concertos for guitar and orchestra.

The next work we will study is Giuliani's Grande Sonata no. 85 for flute and guitar, third movement. The flute part was composed so that a violinist could also play it with the guitar part. While the work was technically composed at the beginning of the next era, the romantic period (1817), it was composed in a classical style so it fits the subject of classical chamber music.

 Listening Guide

 CONNECT CD 4: Track 30

Grande Sonata no. 85 for flute and guitar, third movement, Scherzo MAURO GIULIANI

Date: ca. 1817

Genre: Flute and guitar music

Tempo: Vivace

Form: Scherzo and trio

Texture: Homophonic

Instruments: Flute and guitar

Meter: Triple

Duration: 3:37

Context: Giuliani was an Italian guitarist who moved to Vienna where he was acclaimed for his virtuosic playing. This is the third movement of a four-movement sonata composed in traditional classical form. The first movement is an allegro, the second an andante, the third a scherzo and trio, and the last an allegretto.

	Timing	Form	What to listen for
30	0:00	A	*Scherzo:* The flute's repeated melody notes are decorated with *grace notes* (fast little notes) on a repeat; the guitar begins by playing a countermelody below the flute and then changes to a "bass, chord, chord" kind of accompaniment.
	0:12	A	
	0:25	B	The guitar plays mostly a "bass, chord, chord" accompaniment to a very free-sounding flute melody.
	0:54	B	
	1:24	C	*Trio:* The guitar and flute begin by exchanging melodies, and then the guitar returns to an accompaniment pattern.
	1:37	C	
	1:50	D	The flute slows down and even rests some to allow the guitar to be featured.
	2:20	D	
	2:51	A	*Scherzo*

Summary

Chamber music is usually composed for two to nine instrumentalists, each playing his or her distinct part. Classical composers wrote chamber works for any number of combinations of instruments, their choices often being dictated by their patron or their knowledge of what instrumentalists were available. String quartets were among the most popular of the chamber ensembles.

Haydn was a master of string quartet composition. His primary patron, Prince Nikolaus Esterházy, played the cello and an instrument similar to the cello, the baryton.

The prince enjoyed playing music himself, and many of Haydn's string quartets or chamber works for baryton were composed for his patron.

The string quartets in Haydn's opus 33 are called the Russian Quartets because they were first performed for an audience that included the Russian Grand Duke Paul (later Tsar Paul I) and his wife, who were visiting Vienna.

Classical chamber works included many other compositions for small groups of instrumentalists such as the Grande Sonata for flute and guitar by Mauro Giuliani.

New People and Concepts

chamber music, 132

clavier, 133

Franz Joseph Haydn, 133

Mauro Giuliani, 138

opus, 136

piano quartet, 132

piano quintet, 132

piano trio, 132

première, 136

rondo, 137

sonata rondo, 137

string quartet, 133

Finale

CD 1: Tracks 29–36

Listen again to the recording of String Quartet op. 33, no. 3, fourth movement, by Haydn and compare your impression now with your notes from your First Hearing. Consider the following questions:

- What instruments are playing this work?
- How many times is the A theme played? How many times is the B theme played?
- When do you hear an imitation of bird sounds? What do you hear between the sections of bird sounds?
- What is the tempo? What is the meter?
- If you were going to describe this music to a friend, what would you say?

Further Listening

Joseph Haydn, String Quartet op. 33, no. 3 ("The Bird"). As with many other works represented in this book, only one movement was discussed in detail in this chapter. Haydn's string quartet is much better appreciated in its entirety. The movements are (1) Allegro moderato, (2) Scherzo: Allegretto, (3) Adagio ma non troppo, and (4) Finale: Rondo-Presto. If you remember the classical four-movement plan, you will notice that Haydn has varied the standard plan by putting the scherzo (often used in place of the minuet) as the second movement and the slow movement as the third.

Mauro Giuliani, Grande Sonata no. 85 for flute and guitar. Flute and guitar sound wonderful together because

the plucked strings on the guitar contrast well with the smoothness of the flute. The entire sonata follows the classical four-movement plan: (1) Allegro maestoso, (2) Andante molto sostenuto, (3) Scherzo-Vivace, and (4) Allegretto espressivo.

Wolfgang Amadeus Mozart, Piano Trio in E Major, K. 542. Chamber works called "piano trios" are usually not for three pianos but for piano and two other instruments. A particularly popular combination is this one composed for piano, violin, and cello. This is a late work by Mozart and composed to fit the classical three-movement plan. The movements are (1) Allegro, (2) Andante grazioso, and (3) Allegro.

Classical Vocal Music

> No good opera plot can be sensible, for people do not sing when they are feeling sensible.
>
> —POET W. H. AUDEN (1907–1973)

))) First Hearing   CONNECT   CD 1: Track 37

Listen to the recording of "Non più andrai" ("No More Will You") from *Le Nozze di Figaro (The Marriage of Figaro)* by Mozart and take notes on what you hear. Even if you are working with other students in a paired or group listening session, keep your own notes. Give some attention to the following:

- This is an aria from an opera. What kind of mood does it have? Can you imagine what the text might be about?

- What is the voice type and gender of the singer? Soprano, alto, tenor, or bass-baritone (not an extremely low bass)?

- Listen for repeated sections in the singer's melody. Is it the beginning melody that repeats or some later section? When does it repeat? Does the singer repeat the same melody over and over, or are there sections of contrast between repeated sections?

- Can you tell the language of the text? What is it?

- What instruments can you hear accompanying the singer?

- Can you guess at the tempo and meter?

Keep your notes from this First Hearing to compare with your impressions about the piece after you study the information in this chapter.

14

Composers of the classical era tended to concentrate more on instrumental music than on vocal music. The lieder (songs) written by Haydn, Mozart, and Beethoven are considered a relatively secondary part of their compositional efforts. The operas composed by Haydn to entertain the guests at the Esterházy palace were popular in their day but are not performed today. Beethoven wrote only one opera, *Fidelio*. The age was not, however, completely without significant and lasting achievements in the area of vocal music. Some of the large choral works of Mozart, Haydn, and Beethoven, and many of Mozart's operas, made lasting contributions to vocal literature.

Haydn's Vocal Music

Opera was a highly important part of musical activity at the Esterházy palace, and for a long time Haydn was quite proud of his more than twenty stage works. Austrian Empress Maria Theresa reputedly said, "If I want to hear a good opera, I go to Esterházy." However, when Haydn became familiar with Mozart's incomparable genius for opera composing, he realized that his own works were of lesser quality. Today they are all but forgotten.

Haydn composed Masses based on the same religious texts as those discussed in Chapter 4. Those Masses and his oratorios present a different story. The last six of his twelve Masses, composed between 1796 and 1802, are his crowning achievement as a church composer. One of those, his *Missa in Angustiis (Mass in Time of Peril),* was composed as a tribute to a naval battle. It is also called *The Nelson Mass,* because it was written in 1798 during the Battle of the Nile in which Lord Nelson led the British fleet to defeat Napoleon. Martial fanfares in the Benedictus (second part of the Sanctus in the Mass Ordinary) served to represent that victory. When Lord Nelson visited the Esterházy Castle at Eisenstadt in 1800, this mass was among the works performed in his honor.

The orchestration of Haydn's Masses varied from work to work, depending on the instruments and players available to him at the time. *The Nelson Mass* is scored for a comparatively small orchestra consisting of three trumpets, timpani, organ, and strings, together with four solo voices (SATB) and an SATB chorus.

Stimulated by Handel's oratorios, some of which he had heard during his London visits, Haydn produced three of his own. One of the most widely performed today is *The Creation*. It depicts the story of the creation of the world. From the overture ("Representation of Chaos") to the final triumphant chorus, Haydn uses soloists, chorus, and orchestra to impart the story vividly and dramatically. Together with his Masses, Haydn's oratorios constitute his most important contribution to vocal music.

Classical Opera

The greatest composer of opera in the classical era was Wolfgang Amadeus Mozart, who, with his finest works, took each type of operatic form to its epitome. Each type of opera composed during the classical period can be illustrated by Mozart's most famous works:

Opera seria (serious opera)
Idomeneo, 1781

> **Opera buffa** (Italian comic opera)
> *Le Nozze di Figaro (The Marriage of Figaro)*, 1786
> *Don Giovanni*, 1787
> *Così Fan Tutte (Thus Do They All)*, 1790
>
> *Singspiel* (German opera)
> *Die Entführung aus dem Serail (The Abduction from the Seraglio)*, 1782
> *Die Zauberflöte (The Magic Flute)*, 1791

Notice that most of those operas were composed in Italian even though they were intended for an Austrian audience whose language was German. Opera was still thought of as an Italian art form. Today, it does not matter what language the singers sing because modern opera houses have a translation in English lit up across the top of the stage or elsewhere. These are called supertitles, because they are above, just as subtitles are shown below the screen in foreign movies. In Mozart's day, the audiences probably knew the opera plots before they saw the opera, and it is advisable for modern operagoers to read the plot in advance as well. It is usually provided in a program given to audience members when they enter the hall where the opera will be performed.

Operas are often based on plays, and, like plays, their action is divided into large sections called **acts.** Those acts are sometimes further subdivided into **scenes.** Usually, a performance will have an intermission between acts, but not between scenes. Scenes sometimes require different sets—a first scene might be in one room of a palace, and the second in another room, for example—but the staging is planned so that the changes take a minimal amount of time during which the audience must wait in their seats. Major set changes, if necessary at all, happen between acts. Operas written during the classical period and later usually have two or three acts and one or two intermissions. *The Marriage of Figaro,* however, is particularly long in having four acts. Performances sometimes have three intermissions or just two, with the third and fourth acts performed without a break. Those decisions are made by the director. A full performance of *The Marriage of Figaro* with intermissions usually lasts well over three hours.

"MusiCurious: Classical and Romantic Opera (The Castrato Bows Out)" gives a brief overview of operatic performers.

The Marriage of Figaro

The opera *Le Nozze di Figaro (The Marriage of Figaro)* is based on a French play by Beaumarchais (real name, Pierre Augustin Caron, 1732–1799), translated into Italian and cast in the form of an opera libretto by Lorenzo da Ponte, a popular librettist at the time. On the surface, the plot is typically intricate and amusing, including a pair of lovers, intrigues between servants and masters, a case of discovered identity, and a few unlikely coincidences. The play on which the opera was rather closely based, however, was extremely controversial. It was first produced in 1782, just seven years before the beginning of the French Revolution. In many ways the play represented the antiaristocratic attitudes that erupted in the revolution, a fact that displeased French King Louis XVI, who would ultimately end up beheaded by his people.

The play portrays Count Almaviva as both abusive to his servants and stupid enough to be fooled by them. The abuse is evident in his desire to take advantage of a feudal right (going back to the medieval period) to deflower any young bride on her wedding night. The stupidity is shown by the fact that Susanna and the countess are able to fool him into an embarrassing situation in which he must ask his wife for forgiveness.

Louis XVI tried to keep the play from being produced, banning one production after another just before its performance. Beaumarchais, however, was able to

 **MusiCurious**

CLASSICAL AND ROMANTIC OPERA (THE CASTRATO BOWS OUT)

I know it is hard to stage baroque operas today because castrati no longer exist. Is it also hard to find singers for classical and romantic operas?

No. By the late eighteenth century most female operatic roles were sung by women and most male ones by men. One exception was what is generally referred to as a "trouser role," or a "pants role," for which a female singer, usually a mezzo soprano, sings the part of a young man. There are plenty of sopranos around today to sing such roles.

Did the "trouser" role develop out of the baroque use of castrati?

No. Actually the use of a female singer as a young man started because it was thought that "real men," even tenors with high voices, did not have light enough voices to sound as if they were in their teens or barely beyond. In Mozart's opera *Le Nozze di Figaro (The Marriage of Figaro)* the young court page Cherubino is sung by a woman. Other famous trouser roles include Ottavian in Strauss's *Der Rowenkavalier (The Knight of the Rose),* Siebel in Gounod's *Faust,* and Hänsel in Humperdinck's *Hänsel and Gretel.*

How specialized are opera singers' voices? Can any really good singer sing whatever role he or she wants to?

Opera singers' voices are very specialized, and the roles they can sing must fit their voices and their training. Teachers of opera singers usually begin by testing their students for their natural abilities and then proceed to train them to develop their voices to fit their best vocal range. For example, if a soprano has a naturally high voice, she might work to develop her voice so that she can sing the florid, high-pitched roles known as *coloratura soprano* roles.

I have heard that opera singers have really big egos and are very demanding. Is that true?

Sometimes, yes. The term *diva* means "goddess." In opera, divas are sopranos who are accustomed to singing the lead role and being the "star" of the show. They may feel that everything revolves around them. Perhaps the most famous diva was Nellie Melba (1861-1953), who sang for London's Covent Garden opera company for thirty years. She always insisted on being paid more than any other singer in the company, and she refused to allow any other singer to use her dressing room—even on nights when she was not singing. Male lead roles tend to be written for tenors, and as a result they often have the same reputation as diva sopranos. Of course, not all sopranos and tenors are like that, but the diva stories are part of the color of opera as a dramatic art form.

get enough private readings performed that the play became well known despite the king's resistance. Public pressure on the king forced him to allow sixty-eight public performances, with the audiences applauding almost every line.

Napoleon, who proclaimed himself emperor of France after the French Revolution, said of the play, "If I had been a king, a man such as he [Beaumarchais] would have been locked up. . . . *The Marriage of Figaro* is already the revolution in action."

In the movie *Amadeus,* the Austrian emperor displays his anger at Mozart for having composed an opera on the play that he had banned out of support for the French monarchy. Mozart defends himself by saying that he took all of the politics out of the plot and made it into a love story, but anyone who sees the entire opera can tell that the political controversy was not removed.

The Characters

Count Almaviva, a Spanish nobleman (baritone)

Countess Almaviva, his wife (soprano)

Susanna, the countess' maid (soprano), promised in marriage to Figaro

Figaro, the count's servant (bass)

Cherubino, the count's page (female soprano singing the role of a young man)

Marcellina, housekeeper (soprano)

Bartolo, a doctor from Seville (bass)

Basilio, a music teacher (tenor)

Don Curzio, a lawyer (tenor)

Barbarina, a daughter of Antonio (soprano)

Antonio, the count's gardener and Susanna's uncle (bass)

Chorus of country people and peasants

Note: Cherubino is a young male page at the court, and the role is composed to be sung by a female soprano dressed in male clothing.

Mozart's *The Marriage of Figaro* includes the role of Cherubino, seen here in a performance at the Royal Opera House in London.

The Plot

The opera is set in Count Almaviva's country house near Seville. Figaro, a valet to Count Almaviva, is preparing to marry Susanna, the countess's chambermaid. Figaro has borrowed a large sum of money from Marcellina, the old castle housekeeper, promising to repay it by a certain date or marry her if he defaults. The count has designs on Susanna and tries to seduce her, but she tells Figaro and the countess, and together they scheme to frustrate the count's plans.

Because Susanna will not yield to him, the count decides to take Marcellina's side in the financial dispute and force Figaro to marry her. This plot is foiled by the discovery that Marcellina and her advocate, Dr. Bartolo, are actually Figaro's long-lost parents, from whom he was kidnapped as an infant.

Meanwhile, Susanna and the countess have been conniving; their trick involves a case of disguised identity. Susanna promises to meet the count in the garden that night, but it is the countess, dressed as Susanna, who actually keeps the appointment. Figaro learns of the meeting and thinks that Susanna is deceiving him. The count is caught red-handed by his wife, confesses his attempted infidelity, and begs forgiveness, which she laughingly grants. It all ends happily when Figaro marries Susanna and Marcellina and Dr. Bartolo decide to marry as well.

In the first aria we will hear, the count's page, Cherubino, has discovered women and has been falling in love with every female at the palace, including the countess. By the second aria, the count has told Cherubino that he must join the military. In this aria, Figaro sings to him about how his life will now change.

"Non so più cosa son" ("I Don't Know What I Am Anymore") from
Le Nozze di Figaro (The Marriage of Figaro) WOLFGANG AMADEUS MOZART

Date: 1786

Genre: Opera aria

Tempo: Allegro vivace

Form: ABACC-Coda (beginning section repeats with contrast between the repetitions, then the next contrasting section is sung and repeats with contrasting ending)

Texture: Homophonic

Voices and Instruments: Female soprano singing the role of a young man, accompanied by orchestra

Language: Italian

Meter: Duple

Duration: 2:45

Context: This aria is sung by Cherubino, the count's page. Cherubino has just discovered an attraction to women, and he falls in love with every woman he meets. His confusion about his feelings is expressed by repetitions of sections of text and by several dramatic long-held notes, pauses, and a much slower section before a fast ending.

	Timing	Italian text	English translation	Form	Musical events
1	0:00	Non so più cosa son, cosa faccio, or di foco, ora sono di ghiaccio, ogni donna cangiar di colore. Ogni donna mi fa palpitar. Ogni donna mi fa palpitar. Ogni donna mi fa palpitar.	I don't know what I am, or what I am doing, now I am on fire, or now I am freezing, every woman makes me change color. Every woman makes my heart flutter. Every woman makes my heart flutter. Every woman makes my heart flutter.	A	
	0:18	Solo ai nomi d'amor, di diletto, mi si turba, mi s'altera il petto e a parlare mi sforza d'amore un desio, un desio ch'lo non posso spiegar. Un desio, un desio ch'lo non posso spiegar.	When of love there is just a mention, I am upset, and my heart beats faster and I find myself talking of love from a need, from a need I can't explain. From a need, from a need I can't explain.	B	
	0:44	(Repeat of the music and lyrics of the A section)		A	
	1:04	Parlo d'amor vegliando, parlo d'amor sognando, all'acque, all'ombre, ai monti, ai fiori, all'erbe, ai fonti, all'eco, all'aria, ai venti' che il suon de' vani accenti'	I talk of love when walking. I talk of love when dreaming, to the water, to the shadows, to the mountains, to the flowers, to the grass, to the fountains, to the echoes, to the air, to the winds, and the sound of my useless words	C	 Long-held note at end of phrase

(continued)

Timing	Italian text	English translation	Form	Musical events
	portano via con sé.	is carried away with them.		Long-held note at end of phrase
	Portano via con sé. (Repeat of the music and lyrics of the C section)	Is carried away with them.	C	
2:19	E se non ho chi m'oda, e se non ho chi m'oda,	And if I don't have anyone to hear me, and if I don't have anyone to hear me,		Coda, much slower tempo
	parlo d'amor con me, con me,	I talk of love to myself, to myself,		Long-held note at end of phrase
	parlo d'amor con me.	I talk of love to myself.		Original fast tempo returns

))) **Featured Listening**

 CD 1: Track 37

"Non più andrai" ("No More Will You") from *Le Nozze di Figaro* (*The Marriage of Figaro*) WOLFGANG AMADEUS MOZART

Date: 1786

Genre: Opera aria

Tempo: Vivace (Fast and lively)

Form: ABACA-Coda

Voices and Instruments: Bass-baritone voice and full orchestra

Language: Italian

Meter: Quadruple

Duration: 3:39

Context: At the end of Act One, Figaro tells Cherubino how much his life will change when he enters the military. Opera staging and action varies with the director, but in some traditional versions of the opera, Figaro has Cherubino dress in his military uniform during the aria, handing him his saber or musket and drawing a mustache on him.

	Timing	Italian text	English translation	Form	Musical events
37	0:00	Non più andrai, farfallone amoroso, notte e giorano d'intorno girando, delle belle turbando il riposo, Narcisetto, Adoncino d'amor, delle belle turbando il riposo, Narcisetto, Adoncino d'amor.	No more will you, amorous butterfly, flit around the castle night and day, upsetting all the pretty girls, love's little Narcissus and Adonis, upsetting all the pretty girls, love's little Narcissus and Adonis.	A	
	0:26	Non più avrai questi bei pennacchini, quell cappello leggiero e galante,	No more will you have those fine plumes, that soft and stylish hat,	B	

Timing	Italian text	English translation	Form	Musical events
	quella chioma, quell'aria brillante,	those fine locks, that striking air,		
	quell vermiglio donnesco color.	those rosy, girl-like cheeks.		
	Quell vermiglio donnesco color!	Those rosy, girl-like cheeks!		
	Non più avrai quei pennacchini,	No more, those fine plumes,		
	quell cappello, quella chioma,	the hat, or the fine locks,		
	quell' aria brillante!	that striking air!		
0:57	(Repeat of the music and lyrics of the A section)		A	
1:20	Fra guerrieri, poffar Bacco!	Among warriors swearing by Bacchus!	C	
	Gran mustacchi, stretto sacco,	Great mustachios, holding your pack,		
	schioppo in spalla, sciabla al fianco,	a gun on your shoulder, a saber hanging		
	collo dritto, muso franco,	at your right, musket ready,		
	o un gran casco, un gran turbante,	or some great cask, or a turban,		
	molto onor, poco contante,	winning honors, but caring little,		
	poco contante, poco contante.	winning honors, but caring little.		
	Ed invece del fandango,	And in place of the fandango,		
	una marcia per il fango.	a march through the mud.		
	Per montagne, per valloni,	Over the mountains, over valleys,		
	colle nevi e I sollioni.	through the snow and the burning sun.		
	Al concerto di trombone,	To the music of trumpets,		
	di bombarde, di cannoni,	of shells and cannons,		
	che le palle in tutti tuoni,	with balls sounding thunder,		
	all'orecchio fan fischiar.	making your ears ring.		
	Non più avrai quei pennacchini.	No more, those fine plumes.		
	Non più avrai quell cappello.	No more the fine hat.		
	Non più avrai quella chioma.	No more the fine locks.		
	Non più avrai quell'aria brillante!	No more that striking air!		
2:24	(Repeat of the music and lyrics of the A section)		A	
2:47	Cherubino, alla vittoria,	Cherubino, on to victory,	Coda	
	alla gloria militar.	on to victory in war.		
	Cherubino, alla vittoria.	Cherubino, on to victory.		
	Alla gloria militar.	On to victory in war.		
	Alla gloria militar.	On to victory in war.		
	Alla gloria militar!	On to victory in war!		
				Extended instrumental ending to both the aria and Act One

Figaro's aria is quoted in another of Mozart's operas, *Don Giovanni*, at the beginning of Act Two, Scene 5, when Don Giovanni is seated at his dinner table and some of his "favorite music" plays.

Summary

Although the main area of concentration for most classical composers was instrumental music, the age did pro-duce lasting achievements in vocal music as well. Haydn's *Nelson Mass* well represents the classical treatment of the Mass. Considered a masterpiece, this work is a favorite in contemporary choral repertoires.

The greatest composer of opera in the classical era was Mozart. His first comic opera, *The Marriage of Figaro*, stands out among *opera buffa* for its realistic characters, amusing libretto, delightful solo and ensemble music, and skillful use of orchestral devices to enhance the characterization. Despite its entertainment value, *The Marriage of Figaro* was controversial when it was composed. It was based on a French play of the same name that made fun of a count who was trying to take advantage of his wife's maid. The maid, Susanna, and her fiancé, Figaro, collaborated with the countess to fool the count. For a play to show a member of the aristocracy in such an unflattering light did not sit well with King Louis XVI, because the king was aware of the antiaristocratic sentiments that were building in France. Those sentiments exploded in the French Revolution of 1789, during which Louis XVI was beheaded.

New Concepts

act, 142

opera buffa, 142

opera seria, 141

scene, 142

Finale

   CD 1: Track 37

Listen again to the recording of "Non più andrai" ("No More Will You") from *Le Nozze di Figaro (The Marriage of Figaro)* by Mozart and compare your impression now with your notes from your First Hearing. Consider the following questions:

- What is this aria about, and when is it placed in the opera?
- What is the voice type of the singer? What character is singing, and to whom is he singing?
- What is the form (placement of repeated and contrasting sections) of the aria?
- What is the language of the text?
- What instruments accompany the singer?
- What is the tempo and meter of the aria?
- If you were going to describe this music to a friend, what would you say?

Further Listening

Joseph Haydn, *Die Schöpfung (The Creation)*. As wonderful as the drama of opera is, one should not limit one's listening to vocal music only to opera. Haydn's *Creation* is an oratorio based on the biblical books of Genesis and Psalms, as well as John Milton's *Paradise Lost*. Its telling of the creation of the world begins with an overture that represents total darkness and chaos (see Genesis 1:2) and leads to a triumphant ending, about ninety minutes later.

Wolfgang Amadeus Mozart, Requiem in D Minor, K. 626. This is Mozart's final work as a composer. It is often thought of as his own requiem, but one that he did not live to complete. Because Mozart was dying, he dictated some sections to a student of Antonio Salieri—Franz Süssmayr—who completed the work after Mozart's death. There is no way for scholars today to know exactly which sections of the music in Süssmayr's notation were dictated by Mozart and which ones were his own. The Requiem was commissioned by composer Franz von Walsegg, who asked Mozart to keep the work a secret because Walsegg planned to claim it as his own. In the 1984 movie *Amadeus,* Salieri himself was portrayed as the person who commissioned the Requiem and also the person to whom it was dictated. Salieri really had nothing to do with either of those roles. Despite the intrigue, this Requiem is one of the great masterpieces of music for vocal soloists, chorus, and orchestra.

The Music of Beethoven

15

))) **First Hearing**

  CONNECT   CD 1: Tracks 38–43

Listen to the recording of Symphony no. 5 in C Minor, first movement, by Beethoven and take notes on what you hear. Even if you are working with other students in a paired or group listening session, keep your own notes. Give some attention to the following:

- This symphony is so famous that you might have heard this first movement before. What is noticeable about the opening theme? Is it long or short? When it repeats, does it repeat at the same pitch level, or does it change with each repetition?

- What is the rhythm pattern of the first theme? Short-long, or short-short-long, or short-short-short-long, or short-short-short-short-long?

- Do you hear another theme that is smoother than the famous opening theme? When is that theme first played?

- Write down the instruments that you hear as you hear them.

- Do the first two themes return near the end of the movement?

- Can you guess at the tempo and meter?

Keep your notes from this First Hearing to compare with your impressions about the piece after you study the information in this chapter.

Ludwig van Beethoven

Probably no single composer has influenced the course of musical events more than **Ludwig van Beethoven** ("Bay-toe-ven," 1770–1827). His evolving style had a profound effect on the musicians of his time, and the music he left to the world has continued to influence musicians and to have great public appeal. His greatest contribution was carrying forward the tradition of Mozart and Haydn, building on the structures they had developed and elevating them to new heights of power and expressiveness.

In comparison with the productivity of Mozart and Haydn, Beethoven's works seem surprisingly few. This was partly due to his method of composing. Mozart never lacked musical inspiration, and ideas flowed from his pen with miraculous ease; Haydn also kept to a regular schedule of composition, providing whatever music his patron wanted in time for the performance. Beethoven, however, had to struggle. Ideas did not come easily, and he filled innumerable pages with slowly evolving sketches. Even his finished compositions were continually rewritten and revised. Another reason for

LUDWIG VAN BEETHOVEN
(1770–1827)

- Born in Bonn, Germany; died at age 57 in Vienna, Austria.

- Major, prolific composer, best known for nine symphonies and other orchestral music, chamber music, *Missa Solemnis* and other choral works, piano sonatas including "Moonlight," and one opera, *Fidelio.*

his limited production was his attitude toward composition. Above all, he regarded music as art, and he generally took on only those commissions that he personally wished to fulfill.

If Beethoven's works took longer to write than was usual at the time, they were also more substantial, in both content and length. His works include nine symphonies; nine concert overtures; five piano concertos; one violin concerto; sixteen string quartets; ten sonatas for violin and piano; five sonatas for cello and piano; thirty-two sonatas for solo piano; twenty-one sets of variations for piano; one opera, *Fidelio;* one oratorio, *Christus am Ölberg (Christ on the Mount of Olives); Choral Fantasia* for piano, chorus, and orchestra; and two Masses.

Most musical scholars divide Beethoven's career into three periods: the first extending to about 1802, the second to 1814, and the last ending with his death in 1827. The first period was a time of assimilation of the classical tradition of Mozart and Haydn and includes his string quartets composed before 1800, the First Symphony (1799), and his first three piano sonatas.

The second period was perhaps the happiest of Beethoven's life, and certainly the most productive. During this period he wrote masterpiece after masterpiece: seven more symphonies; the *Rasoumovsky* string quartets of 1806; his opera, *Fidelio;* and two important and popular piano sonatas, the "Waldstein" and the "Appassionata" (both 1804).

Beethoven's last creative period, a time of great personal troubles including his deafness, was less productive, but in many ways it was the most important of the three. This period culminated in his monumental Ninth Symphony (1823), the equally immense *Missa Solemnis* (completed in 1824), and his late string quartets and piano sonatas. In these works he developed many of the musical ideas that influenced the style period that would follow him, the romantic era.

Ludwig van Beethoven was born in the Rhineland city of Bonn, Germany. His father, a singer in the Electoral Court chapel, hoped to make his boy into a child prodigy like Mozart. Although he didn't fulfill his father's aspirations, young Beethoven did learn piano and violin quickly. He received instruction from several musicians at the court, and by age 12 was substituting at the chapel organ. In 1784 he was appointed to a permanent position as assistant organist and had become known for his virtuoso improvisations at the piano. While Beethoven was gaining recognition for his musical talents, personal problems arose. His mother died in 1787, his father's alcoholism grew worse, and Beethoven's home life became increasingly unbearable.

The year 1790 marked a turning point in the young composer's career. Haydn heard Beethoven play when he passed through Bonn on his way to London. Impressed with Beethoven's talent, Haydn urged Elector Max Friedrich, for whom Beethoven worked, to send him to Vienna for further study. Two years later, at age 22, Beethoven moved to Vienna, where he remained the rest of his life. At first he studied composition with Haydn, but, unsatisfied with the older man's methods, he turned to other composers for instruction. Though he was a frequent performer at musical evenings held by prominent Viennese nobility, Beethoven did not play in public until 1795, when he performed one of his early piano concertos.

Unlike Mozart, Beethoven always retained his popularity with both the general public and the aristocracy of Vienna. Unlike Haydn, he never had to endure the rigors of the eighteenth-century system of musical patronage. Though he may have yearned at times for the prestige and security of a court position, he remained proudly and fiercely independent throughout his life. During most of his career he was able to count on annual stipends from a small circle of aristocratic friends and admirers. He seemed to enjoy moving about in the upper echelons of Viennese society, once remarking that "it is good to mingle with aristocrats, but one must know how to impress them."

Beethoven was one of the first composers to demand and obtain an equal footing with this aristocracy solely on the basis of his genius. It was his fortune to come on the world in a time of rapidly changing values and increasing social mobility. The emerging middle-class audience and the growth of public concerts provided ample opportunities for performance of his music. Rising demand for his works enabled him to live off the sale of his music to publishers.

During the first years of the nineteenth century, when Beethoven seemed to be approaching the height of his career, he became aware that he was growing deaf. He became deeply depressed when he realized that his career as a performer would end. In a moving letter to his two brothers, written from the small town of Heiligenstadt outside Vienna and intended to be read after his death, Beethoven confessed,

> My misfortune pains me doubly, in as much as it leads to my being misjudged. For me there can be no relaxation in human society, no refined conversation, no mutual confidences; I must live quite alone and may creep into society only as often as sheer necessity demands; I must live like an outcast. If I appear in company I am overcome by a burning anxiety, a fear that I am running the risk of letting people notice my condition. . . . Such experiences almost made me despair, and I was on the point of putting an end to my life—the only thing that held me back was my art. For indeed it seemed to me impossible to leave this world before I had produced all the works that I felt the urge to compose, and thus I have dragged on this miserable existence.

After his affliction became painfully obvious, Beethoven gave up conducting and playing in public. His principal means of communication became a notebook in which his few visitors were invited to write their remarks. As he withdrew into his art, his works became more complex, more abstract, and more incomprehensible to his fellow musicians. He never married, and when total deafness set in after 1820, he became almost a recluse. Beethoven died in 1827 at age 57.

In many ways Beethoven was a real romantic. Part of the reason he never married was that he fell in love with women who either were already married or were of such a high economic class that their fathers would not have allowed them to marry a working composer, regardless of his fame. Beethoven's only opera, *Fidelio,* is based on a character that Beethoven considered to be the perfect wife. It is about a woman who risks her life and everything she has to save her husband, who has been wrongly imprisoned. The 1994 movie *Immortal Beloved* portrayed Beethoven as a man who had lusted after many women and written a letter to the "immortal beloved," which was found among his things after he died. Such a letter was really written and found, but many other details about the movie are incorrect. Beethoven was probably not as insane as the movie suggests, and it is unlikely that he had the real-life affairs the movie uses to attract modern audiences. At the risk of giving away the mystery-like plot, the woman the movie represents as the "immortal beloved" is unlikely to ever have been Beethoven's lover.

In general, Beethoven's works tend to be longer than those of Haydn or Mozart. He lengthened the development section of movements in sonata form and added further development to his codas. He added more instruments to the orchestra, giving it a more powerful and dramatic sound than the orchestras for which Mozart or Haydn wrote. He also changed the ways some of the instruments were used, writing independent timpani parts, for example. He added more players to the string section, giving it a fuller sound, and used two trumpets as a standard part of the orchestra. A comparison of the orchestra Mozart used for his Fortieth Symphony with the one Beethoven used in his Fifth Symphony follows:

Mozart's Fortieth Symphony	Beethoven's Fifth Symphony
—	one piccolo (fourth movement)
one flute	two flutes
two oboes	two oboes
two clarinets	two clarinets
two bassoons	two bassoons
—	one contrabassoon (fourth movement)
two horns	two horns
—	two trumpets
—	three trombones (fourth movement)
—	timpani
first violins	first violins
second violins	second violins
violas	violas
cellos	cellos
double bass	double bass

Working with this expanded orchestra, Beethoven made important contributions to the craft of **orchestration**—writing and arranging music for orchestra to achieve the most effective overall combination. In this area he greatly influenced composers of the romantic era, for whom orchestration became a major component of musical composition.

Beethoven's Fifth Symphony, which he began in 1804, was first performed in Vienna in December 1808. It is probably the most popular of Beethoven's symphonies, not only for its famous opening but also for its unity. Until this symphony, separate movements in multimovement works had no themes in common. With his Fifth Symphony, Beethoven introduced the idea of a common thread that can be heard in all four movements, an idea that was expanded and often used in the romantic period.

The famous theme that opens Beethoven's Fifth Symphony is a rhythmic motive (a short melodic or rhythmic idea): three short notes, followed by one long note. That rhythm pattern is stated in the first theme of the first movement. It returns in the second theme of the second movement, and again in the scherzo (faster than a minuet) theme of the third movement. It reappears as a quote from the third movement during the development section of the fourth movement. This unification of a symphony with a musical idea that appears in each movement is referred to as **cyclic form** and is something that nineteenth-century composers used often.

Featured Listening

 CD 1: Tracks 38–43

Symphony no. 5 in C Minor, first movement LUDWIG VAN BEETHOVEN

Date: 1808

Genre: Symphony

Tempo: Allegro con brio (fast, with vigor and spirit)

Form: Sonata

Instruments: Two flutes, two oboes, two clarinets, two bassoons, two French horns, two trumpets, timpani, first violins, second violins, violas, cellos, double basses

Meter: Duple

Duration: 7:18

Context: Beethoven first admitted to friends that he was going deaf in 1801. No one knows how much he could hear seven years later when this symphony was completed, but his hearing problems were certainly a focus of concern. After Beethoven's death, a friend wrote that Beethoven had told him that the first theme of his Fifth Symphony represented "fate knocking at the door." The rhythm of the opening motive—three short notes and one long one—is an organizational feature that is used in all four movements of the symphony. That motive is called the "basic motive" in the Listening Guides. Remember, there is no piano as an instrument in the orchestra. "Piano" means soft.

	Timing		Instrumentation
	Exposition		
38	0:00	Theme 1	Basic motive stated twice, forte (loud)
	0:07		Piano (soft), motive sounds throughout strings; crescendo, three forte, separated chords, long-held note by violins on last chord
	0:19	Bridge	Motive, fortissimo (very loud); piano, motive builds theme in strings; instruments gradually enter, crescendo, pitch rises; two separate chords, fortissimo
	Bridge		
39	0:00	Theme 2	Horn call, basic motive with extension, fortissimo
	0:02		Legato theme in violins, then clarinet, then flute; basic motive in low strings; fragment of theme in strings, other instruments gradually enter, crescendo
	0:22		Loud chord, strings in strong descending passage, repeated
	0:32		Basic motive descends in winds answered by strings; repeated; two separate statements of motive
	(Exposition is repeated.)		
	Development		
40	0:00		Basic motive in horns, strings, fortissimo; motive developed among instruments, piano, slight crescendo, return to piano for further development
	0:04		Strings and winds toss motive back and forth, crescendo to strings hammering on repeated note
	0:35		"Horn call" from theme 2 developed, with answer from low strings; reduced to two-note fragment echoed between winds and strings; reduced to one-note echo, suspense builds through diminuendo to pianissimo
	1:05		Horn call erupts in full orchestra; one-note echo resumes; basic motive repeated fortissimo, directly into:
	Recapitulation		
41	0:00	Theme 1	Trumpets and timpani added for two statements of basic motive
	0:07		Motive through strings with countermelody in oboe, piano; three separated chords, oboe cadenza concludes countermelody on last chord
	0:31		Motive, piano, build theme in strings; instruments gradually enter, crescendo, pitch rises; two separate chords, fortissimo

(continued)

	Timing		Instrumentation
42	0:00	Theme 2	Horn call played by bassoon, basic motive with extension, fortissimo
	0:03		Legato theme traded between violins and flute, basic motive in low strings; fragment of theme divided between strings and flute, crescendo in strings as other instruments gradually enter
43	0:00	Coda	Loud chord, strings in strong descending passage, repeated
	0:09		Basic motive descends in woodwinds answered by strings; repeated
	0:14	Second development	Separate statements of motive extended fortissimo to hammer on repeated note, basic motive piano, repeated note forte, motive piano
	0:31		Horn call from theme 2 in cellos and violas, new countertheme in violins; repeated; countertheme vigorously developed, full orchestra
	0:40		Fragment of countertheme tossed between winds and strings; repeated note leads directly into:
	1:04	Second coda	Basic motive stated twice, fortissimo
	1:14		Piano, basic motive in strings; fortissimo, full orchestra states basic motive three times with final chords

Beethoven particularly liked composing and improvising variations on themes. For the second movement of his Fifth Symphony, he composed two themes, both of which are varied through the movement. Notice that the second theme contains the short-short-short-long rhythmic motive that was the primary theme of the first movement of the same symphony.

CD 5: Tracks 2–4

Symphony no. 5 in C Minor, second movement LUDWIG VAN BEETHOVEN

Date: 1808

Genre: Symphony

Tempo: **Andante con moto** (walking pace with a sense of motion)

Form: Theme and variations with two themes

Instruments: Two flutes, two oboes, two clarinets, two bassoons, two French horns, two trumpets, timpani, first violins, second violins, violas, cellos, double basses

Meter: Triple

Duration: 10:40

Context: Theme 2 includes the basic rhythm of three short notes and one long one, unifying it with the first movement.

	Timing		Instrumentation
2	0:00	Theme 1	Lyrical melody, low strings, piano; theme continues with violins and flute
3	0:00	Theme 2	Clarinets, piano; violins, piano; full orchestra, fortissimo
	0:23		Trumpets, fortissimo; violins, pianissimo

Timing		Instrumentation
1:09	Variation 1A	Lyrical melody of theme 1, embellished with faster melody
2:05	Variation 1B	Theme 2 with active accompaniment; soft, long-held chords; cadence
3:12	Variation 2A	Theme 1 embellished with an even faster melody than in variation A
3:49		Theme played by low strings, ends rising to a high note
4:12	Middle section	Strings repeat chords; clarinet, bassoon, and then flute play theme 1;
5:12		brass fanfare based on theme 2; timpani rolls, strings, then staccato wood-winds and crescendo in strings leads into:
6:01	Variation 3A	Theme 1 played by full orchestra, fortissimo
4 0:00	Coda	Tempo faster, soft bassoon responded to by oboe; strings crescendo
0:27		Beginning tempo returns; flute and strings play part of theme 1.
1:06		Clarinets vary theme 1; beginning of theme 2 in strings builds to fortissimo cadence.

The third movement is a scherzo and trio, which is structured like the minuet and trio we heard earlier but flows a bit faster. Actually, the word *scherzo* means "joke," and the joke was that one could not dance a minuet to a scherzo even though the scherzo is also in triple meter. A scherzo is not only faster than a minuet, but it also has more of a stress on the first beat of each three-beat measure and less accent on the second and third beats. A minuet is danced to all three beats.

CONNECT   **CD 5: Track 5**

Symphony no. 5 in C Minor, third movement LUDWIG VAN BEETHOVEN

Date: 1808

Genre: Symphony

Tempo: Allegro

Form: Scherzo and trio

Instruments: Two flutes, two oboes, two clarinets, two bassoons, two French horns, two trumpets, timpani, first violins, second violins, violas, cellos, double basses

Meter: Triple

Duration: 4:54

Context: The short-short-short-long rhythm from the first movement is played as a new melody just nineteen seconds after the opening of the movement. This movement is tied to the next movement by a transition that has no sense of meter and seems to just float until the drama of the beginning of the fourth movement hits.

Timing	What to listen for
Scherzo	
5 0:00	Main theme rises from low to higher notes on strings, followed by a response in high strings
0:20	Short-short-short-long rhythm is made into a new melody played first by horns

(continued)

Timing	What to listen for
Trio	
1:48	Main trio theme begins in string basses with imitation
Scherzo	
3:13	Main scherzo theme returns with lighter-sounding orchestration; strings play pizzicato (plucked) melody with short-short-short-long rhythm
3:31	Short-short-short-long rhythm
4:18	Transition section without regular meter, but short-short-short-long rhythm softly in timpani; leads to fourth movement

The fourth movement of Beethoven's Fifth Symphony is connected directly to the third, with no pause between the movements. There is a transitional section in which the triple meter of the scherzo is no longer played and the quadruple meter of the fourth movement has yet to begin. The fourth movement is in sonata form, and the first theme is triumphant. Beethoven helped create this triumphant effect by adding the piccolo, contrabassoon, and three trombones.

CONNECT   CD 5: Track 6

Symphony no. 5 in C Minor, fourth movement LUDWIG VAN BEETHOVEN

Date: 1808

Genre: Symphony

Tempo: Allegro

Form: Sonata

Instruments: Piccolo, contrabassoon, and three trombones added to the instruments in the earlier movements

Meter: Quadruple

Duration: 10:09

Context: The dramatic sound of this movement is aided by the addition of a piccolo, a contrabassoon, and three trombones. The short-short-short-long rhythm comes in near the end, giving the entire symphony a sense of balance.

Timing	What to listen for
Exposition	
0:00	Theme 1, triumphant sound led by trumpets
0:34	New theme serves as a bridge to second theme.
1:00	Theme 2, played by bowed strings
1:26	Closing theme 1 strings and woodwinds
1:54	(The exposition is repeated.)

Timing	What to listen for
Development	
3:53	Theme 2 is the focus of the development.
5:17	Short-short-short-long rhythm quoted as heard in movement 3
Recapitulation	
5:52	Theme 1 returns.
6:26	Bridge theme returns.
6:55	Theme 2 returns.
7:20	Closing theme returns.
7:49	Coda begins with theme 2, then quotes from other themes; coda often sounds like it is ending and then continues on to be ended by the full orchestra playing the tonic note, C

See "Hearing the Difference: Haydn's Symphony no. 94, second movement, and Beethoven's Symphony no. 5, second movement" to examine how two second movements in theme and variations form can differ from each other.

The Classical Piano

In the classical period, the harpsichord of the baroque period gave way to the new **pianoforte,** or simply **piano,** as the preferred keyboard instrument. Recall that the harpsichord is a keyboard instrument that plucks the instrument's strings, giving it a crisp tone quality. But there is no way for the player to control dynamic changes on the harpsichord other than to play fewer or more notes at one time, more notes

 **Hearing the Difference**

HAYDN'S SYMPHONY NO. 94, SECOND MOVEMENT, AND BEETHOVEN'S SYMPHONY NO. 5, SECOND MOVEMENT

Both of these works are second movements in theme and variations form, but there are a number of differences in the way they each follow the form (see Featured Listening on page 122 and Listening Guide on page 154). Answer the following questions as you listen from one work to the other:

- Both movements begin with strings. Which begins with staccato playing, and which begins with legato playing?

- Which movement is based on one theme, and which has two themes? Can you tell which theme you are hearing when listening to the movement with two themes?

- Can you keep track of exactly when each variation begins in either work? Is hearing the variations easier in the work with one theme, or is it just as easy in the work with two themes?

- Both movements are given the tempo marking of *andante.* What does that mean? Are either or both movements played at what seems to be that tempo?

- The movements are in different meters. Which is duple, and which is triple?

The pianoforte emerged during the classical period as the keyboard instrument of choice for composers like Beethoven.

creating more sound than one or two. No matter how hard or gently the player pushes the keys down, exactly the same sound comes out of the instrument. That sound was fine when used for baroque music that often had terraced dynamics, not requiring a lot of crescendos or diminuendos in a single phrase, but classical style required dynamic versatility.

Pianos are different from harpsichords in that their sound is produced by hammers that hit the strings to make them vibrate. The hammers can hit lightly or hard, depending on the force the player uses on the keyboard, and the instrument will sound soft or loud accordingly. The piano's ability to be played using contrasting dynamic levels gave it its name. Originally, the instruments were called *pianoforte* (soft/loud) or *fortepiano* (loud/soft). In later years, the name was shortened to *piano*.

Early experiments in piano building were being made at the end of the baroque period, but makers had many problems controlling the bounce of the hammers after they hit the strings. Many experimental instruments were made through the 1750s and 1760s. A piano with improved hammer action was invented in England in 1777, and that was followed by better instruments made in Germany and Austria. Mozart, Haydn, and Beethoven all saw the musical advantages of the piano and composed works that made good use of the piano's dynamic range and ability to sustain sounds for a longer period of time than was possible on the old harpsichord. By the late classical period, the piano was popular as a solo instrument, a chamber music participant, and a solo concerto instrument.

We will listen to the first movement of Beethoven's "Moonlight" sonata. (That title was given to the sonata by a publisher, not by Beethoven.)

 **Listening Guide**

"Moonlight," Piano Sonata no. 14 in C-Sharp Minor, op. 27, no. 2, first movement LUDWIG VAN BEETHOVEN

Date: 1798–1799

Genre: Piano sonata

Tempo: Adagio sostenuto (a sustained, leisurely pace)

Form: Fantasia-like with no regular repeated or contrasting sections

Instruments: Solo piano

Meter: Duple, with each beat having a *triplet,* or three notes fit into it (you can count the beats in each measure by saying "1 trip-let, 2 trip-let, 3 trip-let, 4 trip-let")

Duration: 6:28

Context: This sonata is not composed in the standard three-movement format often followed by classical sonatas. Here, the first movement is slow, the second is faster, and the third is even faster. The beauty and long-lasting popularity of this first movement speaks to Beethoven's brilliance in breaking the traditional format.

	Timing	What to listen for
7	0:00	Soft, slow, arpeggiated chords in triplet rhythm (three notes to each beat), very low sustained bass notes in octaves
	0:28	Main theme played just above triplet pattern (on G sharp)
	0:56	Main theme enters again, a little lower (G natural), but continues differently from before.
	2:07	Main theme returns at a higher pitch level than before (C sharp).
	3:48	Main theme back at original pitch (G sharp)
	4:11	Main theme again, but a little higher than the original pitch (B natural)
	5:26	Main theme keeps repeating in bass (low G sharp), final two chords

Summary

Beethoven expanded nearly every aspect of classical composition. His works are longer and larger in scale than those of his predecessors and contemporaries. Beethoven's compositions place great emphasis on developmental procedures and use such effects as dynamics to reach new heights of expressiveness. Beethoven often used a lively scherzo rather than a minuet in third movements of multi-movement works. He also used a single theme or motive in more than one movement to unify longer works. He used this idea in his Fifth Symphony when the rhythm of three short notes, followed by a long note, was featured in all four movements.

Improvements in instruments and instrumental techniques directly influenced Beethoven's compositions. He increased the size of the orchestra from that used by Mozart and Haydn. He was a virtuoso pianist, and his piano works fully exploited the brilliance and power that the newer pianos of his time were capable of achieving.

New People and Concepts

allegro con brio, 153

andante con moto, 154

cyclic form, 152

Ludwig van Beethoven, 149

orchestration, 152

piano, 157

pianoforte, 157

Finale

CD 1: Tracks 38–43

Listen again to the recording of Symphony no. 5 in C Minor, first movement, by Beethoven and compare your impression now with your notes from your First Hearing. Consider the following questions:

- What is the rhythm of the first theme, and how is it handled at the beginning of this movement?
- In what way does the second theme contrast with the first?
- What orchestral instruments do you hear?
- What is the form of the movement?
- What are the tempo and the meter?
- If you were going to describe this music to a friend, what would you say?

Further Listening

Ludwig van Beethoven, Piano Sonata no. 14 in C-Sharp minor, op. 27, no. 2, "Moonlight." Despite what many people think, the Moonlight Sonata has three movements, not just one. In this sonata, Beethoven departed from the standard classical three-movement plan and started with a slow first movement, "Adagio sostenuto." He followed that with a faster, Allegretto, second movement and then a Presto finale.

Ludwig van Beethoven, Piano Sonata no. 8 in C minor, op. 13, "Pathétique." This sonata *does* follow the standard classical three-movement plan, although its first movement has a *grave* introduction before it changes tempo to Allegro di molto e con brio. The second move-ment is Adagio cantabile, and the third is a Rondo: Allegro.

Ludwig van Beethoven, Violin Concerto in D major, op. 61. Beethoven took such a long time composing this concerto that it has been said that the violinist had to sight read it in the first performance. The movements are (1) Allegro ma non troppo, (2) Larghetto, and (3) Rondo: Allegro. The concerto was all but forgotten until 1844 when Felix Mendelssohn, whose own violin concerto we will hear later, conducted a performance of it with Joseph Joachim playing the solo violin part. Since that acclaimed performance, the concerto has remained a favorite and is often performed today.

CHARACTERISTICS OF CLASSICAL MUSIC

Texture	Largely homophonic, but flexible, with shifts to polyphony
Tonality	Major-minor system with frequent modulations to related keys; heavy dependence on tonic-dominant relationship
Rhythm	Variety of rhythmic patterns within a work
Melody	Composed of short, balanced phrases; melodic phrases often contrasted with each other
Mood	Expression of variety of moods within a work and sudden changes of mood
Dynamics	Gradual dynamic changes
Large works	Sonata, symphony, concerto, string quartet, Mass, oratorio, opera
Musical instruments	Piano and violin favored for solo concerto; makeup of orchestra becomes standardized; development of orchestra favors growth of symphonic works
Formal structures	Sonata principle (multimovement structure for long pieces); single-movement sonata form; rondo; minuet and trio; scherzo and trio; theme and variations; cadenza and double exposition used in concertos
Symphonic style	Follows four-movement plan, with first movement in sonata form; each movement self-contained; clarity and balance are major stylistic features

Prelude

Music of the Romantic Era

The word *romantic* as it is applied to the arts in the 1800s means much more than our common use of the term, which conjures up visions of lovers dining with candles on the table or strolling hand-in-hand on the beach. Nineteenth-century romanticism describes a school of thought that encapsulated much of the philosophy, literature, and visual arts of an era that rejected the Enlightenment's *reasoned* view of the world. Instead, romantics were drawn to the exception to the rule. They were excited by the turbulence that followed the French Revolution. They were fascinated by the power of the individual, especially the man or woman of feeling who dwelt in a private world of emotions and solitary dreams, and the hero, who represented the grandest possibilities of the individual. They searched for the exotic, the mysterious, and the unfamiliar. They were adventurers drawn to experience that affected their senses and stimulated their passions.

The Role of Nature

The romantics were preoccupied with nature. In the past, landscapes had been painted only as backgrounds for portraits or other subjects. Nineteenth-century artists made scenes of meadows, trees, clouds, lakes, and mountains the primary subjects of much of their work. At times they showed the power nature could have over mankind through storms, fires, or other uncontrollable natural occurrences. The English painter J. M. W. Turner (1775–1851) painted many such scenes.

Writers sought inspiration in nature and found in its changes metaphors for their own moods and emotions. For some romantics, such as the poet Wordsworth (1770–1850), nature was elevated into a religion. Rejecting absolutely the Age of Reason, William Wordsworth wrote,

> One impulse from a vernal wood
> May teach you more of man,
> Of moral evil and of good,
> Than all the sages can.
> Sweet is the lore which Nature brings;
> Our middling intellect
> Misshapes the beauteous forms of things:
> We murder to dissect.

Political Developments

The French Revolution and the political turbulence that followed it discredited the Enlightenment ideal of the supremacy of reason. After Napoleon's armies brought much of Europe under French control, he was finally defeated and had to resign as emperor of France in 1815. European leaders then began to regroup their people under new governments. The growing middle class of citizens in some of the major areas of power pressured for representative governments. By the end of the century, France, Germany, and Italy were all organized as countries with elected parliaments.

As countries unified, there was a great sense of nationalism that can be seen in many of the arts of the era. Composers expressed their pride in their countries in a variety of ways. For example, Frédéric Chopin

The Fall of an Avalanche in the Grisons, by J. M. W. Turner (1775–1851). This painting displays nature as an uncontrollable power, a subject of great interest to artists in the romantic era.

displayed his love for his native Poland by using the rhythms of Polish dances as the basis of solo piano works. Bedřich Smetana composed orchestral works about the beauty of his Bohemian homeland. He and many other composers wrote operas about their countries' histories or that told stories based on the favorite folktales of their countries.

Other major changes took place during the 1800s. The populations of most areas of Europe grew dramatically. Part of the reason was improvements in medicine and in food supply. The first vaccine was invented in 1798, for smallpox, a disease that had ravaged eighteenth-century Europe. Cholera deaths decreased after the 1850s when it was learned that the disease was spread by the drinking of polluted water. The discovery that minerals could be added to land in the form of fertilizer increased and improved food production.

The Industrial Revolution

The Industrial Revolution had begun during the 1700s, but its effects were most universally felt in the 1800s. Some of the most important inventions at the beginning of the Industrial Revolution were the spinning jenny (1767), which spun sixteen threads of cotton during the time a spinning wheel could spin only one, and the cotton gin (1793), which made removal of seeds from fibers needed for cloth easier and faster. A simple type of steam engine had been used to drain mines for years, and in the 1780s improvements were invented to make it efficient enough to power entire factories. In the early 1700s, the primary source of power was running water. Machines that needed power had to be built near rivers. Once the steam engine was put into regular use, large factories could be built anywhere. The factories hired workers to each do one particular task,

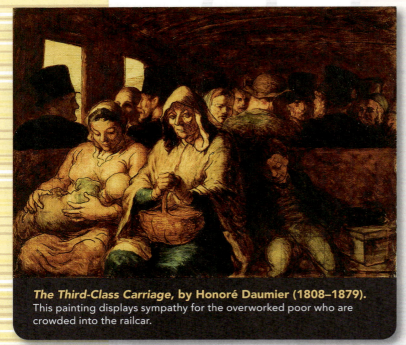

The Third-Class Carriage, by Honoré Daumier (1808–1879).
This painting displays sympathy for the overworked poor who are crowded into the railcar.

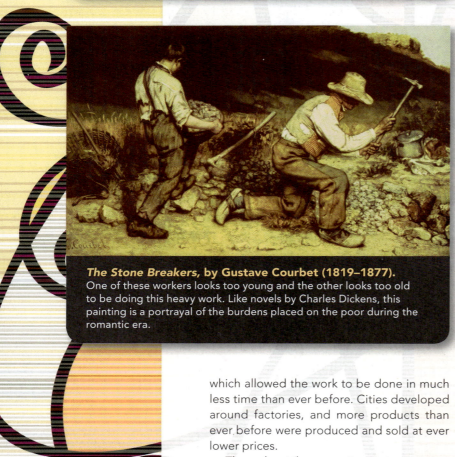

The Stone Breakers, by Gustave Courbet (1819–1877).
One of these workers looks too young and the other looks too old to be doing this heavy work. Like novels by Charles Dickens, this painting is a portrayal of the burdens placed on the poor during the romantic era.

sewing machine was invented in the 1850s, bringing down the cost of clothing. The telephone, phonograph, and electric lightbulb followed in the 1870s. All of these inventions made the world more comfortable for the growing middle class.

The downside of the Industrial Revolution was that people were often forced to work extremely long hours, and poor and lower middle-class children were added to the workforce. The novels of Charles Dickens (1812–1870) depicted the mistreatment of children and the abuse of the poor that were part of this era. Artists portrayed the situation too. The painting, *The Third-Class Carriage* (ca. 1862) by Honoré Daumier sympathetically depicts poor people crowded into a railcar, most not really paying any attention to one another. Gustave Courbet's *The Stone Breakers* (1849) shows two men breaking stones to build a road, but the one on the left looks far too young, and the one on the right looks too old to be doing such heavy work.

The Passion of Romanticism

In the literature of the romantic era, one can see a great interest in the exotic, the mysterious, and even the occult. Edgar Allan Poe (1809–1849) told any number of terrifying tales in his short stories and poems; Emily Brontë's *Wuthering Heights* (1847) was about a brooding and tormented man who unfairly controlled those around him. Emily Brontë's sister Charlotte wrote the novel *Jane Eyre* (1847), in which one of the main characters secretly keeps his insane wife hidden away from the world. Artworks such as *The Sleep of Reason Produces Monsters* by Francisco Goya (1746–1828) reflect similar preoccupations.

In music, we will hear part of Hector Berlioz's *Symphonie fantastique* (1830), which depicts a young musician who dreams that he has killed his beloved and must die for the crime only to then find himself at a witches' sabbath attended by fearful monsters, all awaiting his burial. One of Franz Schubert's best-loved songs, "Erlkönig" ("King of the Elves"), tells the story of a father riding through a storm on horseback carrying his son in his arms. The boy sees and is tempted

which allowed the work to be done in much less time than ever before. Cities developed around factories, and more products than ever before were produced and sold at ever lower prices.

Throughout the romantic era, towns grew, interregional trade quickened, fortunes were made, and the middle class enjoyed a certain amount of economic power. By 1825, the steam engine was used to power trains to carry both freight and passengers. The

by the Elf King and cries out to the father. Legend has it that if the Elf King touches the child, he will die. The father does not believe the child, ignores his cries, and the child dies. The idea that innocent children know more than adults who have been corrupted by the world is essentially romantic.

Birth of the Superstar

In this era of a growing middle class, public concert halls were built to allow the average person to hear music outside of church. That brought about the beginning of the superstar performer. Musical virtuosos such as violinist Niccolò Paganini (1782–1840) would do almost anything to thrill their audiences. Paganini sometimes cut partway through a string on his violin before the concert so that it would break while he was playing, and he could amaze the audience by finishing the piece on the three remaining strings. At times, he would play on a single string, dramatically moving his fingers up and down the string instead of shifting over to another. The rumor spread that Paganini had sold his soul to the devil in order to play as well as he did.

Women Composers

Women composers and instrumentalists began to have careers that brought them international fame. Women composers and instrumentalists prior to the romantic era were usually connected to a particular royal court and were able to perform for court patrons and guests, but they were not necessarily free to tour all over Europe independently. Clara Schumann (1819–1896) spent much of her life on stage and was still performing on concert tours into her 70s.

Despite the new opportunities for women in some professions, women writers found that they could have more success getting works published and bought by the public if they used men's names. Emily Brontë first published her books under the name Ellis Bell. Chopin's long-time mistress, Amandine-Aurore-Lucile Dudevant, published novels under the name George Sand. Franz Liszt's mistress, Marie d'Agoult, published under the name Daniel Stern.

The Sleep of Reason Produces Monsters, by Francisco Goya (1746–1828). Romantics were interested in throwing aside reason and concentrating on dreams and mysterious powers, as seen here.

The romantic era includes, for the most part, the entire nineteenth century. Various inventions that led to the Industrial Revolution in the late 1700s and many romantic attitudes resulted from the reaction to the French Revolution that began in 1789. By 1800, the romantic era was well on its way to becoming one of the most dramatic eras in the history of the arts. Some aspects of romanticism continued on into the twentieth century; but, in many ways, composers late in the century began to reject traditional harmony and move toward the new sounds and attitudes of the next era. Certainly, the romantic period allowed more people to live fuller lives and to have more control over their lives than ever before in European history. Music of the era reflected on individual emotions and experiences, and much of that music is still being enjoyed today.

Romantic Songs

No one understands another's grief, no one understands another's joy. . . . My music is the product of my talent and my misery. And that which I have written in my greatest distress is what the world seems to like best.

—COMPOSER FRANZ SCHUBERT
[1797–1828]

First Hearing

 CONNECT   CD 1: Track 44

Listen to the recording of "Erlkönig" ("King of the Elves") by Schubert and take notes on what you hear. Even if you are working with other students in a paired or group listening session, keep your own notes. Give some attention to the following:

- What kind of mood is created by the piano introduction? Soft and gentle? Music to dance to? Intense and moody? Something else? Does the mood change after the singer begins? If so, how does it change?

- What is the language of the text? Can you understand any of it? If so, what is the song about? If not, can you make a guess about what the text might be?

- Actually, the singer is trying to change his voice to sing the roles of several different people. What roles might he play? Man and woman? Father and son? Mother and daughter? Child and ghostly being?

- Do whole sections of the melody repeat, or does the melody seem to keep changing as the song progresses?

- Can you tell the meter and guess at the tempo?

Keep your notes from this First Hearing to compare with your impressions about the piece after you study the information in this chapter.

16

The Salon

The Industrial Revolution helped to create a large middle class, including an upper middle class who were not born to wealth but were able to afford a good life. These people could afford pianos for their homes, and it became common for families to invite guests in for intimate concerts at which the children or other members of the household would perform. The concert might be followed by the serving of dessert and tea or coffee, as well as polite conversation. Upper-middle-class people sometimes contracted musicians to perform for their guests at catered gatherings.

Upper-class people, including the aristocracy, held *salons* in their homes. These informal literary or musical gatherings were not unlike the kind of entertainment put on by aristocratic patrons such as the Esterházy family for whom Haydn worked for so many years, though on a much smaller scale. The painting *Liszt at the Piano*

***Liszt at the Piano,* by Josef Danhauser (1805–1845).** Liszt is seated at the piano with his mistress, Marie d'Agoult, on the floor to his right. The woman seated behind Liszt is George Sand. Writer Alexandre Dumas is seated next to her. The three men standing behind Sand are (left to right) writer Victor Hugo, violinist Niccolò Paganini, and composer Gioacchino Rossini.

by Josef Danhauser shows a salon scene in which some famous people of the time are gathered to hear the great pianist Franz Liszt play: novelists Alexandre Dumas, Victor Hugo, George Sand (Amandine-Aurore-Lucile Dudevant), and Daniel Stern (Marie d'Agoult), along with opera composer Gioacchino Rossini and violinist Niccolò Paganini. "MusiCurious: How Does a Composer Write a Piece of Music?" discusses some of the things these and other composers had to know to write their compositions.

Art Song

Many songs with piano accompaniment, as well as solo piano works, were composed for performance in salons in elegant homes such as that portrayed in the painting *Liszt at the Piano*. The **art song** is a musical setting of a poem for solo voice and piano. In Germany and Austria the words *lied* ("leed") and *lieder* (pl.) became the standard terms for this type of song.

In the mid-1700s, the lied had been a simple song with keyboard accompaniment. The musical setting used strophic form—that is, the same melody repeated for every stanza (or strophe) of the poem. The text was treated syllabically (one note for each syllable), and the accompaniment served merely to support the singing voice.

Toward the end of the 1700s, the *ballad,* a narrative poem set to music, became popular in Germany. The ballad was long, emphasized dramatic situations, and alternated in structure between narration and dialogue. These characteristics required greater musical resources than the strophic form. Ballads were in **through-composed form;** that is, each section of the text had music that was different from the music preceding and following.

 **MusiCurious**

HOW DOES A COMPOSER WRITE A PIECE OF MUSIC?

What does a composer do to begin writing a piece of music?

You have to begin by thinking about the sound you want to hear. Much music is based on some kind of melody, so composers of instrumental music often begin by singing or playing with new melodies until they come up with one or several that they like. If you are starting with one melody, you might then try to come up with another one to use as a contrasting melody or *theme*, as Mozart often did. You also need to decide what instrument(s) or voice(s) should play or sing your melody. What kind of accompaniment do you want to use with it? If you are writing for singers, you might want to write or find a text. In fact, many song composers start with a poem they like and then write their melody and accompaniment to fit the text of the poem. After you come up with the theme(s) you want, you will have to write your melody in standard music notation if you want live musicians to play or sing it. You can use computer software to do that notation and even play it back to get an idea of what it will sound like when played.

I know that rock and jazz musicians play live without bothering with music notation. Why can't an orchestra or other classical group work that way?

Well, first of all an orchestra is too big to work with in such a casual way. Also, orchestral musicians are not usually trained to memorize lines and play them over and over, and they are not trained to improvise. Their concentration is usually based on reading and interpreting the music in a way that sounds best. Classical music, in general, is more of an *interpretative* art for the player or singer than it is an *improvisational* one.

Do composers have to be able to play every instrument they write for?

No, but the composer needs to know exactly what each instrument or voice can and can't do. Take a pianist, for example. You can't write just any combination of notes on the instrument for one pianist to play because the pianist has only two hands with four fingers and one thumb on each. If the hands are positioned far apart,

you cannot expect them to play a note in the middle of the keyboard at the same time. If both hands are in the high range of notes on the keyboard, you cannot expect the pianist to add a bass note without giving him or her enough time to move a hand down to that note. Wind instruments have a range of notes above and below which they cannot play. They also have some combinations of notes that are difficult to play one after another. The composer needs to know those things to avoid creating problems for the players. Singers also have vocal ranges and some parts of those ranges that sound better than others. Even if a singer has the ability to sing very high, you cannot expect him or her to stay in the highest range for too long a time without tiring.

Does my music have to follow the kinds of forms we are studying in this book?

Not at all. Your music should be *your* music. You might keep in mind, however, that using repetition, contrast, and variation the way many composers of the past have done has proven to be appealing to listeners. People tend to like to hear one theme contrast with another, or one theme played, and then varied, in interesting ways. People also like to hear a theme or melody from early in a piece of music return at the end. This gives the piece a sense of balance. Of course, it is not just classical styled music that follows such formal ideas. Lots of popular music does these things too.

So, to write a piece of music in a classical style, I need to learn standard music notation, learn what the instruments and voices can and cannot do, and come up with some interesting themes and ways to structure them.

Yes, you need to do all of that, and more. You also need to find and hire musicians to play your music and hope that people will want to listen to it. You could make some money from your music if you get a music publisher to print, publish, and distribute it. You could also just get musicians to play it, record their playing, and sell the recordings. If you want to be a composer, it is time to get started, perhaps by taking a class in music theory and musicianship and then taking one in composition.

Both the strophic and through-composed forms were used in the lieder of the 1800s. A variant of the strophic form, called **modified strophic,** was also used. In it, some verses of the poem were sung to the same melody, and others were not. The composer chose the form that would best suit the poem. If the poem's verses all fit the same melody and also had similar moods, the strophic form was perfect. If some verses repeated but others changed in mood or number of words so that they needed to be sung to a new melody, then modified-strophic form was used. If, on the other hand, the poem told a story that changed in mood or character, then the composer would most likely use the through-composed form to vary the mood and melody. The earliest, and in many respects the most important, lieder composer was **Franz Schubert** ("Shoo-bert," 1797–1828).

Franz Schubert

In many ways, the circumstances of Franz Schubert's life were the very essence of the romantic's view of an artist's condition. During his brief and troubled lifetime, Schubert lived in poverty and never gained the recognition his talent deserved. He was born in a suburb northwest of Vienna, the fourth surviving son of an industrious and pious schoolmaster. His formal musical training, never very systematic, began with violin lessons from his father and piano instruction from an older brother.

In 1808, at age 11, Schubert obtained a place in the choir of the Imperial Court Chapel and was thereby privileged to attend the City Seminary, one of Vienna's most prestigious boarding schools. In addition to his regular studies and music lessons, he became a violinist in the school orchestra, later assuming the duties of conductor on various occasions. The numerous works he composed during these years at the seminary include songs, overtures, religious works, part of a singspiel (light opera), and six string quartets. His first symphony was written in 1813, the year he left the seminary, and his first Mass was successfully performed in 1814.

After leaving the seminary, Schubert returned home to live, first attending a training college for primary school teachers and then teaching at his father's school. The regimen of the classroom did not suit his temperament, and in 1816 he resolved to earn his living by taking music students, selling his compositions, and writing for the theater. In 1817, he moved to Vienna.

During the early 1820s, two of Schubert's singspiel were produced with moderate success, and a number of songs and piano works were published. These successes were offset by his continuing inability to obtain a salaried position. In 1822, a serious illness necessitated a stay in the hospital and a prolonged period of recuperation. The following year, *Rosamunde,* a play with his incidental music, failed dismally, closing after only two performances. It was his last work for the theater.

Despite his ill health and poverty, Schubert was an extremely prolific composer. Between 1811 and 1828 he composed about a thousand works. They include nine symphonies, fifty chamber works and piano sonatas, a large number of short piano pieces, several operas and operettas, six Masses and about twenty-five other religious works, nearly one hundred choral compositions, and more than six hundred songs.

The last four years of Schubert's life were a continual struggle. Though his music, particularly the songs, continued to draw high praise from fellow musicians, including Beethoven, it was not until 1828 that a public concert of his works was given. He was unable to live on the pitifully small income from his music publications, but he continued to compose at a feverish pace. In the fall of 1828, Schubert died at age 31. His last wish, to be buried near Beethoven, was granted, and on his tombstone was written, "The art of music here entombed a rich possession, but even far fairer hopes."

Schubert is best remembered for his abundant body of songs. The song we are going to listen to is one of his most famous, "Erlkönig" ("King of the Elves"). The poem on which it is based is a ballad by Goethe. The story maintains the legend that the King of the Elves represents death and that anyone who is touched by the Elf King will die.

FRANZ SCHUBERT
(1797–1828)

- Born in Vienna, Austria; died at age 31 in Vienna, Austria.

- Prolific composer best known for more than 600 lieder including "Erlkönig," song cycles "Die Schöne Müllerin" and "Winterreise," chamber works including "Trout" piano quintet, and his eighth "unfinished" symphony.

A painting inspired by Schubert's "Erlkönig." The painter, Moritz von Schwind, was a friend of Schubert.

 ))) **Featured Listening**

CONNECT   **CD 1: Track 44**

"Erlkönig" ("King of the Elves")   FRANZ SCHUBERT

Date: 1815

Genre: Lied

Tempo: Schnell (fast)

Form: Through-composed

Voices and Instruments: Solo voice and piano

Language: German

Meter: Quadruple

Duration: 4:00

Context: The text of this song is a poem by Johann Wolfgang von Goethe. The song remains one of Schubert's most popular. The text calls for the singer to take the roles of a narrator, father, son, and the Elf King. Notice how the range of notes changes, with the father singing lower notes than the son, and how the Elf King sounds lighter in tone quality.

German text	English translation	Musical events
NARRATOR Wer reitet so spät durch Nacht und Wind? Es ist der Vater mit seinem Kind; Er hat den Knaben wohl in dem Arm, Er fasst ihn sicher, er hält ihn warm.	Who rides so late through the night and the wind? It is the father with his child; he holds the boy in his arm, He grasps him securely, he keeps him warm.	Repeated low patterns in the piano part set the mood for a tense drama.
FATHER "Mein Sohn, was birgst du so bang dein Gesicht?"	"My son, why do you hide your face so anxiously?"	

German text	English translation	Musical events

SON

"Siehst, Vater, du den Erlkönig nicht?
Den Erlenkönig mit Kron' und Schweif?"

FATHER

"Mein Sohn, es ist ein Nebelstreif."

ELF KING

"Du liebes Kind, komm, geh' mit mir!
Gar schöne Spiele spiel' ich mit dir;
Manch' bunte Blumen sind an dem Strand,
Meine Mutter hat manch' gülden Gewand."

SON

"Mein Vater, mein Vater, und hörest du
nicht,
Was Erlenkönig mir leise verspricht?"

FATHER

"Sei ruhig, bleibe ruhig, mein Kind:
In dürren Blättern säuselt der Wind."

ELF KING

"Willst, feiner Knabe, du mit mir gehn?
Meine Töchter sollen dich warten schön;
Meine Töchter führen den nächtlichen
Reihn'
Und wiegen und tanzen und singen dich
ein."

SON

"Mein Vater, mein Vater, und siehst
du nicht dort
Erlkönigs Töchter am düstern Ort?"

FATHER

"Mein Sohn, mein Sohn, ich seh' es genau:
Es scheinen die alten Weiden so grau."

ELF KING

"Ich liebe dich, mich reizt deine schöne
Gestalt;
Und bist du nicht willig so brauch' ich
Gewalt."

SON

"Mein Vater, mein Vater, jetzt fasst er
mich an!
"Erlkönig hat mir ein Leids gethan!"—

NARRATOR

Dem Vater grauset's, er reitet geschwind,
Er hält in den Armen das ächzende Kind,
Erreicht den Hof mit Müh' und Not;

In seinen Armen das Kind—
                                    war tot.

"Father, do you not see the Elf King?
The Elf King with his crown and train?"

"My son, it is only a streak of mist."

"Darling child, come away with me!
I will play fine games with you;
Many gay flowers grow by the shore,
my mother has many golden robes."

"Father, father, do you not hear

what the Elf King softly promises me?"

"Be calm, dear child, be calm—
the wind is rustling in the dry leaves."

"You beautiful boy, will you come with me?
My daughters will wait upon you;
my daughters will lead the nightly round,

they will rock you, dance to you, sing you
to sleep."

"Father, father, do you not see there

the Elf King's daughters there, in that
dark place?"

"My son, my son, I see it clearly: it is the
grey gleam of the old willow-trees."

"I love you, your beauty allures me;

and if you do not come willingly, I shall
use force."

"Father, father, now he is seizing me!

The Elf King has hurt me!"—

Fear grips the father, he rides swiftly,
holding the moaning child in his arms;
with effort and toil he reaches the
house—
the child in his arms—
                                    was dead.

ROBERT SCHUMANN
(1810–1856)

- Born in Zwickau, Germany; died at age 46 in Endenich, near Bonn, Germany.

- Prolific composer best known for song cycles including "Frauenliebe und Leben," piano music including character pieces such as "Carnaval," concertos, and four symphonies.

CLARA SCHUMANN
(1819–1896)

- Born in Leipzig, Germany; died at age 76 in Frankfurt am Main, Germany.

- Best known as a concert pianist. Her compositions include lieder, solo piano music, one piano concerto, and chamber music.

Schubert portrays the characters and sets them off from each other by a number of devices, particularly by manipulating the piano accompaniment. Whenever the Elf King enters, for example, the dynamic level drops to *pianissimo,* the accompaniment changes, and the vocal line becomes smooth and alluring. Schubert reflects the son's mounting terror by repeating the same melody at successively higher pitch levels each time he cries out to his father. The last verse demonstrates Schubert's sense of drama and his technique of manipulating the song's elements to heighten the emotional impact. The piano is silent as the narrator sings, "the child in his arms," a single chord sounds, increasing the feeling of suspense, and the narrator concludes, "was dead."

Schubert wrote two **song cycles** (a series of art songs that tell a story or are otherwise related to one another), *Die Schöne Müllerin (The Maid of the Mill,* 1823) and *Die Winterreise (Winter Journey,* 1827).

Robert and Clara Schumann

Another romantic composer who is well remembered today for his songs and song cycles is **Robert Schumann** (1810–1856). Robert Schumann was born in Zwickau, a town in central Germany, in 1810. His father was a writer, publisher, and bookseller, and young Robert took great interest in literature, as well as in music. He had studied music as a child but began his university education majoring in law. He gave up the study of law to concentrate on music and, in 1830, began taking lessons from a well-known piano teacher in Leipzig, Friedrich Wieck ("Veek").

Wieck had many students, but his primary concentration was on his extremely talented daughter, Clara, who was 11 years old when she first met Robert Schumann. By that age, **Clara Wieck** had performed many times in Leipzig, and within the next two years she gave concerts across Europe to Paris and back to Germany. She had composed many small pieces for the piano and undertook her largest composition, a Concerto for Piano and Orchestra in A Minor, op. 7, in 1836. Clara had not studied orchestration, but Robert Schumann had. The two had become friends, and Clara asked Robert to help her in writing the orchestral parts. He did that, and Clara premiered the work in November of 1835 with Felix Mendelssohn conducting the Gewandhaus Orchestra in Leipzig. She joined Mendelssohn and another pianist in the performance of a concerto for three keyboard instruments by J. S. Bach on that same concert program. In the next few years, Clara continued to perform her concerto in concerts all over Germany and Austria. The work was published in 1837. It was performed by other pianists throughout the 1800s.

Successful as her concerto showed her to be as a composer, Clara Wieck's primary concentration was on performing. By 1832, Robert had lost his ability to perform as a pianist because of a problem with his hands. Modern historians are not certain, but he is thought to have damaged them by practicing too much or by overusing a device intended to strengthen his hands. Whatever the case, Robert turned his concentration to composition, and Clara became the first great interpreter of his music.

Robert also turned his attentions back to writing and, in 1834, cofounded and edited a successful music journal, the *Neue Zeitschrift für Musik (New Journal of Music),* which is still being published in Germany today.

Robert and Clara's friendship developed into love and a desire to marry. Clara's father did everything he could to prevent their marriage because he thought it would interfere with her career in music. After Clara turned 21, her father could no longer prevent it, and she married Robert in 1840. That year became known as "the year of the song" for Robert because he composed so many songs about love. The song we will listen to is from his 1840 song cycle, *Dichterliebe (A Poet's Love).* The songs in *Dich-*

terliebe all relate to love and love relationships. The cycle opens with a short, strophic song, "Im wunderschönen Monat Mai" ("In the Wonderfully Lovely Month of May"). The entire cycle comprises sixteen songs. After that we will listen to a song Clara Schumann composed, "Liebst du um Schönheit" ("If You Love for Beauty's Sake").

CD 5: Tracks 8–9

"Im wunderschönen Monat Mai" ("In the Wonderfully Lovely Month of May"), from *Dichterliebe (A Poet's Love)* ROBERT SCHUMANN

Date: 1840

Genre: Lied

Tempo: Langsam, zart (slow)

Form: Strophic

Voices and Instruments: Solo voice (baritone, in this recording) and piano

Language: German

Meter: Duple

Duration: 1:33

Context: The text of this and of all of the sixteen songs in the cycle *Dichterliebe (A Poet's Love)* was written by Heinrich Heine. Schumann composed the cycle in 1840, the year he and Clara were married. The pianist and singer on this recording use a lot of *rubato,* or "robbed time," which means that they slow down and speed up the tempo to make the musical phrases more expressive. The final chord does not sound completely final because it is intended to lead into the next song in the cycle.

	German text	English translation	Form	Musical events
8	Im wunderschönen Monat Mai, als alle Knospen sprangen, da ist in meinem Herzen die Liebe aufgegangen.	In the wonderfully lovely month of May, when all buds were burgeoning, then in my heart did love arise.	A	Much rubato (slowing down and speeding up to fit the expressiveness of the text) used by the singer and the pianist.
9	Im wunderschönen Monat Mai, als alle Vögel sangen, da hab' ich ihr gestanden mein Sehnen und Verlangen.	In the wonderfully lovely month of May, when all birds sang, then I told her of my desire and longing.	A	The final chord does not sound completely final because it is intended to lead into the next song in the cycle.

CD 5: Track 10

"Liebst du um Schönheit" ("If You Love for Beauty's Sake")

CLARA WIECK SCHUMANN

Date: 1841

Genre: Lied

Tempo: Tenderly

(continued)

Form: Mostly strophic

Texture: Homophonic

Voices and Instruments: Female soprano and piano

Language: German

Meter: Quadruple

Duration: 2:28

Context: The text for this song is a poem by Friedrich Rüchert. Clara composed the song for her husband, Robert Schumann, for his thirty-first birthday.

	Timing	German text	English translation	Musical events
10	0:00			Slow, gentle piano introduction
	0:06	Liebst du um Schönheit, o nicht mich liebe! Liebe die Sonne, sie trägt ein gold'nes Haar!	If you love for beauty's sake, do not love me! Love the sun, she had golden hair!	
	0:34	Liebst du um Jugend, o nicht mich liebe! Liebe den Frühling, der jung ist jades Jahr!	If you love for youth's sake, do not love me! Love the spring, who every year is young!	Second verse, same melody
	1:00	Liebst du um Schätze, o nicht mich liebe! Liebe die Meerfrau, sie hat viel Perlen klar!	If you love for treasures' sake, do not love me! Love the mermaid, for she has many pearls!	Third verse, same melody
	1:28	Liebst du um Liebe, o ja, mich liebe. Liebe mich immer, dich lieb' ich immer dar!	If you love for love's sake, then love me. Love me for ever, for I love you eternally!	Fourth verse, melody changes at end to fit the new mood of the text

Robert and Clara Schumann had eight children, but her career as a performer did not end. Robert was very supportive and often hired people to watch the children so that he could accompany Clara on her many concert tours. Robert continued to compose orchestral works, string quartets, a variety of chamber works with piano, and solo piano works.

Robert Schumann had experienced bouts of depression in his twenties. By 1845 these bouts became much more severe and more frequent. In 1850, he took a position as music director of the municipal orchestra in Düsseldorf, Germany. He was not good at the administrative duties that were required by the job and resigned from the position in 1853. His mental condition worsened, and he tried to commit suicide in 1854. Clara was forced to put him into an asylum because she could no longer care for him herself. He died two years later at age 46.

Clara's concert career continued to be successful, with tours that included many parts of Europe and took her as far as Russia. She became the principal teacher of the piano division of the Hoch Conservatory of Music in Frankfurt, Germany, in 1878. She died in 1896 at age 76.

Summary

The Industrial Revolution created a large middle and upper-middle class of people who could afford to have pianos in their homes and take piano and singing lessons. It became popular for such people to invite friends in to hear small-scale concerts performed by family members or by hired musicians. Many songs with piano accompaniment, as well as solo piano pieces, were composed for such settings.

Franz Schubert and Robert and Clara Schumann composed many art songs for performance in intimate settings. Of those three composers, Schubert and Robert Schumann focused most directly on composing. Clara Schumann composed music but made her primary career that of a performer. She was among the first women to tour internationally.

New People and Concepts

art song, 167

Clara Wieck Schumann, 172

Franz Schubert, 169

modified-strophic form, 168

Robert Schumann, 172

song cycle, 172

through-composed form, 167

)))) **Finale**  CONNECT **CD 1: Track 44**

Listen again to the recording of "Erlkönig" ("King of the Elves") by Schubert and compare your impression now with your notes from your First Hearing. Consider the following questions:

- What is the mood of the song? What is it about? Does the mood change?
- What roles is the singer singing? Which roles are lighter, and which role(s) deeper and more authoritative?
- What is the form, and how does it compare to a song form with repeated verses?
- What are the meter and tempo?
- If you were going to describe this music to a friend, what would you say?

Further Listening

Franz Schubert, "Die Forelle" ("The Trout"). The first two verses of this song are "strophic" (sung to the same melody), but the beginning of the third verse changes and becomes more agitated in mood because a fisherman has finally caught the trout. That third verse then ends with the earlier melody to give the song a sense of balance. The poem emphasizes the fish's struggle and the tragedy of its death. The sympathy for the fish supports the love of nature found in the arts of the romantic era.

Franz Schubert, Quintet in A Major, op. 114, "The Trout Quintet." This quintet for piano, violin, viola, cello, and double bass is named after Schubert's lied "The Trout" because its fourth movement is a theme and variations on the melody of his "trout" song. The quintet has five movements: (1) Allegro vivace, (2) Andante, (3) Scherzo: Presto, (4) Andantino-Allegretto, and (5) Allegro giusto.

Robert Schumann, *Dichterliebe (A Poet's Love)*. We heard only the first of the sixteen songs in this cycle about love and the many complex feelings it brings to life. The cycle was composed in 1840, the year Robert and Clara Schumann were married.

Clara Schumann, Piano Concerto in A Minor, op. 7. This concerto was composed by Clara Wieck (Clara Schumann's name before her marriage) when she was only a teenager. She was sixteen years old when she performed it with Felix Mendelssohn's Leipzig Gewandhaus Orchestra in 1835. The movements are (1) Allegro maestoso, (2) Romanze: Andante non tropo, con grazia, and (3) Finale: Allegro non troppo.

Romantic Piano Music

Bach is like an astronomer who, with the help of ciphers, finds the most wonderful stars. . . . Beethoven embraced the universe with the power of his spirit. . . . I do not climb so high. A long time ago, I decided that my universe will be the soul and heart of man.

—COMPOSER FRÉDÉRIC CHOPIN
[1810–1849]

17

))) **First Hearing**

 CONNECT   CD 1: Track 45

Listen to the recording of Nocturne, op. 9, no. 2, by Chopin and take notes on what you hear. Even if you are working with other students in a paired or group listening session, keep your own notes. Give some attention to the following:

- How would you describe the melody at the beginning of the piece? Moody? Bouncy and dancelike? Light and graceful?

- How many times does that beginning melody, theme 1, repeat? Is it played exactly the same way each time it repeats, or is it embellished when it returns?

- How many other melodies do you hear? Do they repeat?

- Are there places where the pianist uses rubato (gradual speeding up or slowing down to fit the expressiveness of the music)? When do you hear rubato used? Do you think that it enhances the performance, or would you rather hear a steady beat throughout the piece?

- The piece is called "nocturne." What might that mean, and what general mood does the piece have?

- Can you guess at the tempo and meter?

Keep your notes from this First Hearing to compare with your impressions about the piece after you study the information in this chapter.

Piano builders of the late classical period worked hard to improve the tone quality and dynamic range of the instruments they produced. By 1800, both high and low notes had been added. Felt hammers replaced the old leather ones, allowing for more depth to the tone. Cast iron frames were made to increase the volume of sound.

Although such improvements gave concert pianos more and better sound, the standard size and shape of the piano took up too much room to fit into the parlors of middle-class homes. By the 1840s, piano designers had developed the upright piano with the strings in a box that could fit against a wall instead of being parallel to the floor. Upright pianos were manufactured on a large scale, and it became as important

The Pleyel piano factory in Paris, where upright pianos were manufactured for nineteenth-century homes.

for a socially conscious middle-class family to own a piano and for the children to learn to play it as it is for some to have a computer and video games today.

With so many people learning to play the piano, the demand for new music and teachers increased dramatically. Music publication became a more lucrative business than ever before. The general music literacy brought about by so many people learning to play an instrument also increased the public's interest in attending live concerts.

Frédéric Chopin and Franz Liszt

Two romantic pianist-composers who stand out for their many compositions still in the repertoire of performing pianists today are **Franz Liszt** ("List," 1811–1886) and **Frédéric Chopin** ("Show-pan," 1810–1849). The personalities of these two men were quite opposite. Liszt loved performing to large audiences, and he dramatized his playing by turning the piano sideways so that the listeners could see his hands. He also memorized his music so that it seemed to flow out of him and not just appear as an interpretation of music notation in front of him. Both the position of the piano and the practice of memorization have become common practice today.

Chopin, though also a fine pianist, did not enjoy large-scale performing as Liszt did. He did perform in public, but not any more often than required to maintain his reputation as a composer and teacher. Rather than the large-scale public concerts that Liszt and other performers such as Clara Schumann often played, Chopin preferred to play in the more intimate salon settings.

Liszt was Hungarian and moved to Paris in 1827, where he remained until 1848, when he moved to Germany to take a job as music director at the court of Weimar. Chopin was born in Poland, moved to Paris in 1831, and remained there until his death in 1849. Liszt and Chopin knew each other and shared many of the same friends and acquaintances. The painting *Liszt at the Piano* on page 167 shows Liszt in a salon with, among others, George Sand, who was, at the time, Chopin's mistress. It was Chopin's association with Sand that helped to introduce him to the intellectual elite of Paris. The other woman in the painting, Marie d'Agoult, was, like Sand, a novelist who used a man's name—Daniel Stern. She was Liszt's mistress during the late 1830s and the mother of Liszt's three children, one of

FRÉDÉRIC CHOPIN
(1810–1849)

- Born in Żelazowa Wola, near Warsaw, Poland; died at age 39 in Paris, France.

- Best known for solo piano music including nocturnes, études, preludes, polonaises (based on a Polish dance), mazurkas (based on a Polish dance), waltzes (including the "Minute Waltz"), and two piano concertos.

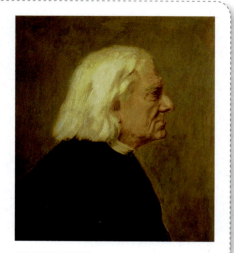

FRANZ LISZT
(1811–1886)

- Born in Raiding, Hungary; died at age 74 in Bayreuth, Germany.

- Best known for solo piano music (including six Transcendental Études, transcriptions of songs such as "Erlkönig," and Sonata in B Minor), two piano concertos, and symphonic poems for orchestra including *Les Préludes*.

- In addition to being a composer, Liszt was a virtuoso performer.

whom, daughter Cosima, later married composer Richard Wagner. Liszt and d'Agoult could not have married even if they had wanted to because she had left, but not divorced, her husband.

Franz Liszt was involved with music beyond his work as a pianist and teacher. After his move to Weimar, he worked with orchestras as a composer and conductor. He wrote symphonies and piano concertos and developed a new orchestral form that became widely popular in the romantic period—the **symphonic poem,** also sometimes called a **tone poem.** The symphonic, or tone, poem is a single-movement work for orchestra that is composed to tell a story or to go along with the events or moods in a particular poem. Liszt wrote twelve of these, the best known of which is *Les Préludes.*

Liszt's piano music includes variations on well-known symphonic works, brilliant showpieces, and technical studies. The *Transcendental Études,* the *Hungarian Rhapsodies,* and *Liebestraum (Love Dream),* along with the Sonata in B Minor, were important contributions to the literature for solo piano. His works for piano and orchestra include two concertos, *Hungarian Fantasia* and *Totentanz (Dance of Death),* the latter of which is a large-scale paraphrase of the medieval funeral chant, the "Dies irae."

In his contributions to piano repertoire, Liszt created a grand and dramatic style that exploited the orchestral possibilities of the instrument and demanded enormous technical skill on the part of the performer.

In 1861, Liszt left his position at Weimar and moved to Rome to pursue religious training. He studied under church leaders and, in 1865, was given the honorary title of abbé. He composed religious music during that time. His compositions for the church included psalm settings, Masses, a requiem, oratorios, and other works for chorus and orchestra. Liszt died in 1886 at age 74.

Unlike Liszt, Chopin limited himself to composing for the piano. He was born near Warsaw, Poland. His mother was Polish. His father was French and had come to Poland to teach the French language to Polish nobility. The young Frédéric showed great talent for the piano and gave his first public concert at age 7. By age 15, he had already published some compositions, and, by 19, he had achieved eminence in both composition and performance. He traveled widely throughout Europe and was received enthusiastically wherever he played. So cordial was the reception at Chopin's first concert in Paris in 1831 that he decided to make that city his home. He expressed his Polish nationalism by composing a number of **polonaises** and **mazurkas** that were based on the rhythms of Polish dances of the same names.

Most of Chopin's music is for solo piano. He did write two piano concertos, a few chamber works for piano and other instruments, and some songs based on Polish poems with piano accompaniment. Listening Guides to a **nocturne** by Chopin and Liszt's Transcendental Étude no. 10 in F Minor follow.

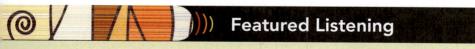

Featured Listening

CONNECT   CD 1: Track 45

Nocturne, op. 9, no. 2 FRÉDÉRIC CHOPIN

Date: 1830–1831

Genre: Solo piano music

Tempo: Andante

Form: No repeated sections; three themes that are embellished each time they repeat

Instruments: Piano

Meter: Twelve beats in each bar, divided into four beats with three notes each (the effect is similar to that of Beethoven's "Moonlight" Sonata, first movement)

Duration: 4:12

Context: Chopin was only 20 years old when he composed this nocturne. A nocturne is a "night piece" and is gentle and reflective.

	Timing	What to listen for
45	0:00	Theme 1
	0:28	Theme 1 returns in an embellished version
	0:54	Theme 2
	1:22	Theme 1 returns further embellished
	1:48	Theme 2 returns embellished
	2:16	Theme 1 returns again further embellished
	2:43	Theme 3
	3:11	Theme 3 returns embellished

CD 5: Track 11

Transcendental Étude no. 10 in F Minor FRANZ LISZT

Date: 1851

Genre: Solo piano music

Tempo: Allegro agitato molto (fast and very agitated)

Form: Sonata with three themes

Instruments: Solo piano

Meter: Duple

Duration: 4:51

Context: Our recording is the third and last version of this étude. Liszt dedicated it to his teacher Carl Czerny. It is full of emotional outbursts and extremes of range and dynamic changes, and extremely difficult to play. Thus, it is also impressive to watch being played. The A section has three primary themes, and the development is based in part on the first theme of A with varied rhythms.

	Timing	What to listen for
	Exposition	
11	0:00	Flourish of descending runs
	0:08	First theme in octaves
	0:52	Second theme, very high, again in octaves, accompanied by much activity in the left hand
	1:26	Third theme, also in octaves, but at a lower pitch level and a heavier sound with ascending runs above it

(continued)

Timing	What to listen for
Development	
1:40	Suddenly quiet, then first theme with varied rhythms leads to very loud and excited music
Recapitulation	
2:12	Repeat of opening flourish of descending runs
2:17	First theme begins, rather soft and light.
2:36	Second theme, followed by dramatic extension
4:00	Third theme, pounding and low
Coda	
4:23	Faster tempo and crescendo to loud chords and dramatic finale

In this chapter we have emphasized Chopin and Liszt, both of whom were performing pianists. Robert Schumann, whom we discussed in Chapter 16 as a composer of romantic songs, also contributed much to the piano repertoire of the period. Almost all of his most popular and greatest works for piano date from his early years as a composer. They range from miniature **character pieces** (pieces portraying a single mood, emotion, or idea) whose titles establish them as wholly romantic—"Papillons" ("Butterflies"), "Carnaval," "Kinderscenen" ("Scenes from Childhood")—to large, classically oriented, works such as the three piano sonatas, the Fantasy in C Minor, the Symphonic Études (**études,** or study pieces), and the Piano Concerto in A Minor. Schumann considered the *Fantasiestücke (Fantasy Pieces)* to be among his best works for piano.

Clara Schumann also composed a number of works for solo piano, including extended works such as multimovement sonatas. She also wrote chamber works with piano and a large number of songs for voice and piano. As mentioned earlier, however, she concentrated on performing more than on composing. In a world before recording equipment was invented, those performances, as well as those of Chopin and Liszt, unfortunately, have been lost to history.

Summary

By the early 1800s, the piano had taken over as a popular musical instrument to be played by both professional performers and many middle-class people in their homes. The upright piano was invented to fit into people's parlors, and the prices of those instruments were low enough that they were easily affordable. Pianos had been greatly improved to allow for more dynamic range. More notes were added, expanding the keyboard to the eighty-eight keys still in use today. With more people learning to play the piano, more composers and teachers were needed.

Chopin and Liszt stand out as virtuoso performers who also composed for and taught piano. Chopin preferred to play in intimate, salon settings, whereas Liszt enjoyed entertaining large audiences. Along with Robert and Clara Schumann, they added much to the piano repertoire still being performed today.

New People and Concepts

character pieces, 180

étude, 180

Franz Liszt, 177

Frédéric Chopin, 177

mazurka, 178

nocturne, 178

polonaise, 178

symphonic poem, 178

tone poem, 178

))) Finale

CONNECT   CD 1: Track 45

Listen again to the recording of Nocturne, op. 9, no. 2, by Chopin and compare your impression now with your notes from your First Hearing. Consider the following questions:

- What is the character of theme 1?
- How many times does the opening theme repeat? Is it played the same each time, or is it embellished?
- What other themes do you hear? Do they repeat? Are they repeated as they were first played, or are they embellished?
- How is rubato used by the pianist, and what effect does it have?
- What is the mood of the piece, and how does that relate to its title?
- If you were going to describe this music to a friend, what would you say?

Further Listening

Frédéric Chopin, Ballade no. 1 in G Minor. This beautiful solo piano work is based on three contrasting themes, each of which returns one or two times after being first presented. The first theme is waltzlike, the second tender and lyrical, and the third faster with the insertion of triplets to free the steadiness of the beat. The overall effect is free-flowing and a perfect example of the romantic spirit.

Franz Liszt, *Les jeux d'eaux à la Villa d'Este (The fountains at Villa d'Este)*. Liszt loved to visit the beautiful Villa d'Este in Tivoli, near Rome, Italy. The fountains in the villa's Re-naissance garden have over a hundred jets and water spraying into pools and running in troughs. The sound of the fountains inspired this work.

Robert Schumann, *Carnaval*. This set of twenty character pieces for solo piano represents Schumann and his friends at a carnaval celebration (a feast before Lent). "Eusebius" is Schumann in a dreamy introspective state and "Florestan" shows him to be playful and impetuous. "Chiarina" is his future wife Clara, and "Chopin" is the composer/pianist Frédéric Chopin.

Romantic Program Music

))) **First Hearing**

 CONNECT CD 2: Tracks 1–3

Listen to the recording of *Symphonie fantastique,* fifth movement, "Dream of a Witches' Sabbath," by Berlioz and take notes on what you hear. Even if you are working with other students in a paired or group listening session, keep your own notes. Give some attention to the following:

● What is the mood of the opening of the movement? Does that mood continue or change to something else?

● This movement is the conclusion of a rather long symphony. What is your impression about the mood at the end?

● This work is scored for a large orchestra. Do you hear any instruments that you have not heard in orchestras before this? If so, what is new? When do you hear it?

● A melody called the "Dies irae" plays about three minutes into the movement. Do you recognize that melody, and do you know what it represents? (We studied it in Chapter 4 on music in the medieval period.) What does that melody tell you about the symphony?

● Do you hear any repeated sections of music?

● Can you guess the tempo and meter?

Keep your notes from this First Hearing to compare with your impressions about the piece after you study the information in this chapter.

18

The romantic era gave rise to the establishment of a fascinating genre of music that has become known as *program music.* We heard one program piece in the baroque period—Vivaldi's *The Four Seasons,* in which the music portrayed sounds of birds, a stream, and a storm to represent those images in a poem. This imagery through music was unusual in the baroque period, during which most instrumental music was what we call *absolute.* Absolute music is composed for the appreciation of the musical sound and does not attempt to tell a story or depict a scene in nature. Program music was somewhat rare until the romantic period.

Romantic program music depicts or portrays an extramusical phenomenon such as a dramatic incident, a poetic image, a visual object, or some element in nature. Romantic composers planned everything about the music, including its form, around the program, which the listener should know in advance of listening to the music. "MusiCurious: Does the Listener Need to Know the Program in Program Music?"

 **MusiCurious**

DOES THE LISTENER NEED TO KNOW THE PROGRAM IN PROGRAM MUSIC?

What is program music?

Program music is instrumental music that is composed to portray something beyond just the sound of the music. It is used to tell some story, describe a picture or a scene, support the emotions in a literary work, or otherwise communicate something to the listener without the use of sung or spoken text.

Do I need to know the program to enjoy a piece of program music?

It is not essential, but it helps. If you remember listening to Vivaldi's "Spring" violin concerto back in the baroque period, you read the poem on which the music was based before listening to the music. Didn't knowing to listen for the birds, the stream, the thunder, and the lightning help you to appreciate what was going on in the first movement? You might well have enjoyed the sound of the music anyway, but knowing what Vivaldi had in mind when he wrote it probably helped you understand what you heard.

If I just buy a CD or hear program music on the radio, how will I know the program?

Usually, a CD will have an insert that tells you the program. If you hear the music some other way, you might not know that the music has a program. Often, however, when you listen to program music, you will hear changes of mood and even sound effects that give you a hint that the music is composed to express some kind of idea that goes beyond the music.

The title "Dream of a Witches' Sabbath" was a good clue that there was some kind of story behind the piece in this chapter. Might just that title be enough to know?

It might be, and you might guess that the piece has something to do with the dead. Knowing the theme of death might allow you to connect the sound of the chimes with the tolling of church bells. Beyond that, if you know that the "Dies irae" melody is from a medieval chant that has always been used to represent death, you realize how the piece emphasizes that theme by using the chant and repeats it so many times at low pitch levels.

Knowing the program would also help you be aware of the significance of the *idée fixe* in this symphony. If you hear the entire *Symphonie fantastique*, you can appreciate that it is a story of the composer's love for a woman who has rejected him and his dream of killing her and then being executed for her murder. The *idée fixe* keeps returning because it represents the woman who constantly haunts him. The composer and his lover are both dead at a witches' Sabbath in the last movement.

Did or do composers write program music very often, or is this an unusual work?

Many program works have been composed through the ages. The idea of telling stories through instrumental music has always held a certain amount of appeal, but it was particularly popular during the nineteenth century when the expression of strong emotions was an important aspect of artistic creation.

explains why knowing the story behind the music is helpful. Usually, the program is told in an insert with a recording or in the program provided at a live concert. Many romantic composers wrote program music, and one that stands out early in the period was the French composer **Hector Berlioz** ("Bear-lee-ohz," 1803–1869).

Hector Berlioz

Hector Berlioz grew up in a small town near Grenoble, France. He was expected to follow his father's profession and was sent to medical school in Paris. However, he was drawn to the opera and the music library. When he appeared in class, he would annoy his fellow students by humming at the dissecting table. Finally, to the fury of his father, he quit the study of medicine to become a composer.

At 23, Berlioz began what he called "the great drama of my life." At a performance of *Hamlet,* he was overwhelmed, both by "the lightning-flash" of Shakespeare's genius and "the dramatic genius" of Harriet Smithson, who played Ophelia. Berlioz tried to meet the actress, but his wild letters convinced her that he was a lunatic.

In 1830, on his fifth attempt, Berlioz won the Prix de Rome, a composition prize offered at the Paris Conservatory. In that year he also wrote the *Symphonie fantastique,* the outpouring of his passion for Smithson. When the composition was performed in Paris two years later, Harriet Smithson was in the audience. Having been told that the music was about her, she felt (according to Berlioz) "as if the room reeled." They were married a year later. The marriage was not particularly happy, although they stayed together for nine years and had one son. Berlioz continued to support his wife until her death in 1854.

Although he had become successful, Berlioz had difficulty getting his works performed. His music soon ceased to appeal to most of "the frivolous and fickle public." Both to support his family and to promote an understanding of the kind of music he advocated, Berlioz wrote musical criticism. He also wrote a fascinating prose autobiography. In it he emerges as a romantic hero, falling in love, scheming murder, talking politics, and passionately composing. He conducted performances of his works throughout most of Europe, but in Paris he was overlooked for various honors and conducting posts. However, he was recognized as a gifted orchestrator, and his book *Treatise on Instrumentation and Orchestration* (1843) sold well for years and was translated into several languages. It is still in print today. Berlioz became the librarian of the Paris Conservatory in 1852. He died at age 65.

HECTOR BERLIOZ
(1803–1869)

- Born in La Côte St-André, France; died at age 65 in Paris, France.
- Best known for program symphonies including *Symphonie fantastique, Harold en Italie,* and *Roméo et Juliette, Messe des morts (Requiem Mass),* and the grand opera *Les Troyens (The Trojans).*

Symphonie fantastique

Berlioz's *Symphonie fantastique,* subtitled "An Episode in the Life of an Artist," is a **program symphony** in five movements. It is based on a story supplied by Berlioz out of his personal experience meeting and falling in love with Harriet Smithson.

Program of the Symphony

The prelude to the story of the symphony is not part of the music but is usually included in program and liner notes. A young musician of morbidly sensitive temperament and fiery imagination poisons himself with opium in a fit of lovesick despair. The dose of the narcotic, too weak to kill him, plunges him into a deep slumber accompanied by the strangest visions, during which his sensations, his emotions, and his memories are transformed in his sick mind into musical thoughts and images. The loved one herself has become a melody to him, an **idée fixe** ("fixed idea") that he encounters and hears everywhere. The use of a melody that appears in each movement unifies Berlioz's composition in much the same way that the rhythmic motive of Beethoven's Fifth Symphony unifies that work.

Part I: Reveries, Passions   He recalls the soul sickness, passion, and depression that he experienced before he first met his beloved. The idée fixe plays, representing their

A detail of *Witches' Sabbath*, by Francisco Goya (1746–1828). A scene like this one is musically expressed in Berlioz's *Symphonie fantastique.*

first meeting. It is followed by a grand expression of the passion that she inspired in him. The movement ends with tenderness and religious consolation.

Part II: A Ball   At a dance in the midst of a brilliant party, he encounters the loved one, again represented by the idée fixe melody.

Part III: Scene in the Country   One summer evening in the country, he hears two shepherds piping melodies to one another across the fields. This pastoral duet combines with the quiet rustling of the trees, gently brushed by the wind, and his newly entertained hopes to be able to give his heart an unaccustomed calm and his ideas a more cheerful color. But she (the idée fixe) appears again, and he feels a tightening in his heart and the fear that she might be deceiving him. One of the shepherds takes up his simple tune again, but the other no longer answers. The movement ends as the sun sets to the distant sounds of thunder. The mood is lonely and quiet.

Part IV: March to the Scaffold   He dreams that he has killed his beloved. He is condemned to death and led to the scaffold. The procession moves forward to the sounds of a march that is at times somber, fierce, and solemn. The muffled sound of heavy steps gives way, without transition, to a noisy clamor from the crowd. At the end, the idée fixe returns for a moment, like a last thought of love interrupted by the fatal blow. Brilliant fanfares follow the public execution.

Part V: Dream of a Witches' Sabbath   He sees himself at the Sabbath, amid a frightening troop of ghosts, sorcerers, and monsters of every kind. They have all come together for his funeral. His beloved appears again, but the idée fixe has changed. It sounds mean and trivial. It represents his beloved coming to join the Sabbath. Bells toll for him as a dead man, and a melody from a medieval chant that represented judgment day, the "**Dies irae**" ("Day of Wrath"), is played.

The five movements are linked together by the use of one melody that represents the hero's image of his beloved. This melody, the idée fixe, appears in each movement of the symphony in various transformations—in the second movement, it is a waltz tune; in the fourth, it appears fleetingly just before the fall of the executioner's blade; and, in the fifth movement, it becomes a grotesque witches' dance. The technique of using one theme that changes throughout a composition is called **thematic transformation,** and it was used by many later romantic composers to unify their works.

Throughout the work, Berlioz uses the orchestra to portray a wide range of images and emotional states. The orchestra in our recording is not quite as large as the one Berlioz wanted, which would have had at least fifteen first violins, at least fifteen second violins, ten violas, eleven cellos, and nine double basses. That large an orchestra is seldom assembled, even for Berlioz's masterwork. The tuba was not invented until

1835 in Germany, so Berlioz's orchestra would have had the low brass parts played on ophicleides and/or serpents, neither of which is in common use today.

This fifth movement of Berlioz's *Symphonie fantastique* tells only part of the story of the symphony, but it is often performed without the other movements. It helps to know the entire story to appreciate it. "Hearing the Difference: Beethoven's Symphony no. 5, first movement, and Berlioz's *Symphonie fantastique*, fifth movement," compares a piece of absolute music with a program symphony.

 **Featured Listening**  CONNECT CD 2: Tracks 1–3

Symphonie fantastique, fifth movement, "Dream of a Witches' Sabbath" HECTOR BERLIOZ

Date: 1830

Genre: Program symphony

Tempo: Larghetto-allegro (larghetto is not as slow as largo)

Form: No major sections repeat

Instruments: Two flutes, two oboes, two clarinets, four bassoons, four French horns, two trumpets, two cornets, three trombones, two tubas, timpani, bass drum, snare drum, cymbals, three sets of bells, first violins, second violins, violas, cellos, double basses

Meter: Sextuple

Duration: 9:46

Context: Berlioz was 27 years old and much in love with an actress he really did not know when he composed this work. She was impressed by him and agreed to meet and eventually marry him. This might seem a little strange to us since he killed his lover in the story of the symphony, and they are both dead in this final movement, but great extremes of emotion portrayed in musical compositions were one of the characteristics of the romantic period. The melody called the idée fixe has played in all four of the preceding movements to represent the composer's love, and, in this movement, it has been transformed into a grotesque, mocking little melody.

	Timing	Musical events
1	0:00	Larghetto—soft, muted strings create a mysterious atmosphere and basses repeat an ascending motive; muted horns and high woodwinds enter, playing playful but ominous lines that fall to lower notes as if dead; rumbling timpani accompany
2	0:00	Allegro—A high clarinet plays a grotesque, mocking form of the idée fixe; the strings bring forth a strong response; the idée fixe repeats and bassoons enter with a countermelody; intensity builds, then subsides
	1:16	Bells toll for the dead.
3	0:00	The "Dies irae" ("Day of Wrath") melody is played first by tubas and bassoons, then repeated faster, played by horns and trombones; the melody continues to repeat in different instrumental groups.
	1:53	Witches' dance—a melody played by low strings is imitated by three other groups of instruments in fuguelike counterpoint
	3:37	The "Dies irae" returns in string basses; tension builds.
	4:39	The "Dies irae" is played again, this time by high brass.
	5:06	The strings are played with the wood of the bows, creating an eerie sound as the woodwinds play a dance melody; crescendo with repeat of the "Dies irae"; strong cadence.

**BEETHOVEN'S SYMPHONY NO. 5, FIRST MOVEMENT,
AND BERLIOZ'S *SYMPHONIE FANTASTIQUE*, FIFTH MOVEMENT**

Beethoven was a classical composer, and Berlioz was a romantic one (see Featured Listening on page 152 and page 186). If you think about the general interests and attitudes of each of those periods, you can hear how the music reflected the composers' and the audiences' thoughts of the times. (Refer back to the Preludes for a reminder of these historical periods.) Answer the following questions as you listen from one work to the other:

- Consider the formal structure of each of these movements. Which movement displays a sense of balance, and which concentrates more on a display of emotion?

- How do the orchestras playing these two symphonies compare? Which is larger? What instruments are added to the larger orchestra? What is the purpose of adding instruments?

- Beethoven's Symphony no. 5 and Berlioz's *Symphonie fantastique* each have a musical characteristic that appears in every movement. Which is a rhythmic idea, and which is a melody? What did each of those repeating ideas represent in the symphonies?

- How do the tempos differ?

- How do the meters differ?

Other Program Music

Most romantic composers who wrote for orchestra also wrote program music. The desire to use music to tell life stories, real or imagined, was irresistible in the era. Some other programmatic works by Berlioz included the dramatic symphony *Roméo et Juliette* (1839); the *King Lear* Overture (1831); the *Waverley* and *Rob Roy* overtures (ca. 1827 and 1831), both of which are based on novels of Sir Walter Scott; and the symphony *Harold en Italie* (1834), based on the poem by Byron.

The pianist Franz Liszt developed the symphonic poem, or tone poem. For his symphonic poems, Liszt ignored the tradition of having symphonic works organized into several movements. He also avoided the idea that sonata form provided necessary balance for a first movement of a symphonic composition. He often unified his works by using a single theme or melody that he continuously transformed as the piece progressed. This technique is much like that used by Berlioz with the idée fixe. Liszt's *Les Préludes* (1853) is a single-movement work that follows the events and emotions in a poem called *Méditations poétiques* by Alphonse de Lamartine. Liszt wrote it to be played by a large orchestra that included a harp and several percussion instruments besides timpani. The manner in which the orchestra is used is also typically romantic. The winds are often used as solo instruments; the horn, a favorite romantic instrument, is particularly prominent; fluctuations in tempo and dynamics occur frequently, something that would not have happened in the classical period.

Liszt composed twelve symphonic poems. For some he drew on Greek myths such as *Orpheus* (1853) and *Prometheus* (1850). Another of his symphonic poems that is often performed today is *Hamlet* (1858), based on Shakespeare's play. His two symphonies tell the stories of other literary works. *Faust* (1854–1857) is from a play of that name by Johann Wolfgang von Goethe (1749–1832), and *Dante* (1855–1856) was composed in three movements to fit the structure of *The Divine Comedy* (ca. 1307) by Dante (1265–1321).

Another important composer of program music was **Richard Strauss** (1864–1949). Although Strauss's life extended nearly halfway through the twentieth century, the bulk of his tone poems were written in the nineteenth century. Some of his works, such as *Also sprach Zarathustra* (*Thus Spake Zarathustra*, 1896, used in the 1968 movie *2001:*

A *Space Odyssey*), have general, philosophical programs, whereas the comic *Till Eulenspiegels lustige Streiche* (*Till Eulenspiegel's Merry Pranks*, 1895) and *Don Quixote* (1897) have more specific programs.

Summary

Romantic composers who chose to abandon the classical forms found new ways of unifying their larger instrumental works. A favorite method was to compose the music to fit a nonmusical idea, frequently a story. Such music is known as program music.

The more radical romantic composers, such as Hector Berlioz, composed dramatic major works that were often inspired by literary texts. His *Symphonie fantastique* was based on his life and feelings. It derives its unity from the idée fixe, a melodic idea appearing in various transformations throughout the five-movement symphony.

Franz Liszt and Richard Strauss also composed many programmatic works for orchestra that are still performed often today. The idea of having a theme change or transform as the piece is played was also employed by other romantic composers.

New People and Concepts

"Dies irae," 185

Hector Berlioz, 183

idée fixe, 184

program symphony, 184

Richard Strauss, 187

thematic transformation, 185

Finale

CD 2: Tracks 1–3

Listen again to the recording of *Symphonie fantastique*, fifth movement, "Dream of a Witches' Sabbath," by Berlioz and compare your impression now with your notes from your First Hearing. Consider the following questions:

- What is the mood of this fifth movement, and how does it fit into the story of the symphony?
- What instruments do you hear added to the orchestra in this movement, and what do they represent in the story of the symphony?
- What is the "Dies irae," and what does it represent in music? How does that fit the story of this symphony?
- What is the form of this movement?
- What are the tempo and meter?
- If you were going to describe this music to a friend, what would you say?

Further Listening

Franz Liszt, *Les Préludes*. Liszt was a brilliant pianist, but he also composed much music for orchestra. *Les Préludes* is one of twelve symphonic poems he composed. It is based on the events and emotions in a poem called *Méditations poétiques* by Alphonse de Lamarine.

Richard Strauss, *Don Quixote*. This work portrays episodes from the novel *Don Quixote* by the Spanish writer Miguel de Cervantes. Strauss even used particular instruments to represent the two main characters: Quixote is played by a solo cello and his squire Sancho Panza is played by a solo viola.

Modest Mussorgsky, *Pictures at an Exhibition*. This work was composed for solo piano, but it has been transcribed to be played by an orchestra, and even the rock band Emerson, Lake and Palmer did a version of it. The music is about the composer's reactions to viewing pictures at an art exhibition and includes the returning sound of a "promenade" that represents the composer walking from one painting to another.

Nationalism in the Romantic Era

 ))) **First Hearing**

 CONNECT   CD 2: Tracks 4–11

Listen to the recording of "The Moldau" by Smetana and take notes on what you hear. Even if you are working with other students in a paired or group listening session, keep your own notes. Give some attention to the following:

- This composition is about a river called the Moldau. What do you hear that sounds like water? What instruments are playing to give it that sound?

- Listen for a melody that repeats. When do you first hear that melody? At the very beginning, or a little after the beginning? How many times does it repeat?

- The mood changes throughout the work. List what moods you hear as you listen. What is the mood at the end? Sad and lonely? Happy and lighthearted? Proud, thoughtful, or some other mood?

- Is a constant tempo kept throughout the work, or does the tempo seem to vary?

- Is the meter stressed in a very regular pattern, or is the meter difficult to determine?

Keep your notes from this First Hearing to compare with your impressions about the piece after you study the information in this chapter.

19

During the later part of the romantic era, nationalism became an important force in music. *Nationalism* in this context refers to any musical expression that is intended to emphasize the unique character and interests of a particular nation. There had been some stylistic differences in the music of different nations in previous eras. Certainly, J. S. Bach's music was composed in a Germanic style, whereas opera was generally thought of as an Italian art form into the classical period. For the most part, however, the classical style of Mozart, Haydn, and Beethoven was international and cosmopolitan.

During the romantic era, however, self-conscious and even aggressive nationalistic feeling flared up in both literature and music. Common musical expressions of nationalism ranged from the use of historical or other national subjects to the quoting of folk melodies and rhythms in new works.

Russia had been isolated from the influence of Western European culture until the reign of Peter the Great (1672–1725). Peter forced Western customs and ideas on his people to the point of eliminating many of their own traditions. Italian opera became particularly popular at the Imperial Court. Most of the musicians were brought in from the West, and performances were available only for the upper classes.

In the nineteenth century, a new sense of national pride began to grow, demanding that there be something "Russian" about the music played in Russia. One of the early romantics to do this was Mikhail Glinka (1804–1857) who composed the opera *A Life for the Tsar* (1836). The work was full of Russian folk melodies and expressed a proud Russian spirit.

Later in the century, a group of five Russian composers shared the feeling that musical influences from the West should be completely abandoned. They referred to themselves as "the Five." Of these composers, the most significant were Alexander Borodin (1833–1887), who is best known for his opera *Prince Igor;* Nikolai Rimsky-Korsakov (1844–1908), well remembered for his orchestral tone poem *Scheherazade;* and Modest Mussorgsky (1839–1881), who wrote *Pictures at an Exhibition* for solo piano and the opera *Boris Godunov.*

The distinctive nature of Russian folk music and Slavic culture made the nationalist movement in Russia obvious. But Russia was not the only country in which nationalistic forces influenced the musical scene. Ralph Vaughan Williams and Edward Elgar of England, Jean Sibelius of Finland, Edvard Grieg of Norway, Manuel de Falla of Spain, and Ottorino Respighi of Italy each reflected in some way the particular nationalistic flavor of their native countries.

The forces of nationalism also influenced musical developments in Bohemia, an area that is now part of the Czech Republic. Bohemia had been an Austrian colony for centuries and thus had always been in touch with the mainstream of European music. Many fine musicians were produced in this region, but until the romantic era, no distinctively Czech national style had developed. Even when a nationalist movement did arise, no extreme effort was made to avoid Western influence.

Bedřich Smetana

Regarded as the founder of the Czech national school, **Bedřich Smetana** (1824–1884) was a composer dedicated to merging the spirit of Bohemian folk music with the innovations of the European musical pioneers of his day. A gifted pianist from childhood, Smetana performed the works of the classical masters. His traditional orientation was supplanted, however, when on a visit to Prague he had the opportunity to hear Liszt and Berlioz. Smetana came to share with these men not only a fascination with progressive musical ideas but also a spirit of nationalism and a dream of a Bohemia free from Austrian rule.

The spirit of Czech nationalism was widespread in Austrian-ruled Bohemia, and rising unrest culminated in the revolution of 1848. The uprising was a failure and left in its wake a long period of repression that Smetana eventually found unbearable. In 1856, he traveled to Sweden, where he worked as a teacher and conductor. He returned to his homeland six years later, this time finding a new and dynamic liberalism in the air. Shortly after his return, a Czech national theater for opera, drama, and ballet was established, and Smetana began work on an opera in the Czech language.

Over the next twenty years, the composer produced ten operas, eight of them on patriotic themes. *The Bartered Bride* (1866), which told of a village romance and recounted the comic antics of local Bohemian peasants, was instrumental in establishing his reputation.

In 1874, Smetana suddenly became deaf. But, like Beethoven before him, he continued to compose until close to the end of his life. He died at age 60.

Aside from his operas, Smetana is best known for his famous cycle of symphonic poems, *Má Vlast* (*My Country*, 1879). The six works in this

BEDŘICH SMETANA
(1824–1884)

- Born in Litomyšl, Bohemia; died at age 60 in Prague; Bohemia (Czech Republic).

- Best known for "The Moldau," which is one of six symphonic poems in *Má Vlast (My Country)*, and the opera *The Bartered Bride.*

cycle celebrate his country's legendary past, its splendid rivers and hillsides, and great moments in Bohemian history. One of the finest of the six is called "Vltava" ("The Moldau"). It traces musically the course of the river Moldau from its sources through central Bohemia to Prague and on to join another river, the Elbe.

))) **Featured Listening**  CONNECT   CD 2: Tracks 4–11

"The Moldau" BEDŘICH SMETANA

Date: 1874

Genre: Symphonic poem

Tempo: Allegro commodo non agitato (fast, but unhurried and not agitated); the tempo varies according to the program

Form: Through-composed to fit the program, with one returning theme that represents the river

Instruments: One piccolo, two flutes, two oboes, two clarinets, two bassoons, four French horns, two trumpets, three trombones, one tuba, timpani, bass drum, triangle, cymbals, harp, first violins, second violins, violas, cellos, double basses

Meter: Mostly duple; the Moldau theme is sextuple

Duration: 11:32

Context: The piece begins with flutes playfully sounding like two streams, one warm and one cold, joining together to become a river that flows through the beautiful land of Bohemia. French horns soon represent people hunting along the shore of the river, then a series of scenes appear one at a time, including a wedding dance, moonlight and water nymphs, rapids, an ancient royal castle Vysihrad, and arrival at the capital city of Prague. At the very end, the mood quiets as the river flows on beyond the Bohemian border. As you listen, imagine yourself on a boat on the river and visualize the scenes as you hear them.

	Timing		What to listen for
4	0:00	Two Springs, Sources of the River	Flutes portray a cold spring bubbling up; harp and pizzicato (plucked) strings accompany.
	0:28		Clarinets enter to portray a warm spring; two springs remain separate, then blend together to form a single stream.
5	0:00	The Moldau	A triangle note; flowing accompaniment suggests movement of water
	0:07		The Moldau theme
6	0:00	Forest Hunt	Hunting horns are suddenly heard from the forests along the river, as flowing accompaniment continues; louder trumpet calls increase excitement; calls and accompaniment die away.
7	0:00	Peasant Wedding	Music in the style of a Czech folk dance portrays a peasant wedding celebration on the banks of the river; dies away to single notes in bass.
8	0:00	Moonlight, Dance of Water Sprites	Woodwinds hold long notes like beams of moonlight; serene melody high in violins; quietly undulating woodwind accompaniment, occasional harp arpeggios portray the calm of the river in the moonlight.
	1:50		Distant brass fanfares, pianissimo, recall the ruins of ancient castles reflected in the water and bygone days of chivalry; timpani roll and crescendo in woodwinds lead to:

(continued)

	Timing		What to listen for
	2:41	The Moldau	Return of the Moldau theme, flowing accompaniment
9	0:00	St. John Rapids	Sudden brass calls, fortissimo, cymbal roll signal the white-water turbulence of the St. John Rapids; sudden drop to pianissimo, then upward rushing crescendo
	1:14	The Moldau	The Moldau theme; the river flows majestically through the great city of Prague
10	0:00	Vysihrad Castle	Brasses peal forth the theme of Vysihrad Castle, home of great heroes of Bohemia's past.
11	0:00	Coda	Fragment of the Moldau theme sweeps up and down through the strings, gradually softening and slowing as the river flows into the distance; two closing chords, forte.

"The Moldau" is nationalistic not only because it portrays the beauty of the famous Bohemian river; it is also nationalistic in the particular events Smetana chose to put into the work. The portrayal of a hunt represented a land of plenty that provided for its people, and the wedding represented the beginning of a family and all of the related values.

It is interesting to notice how beautifully Smetana gave sound to moonlight. His long-held notes in the woodwinds can easily be heard as beams of light coming from the moon, and yet moonlight itself is without sound. Modern movie composers like to steal ideas from programmatic composers of the romantic era because the romantics did such a wonderful job of giving sound to the soundless things.

Summary

Nationalism refers to any musical expression that is intended to emphasize the unique character and interests of a particular nation. Common musical expressions of nationalism range from the use of historical or other types of national subjects for operas and symphonic poems to the occasional quoting of folk melodies and rhythms in new works.

Early in the nineteenth century, Russia began to produce nationalistic music. Glinka drew from his country's vast supply of folk music and liturgical chant to write the opera *A Life for the Tsar*, first performed in 1836. A group of Glinka's successors formed a nationalistic school known as "the Five." The outstanding members of this group were Alexander Borodin, Nikolai Rimsky-Korsakov, and Modest Mussorgsky.

The forces of nationalism were also felt in other European countries. In particular, a national style developed in Bohemia through the efforts of Bedřich Smetana. Nationalistic influences were also felt in Spain, Italy, Finland, the Scandinavian countries, and England.

New People

Bedřich Smetana, 190

Finale

CONNECT   **CD 2: Tracks 4–11**

Listen again to the recording of "The Moldau" by Smetana and compare your impression now with your notes from your First Hearing. Consider the following questions:

- What instruments are used to imitate the sound of water at the beginning of the work? How is water represented later?
- What is the character of the returning Moldau theme? Soft and gentle? Proud, playful, angry? How many times is the theme played?
- What instruments represent the hunt?
- What kind of music represents the wedding? How is moonlight "played" by the orchestra?
- How are the rapids represented?
- During which scenes (hunt, wedding, moonlight, or rapids) is the percussion section of the orchestra the most important, and why do you think percussion is effective in that scene?
- What is the mood on reaching the city of Prague? Does the music sound like Smetana was proud of Prague or unhappy to arrive there?
- Are the tempo and meter regular and obvious, or does the music obscure either or both of them for the sake of the dramatic story behind the music?
- If you were going to describe this music to a friend, what would you say?

Further Listening

Modest Mussorgsky, *Boris Godunov.* This is an opera loosely based on the novel *Boris Godunov* by the Russian writer Alexander Pushkin. The story is about the Tsar Boris Godunov, who took the Russian throne after the suspicious death of the real heir who was the ten-year-old son of the previous tsar. The Coronation Scene in which the Russian people praise their new Tsar to the ringing of many church bells is full of patriotic spirit.

Jean Sibelius, *Finlandia.* This symphonic poem was composed while the Russians dominated Finland. It was seen to represent the pride and independence of the Finnish people.

Bedřich Smetana, *The Bartered Bride.* This opera is based on a comic story of a village romance among Bohemian peasants. It captures the Bohemian spirit using folk melodies and dances such as the polka and the furiant.

The Concert Overture

> Music is a code that opens a door to a world everybody interprets differently because our aesthetic and sensory values are different and each generation has to discover its own.
>
> —CELLIST YO-YO MA (B. 1955)

))) First Hearing

 CD 2: Tracks 12–18

Listen to the recording of the *Romeo and Juliet* Overture by Tchaikovsky and take notes on what you hear. Even if you are working with other students in a paired or group listening session, keep your own notes. Give some attention to the following:

- This is a long composition, but you can begin by concentrating on just the first nine minutes where the main themes (melodies) are introduced. There is an introduction and then two themes that contrast with each other. What is the mood of the introduction? What kind of mood comes next? What kind of mood follows?

- If you know the story of Shakespeare's play *Romeo and Juliet,* can you connect any of the themes to events or characters in the story? If you can, what theme fits with the mood of which character or event?

- As you listen to the rest of the composition, notice when those themes from the first nine minutes repeat. When you hear them again, do they repeat totally, or just partially? Are they heard near the end of the work?

- Given the way or ways themes repeat, try to guess at the form (sonata, minuet and trio, rondo, theme and variations, through-composed, and so on). (Note: the form is a bit difficult to follow in this work, so you can feel very good about your listening skills if you get it right.)

- Can you guess at the tempo or the meter?

Keep your notes from this First Hearing to compare with your impressions about the piece after you study the information in this chapter.

20

Prior to the nineteenth century, the overture had been an instrumental piece that functioned as an introduction to a longer musical work (such as an opera or oratorio) or, in some instances, as **incidental music** to a play. Although this type of overture continued to be written during the nineteenth century, the romantic period gave rise to a new type of overture, one that was not an introduction to something else. The **concert overture** was a one-movement, self-contained musical work intended for performance in the concert hall.

Some concert overtures were written for specific festive occasions. Beethoven's "Consecration of the House" is one such work. Others, such as Mendelssohn's "Hebrides Overture," attempted to evoke some aspect of nature. And still others, including Brahms's "Tragic Overture," expressed a generalized mood or human condition.

Many concert overtures have programmatic and descriptive elements and in some respects resemble the symphonic poem. But unlike the symphonic poem, the concert overture retains the strong musical organization embodied in sonata form. In this respect, the concert overture is much like the first movement of a symphony, except that it is complete in itself.

Peter Ilyich Tchaikovsky

One of the most popular concert overtures written during the romantic era, *Romeo and Juliet,* was composed by the Russian **Peter Ilyich Tchaikovsky** ("Chy-koff-skee," 1840–1893). During the romantic period there were two schools of musical thought in Russia. The nationalists, such as Glinka and his successors, "the Five," attempted to create a music that was totally Russian in character and style. Other composers, such as Tchaikovsky, were more cosmopolitan and looked to Western European traditions for their inspiration while still incorporating Russian elements into their music. Tchaikovsky was the first Russian composer to gain an international reputation.

Tchaikovsky was born in Votkinsk, in a remote province of Russia. He received his earliest musical training from a French governess. When he was 10, his family moved to St. Petersburg. On graduating from school at age 19, he became a government clerk but soon decided to give that up to pursue a musical career. He was accepted into the newly established St. Petersburg Conservatory, where he began serious composition under Anton Rubinstein (1829–1894), the institution's founder and an eminent pianist and composer.

Tchaikovsky graduated in 1865, winning a gold medal for a cantata based not on a Russian subject but, significantly, on a German one—Schiller's *Hymn to Joy.* The following year he became a professor of harmony at the Moscow Conservatory, a position he was to hold for twelve years. His early works, which included overtures, string quartets, and a programmatic symphony, demonstrated little of the individual style that marked his later achievements. He widened his experience, however, through frequent trips abroad.

In 1876, Tchaikovsky acquired the support of an unusual benefactress, Nadezhda von Meck, a widow who had inherited an immense fortune. Impressed by his music and informed that the composer was in financial need, she commissioned several works at large fees. She arranged to pay him a fixed annuity so that he could devote himself completely to composition. Their relationship, lasting thirteen years, was carried on entirely by letter. They agreed never to meet, and except for several accidental encounters in public places, the bargain was kept.

In 1877, Tchaikovsky married Antonina Milyukova, a conservatory student who threatened suicide if he would not marry her. The marriage was a disastrous failure, for Tchaikovsky's sympathy for the girl quickly turned to revulsion, in part because of his homosexuality. After he attempted suicide by plunging into the Moscow River, a legal separation was arranged. With the financial help of von Meck, he embarked on a trip to Italy, Paris, and Vienna.

Despite an increasing tendency toward depression, Tchaikovsky remained a highly productive composer. His Fourth and Fifth Symphonies (1877 and 1888) and the ballets *Swan Lake* (1876) and *The Sleeping Beauty* (1889) were soon performed all over Europe. By the 1880s he had reached the height of his career. Suddenly, for reasons that have never been fully explained, von Meck withdrew her support and friendship. Though her action was a severe blow to his pride, Tchaikovsky was by then able to afford the financial loss, and his capacity for work remained undiminished. During 1891 and 1892, he undertook several concert tours in America, Poland, and Germany.

PETER ILYICH TCHAIKOVSKY
(1840–1893)

- Born in Votkinsk, Russia; died at age 53 in St. Petersburg, Russia.

- Prolific composer best known for his last three symphonies (nos. 4, 5, and 6), orchestral works including *Romeo and Juliet,* three ballets—*Swan Lake, Sleeping Beauty,* and *The Nutcracker*—and eleven operas including *Eugene Onegin* and *The Queen of Spades.*

He went to St. Petersburg in 1893 to conduct the premiere of his Sixth Symphony, the *Pathétique.* He died just nine days after that performance.

Much mystery has surrounded Tchaikovsky's death. It was initially reported that he had fallen victim to a cholera epidemic that had been raging in the city, but it was later thought by some that he might have committed suicide by taking arsenic. The truth will probably never be known. He was 53 years old.

Romeo and Juliet Overture

Many of Tchaikovsky's works are often performed today. His last three symphonies, his operas, his first piano concerto, his violin concerto, and particularly his ballets *Swan Lake, The Sleeping Beauty,* and *The Nutcracker* are among the most popular works in the concert repertoire today. His concert overture *Romeo and Juliet,* sometimes referred to as a *fantasy overture,* was a relatively early work, composed in 1870 (revised in 1881). It is based on Shakespeare's play of the same title, although it was not intended to be performed with the play. Its themes are based on characters and events in the play, making it necessary to know the play to fully appreciate the music.

The primary characters and events represented in the overture are

Tchaikovsky used Shakespeare's most famous drama as the basis for the concert overture *Romeo and Juliet.*

Romeo Montague—a young man who falls in love with the daughter of a family that is hated by his family

Juliet Capulet—loved by Romeo and falls in love with him

Friar Laurence—who secretly performs the marriage of Romeo and Juliet

Romeo is banished from the town because he killed Juliet's cousin in a street fight. Unaware of the marriage between Romeo and Juliet, Juliet's family plans for her to marry someone else. To escape her family and attempt to be united with Romeo, Juliet obtains a sleeping potion from Friar Laurence that makes her seem to be dead. The Friar then sends a messenger to find Romeo to tell him that she is not dead and that Romeo should meet her at her family's tomb when she wakes up from the potion. That message never reaches Romeo, but the news of Juliet's death does. He finds her body at the tomb, thinks she is dead, takes poison, and dies. She then wakes up to find Romeo dead and fatally stabs herself.

The point was made earlier that Tchaikovsky's overture was not intended to be played during a performance of the play, although a movie version of the play made in 1968 used Tchaikovsky's themes in the score. The overture represents the essence of the play in some interesting ways, however. The foreboding music at the beginning sets the mood for a tragedy; the feud theme almost sounds like swords clashing in a street fight; and the love theme is beautiful and gentle. Tchaikovsky's coda is brilliant in that the feud and love themes compete with each other, then the feud theme takes over, to be followed by a funeral march. It was the feud that separated the lovers and caused their deaths. "MusiCurious: *Romeo and Juliet:* The Alternate Endings" describes how powerful stories can be presented for numerous audiences.

 **MusiCurious**

ROMEO AND JULIET: THE ALTERNATE ENDINGS

Did Shakespeare write the story of *Romeo and Juliet*?

No. Shakespeare's play was based on an old classic tale. The origins of the story are unknown, but the basic plot was written in the 1400s in an Italian collection of stories called *Novella*. The authors of the stories in *Novella* were anonymous, and various writers through the ages, including William Shakespeare, used them as plots for their work. In fact, there are many operas and ballets, musicals, and films based on the story of Romeo and Juliet.

Do all of the versions tell exactly the same story?

No. Some writers have thought that their audiences would prefer a happy ending and have rewritten the story so that Juliet wakes up before Romeo drinks the poison, which allows the two lovers to live happily ever after just as Friar Laurence planned for them in the play.

The most popular *Romeo and Juliet* opera performed today was composed in France in 1867 by Charles-François Gounod using a libretto by Jules Barbier and Michel Carré. It follows Shakespeare's plot more closely, but the final scene is extended to allow the characters to sing as they die. In the play, Romeo dies, then Juliet kills herself. In the opera, Romeo takes the poison but is still alive when Juliet wakes up. This provides the two an opportunity to sing to each other. It is only when Romeo begins to weaken from the poison that Juliet takes out a sword and stabs herself with it. Then, the two continue to sing to each other as they pray for God's goodwill. Then they die together. This is, after all, opera, which is about singing.

Are the characters always called Romeo and Juliet?

No. There have been versions loosely based on the story in which the names were changed. The most famous musical based on the story is Leonard Bernstein's *West Side Story* (1957), by Arthur Laurents (book) and Stephen Sondheim (lyrics). In that version, the lovers are named Tony and Maria and they come from two different feuding street gangs in New York. Tony, like Romeo, is under the mistaken impression that his lover has been killed. Overcome by grief, Tony asks the person he thinks killed Maria to kill him as well—like Romeo, he is the author of his own death. Maria appears alive just as Tony is shot, but it is too late to save Tony, who dies in her arms. In the play, Juliet kills herself after she sees that Romeo is dead. In *West Side Story*, Maria tries, but is unable to kill herself. After Tony's death, the feuding gang members gather together and stop their fighting.

))) **Featured Listening**    CONNECT   **CD 2: Tracks 12–18**

***Romeo and Juliet* Overture**   PETER ILYICH TCHAIKOVSKY

Date: 1870

Genre: Concert overture

Tempo: Slow introduction, faster with some variation later

Form: Sonata with an introduction

Instruments: Two flutes (piccolo), two oboes, two clarinets, one English horn, two bassoons, four horns, two trumpets, three trombones, one tuba, timpani, cymbals, bass drum, harp, first violins, second violins, violas, cellos, double basses

Meter: Quadruple

Duration: 19:20

Context: Notice how well the themes fit the characters or emotions in the play: The Friar Laurence theme is serious and sounds like it might be played in a church, the feud theme sounds like a street fight, and the love theme is beautiful and gentle.

(continued)

Timing		What to listen for

Introduction

12	0:00	Friar Laurence	Hymnlike, homophonic theme softly in clarinets and bassoons
	0:38		Foreboding fragments begin in low strings, build gradually to winds with harp.
	2:05		Strings pizzicato, Friar Laurence theme more agitated in woodwinds
	2:35		Foreboding music returns, then with harp arpeggios.
	3:51		Timpani roll introduces intense, threatening motives climaxing in loud, fast passage.
	4:28		Timpani, threatening motives: woodwind-string echoes build directly to:

Exposition

13	0:00	Theme 1: Feud	Agitated feud theme in orchestra; strings rush up and down; agitated feud theme; rising three-note motive tossed between strings and winds
	0:23		Fragments of feud theme and rushing strings combined, developed with three-note motive; full orchestra with cymbal crashes in loud chords and rushing strings builds to climax
	1:00		Feud theme explodes in full orchestra; transition with rushing strings; feud theme builds to close
	1:22	Bridge	Energy released in woodwind development of three-note motive; low strings take over
14	0:00	Theme 2: Love	Flowing love theme in English horn and muted violas, pulsating horns accompany
	0:19		Harp arpeggio introduces muted strings with tender love music
	1:04		Flutes and oboes surge upward to love theme with countertheme in French horn creating a love duet; greatly extended with lush orchestration.
	2:05	Closing	Harp chords and soft tones in strings and winds subside to restful close.

Development

15	0:00		Fragments of feud theme; fast scales in strings accompany Friar Laurence theme intoned softly in horn; theme extended and developed
	1:11		Three-note motive interrupts in cellos and basses, with fragments of feud theme; downward rushing strings added and build to climax
	1:27		Cymbal crash, full orchestra develops both feud and Friar Laurence themes, forte in trumpet; rushing strings with loud chords in orchestra lead directly into:

Recapitulation

16	0:00	Theme 1	Agitated feud theme in full orchestra with cymbal crashes; strings rush downward
17	0:00	Theme 2	Tender love music in oboes and clarinets; intensity grows as other winds enrich the sound; strings rise intensely upward into:
	0:36		Love theme soars in strings and flute with countertheme in horn and throbbing woodwind accompaniment; grows to full, rich orchestration.
	1:32		Love theme fragment in cellos answered by flute; extended with fragments and horns answered by flute and oboe; strings begin love theme but it dissolves

	Timing		What to listen for
18	0:00	Coda	Fragments of feud and love themes vie with each other in full orchestra; feud theme emphatically takes over, then combines with Friar Laurence theme in brass; extended development as feud music takes over; furious activity decreases to ominous timpani roll.
	1:18		Drumbeat continues as in a funeral march; fragments of love theme sound brokenly in strings, drumbeat ceases as woodwinds answer with a variation of tender love music; rising harp arpeggios signal union of the lovers, strings yearningly sing fragment of love theme.
	3:48		Drum roll crescendo to strong final chords, recalling the feud theme

Summary

The romantic era gave rise to a new type of overture, one that did not introduce a longer work but was instead a self-contained work in one movement, intended for performance in the concert hall. The concert overture, ex- emplified by Tchaikovsky's *Romeo and Juliet,* often had programmatic elements but retained the sonata form of organization.

New People and Concepts

concert overture, 194

incidental music, 194

Peter Ilyich Tchaikovsky, 195

Finale

 CD 2: Tracks 12–18

Listen again to the recording of the *Romeo and Juliet* Overture by Tchaikovsky and com- pare your impression now with your notes from your First Hearing. Consider the following questions:

- What characters or events from *Romeo and Juliet* do the primary themes presented in the exposition (first nine minutes) represent? What moods are connected with each character and theme?
- In the coda, Tchaikovsky brilliantly has the love theme and the feud theme fighting each other. Which theme takes over the other, and how does that fit the story of the play?
- The work is in sonata form, but the themes in the exposition do not repeat in the recapitulation as a work by Mozart or Beethoven would. What is it about the romantic period that encouraged composers to break formal conventions that were so popular during the classical period?
- What is the tempo?
- What is the meter?
- If you were going to describe this music to a friend, what would you say?

Further Listening

Felix Mendelssohn, *A Midsummer Night's Dream* Overture. This concert overture was first composed as a concert work, not associated with any production of Shakespeare's play, *A Midsummer Night's Dream*. Later, however, Mendelssohn rewrote it to go with incidental music for the play. That incidental music includes the famous "Wedding March," which might be Mendelssohn's most familiar composition. The Overture is based on sounds from the play, including dancing fairies and the braying of Bottom as a donkey.

Gioachio Rossini, The *William Tell* Overture. This overture was composed as the overture to Rossini's opera *William Tell,* but it also became popular as a concert work without the opera. It includes the famous theme used in the *Lone Ranger* radio programs of the 1930s and television shows of the 1950s.

Peter Ilyich Tchaikovsky, The 1812 Overture. Tchaikovsky composed this overture in 1882 to commemorate Russia's having successfully defeated Napoleon in 1812. Cannons and chimes bring the work to a dramatic conclusion, causing it to be popular for performance at American Fourth of July concerts.

Johannes Brahms, The Academic Festival Overture. This overture was composed by Brahms to thank the University of Breslau for having given him an honorary doctorate degree. It includes melodies often sung by university students of the time, including "Gaudeamus igitur" ("Let Us Rejoice"), which was traditionally sung at graduation ceremonies.

The Romantic Concerto

))) First Hearing

Listen to the recording of Violin Concerto in E Minor, op. 64, first movement, by Mendelssohn and take notes on what you hear. Even if you are working with other students in a paired or group listening session, keep your own notes. Give some attention to the following:

- In Mozart's Piano Concerto no. 23 in A Major, first movement, we heard the orchestra play for two full minutes before the piano soloist came in. Does the beginning of this concerto sound like Mozart's concerto, or is the violin soloist featured earlier?

- The term *virtuoso* means that the musician has excellent technical control of his or her instrument. Knowing that it tends to be difficult to play very high notes in tune on the violin, would you call this solo violin part a virtuoso solo (cadenza)? Is the solo up very high, or does the violinist play within the pitch range of the orchestral violinists?

- Mozart's piano concerto had a cadenza in which the soloist played without orchestral accompaniment. Do you hear a cadenza in Mendelssohn's violin concerto?

- Do the themes at the beginning of the movement repeat at or near the end? What might the form of the movement be?

- Can you guess at the tempo and meter?

Keep your notes from this First Hearing to compare with your impressions about the piece after you study the information in this chapter.

21

As we have already pointed out, romantic audiences were dazzled by exhibitions of virtuosity. All through the romantic era there was a steady growth of virtuoso technique, particularly on the piano and the violin. The trend was begun by Beethoven, whose works were very advanced for his time. It was spurred on in 1820 by the arrival on the European concert stage of Niccolò Paganini (1782–1840); this phenomenal Italian violinist astounded and enchanted all who witnessed the incredible speed and brilliance of his playing.

The concerto for solo instrument and orchestra, with the improvised quality of its cadenza (an unaccompanied or solo section) lent itself especially well to displays of technical skill. The master composers of the period include Robert Schumann, Johannes Brahms, Felix Mendelssohn, and Peter Ilyich Tchaikovsky, all of whom wrote outstanding concertos with memorable solo parts.

Felix Mendelssohn and Fanny Mendelssohn Hensel

Unlike most of the great composers of his generation, **Felix Mendelssohn** (1809–1847) not only achieved artistic success but also lived a life of relative ease and financial security. Born into a wealthy and cultured Jewish family—his father was a banker, and his grandfather Moses Mendelssohn was a distinguished philosopher—he and his brother and two sisters were brought up as Christians. The remarkable musical abilities of Felix and his elder sister, Fanny, were quickly recognized by their mother, Leah, who began teaching the children piano when they were quite young. After the family moved to Berlin in 1812, Felix and Fanny's formal musical training was entrusted to Carl Zelter, an eminent composer and teacher.

The Mendelssohn home was a meeting place for musicians and poets. Leah Mendelssohn organized concerts of chamber music for the enjoyment of their guests. Felix and Fanny's earliest compositions were performed at these gatherings.

By 1821, Felix had composed trios, quartets, sonatas, and operettas. His debut as a concert pianist had been made even earlier—at age 9—and he mastered both violin and viola while still in his teens. The first striking demonstration of Felix's genius as a composer was the overture to Shakespeare's *A Midsummer Night's Dream,* composed in 1826, when he was 17. Three years later, he made his mark as a conductor when he revived J. S. Bach's *St. Matthew Passion.* This performance of the *Passion,* a great triumph for Mendelssohn, was the first since Bach's death almost eighty years earlier and began a wide-scale revival of Bach's music.

Mendelssohn's long-standing appreciation of Bach's music shows up in his several collections of preludes and fugues for piano. The bulk of his piano music, however, consisted of short character pieces in a highly romantic vein. Although he composed many religious works, he is best remembered for two oratorios, *St. Paul* (1836) and *Elijah* (1846). In them, Mendelssohn incorporated elements of Bach's Passion style and Handel's oratorio form. They are generally considered the most successful nineteenth-century works of their kind.

Early in the 1830s, Mendelssohn traveled extensively throughout Europe. He conducted his concert overture *Fingal's Cave (The Hebrides)* in London and met Hector Berlioz in Italy. Returning to Berlin in 1833, Mendelssohn decided to seek a permanent post as a music academy director. He was turned down—due to local politics—but in the same year he accepted the position of town musical director and conductor at Düsseldorf. Two years later, he accepted an offer to become conductor of the famous Gewandhaus Orchestra in Leipzig. During the time he conducted the orchestra, he hired Clara Schumann to play more than twenty concerts with them.

FELIX MENDELSSOHN
(1809–1847)

- Born in Hamburg, Germany; died at age 38 in Leipzig, Germany.

- Prolific composer best known for Violin Concerto in E Minor, incidental music for *A Midsummer Night's Dream,* five symphonies, including no. 3 "Italian" and no. 4 "Scottish," and the oratorio *Elijah.*

- Brother of pianist and composer Fanny Mendelssohn Hensel.

FANNY MENDELSSOHN HENSEL
(1805–1847)

- Born in Hamburg, Germany; died at age 41 in Berlin, Germany.
- Best known for *lieder* (songs) and the choral works in *Gartenlieder*.
- Sister of composer Felix Mendelssohn.

In 1837, Mendelssohn married Cécile Jeanrenaud, the daughter of a French Protestant clergyman. In 1841, they moved to Berlin, where, at the request of Kaiser Friedrich Wilhelm IV, Mendelssohn took charge of the music division of the newly established Academy of Arts. The position did not require close supervision, and he was able to develop his plans for a conservatory at Leipzig. In 1843, the conservatory opened with a distinguished faculty that included both Robert and Clara Schumann. Several years later, Mendelssohn moved his family back to Leipzig.

Though his health began to deteriorate, Mendelssohn continued to immerse himself in his work. The unexpected death of Fanny, to whom he was deeply attached, was a major shock. Falling into a severe depression, he died of a stroke in Leipzig at age 38.

Fanny Mendelssohn Hensel's (1805–1847) musical life was not as public or all-encompassing as was Felix's. Their father, Abraham Mendelssohn, did not want her to perform in public. Felix agreed with their father, although he was supportive of Fanny as a composer. He did not think that her name should appear on published music, so he put some of her songs in a collection of his. This sounds to us as if he was taking advantage of her, but the general feeling of the time was that a woman of her relatively high social and economic class should not write music for sale or perform for the general public.

In 1829, Fanny married Wilhelm Hensel, who was a more liberal-minded court painter. He encouraged her to play the piano, write music, and perform when she could. After her father's death, she was able to publish some of her works. She performed Felix's Piano Concerto no. 1 in 1838, and she continued to compose on a regular basis. Fanny continued the tradition of planning and playing in concerts at the Mendelssohn home. She performed in public occasionally as a pianist and directed and composed music for a local choral group. Most of her compositions are songs, but she also composed solo piano music, chamber works, a cantata, an oratorio, and a collection of choral works. She died in 1847, at age 41, apparently from a stroke.

Mendelssohn's Concerto

One of Felix Mendelssohn's greatest concertos is the Violin Concerto in E Minor (op. 64, 1844). Mendelssohn composed the concerto for his good friend Ferdinand David. The two had met when Mendelssohn was 16 and David 15. Both were child prodigies and were already highly respected performers at that time. Mendelssohn appointed David to be concertmaster of his Gewandhaus Orchestra in 1836. In 1838, Mendelssohn told David that he was planning to compose a concerto for him and that he already had such a clear idea of what he wanted it to sound like that the opening melody "sticks in my head, the beginning of which will not leave me in peace." The concerto was not completed until 1844. The first performance was such a success that the work continued to be popular, receiving many other performances during the rest of Mendelssohn's life, and it remains one of the most popular violin concertos to this day.

The concerto retains the fast-slow-fast movement structure of the classical concerto but has a solo bassoon hold a note between the first and second movements to connect them. Classical concertos, such as the Mozart piano concerto we listened to earlier (see page 128), usually had the orchestra introduce the themes before the soloist played at all. For this concerto, Mendelssohn featured the soloist by having him or her introduce the first theme before it was played by the orchestra. Mendelssohn also wrote the cadenza, as did most romantic composers. The Mendelssohn concerto is scored for solo violin and a fairly small orchestra.

"Hearing the Difference: Vivaldi's 'La Primavera,' first movement, and Mendelssohn's Violin Concerto, first movement," examines two violin concertos from different musical eras.

))) **Featured Listening**  CD 2: Track 19
CONNECT

Violin Concerto in E Minor, op. 64, first movement FELIX MENDELSSOHN

Date: 1844

Genre: Concerto

Tempo: Allegro molto appassionato (fast and quite passionate)

Form: Double-exposition sonata

Instruments: Two flutes, two oboes, two clarinets, two bassoons, two French horns, two trombones, timpani, solo violin, first violins, second violins, violas, cellos, double basses

Meter: Duple

Duration: 11:59

Context: While Mendelssohn was composing this concerto, he often asked his violinist friend Ferdinand David for advice about the violin part. David was a virtuoso player, and Mendelssohn wanted to be certain that the music was playable, challenging, and yet also passionate. David played the solo in the first performance of the concerto.

Timing		What to listen for
Exposition		
0:00	Theme 1 (soloist)	After a brief introduction, the violin soloist plays theme 1 with orchestral accompaniment; orchestral chords.
0:53	Theme 1 (orchestra)	Orchestra plays first theme, then goes into a transition while the soloist plays an extension of the theme with orchestra accompaniment.
1:21	Theme 2	Woodwinds play second theme; violin soloist plays and extends the theme.
3:52		Soloist returns to theme 1, played with brilliant display of virtuoso technique; stressing runs up to very high notes accompanied by pizzicato strings; orchestra plays fortissimo chords.
Development		
5:00		Fragments of both themes are played by orchestra and soloist with dynamic contrasts.
6:27	Cadenza	Soloist plays alone using arpeggios, trills, *quadruple stops* (all four strings played together), and other virtuoso techniques, ending on extremely high notes.

The number **19** appears in a box at the left of the 0:00 row.

Timing		What to listen for
Recapitulation		
8:01	Theme 1	Orchestra plays theme; soloist plays brilliant passage that includes parts of the theme.
8:47	Theme 2	Woodwinds play theme; soloist joins in and extends the theme.
10:04		Fragments of theme 1 return in the orchestra; soloist is accompanied by pizzicato strings; orchestra plays chords; intensity builds.
10:50	Coda	Soloist plays transitional passage alone; tempo gets faster, building intensity to end.

 # Hearing the Difference

VIVALDI'S "LA PRIMAVERA," FIRST MOVEMENT, AND MENDELSSOHN'S VIOLIN CONCERTO, FIRST MOVEMENT

Both of these works are violin concertos (see Featured Listening on page 104 and page 204). Vivaldi's "La Primavera" was composed in the baroque period (in 1725), and Mendelssohn's concerto was composed 119 years later (in 1844) during the romantic period. In comparing them, we are also comparing aspects of style between those two somewhat distant musical eras. Answer the following questions as you listen from one work to the other:

- The instrumentation of these concertos is quite different. They both have solo violins, but what other instruments do you hear in each? Which orchestra is larger? Which includes the distinctive sound of the harpsichord?

- The formal structure of the two concertos is different. Which is in *ritornello* form (introductory theme that keeps repeating) and which is in double-

exposition sonata form (two themes from the exposition repeating near the end)?

- Which concerto does more to feature the violin soloist? In what ways is that soloist featured more than the other concerto's soloist?

- Which concerto is programmatic in that it is composed the way it is to tell the story in a poem? Does the other concerto have any program, or is it absolute music (to be appreciated for the music itself without any story line)?

- Are the tempos at all similar, or do they contrast with each other? Given that we are only hearing the first movements of both concertos, do the tempos fit any multimovement structure that is familiar to us by now? What might we assume the general tempos of the next two movements would be?

Summary

The interest of romantic audiences in virtuosity encouraged composers to write concertos containing intricate solo parts. Most concertos were still composed in three movements, fast-slow-fast, as they had been since the baroque period, and they continued to use the classical tradition of a double-exposition sonata form as the

basic structure of the first movement. Some composers, such as Felix Mendelssohn, featured their soloists by having them introduce the first theme before the orchestra played it. Romantic composers usually wrote their cadenzas instead of allowing performers to improvise them as had been the practice in the classical period.

New People

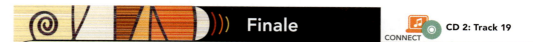

Finale

Listen again to the recording of Violin Concerto in E Minor, op. 64, first movement, by Mendelssohn and compare your impression now with your notes from your First Hearing. Consider the following questions:

- When does the soloist begin to play?

- Does this solo violin part require a virtuoso to play it? Can you identify any particularly difficult things that the player does?

- When is the cadenza played? Is it effective in featuring the soloist?

- What is the form?

- What are the tempo and meter?

- If you were going to describe this music to a friend, what would you say?

Further Listening

Peter Ilyich Tchaikovsky, Piano Concerto no. 1 in B-flat Minor, op. 23. One of Tchaikovsky's most often performed works today, this piano concerto lives up to Tchaikovsky's reputation for composing beautiful melodies. The movements are (1) Allegro non troppo e molto maestoso-Allegro con spirito, (2) Andantino simplice, and (3) Allegro con fuoco.

Antonín Dvořák, Cello Concerto in B Minor, op. 104, B. 191. This is a late work of Dvořák's, composed for his friend, cellist Hanuš Wihan. The movements are (1) Allegro, (2) Adagio, ma non troppo, and (3) Finale: Allegro moderato-Andante-Allegro vivo.

Johannes Brahms, The Double Concerto in A Minor, op. 102. This double concerto for violin, cello, and orchestra was composed for two friends of Brahms, violinist Joseph Joachim and cellist Robert Hausmann. It was the composer's last orchestral composition. The movements are (1) Allegro, (2) Andante, and (3) Vivace non troppo.

Romantic Choral Music

))) First Hearing

CD 2: Track 20
CONNECT

Listen to the recording of *Ein Deutsches Requiem* (*A German Requiem*), op. 45, fourth movement, by Brahms and take notes on what you hear. Even if you are working with other students in a paired or group listening session, keep your own notes. Give some attention to the following:

- What is the mood of this movement? Light and happy? Passionate? Depressed? Stable and reassuring? Does the title of the work indicate anything about the subject of the text?

- How does Brahms use the choir and orchestra? Does the orchestra always accompany the choir, or are the two separate at times and responsive to each other?

- Does the texture of the choral sections stay homophonic (all in the same rhythm), or are some sections polyphonic (voice parts separate and imitating one another)?

- Do you hear any sections that repeat? Do you hear sections that contrast with the beginning melody and mood?

- Can you guess at the meter?

Keep your notes from this First Hearing to compare with your impressions about the piece after you study the information in this chapter.

22

The choral literature of the nineteenth century presents a fascinating array of compositions, ranging from short, modest pieces for unaccompanied chorus to colossal works that use both a large chorus and orchestra. Choral festivals were popular during the romantic period, and virtually every major composer made significant contributions to choral literature and the choral tradition.

The oratorio tradition established in the baroque period by Handel and continued through the classical era by Haydn received the attention of such composers as Franz Liszt (*Legend of St. Elizabeth*), Hector Berlioz (*Childhood of Christ*), and Felix Mendelssohn, whose oratorio *Elijah* became very popular and is still often performed today. In other instances a chorus was incorporated into symphonic works, such as Robert Schumann's *Scenes from Faust,* Franz Liszt's *A Faust Symphony,* and Hector Berlioz's *Romeo and Juliet.*

Also, the great religious texts of the Catholic Church, including the Mass, Requiem, Te Deum, and Stabat Mater, were set for soloists, chorus, and orchestra by a wide variety of composers, such as Anton Bruckner, Franz Schubert, Antonín Dvořák, and Gioacchino Rossini. Verdi's *Requiem,* in memory of the author Alessandro Manzoni, is a large and dramatic setting of the moving requiem text, and the work is still familiar to modern-day concertgoers.

When we listened to Berlioz's *Symphonie fantastique* in Chapter 18, we saw what a large orchestra Berlioz had hoped to use for it. He thought "big" in other compositions, as well. In three great works, *The Damnation of Faust,* the *Requiem (Grande Messe des Morts),* and the *Te Deum (Praise to God),* Berlioz reached the epitome of the colossal romantic choral style. The musical forces involved in these works are huge. The *Requiem* was written for 210 singers, a large orchestra, and four brass bands positioned in various locations around the concert hall to represent the summons to the Last Judgment. The *Te Deum* requires two choruses of 100 singers each, 6 children's voices, and an orchestra of 150 players.

Johannes Brahms

Johannes Brahms (1833–1897) composed some of the most enduring choral music of the romantic period. He wrote in diverse styles for a wide variety of choral combinations. Smaller works include a cappella choruses for various voice combinations, motets, canons, part songs, and psalm settings, many employing various types of instrumental accompaniment. One of the most popular of these works is the "Liebeslieder Walzer" ("Lovesong Waltzes") for **piano, four hands** (two players on one piano) and either a vocal quartet or a four-part chorus. Brahms composed several large works for chorus and orchestra, some with soloists. Among these are the cantata "Rinaldo," "Schicksalslied" ("Song of Destiny"), for chorus and orchestra, and "Triumphlied" ("Song of Triumph"). The most important of his large-scale choral compositions was one of his early works, *Ein Deutsches Requiem (A German Requiem).* It was composed over a period of eleven years and was finished in 1868, when Brahms was 35. It not only preceded much of his other choral writing but was written a full eight years before his first symphony.

Brahms was born and raised in Hamburg, Germany. He received his earliest musical training from his father, a double-bass player. The family was not wealthy, and at an early age Brahms had to contribute to the family income by playing the piano in local taverns. At age 20, he met the famed Hungarian violinist Eduard Reményi and toured Germany as Reményi's accompanist. His first attempts at composition were heard by Joseph Joachim, the foremost violin virtuoso of the time, on one of his tours. Through Joachim, Brahms was introduced to Franz Liszt and Robert Schumann, who were greatly impressed by the young composer. Schumann, always eager to do what he could to advance the career of young, promising composers, wrote a laudatory article heralding Brahms as the coming genius of German music.

In his thirties, Brahms took several posts in various German towns, conducting and organizing choral groups and music societies. He spent much of his time in Vienna, finally settling there in 1868. His reputation as a composer grew to international proportions, and Cambridge University offered him the honorary degree of doctor of music. He declined, being reluctant to make a long journey that would require him to cross the English Channel, but in 1880 he accepted a similar honor from the University of Breslau, acknowledging it by writing the celebrated "Academic Festival Overture," which is based in large part on popular German student drinking songs.

Brahms was not a controversial figure, as so many of his contemporaries were, and he had no enemies. Yet, in his dealings with others, his characteristic charm could give way to the most acerbic sarcasm. To one musician who was trying to maneuver Brahms into paying him a compliment, he said, "Yes, you have talent, but very little." But when the daughter of Johann Strauss (the Waltz King of Vienna) presented him with her fan so that he might autograph it, he wrote on it the first few measures of Strauss's "Blue Danube Waltz" and signed it, "Not, alas, by Johannes Brahms."

JOHANNES BRAHMS
(1833–1897)

- Born in Hamburg, Germany; died at age 63 in Vienna, Austria.

- Prolific composer best known for *Ein Deutsches Requiem (A German Requiem),* op. 45, many other choral and solo vocal works, four symphonies, and the Double Concerto, op. 102, for violin and cello with orchestra.

Brahms remained a bachelor all his life, living simply and composing methodically. He enjoyed the respect and admiration of his peers and inspired the noted conductor Hans von Bülow to coin the famous phrase "the Three B's of Music": Bach, Beethoven, and Brahms. After Brahms's death his fame grew, as many societies were founded to publish and perform his works. In the concert repertoire, Brahms's symphonies occupy a place second only to that of his acknowledged master, Beethoven. Brahms died of cancer a month before he would have turned 64.

Brahms's *Requiem*

Unlike the requiems of Mozart, Berlioz, Verdi, and later Fauré, Brahms's setting does not employ the traditional Latin text, which is actually a Mass for the dead. Rather, it is a setting of nonliturgical (not part of Catholic Mass) German texts that Brahms selected from the Lutheran Bible. A comparison of the Brahms text with the Roman Catholic liturgy shows a marked difference in intention and feeling: The Latin text prays for the soul of the dead, whereas Brahms's text is designed to console the living. The opening words of the two texts confirm this:

Roman Catholic text	**Brahms text**
Requiem aeternam dona eis Domine	Selig sind, die da Leid tragen, denn sie sollen getröstet werden
(Give them eternal rest, O Lord)	(Blessed are they that mourn, for they shall be comforted)

Brahms's entire composition conveys this pervasive feeling of consolation in both the text and the music.

Brahms's *Requiem* consists of seven movements and is scored for soprano and baritone soloists, chorus, and orchestra. The chorus and orchestra participate in all seven movements, although the orchestration varies somewhat from movement to movement. By comparison, the role of the soloists is minimal, with the baritone appearing in the third and sixth movements and the soprano appearing only in the fifth. Brahms builds a sense of overall unity into the piece, including themes from the first movement in the last movement.

The first movement begins with "Blessed are they that mourn, for they shall be comforted" (Matthew 5:4), and the seventh and final movement ends with "Blessed are the dead which die in the Lord from henceforth; yea, saith the Spirit, that they may rest from their labors; and their works do follow them" (Revelation 14:13). Perhaps more than any other, this work demonstrates Brahms's unique ability to combine classical design—its carefully balanced and contrasting elements—with the expressive qualities of the romantic spirit.

))) **Featured Listening**    **CD 2: Track 20**
CONNECT

Ein Deutsches Requiem (A German Requiem), op. 45, fourth movement, **"How Lovely Is Thy Dwelling Place"** JOHANNES BRAHMS

Date: 1868

Genre: Lutheran requiem

Tempo: Mässig bewegt (somewhat agitated)

Form: Rondo-like (ABA'CA')

(continued)

Voices and Instruments: SATB choir and orchestra: one piccolo, two flutes, two oboes, two clarinets, two bassoons, one contrabassoon, four French horns, two trumpets, three trombones, one tuba, timpani, first violins, second violins, violas, and cellos

Language: German

Meter: Triple

Duration: 5:47

Context: The fourth of seven movements, this gentle piece expresses the psalmist's longing to be in the presence of God. The text was taken from Psalm 84.

	Timing	German text	English translation	Musical events
20	0:00	Wie lieblich sind deine Wohnungen, Herr Zebaoth! deine Wohnungen, Herr Zebaoth!	How lovely is thy dwelling place, O Lord of Hosts! thy dwelling place, O Lord of Hosts!	A section: a soft, peaceful orchestral introduction is answered by the chorus
		Wie lieblich sind deine Wohnungen, Herr Zebaoth! Wie lieblich sind deine Wohnungen, Herr Zebaoth!	How lovely is thy dwelling place, O Lord of Hosts! How lovely is thy dwelling place, O Lord of Hosts!	Homophonic texture
	1:26	Meine Seele verlanget und sehnet sich nach den Vorhöfen des Herrn. Mein Leib und Seele freuen sich in dem lebendigen Gott. Mein Leib und Seele freuen sich in dem lebendigen Gott.	My soul longs and thirsts for the courts of the Lord. My body and soul rejoice in the living God. My body and soul rejoice in the living God.	B section: some polyphonic texture with imitation in choral part
	2:37	Wie lieblich sind deine Wohnungen, Herr Zebaoth! deine Wohnungen, Herr Zebaoth! Wohl denen, Wohl denen, die in deinem Hause Wohnen,	How lovely is thy dwelling place, O Lord of Hosts! thy dwelling place, O Lord of Hosts! Blessed are those, Blessed are those, who dwell in thy house,	A' section: varied version of the beginning, with added new text
	3:50	die loben dich immerdar, Immerdar.	who praise Thee evermore, Evermore.	C section: a martial sound in the orchestra; imitation in the choir
	4:43	Wie lieblich, Wie lieblich sind deine Wohnungen!	How lovely, How lovely is thy dwelling place!	A' section: beginning peacefulness returns

Summary

The lush sound of a large chorus was well suited to the romantic style, and nearly every composer of the period wrote choral music in some form. Hector Berlioz frequently utilized a large chorus combined with an enormous orchestra in his works. Oratorios and settings of Catholic liturgical texts were written by such composers as Mendelssohn, Liszt, Berlioz, Schubert, Bruckner, and Verdi. Choruses also were used in programmatic symphonic works.

Some of the most enduring choral music of the romantic era was written by Johannes Brahms. The greatness of his most significant work, *Ein Deutsches Requiem (A German Requiem),* rests on its masterful and eloquent marriage of the music and texts. In contrast with the traditional Catholic funeral Mass, Brahms's *Requiem* uses texts from the Old and New Testaments that give a message of comfort and consolation to the bereaved mourners.

New People and Concepts

Johannes Brahms, 208

piano, four hands, 208

Finale

CD 2: Track 20
CONNECT

Listen again to the recording of *Ein Deutsches Requiem (A German Requiem),* op. 45, fourth movement, by Brahms and compare your impression now with your notes from your First Hearing. Consider the following questions:

- What is the text of this movement about? Does the music fit that mood?
- Describe how the choir and orchestra work together and in response to each other.
- What textures are used for the choral parts at the beginning and ending? What textures do you hear in other sections?
- What sections repeat, and when does that happen? What is the name of the form?
- What is the meter?
- If you were going to describe this music to a friend, what would you say?

Further Listening

Johannes Brahms, *Ein Deutsches Requiem (A German Requiem),* op. 45. In this chapter we discussed only the fourth of seven movements of this magnificent work for soloists, chorus, and orchestra. Just before the quiet consolation of the seventh movement is the dramatic sixth movement in three sections that concludes with an extended fugue for chorus and orchestra. The entire requiem lasts over an hour, although the exact time varies with the tempos taken by the conductor.

Felix Mendelssohn, *Elijah.* This oratorio is based on the biblical prophet Elijah who was written about in Kings 1 and 2 in the Old Testament of the Bible, called "Kings"

in the *Torah.* Mendelssohn enjoyed reviving works by baroque composers such as J. S. Bach and G. F. Handel, and this oratorio was composed with their works in mind, but in a romantic style.

Giuseppe Verdi, *Requiem.* Unlike the Brahms Requiem, this is a setting of the Roman Catholic Requiem Mass. For that reason, it includes the standard Latin texts used for requiems in the Roman Catholic religion. The work is performed by four solo voices—soprano, alto, tenor, and bass—as well as a double chorus and a large orchestra.

The Late Romantic Symphonies

How can one express the indefinable sensations that one experiences while writing an instrumental composition that has no definite subject? It is a purely lyrical process. It is a musical confession of the soul, which unburdens itself through sounds, just as a lyric poet expresses himself through poetry. . . . As the poet Heine said, "Where words leave off, music begins."

—COMPOSER PETER ILYICH TCHAIKOVSKY [1840–1893]

))) First Hearing

CONNECT CD 2: Tracks 21–31

Listen to the recording of *From the New World*, Symphony no. 9 in E Minor, fourth movement, by Dvořák and take notes on what you hear. Even if you are working with other students in a paired or group listening session, keep your own notes. Give some attention to the following:

● This symphony is titled *From the New World* and, indeed, Dvořák was living in New York City when he composed it. Do you hear any themes that sound like they might have been influenced by American music, or does it sound like music from the Czech Republic?

● How would you describe the beginning theme? What instruments play it first?

● How many other themes do you hear near the beginning, and how would you describe them?

● Do the themes you hear at the beginning repeat near the end? What does that tell you about the form?

● Can you guess at the tempo and the meter?

Keep your notes from this First Hearing to compare with your impressions about the piece after you study the information in this chapter.

23

Among romantic composers, attitudes toward the classical forms that had been developed by Haydn and Mozart and expanded by Beethoven varied considerably. As we have seen in earlier chapters, some of the more radical composers abandoned these traditions altogether, turning instead to other sources of inspiration and organization. For example, Berlioz's *Symphonie fantastique,* with five movements all organized around the tale of a drugged and dreaming lovesick man, broke most classical symphonic traditions. Some romantic composers, however, continued to follow more classically oriented forms, usually also expanding the forms in some ways. In doing so, they utilized elements from both the classical and the romantic eras.

The Romantic Symphony

The romantic symphony grew in the shadow of Beethoven's symphonic writing. Virtually all the early romantic composers were affected by Beethoven's music, some by his use of the orchestra, others by the ways he expanded the forms, lengthening developments and adding development sections to codas.

The symphonies of Franz Schubert, whose song "The Erlkönig" we heard earlier, displayed a romantic gift for lyric melody but were written in the traditional classical forms. He composed nine symphonies in all. His famous Symphony no. 8 was written in 1822, when the composer was 25 years old, but he never chose to extend it beyond the original two movements. Nicknamed "The Unfinished," the work was not performed until 1865, forty-three years after Schubert's death. Today it is better known than any of his other symphonies.

If Schubert was the outstanding symphonist of the beginning of the romantic period, Johannes Brahms deserves that honor for the latter part of the century. Brahms occupies a unique place in the history of the romantic era. Although he was much admired by his contemporaries, he disagreed with the popular romantic notion—championed by more radical composers such as Berlioz and Wagner—that literature, the visual arts, and philosophy should be united with music. In a period of experimentation and change, he looked back to Beethoven and the classical era, finding in traditional forms new and worthwhile ideas to express. His four symphonies rank with Beethoven's as masterworks of the symphonic repertoire. A Listening Guide to the fourth movement of Brahms's Fourth Symphony follows.

CD 5: Track 12

Symphony no. 4 in E minor, fourth movement JOHANNES BRAHMS

Date: 1885

Genre: Symphony

Tempo: Allegro energico e passionato (fast, energetic, and passionate)

Form: ABA'-Coda based on a *chaconne* (a series of variations on a slow-moving chord progression as a theme)

Instruments: Two flutes, two oboes, two clarinets, two bassoons, one contrabassoon, four French horns, two trumpets, three trombones, first violins, second violins, violas, cellos, double basses, and timpani

Meter: Triple

Duration: 10:35

Context: The type of variation form Brahms used for this movement was popular during the baroque period, and, in fact, Brahms took the theme from the continuo line in the last movement of J. S. Bach's Cantata no. 150, *Nach dir, Herr, verlanget mich (To Thee, Lord, I Lift my Soul).*

(continued)

Timing	What to listen for

A Section

	Timing	What to listen for
12	0:00	Chaconne theme (eight measures long), one sustained chord in each measure
	0:16	Variation 1—timpani rolls on first beats followed by strings accenting on second beats
	0:30	Variation 2—gentle melody in woodwinds
	0:47	Variation 3—staccato accents on all three beats in each measure
	1:01	Variation 4—sustained chaconne chords in low strings, new melody and rhythms in violins
	1:18	Variation 5—speed of new melody builds higher
	1:33	Variation 6—intensity builds
	1:48	Variation 7—crisp, dotted rhythms (short-long, short-long, short-long) alternate between high and low strings
	2:05	Variation 8—faster motion, then smoother finish
	2:20	Variation 9—suddenly loud and fast rhythms, ends with descending scale
	2:36	Variation 10—long-held chords alternate between strings and woodwinds
	2:54	Variation 11—new melody in violins, then flute begins descending melody that continues in next variation

B Section

Timing	What to listen for
3:14	Variation 12—tempo slower, each measure twice as long as before, flute solo with strings
3:58	Variation 13—clarinet and oboe melodies alternate with strings
4:37	Variation 14—chords in low brass with string accompaniment
5:21	Variation 15—brass and strings continue, descending melody flute brings variation to close, short pause

A' Section

Timing	What to listen for
6:03	Variation 16—opening chaconne theme accompanied by violins
6:17	Variation 17—strings continue, woodwinds accent beats two and three of each measure
6:28	Variation 18—brass join woodwinds
6:40	Variation 19—loud, crisp accents on half beats (space between the main three beats in each measure)
6:53	Variation 20—faster rhythms
7:06	Variation 21—strings and brass alternate
7:19	Variation 22—soft syncopated rhythms
7:31	Variation 23—loud theme played by French horns
7:44	Variation 24—timpani rolls on first beats, string accents on second beats of each measure
7:58	Variation 25—gentle melody from variation 2 repeats
8:12	Variation 26—gentle accents on all three beats of each measure, like variation 3
8:26	Variation 27—winds hold chords, strings active above
8:40	Variation 28—strings and woodwinds increase activity
8:54	Variation 29—strings play pizzicato (plucked notes) between beats
9:08	Variation 30—loud accents on and between beats, extension of four extra measures

Coda

Timing	What to listen for
9:29	Chaconne theme, increasing intensity, pauses, build to concluding chords

Antonín Dvořák

Another late romantic composer, **Antonín Dvořák** ("Dvor-zhak," 1841–1904) composed nine symphonies based on classical forms. Like Bedřich Smetana, whose symphonic poem "The Moldau" we heard earlier, Dvořák was Bohemian. He was born in a small village near Prague and moved to that city at age 16 to study music of the German classical tradition. The Prague public first became aware of Dvořák with the performance of his patriotic choral work *Hymnus* in 1873. This success prompted a grant from the Austrian Ministry of Fine Arts, which supplied the composer with a small income. However, it was the patronage of Brahms, whom he met a year later, that thrust Dvořák into musical prominence. In 1877, Brahms persuaded a German music publisher to print the composer's *Moravian Duets* and *Slavonic Dances*. This allowed Dvořák to spend the 1880s touring Europe conducting his own works. He eventually obtained the position of professor of composition at the Prague Conservatory.

Dvořák's career ultimately brought him to America, where he served from 1892 to 1895 as artistic director of the National Conservatory of Music in New York. One of his students at the conservatory was Henry T. Burleigh, an African American composer and baritone who introduced him to African American spirituals. Dvořák was also introduced to the melodies of American Natives. In these traditions, he believed, lay the basis of a new musical school capable of expressing the unique spirit of the American people. His own nationalistic fervor impelled him to urge his American students toward the creation of a national style that would draw on these musical resources.

Homesick for his native country, Dvořák spent only three years in the United States. In 1901, he was appointed to the directorship of the Prague Conservatory. His death in 1904 at age 62 was mourned throughout his beloved Bohemia.

Dvořák's versatility is reflected in his legacy of concertos for violin, cello, and piano; his fourteen string quartets; his four great oratorios; his five symphonic poems; his cantata; his four piano trios and two quintets; and his eleven operas and nine symphonies, among a multitude of other works.

As mentioned above, Dvořák was very much interested in the music of African Americans and Native Americans. Indeed, these elements helped shape his "American style" and gave his Symphony no. 9, titled *From the New World,* much of its particular flavor. In a letter written while he was composing the symphony, he declared, "I should never have written the symphony like I have, if I hadn't seen America." However, the influence of American music was general rather than specific. Some of the melodies were not quoted from but suggested by Native or African American sources. The influences of Czech and American music are also evident in the folklike character and syncopated rhythms of portions of the work.

Although we did not listen to the first three movements of Dvořák's symphony, you might notice the many references to themes from these movements in the Listening Guide to the fourth movement. This technique of unifying long musical works with recurring themes is cyclical in much the same way in which Beethoven's rhythmic motive returns in each movement of his Fifth Symphony. Many romantic composers used this technique in their longer works. The idea is much like the thematic transformation we discussed in Berlioz's *Symphonie fantastique* in which the idée fixe kept returning in each movement. The difference is that Berlioz changed, or transformed, the theme for each of its returns, whereas Dvořák quoted the old themes much the way they had been played before.

ANTONÍN DVOŘÁK
(1841–1904)

- Born in Nelahozeves, Bohemia; died at age 62 in Prague, Bohemia (now the Czech Republic).

- Prolific composer, best known for his Symphony no. 9, *From the New World,* concertos for violin and cello, *Slavonic Dances* for orchestra, and many string quartets and other chamber music.

Featured Listening

CONNECT   CD 2: Tracks 21–31

From the New World, Symphony no. 9 in E Minor, fourth movement   ANTONÍN DVOŘÁK

Date: 1893

Genre: Symphony

Tempo: Allegro con fuoco (fast, with fire)

Form: Sonata

Instruments: One piccolo, two flutes, two oboes, two clarinets, two bassoons, four French horns, two trumpets, three trombones, timpani, first violins, second violins, violas, cellos, double basses

Meter: Quadruple

Duration: 10:27

Context: This symphony was composed while Dvořák was living in the United States and working as director of the National Conservatory of Music in New York.

	Timing		What to listen for
	Exposition		
21	0:00	Introduction	Two-note motive stated, expanded with faster rhythms, timpani roll
22	0:00	Theme 1	Emphatic, marchlike theme in brass, powerful chords from orchestra, repeated
	0:28		Strings state contrasting second phrase of theme.
	0:42		First phrase returns in orchestra, brass chords
	0:59	Bridge	Jaunty **triplet** (three notes per beat) theme in violins, woodwinds, violins; energy dissipates, soft cymbal crash
23	0:00	Theme 2	Clarinet sings tender melody, comments from cellos with triplet motive from bridge; violins take over melody; drum roll leads to:
24	0:00	Theme 3	Czech village dance theme, first phrase closes with three-note motive moving down scale; repeated
	0:13		Second phrase closes with same three-note motive descending
	Development		
25	0:00		Three-note motive continues in low strings, vigorous new countermelody in violins; three-note motive shifts to winds, returns to low strings with countermelody; countermelody winds down to pianissimo
	0:26		Three-note motive in pizzicato strings, then woodwinds with high trills; horns suddenly intone opening theme, forte
	0:37		Three-note motive softly in woodwinds; opening motive forte in horns
	1:05		Opening motive in faster notes alternates with triplet motive from bridge.
	1:23		Flutes softly sing "Goin' Home" (an African American spiritual-like theme from second movement); strings alternate in fragment from third movement.
26	0:00		Crescendo with faster rhythm; brass blares out "Goin' Home" fragment; these two ideas then repeated
	0:22		Opening motive developed in simultaneous fast and slow rhythms, crescendo into forte statement of fragment from first movement; development of opening motive takes over with powerful chords, crescendo

	Timing		What to listen for
		Recapitulation	
27	0:00	Theme 1	Trombones proclaim marchlike theme; rhythmic motive developed as energy subsides
28	0:00	Theme 2	Tender melody in strings, answered by woodwinds with triplet melody; intensity grows, then fades
29	0:00	Theme 3	Village dance theme now in slower, reflective version
	0:16		Second phrase, closes into horn call softly recalling theme from first movement; three-note motive excitedly developed as transition
		Coda	
30	0:00	Second development	Brass proclaims opening marchlike theme, strings respond with triplet theme from bridge
	0:16		Trombones triumphantly blast out theme from first movement; orchestra continues to develop opening motive with powerful chords; timpani figure and rushing strings lead to climactic chord; energy dissipates
	0:55		Clarinet in "Goin' Home" theme of second movement set against fragment from third movement
31	0:00	Second recapitulation and coda	Horn softly intones opening marchlike theme; orchestra restates theme forte.
	0:31		Themes of first and fourth movements boldly stated simultaneously
	0:42		Triumphant cadence closes movement; long-held chord dies away.

Other Late Romantics

Anton Bruckner (1824–1896), an Austrian composer and organist, joined Brahms in the effort to use classical forms within an expanded framework. Bruckner was a simple, religious man, deeply involved with Catholic beliefs. His three Masses are of sufficient caliber to rank Bruckner as the most important church composer of the late nineteenth century.

Bruckner's nine symphonies show his kinship to classical tradition in their formal design, but their exceptional length and weighty orchestration mark them as romantic works. The German romantic opera composer Richard Wagner was one of Bruckner's idols. Bruckner influenced later composers in Vienna, particularly Mahler and Schoenberg.

The Austrian **Gustav Mahler** (1860–1911) was a conductor, as well as a symphonic composer. His nine completed symphonies are immense and complex and encompass a vast emotional range. Although the symphonies follow the classical outline and have separate movements, their style incorporates many elements from vocal music, including opera. His symphonies contain long, lyrical melodies; four of them have parts for voices, as well as instruments. Mahler's works span the spectrum of emotions, from ecstasy to despair. He tried to make each symphony a complete world in itself, with all types of themes and techniques. These large-scale works are unified by the use of recurring themes and motives.

The world Mahler created for his first symphony was one that charted experiences of the human soul. It begins with two movements that express springtime, full of flowers and joyous dancing. The mood changes in the third movement, which begins

GUSTAV MAHLER
(1860–1911)

- Born in Kalište, Bohemia (now the Czech Republic); died at age 50 in Vienna, Austria.

- Best known for nine symphonies, the eighth of which is called "Symphony of a Thousand" because of its extremely large chorus and orchestra, and two song cycles for voices and orchestra: "Kindertotenlieder" (Songs on the Death of Children) and "Das Lied von der Erde" (The Song of the Earth).

with a mock funeral march that was inspired by an engraving titled *The Huntsman's Funeral Procession*. The engraving was a popular children's image in which forest animals cry as they carry the casket of a hunter to his grave. The third movement also uses the melody of the children's song "Frère Jacques," which Germans and Austrians called "Brüder Martin" ("Brother Martin"), as a primary theme. Mahler varied the melody slightly and set it in a minor mode, changing it from what was originally a cheerful song into a lament. A dancelike melody is played in the first contrasting section, followed by another section that introduces a slightly faster and lighter but lonely sounding melody. The funeral march and "Frère Jacques" melody return in the final section. The symphony's last movement is vigorous, dramatic, and then reflective as a deeply wounded soul moves toward paradise. We will listen to the third movement.

Listening Guide

CONNECT   **CD 5: Tracks 13–16**

Symphony no. 1 in D Major, third movement GUSTAV MAHLER

Date: 1888

Genre: Symphony

Tempo: Solemn, measured, not hurried

Form: Sectional with a return of the first theme near the end, giving the movement a feeling of balance

Instruments: Four flutes, four oboes, four clarinets, four bassoons, seven French horns, five trumpets, four trombones, one tuba, percussion, first violins, second violins, violas, cellos, double basses, and harp

Meter: Quadruple

Duration: 10:19

Context: Listen carefully to the way each melody enters imitating the earlier one at the beginning, and then notice the way the oboe enters, playing a contrasting melody. The timpani keeps a somber mood through it all, giving the movement the mood of a funeral march.

	Timing		What to listen for
13	0:00	Section 1	Timpani establish a steady beat with two alternating notes, suggesting a funeral march
	0:07		Minor version of "Frère Jacques" is played as a round; double bass (solo) begins.
	0:28		Bassoon enters with round melody.
	0:48		Tuba enters with round melody.
	1:02		Oboe adds a contrasting melody above the round and drumbeat (volume somewhat louder).
	1:16		Flute enters with round melody.
	1:35		Oboe repeats contrasting melody (gradual decrease of volume).
	2:02		Round concludes; long-held chord (*piano*) leads into next section.
14	0:00	Section 2	A dancelike melody is played by soft oboes joined by trumpets accompanied by pizzicato strings; high clarinets, bass drum, and cymbals are added, playing slightly faster and louder.
	0:50		The dancelike melody is repeated by strings and woodwinds with a contrasting melody by trumpets.
	1:15		A varied version of the dancelike melody returns a bit slower; the funeral march beat continues and then finishes with the end of the "Frère Jacques" melody (*diminuendo*) and then sustained notes.
15	0:00	Section 3	A slightly faster and lighter, but somewhat lonely sounding melody is played by muted strings, then joined by flute, two violins, clarinet and horns, and finally oboe; that melody gets slower and softer.
	1:40		Flutes play a slower concluding melody.
16	0:00	Section 4	Faster timpani beat and "Frère Jacques" march returns and are joined by contrasting melody from section 1 played by high clarinet and then taken over by flute and strings.
	0:34		Trumpets enter march.
	0:58		Dancelike melody from section 2 is played by clarinets, cymbals, and drums.
	1:18		Clarinets play suddenly faster and louder, then the tempo retards with descending fragments of melody bringing a sense of quiet conclusion.
	2:36		Low bassoon plays the contrasting melody from section 1, decrescendo, gong

Mahler composed eight other symphonies and had not yet finished a tenth when he died at age 50. He is also well remembered for his songs and song cycles; the "Kindertotenlieder" ("Songs on the Death of Children"), composed in 1902, and "Das Lied von der Erde" ("The Song of the Earth") from 1908 are particularly outstanding. Themes from his songs are often echoed in his symphonic works, including the one we just listened to. Mahler's first symphony used melodies from "Lieder eines fahrenden Gesellen" ("Songs of a Wayfarer"), composed in 1884, in both the first and third movements.

Summary

Although many composers of the romantic era broke away from classical forms and traditions to base their works on stories or other extramusical ideas, others stayed closer to the classical traditions established by Haydn, Mozart, and Beethoven. Of the various types of works composed during the romantic period, symphonies tended to be the most traditional. Composers who adhered the most closely to traditional forms include Franz Schubert, Johannes Brahms, Antonín Dvořák, Anton Bruckner, and Gustav Mahler.

Using Dvořák's Symphony no. 9 (*From the New World*) as an example, we saw that the fourth movement was composed in a fairly standard structuring of sonata form, except that Dvořák had three main themes when two were more common in the classical period. He also extended the coda to include a second development section followed by a second recapitulation and coda. As we have heard before in Beethoven's Fifth Symphony and in Berlioz's *Symphonie fantastique,* Dvořák unified the entire symphony by having themes from earlier movements return in the fourth movement.

The formal structure of the third movement of Mahler's first symphony, with its marchlike beginning and ending sections and two lighter contrasting sections between them, is based on the classical forms of the minuet and trio and the scherzo and trio. Both forms, commonly used for third movements of classical symphonies, were structured ABA, with the minuet or scherzo as the A sections, and the trio as the B. If you see Mahler's march sections as A and the contrasting sections as B and C trios, then Mahler's third movement is an expansion of the classical form from ABA to ABCA. Of course, minuets and scherzos are in triple meter and the march is in quadruple, but the structure is still an expansion of the classical one. Many romantic composers were similarly influenced by classical traditions but felt the need to expand them.

New People and Concepts

Anton Bruckner, 217

Antonín Dvořák, 215

Gustav Mahler, 217

triplet, 216

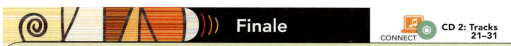

Finale CD 2: Tracks 21–31

Listen again to the recording of *From the New World,* Symphony no. 9 in E Minor, fourth movement, by Dvořák and compare your impression now with your notes from your First Hearing. Consider the following questions:

- What North American influences can you identify in this movement?
- Describe the very beginning theme. What instruments play it first?
- Describe the next two themes.
- What is the form?
- What is the tempo?
- What is the meter?
- If you were going to describe this music to a friend, what would you say?

Further Listening

Johannes Brahms, Symphony no. 4. The movements of this last symphony by Brahms are (1) Allegro non troppo, (2) Andante moderato, (3) Allegro giocoso, and (4) Allegro energico e passionato.

Antonín Dvořák, Symphony no. 9, "From the New World." The movements are (1) Adagio—Allegro molto, (2) Largo, (3) Scherzo: Molto vivace—Poco sostenuto, and (4) Allegro con fuoco.

Gustav Mahler, Symphony no. 1. The movements are (1) *Langsam, schleppend* (slowly, dragging), (2) *Kräftig bewegt, doch nicht zu schnell* (moving strongly, but not too quickly), (3) *Feierlich und gemessen, ohne zu schleppen* (solemn and measured, without dragging), and (4) *Stürmisch bewegt* (stormily agitated).

Nothing primes inspiration more than necessity, whether it be the presence of a copyist waiting for your work, or the prodding of an impresario tearing his hair. In my time, all the impresarios of Italy were bald at 30.

—COMPOSER GIOACCHINO ROSSINI
[1792–1868]

Romantic Opera in France and Italy

  **))) First Hearing**

 CONNECT ○ CD 2: Track 32

Listen to the recording of "O terra, addio" ("Oh Earth, Goodbye") from *Aida*, by Verdi, and make notes about what you hear. Even if you are working with other students in a paired or group listening session, keep your own notes. Give some attention to the following:

● What is the general mood of this music? What might the title tell you about the subject? How does the mood change from the beginning to the end?

● There are three soloists and a chorus in this section of the opera. What solo voice types do you hear—soprano, mezzo soprano, alto, tenor, baritone, bass? When does the chorus come in? Does it sound like the last solo singer is the same person who sang first?

● In this example, does the orchestra's role sound more important than the voices, or is it mere support for the voices?

● Does this sound to you like the introduction to the opera, a point somewhere in the middle, or the end? What is it about the mood that supports your answer?

Keep your notes from this First Hearing to compare with your impressions about the piece after you study the information in this chapter.

24

French Opera

Opera was one of the most important musical genres of the romantic period. During the first half of the era, Paris was the operatic capital of Europe. Beginning about 1820, with the rise of a large and influential middle class, a new type of opera developed. Called *grand opera,* it concentrated on the spectacular elements of the production: crowd scenes, ballets, choruses, and elaborate scenery. The integrity of the drama and the music was often sacrificed for these special effects. Giacomo Meyerbeer (1791–1864), a German composer who had studied and worked extensively in Italy before going to France, introduced grand opera to Paris with operas such as *Les Huguenots* (1836) and *Le Prophète* (1849). One of the longest grand operas of the early romantic period was *Guillaume Tell (William Tell,* 1829) by an Italian, Gioacchino Rossini. The overture to *William Tell,* which includes the famous "Lone Ranger" theme, remains popular today.

Although grand opera received the lion's share of Parisian attention, the less pretentious *opéra comique* (comic opera) continued to be popular. The distinguishing feature of *opéra comique* was its use of spoken dialogue rather than sung recitative. Both the music and the plot tended to be simpler than in grand opera. Despite the word *comic,* many operas in this form had serious plots. Georges Bizet's *Carmen,* for example, has some light and entertaining moments, but the main character ends up being stabbed to death by her former lover.

Later in the nineteenth century, a new form developed as a compromise between the overwhelming spectacle of grand opera and the lightness of *opéra comique.* Called *lyric opera,* it evolved from the more serious type of *opéra comique.* Using plots taken from romantic drama or fantasy, these works relied primarily on the beauty of their melodies. One of the finest lyric operas of the period, Charles Gounod's *Faust* (1859), was first performed with spoken dialogue, but Gounod decided to replace the dialogue with recitative, moving the opera into the lyric category for performances in 1860 and after. The opera was based on the first part of Goethe's famous play, *Faust,* in which the lead character sells his soul to the devil in return for youth and romance. As one might assume, the romance ends with tragedy and the deaths of Faust, his infant son, and his lover Marguerite, although Marguerite manages to avoid hell by calling for divine mercy and then ascending to heaven.

Toward the latter part of the century, a new literary movement, *naturalism,* developed in France. Naturalist writers rebelled against the romantic tendency toward escapism and artificially poetic language. They sought to depict life as it was, objectively and truthfully. Often they portrayed characters from the lower classes whose lives were controlled by their passions.

Bizet (1838–1875) introduced naturalism to opera in his *opéra comique* masterpiece *Carmen* (1875). Whereas grand operas often portrayed historical and mythological figures, with the performers using stylized gestures to express their feelings, Bizet's main character was a gypsy girl whose fiery temper and passionate nature were dramatized realistically. The language she used was crass and realistic for her character type. Bizet's brilliant and memorable melodies and colorful Spanish rhythms effectively complemented the characterization and dramatic action.

Italian Opera

By the nineteenth century, opera was virtually the only important musical form being cultivated in Italy. The classical distinctions between *opera seria* and *opera buffa* were still maintained, although both were influenced by French grand opera, and the orchestra began to play a more important and colorful role.

One of the most outstanding Italian opera composers of the early part of the nineteenth century was Gioacchino Rossini (1792–1868). His sense of melody and effective staging made him an instant success. *Opera buffa* seemed to be a natural outlet for his talents, and *Il Barbiere di Siviglia (The Barber of Seville,* 1816) ranks with Mozart's *The Marriage of Figaro* (1786) as a supreme example of Italian comic opera. The two operas are based on plays by Beaumarchais and include many of the same characters. Rossini's retelling of the Cinderella fairy tale in *La Cenerentola* (1817) further strengthened his popularity and success as a composer of comic operas.

In his operas and oratorios, Rossini sought to cultivate the aria to its highest possible level. Its function was to delight audiences with melodious and spontaneous music. This **bel canto** style, emphasizing beauty and purity of tone and an agile vocal technique, was also exemplified in the work of two of Rossini's contemporaries. Gaetano Donizetti (1797–1848) composed some seventy operas, including *The Elixir* *of Love* (1832), *Lucia di Lammermoor* (1835), *The Daughter of the Regiment* (1840), and *Don Pasquale* (1843). Vincenzo Bellini's (1801–1835) lyric and expressive style is particularly evident in *Norma* (1831). All of the operas just mentioned are often performed today.

Giuseppe Verdi

No composer is better represented in the repertoire of today's opera companies than **Giuseppe Verdi** ("Vair-dee," 1813–1901). Verdi was born into a poor family in a little hamlet near Busseto, Italy. He began his musical training as the apprentice of the local church organist. His hard work and talent were rewarded with a stipend contributed by his town to enable the continuation of his studies at the Milan Conservatory. He was subsequently turned down by the examiners; but, through the financial aid of a friend, he continued his studies by means of private lessons.

Verdi's first opera, *Oberto* (1839), written when he was 26, was an instant success. To this musical triumph he added another with the presentation of his third opera, *Nabucco,* in 1842, based on a plot taken from the Old Testament of the Bible, Daniel 4:29–33. It was this work that brought him not only musical recognition but national fame. The story dealt with the plight of the Jews in Babylon, but the parallel with the Milanese crusade for freedom from Austrian rule was so striking that Verdi was exalted as a patriot and champion of the Italian cause. His name soon became linked with the cry for independence, and his evident sympathies, as they were reflected in his works, brought him under police suspicion.

After producing a number of successful works, Verdi settled on a country estate in 1849. There he continued to pursue his political activities and produced, in succession, three of his best-known works: *Rigoletto* (1851), *Il Trovatore* (1853), and *La Traviata* (1853). These productions are regarded as the culmination of his first creative period.

Many years of intensive musical productivity followed, during which such memorable works as *Un Ballo in Maschera (The Masked Ball,* 1859) and *Don Carlos* (1867) were created. In 1871, Verdi's masterpiece of spectacular grand opera, *Aida,* was written. With its pageantry, grand crowd scenes, and tragic but beautiful ending, this work is regarded as the height of his second creative phase.

Following this triumph, Verdi produced no operatic work for sixteen years. Then, in 1887, *Otello,* based on Shakespeare's play *Othello,* was performed in Milan. It is regarded by many critics as the pinnacle of Italian tragic opera. Verdi's last opera, *Falstaff,* also based on a Shakespearian character, was written in 1893 when the composer was nearly 80 and is one of the finest in the comic opera style. Verdi was 87 years old when he died.

Verdi's style is frequently contrasted with that of his German contemporary Richard Wagner, whose music we will study in the next chapter. Although each of these composers brought romantic opera to its height in his native country, they used quite different approaches. Wagner's plots usually involved larger-than-life, mythological characters whose activities were meant to symbolize underlying philosophical issues. Verdi's plots more often involved real people cast in dramatic, action-filled situations and are notable for their spontaneity and sure sense of effective drama.

Verdi and Wagner disagreed on the relative importance of the singers and the orchestra. Wagner used orchestration to convey his philosophical ideas, sometimes overshadowing the singers, whose role was to move the surface action along. In contrast, Verdi's operas are dominated by the singing voice. Melody is the vehicle for expressing

GIUSEPPE VERDI
(1813–1901)

- Born in Le Roncole, near Busseto, Italy; died at age 87 in Milan, Italy.

- Best known for one *Requiem Mass* and many popular operas including *Rigoletto, Il Trovatore, La Traviata, Aida, Otello,* and *Falstaff.*

a vast range of emotions, and singers are rarely forced to compete with the orchestral background.

As an example of an opera by Verdi, we will listen to the finale of one of the grandest of his operas, *Aida.* It was first performed in Cairo, Egypt, on Christmas Eve in 1871, and the next year it was produced at La Scala in Milan. Today, it is performed all over the world. "MusiCurious: Attending an Opera" describes what it is like to see such a performance.

Aida

The Primary Characters

> The Pharaoh, King of Egypt (bass)
>
> Amneris, the Pharaoh's daughter who wants to marry Radamès (mezzo soprano)
>
> Aida, Ethiopian princess, but slave to Amneris and in love with Radamès (soprano)
>
> Radamès, Egyptian military captain, in love with Aida (tenor)

Amonasro, King of Ethiopia, and Aida's father (baritone)

Other singers play priests, priestesses, soldiers, Ethiopian slaves and prisoners, and the Egyptian court and people.

The Plot   The opera is set in ancient Egypt at the beginning of a war against Ethiopia. The god Isis has been consulted for advice about who should lead the Egyptian army in battle, and the young Egyptian military captain Radamès is hoping that he might be chosen. With that in mind, he visits with the high priest Ramfis. Aida is really the princess of Ethiopia, but she was captured in a former battle, and the Egyptians do not know of her status. She has been made the slave of Princess Amneris. The plot is complicated by the fact that Radamès has a smoldering attraction for Aida, who also loves him, but Amneris, who loves and wants to marry Radamès, is suspicious and jealous.

The Pharaoh—surrounded by his guards, ministers, and priests—announces that Isis has chosen Radamès to lead the Egyptian armies in war. Aida has conflicting feelings—hoping that her lover Radamès is successful but also fearful about what the war might do to her father Amonasro, the king of Ethiopia. She contemplates death. A solemn consecration ritual takes place in the temple as Radamès is given his sacred sword and armor to begin his fight.

Radamès is victorious in battle, and a great ceremony is arranged for his homecoming. Amneris tricks Aida into confessing that she loves Radamès. Amneris shows her jealousy by requiring Aida to attend the victory celebration with her, knowing that her father, the Pharaoh, will announce that Amneris will marry Radamès.

The victory celebration is very elaborate and attended by the Pharaoh and his daughter, the priests, and crowds of onlookers. Dancers lead in the Egyptian armies, and the newly captured prisoners from Ethiopia are led across the stage in chains. Live animals are sometimes brought on stage as part of the victory parade. Aida recognizes her father, King Amonasro, among the captives. He tells her not to reveal his identity and explains to the crowd that he is a simple soldier who saw his king die in battle. Radamès requests the release of the Ethiopians, because he believes their king is dead. All are released except, ironically, Aida's father, who is kept as a hostage. He secretly assures Aida that revenge will come. The Pharaoh announces the marriage of Radamès and Amneris.

On the night before her wedding to Radamès, Amneris enters the Temple of Isis to pray. Aida is outside the temple to meet with Radamès and is surprised by her father, Amonasro. He promises to take her back to Ethiopia if she can get Radamès to divulge the route the Egyptian army plans to take against the Ethiopians. Aida is horrified at the idea of betraying her lover. However, her father declares that she is no daughter of his, and Aida, shamed, agrees to trick Radamès into revealing the information.

Amonasro hides, and when Radamès meets with Aida to go away with her, she asks where the troops are so that they can avoid them. When Radamès responds, Aida's father then shows himself and offers Radamès a good life in Ethiopia. Amneris emerges from the temple, hears this, and accuses Radamès of treason for giving a military secret to the enemy. Radamès is arrested while Aida and her father escape.

Radamès is imprisoned and condemned as a traitor. He says nothing in his defense. Amneris promises that she will convince her father to save him if he will give up Aida and love her. Radamès chooses death instead. Amneris blames herself for his capture and curses the bloodthirsty priests. Radamès is condemned to death. He is to be sealed alive in a tomb under the temple and left to suffocate.

Aida has decided to die with Radamès and has hidden in the tomb to be sealed in with him. In the final scene, Aida and Radamès are in the tomb, and the priests and priestesses are in the temple above them. The lovers bid goodbye to the earth and life. Amneris has thrown herself on the stone that entombs them and prays for peace. We will now listen to that finale.

Featured Listening

"O terra, addio" ("Oh Earth, Goodbye") from *Aida*   GIUSEPPE VERDI

Date: 1871

Genre: Opera aria, duet, trio, and chorus

Tempo: Meno mosso (slow)

Voices and Instruments: Soprano soloist, tenor soloist, mezzo soprano soloist, chorus, and orchestra

Language: Italian

Meter: Quadruple

Duration: 5:13

Context: This is the very end of the opera. Radamès has been sealed in the tomb to die, and Aida has appeared, having hidden there earlier to die with him. Amneris feels guilty for having caused Radamès's death and has thrown herself on the stone that seals his tomb and begs for peace. The choir represents priests and priestesses who are present at the tomb.

Timing	Italian text	English translation	Musical events
	AIDA		
32 0:00	O terra, addio, addio valle di pianti,	O earth, goodbye, goodbye vale of tears,	The singing is very dramatic with many dynamic contrasts.
	sogno di gaudio che in dolor svanì.	dream of joy which in sorrow faded.	
	A noi si schiude, si schiude il ciel,	For us heaven opens, yes heaven opens.	
	si schiude il ciel e l'alme erranti,	Heaven opens and our wandering souls	
	volano al raggio dell'eterno dì.	fly to the light of eternal day.	
	RADAMÈS		
1:10	O terra, addio, addio valle di pianti,	O earth, goodbye, goodbye vale of tears,	
	sogno di gaudio che in dolor svanì.	dream of joy which in sorrow faded.	
	RADAMÈS AND AIDA ALTERNATE		
	A noi si schiude, si schiude il ciel,	For us heaven opens, yes heaven opens.	
	si schiude il ciel e l'alme erranti	Heaven opens and our wandering souls	
	volano al raggio dell'eterno dì.	fly to the light of eternal day.	
	CHORUS		
2:12	Immenso Fthà, noi t'invochiam, noi t'invochiam, t'invochiam, t'invochiam!	Mighty Phtha, we invoke thee, we invoke thee, we invoke thee, we invoke thee!	The chorus sings together, giving the effect of unity.
	AIDA AND RADAMÈS (over the chorus) Ah! Si schiude il ciel! (together) O terra, addio,	Ah! Heaven is opening for us! O earth, goodbye,	

Timing	Italian text	English translation	Musical events
	addio valle di pianti,	goodbye vale of tears,	
	sogno di gaudio che in dolor svanì.	dream of joy which in sorrow faded.	
	A noi si schiude, si schiude il ciel,	For us heaven opens, yes heaven opens.	
	si schiude il ciel e l'alme erranti,	Heaven opens and our wandering souls	
	volano al raggio dell'eterno dì.	fly to the light of eternal day.	
	Il ciel, il ciel, si schiudi il ciel,	Heaven, heaven, heaven opens for us,	
	si schiude il ciel.	heaven opens!	
	AMNERIS		
	(during the duet between Aida and Radamès)		
	Pace t'imploro, salma adorata,	Peace, I beg, beloved corpse,	Amneris's voice is lower than Aida's and her mood more solemn.
	Isi placata, Isi placata	May Isis, placated, Isis placated	
	ti schiuda il ciel!	open heaven to you!	
4:19	Pace t'imploro. Pace t'imploro.	Peace, I beg. Peace, I beg.	
	Pace, pace, pace!	Peace, peace, peace!	
	CHORUS		
	Noi t'invochiam, noi t'invochiam,	We invoke thee, we invoke thee,	The chorus is, again, together and unified.
	immenso Fathà! immenso Fathà!	mighty Phtha! mighty Phtha!	
	immenso Fathà!	mighty Phtha!	

The 1998 musical version of *Aida* by Elton John and Tim Rice was based on the same general plot as Verdi's opera, and, of course, the music was new. The musical begins in the present time where the singers who have the roles of Radamès and Aida are visiting an Egyptian wing of a museum. The story then goes back to ancient Egypt where it is changed so that Aida is condemned along with Radamès, so her death is not a suicide as it was in the opera. The two die in the tomb together, but then the scene returns to the contemporary museum where they have been reincarnated and are singing of their new beginning together.

Giacomo Puccini

Toward the end of the nineteenth century, a movement toward naturalism and realism also took place in Italian literature. Called **verismo** (realism), it quickly penetrated Italian opera. Bizet's *Carmen* served as a model for the three Italian composers who led the movement: **Giacomo Puccini** ("Poo-chee-nee," 1858–1924), Ruggiero Leoncavallo (1857–1919), and Pietro Mascagni (1863–1945). Leoncavallo is remembered for *I Pagliacci (The Players,* 1892*)* and Mascagni for *Cavalleria Rusticana (Rustic Chivalry,* 1890*)*. Puccini, the most successful of the verismo composers, effectively united grand opera and realism.

Puccini was descended from a line of musicians that stretched back over five generations. During most of his childhood, Puccini showed only a modest talent for music; nevertheless, his mother insisted that he continue his studies, and by age 16 he was composing in earnest—chiefly organ music for church services.

In 1880, Puccini obtained a scholarship to enter the Milan Conservatory. Once graduated from the Conservatory, he entered an opera competition with *Le Villi* (1884),

GIACOMO PUCCINI
(1858–1924)

- Born in Lucca, Italy; died at age 65 in Brussels, Belgium.

- Best known for his operas, including *Manon Lescaut, La Bohème, Tosca, Madame Butterfly, The Girl of the Golden West,* and *Turandot.*

a work based on a Slavonic legend. He failed to win the contest, but the opera was produced in Milan on May 31, 1884. The success of the premiere persuaded the well-known publisher Giulio Ricordi to commission a second opera by Puccini. Largely because of a poor libretto, *Edgar* (1884–1888) was not a success; however, Ricordi continued to support the composer, and both men worked over the book for the next work, *Manon Lescaut,* based on the 1731 novel by Abbé Prévost. Its premiere on February 1, 1893, was an immense triumph.

Although *Manon Lescaut* made Puccini famous in Italy, it was his next opera, *La Bohème* (*Bohemian Life,* 1893–1896), that brought him worldwide fame. Ironically, Puccini's only serious failure was his favorite opera, *Madame Butterfly* (1904). Despite the hisses and catcalls at the premiere, however, the work became quite popular outside Italy and continues to be popular today. The main story of the modern musical *Miss Saigon* (1989) moves the story of *Madame Butterfly* from early twentieth-century Japan to Vietnam in 1975 when U.S. troops were leaving the country.

Puccini's next opera, *La Fanciulla del West* (*The Girl of the Golden West,* 1910), was based on a play by David Belasco, as was *Madame Butterfly.* The premiere of *The Girl of the Golden West* at the Metropolitan Opera in New York was one of the most glittering events of 1910, with Arturo Toscanini conducting and the famous tenor Enrico Caruso singing the lead male role.

During World War I, Puccini remained in Italy, working quietly on more operas. His last work, *Turandot,* was left incomplete at his death. In 1923 he began suffering from what turned out to be throat cancer, and the following year he died of a heart attack. He was 65 years old. The task of finishing the final scenes of *Turandot* was entrusted to Franco Alfano, a distinguished younger composer. The opera was produced under Toscanini at La Scala, Milan, on April 25, 1926. In the early twenty-first century another Italian composer, Luciano Berio (1925–2003), undertook to remove Alfano's ending and compose a new one that he thought was more in line with Puccini's original plan. The new ending has met with mixed reviews.

Puccini's operas reflect his realistic bent and his fascination with exotic settings. *Madame Butterfly,* for example, is set in Japan, and *Turandot* in China. The opera that brought him international acclaim, *La Bohème* ("La Bow-em"), combines rich and sensuous romantic melodies with realistic details of plot and characterization.

La Bohème

The Primary Characters

Rodolfo, a poet who falls in love with Mimi (tenor)

Mimi, a seamstress sick with tuberculosis and in love with Rodolfo (soprano)

Marcello, a painter (baritone)

Schaunard, a musician (baritone)

Colline, a philosopher (bass)

Musetta, a singer (soprano)

Other singers play the landlord, townsfolk, street vendors, soldiers, waiters, and children.

The Plot   The opera begins on Christmas Eve in the Latin Quarter of Paris (the artists' district on the Left Bank) in the 1830s. Rodolfo (a struggling young poet) and his friend Marcello (a painter) are freezing in their attic studio on Christmas Eve. Suddenly a friend enters with money, groceries, and firewood and insists they all go out to celebrate. Rodolfo stays to finish an article he is writing but is interrupted by a knock

A scene from Puccini's opera *La Bohème.*

at the door. The caller is Mimi, a neighbor, whose candle has blown out. She asks for a light, and he invites her in. She is ill and faints. When she feels strong enough to leave, they discover that her key has fallen. As they search for it on the floor, their hands meet, and they give up the search to wait for more light from the moon. Rodolfo tells Mimi about his life and hopes. She describes her life as a maker of artificial flowers and talks about her longing for spring and sunshine. Rodolfo declares his love, and Mimi responds passionately. As the act ends, they leave to join his friends at the café.

Act Two opens with a holiday crowd in the streets near the café. Marcello sees his old flame, Musetta, with a wealthy old codger in tow. She tries to attract Marcello's attention, embarrassing her escort and amusing the spectators. Finally she sings a provocative waltz and, having sent her escort off on a fool's errand, leaps into Marcello's eager arms.

Act Three is set some months later. Rodolfo's jealousy has caused Mimi to leave him. She seeks out Marcello to ask his help and tells him of Rodolfo's unbearable behavior; Rodolfo arrives, and Mimi hides. He starts to complain to Marcello of Mimi's flirting but admits that he is actually in despair over her failing health. When Mimi's coughing reveals her presence, Rodolfo begs her to stay with him until spring, and she agrees.

Act Four is set back in the garret shared by Rodolfo and Marcello the following fall. Rodolfo and Marcello are there. Fellow artist friends arrive for dinner, and a hilarious evening begins. Musetta interrupts their gaiety, announcing that Mimi has collapsed on the stairs. They carry her in; all except Rodolfo leave to pawn their treasures to buy medical supplies for Mimi. Rodolfo and Mimi recall their first meeting. Their friends return, and Mimi drifts off to sleep. She dies, and Rodolfo embraces her while the others weep.

Notice how different this plot is from Mozart's *The Marriage of Figaro.* Mozart's opera was about French aristocrats and their dealings with servants. Classical opera plots often dealt with aristocratic lifestyles or the old Greek or Roman plots that were most common in the baroque era. With *La Bohème,* we have an opera about starving artists and a sweet and innocent woman who is dying of tuberculosis, a common cause of death in the nineteenth century. The reality of the verismo movement and its connection to the large, romantic middle class is clear. This is a story that most people can relate to and identify with on every level. "Hearing the Difference: Mozart's 'Non più andrai' and Puccini's 'Si, mi chiamano Mimì'" explores the different qualities of these two arias.

The aria that is discussed here is from Act One. Rodolfo has touched Mimi's hand for the first time and then told her about himself. Now it is Mimi's turn to tell Rodolfo about herself.

 Listening Guide

CONNECT  CD 2: Track 33

"Sì, mi chiamano Mimì" ("Yes, They Call Me Mimi") from *La Bohème* GIACOMO PUCCINI

Date: 1896

Genre: Opera aria

Tempo: Slow, but varies with the mood of the text

Form: Some short repeating phrases, but not structured

Voices and Instruments: Soprano soloist with orchestra

Language: Italian

Meter: Mostly duple and sung with much rubato to fit the text

Duration: 4:45

Context: *La Bohème* is one of the most popular and often performed operas in the repertoire, and this is one of its most moving arias. Notice how sweet, innocent, and fragile Mimi appears in her story about herself. That sets us up for the tragedy of her death at the end of the opera.

Italian text	English translation	Musical events
33 Sì. Mi chiamano Mimì, ma il mio nome è Lucia. La storia mia è breve. A tela o a seta ricamo in casa e fuori. Son tranquilla e lieta, ed è mio svago far gigli e rose. Mi piaccion quelle cose che han si dolce malia, che parlano d'amor, di primavere, che parlano di sogni e di chimere—quelle cose che han nome poesia. Lei m'intende?	Yes. They call me Mimi, but my name is Lucia. My story is brief. I embroider silk or linen at home and outside. I'm contented and happy, and it's my pleasure to make lilies and roses. I like those things that have sweet charm, that speak of love, of springtimes, that speak of dreams and fancies—those things that are called poetry. Do you understand me?	The orchestra is soft and gentle in support of the text.
Mi chiamano Mimì, il perchè non so. Sola, mi fo il pranzo da me stessa. Non vado sempre a messa, ma prego assai il Signor. Vivo sola, soletta, là in una bianca cameretta; guardo sui tetti e in cielo, ma quando vien lo sgelo il primo sole è mio—il primo bacio dell'aprile è mio! Il primo sole è mio! Germoglia in un vaso una rosa. Foglia a foglia l'aspiro! Così gentil è il profumo d'un fior! Ma i fior ch'io faccio, ahimè, i fior ch'io faccio, ahimè, non hanno odore! Altro di me non le saprei narrare: sono la sua vicina che la vien fuori d'ora a importunare.	They call me Mimi, but I don't know why. All alone, I make dinner for myself. I don't always go to Mass, but I often pray to the Lord. I live alone, all by myself, in a little white room over there; I look on the roofs and into the sky, but when the thaw comes, the first sunshine is mine—the first kiss of April is mine! The first sunshine is mine! A rose opens in a vase. Leaf by leaf I sniff its fragrance. So lovely is the perfume of a flower. But the flowers that I make—alas! the flowers that I make—alas! have no odor. I wouldn't know anything else to tell you about myself—I'm your neighbor who comes at this odd hour to trouble you.	Energy builds. The gentle mood returns.

Hearing the Difference

MOZART'S "NON PIÙ ANDRAI" AND PUCCINI'S "SI, MI CHIAMANO MIMÌ"

These two arias (see Featured Listening on page 146 and Listening Guide on page 230) come from different style periods—classical and romantic. As we discussed in the Preludes, classical music tends to favor more structure in terms of form, while romantic music favors passion and feelings over structure. The two operas from which these arias are taken also represent differences between the periods. Mozart's *The Marriage of Figaro* details the happenings in the lives of people at a royal classical court, while Puccini's *La Bohème* tells the story of four starving artists and a gentle, dying woman. Answer the following questions as you listen to one work and then the other.

- One of these arias jokingly tells a young man who is about to enter the military how his life is going to change, and the other introduces a sensitive and beautiful woman who has just met the man in whose arms she will eventually die. What things about the sound of the music and the singers' voices tell you the difference?

- One of these arias is much more structured than the other, with a sectional form with a returning theme that can be outlined as ABACA-Coda. The other has some short repeating phrases but is otherwise unstructured. Why do you think these structures differ?

- What might you say about the size and instrumentation of the orchestra that would indicate the period in which each of the arias was composed?

- The tempos of these works are different. Which is fast and lively, and which is slow? Which has a more regular beat, and which varies the speed of the beat to fit the mood of the text?

- Consider the meters of each. Which is quadruple (you can count a clear four beats in each measure), and which is mostly duple but not easy to count?

The musical *Rent* (1996) by Jonathan Larson is based on the story of *La Bohème*. *Rent* is set in New York instead of Paris, and Mimi has AIDS instead of tuberculosis. Rodolfo is renamed Roger and is an HIV-positive songwriter.

Summary

Opera was one of the most important musical genres of the romantic period because its combination of music and drama was greatly appealing to the large middle class, as well as to the aristocracy. In Paris, grand opera was composed to be performed on a large scale with crowd scenes, ballets, choruses, and elaborate scenery. *Opéra comique* was a lighter type of opera set on a smaller scale than grand opera. It also made use of spoken dialogue. Lyric opera developed as a more serious type of opera than *opéra comique* but was still set on a smaller scale than grand opera. In France, the naturalist literary movement brought about an interest in creating operas based on natural and realistic characters who often were poor.

Italian composers continued to write in the *opera seria* and *opera buffa* styles and developed the bel canto (beautiful singing) vocal style. Of the many successful opera composers of the era whose works are still often performed today, the two Italians—Giuseppe Verdi and Giacomo Puccini—lead the list; their works have continuously provided audiences with laughter, tears, and every emotion in between. Elton John and Tim Rice's *Aida* is based on Verdi's opera, and the modern-day musicals *Miss Saigon* and *Rent* are based on Puccini's operas *Madame Butterfly* and *La Bohème*, respectively.

New People and Concepts

bel canto, 222

Giacomo Puccini, 227

Giuseppe Verdi, 223

verismo, 227

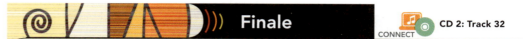

Finale

CONNECT   CD 2: Track 32

Listen again to the recording of "O terra, addio" ("Oh Earth, Goodbye") from *Aida*, by Verdi, and compare your impression now with your notes from your First Hearing. Do you hear more now than you did before? Consider the following questions:

- What is happening in this section of the opera? How does the music support the story?
- What characters sing the solo parts heard here, and what are their voice types?
- What is the role of the orchestra in this section?
- Where is this section in the opera?
- If you were going to describe this music to a friend, what would you say?

Further Listening

Georges Bizet, *Carmen*. Bizet was French, but the opera *Carmen* is set in Spain. Carmen is a gypsy woman who convinces a soldier to leave his regiment and girlfriend to go away with her. As soon as he does, she dumps him. Nothing is left of his former life. The opera is full of colorful Spanish dancing and music. Because of its many hummable tunes and passionate theme, *Carmen* continues to be very popular and is often performed today.

Gioacchino Rossini, *Il Barbiere di Siviglia (The Barber of Seville)*. This wonderful and fun opera is based on a play by the French writer Beaumarchais (Pierre Augustine Caron), who also wrote the play on which Mozart's *Le Nozze di Figaro (The Marriage of Figaro)* was based. In fact, the barber is Figaro, the same character who gets married in Mozart's opera.

Romantic German Opera

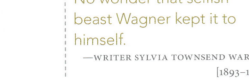

))) First Hearing

 CONNECT — CD 3: Track 1

Listen to the recording of "Grane, mein Ross!" ("Grane, My Horse!") and finale by Wagner and take notes on what you hear. Even if you are working with other students in a paired or group listening session, keep your own notes. Give some attention to the following:

- What is the mood of this scene?

- Does the orchestra sound large? What instruments can you pick out?

- What is the voice type of the singer? Soprano, mezzo soprano, alto, tenor, baritone, or bass?

- There is a fire on stage at this point in the drama. What instruments are used to give you a sense of fire?

- Can you count the meter at any point in this scene? What meter(s) do you hear?

- Do you hear any melodies that repeat?

Keep your notes from this First Hearing to compare with your impressions about the piece after you study the information in this chapter.

25

Whereas the Italian verismo composers were influenced by the realist movement in literature, nineteenth-century German opera drew its inspiration from the passionate, heroic, and adventurous ideals of the romantic era. The first significant composer of romantic German opera was Carl Maria von Weber (1786–1826). A nationalist and romanticist, he built his style on the legends and songs of the German people and on romantic elements. His opera *Der Freischütz* (*The Freeshooter*, 1821) features supernatural elements such as magic bullets and a pact with the devil, a typically romantic fascination.

Romantic German operas, such as *Der Freischütz*, tended to stress mood and setting. Nature was represented as a wild and mysterious force. Supernatural beings mixed freely with ordinary mortals. Human characters often symbolized good and evil, and the hero's victory meant salvation or redemption.

RICHARD WAGNER
(1813–1883)

- Born in Leipzig, Germany; died at age 69 in Venice, Italy.
- Best known for his operas, which he called *music dramas*, including *Der fliegende Holländer (The Flying Dutchman), Tannhäuser, Lohengrin, Der Ring des Nibelungen, Tristan und Isolde, Die Meistersinger von Nürnberg (The Mastersingers of Nuremberg),* and *Parsifal.*

Richard Wagner

In the latter part of the nineteenth century, one of the most powerful personalities in the history of music emerged—**Richard Wagner** ("Ree-card Vaug-ner," 1813–1883). In his works, romantic German opera reached its highest point. Born in Leipzig, Wagner was the son of a clerk in the city police court who died when his son was only 6 months old. Richard's mother later married Ludwig Geyer, a gifted actor, playwright, and painter. It was rumored that Geyer was Wagner's real father, and Wagner himself considered this likely. Wagner was a precocious child who showed an early interest in literature, writing a tragedy in the style of Shakespeare at age 14.

In his formal musical training Wagner was among the least systematic of the great nineteenth-century composers. He began piano lessons at age 12 but never became a first-rate performer on any instrument. Lack of adequate technical preparation, however, did not prevent Wagner from making early attempts at composition. By 1832, several of his works—including two overtures and a symphony—had been performed publicly. The following year, at age 20, he began his professional career, becoming chorusmaster for the Würzburg Theater. Other, similar jobs followed, and he began combining his interest in music with his interest in theater by composing operas.

He married an actress, Minna Planer, and began work on an opera based on a historical novel set in Rome during the middle 1300s. The opera was called *Rienzi, Last of the Tribunes,* and with it Wagner tried to outdo every French or Italian grand opera of the past. The story dealt with Rienzi's rise and fall as the ruler of Rome and had such a large cast performing marches, processions, and ballets that it could be played only in the largest theater. Wagner spent the years 1839 to 1842 in Paris, where he tried vainly to get the work performed. His financial situation became desperate—partly because of his increasingly spendthrift ways—and he even landed in a debtors' prison for a short time. Although there had been problems in their marriage, Minna stood by him through the difficulties of the time.

Rienzi was finally accepted, but not in Paris. It was in Dresden, Germany, that it was first performed in 1842. Wagner returned to Germany to supervise the production. The première performance was over six hours long, including several intermissions. It was eventually split to be shown in two evenings and received hundreds of performances in Germany over the course of the next sixty years.

The success of *Rienzi* and that of Wagner's next opera, *Der fliegende Holländer (The Flying Dutchman,* 1843), based on an old German legend about a Dutchman who was condemned to sail the seas until he could find a faithful woman, led to his appointment as music director at the Royal Opera House in Dresden. For the next six years, Wagner busied himself producing operas and writing two more himself: *Tannhäuser* (1842–1844), about a German singer from the medieval era, and *Lohengrin* (finished 1848), based on a Grimm brothers fairy tale. Wagner's active participation in the revolutionary uprising of 1848–1849 caused a warrant to be issued for his arrest and forced him to flee to Switzerland.

While in exile, he turned to literary activity and wrote a number of essays, the most influential of which were "Das Kunstwerk der Zukunft" ("The Art-Work of the Future," 1850) and "Oper und Drama" ("Opera and Drama," 1851). In these he laid the foundations for **music drama,** the term he used for his unique type of opera.

During his ten years in Switzerland, Wagner began putting his artistic theories into practice. By 1852 he had completed the poems of an epic cycle of four music dramas, entitled *Der Ring des Nibelungen (The Ring of the Nibelung),* based primarily on the struggle of characters from Scandinavian and Germanic legends—gods, humans,

 **MusiCurious**

OPERA PRODUCTIONS

I have seen a few bits of operas on YouTube and found that performances of the same opera look very different from one another. Why?

What you have seen is parts of different *productions* of the same opera. Although a given opera will have the same characters, songs, texts, and music in each production, the look of the scenery, lighting, costumes, and even the action of the characters can vary greatly. Operas are based on a libretto, or "the book," which sometimes has a few stage directions that indicate when a character should come out on stage or to whom they should sing an aria. The libretto may also note items that are necessary in the action, such as a particular piece of furniture or some other prop. Beyond that, the artistic director of the company makes the decisions about what the furniture and the room it is in should look like and how the singers should be dressed.

How much variation is there among different productions?

Sometimes a lot, but not always. There are certain conventions for some operas such as, for example, Mozart's *The Marriage of Figaro*. Figaro is usually set in a classical-looking palace, but the palace furnishings vary in elaborateness. Directors usually don't set Figaro on the moon or out in the desert because of the specific historical nature of the plot and characters. Operas that have no established historical place or time, like Wagner's *Ring* cycle, are sometimes set in very nontraditional places and unidentifiable times.

Why is Wagner's *Ring* cycle so nonspecific regarding place and time?

The *Ring* cycle is set in an undated time and in a world full of humans, gods, and numerous fantastical creatures. It is, in that respect, like *Star Wars* or Tolkien's *Lord of the Rings*, to which it is often compared.

As an illustration, we can compare two very different recorded productions of the cycle. The 1976 production at Wagner's own opera house—the *Festspielhaus* in Germany—was shockingly modern. The Rhine River was represented by a modern-looking water-processing plant, and the Rhine maidens were dressed like prostitutes. The production deliberately looked very industrial. The recording of that production made in 1980 is available on DVD. On the other hand, the 1990 production by the Metropolitan Opera Company in New York was far more traditional. The overall look of that production was reminiscent of Norse mythology with ugly dwarves, hulking giants, beautiful Rhine maidens, and gods in gowns with breastplates.

Which production is better?

Your choice. Most people prefer one over the other, but some people just love the music so much that they see the *Ring* cycle as often as they can and don't care about the sets. The important point is that when you watch an opera, you are experiencing several levels of creative work. Directors like to put their own ideas in their productions, and each new singer tends to interpret his or her role a bit differently from what other singers have done.

and various types of mythical beings—to gain possession of a powerful gold ring. It took Wagner seventeen years to complete the entire cycle (referred to as the *Ring* cycle). These works lay heavy demands on the performers, and because the individual dramas last from three to five hours each, the whole set requires four evenings for its performance. "MusiCurious: Opera Productions" examines the idiosyncratic demands of presenting this musical form.

In the intervening years, Wagner wrote two other works that remain perhaps his most popular and frequently performed: *Tristan und Isolde* (1856–1859) and *Die Meistersinger von Nürnberg* (*The Mastersingers of Nuremberg*, 1862–1867).

Although highly prolific, Wagner experienced great difficulty in arranging performances of his works. Most were formidable in scale, requiring theatrical and musical resources beyond the means of even the largest opera houses. As he approached age 50, he became discouraged. His debts continued to pile up, and he separated from his wife and even contemplated suicide.

Richard Wagner with Franz Liszt and Liszt's daughter, Cosima.

Then in 1864, his fortunes changed. The new king of Bavaria, Ludwig II, a devoted admirer of Wagner's music, invited him to Munich with the promise of financial and artistic support. At this time, Wagner fell in love with Cosima von Bülow, the daughter of the great pianist and composer Franz Liszt and wife of one of Wagner's close associates, Hans von Bülow. Cosima left her husband to be with Wagner, completely devoting herself to his career. They were finally married in 1870, and with help from Ludwig II they raised enough money to build an opera house. Located in the small Bavarian town of Bayreuth, the *Festspielhaus* ("festival drama house"), as it was called, was constructed especially for Wagner's works. He liked to use such a large orchestra that, in regular opera houses with the orchestra pit in front of the stage, the orchestra sometimes covered the sound of the singers, who were behind it. The *Festspielhaus* was designed with most of the orchestra set under the stage so that the sound of the orchestra and that of the singers came out to the audience together. The *Festspielhaus* is still run by the Wagner family and is used for performances of his works.

The *Festspielhaus* was the scene of the first complete performance of the *Ring* cycle, in 1876. One of the great artistic events of the century, this performance was the fulfillment of Wagner's lifelong dream. He completed one more work, *Parsifal* (1882), before illness forced him to travel to Italy in hope of regaining his health. He died of a heart attack, in Venice, in 1883 at age 69.

Wagner believed that a music drama should be a *Gesamtkunstwerk* (universal artwork), combining elements from all the arts. The most important element should be drama, with the music serving to reinforce the dramatic expression. This view was different from that held by many earlier opera composers, including Mozart, who believed that music was the most important element in opera because it is the music that creates the drama.

In Wagner's works the music is essentially continuous throughout each act, with one section moving smoothly into the next. In place of the traditional arias and recitatives, Wagner developed a musical line he called *Sprechsingen* (singing speech). This

A scene from *Die Walküre,* from Wagner's *Ring* cycle. In this scene, two giants have been promised the goddess Freia in payment for building Valhalla, a promise Wotan does not keep.

style combined the lyric quality of the aria and the speaking quality of the recitative and permitted a continuous musical flow that Wagner termed *endless melody.*

To allow the music to support the drama as much as possible, Wagner used melodies or fragments of melodies to identify particular characters, objects, or ideas. These melodies are called **leitmotifs** (pronounced "light moteefs"; "leading melodies" or signature tunes). Berlioz used this technique in the idée fixe that represents the beloved in *Symphonie fantastique,* but Wagner attached leitmotifs to many characters, objects, or ideas in an opera, not just one. Indeed, some characters had several leitmotifs depending on their different moods or activities. Movie composers often use this idea. In *Star Wars* (1977), for example, composer John Williams gave each main character his or her melody, which becomes obvious to the listener during the movie. In fact, *Star Wars* has many connections with Wagner's *Der Ring des Nibelungen.* Another movie, *Excalibur* (1981), used not only the leitmotif idea but also the same melody that Wagner did in the *Ring* cycle to represent the sword Nothung.

A story with an even closer story-line connection to Wagner's *Ring* cycle is J. R. R. Tolkien's (1892–1973) *The Lord of the Rings* trilogy. Both cycles are based on similar mythical themes of loss and recovery and a quest for magical power. In fact, Tolkien took his story from legends similar to those Wagner had used.

The first music drama in Wagner's cycle is *Das Rheingold (The Gold of the Rhine).* That opera begins in the Rhine River, where a pile of magic gold is being guarded by the Rhine maidens. The gold is stolen, and part of it is made into a ring by a hunchbacked dwarf of the race of the Nibelungs. The ring becomes the center of attention for much of the cycle of dramas because anyone who possesses it and renounces love will rule the world. Various characters steal or kill to get the ring as the dwarf tries to get it back.

The second music drama is *Die Walküre (The Valkyries).* The Valkyries are the daughters of the father of the gods, Wotan. Their primary job is to ride their horses above battlegrounds and take fallen heroes to Valhalla, the home of the gods. Wotan has told one of the Valkyries, Brünnhilde, to intercede in a sword fight, and Brünnhilde does so but tries to save the wrong person. Both men end up dead, and Brünnhilde is punished by losing her status as a goddess and by being put to sleep on a rock surrounded by fire. Only a hero will be able to wake her.

The third music drama is named for Wotan's heroic grandson, *Siegfried*. Siegfried's mother, Sieglinde, had died in childbirth and had asked a Nibelung, Mime, to raise her son. Like most other creatures in the cycle, Mime would like to gain control of the ring, which was made by and stolen from his brother. Siegfried fixes the sword that was shattered when his father died as Mime plots to get the ring. The name of the sword is Nothung.

As *Siegfried* continues on, Siegfried uses his sword to slay both the dragon and Mime. A bird leads him to Brünnhilde, who is asleep on her rock. On his way to find Brünnhilde, Siegfried is challenged by Wotan, and Siegfried's sword breaks Wotan's spear, causing Wotan to lose his power. Finally, Siegfried awakens Brünnhilde, and the two fall in love.

The fourth, and final, music drama is *Die Götterdämmerung (The Twilight of the Gods)*. In it, Siegfried is killed while attempting to steal the ring, and Brünnhilde commits suicide by riding her horse into his funeral pyre. But, before dying, Brünnhilde promises that the ring will be returned to the Rhine maidens, which it is. Brünnhilde's death, however, causes a flood and then a fire that destroys Valhalla and all of the gods and heroes in it. The ring, therefore, ends up exactly where it was at the beginning of the cycle, over fifteen hours earlier. The Featured Listening to this finale follows.

))) Featured Listening

 CD 3: Track 1

"Grane, mein Ross!" ("Grane, My Horse!") and finale to *Die Götterdämmerung (The Twilight of the Gods)* from *Der Ring des Nibelungen (The Ring of the Nibelung)* RICHARD WAGNER

Date: First performed in 1876

Genre: Opera

Tempo: Varies to fit the events

Voices and Instruments: Soprano and large orchestra

Language: German

Meter: Changes often

Duration: 7:20

Context: This is the final scene from the four-part opera set called *Der Ring des Nibelungen (The Ring of the Nibelung)* by Wagner. In it, Brünnhilde rides into the fire that has destroyed Valhalla, the castle of the gods and heroes. Her husband, Siegfried, has also died. The Rhine River rises, and the Rhine maidens recover the ring, which was made from the gold that was stolen from them at the beginning of the first opera. The final melody represents redemption by love. Themes (leitmotifs to Wagner) heard in this finale come from earlier operas in the set. They represent Brünnhilde (herself a Valkyrie), redemption by love, and the Rhine maidens.

German text	English translation	Musical events
1		Swirling strings represent fire raging all around, "Ride of the Valkyries."

German text	English translation	Musical events
BRÜNNHILDE		
Grane, mein Ross, sei mir gegrüsst!	Grane, my horse, I greet you!	
Weisst du auch, mein Freund, wohin ich dich führe?	Do you know, my friend, where I lead you?	
Im Feuer leuchtend, liegt dort dein Herr, Siegfried, mein seliger Held.	In fire radiant, lies there your lord, Siegfried, my blessed hero.	Flute and voice, "Redemption by Love"
Dem Freunde zu folgen.	Then follow your friend.	
Wieherst du freudig?	Are you neighing with joy?	
Lockt dich zu ihm die lachende Lohe?	Are you lured to the laughing light?	Gentler mood
Fühl' mein Brust auch, wie sie enthrennt.	Feel my breast, how it burns.	
Helles Feuer das Herz mir erfasst.	Glowing flames now hold my heart.	
Ihn zu umschlinge, umschlosse, von ihm,	Fast to embrace him, be embraced by him,	
In mächtigster Minne vermählt ihm zu sein!	In powerful love we are united!	Intensity builds.
Hei-a-ja-ho! Grane! Grüss deinen Herren!	Hei-a-ja-ho! Grane! Give him your greeting!	
Siegfried! Siegfried! Sieh!	Siegfried! Siegfried! See!	
Selig grüsst dich dein Weib!	Your wife greets you with bliss!	
		Brass play "Ride of the Valkyries."
		The Rhine maidens have recovered the ring.
		Fire motion backs off as the Rhine River rises.
		Brass plays "Valhalla" (the castle that is burning).
		Rhine maidens leitmotif, "Redemption by Love"

Brünnhilde and her sisters, the Valkyries, are usually dressed with breastplates and sometimes wear helmets with wings on the sides. When one sees cartoons that make fun of opera, it is often that image that is portrayed.

One subject that cannot be ignored in a discussion about Wagner is the fact that he was anti-Semitic and was Hitler's favorite composer. In 1850, Wagner wrote an essay called "Jewishness in Music" in which he blamed Jewish musicians for commercializing music and stated that music by Jewish composers was not up to the quality of music by other Germans. He continued that any popularity of their works was the result of a corrupting of the tastes of the general public. Wagner published the original essay under a pseudonym, but he added comments about the "yoke of the ruling Jewish society" to it and republished it under his own name in 1869. Some modern listeners have responded to this by saying that Wagner's music is so great that it transcends his personal flaws; others say that the music is destroyed for them because they can see Wagner's anti-Semitic views in his works. Much controversy arises whenever a conductor tries to present anything by Wagner in Israel.

Summary

Romantic opera in Germany was strongly influenced by the romantic movement itself. The composer who first established a genuinely Germanic style was Carl Maria von Weber. The most important composer in romantic German opera was Richard Wagner, who wrote *music dramas* that encompassed all the arts in a unified whole. To Wagner, the most important element was the drama, with the music serving the dramatic expression. Dramatic unity was enhanced by the use of leitmotifs, or melodic fragments associated with persons, objects, or ideas.

One of Wagner's greatest accomplishments was the composition of a cycle of four music dramas, *Der Ring des Nibelungen (The Ring of the Nibelung)*. Not unlike J. R. R. Tolkien's trilogy, *The Lord of the Rings*, which was also based on legends, the cycle tells of loss, recovery, and a quest for magical power.

New People and Concepts

leitmotif, 237 music drama, 234 Richard Wagner, 234

))) **Finale** CONNECT **CD 3: Track 1**

Listen again to the recording of "Grane, mein Ross!" ("Grane, My Horse!") and finale by Wagner and compare your impression now with your notes from your First Hearing. Consider the following questions:

- What is happening in this scene? What is the mood, and how does it change?
- What size is the orchestra? What instruments can you pick out?
- Who is singing? What is the voice type?
- What instruments represent the sound of fire?
- What can you say about the meter(s) used for this scene?
- What melodies repeat, and what do they represent?
- If you were going to describe this music to a friend, what would you say?

Further Listening

Richard Wagner, *Tristan und Isolde*. This opera is one of the most often performed of Wagner's music dramas. The plot is based on the tale of two lovers, Tristan and Isolde, who cannot give themselves to one another because of Isolde's marriage to King Marke of Cornwall. In the end, Tristan dies with Isolde at his side, and she dies of a broken heart. The libretto was written by Wagner and based on an affair of his own.

Richard Wagner, *Der fliegende Holländer (The Flying Dutchman)*. This is another of Wagner's music dramas that is often performed today. Wagner based the libretto on an old legend about a ghost seaman, described as a Dutchman in some versions of the legend, who was condemned to sail the seas until he could find a faithful woman. Only once every seven years is he allowed to return to shore for that search. When he finally does find that woman, the two of them ascend into heaven together. Such redemption through true love is a common theme in Wagner's work.

CHARACTERISTICS OF ROMANTIC MUSIC

Texture	Variety of textures
Tonality	Major-minor system with less firm sense of tonal center
Rhythm	Frequent fluctuations in tempo; use of rubato
Pitch	Greatly expanded pitch range
Tone color	Fascination and experimentation with instrumental color
Melody	Lyrical, expressive, flowing; sometimes ornamented
Dynamics	Wide range of dynamics; frequent fluctuations in dynamic levels; dynamics used for dramatic effect
Small works	Art song (lied); character pieces and miniatures for piano; chamber music
Large works	Concerto, symphony, program symphony, symphonic poem (tone poem), opera, choral works, concert overture
Musical instruments	Piano was a favorite instrument; large orchestra; unusual instrument groupings; emphasis on orchestration and color
Performance style	Steady growth of virtuoso technique
Formal innovations	Carefully constructed classical forms were freely manipulated and expanded; cyclical procedure; thematic transformation; development of programmatic and descriptive music as manifested in the program symphony and tone poem; verismo movement in opera; development of nationalism in music

Prelude | The Early Twentieth Century

Impressionism

As we have seen with past eras, new periods often begin as reactions against the excesses of the previous ones. The classical period began with simple, direct, and well-balanced musical phrases in contrast with the great amount of activity and complexity of late baroque music, and the romantic period provided an emotional reaction against the intellectualism of the classical period. At the end of the romantic era, the extremes of emotion that were commonly portrayed in the arts of the mid-nineteenth century gave way to much experimentation in the new century. This happened in all the arts, usually with music following the visual arts.

Technological advances also affected the development of new styles. By the mid-nineteenth century, artists were able to buy oil paint in tubes instead of having to mix their colors in their studios. That was a tremendous boon, because the use of easily transported premixed paints allowed artists to paint outdoors while they were viewing their subjects. In some cases, it allowed them to concentrate not only on the subject of their work but also on the sunlight illuminating it. Gradually, many artists, particularly in France, began applying their paint in small brushstokes or even just tiny flecks of pure colors to show reflected light. Sometimes those brushstrokes created blurred or distorted images, as in Claude Monet's *Impression: Sunrise*, on page 248, a look that lacked the detail common in earlier styles of painting. This style was widely criticized at first because its lack of detail caused it to look like a mere impression of a scene instead of being a realistic portrayal of it. Those criticisms gave the name *impressionism* to the style.

Music followed impressionistic art with compositions by Claude Debussy and others during the late nineteenth and early twentieth centuries. In this music we hear flowing rhythms that do not follow a steady beat and melodies that seem to come out of nowhere and then disappear without a strong conclusion. Those aspects of the music gave it a vagueness that is similar to what we see in the impressionistic style in the visual arts.

Ways of reflecting and preserving images had been experimented with since Leonardo da Vinci's scientific work of the sixteenth century. The first photograph was made in 1826, and by 1839 photographs could be printed on paper. With improvements in cameras and photographic techniques being made during the rest of the 1800s, it became less necessary for artists to realistically portray people or scenes. That gave artists more freedom to experiment in new, less realistic, directions.

Non-Western Art and Music

Another factor that helped bring about changes in artistic styles at the turn of the century in Europe was the growing awareness and influence of non-Western art and music. In Paris in 1889, the French celebrated the one hundredth anniversary of the French Revolution by inviting musicians, dancers, and other performers from all over the world to a World

***The Starry Night,* by Vincent van Gogh (1853–1890).** As is typical of the style called expressionism, this painting is as much about inner feelings of conflict and unrest as it is about stars in a nighttime sky.

Exhibition. French artists and composers were able to see and hear dances, costumes, and music from places as distant as Asia, the Middle East, and Africa. The influence of those sights and sounds was expressed in art that included facsimiles of African masks, decorations from Asian costumes, and, in the case of music, non-Western instruments, particularly percussive instruments.

We hear a proliferation of non-Western influences as composers begin to do away with the traditional major and minor scales and use new or non-Western scale structures. Traditional European music tends to use relatively repetitious rhythmic patterns, concentrating more on melody than on rhythm. Much non-Western music uses complex rhythms, including several different rhythms played simultaneously.

Expressionism

Expressionism was a style that developed out of impressionism. Expressionism concentrated on the expression of inner feelings of conflict and unrest. Expressionism began with Vincent van Gogh's (1835–1890) late paintings, such as *The Starry Night* (1889). *The Scream* (1893), by Norway's Edvard Munch (1863–1944), is another famous example. After World War I, German artists developed their own type of expressionism, because it readily lent itself to the reflection of inner thoughts and torments felt by a people torn by war and social injustice. Later in the twentieth century, Arnold Schoenberg (1874–1951) composed musical counterparts to Germanic (German and Austrian) expressionism in art.

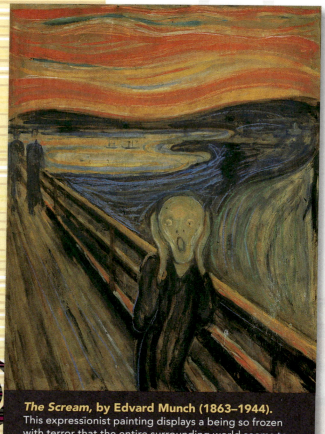

The Scream, by Edvard Munch (1863–1944). This expressionist painting displays a being so frozen with terror that the entire surrounding world seems to be screaming also.

Without Title, by Wassily Kandinsky (1866–1944). This is an example of abstract art because it does not represent any particular figure or view of the world. It is an abstraction of colors and shapes.

Abstract Art

Abstract art also developed out of impressionism. Abstract art is appreciated for its shapes, color, and/or texture but is not meant to represent any particular scene or being. An important leader in the development of abstract art was Russian-born artist Wassily Kandinsky (1866–1944), who left Russia to study art in Germany in 1896. After seeing an exhibit of paintings by Claude Monet in which he found it difficult to determine the subject, Kandinsky took the drastic step of completely abandoning representational painting. By 1903 he had come to be considered the founder of abstract art. Kandinsky's works, such as *Without Title*, were displayed all over Western Europe and influenced many other artists to develop their own nonrepresentational styles.

While Kandinsky was enjoying the praise of artists in Germany and also in France, where he spent the last eleven years of his life, the Soviet government in Russia outlawed abstract art altogether. Early in the twentieth century the Russian government had refused to allow the performance of any artwork that was not supportive of the tsar's

regime. For example, composer Rimsky-Korsakov's opera *Le Coq d'Or* (1908) was banned because the story made fun of autocrats. The opera is still missing from many lists of the composer's works.

After the Bolshevik Revolution of 1917, artists and composers had hoped for more freedom, but government control of the arts became even tighter. The new Soviet government required artists to realistically portray workers doing manual labor, including scenes that indicated that Russia was advancing industrially. They also wanted works that showed their communist leaders doing kind acts for their people. Works that did not do that were banned. In music, it was necessary that compositions be "understood" at first hearing. Some compositions were banned because they were too religious or because they used musical elements deemed unsuitable. Even triple meter was to be avoided because music should be "marchable," which requires duple or quadruple meters.

Composers such as Sergei Prokofiev (1891–1953) and Dmitri Shostakovich (1906–1975) managed to work within the Soviet system enough to create brilliant compositions that were allowed to be performed both within and outside of Russia. Even these composers had problems with censorship, however. Shostakovich's opera *Lady Macbeth of Mtsensk* (1934) was praised when it was first performed. Unfortunately, Stalin went to see the opera in 1936 and described it as "chaos instead of music." The work was eventually banned (although it has been revived in recent years).

Modernism

In Western Europe, artists and composers were experimenting with new techniques and creating new styles one after another. The general term *modernism* refers to a number of these new styles. Pablo Picasso's (1881–1973) *Les Demoiselles d'Avignon* (1907) was viewed as *primitive*, not only because of its use of African-type masks for some of the faces, but also because the women's figures are sectioned into planes of geometric shapes, a style that later became known as *cubism*. Music we will hear by Igor Stravinsky (1882–1971) also contains primitive elements, such as complex rhythms influenced by non-Western music.

During World War I, expressionistic German artists such as Otto Dix (1891–1969) personally experienced the horrors of war while serving as soldiers. After the war they responded by exhibiting paintings that portrayed those horrors, calling their exhibition "No More War!" When Adolf Hitler came to power in 1933, he said that the works were too likely to influence the German people against fighting, and he had many of those paintings destroyed. *Trench Warfare* (1932) on page 270 is one of Dix's antiwar paintings that survived Hitler's fires. Dix survived as an artist in Germany only because he agreed to paint nothing other than landscapes until he was forced to fight again in World War II.

It is ironic that the Soviets and the Nazis were absolute enemies (except for a treaty in 1939 that did not last), and yet they both used the arts in similar ways to control and "educate" their people about advantages of life under their systems of government. Like the Soviets, the Nazis opposed modern art for reasons that went beyond its antiwar content. They wanted the world to see Germanic peoples as perfect and proud, and so allowed only classic or sentimental portray-

Les Demoiselles d'Avignon, by Pablo Picasso (1881–1973). This is seen as "primitive" because of the use of African-type masks for some faces and also the sectional shapes of the figures.

als of life. Wagner's operas and music dramas were favorites because Wagner used Germanic lore and legends and because he had the reputation of believing that the German race should remain "pure."

In 1937, Nazi leaders took expressionistic and other works that they deemed corrupting out of museums and galleries and put 650 of them in a special exhibit they called "Degenerate Art." The exhibit toured throughout much of Germany and Austria, showing the works on walls covered by graffiti with signs that encouraged people to ridicule both the work and the artists who created it. Painters and art professors who refused to work within the subject and style constraints of the Third Reich were fired from their teaching positions and not allowed to display their works in public. The government also destroyed many works that included personal expressions or that did not support and reflect Nazi attitudes.

Dadaism

In the freer environment of Switzerland, another movement in art came about as a reaction to World War I, called Dadaism. The

The Persistence of Memory, by Salvador Dali (1904–1989). This is an example of surrealism in art because it portrays things from the real world in ways they could not really exist in that world. Surrealism means "beyond the real."

statement behind most Dadaist works was that modern warfare had shown human life to be meaningless. Dada works were sometimes fashioned out of trash. A famous Dada sculpture by Marcel Duchamp (1887–1968) was a real urinal, placed in an art exhibit and called *Fountain* (1917).

Surrealism

Surrealism developed out of Dadaism and expressionism and was inspired by Sigmund Freud's (1856–1939) early-twentieth-century studies of the unconscious or the dream state. Surrealistic works portrayed things from the real world but put them into forms that could not really exist, making them "beyond the real," or things that could only be dreamed—such as Salvador Dali's (1904–1989) *The Persistence of Memory* (1931).

Neoclassicism

Other new styles emerged as artists and composers attempted to go beyond classical and romantic traditions and try new techniques and sounds. In some cases, however, artists and composers chose not to reject the past altogether but to base their works on older forms while still using newer ideas. One such style was called *neoclassicism* because new works were constructed using old (from any past era) types of images or, in the case of

music, forms such as sonata or rondo. Before he worked with primitivism, Pablo Picasso spent some time painting figures that were suggestive of earlier styles, even those of ancient Greece. The composer Igor Stravinsky, whose works continued to change in style throughout his life, composed the oratorio *Oedipus Rex* (1927), based on the Greek tragedy of that same title. In 1950 he composed music for another opera, *The Rake's Progress*, in which he used the singing styles of arias and recitatives much the way Mozart had. The opera was based so closely on Mozart's style that Stravinsky even used harpsichord accompaniment for the recitatives.

In summary, the early twentieth century introduced many new sights and sounds to the arts. Some we might find beautiful and excitingly new, whereas others we might find disturbing. In the case of expressionism, the music is often meant to be disturbing. The people who created in that style were not living happy and free lives. Their art and music reflected their discontent. Censorship by Soviet and Nazi governments controlled artists and composers in Russia and Germany, but many artists and composers who wanted to freely produce works that were not dictated by governments were able to leave and pursue successful careers in other countries.

Impressionism and Symbolism

))) First Hearing

CONNECT   CD 3: Tracks 2–6

Listen to the recording of *Prélude à "L'après-midi d'un faune"* (*Prelude to "The Afternoon of a Faun"*) by Debussy and take notes on what you hear. Even if you are working with other students in a paired or group listening session, keep your own notes. Give some attention to the following:

- What instrument plays the opening melody? What other instruments come in after that? Which, if any, brass or percussion instruments do you hear in the piece?

- When does the opening melody repeat? Near the beginning, the middle, and/or the end? Does it repeat just as you heard it the first time, or is it varied?

- How would you describe the mood of the piece? Does it have a single mood throughout, or does the mood seem to change often?

- Can you guess at the tempo, or does that seem to vary?

- Can you guess at the meter, or is it difficult to count?

Keep your notes from this First Hearing to compare with your impressions about the piece after you study the information in this chapter.

26

The musical culture of France was closely connected to the other arts, particularly painting and literature. One of the outstanding artistic movements of the turn of the century was **impressionism,** in which painters sought to capture the visual impression, rather than the literal reality, of a subject. Although their work and methods were at first ridiculed by the critics, the impressionists persisted in their exploration of the play of light and their use of patches and dabs of color to build up an image. They also continued their habit of working outdoors and utilizing bright afternoon light; mood and atmosphere and the richness of nature were among their major inspirations, as can be seen in Claude Monet's *Impression: Sunrise.* Meanwhile, poets were experimenting with rhythm, sound, and the clustering of images to suggest moods or emotions. This poetic style came to be known as **symbolism.**

Coming slightly later than the movements in art and literature, the impressionist movement in music was similarly characterized by experimentation and the rejection of past viewpoints. It, too, emphasized mood and atmosphere more than structure, and it, too, adopted nature as a frequent subject. Impressionist music is recognizable by its fragile and decorative beauty, its sensuous tone colors, its subdued atmosphere, its elegance and refinement, and its rhythmic fluidity. It cast off the more pompous,

***Impression: Sunrise*, by Claude Monet.** The lack of detail in this painting makes it appear more like an impression of a scene than what we might see in real life. The colors and the reflection of light are as much the subject of the painting as are the water, boats, and sun.

heavy, and serious quality of the romantic German tradition. The influence of impressionism extended to England, Spain, Italy, and America, but France produced the most important composers: Claude Debussy ("Deb-you-see") and Maurice Ravel.

Claude Debussy

Claude Debussy (1862–1918) was born in St. Germain-en-Laye, near Paris, and was educated at the Paris Conservatory, where he received traditional training in the cosmopolitan late-romantic style of composition. He absorbed it well enough to win the Prix de Rome at age 22, but soon afterward he began to reject the Germanic tradition in general and Wagner's philosophy in particular.

Debussy was put off by what he heard as the grand themes and ponderous quality of German romantic music. For him the primary goal of music was to give pleasure, to appeal to the senses. An incisive critic, Debussy wrote articles on music that were published in the leading French journals. His reaction to Wagner's use of the leitmotif is characteristically witty and caustic: Wagnerian characters "never appear unless accompanied by their damnable leitmotiv, and there are even those who sing it! It's rather like those silly people who hand you their visiting cards and then lyrically recite key information they contain."

Opera was one of Debussy's lifelong interests, and his operatic style was very much a reaction against Wagner's influence. *Pelléas et Mélisande* (1902), which Debussy worked on during the 1890s, was taken from a symbolist play by Maurice Maeterlinck. It contains vague references and images of text that Debussy matched by restrained orchestral tone colors. Throughout the work, the voices dominate over a continuous orchestral background. The first performance of the opera received mixed reactions. Some critics attacked it for its lack of form and melody, and others were enchanted by its subtle, elusive quality. Eventually, the opera caught on and established Debussy as the leader of the impressionist movement in music.

World War I and its devastating effects on France disturbed Debussy so profoundly that for a time he felt incapable of writing music. It was his sense of nationalism that impelled him to return to his art, and he began composing again with furious energy—an effort spurred on by the fact that he was slowly dying of cancer. His death came in March 1918, as Paris was being bombarded by German artillery. He was 55 years old.

Debussy was an accomplished pianist, and his piano compositions are among the most significant for his era. His early works were not impressionistic, but by 1903 he was well established in that style, with two collections of *Préludes* and two of *Images*.

His orchestral works are all impressionistic. We will listen to and discuss the first of those, *Prélude à L'après-midi d'un faune (Prelude to The Afternoon of a Faun)*. This piece is programmatic but in a general way. There is little attempt to tell a story or express specific feelings. Rather, it creates a mood or atmosphere to correspond with its program. The basis of the program is a poem by the symbolist writer Stéphane Mallarmé. Debussy described the prelude as a "very free illustration of Mallarmé's poem." In the poem, the faun (a sensual forest deity of pagan mythology, half man, half goat) awakens from sleep, his mind befuddled by wine. The faun recalls two nymphs he had seen earlier in the day. Did he carry them off to his lair or was it only a fantasy? "Is it a dream that I love?" he asks. But the afternoon is warm and the effort to remember too great, so once again he drifts off to sleep. Without following the events of the poem literally, Debussy evokes a musical impression of the poem.

The vague events in the poem on which Debussy's prelude is based makes it a very different work from programmatic works we heard in the romantic period, particularly those that told specific stories. "Hearing the Difference: Smetana's 'The Moldau' and Debussy's *Prélude à L'après-midi d'un faune*" examines some of these differences.

CLAUDE DEBUSSY
(1862–1918)

- Born in St. Germain-en-Laye, France; died at age 55 in Paris, France.

- Best known for piano works such as *Suite Bergamasque* (which includes "Clair de lune"), the orchestral works *Prélude à L'après-midi d'un faune* and "La mer," the opera *Pelléas et Mélisande*, and the ballet *Jeux (Games)*.

 ))) **Featured Listening**

 CD 3: Tracks 2–6

Prélude à L'après-midi d'un faune (Prelude to The Afternoon of a Faun) CLAUDE DEBUSSY

Date: 1894

Genre: Symphonic poem

Tempo: Moderate tempo, changing throughout work

Form: Modified ternary (AA'BA") with no literal repetition; sections indicated as being repeated merely contain suggestions of the melodies of the earlier ones

Instruments: Three flutes, two oboes, one English horn, two clarinets, two bassoons, four French horns, two harps, antique cymbals, first violins, second violins, violas, cellos, double basses. (*Note:* The only brass instruments are the mellow-sounding French horns, and the only percussion instruments are two antique cymbals, which produce a delicate sound.)

Meter: Irregular and unclear

Duration: 9:40

(continued)

Context: It might be helpful to look again at the painting *Impression: Sunrise* by Claude Monet on page 248 before listening to this piece. The painting has a different subject from the orchestral work, but you might notice that the lack of clear outlines in the painting and the lack of complete and resolved melodies display a similar mood. The painting was also created by brushstrokes of pure colors that the viewer's eye must combine to see the subject. In Debussy's *Prélude*, a single melody often begins played by one instrument, then by another, and then another. The music moves from one tone color to another in much the same way that the painting moves from one brushstroke to another.

	Timing		What to listen for
2	0:00	A	Languid, sensuous flute melody floats down and up; horn calls and harp **glissandos;** sensuous melody again in flute with quiet tremolo (fast, repeated notes) in strings; crescendo in orchestra as intensity builds, then fades away
3	0:00	A'	Sensuous melody, flute, with added decoration, accompanied by occasional harp arpeggios
	1:03	Bridge	Splashes of instrumental color through the orchestra grow in volume and animation, suggest the faun's awakening senses, then subside; slow, dreamlike clarinet solo with delicate strings moves directly into:
4	0:00	B	Lyric, long-breathed melody in woodwinds with gently pulsing string accompaniment, crescendo; suddenly soft as lyric melody repeats in strings with harp arpeggios and pulsing woodwinds
	0:50	Bridge	Fragments from previous bridge in strings, then in various woodwind colors; solo violin longingly sings beginning of lyric melody
	1:48		Harp arpeggios accompany flute in anticipation of sensuous melody; woodwind fragments of melody and staccato chords interrupt; harp arpeggios accompany opening of sensuous melody in oboe; again soft interruptions
5	0:00	A''	Sensuous melody in flutes, with the delicate ring of antique cymbals and subdued tremolo in strings, yearning solo violin counterpoint; melody repeated in flute and cello, flute wanders drowsily off, melody completed by oboe
6	0:00	Coda	Harp and strings in floating, static notes, fragment of sensuous melody in horns, ringing antique cymbals, pizzicato in low strings

Maurice Ravel

Maurice Ravel (1875–1937) is often linked with Debussy as the other major figure who most fully realized the possibilities of musical impressionism. But Ravel's music, especially the compositions written in his later years, combines the sonorous impressionism of Debussy with a classical orientation toward form and balance.

Philosophically, Ravel had much in common with Debussy. Both composers agreed that music should serve an aesthetic purpose and that the creation of beautiful sound was the ultimate aim. They considered themselves rebels against German romanticism and the Wagnerian school. They shared an attraction to the rhythms of Spanish dance music, as well as non-Western modes, scales, and instrumental tone colors.

SMETANA'S "THE MOLDAU" AND DEBUSSY'S *PRÉLUDE À L'APRÈS-MIDI D'UN FAUNE*

Both of these works are symphonic poems composed in the nineteenth century, although twenty years apart (see Featured Listening on page 191 and page 249). Despite that closeness, Smetana's work is considered very romantic and Debussy's is viewed as foreshadowing the artistic movements of the twentieth century. We will compare them to help us appreciate some of the differences in compositional styles as we move into the new century. Answer the following questions as you listen from one work to the other:

- Both works are programmatic, which means that they are composed to portray a story through music. What kinds of places or events are portrayed in each story? Look back at the Listening Guides for reminders of the stories.)

- How are the instruments in the orchestra used to portray the events in the stories? Is one work clearer in telling its story? Which one?

- Which work uses more percussion instruments? How do those instruments fit the story?

- Which work has a specific melody that clearly repeats several times? When the other has a melody repeat, is it much the same each time, or is it more of a suggestion than a full repeat?

- Which work fits the mood of the painting *Impression: Sunrise* by Monet? What is it about the sound of the music that corresponds to the general style of that painting?

Ravel created many compositions for the piano, as well as a number of songs for voice and chamber ensembles or voice and orchestra. He is best known for his orchestral works, however. His interest in Spanish dance rhythms can be heard in his most famous work, "Boléro" (1928), which employs a gradual uninterrupted crescendo and a repetitive single melody.

Summary

Around the beginning of the twentieth century, the musical culture of France was closely related to the other arts. Two of the dominant movements at the time were impressionism in painting and symbolism in literature, both of which influenced the development of impressionism in music. Impressionist music is characterized by its fragile beauty, sensuous tone colors, subdued atmosphere, and elegance. It cast off the more pompous, heavy, and serious quality of the German tradition. Claude Debussy is the composer primarily associated with musical impressionism. His use of free-flowing rhythms and light instrumental colors are characteristic of the style. Maurice Ravel, who is often linked with Debussy, incorporated many impressionistic devices into his music, but he also displayed a classical orientation toward form and balance.

New People and Concepts

Claude Debussy, 248

glissando, 250

impressionism, 247

Maurice Ravel, 250

symbolism, 247

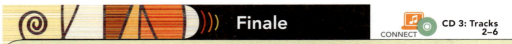

Finale

CD 3: Tracks
2–6

Listen again to the recording of *Prélude à L'après-midi d'un faune (Prelude to The After-noon of a Faun)* by Debussy and compare your impression now with your notes from your First Hearing. Consider the following questions:

- What instrument plays the opening melody? What instruments do you notice most in this piece? Which instruments that are common to most orchestras are *not* present here?
- When does the opening melody repeat? What is the general form of the piece?
- What is the mood, and how does that relate to the general style of impressionism?
- How would you describe the tempo?
- How would you describe the meter?
- If you were going to describe this music to a friend, what would you say?

Further Listening

Claude Debussy, *La cathédrale engloutie (The Sunken Cathedral).* This prelude for solo piano conveys images from a Breton myth. In the myth, a cathedral on an island has sunken below the water, and it rises from the sea on a clear morning. The sounds of the cathedral rising from the sea, medieval chants, the ringing of the cathedral's bells, and the cathedral organ are all part of the impressionistic vision.

Claude Debussy, *La mer (The Sea).* Sounds of the sea are the focus of this three-movement orchestral work. The movements are (1) "De l'aube à midi sur la mer—très lent" ("From dawn to noon on the sea—very slowly"), (2) "Jeux de vagues—allegro" ("Play of the waves—fast"), and (3) "Dialogue du vent et de la mer—animé et tumultueux" ("Dialogue of the wind and the sea—animated and stormy").

Maurice Ravel, *Jeux d'eau.* This solo piano work depicts water fountains. It was inspired by *Jeux d'eau a la Villa d'Este (The fountains of the Villa d'Este)* by Franz Liszt.

Maurice Ravel, *Pavane pour une infant défunte (Pavane for a Dead Princess).* This is a slow processional dance for a Spanish princess who has died. It was composed for solo piano, but Ravel also published an orchestral version.

Primitivism and Neoclassicism

> I don't write modern music.
> I only write good music.
>
> —COMPOSER IGOR STRAVINSKY
> (1882–1971)

))) First Hearing

CONNECT   CD 3: Tracks 7–8

Listen to the recording of *Le Sacre du printemps (The Rite of Spring)*, Introduction, by Stravinsky and take notes on what you hear. Even if you are working with other students in a paired or group listening session, keep your own notes. Give some attention to the following:

● What instrument plays the introductory melody? What instruments join the soloist in the beginning? What instruments can you identify later in the work?

● We are listening to three sections of a long work. What kinds of moods do you hear in those sections? Are they all similar, or do they contrast with one another? If you hear contrasts, try to describe the mood of each section.

● This is music for a ballet. What can you imagine about the dance that would go with this music? What costumes might the dancers be wearing?

● Does the work seem to have a steady tempo and meter? If not, do you think it would be difficult to dance to?

● This work was first performed in 1913. What reaction do you think the first audience would have had?

Keep your notes from this First Hearing to compare with your impressions about the piece after you study the information in this chapter.

27

Primitivism

The French World Exhibition of 1889 introduced visual images, music, and dance from many non-Western cultures to artists and composers in Paris. Artist Paul Gauguin (1848–1903) was so impressed with what he saw as an "honest exoticism" that, in 1891, he moved to the South Sea island of Tahiti. There, he painted many wonderful lush and colorful scenes of islanders enjoying a relaxed life in the tropics, such as *Mahana no Atua* (*Day of the Gods,* 1894).

This style came to be known as **primitivism.** The term *primitive* refers to more than the portrayal of technologically underdeveloped people. It also refers to flat shapes, lack of traditional sense of perspective, and colors so vivid that they are beyond what might look real. Without perspective, the figures in the background are not all that much smaller than those in the foreground. The viewer can tell they are in the background only because they are slightly smaller and higher on the canvas. Many artists, such as Gauguin and Henri Rousseau, whose works are also categorized as primitive, were self-taught and were interested in breaking away from traditional realistic styles while still representing live subjects. Much folk art is also considered primitive. Primitivist

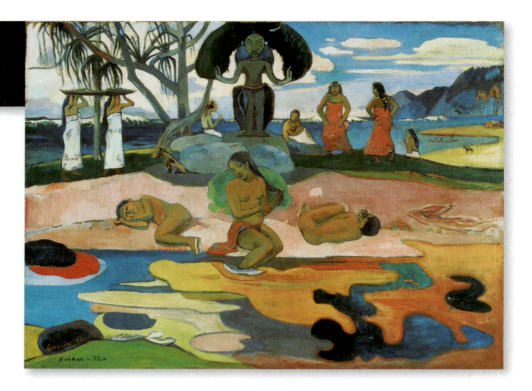

Mahana no Atua (Day of the Gods), by Paul Gauguin. This painting portrays the relaxed life of Tahitian natives.

influences manifested themselves in Pablo Picasso's painting *Les Demoiselles d'Avignon* (*The Young Women of Avignon,* page 245).

Igor Stravinsky

IGOR STRAVINSKY
(1882–1971)

- Born in Oranienbaum, Russia; died at age 88 in New York.

- Best known for the ballets *L'oiseau de Feu (The Firebird), Petrouchka,* and *Le Sacre du printemps (The Rite of Spring)*; the opera/oratorio *Oedipus Rex*; the choral and orchestra work *Symphony of Psalms*; the Symphony in C; and the opera *The Rake's Progress.*

Like Picasso in the visual arts, composer **Igor Stravinsky** (1882–1971) had a long, successful career that encompassed many twentieth-century styles, including primitivism. Stravinsky, the third son of one of the most celebrated bass baritones in the Imperial Opera, was born in a small Russian town on the Gulf of Finland near St. Petersburg. He began piano lessons at age 9; but his parents, though encouraging his piano studies, regarded his musical activity as a sideline and decided that he should study law at the University of St. Petersburg, where he had the good fortune to make friends with the youngest son of Nikolai Rimsky-Korsakov. He soon met the composer himself, at that time the leading figure in Russian music and one of the members of "the Five." By 1903, Stravinsky was studying orchestration with Rimsky-Korsakov. They became close friends, and the elder composer acted as best man at Stravinsky's wedding to a cousin in 1906.

After completing his university studies in 1905, Stravinsky decided on a career as a composer. His earliest serious works were written under Rimsky-Korsakov's supervision. In 1909, he met Sergei Diaghilev, the impresario of the newly formed Ballet Russes, a Russian ballet company in Paris. Diaghilev commissioned the young composer to write music for a ballet based on an old Slavic legend. The work, entitled *L'oiseau de Feu* (*The Firebird*), had its première at the Paris Opera the following year. It was so successful that Stravinsky became a celebrity almost overnight.

Two more ballets quickly followed: *Petrouchka* (1910–1911) and *Le Sacre du printemps* (*The Rite of Spring,* 1912–1913). The first performance of *The Rite of Spring* sparked the most famous riot in music history (some of the reasons for the wild reaction are discussed later in this chapter).

Dancers in costumes from the original production of Stravinsky's *Rite of Spring*.

Despite that temporary setback, Stravinsky continued to compose music that was critically acclaimed. Until the outbreak of World War I, Stravinsky divided his time among Switzerland, Russia, and France. A member of the most distinguished musical and artistic circles of Europe, he came in close contact with Debussy, Ravel, writer Jean Cocteau, and artist Pablo Picasso.

From the outbreak of World War I until 1919, Stravinsky lived in Switzerland. The difficulty in gathering together large groups of performers during this period of world war contributed to his evolving compositional style. He turned from huge orchestral works to compositions scored for instrumental ensembles of more modest size.

Stravinsky had given up his Russian citizenship at the time of the Russian Revolution of 1917. At the end of World War I, he returned to Paris, where he became a French citizen. Much of his time during the 1920s and 1930s was spent on tour through the principal cities of Europe and America. When World War II began, he moved again, this time to Hollywood, California. Deciding to remain in the United States permanently, he gave up his French citizenship to become a naturalized American in 1945.

Stravinsky continued to compose music well into his later years, and he conducted concerts of his music all over the world even into his eighties. He died in 1971 at age 88.

Stravinsky used rhythmically complex ideas from non-Western cultures and combined those with his knowledge of Russian folk music when he was commissioned to compose *The Rite of Spring* for the Ballet Russes de Monte Carlo. The ballet was subtitled *Pictures of Pagan Russia,* and it depicts the Russian peasants' pagan (pre-Christian) rites to convince the gods to end the winter and bring the earth back to life with spring. The rite culminates in the sacrifice of a young virgin, who dances herself to death while the tribal elders watch. Stravinsky's music incorporated the idea of paganism by stressing angular melodies and offbeat, primitive rhythms. Not only were the subject matter and the music unexpected by the audience, but the costumes were brightly colored and bulky, and the choreography by Vaslav Nijinsky was even more shocking. Nijinsky's wife, Romola, danced in the first performance, and she described the dancers as follows:

> The men in *The Rite of Spring* are primitive. There is something almost bestial in their appearance. Their legs and feet are turned inwards, their fists clenched, their heads held down between hunched shoulders; their walk, on slightly bent knees, is heavy as they laboriously straggle up a winding trail, stamping in the rough, hilly terrain. The women are also primitive, but in their countenances one already perceives the awakening of an awareness of beauty. Still, their postures and movements

 **MusiCurious**

MUSIC FOR BALLET

Is it common for music composed for a ballet to become famous without the dance?

Yes. It hasn't always been that way, however. Before Tchaikovsky began to write ballet music in the late nineteenth century, ballet music was composed without thought of its value beyond the dance. Operas often had little sections of dance, but the dance served as a break within the drama. It certainly wasn't the central concentration of the opera. In fact, it was not until the early nineteenth century that dance technique developed to allow for the kinds of expression we think of as ballet today. Early dancers wore hard shoes, and their movements were not at all fluid. Once toe shoes were invented, dancers could move more smoothly, twirl on their toes, and be lifted into the air to follow the lines and rhythms of an orchestra playing dramatic music. Tchaikovsky's *Swan Lake* was the first major work to effectively combine the new classical ballet style of dance with orchestral music of symphonic quality.

Didn't Tchaikovsky also compose music for *The Nutcracker?*

Yes. His music for *Sleeping Beauty* and *The Nutcracker,* as well as *Swan Lake,* is often performed today. For concert performances without dancers, composers rearrange the music so that it concentrates on the primary melodies, without the sections needed only to allow the dancers to move around the stage. Those rearrangements are usually called "suites." We heard dances from suites in our study of the baroque period, and that is the source of the term for instrumental works based on dance rhythms.

What about Stravinsky's ballets?

By the early twentieth century when Stravinsky took a job as composer for Sergei Diaghilev's Russian ballet company in Paris, ballet had become very popular. Parisian audiences in particular expected ballets to feature beautiful costumes, scenery, and music that allowed the dancers to move smoothly and dramatically. Diaghilev and Stravinsky provided exotic and beautiful choreography and music for their first two ballets, *L'Oiseau de Feu (The Firebird)* and *Petrouchka.* However, audiences were shocked to the point of rioting during the first performance of their next ballet, *The Rite of Spring,* with its pagan story, clumsy dance movements, and heavy, primitive costumes. Stravinsky did, indeed, imitate the pagan story about a human sacrifice in his dissonant and angular music, but it was the ballet that most shocked the audience.

Did *The Rite of Spring* destroy interest in ballet?

Not at all. Many ballets with music by major composers were written during the twentieth century, and ballet companies continue to perform new works today. Ballet dance styles have changed considerably and reflect the story being danced. For example, American composer Aaron Copland worked with choreographer Agnes DeMille to compose the cowboy-sounding music for *Rodeo,* which had a frontier setting. Copland also worked closely with modern dance choreographer Martha Graham to compose the music for *Appalachian Spring.* After a century of innovation, ballet audiences no longer are shocked or angry to witness dance styles or techniques that are different from what they have seen before.

are uncouth and clumsy, as they gather in clusters on the tops of small hillocks and come down together to meet in the middle of the stage and form a large crowd.

This was not the kind of dance that Parisian ballet audiences in 1913 expected to see. The audience was not only shocked but angry. There were boos and catcalls followed by actual fighting. The dancers could not even hear the music, and Nijinsky had to call out beats and cues to keep the performance going. Stravinsky was accused of "destroying music as art." Actually, the very same music was well received when it was played without the dancing only a year later. By the 1920s the work was lauded as a great achievement. The music then got another boost of popularity in 1940, when the Walt Disney Company used part of it in the movie *Fantasia* to accompany visions of animated dinosaurs. For more background on what the Parisian audience expected and why, see "MusiCurious: Music for Ballet."

The Rite of Spring takes about thirty-five minutes to perform. It has two large parts, the first of which features a series of pagan rituals involving the adoration of the earth and the choosing of the maiden who is to die. The second part includes dances with the chosen one and the tribal ancestors, as well as the final sacrificial dance. We will listen to the Introduction, "Auguries of Spring—Dances of the Young Girls," and "The Ritual of Abduction."

 ))) **Featured Listening**   CD 3: Tracks 7–8

Le Sacre du printemps (The Rite of Spring), **Introduction, "Auguries of Spring—Dances of the Young Girls," and "The Ritual of Abduction"** IGOR STRAVINSKY

Date: 1913

Genre: Ballet music

Tempo: Varies throughout the work

Form: Sectional, following the program

Instruments: Two piccolos, three flutes, one alto flute, four oboes, two English horns, four bassoons, two contrabassoons, eight French horns, five trumpets, one bass trumpet, three trombones, four tubas, a very large percussion section, first violins, second violins, violas, cellos, double basses

Meter: Irregular and changing

Duration: 8:22

Context: In order to fully appreciate the irregularity of the rhythms, try counting duple or triple metric patterns while you listen to the music and notice how unexpected the placement of the accented beats is.

	Timing	What to listen for
	Introduction	
7	0:00	Gentle, springlike melody in high bassoon; clarinet, high bassoon; new melody begins in English horn; bassoon; English horn completes its melody
	1:55	Additional melodies polyphonically in woodwinds; trill in violin; woodwind polyphony continues at length
	2:25	Oboe introduces fragment, high woodwinds only; clarinet squeals answer.
	2:39	Low chord in double basses supports woodwind polyphony of previous fragments.
	3:03	High bassoon alone in gentle opening theme; clarinet trill; back-and-forth motive in pizzicato violins, directly into:
	"Auguries of Spring—Dances of the Young Girls"	
8	0:00	Pounding barbaric rhythm in strings, loud horn punctuations; back-and-forth motive, English horn; barbaric rhythm, flirtatious melody in muted trumpet, oboes
	0:25	Back-and-forth motive, violent trumpet fanfares and woodwind shrieks
	0:39	Barbaric rhythm; mocking melody in bassoons, echoed in trombone, bassoons, bassoons again, oboes, trombone, oboes
	1:19	Violent interruption, drumbeats, long note in trombone
	1:24	Shrieks down through winds, violin solo trill, back-and-forth motive in English horn, with interruptions
	1:31	Back-and-forth motive in strings, smooth melody in horn, answered by flute; flirtatious melody in oboes and trumpet; smooth melody in alto flute

(continued)

Timing	What to listen for
2:15	Activity mounts; heavy melody in trumpets, added triangle and cymbals
2:36	Sudden piano, strings loud punctuations; smooth melody in piccolo, extended and developed, mounting whirling activity, full orchestra, crescendo

"The Ritual of Abduction"

3:20	Very fast, sustained brass chord, violent drumbeats, shrieking woodwinds, raucous trombones
3:31	Horn calls answered by woodwinds and strings; violent drumbeats, raucous trombones return; violent, polyphonic activity continues
3:57	Full orchestra suddenly comes together playing frantic rhythms.
4:06	Suddenly reduced, softer, horn calls; loud, descending interruption
4:19	Fanfare-like brass, drum interruptions; whirling strings, violent interruptions; solitary trill in flute continues into the next section, "Roundelays of Spring"

In this chapter we have concentrated on the style of primitivism because that is the style of *The Rite of Spring.* However, rather like the artworks of Picasso, Stravinsky's music cannot be generally categorized as primitive. His work includes a great variety of styles. With his ballet *Pulcinella* (1919), based on music by the eighteenth-century composer Giovanni Battista Pergolesi, and the *Octet for Wind Instruments* (1923), Stravinsky began working in a style called *neoclassicism.*

Neoclassicism

As we saw in the introduction to the medieval period, the term *classical* is used to describe the civilization of ancient Greece. In music, we call the late eighteenth century classical because of its concentration on symmetrically balanced forms reminiscent of ancient Greek art. When the term appears in the early twentieth century, this time called **neoclassical,** it refers to art or to music that is based on the objectivity, balanced formal structure, and emotional restraint of the works of an earlier period, usually ancient Greece, the baroque, or classical.

Much of Stravinsky's music through about 1950 is neoclassical, including his chamber work for winds and strings, the Dumbarton Oaks Concerto (1938). The texture and rhythms of the concerto were strongly influenced by Bach's Brandenburg Concertos. A Listening Guide to the first movement of the Dumbarton Oaks Concerto follows.

***La Toilette,* by Pablo Picasso.** This is an example of neoclassical art in that the figures are reminiscent of ancient Greek vase painting.

Concerto in E-Flat Major, the Dumbarton Oaks Concerto, first movement IGOR STRAVINSKY

Date: 1938

Genre: Chamber concerto

Tempo: Tempo giusto (precise, not flexible)

Form: No clear repeating sections

Instruments: One flute, one clarinet, one bassoon, two horns, three violins, three violas, two cellos, two string basses

Meter: Varies

Duration: 4:21

Context: This is the first movement of a three-movement work stylized after Bach's concerto grossos, particularly the third Brandenburg. It is mostly polyphonic, and the instruments take turns playing solos or playing in the ripieno, or backup group. "Dumbarton Oaks" was the name of the mansion home of the people who commissioned the work. For history buffs, that home was also the place where the Dumbarton Oaks Conference took place in 1944, beginning the United Nations.

Timing	Musical events
17 0:00	Strings and flute begin with fast and active counterpoint influenced by Bach's concerto, but with off-beat accents and dissonances not found in baroque music.
1:00	Fanfare-like exchange between horns and bassoon
1:12	Strings join the exchange.
2:04	Violas play a fugue subject imitated by violins, string basses, and then cellos.
2:35	Loud, horns and strings, much activity follows
2:50	Loud again, flute plays a high countermelody above the rest of the group
3:38	Fast descending lines give a sense of an ending.
3:58	Long-held chords end the movement and lead directly into the second, slower movement.

Other neoclassical works by Stravinsky include his opera-oratorio *Oedipus Rex* (1927), based on the Greek tragedy of the same title, and the opera *The Rake's Progress* (1950), titled after a series of engravings by the English artist William Hogarth.

The Rake's Progress features Stravinsky's brilliant musical language of varied rhythms and his colorful use of woodwinds, but it is also much like Mozart's operas in many ways. Like Mozart, Stravinsky had the orchestra accompany emotional arias, and he had the harpsichord accompany recitative-styled dialogue. Romantic opera composers had done away with the harpsichord and had composed more melodic singing for sections of dialogue, so Stravinsky's style and instrumentation marked a return to the older classical style, making it neoclassical. Mozart's operatic style can again be heard at the end of *The Rake's Progress* when the lead singers come out on stage to sing the moral of the tale, "For idle hands / And hearts and minds / The Devil finds / A work to do." Mozart ended *Don Giovanni* by having the characters who remain after Don Giovanni's death stand and sing the opera's moral lesson: "This is the end of the evil-doer: His death is as bad as his life."

Summary

In this chapter we have discussed two styles of the early twentieth century, primitivism and neoclassicism. Composer Igor Stravinsky wrote in both styles. The development of primitivism was heavily influenced by non-Western art and music. In the case of Stravinsky's ballet *The Rite of Spring*, the subject was a pagan ritual in which a young maiden was sacrificed to encourage the gods to awaken the world with the new life of spring. The music is full of syncopated, jarring rhythms and angular themes.

The dance was even more shocking to the Parisian ballet audience in 1913 because the dancers were hunched over with clenched fists to look like a pagan tribe. The audience rioted at the first performance, but the music was eagerly accepted only one year later. Stravinsky's neoclassical works followed *The Rite of Spring*. They took various forms, but all were based in some way on forms or subjects from earlier periods.

New People and Concepts

neoclassicism, 258   primitivism, 253   Igor Stravinsky, 254

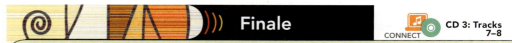

Finale

CD 3: Tracks 7–8
CONNECT

Listen again to the recording of *Le Sacre du printemps (The Rite of Spring)*, Introduction, by Stravinsky and compare your impression now with your notes from your First Hearing. Consider the following questions:

● What instrument plays the introductory melody, and what instruments join that? What other instruments or sections of instruments stand out later in the work?

● What kinds of moods are portrayed in these three sections of the ballet? How do those fit the story behind the ballet?

● What kind of costumes did the dancers wear? How did the audience react to them? What was unusual about the dancing?

● Does the work have one steady tempo and meter? How would you describe it?

● How did the first audience react to the sound of the music?

● If you were going to describe this music to a friend, what would you say?

Further Listening

Igor Stravinsky, *Le Sacre du printemps (The Rite of Spring)*. We heard only the beginning of this ballet, which should be enjoyed in its entirety. Some of the music was featured in Disney's 1940 version of *Fantasia*.

Igor Stravinsky, Concerto in E-Flat Major, the "Dumbarton Oaks Concerto." J. S. Bach's *Brandenburg Concertos* were the model for this chamber work whose first movement we heard in this chapter. The movements are (1) Tempo giusto, (2) Allegretto, and (3) Con moto, but the three are performed without any pauses between them.

Igor Stravinsky, *Petroushka*. This is a ballet about a Russian puppet named Petroushka who is made of bagged sawdust and straw, but who develops emotions when he

comes to life and falls in love. The music from the ballet is available as a suite.

Igor Stravinsky, *Symphony of Psalms*. As Stravinsky said of this work, "It is not a symphony in which I have included *Psalms* to be sung. On the contrary, it is the singing of the *Psalms* that I am symphonizing." The work was commissioned by the Boston Symphony Orchestra on its fiftieth anniversary. It is scored for orchestra without violins or violas, but with two pianos and harp, along with a full choir. Its three "parts" are performed without a pause.

Igor Stravinsky, *The Rake's Progress*. This opera was discussed in this chapter and is available on DVD.

The sacredness of church music, the joyfulness and soulfulness of folk songs are the two pivots around which revolve true music. A nation creates music . . . the composer only arranges it.

—COMPOSER BÉLA BARTÓK (1881–1945)

Eastern European Nationalism

 ))) **First Hearing**

CONNECT CD 3: Track 9

Listen to the recording of Concerto for Orchestra, fourth movement, by Bartók and take notes on what you hear. Even if you are working with other students in a paired or group listening session, keep your own notes. Give some attention to the following:

- How would you describe the mood of this piece? Somber? Light and cheerful? Passionate? Something else?

- How many different themes do you hear? If a theme repeats, does it sound the same as it did before, or is it changed somewhat? Can you describe the change?

- Do you hear the same instruments playing over and over again, or does the instrumentation vary? Do the instruments that play solo melodies change fairly often?

- Do you hear any instruments playing sounds that seem disturbing or unpleasant?

- Can you guess at the tempo?

- Can you guess at the meter?

Keep your notes from this First Hearing to compare with your impressions about the piece after you study the information in this chapter.

28

As we discussed in earlier chapters, one aspect of nationalism is the expression of pride in one's country. We saw Chopin exhibit a sense of nationalism when he composed mazurkas and polonaises based on Polish dance rhythms. Smetana displayed similar pride in his country of Bohemia when he composed "The Moldau," using it to describe the beauty of that Bohemian river. Many other composers have created works, particularly operas, based on national folklore or historical events. Modest Mussorgsky's opera *Boris Godunov,* for example, took its libretto from a drama by Pushkin about a tsar in Russia's past. Composers have usually tried to look at what the people in the small villages of their country sang, danced, and cared about, the theory being that such people are not "tarnished" by having traveled to foreign places. They were villagers and farmers who took pride in their work and lifestyles.

Before recording machines were invented, it was difficult for people outside of these small villages to hear and appreciate the music played and sung by villagers, but by the early twentieth century it had become possible for recordings to be made. The earliest experiments in sound recording were conducted during the mid-nineteenth century, and in 1877 Thomas Edison (1847–1931) patented the first phonograph. It was a mechanical device that gathered sound in a horn and then transferred the sound

Bartók visiting a Hungarian village in 1907 to record local folk-songs on a machine that captured sound waves in the horn and engraved them on a wax-covered cylinder. The machine was hand-cranked and could play the songs back. Bartók's music was much influenced by the folk traditions of such villages.

waves onto a wax-covered cylinder. The same device could then play back the sounds that had been recorded. Flat discs soon replaced the cylinders. It was not until the 1920s that the devices were made to run on electricity. Though the quality of sound was primitive at best, the phonographs did at least reproduce a melody or rhythm pattern that allowed composers to record what they heard in villages and then play that music back for further study whenever they wanted. Hungarian composer Béla Bartók was the first major composer to study folk music by making field recordings and using the ideas he gained in his compositions.

Béla Bartók

Béla Bartók (1881–1945) was the son of the director of a government agricultural school. His first piano lessons, begun at age 5, were given by his mother. Following the death of his father in 1888, the family moved to Bratislava (now the capital of Slovakia), where Bartók began formal studies in music. In 1892, he made his first public appearance as a composer and pianist, playing one of his own works, and he formed a close friendship with Ernö Dohnányi, in later years one of Hungary's most noted pianists and composers.

In 1899, though admitted to the prestigious Vienna Conservatory, Bartók decided to follow Dohnányi to the Royal Academy of Music in Budapest. There he became strongly attracted to the music of Wagner and Richard Strauss. He also was caught up in the nationalistic movement in politics, literature, and the arts then sweeping through Hungary. His first major composition, an immense orchestral tone poem entitled *Kossuth* (1903), commemorated the nationalist leader of the unsuccessful revolution of 1848. Bartók became friends with Zoltán Kodály (1882–1967), the third member (with Dohnányi and Bartók) of the great trio of modern Hungarian composers.

Both Bartók and Kodály developed a strong interest in the problem of creating a national music and began collecting and analyzing Hungarian folk music. The earliest product of their research was a joint publication of arrangements, *Twenty Hungarian Folksongs* (1906). Bartók's interest in folk music began to have an immediate effect on his work; folk-derived rhythms and melodic patterns appeared side by side with the most current devices in composition.

Following his graduation in 1902 from the Royal Academy, Bartók began a series of concert tours throughout major European cities that lasted for the next several years. During this period, he became increasingly influenced by the French impressionistic music of Debussy and his contemporaries. Bartók's efforts at composition, however, did not seem to get off the ground during this period, and for a while he leaned toward a career as a concert pianist rather than a composer.

In 1907, Bartók accepted an appointment as a piano teacher at the Budapest Academy, a post that he held for nearly thirty years. In 1909, he married Márta Ziegler, one of his pupils, and settled into a routine of teaching, composing, and making extensive concert tours. He also continued his research and study of Hungarian folk music, which continued to influence his compositions. In 1923, he was divorced and married another of his piano students, Ditta Pásztory. They often toured together, playing works for two pianos; and, in 1927, they traveled to America for a series of solo recitals and appearances with various orchestras.

By the late 1930s, Nazi Germany had designs on Hungary, and the political turmoil brought on by the conflict convinced Bartók to leave Hungary. In 1940, he immigrated to the United States, where he was given an appointment at Columbia University. While in New York, however, he developed leukemia, and his health began declining seriously. He died in September 1945 at age 64.

Béla Bartók's works include music for solo piano, chamber music for strings (often with piano), concertos, orchestral works of various types, and such vocal works as *Duke Bluebeard's Castle* and *Cantata Profana*.

Throughout his life, Bartók studied the folk music of Eastern Europe. His studies influenced his style of writing melodies, which sometimes had a folklike character. He rarely used actual folksongs in his compositions, but he understood how they were constructed and effectively imitated them. The diverse, irregular rhythms of Hungarian folk music also had a significant impact on his work. In individual passages of much of his music, the meter changes so often as to have the effect of a strongly complex rhythmic impulse.

In many ways Bartók's music can be categorized as neoclassical because he often used traditional compositional devices such as fugue and canon, as well as sonata form. In his *Music for Strings, Percussion, and Celesta* (1936), Bartók used an *arch form,* in which the beginning and ending of the piece are related, the second and second-to-last sections are related, the third and third-from-last are related, and the middle section stands alone, like the keystone on an archway. He also used another idea sometimes characteristic of some baroque religious music when he gave instructions for the two string ensembles to sit on opposite sides of the stage so that they might be heard in an antiphonal, or stereo, effect.

We will listen to the fourth movement of Bartók's Concerto for Orchestra. This work was premiered by the Boston Symphony Orchestra in 1944. The work features various solo instruments, hence the title "Concerto."

BÉLA BARTÓK
(1881–1945)

- Born in Nagyszentmiklós, Hungary; died at age 64 in New York City.

- Best known for the opera *Duke Bluebeard's Castle, Mikrokosmos* (six books) for piano, the ballet *Miraculous Mandarin,* and Concerto for Orchestra.

 ))) **Featured Listening**    CD 3: Track 9

Concerto for Orchestra, fourth movement, "Interrupted Intermezzo" BÉLA BARTÓK

Date: 1943

Genre: Concerto

Tempo: Allegretto

Form: Rondo-like (ABA-interruption-BA)

Instruments: One piccolo, three flutes, three oboes, one English horn, three clarinets, three bassoons, one contrabassoon, four horns, three trumpets, three trombones, one tuba, first violins, second violins, violas, cellos, string basses, two harps, timpani, triangle, side drum, bass drum, cymbals, and gong

Meter: Varies

Duration: 4:14

Context: Bartók composed this work after his move to the United States. He called it a concerto instead of a symphony because different instruments and groups of instruments in the orchestra are featured, much as a soloist is featured in a solo concerto. We are hearing the fourth of five movements.

(continued)

	Timing		Musical events
9	0:00	A	Short string introduction, then oboe plays the folklike A theme; clarinet, then flute, then horn follow; oboe returns playing the theme
	1:02	B	Violas introduce the gentle B theme; violins join with English horn accompaniment in background.
	1:42	A'	Woodwinds play varied version of A theme.
	2:06	Interruption	Clarinet plays light, bouncy C theme with interruptions from trumpets, woodwinds.
	2:29		Violins imitate the C theme; more interruptions follow.
	2:42		Strings begin C theme upside down, more interruptions.
	2:55	B'	Muted violins and violas (mutes subdue the sound) play gentle B theme.
	3:12	A"	Woodwinds exchange fragments of A theme, flute follows with a cadenza; woodwinds rejoin; soft ending with three short notes

Summary

Composers have often expressed nationalistic ideals in their music by basing their work on the melodies and dance rhythms of traditional folk music. Béla Bartók was the first major composer to do a detailed study of the folk music of his native Hungary by actually taking recording equipment to Hungarian villages. Recording the music allowed him to replay it later in his home studio. His compositions did not exactly quote folk melodies or rhythms, but his music was strongly influenced by them.

In the work we heard, Concerto for Orchestra, fourth movement, the irregular metric patterns and rhythms were influenced by the asymmetrical rhythms found in much Hungarian folk music.

Much of Bartók's music fits into both the categories of primitivism and neoclassicism because of his use of strong, primitive rhythms and reliance on formal structures from the baroque and classical periods.

New People

Béla Bartók, 262

))) **Finale**   CD 3: Track 9
CONNECT

Listen again to the recording of Concerto for Orchestra, fourth movement, by Bartók and compare your impression now with your notes from your First Hearing. Consider the following questions:

- What is the mood of this piece?
- How many primary themes do you hear? Is any variation used when themes repeat?
- How would you describe the use of instruments that play solos?
- What kind of instrumental sounds do you hear as "interruptions"?
- What is the tempo?
- Is there one clear and steady meter, or does the meter change often?
- If you were going to describe this music to a friend, what would you say?

Further Listening

Béla Bartók, Concerto for Orchestra. We heard only the fourth movement of this important work. Bartók called it a concerto instead of a symphony because of the way individual instruments are treated as soloists. The movements are (1) Introduzione (Introduction)—Andante non troppo—Allegro vivace, (2) Giuoco delle coppie (Game of Pairs)—Allegretto scherzando (light and playful), (3) Elegia (Elegy)—Andante non troppo, (4) Intermezzo interrotto (Interrupted Intermezzo)—Allegretto, and (5) Finale—Pesante–Presto (heavy and ponderous–very quick).

Béla Bartók, *Music for Strings, Percussion, and Celesta.* Bartók used special effects in this work. The score directs the two string quintets to be separated and placed on either side of the center instruments, which include a harp, celesta, piano, and a variety of percussion instruments. The spatial separation is used for its antiphonal effects. The movements are (1) Andante Tranquillo, (2) Allegro, (3) Adagio, and (4) Allegro Molto.

Béla Bartók, String Quartet no. 4. This quartet is constructed in an *arch* form in that the first and fifth movements share a similar theme, the second and fourth have similarities, and the third movement contrasts with the other movements as the keystone of the arch. In this and others of his quartets, Bartók used a number of special effects including pizzicato in which the strings are slapped against the fingerboard, muting of all instruments for extended periods, and many glissandi (sliding along the strings). The movements are (1) Allegro, (2) Prestissimo, con sordino (as fast as possible, with mute), (3) Non troppo lento, (4) Allegretto pizzicato, and (5) Allegro molto.

Germanic Expressionism and the Development of Serialism

))) First Hearing

CONNECT CD 3: Track 10

Listen to the recording of "Der Mondfleck" ("Moonfleck"), no. 18, from *Pierrot Lunaire (Moonstruck Pierrot)* by Schoenberg and take notes on what you hear. Even if you are working with other students in a paired or group listening session, keep your own notes. Give some attention to the following:

- What is your overall impression about this work? What kind of mood does it have? Can you tell the language of the text? What might the text be about?

- What kind of voice type is the singer? Soprano, mezzo soprano, alto, tenor, baritone, or bass?

- What instruments do you hear?

- Do you hear any repeated melodies?

- Can you guess at the tempo and meter?

Keep your notes from this First Hearing to compare with your impressions about the piece after you study the information in this chapter.

29

Expressionism in art generally represents the tormented feelings of people stuck in a world of pain and conflict. The artworks often used harsh colors and distorted images to achieve intense emotional effects. The subject matter of expressionism was modern humanity in its varied psychological states: isolated, irrational, rebellious, and tense. Expressionistic artists did not attempt to produce beautiful or realistic art but only to penetrate and reveal inner feelings. Several early twentieth-century composers shared the goals of the artists. To better understand the use of art and music to express emotions, see "MusiCurious: How Can Art Be Great If It Is Ugly?"

In their efforts to create a new kind of tonality, it occurred to twentieth-century composers that they might be able to avoid the traditional concept of tonality completely. But the idea of the tonal center (a note such as the "key" note of the piece that, when played at the end of a phrase, can give the music a sense of finality) was so fundamental to musical organization that it could not simply be dropped. Rather, it had to be replaced by an organizing principle of equal strength. One of the most effective of the systems developed to replace traditional harmony and tonality was **serialism,** developed by the Austrian composer Arnold Schoenberg.

 **MusiCurious**

HOW CAN ART BE GREAT IF IT IS UGLY?

What is so great about ugly paintings and music that express pain and inner conflict?

Nothing, necessarily. No one says you have to like them or even appreciate them. But some people look to the arts as a way of getting in touch with a variety of emotions, including anger, despair, and general angst. Please also bear in mind that much expressionistic art and music was created around the time of World War I. That war was a truly horrific experience. Few of us can imagine the misery endured by ordinary soldiers. For example, the painting *Trench Warfare*, by Otto Dix, is, indeed, ugly in that it shows some of the horrors of that war. Dix had served in the German army and used his art as an outlet for releasing the emotional trauma he had experienced.

What about Schoenberg's music? Did he fight in World War I too?

Yes. He was put in the army, even though he was 42 years old and a well-known, successful composer. On the other hand, the currents behind expressionism had already been manifesting themselves in Schoenberg's work before the war. The work we heard, "Moonfleck," from *Pierrot Lunaire*, was composed in 1912, two years before World War I started.

So the style known as expressionism was not really caused by the war.

Right, but it is often associated with World War I because the style of expressionism fit the emotions of people in Germany and Austria around the time of that war, and the style grew in influence and popularity as a result. In art, expressionism started with Vincent van

Gogh in the late nineteenth century. If you look at his painting *The Starry Night*, you can see a certain amount of his own internal conflict and unrest. In other words, it was a painting of stars at night, but it also expressed his personal emotions. That is why the style came to be called "expressionism." Another early expressionist was the Norwegian artist Edvard Munch, who painted *The Scream*, which also shows unrest, even terror. Wassily Kandinsky, who painted *Without Title*, broke away from portraying anything of the real world in his work well before the war. He and Schoenberg became friends before Schoenberg composed *Pierrot Lunaire*, and both were interested in breaking away from past traditions. They wanted to redefine what art and music was and come up with completely new ideas and sounds. Those paintings and sounds fit into, and even reflected, the emotions in the style of expressionism so they became associated with it.

Does expressionism exist only in art and music?

No. By around 1910, German writers such as Georg Heym wrote poetry that rebelled emotionally against cultural traditions of the time. Playwrights such as Bertolt Brecht wrote plays that rejected the values and traditions with which they had been raised. Early filmmakers such as Robert Wiene, particularly in his film, *The Cabinet of Dr. Caligari* (1919), used dramatic camera and lighting techniques such as shooting from awkward angles and capturing extremes of light and dark to express horror and pain. Those techniques influenced the work of later movie directors such as Orson Welles and Alfred Hitchcock.

Arnold Schoenberg

At the start of his career, **Arnold Schoenberg** (1874–1951) was closely allied with late German romanticism, although he moved further from it than almost any of his contemporaries. With two of his students, Alban Berg and Anton Webern, Schoenberg devised a way to reject tonality, creating a style that was **atonal.** His new system of musical organization involved arranging the twelve chromatic tones in a chosen (non-scalelike) order, called a *tone row*, and then writing the music using different versions of that row one after another. The notes of the row could be used in sequence, forming a melody or theme, or simultaneously in groups to form chords. This system is called **twelve tone** or *dodecaphony* (a dodecagon has twelve sides). The repeated use of the twelve-tone row over and over created a type of series and is, therefore, called *serialism.* Twelve-tone music opened the door to new methods of composing and new ways of constructing harmonies.

ARNOLD SCHOENBERG
(1874–1951)

- Born in Vienna, Austria; died at age 76 in Los Angeles, California.

- Best known for the invention of the twelve-tone system of composition and the works *Verklärte Nacht (Transfigured Night)*, Pierrot Lunaire (Moonstruck Pierrot), Suite for Piano, Ode to Napoleon, and *Moses and Aaron*.

Schoenberg was born into a Viennese middle-class family; although both of his parents loved music, neither provided much guidance in his early training. While in grammar school, he studied the violin and cello and was soon composing and playing in chamber ensembles. When Schoenberg was in his late teens, a friend who directed an amateur orchestral society, Alexander von Zemlinsky, first interested him in serious musical study. After working several years as a bank employee, Schoenberg decided in 1895 to embark on a musical career.

The two great influences on his early compositions were the giants of late-nineteenth-century German music: Brahms and Wagner. During the 1890s Schoenberg wrote several string quartets and piano works and a small number of songs. In 1901 he married his friend's sister, Mathilde von Zemlinsky. Shortly afterward, he was hired as a theater conductor in Berlin. There he became acquainted with composer Richard Strauss, who helped him obtain a teaching position and expressed great interest in his work. In 1903, Schoenberg returned to Vienna to teach musical composition. Composer Gustav Mahler became a supporter of his music, and, more important, Schoenberg took on as students two younger men, Alban Berg and Anton Webern. Both pupils would later adopt Schoenberg's twelve-tone methods and would develop them in their individual ways; Webern would decisively influence the future course of music.

It was during the first decade of the twentieth century that Schoenberg began turning away from the late romantic style of his earlier works and gradually developed his new twelve-tone method. Although his name spread among composers and performers, public acclaim eluded him. His famous song cycle *Pierrot Lunaire* (*Moonstruck Pierrot*, 1912) drew invective from critics but praise from **avant-garde** (new and experimental) sympathizers. *Pierrot Lunaire* employed a half-sung, half-spoken vocal technique called **Sprechstimme** (literally, "speech voice").

Schoenberg based *Pierrot Lunaire* on a set of twenty-one poems published in French by a Belgian poet, Albert Giraud, in 1884. The poems were translated into German by Otto Erich Hartleben in the 1890s. Schoenberg used that German translation for his work. Rondeaux form—in which lines 1 and 2 of a thirteen-line poem are repeated as lines 7 and 8—was used for most of the poems, including the one we will listen to, "Der Mondfleck" ("Moonfleck"), no. 18. The overall work is about Pierrot, who represents the classic "crying clown" figure. The poems are organized in three sections of seven poems each. The first set is about ecstasy, the second about weakness and despair, and the third about Pierrot being haunted by his past.

Pierrot Lunaire is composed for soprano voice and five instrumentalists playing piano, flute/piccolo, clarinet/bass clarinet, violin/viola, and cello, although some songs do not use all five musicians. The work is atonal, but not twelve tone. Schoenberg did not develop the twelve-tone system of composition until the 1920s, so this work predates that system.

Featured Listening

CONNECT CD 3: Track 10

"Der Mondfleck" ("Moonfleck"), no. 18, from *Pierrot Lunaire* (*Moonstruck Pierrot*) ARNOLD SCHOENBERG

Date: 1912
Genre: Chamber music

Tempo: Sehr rasche (very fast)

Form: Through-composed (no repeating sections) with some use of imitation (such as that used in canons and fugues) that is difficult to identify by ear

Voices and Instruments: Soprano voice, piano, piccolo, clarinet, violin, and cello

Language: German

Meter: Triple

Duration: 0:54

Context: The sad clown, Pierrot, is obsessed with the moon and its light. The *Sprechstimme* (speech song) vocal technique gives the text an eerie effect. The melodies, both sung and played, jump around, in an attempt to give the effect of flickering light.

	Timing	German text	English translation	Musical events
10	0:00	Einen weissen Fleck des hellen Mondes	A white fleck of bright moonlight	The piccolo begins by imitating the clarinet.
		Auf dem Rücken seines schwarzen Rockes,	on the back of his black jacket,	
		So spaziert Pierrot im lauen Abend,	Pierrot strolls in the mild evening air,	
		Aufzusuchen Glück und Abenteuer.	To search for good fun and adventure.	
	0:18	Plötzlich stört ihn was an seinem Anzug.	Suddenly, something about his clothing seems wrong,	
		Er beschaut sich rings und findet richtig—	He checks himself and, indeed, finds—	
		Einen weissen Fleck des hellen Mondes	A white fleck of bright moonlight	As the text repeats, the melody does not.
		Auf dem Rücken seines schwarzen Rockes.	on the back of his black jacket.	
	0:32	Warte! Denkt er: das ist so ein Gipsfleck!	Wait! He thinks: that is a fleck of plaster!	
		Wischt und wischt, doch—	He wipes and wipes, still—	
		bringt ihn nicht hurunter!	he can't get rid of it!	
		Und so geht er, giftheschwollen, weiter.	And so he goes on, filled with poison.	
		Reibt und reibt bis an den frühen Morgen—	He rubs and rubs until dawn comes—	
		Einen weissen Fleck des hellen Mondes.	at a white fleck of bright moonlight.	

Schoenberg's reputation was beginning to grow when his career was interrupted by World War I, in which he served with the Austrian army. Soon after, however, he was again active as a composer, a lecturer on theory, and a teacher. The 1920s marked a new direction. He went to Berlin in 1925 to teach composition at the State Academy of the Arts, taking with him his second wife, Gertrude Kolisch. (His first wife had died in 1923.)

In 1933, Schoenberg's career again took another direction. When the Nazi Party assumed power, Schoenberg, being Jewish, was dismissed from his post. He immigrated first to France, then to the United States. Although his reputation as a teacher and a modernist preceded him, he nevertheless had financial difficulty. After working

Trench Warfare, by Otto Dix. This painting expresses some of the horrors of World War I. War shadowed the first half of the twentieth century and had a strong impact on all the arts.

in Boston and New York, he joined the faculty of the University of California at Los Angeles. He died in Los Angeles at age 76.

Other Serial Composers

ANTON WEBERN
(1883–1945)

- Born in Vienna, Austria; died at age 61 in Mittersill, Austria.
- Best known for Five Pieces for Orchestra, op. 10; Symphony, op. 21, and Variations for Orchestra, op. 30.

Schoenberg's student **Alban Berg** (1885–1935) adopted most of Schoenberg's twelve-tone system of composition but used it with a great deal of flexibility. His works allow for a sense of tonality and combine twelve-tone techniques with established formal procedures from earlier musical periods, including the suite, the march, and the rondo. Much of his music has a warmth and lyricism that stem from the romantic tendencies of earlier composers, like Mahler. In addition, such elements as his ability to sustain large forms and his use of large orchestras reflect the romantic aspect of his style.

The opera *Wozzeck* (1917–1921) is considered by many to be Berg's greatest work. It was unquestionably influenced by the environment created in Europe by World War I. The central character is Wozzeck, a soldier who is belittled and abused by his superior, the captain, and used as a hired guinea pig in medical "experiments" by his doctor. He is betrayed by his mistress, Marie, and eventually driven to murder and suicide by a completely hostile society.

The vocal style of *Wozzeck* depends heavily on Schoenberg's *Sprechstimme* technique, which alternates with ordinary speech and conventional singing in an extremely expressive manner. The prevailing mood of the opera is one of cynicism, irony, helplessness, and depression. Few portrayals of life are as hopeless as that of *Wozzeck*.

Schoenberg's other important and influential student was **Anton Webern** ("Vayburn," 1883–1945). Whereas Berg came to represent a link to the past among the followers of Schoenberg, Webern's music represents a more radical denial of and departure from established compositional procedures and concepts. His mature works crystallize the serialist constructionist approach to musical composition inherent in the twelve-tone system as originally postulated by Schoenberg.

Whereas Berg was writing in complex forms for large musical forces, Webern was striving for economy of material and extreme compactness of form. He felt strongly that each individual note in a composition was important in itself; he added nothing for general effect. As a result of this preoccupation, most of his works are "miniatures." Webern's music is the epitome of clarity, economy of material, spareness of texture, and brevity.

The third movement from Five Pieces for Orchestra, op. 10, will serve as our example of Webern's style.

 CD 5: Track 18

Five Pieces for Orchestra, op. 10, third movement ANTON WEBERN

Date: 1928

Genre: Orchestral music

Tempo: Sehr langsam und äußerst ruhig (very slow and extremely quiet)

Form: The pulsating tones of the beginning and ending with a faster middle section give the effect of an ABA form, but the beginning music does not repeat to fit that form

Instruments: One clarinet, one French horn (muted), one trombone (muted), one harmonium (a keyboard instrument with reeds), one mandolin, one classical guitar, one celesta (a keyboard instrument with hammers that strike metal bars), one violin, viola (muted), one cello (muted), one harp, bass drum, snare drum, chimes, and cowbells

Meter: Mostly slow sextuple, varies in center section

Duration: 1:29

Context: When you look at the list of instruments, it is obvious that Webern's idea of an orchestra is a group of instruments from woodwind, brass, string, and percussion families along with other plucked string and keyboard instruments. It is not the usual grouping of full string sections and other instruments that we have generally heard as orchestras.

	Timing	What to listen for
18	0:00	Very soft, pulsating sound created by mandolin, guitar, celesta, harp, chimes, and cowbell
	0:07	Violin softly enters, skipping from very high to very low and back to high notes.
	0:28	Horn enters, then chimes.
	0:39	Faster, triple then duple meter, clarinet enters while cello and viola skip from high to low and back
	0:50	Very soft, pulsating sounds return.
	0:58	Horn enters; a very soft roll by the snare drum ends the movement.

It is not surprising, then, that Webern wrote little music and that all of his works tend to be quite short, some individual pieces lasting less than a minute and some of the longest works not exceeding ten minutes. His complete output totals less than five hours of music.

During his lifetime, Webern suffered the same lack of public recognition as Schoenberg, but his music, like that of his teacher, became increasingly influential after World War II. In particular, in the 1970s and 1980s, many young composers, such as Pierre Boulez and Milton Babbitt, captivated by the lean character of his style and his isolation of the single note as an important musical event, adapted features of his music and expanded the techniques of serialism to suit their own purposes. The twelve-tone system initiated by Schoenberg and advanced by Berg and Webern became a powerful force in the world of music and still influences some composers today.

Summary

The development of the atonal style was led by Arnold Schoenberg, a Viennese composer. Schoenberg rejected the concept of tonality completely and devised the twelve-tone system of arranging the twelve notes of the chromatic scale in an order that could be used in a series. The general system is called *serialism.* Under the system, the notes of the tone row could be used in sequence, forming a melody or theme, or simultaneously in groups to form chords. "Der Mondfleck" was an early, atonal work by Schoenberg that was composed before he had fully developed his twelve-tone system.

Schoenberg has had a major influence on contemporary composition. Much of that influence has been transmitted through the music of his pupils and colleagues. Alban Berg and Anton Webern represent the further development of two divergent aspects of Schoenberg's style: Berg was more romantic and produced the great opera *Wozzeck.* Webern's music was abstract, as we heard in the third movement of Five Pieces for Orchestra.

New People and Concepts

Alban Berg, 270

Anton Webern, 271

Arnold Schoenberg, 267

atonal, 267

avant-garde, 268

expressionism, 266

serialism, 266

Sprechstimme, 268

twelve tone, 267

))) **Finale**   CONNECT   CD 3: Track 10

Listen again to the recording of "Der Mondfleck" ("Moonfleck"), no. 18, from *Pierrot Lunaire (Moonstruck Pierrot)* by Schoenberg and compare your impression now with your notes from your First Hearing. Consider the following questions:

● What is the language of the text? What is the poem about? Does the mood of the music fit the text?

● What kind of singer is singing, and what is the vocal style being used?

● What instruments are playing? What do they do that supports or imitates the obsession with moonlight in the text?

● Does the form involve repeated sections of text and/or music?

● What is the tempo? What is the meter?

● If you were going to describe this music to a friend, what would you say?

Further Listening

Arnold Schoenberg, *Pierrot Lunaire,* op. 21. We heard only one of the twenty-one songs in this cycle. As was the case with the one song we heard, all of the songs are atonal and *sprechstimme* ("speech voice") vocals are used by the soprano. Both of those characteristics might be unpopular with some listeners, but the entire cycle is interesting to hear because it creates a little melodrama in which the moonstruck Pierrot (the "crying clown") experiences extremes of emotion and a return home.

Arnold Schoenberg, *A Survivor from Warsaw,* op. 46. This is a late work by Schoenberg, one composed in 1947 while he was living in southern California. It uses twelve-tone technique and is performed by a narrator, a male chorus, and an orchestra. It is based on the story of Jews in the Warsaw ghetto who were being counted to be sent to a death camp and responded by unifying to sing the prayer, *Shema Yisroel (Hear, Israel).* The three languages used are English, German, and Hebrew.

Alban Berg, *Wozzeck.* For the most part, this opera by a student of Schoenberg's is atonal, but not completely twelve-tone. In fact, there are sections with rich orchestral accompaniments to atonal vocals. The plot was discussed in this chapter, so it is enough to say here that it is an effective portrayal of the hostile environment created in the aftermath of World War I in Europe.

Anton Webern, Five Pieces for Orchestra, op. 10. Webern was another student of Schoenberg's who also composed atonal music. As is true of most of Webern's music, the works are very brief but full of colorful instrumental sounds, including instruments not usually part of an orchestra such as the harmonium, mandolin, and classical guitar. The entire set of five pieces is less than five minutes long.

CHARACTERISTICS OF TWENTIETH-CENTURY MUSIC (TO WORLD WAR II)

Texture	Both homophonic and contrapuntal textures employed; variety of textures within a single composition
Tonality	Major-minor system retained by some composers, but methods of establishing tonal centers altered; other composers employed atonal systems, including serialism
Rhythm	Complex rhythms; rhythmic patterns used; frequent absence of well-defined beat; frequent changes of meter
Harmony	High dissonance levels; new methods of chord construction in addition to triadic harmony
Tone color	Instruments sometimes played in extreme registers; unusual instruments and instrument groupings
Melody	Melodies sometimes derived from very short motives; melodies often not easy to sing because of extreme range and melodic intervals
Dynamics	Dynamic extremes employed; rapid dynamic fluctuations
Ensembles	Wide variety in size of ensembles from very small to gigantic
New organizational procedures	Serialism (twelve tone)
General stylistic trends	Impressionism, primitivism, neoclassicism, expressionism
Vocal style	Combination of ordinary speaking, conventional singing, and *Sprechstimme*

Prelude

American Innovations in the Arts

The Seventeenth Century

In the seventeenth century, Europeans colonized and settled parts of North America, including the eastern seaboard of what is now the United States. By 1700, more than a million colonists were scattered up and down the Atlantic coast, living mainly on farms, sometimes in villages, and occasionally in trading towns such as Boston, New York, and Charleston. The music performed in this New World was of European origin. English ballad operas (spoken dialogue and songs with simple melodies) were particularly popular. One example was John Gay's *The Beggar's Opera.*

The Eighteenth Century

American artworks and styles of clothing were much simpler than those in Europe. When France was leading the fashion world with highly decorative rococo styles, Americans were concentrating more on establishing their cities, negotiating or fighting with the Native Americans, or dealing with their British government. Compare the *Portrait of Paul Revere* by the American artist John S. Copley (1737–1815) with the décor of an eighteenth-century French interior on page 111 to see the differences in style. Remember the reference to the American Yankee (New Englander) in the song "Yankee Doodle," who tried to adopt the French style by merely sticking a feather in his hat? (See the Prelude to the Classical Era.)

Crafts

The American colonies did have a rich local tradition in the crafts. Even today, the names Paul Revere and Duncan Phyfe suggest excellence in silversmithing and furniture making, respectively. Many of the most talented painters in America, however, had to travel to London to make their reputations. For example, John S. Copley moved to England in 1774.

The Glass Harmonica

As far as American music of the eighteenth century is concerned, Francis Hopkinson (1737–1791), whose signature is on the Declaration of Independence, and William Billings (1746–1800) were two of the first American-born composers to gain widespread reputations.

Benjamin Franklin played a number of musical instruments and invented the glass harmonica that was popular in America as well as in Europe. The glass harmonica is based on the sound one can get by running a wet finger around the edge of a crystal glass. The ringing sound that results changes in pitch depending on the size of the glass. Franklin's instrument has a series of different-sized bowls that are stacked on their sides with a bar through them to allow them to spin around in a tub of water. The player had merely to touch the rims of various bowls to sustain a ringing tone. Even Mozart composed a quintet for the glass harmonica and wind instruments.

The Opera House

The first North American city to have an opera house was the culturally diverse city of New Orleans. French, Italian, and German operas were performed there on a regular basis in the late eighteenth century, but such grand events in foreign languages were not all that popular in other American cities. Some composers, however, found that they could use the operatic stories to entertain American audiences by making "Englished" versions of them. The composer would translate the opera into English, replace the recitatives with spoken dialogue, and shorten the arias into something closer to the popular songs from the English ballad operas. Not much of the original opera was left other than the story. This was at a time when the full-scale operas were being performed all over Europe and enjoyed by a growing middle, as well as upper, class.

The Nineteenth Century

In art, purely American scenes did not become fashionable until the early nineteenth century. Then, painters of the newly explored American West found a large and enthusiastic audience. George C. Bingham (1811–1879) painted scenes of Missouri flatboatmen, river ports, and trappers (page 277).

Literature

American literature did share some of the same interests in individual freedom, appreciation of the uncontrollability of nature, and

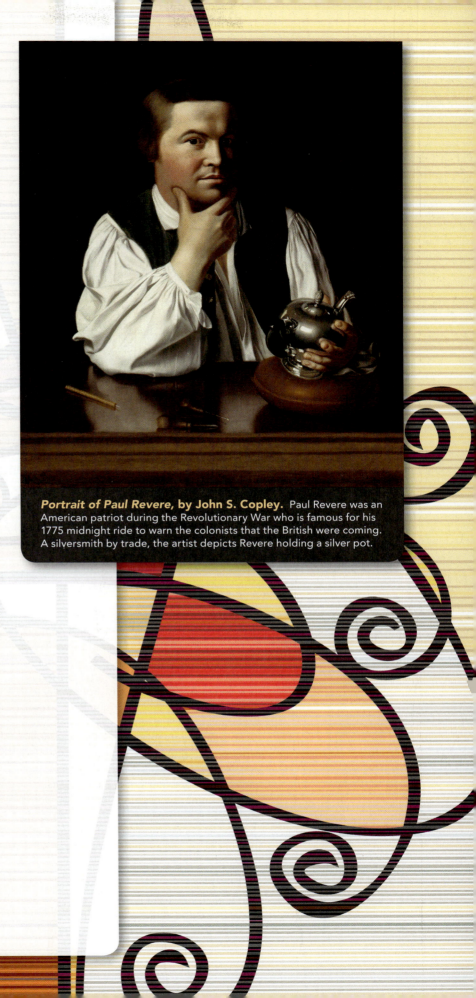

Portrait of Paul Revere, by John S. Copley. Paul Revere was an American patriot during the Revolutionary War who is famous for his 1775 midnight ride to warn the colonists that the British were coming. A silversmith by trade, the artist depicts Revere holding a silver pot.

Drafting of the Declaration of Independence, by Jean Leon Gerome Ferris.

the sense of mystery that were popular in the romantic era in Europe. James Fenimore Cooper (1789–1851), for example, had been born into a wealthy landowning family, but he tossed away his family advantages by getting expelled from Yale University and running off to be a sailor and then a farmer. Both experiences influenced his novels. *The Pilot* drew on his knowledge of the sea, and *The Last of the Mohicans* described Cooper's experiences with Native Americans. The name of American short-story writer Edgar Allan Poe (1809–1849) became synonymous with the words *grotesque* and *mysterious* after such stories as "Murders in the Rue Morgue," "The Pit and the Pendulum," and "The Tell-Tale Heart."

Philosophy

One area in which American writers took the lead in romantic thinking was in the development of the philosophy of transcendental-

ism. Just as the European romantics rejected the scientific rationalism of the Enlightenment, American writers Ralph Waldo Emerson (1803–1882) and Henry David Thoreau (1817–1862) wrote about the need to reject tradition and authority and to see humans and the natural world as divine. Thoreau built a cabin at Walden Pond in Massachusetts in order to experience a quiet life without the material possessions and pressures of the city. He told of his experiences in his book *Walden; or, Life in the Woods* (1854).

Concert Music

Stephen Foster was among the successful popular songwriters of the nineteenth century, but in the field of serious concert music, most American music was still based on European models. The Bohemian composer Dvořák tried to encourage American composers to make use of African American and Native American music in their compositions when he visited the United States in the 1890s. Amy Beach (1867–1944) was one of many American composers to successfully follow his advice.

Taste for European opera eventually spread beyond New Orleans, and opera companies and philharmonic societies were established in large cities nationwide. Another type of music was also gaining popularity, however, and that was music for concert or marching bands. U.S. Marine Band leader John Philip Sousa (1854–1932) composed many works for band that have become American classics. One of the most popular is "Stars and Stripes Forever" (1897).

The Twentieth Century

By the late nineteenth and early twentieth century, the Industrial Revolution was changing the American landscape and transforming the lives of most Americans. Such improvements as a coast-to-coast rail system helped move the United States to a position of world dominance. Many American investors made large sums of money in the process.

Art

At the beginning of the twentieth century, the favored painter in the United States was John Singer Sargent (1856–1925), whose handsome portraits of the landed, powerful, and financially secure were eagerly sought and displayed in the best New York and Boston townhouses. Americans tended to have less interest in the works of European avant-garde artists like Pablo Picasso or composers such as Arnold Schoenberg or Igor Stravinsky.

As a result of the Great Depression that began with the fall of the stock market in 1929, the federal government commissioned murals and decorations for public buildings as part of its public works program. Painters such as Edward Hopper (1882–1967) portrayed commonplace aspects of American life (page 278). Other painters of the depression era were drawn to political subjects. Some, such as Thomas Hart Benton (1889–1975), idealized the worker as the backbone of society and real hero of the American people.

Early Jazz

The music we have been talking about to this point was all written down in notation that we can read today, and therefore we have a fairly good idea of how it sounded. But another great American musical tradition, and one that would eventually gain a great deal of popularity in Europe and the rest of the world, was not written down. It is called *jazz.* Early jazz was primarily an improvised music that was not formally composed using traditional notation. It developed out of the work songs and field hollers of African American slaves, which were further influenced by band music in New Orleans. The earliest jazz developed in that city and is called either *New Orleans jazz* or *Dixieland jazz.*

World War I (1914–1918) opened up many factory jobs in northern cities such as Kansas City, Chicago, and New York, and among the African Americans who moved from the South to those cities were jazz musicians. The instrumentation and style of jazz changed in the North, with bands getting much larger to appeal to large-scale white audiences who wanted to dance to the music. Swing jazz developed through the 1930s and continued to be popular until the end of World War II. Swing experienced a popular revival in the 1990s.

Ragtime

Another style of music that was uniquely American and popular during the 1890s and

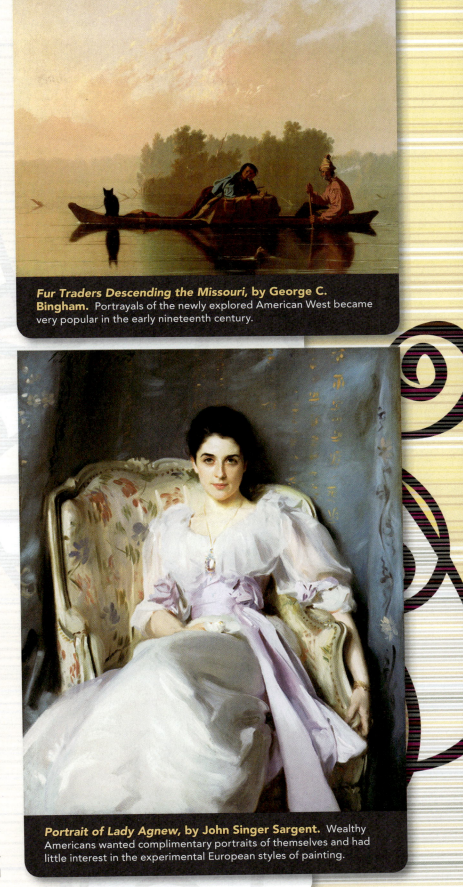

***Fur Traders Descending the Missouri,* by George C. Bingham.** Portrayals of the newly explored American West became very popular in the early nineteenth century.

***Portrait of Lady Agnew,* by John Singer Sargent.** Wealthy Americans wanted complimentary portraits of themselves and had little interest in the experimental European styles of painting.

***Early Sunday Morning,* by Edward Hopper.** This painting portrays a plain and simple American street in the early morning during the Great Depression of the early 1930s.

after was called *ragtime*. Played on the banjo, piano, or by bands, ragtime is named for its "ragged" rhythms. Scott Joplin (1868–1917) was not the first to play the music, but he became the most famous ragtime pianist and composer. Joplin also composed operas, but he could not get the funding to produce them with full costuming, staging, and orchestra during his lifetime. *Treemonisha* (1911) was finally produced in the 1970s, and Joplin's ragtime piano music experienced a revival of popularity after it was featured in the Academy Award–winning movie *The Sting* (1973).

New Styles in Jazz

Jazz continued to develop new styles through the 1940s and beyond, and it also became an important influence on American classical composers such as George Gershwin (1898–1937), William Grant Still (1895–1978), and Aaron Copland (1900–1990).

America's first *modernist* composer was Charles Ives (1874–1954), whose music used tonality in new ways. Whereas some Europeans such as Schoenberg were rejecting tonality completely, Ives wrote music with more than one tonality operating at the same time, as did some Europeans like Stravinsky. This technique created a new, dissonant style. Ives would also, on occasion, have several rhythms going on at the same time, which was new for a music that had developed out of the European traditions. Ives celebrated his American identity in his music by quoting American popular or patriotic melodies in his serious concert works.

Rock

In the field of popular music, American musicians combined African American blues and rhythm and blues with Caucasian American country styles to create rock-and-roll music during the late 1940s and early 1950s. Rock, as well as jazz, soon gained international popularity. Given that so many major performers of both jazz and rock music today are not Americans, it is easy for some to think of both styles as completely international. The fact is that, in their roots, jazz and rock music came into being as the result of the particular American mixture of transplanted Africans and transplanted Europeans.

American Music Before World War II

> When I hear music I fear no danger, I am invulnerable, I see no foe, I am related to the earliest times and to the latest.
>
> —WRITER HENRY DAVID THOREAU
> (1817–1862)

))) **First Hearing**

CONNECT   CD 3: Track 11

Listen to the recording of "When Jesus Wept" by Billings and take notes on what you hear. Even if you are working with other students in a paired or group listening session, keep your own notes. Give some attention to the following:

- What voice types do you hear at the beginning? Are all the voices high? Are they all low? Do you hear a choir with sopranos, altos, tenors, and bass?

- What is the first texture you hear? Monophonic, homophonic, or polyphonic?

- When the texture changes, to what does it change? In what order do the voices enter?

- When you hear a melody repeat, does the complete melody repeat one time after another as if it were a series of verses, or do the repetitions overlap one another as they would in a round or canon?

- Are any instruments accompanying the voices, or is the piece performed a cappella?

- Can you guess at the tempo? Can you guess at the meter?

Keep your notes from this First Hearing to compare with your impressions about the piece after you study the information in this chapter.

30

The Seventeenth Century

Striking contrasts run through the history of music in the United States. Native Americans had musical instruments, traditional melodies, and dance rhythms, but those had little influence on the musical practices of the original European settlers. Similarly, African slaves had rich cultural and musical traditions, but their music did not have much effect on the music in the lives of the settlers. The music of the first settlers came with them from their European homelands.

Some Protestants thought music too distracting to use in their church services. Many of the Pilgrims, however, loved and practiced music, but they had little spare time for much entertainment in their new land. They had come to the New World as religious dissenters, and their music was functional and used mostly for worship in church and at home. It consisted primarily of **psalms** and hymns, with tunes taken from older hymns or folk songs brought over from England and Holland.

The first extant book printed in the Colonies was a new rhymed translation of the psalms called the *Bay Psalm Book* (1640). It was published with musical notation in 1698. Because few of the Pilgrims could read music, a singing practice called *lining out* was developed, in which a leader, usually the preacher or deacon, would sing each phrase of the song alone and then pause for the congregation to repeat what he had just sung. That practice allowed everyone to participate in the musical aspect of the service. A system of notation was eventually developed to help untrained singers read music. It was called *shape note* notation because each note of the scale had a different shape.

The Eighteenth Century

Secular music began to flourish in the Colonies during the 1700s, particularly in major cities such as New York, Boston, Philadelphia, and Charleston. The people in these cities remained in close contact with the artistic life of Europe through shipping and trading contacts. As the cities prospered, a growing middle class acquired both the leisure and the money to support the arts.

Beginning in the 1730s, concerts and other musical events were organized and featured professional musicians with European training. These professionals worked both as performers and as teachers of music. They taught music to gentleman amateurs who, in turn, supported the rapid growth of music in America. These supporters included Thomas Jefferson, one of the outstanding music patrons of his day and an amateur violinist himself, and Benjamin Franklin, who served capably as performer, inventor of an instrument (the glass harmonica), and music critic. Another of the gentleman amateurs, Francis Hopkinson (1737–1791), wrote songs and claimed to be the "first native of the United States who has produced a musical composition."

By 1770, there was a group of American composers with enough in common to be considered a school. The leader of this group was **William Billings** of Boston (1746–1800). Billings and his school of compatriots did not always follow traditional European styles and rules of composition. In fact, Billings was proud to assert that he was "not confined to any Rules for Composition by any that went before him." He went on to say that "Nature is the Best Dictator, for all the hard dry rules will not enable any Person to form an Air without Genius. Nature must inspire the thought." The result of this attitude was a distinctive style of music that some Europeans considered crude and inept but that had its own profound power and grace and had a lasting effect on the development of American music.

Billings, a tanner by trade, published a number of collections of his compositions, among them *The New England Psalm Singer* (1770), engraved by Paul Revere; *Singing Masters Assistant* (1778); and *The Psalm Singers Amusement* (1781). These publications contained hymns, anthems, canons (or rounds), and **fuging tunes**—hymns or psalm tunes with brief polyphonic sections that have imitative entrances. The National Copyright Act of 1790 allowed composers to gain income from the publication and sale of their music.

One of Billings's most beautiful and popular compositions is the round (canon) "When Jesus Wept" from *The New England Psalm Tunes* (highlighted in the Featured Listening below). The song "When Jesus Wept," the anthem "Be Glad then America," and the hymn tune "Chester," all by Billings, were used by the twentieth-century American composer William Schuman in his orchestral work *New England Triptych*.

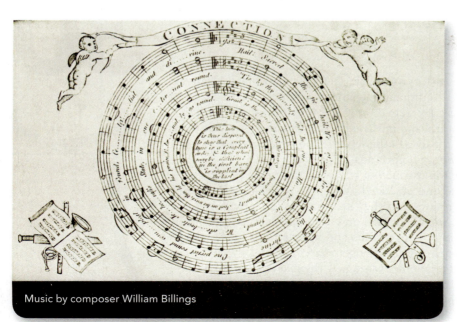

Music by composer William Billings

))) **Featured Listening**    **CD 3: Track 11**

"When Jesus Wept" WILLIAM BILLINGS

Date: ca. 1776

Genre: American fuging tune

Tempo: Moderato

Form: Canon (single melody sung at different times, allowing four parts to be heard at once)

Texture: Monophonic first and last phrases, polyphonic when new voices join in

Voices: SATB

Language: English

Meter: Triple

Duration: 2:00

Context: The simple-sounding song becomes full-sounding and complex when all four voices sing it polyphonically. The texture then thins out as each voice completes its second time through and drops off. This allows the ending to return to the simplicity of the beginning. This would have been sung in early American churches, but it also would have been sung as part of music making in homes of the same era.

	Timing	Text	Voices
11	0:00	When Jesus wept, the falling tear, In mercy flowed beyond all bound; When Jesus groaned, a trembling fear, Seized all the guilty world around.	All sing the complete text together one time.
	0:34	When Jesus wept, the falling tear,	Sopranos (S) begin to sing alone.
	0:42	In mercy flowed beyond all bound;	S continue, altos (A) sing the beginning.
	0:50	When Jesus groaned, a trembling fear,	S and A continue, tenors (T) begin.
	0:58	Seized all the guilty world around.	S, A, T continue, basses (B) begin.
	1:07	When Jesus wept, the falling tear, In mercy flowed beyond all bound; When Jesus groaned, a trembling fear, Seized all the guilty world around.	S begin again and stop when they reach the end; all other voices do the same; recording fades out.

The Nineteenth Century

The musical culture of nineteenth-century America was marked by two significant phenomena. The first was the division between what we now call classical and popular music. Classical music was meant either for serious study and listening or for religious purposes, whereas popular music aimed only to entertain. Earlier music had served both functions. For example, the eighteenth-century fuging tunes were written for worship and enlightenment, but they also served as enjoyable social entertainments.

The second phenomenon of nineteenth-century music was the imitation of German music by American composers, a trend that became most evident after the Civil War. By that time, the pattern of immigration to the United States had changed, as more people came from the European mainland, particularly Germany, and fewer from the United Kingdom. The Europeans brought to America the ideas of the romantic movement, which was strongest in Germany. Soon romanticism influenced every area of American musical life.

Popular music in the years preceding the Civil War included many extremely sentimental songs written and published primarily for use by amateurs in their homes. The greatest songwriter of the period, **Stephen Foster** (1826–1864), did not follow the European lieder tradition in which the songs took a great amount of skill and training to perform, but instead wrote for the amateur players and singers in the parlors of America. Foster wrote his own texts, and his songs articulated the attitudes and thoughts of the average American in a way that no other writer had in the past.

Although his formal musical training was not extensive, Foster had an unmistakable gift for melody. Many of his songs are filled with nostalgic yearning, often for an unattainable love. Both the text and music of his best-known songs, such as "Jeanie with the Light Brown Hair" (see the Listening Guide below), are gentle and tender. Foster also wrote many songs for the minstrel shows that were a popular form of entertainment, both before and after the Civil War. Dance tunes and songs using the dialects of African Americans were the basis of the shows, and Foster contributed many songs, including his well-known "Oh! Susanna" and "Camptown Races."

 **Listening Guide**

 **CD 5: Track 19**
CONNECT

"Jeanie with the Light Brown Hair" STEPHEN FOSTER

Date: 1854

Genre: American popular song

Tempo: Moderato

Form: Strophic

Texture: Homophonic

Voices and Instruments: Soprano voice, alto voice, with hammered and mountain dulcimers

Language: English

Meter: Quadruple

Duration: 3:03

Context: A soprano singer is the main soloist in this recording, but an alto singer joins in to harmonize with the soprano at the ends of the third and fourth verses. The song was probably performed with accompaniment by any number of instruments available in homes of the middle nineteenth century. The dulcimers in this recording add a folk-oriented sound that is most appealing, and quite possibly used at that time.

	Timing	Text
19	0:00	I dream of Jeanie with the light brown hair, Borne, like a vapor, on the summer air; I see her tripping where the bright streams play, Happy as the daisies that dance on her way.
	0:16	Many were the wild notes her merry voice would pour, Many were the blithe birds that warbled them o'er: I dream of Jeanie with the light brown hair, Floating, like a vapor, on the soft summer air.

Timing	Text
1:36	I long for Jeanie with the day dawn smile,
	Radiant in gladness, warm with winning guile;
	I hear her melodies, like joys gone by,
	Sighing round my heart o'er the fond hopes that die:
2:09	Sighing like the night wind and sobbing like the rain,
	Wailing for the lost one that comes not again:
	Oh! I long for Jeanie, and my heart bows low,
	Never more to find her where the bright waters flow.

Whereas Foster wrote in a vernacular style and drew from uniquely American experience, composers of sacred music centered their attention on European styles. The Civil War and Reconstruction years were marked by a growing taste for hymns adapted from the music of the great European composers, from Palestrina to Mendelssohn. Lowell Mason (1792–1872) composed and adapted many such hymns. His efforts also brought music education into the public school curriculum for the first time.

Much American music in the classical tradition included original compositions, arrangements of songs and dances, and sets of variations on well-known tunes written for the piano, the favorite instrument of the romantic era. American piano builders became some of the best in the world. One of the most colorful and talented figures in American music before the Civil War was a virtuoso pianist from New Orleans, **Louis Moreau Gottschalk** (1829–1869), who adopted many of the mannerisms of Liszt and was known in Europe as the American Chopin. He composed numerous works for both piano and orchestra, many of which contained exaggerated sentimentality, and he also used such exotic musical materials as African Caribbean rhythms and Creole melodies. He had the piano imitate strummed chords to sound like a banjo in his piece *The Banjo,* and he quoted "The Star-Spangled Banner," "Yankee Doodle," and "Hail, Columbia" in his solo piano piece *The Union.*

Most of the music performed by American orchestras was written by European composers, although the works of the American George Bristow (1825–1898) gained some attention. Bristow wrote six symphonies in a style similar to Mendelssohn's. The New York Philharmonic, of which he was a member, was founded in 1842. A typical orchestral program in this period carefully mixed heavy music (single movements of symphonies, rarely complete ones) with lighter music (marches and overtures).

After the Civil War

From the end of the Civil War to World War I, German romantic music had its greatest influence. Symphony orchestras were formed in many of the major cities, and large concert halls were built, including Carnegie Hall in New York (1891). Conservatories were established, and music departments appeared in colleges and universities.

A group of romantic composers emerged in Boston under John K. Paine (1839–1906), who became the first professor of music at Harvard. Other talented members of the Boston group were Horatio Parker (1863–1919) of Yale and George Chadwick (1854–1931). These men composed instrumental and choral music: symphonies, sonatas, chamber music, and oratorios. Stylistically, they were closely allied with the early German romantics, such as Schubert, Mendelssohn, and Schumann.

Amy Beach (1867–1944) also lived in Boston and composed in the romantic tradition. Her output included more than a hundred songs, short piano pieces, sacred and secular choral works, a piano quintet, and a symphony (1894). Her compositions for chorus and orchestra, *Three Browning Songs* (1900) and *The Canticle of the Sun* (1928), were among her most widely known works. Beach was recognized as a gifted

Amy Beach and other American female songwriters in April 1924. From left to right: Harriet Ware, Gena Branscombe, Mary Turner Salter, Ethel Glenn Hier, and Amy Beach.

pianist and composer in both the United States and Europe, which she toured from 1910 to 1914. Beginning in 1885, much of her music was published by Arthur P. Schmidt, an early champion of American female composers, including Beach, Margaret Ruthven Lang, Helen Hood, and Clara Kathleen Rogers.

Beach greatly admired the work of the English poet Robert Browning (1812–1889). In 1900, she set three of his poems to music and dedicated the music to the Browning Society of Boston. The group of three songs begins with "The Year's at Spring," with its famous line "God's in His Heaven, all's right with the world!" and ends with an effective musical rendering of "I send my heart up to Thee." As a centerpiece, Beach chose the poem "Ah, Love, but a Day." She manipulated the text by repeating certain words and lines to facilitate the musical structure she designed to convey the overall quality of the poem. The piece consists of two larger sections. Each begins quietly, builds to a climax, then subsides. Between them is the brief refrain, on the words "Ah, Love, but a day, and the world has changed!"

Each successive setting of "Ah, Love" is heard as an increase of musical energy, growing toward a climax. The second "Ah, Love" is louder and higher than the first; the third is louder and longer; the fourth, the loudest, longest, and highest, is the climax of this progress and of the entire song. The craftsmanship exemplified in "Ah, Love, but a Day" made Beach a respected and popular composer during her lifetime.

 CD 6: Tracks 1–3

"Ah, Love, but a Day" AMY BEACH

Date: 1900

Genre: American art song

Tempo: Molto expessione (very expressive), which means that the tempo changes to fit the expressiveness of the text

Form: Two sections with a refrain, or repeated line sung to the same melody

Texture: Homophonic

Voices: Baritone and soprano

Language: English

Meter: Quadruple

Duration: 2:51

Context: This song was composed while Amy Beach was still married and had agreed to perform in public only rarely. She might well, however, have played the accompaniment with a singer in her home, and it might have been performed for a meeting of the Browning Society (Robert Browning wrote the poem on which this song was based), for which it was composed. It was published, allowing others access to it.

	Timing	Text	Musical events and dynamic and tempo changes
	Part I		
1	0:00	1. Ah, Love, but a day,	Baritone singer
		And the world has changed!	
	0:18	2. Ah, Love, but a day,	Soprano singer
		And the world has changed!	
	0:31	The sun's away,	Baritone and soprano together
		And the bird estranged;	crescendo
		The wind has dropped,	crescendo
		And the sky's deranged;	crescendo to forte
	0:43	Summer,	forte
		Summer has stopped,	decrescendo and ritard
		Summer has stopped.	pianissimo, a tempo
	Refrain		
2	0:00	3. Ah, Love, but a day,	decrescendo
		And the world has changed!	
	Part II		
3	0:00	Look in my eyes!	Soprano solo
		Wilt thou change too?	
	0:14	Look in my eyes!	Baritone solo
		Wilt thou change too?	
	0:26	Should I fear surprise?	Soprano solo
		Shall I find aught new	Baritone joins
		In the old and dear,	Baritone solo
		In the good and true,	Soprano joins
		With the changing year?	crescendo
	0:47	4. Ah, Love,	fortissimo, decrescendo
		Look in my eyes.	decrescendo, ritard
		Look in my eyes,	
		Wilt thou change too?	decrescendo, pianissimo, dying away

Edward MacDowell (1860–1908) also came under the influence of German romanticism but avoided the established instrumental forms in favor of program music. Having studied in Germany, he went on to achieve success there as a pianist, composer, and teacher. He wrote several tone poems for orchestra, an often-performed piano concerto, many songs and choral pieces, and a number of small character pieces for piano.

Late in the century, a few American musicians began to react against the domination of German ideals and attitudes. Some American composers decided to make use of Native and African American themes—a challenge put forth by Bohemian composer Antonín Dvořák on his visit to America from 1892 to 1895. Arthur Farwell (1872–1952) was an American composer who accepted Dvořák's ideas and concentrated on using Native American themes in his works. Those who reacted against German influence also took interest in new musical ideas from France and Russia. Charles T. Griffes (1884–1920), whose creative talents were cut short by his premature death, showed the influence of Debussy, Ravel, and Stravinsky in his early works. An interest in Asian music influenced some of his last works.

Canadian Music

Canada's music history is similar in many ways to that of the United States. Both nations began as colonies established by European powers—in Canada's case, by France as well as Great Britain. Studies of many Canadian folk songs have found them to be derived from the ones Europeans brought to Canada, probably around 1650 or earlier. Similarly, musical instrument and dance styles in Canada developed from European models. One particularly notable example is the great tradition of fiddle music in Nova Scotia, which traces its origins to Scotland (*Nova Scotia* means "New Scotland").

In the area of classical music, much printed music by European composers, such as Haydn, Mozart, and Beethoven, was exported to and performed in Canada. As one might guess, chamber music, such as string quartets or small ensembles with piano, were more commonly performed than music that required a full orchestra because it was easier to get such ensembles together. In fact, it was not until the end of the nineteenth century that major cities such as Ottawa (1894), Montréal (1897), and Vancouver (1899) were able to establish orchestras. Québec City (1902), Toronto (1906), and Regina (1908) followed with orchestras at the beginning of the twentieth century.

Canadian choral societies formed as well. The Sacred Harmonic Choir in Toronto performed Handel's *Messiah* in 1857, and, thirty years later, the Philharmonic Society of Montreal performed *Messiah*, Mendelssohn's *Elijah*, and other major works. Musical theater, including operettas such as *H. M. S. Pinafore* and *The Pirates of Penzance* by Gilbert and Sullivan, became widely popular in Canada in the late nineteenth century. Opera companies from the United States toured in Canada, but it was not until the 1940s that Canadian companies began producing operas and touring the United States.

One of the most important early native-born Canadian composers was **Calixa Lavallée** (1842–1891). Besides being a composer, he was a virtuoso at the piano, organ, cornet, and violin. He won competitions and toured in the United States and as far south as Brazil. On his way back through the United States, Lavallée joined the Union army and fought in the American Civil War. He was wounded in 1862 and returned to Québec City, Montréal, although he continued to visit and perform in the United States and later went to France to study. In 1880, back in Québec, he took a song text written in French by Sir Adolphe Basile Routhier for St. Jean-Baptiste Day and set it to music for performance at a Canadian national meeting. The song became quite popular and was translated into English by Robert Stanley Weir in 1908. After several revisions and much controversy, that song, "Oh Canada" in both official languages, was finally declared Canada's national anthem in 1980, a hundred years after its first performance. In addition to that song, Lavallée's works include music for operettas, one symphony, and chamber music, including *Le papillon (The Butterfly)* for flute, clarinet, and piano.

In the twentieth century, support for the arts in Canada was aided by sponsoring organizations such as the Canadian Broadcast Corporation (CBC), which broadcast on radio and television, and the Canadian Music Centre, which promotes and distributes music by Canadian composers. Successful Canadian performers in the fields of popular music from country and folk traditions include Hank Snow, Joni Mitchell, Céline Dion, and Shania Twain. The internationally acclaimed jazz pianist Oscar Peterson was Canadian. Rock musicians Neil Young, Bryan Adams, and Rush are Canadians.

Summary

Music in seventeenth-century America was primarily functional, used mostly for worship in church and at home. Secular music began to flourish in the eighteenth century, especially in the larger cities. Although a group of composers led by William Billings created an American style, most American music continued to be based on European styles.

Nineteenth-century American music was marked by two significant phenomena: a division between classical and popular music and the imitation of German music by American composers. Although the songs of Stephen Foster and the instrumental works of Louis Moreau Gott-

schalk incorporate many uniquely American elements, most composers continued to imitate Europeans. In the post–Civil War years, the Boston area produced several notable composers, including Amy Beach, whose style was much like that of the German romantics. Late in the century, some composers reacted against the domination of German ideals and attitudes. Arthur Farwell used Native American themes in his music, and the works of Charles Griffes were influenced by French impressionists.

The music history of Canada is similar to that of the United States. Music brought by European immigrants formed the basis of what became a rich cultural tradition.

New People and Concepts

Amy Beach, 283

Calixa Lavallée, 286

fuging tunes, 280

Louis Moreau Gottschalk, 283

psalms, 279

Stephen Foster, 282

William Billings, 280

Finale

CD 3: Track 11

Listen again to the recording of "When Jesus Wept" by Billings and compare your impression now with your notes from your First Hearing. Consider the following questions:

- What voice types are singing?
- What is the texture at the beginning and end?
- What is the texture when more than one voice type is singing at the same time?
- What is the form called when one group imitates another as in this piece?
- What is the tempo? What is the meter?
- If you were going to describe this music to a friend, what would you say?

Further Listening

Stephen Foster, "Oh! Susanna" and "Camptown Races." These are just two of many of Foster's songs that captured the American spirit of the middle nineteenth century and remain familiar today.

Louis Moreau Gottschalk, *The Banjo.* The piano imitates the strumming of a banjo in this colorful solo piano piece.

Amy Beach, Symphony in E minor, "Gaelic." Amy Beach lived in Boston and was familiar with the many Irish melodies popular there. She quoted some of those in this

symphony and other themes she composed in a way that captured the spirit of the Irish tunes. The movements are (1) Allegro con fuoco, (2) Alla siciliana–Allegro vivace, (3) Lento con molto espressione, and (4) Allegro di molto.

Calixa Lavallée, *Le papillon (The Butterfly).* A trio for flute, clarinet, and piano by one of the most important nationalistic composers of Canada, who also wrote the Canadian national anthem, "Oh Canada."

Early Jazz Styles

> Maybe our forefathers couldn't keep their language together when they were taken away from Africa, but this—the blues—was a language we invented to let people know we had something to say. And we've been saying it pretty strong ever since.
>
> —GUITARIST-SINGER-SONGWRITER
> B. B. KING (B. 1925)

First Hearing

CONNECT   CD 3: Tracks 12–16

Listen to the recording of "Lost Your Head Blues" by Smith and take notes on what you hear. Even if you are working with other students in a paired or group listening session, keep your own notes. Give some attention to the following:

- What voice type is singing? Soprano, alto, tenor, or bass?

- What instruments do you hear accompanying the singer?

- If you can understand the text, what is the song about? Does the overall mood fit the meaning of the text? What words would you use to describe the mood?

- Where do you hear sections of the text repeat? Does that happen in a regular pattern, just occasionally, or does the beginning text repeat at the end?

- Can you guess at the meter?

Keep your notes from this First Hearing to compare with your impressions about the piece after you study the information in this chapter.

31

Jazz is considered by many to be America's greatest contribution to music. Its impact on American society has been enormous, and its influence on world culture has been far-reaching. Its message has been direct, vital, and immediate, enabling it to hurdle cultural, linguistic, and political barriers.

Origins of Jazz

The precise origins and early history of **jazz** cannot be chronicled because early jazz was neither notated nor recorded; it was improvised and existed only in performance. We know that the music was rooted in the American South, particularly in New Orleans, and that it was created by African Americans and influenced by some characteristics of both African and European music. Before going too deeply into which elements of jazz are African and which are European, we need to discuss something about African music.

Music is considered the rhythm of life by these African dancers.

Africa is a very large continent with many diverse tribal groups and a variety of musical practices in different areas. To find the African roots of jazz, we have to pay attention to musical practices in the Western part of the continent, because that was the homeland of most Africans who were brought to the New World as slaves.

One general point about African music is that it involves everyone. The concept of people sitting quietly as part of a large audience and just listening to performers is not part of the traditional African experience. One can find concert halls there today only because they have been influenced by other cultures of the modern world. Instead of listening passively, an African might dance or tap rhythms to accompany what someone else plays; music is commonly thought of as part of the rhythm of life.

For much of their history, the tribes of northwestern Africa had no written languages. In order to keep track of governmental and historical information, singers called **griots** ("gree-ohs") memorized and repeated songs about their people and history. Griots were highly respected in their societies, and what they sang was extremely important to their cultures.

In addition to the importance of lyrics, characteristics of African music include the following:

- A practice known as **call and response,** in which a phrase sung by a leader is responded to by a group. (This is different from the practice of lining out, discussed in Chapter 30, because the response is not a repetition of the call.)
- **Polyrhythms,** which are several distinctly different rhythm patterns being played at the same time.
- Repetition of individual rhythm patterns. This is essential when music is polyrhythmic because it allows the listeners to hear one rhythm as it repeats and then turn their attention to another as it also repeats itself. Without a lot of repetition, polyrhythmic music would sound chaotic.
- Harmony, such as the chordal accompaniments common in European music, does not exist. Where harmony occurs, it exists mainly as a by-product of several melodies played or sung together.

- A variety of scale patterns are used. Some are five-tone scales and some closer to the seven-tone scales found in European music.
- A great variety of percussion instruments are used.

Our African listening example comes from Sierra Leone, in northwestern Africa. It was recorded in a small village on Christmas Day in 1962. The villagers are entertaining the chairman of the Public Service Commission, who is visiting for the Christmas celebration. (Both the Muslim and the Christian religions are practiced in Sierra Leone.) The male solo singer is probably a farmer from the village.

 CD 6: Track 4
CONNECT

"Village Celebration" MENDE TRIBE OF SIERRA LEONE

Date: 1962

Genre: African tribal music

Tempo: Moderate

Form: No structured repeating sections; our example is only a short section of a much longer celebration.

Voices and Instruments: The primary singer is a male leader. Responses are by the villagers; one *segbure* (a rattle made from a gourd with pebbles inside and netting sewn with beads around the outside; the beads can be snapped against the gourd for a special effect), one *sangbei* (a wooden drum about two feet high with metal rings attached to rattle when the drum is played), and a mouth organ (very soft in the background, probably underrecorded).

Language: Mende

Meter: Quadruple with polyrhythms playing against the basic beat

Duration: 6:16

Context: The responses from the villagers often repeat the same phrase, but occasionally the phrase is varied. The lead vocals are improvised. The villagers are probably dancing along with their singing responses.

We will hear many of these characteristics of African music in the jazz examples we listen to.

Ragtime

Two styles of jazz-related American music that are based on African elements are **ragtime** and the **blues.** Ragtime gets its name from melodies played in *ragged,* or syncopated, rhythms. It is not polyrhythmic as African music often is, but the syncopations come from the rhythms of Africa. An important European characteristic of ragtime is that it has a regular, sectional formal structure that could be diagrammed with repeating and contrasting letters, just as we have outlined form in the European examples earlier in this text.

Ragtime was popularized as the music used for cakewalk dances during the 1890s. It was played on banjos, fiddles (violins), the piano, or by bands. The piano became the preferred instrument for many players, including **Scott Joplin** (1868–1917), whose *rags* are still performed today. Other notable ragtime pianist-composers of the 1890s include James Scott, Tom Turpin, and Joseph Lamb. Ragtime music is not really jazz because it is notated and performed without improvisation. Jazz always involves **improvisation.** The blues is closer to jazz in every respect and is often played by jazz musicians. A Listening Guide to Scott Joplin's "Maple Leaf Rag" follows.

 **Listening Guide**

 CONNECT   CD 6: Track 5

"Maple Leaf Rag" SCOTT JOPLIN

Date: 1899

Genre: Piano rag

Tempo: Tempo di marcia (march tempo)

Form: AABBACCDD

Instruments: Solo piano

Meter: Duple

Duration: 2:25

Context: Piano rags such as this one were very popular, played on riverboats on the Mississippi and in homes and nightclubs during the 1890s and in the early twentieth century.

	Timing	Form	Musical events
5	0:00	A	The pianist's left hand (low notes) keeps a steady tempo, and the right hand plays syncopated rhythms.
	0:17	A	Repeat
	0:33	B	The syncopated right hand part begins higher and then moves lower and closer to the left-hand part.
	0:49	B	Repeat
	1:04	A	Repeat of first section
	1:20	C	Low to high jumps in left hand, new rhythms, still syncopated right hand
	1:36	C	Repeat
	1:51	D	Syncopated right hand part more like the character of the A section
	2:07	D	Repeat

The Blues

As mentioned earlier, music was part of most life experiences in Africa. African slaves would often work to the rhythms of their songs. These *field hollers* (rhythmic free singing among field workers) and *work songs* (singing in rhythm with the work being done) formed the basis of the blues. The earliest type of blues is called *country blues* because it was performed in the rural South. In this type of blues, the singer often accompanies himself or herself on a guitar. The song text is usually personal and full of feeling, although not always sad. It is sung in a rhythmically and structurally loose manner, allowing the singer to improvise new lines of text or more elaborate accompaniments.

IMPROVISATION

I have heard individual songs played by different jazz musicians and they don't sound the same at all. Why?

Jazz musicians don't play each note as it was written, the way classical musicians do. There are different types of jazz, and the musicians in each category approach their playing according to their own style, but as a general rule, jazz musicians improvise around the written notes of the melody. It is a little bit like what we heard from musicians in the Renaissance and baroque periods when they added embellishments to their music, but jazz musicians go much further from the melody than those earlier musicians did.

So what do jazz musicians do when they improvise?

Jazz musicians often treat the given melody as a starting point. They might play it through in what is close to its original form at the beginning, but then they might play it again, adding new notes around those of the melody. After that, they might spontaneously invent a new melody that is based on the original melody, or even play something that has little or no relationship to the original melody. Rhythm is also very important in jazz, and the musicians might make a lot of changes to the rhythms as they play, even sometimes freely leaving the steady beat played by the rhythm section.

If jazz musicians are playing in a group, how do they make all these changes and stay together?

They listen to one another. In fact, the way jazz musicians work together is one of the great pleasures of listening to jazz. If you listen closely, you can often hear one musician improvise something completely new, and then someone else in the group respond by repeating that or by playing something that goes with it. Other musicians in the group might, then, also respond to the new idea. Jazz improvisations can stray pretty far away from the melody and chord progression they started with. The next time the same group plays the same song, they might improvise something completely different to it. There is a freedom in jazz that one doesn't find in most other kinds of music, including rock.

What about the blues? Doesn't it have a set chord progression that the musicians must follow?

Yes. The twelve-bar blues is called that because it is based on a particular twelve-bar chord progression. Interestingly enough, though, the standard blues progression has only three chords in it. There are many other chords that are commonly used as replacements for those chords, and jazz musicians often substitute those for the standard ones. Sometimes the musicians maintain the basic progression and concentrate their improvisation on the melody. In other words, the basic twelve-bar format allows the musicians to improvise around it in many ways.

By around 1900, the blues had developed into a highly structured style, with distinct forms for both the lyrics and the melodies. These forms reflect European musical traditions. African Americans had heard and sung structured songs of European origin with chordal accompaniments in churches, and they worked those types of structures into their music.

The standard blues lyrical pattern consisted of two rhyming lines of poetry, with the first line repeated to create an AAB form, as in the following example:

Now listen baby, you so good and sweet,
Now listen baby, you so good and sweet,
I want to stay 'round you, if I have to beg in the street.

The blues typically follows a twelve-bar harmonic progression with four bars for each of the three sections of text such as those above. Rhythmically, the blues is usually in quadruple meter, with each beat being subdivided unevenly (a flow of long-short-long-short-long-short-long-short pattern for each four beats). This flow creates a more relaxed feel than the evenly subdivided beats that are typically found in music of European traditions.

Blues singers often lower certain notes of the scale (the third, seventh, and, in complex jazz styles, the fifth) to give the melody a relaxed effect. These lowered notes are called **blue notes.** It is not certain whether blue notes were derived from African scale structures or became standard independently in America. Blues singers also use other techniques that add to the relaxed flow of their music, including sliding from one note to another.

The Empress of the Blues was **Bessie Smith** (1894–1937). Smith started her career singing the blues and jazz in minstrel shows, nightclubs, and theaters. She sang and made records with a number of prominent jazz musicians throughout the 1920s and 1930s. In 1929 she appeared in the film *St. Louis Blues.* The musicians at the recording session said that Smith improvised "Lost Your Head Blues" in the studio because they needed one more song to make use of the time they had. By the time of her death in a 1937 auto accident, Smith had recorded close to two hundred songs. "MusiCurious: Improvisation" discusses this quality of jazz and blues music.

Blues singer Bessie Smith

 ))) **Featured Listening**   CONNECT   CD 3: Tracks 12–16

"Lost Your Head Blues" BESSIE SMITH

Date: 1926

Genre: Classic blues

Form: Five choruses of the twelve-bar blues

Voices and Instruments: Bessie Smith with cornet (Joe Smith) and piano (Fletcher Henderson)

Language: English

Meter: Quadruple with uneven beat subdivisions

Duration: 2:54

Context: African roots of the blues can be heard in many ways. The blue notes and sliding between notes come from the way African singers sang. Call and response is heard, although the responses are played on the cornet instead of being sung by a group. European influences are evident in the structure of the music and text, as well as in the chordal accompaniment played by the piano.

(continued)

Text	Sections of the form
12	Cornet and piano introduction
I was with you baby when you didn't have a dime. I was with you baby when you didn't have a dime. Now since you got plenty money you have throw'd your good gal down.	First chorus
13 Once ain't for always, two ain't for twice. Once ain't for always, two ain't for twice. When you get a good gal you better treat her nice.	Second chorus
14 When you were lonesome I tried to treat you kind. When you were lonesome I tried to treat you kind. But since you got money, it's done changed your mind.	Third chorus
15 I'm gonna leave baby, ain't gonna say good-bye. I'm gonna leave baby, ain't gonna say good-bye. But I'll write you and tell you the reason why.	Fourth chorus
16 Days are lonesome, nights are long. Days are lonesome, nights are so long. I'm a good old gal, but I've just been treated wrong.	Fifth chorus

"Hearing the Difference: Foster's 'Jeanie with the Light Brown Hair' and Smith's 'Lost Your Head Blues'" compares these two American songs.

Jazz Styles

New Orleans was abuzz with activity in the early 1900s. It was in the dance halls, gambling places, and brothels of the red-light district known as Storyville that **New Orleans jazz,** also called **Dixieland,** was born and nurtured. New Orleans jazz combos were usually made up of one or two cornets (or trumpets), one clarinet, and one trombone, which formed the **front line** (instruments responsible for playing the melodies); string bass, guitar or banjo, sometimes piano, and sometimes drums made up the **rhythm section** (responsible for the basic beat and accompaniment).

The most outstanding feature of New Orleans jazz was *collective improvisation.* Against a background supplied by the rhythm section, the front-line players improvised on well-known melodies. Usually the cornet played variations of the melody, while the clarinet improvised an upper melodic line, and the trombone supplied yet another improvised melody below the cornet. All three instruments in the front line employed a lively, syncopated style against a steady beat maintained by the rhythm section.

A variety of factors, including the closing of the Storyville district in 1917, led to the migration of jazz musicians and their music to other parts of the country. In the Roaring Twenties, jazz spread over a wide geographic area, including Chicago, which became the scene of some important developments. Whereas the heart of the New Orleans style was collective improvisation, the focus of attention in the Chicago bands shifted to the *individual* soloist. By far the most important jazz soloist in the Chicago style was **Louis Armstrong** (1900–1971), a young cornetist from New Orleans.

Rhythmically, Armstrong's music was the embodiment of what came to be known as **swing.** His horn style—highly embellished, full of swoops, sudden dips, and darts—influenced the performing style of all later cornet and trumpet players and other instrumentalists as well. His brilliant **scat singing,** in which the singer sings nonsense syllables instead of words, has become a basic element of jazz vocal styles. Because the singer does not have to worry about a specific text, scat singing allows singers the same kind of improvisatory freedom instrumentalists have always enjoyed.

 **Hearing** the **Difference**

FOSTER'S "JEANIE WITH THE LIGHT BROWN HAIR" AND SMITH'S "LOST YOUR HEAD BLUES"

These two American songs offer many points of comparison (see Listening Guide on page 282 and Featured Listening on page 293). Stephen Foster's song is a good example of simple popular music of the middle nineteenth century. It was written in music notation and sold in printed form for untrained singers to learn and sing for their own entertainment and that of family and friends, with just a simple accompaniment. Bessie Smith's song is an example of early twentieth-century blues; it was not notated but just sung during a recording session. She might even have improvised as she sang it. Anyone who wanted to sing it later would have to memorize it from Smith's recording. Answer the following questions as you listen from one work to the other:

- These songs are both in English, so you should be able to understand the texts. What are the songs about? Which song uses more slang? What are examples?

- Both of these songs are in quadruple meter. Which is sung to a steadier beat? If you can hear the subdivisions between the beats (the rhythmic flow of the spaces between the accented beats), which song uses even beat subdivisions, and which uses uneven subdivisions (a flow of long-short, long-short, long-short, long-short patterns in each measure)?

- Both of these songs are in strophic form in that their melodies repeat with new verses of text. Which has a regular repetition of text in every verse (AAB form for each verse or chorus)?

- Both songs are sung to instrumental accompaniment. What instruments do you hear in each accompaniment part?

- Does either singer use any rubato (rhythmic freedom) with the tempo? Does either singer ever slide between notes instead of hitting each note exactly on pitch with no pitch variation?

Jazz musician Louis Armstrong and his band

In addition to being an important and influential jazz musician, Armstrong recorded several songs that were hits on the pop charts, including "What a Wonderful World" and "Hello Dolly." In 1990, he was inducted into the Rock and Roll Hall of Fame as an early influence.

By the mid-1930s, with the national economy slowly recovering from the depression, larger ensembles began to make a comeback. Gradually, jazz moved out of the saloons and into ballrooms and dance halls. The *big band sound,* as it became known, soon reached an even larger audience via radio. During this period, New York became the cultural and communication center of America, replacing Chicago as the major jazz city. Thus began the swing era, which lasted roughly from 1935 to 1950.

Swing featured big bands of fifteen to seventeen players, with the old New Orleans front line of cornet, clarinet, and trombone increased to include sections of trumpets and trombones, along with woodwind sections of clarinets and saxophones. The swing band rhythm sections included piano, string bass, sometimes guitar, and drums.

A comparison between a standard New Orleans jazz band of the 1920s and a typical swing jazz band of the 1930s and early 1940s follows:

New Orleans Jazz Band	**Swing Jazz Band**
Front line (soloists)	*Horn section (play as a group and solos)*
one trumpet	Three or four trumpets
one trombone	Three or four trombones
one clarinet	Three or four saxophones of varying sizes
Rhythm section	*Rhythm section*
(accompaniment)	*(accompaniment and solos)*
one piano	one piano
(and/or guitar or banjo)	one string bass
one string bass	one drum set
one drum set	

Jazz musician Duke Ellington

Sometimes the respect musicians and fans had for jazz band leaders caused them to call them by titles of European royalty—for example "Duke" Ellington, "King" Oliver, and "Count" Basie. **Duke Ellington** (Edward Kennedy Ellington, 1899–1974) was born into a middle-class African American family in Washington, D.C. As a child, he studied both art and music; his piano studies included the popular ragtime music. Although an accomplished painter, he opted for a career in music and began to coordinate and lead bands for dances and social events, playing simple arrangements of popular tunes.

After relocating to New York in 1923, Ellington's band began to incorporate some of the new jazz styles that had started to become popular. In 1927, they started a five-year stint as the house band of Harlem's Cotton Club. During this time, Ellington's compositions and arrangements moved him and his band, which he began calling his "orchestra," into the forefront of the emerging big band style. Ellington's music from this era was featured in the 1984 movie *Cotton Club.*

"It Don't Mean a Thing (If It Ain't Got That Swing)" was recorded in New York in 1932, just after Ellington's time at the Cotton Club and just before his orchestra began a long period of touring all over the United States and Europe as one of the most popular of the swing bands.

 **Listening Guide**

 CONNECT CD 6: Track 6

"It Don't Mean a Thing (If It Ain't Got That Swing)" DUKE ELLINGTON

Date: 1932

Genre: Swing jazz

Form: AABA song form

Voices and Instruments: Ivie Anderson singing, three trumpets, two trombones, three saxophones, piano, banjo, bass, drums

Language: English

Meter: Quadruple

Duration: 3:08

Context: This piece was performed in dance halls and nightclubs such as the famous Cotton Club in New York City. The sound of the trumpets is not as brilliant as usual because the players have put mutes in the bells of their instruments to cut down the sound.

Timing	Text	What to listen for
6 0:00		Band introduction with scat vocals
0:11		Improvised solo on muted trumpet with backing and responses by band
0:46	It don't mean a thing if it ain't got that swing.	Vocal with blue note on "ain't"
	It don't mean a thing all you've got to do is sing.	Same melody repeated
1:03	It makes no difference if it's sweet or hot.	New melody (the **bridge**)
	Just keep that rhythm, give it ev'rything you've got.	
1:13	It don't mean a thing if it ain't got that swing.	Beginning melody returns.
1:22		Improvised saxophone solo
2:41		Scat improvisation in vocal
2:49	It don't mean a thing if it ain't got that swing.	Fadeout at end

By the time of his death in 1974, Ellington had heard himself described as one of the great American composers. His large body of work, from popular songs to jazz suites to simple arrangements of the twelve-bar blues, is still popular today.

Other African American swing band leaders included Fletcher Henderson, Count Basie (William Basie), and Cab Calloway. White musicians led swing bands as well. Among them were Benny Goodman, Harry James, Glenn Miller, Artie Shaw, Tommy Dorsey, and Woody Herman. The bands' swing styles varied depending on the tastes of the leaders, the skills of the star soloists, and the types of arrangements that were written for them. In general, swing music was smooth and polished. The aim was to please the audience, for whom listening and dancing was an important part of life during World War II.

Summary

Perhaps the most significant American contribution to music is jazz, a musical language that grew out of the African American experience and musical traditions from Africa. Jazz was also influenced by formal structure and chordal accompaniments of European origin. Two styles of music that informed early jazz were ragtime and the blues. Ragtime is not technically jazz because it is formally composed and is performed without improvisation. Its ragged rhythms do, however, come from the same roots as jazz, and its energy has been an influence on jazz.

The blues developed a structured twelve-bar form with lyrics that follow an AAB pattern of repetition and contrast. African elements in the blues include the use of blue notes, call and response, and uneven beat subdivisions.

Jazz bands first played in New Orleans. They played for all types of private and civic functions, including dances

and entertainment in the red-light district of Storyville. New Orleans jazz bands used collective improvisation among the members of the front line, with accompaniment of a rhythm section.

When Storyville closed in 1917, jazz musicians moved to northern cities, including Chicago, where a new jazz style began featuring individual soloists over the collective improvisation of three or four players playing at the same time. As jazz developed further in New York, jazz bands grew bigger and began playing in a style known as swing. Swing bands played for dancers and at clubs such as the Cotton Club in Harlem. Duke Ellington led one of the most popular of the swing bands, which he called his orchestra.

New People and Concepts

Bessie Smith, 293

blue notes, 293

blues, 290

bridge, 297

call and response, 289

Dixieland, 294

Duke Ellington, 296

front line, 294

griots, 289

improvisation, 291

jazz, 288

Louis Armstrong, 294

New Orleans jazz, 294

polyrhythms, 289

ragtime, 290

rhythm section, 294

scat singing, 294

Scott Joplin, 290

swing, 294

 **Finale** CD 3: Tracks 12–16

Listen again to the recording of "Lost Your Head Blues" by Smith and compare your impression now with your notes from your First Hearing. Consider the following questions:

- What is the voice type of the singer?
- What instruments accompany the singer?
- What is the song about? What is the mood, and does it fit the text?
- What kind of pattern do you hear in the repetitions of sections of text?
- What is the meter?
- If you were going to describe this music to a friend, what would you say?

Further Listening

Django Reinhardt with Stephane Grappelli, *Swing from Paris.* "It Don't Mean a Thing If It Ain't Got That Swing."

The Count Basie Orchestra, *Count Plays Duke.* "It Don't Mean a Thing If It Ain't Got That Swing."

Cab Calloway, *Hi Di Hi Di Hi Di . . . Ho, Minnie the Moocher.* "It Don't Mean a Thing If It Ain't Got That Swing."

Thelonious Monk, *Thelonious Monk Plays the Music of Duke Ellington.* "It Don't Mean a Thing If It Ain't Got That Swing."

Ella Fitzgerald, *Ella Fitzgerald Sings the Duke Ellington Songbook.* "It Don't Mean a Thing If It Ain't Got That Swing."

Mel Tormé, *The Best of Mel Tormé: The Millennium Collection.* "It Don't Mean a Thing If It Ain't Got That Swing."

Nina Simone, *Nina Simone Sings Duke Ellington at Carnegie Hall.* "It Don't Mean a Thing If It Ain't Got That Swing."

Louis Armstrong, *The Essential Louis Armstrong.* This two-CD set includes remastered early recordings with the Hot Five as well as his later hits such as "What a Wonderful World."

Developments in Jazz in the Late Twentieth Century

> This human thing in instrumental playing has to do with trying to get as much human warmth and feeling into my work as I can. I want to say more on my horn than I ever could in ordinary speech.
>
> —JAZZ WOODWIND PLAYER
> ERIC DOLPHY [1928–1964]

))) First Hearing

 CD 3: Track 17

Listen to the recording of "Ko Ko" by Parker and take notes on what you hear. Even if you are working with other students in a paired or group listening session, keep your own notes. Give some attention to the following:

- What does this piece sound like to you?
- What musical instruments do you hear? Which do you think are the primary solo instruments, and which are in the accompanying rhythm section?
- Do any of the rhythm section instruments play solos?
- When do you hear any repetition?
- What would you guess is the tempo? Does the tempo change?
- What might the meter be?

Keep your notes from this First Hearing to compare with your impressions about the piece after you study the information in this chapter.

32

Bebop

At the height of the swing era, an influential group of jazz musicians rebelled against the big band style and its commercialization. These young rebels began to organize small *combos* that offered more opportunity for individual expression. The result was **bebop,** or just *bop.*

In special after-hours clubs young, adventuresome, experimental musicians such as guitarist Charlie Christian (1916–1942), pianist Thelonious Monk (1917–1982), and drummer Kenny Clarke (1914–1985) played music together to explore their personal potentials. These and other musicians, notably trumpeter **Dizzy Gillespie** (1917–1993) and saxophonist **Charlie "Bird" Parker** (1920–1955), would work all night with the swing bands in Manhattan nightclubs and ballrooms, then ride north to Minton's Play House in the early morning to participate in *jam sessions,* in which they experimented with free-form solo work and improvisation. The new style they developed was given the name *bebop* (later shortened to *bop*). The bebop combo consisted of one to three soloists supported by a rhythm section of drums and bass and sometimes piano or guitar.

Bebop players sought to extend the role of the soloist in jazz. They used jagged, uneven phrases, wide melodic leaps, and a great deal of rhythmic variety to develop their new sound. Clarke introduced an extraordinary rhythmic innovation with his technique of "dropping bombs"—that is, placing unanticipated bass drum accents before or after the beat. Almost single-handedly, Clarke moved the focus of jazz drumming away from the objective of simply keeping time. Drummers began to work around an implicit, rather than a stated, beat, and whatever basic timekeeping was necessary usually fell to the bass player.

Bebop songs typically borrowed chord changes from the popular songs of the day and added entirely new melodies to them. Whereas swing melodies were usually vocally conceived, bebop melodies were designed for instruments and were difficult to sing. Another bop innovation was the use of more complicated chords with much more chromaticism (notes outside the scale that are dissonant with the scale) than had been present in earlier jazz styles.

Among the early innovators of bebop, Charlie Parker had the greatest influence on those who followed. His playing brought together all of the important bop innovations—harmonic complexity, rhythmic inventiveness, technical virtuosity—and combined them with a brilliant melodic sensibility. The example we will listen to is "Ko Ko," recorded in 1945. Parker plays the alto saxophone. The other musicians on the recording are trumpeter Miles Davis, pianist and muted trumpeter Dizzy Gillespie, pianist Sadik Hakim, bassist Curly Russell, and drummer Max Roach.

Charlie Parker and Dizzy Gillespie

))) Featured Listening

CD 3: Track 17

CONNECT

"Ko Ko" CHARLIE PARKER

Date: 1945

Genre: Bebop jazz

Tempo: Very fast—if you can pick out the bass player, he is playing one note per beat

Form: Most solos are 8 bars long, and choruses are made up of 4 or 8 of those, to be 32 or 64 bars each; the beginning 32 bars are repeated at the end, giving the recording a sense of balance.

Instruments: Trumpet, muted trumpet, alto saxophone, piano, bass, and drums

Meter: Quadruple

Duration: 2:52

Context: This recording is intense and energetic; it is intended for careful listening, not dancing. "Ko Ko" is based on the harmonic progression of the jazz tune "Cherokee."

(continued)

Timing	What to listen for
0:00	Trumpet and saxophone together (8 bars)
0:07	Trumpet solo (8 bars)
0:13	Saxophone solo (8 bars)
0:19	Trumpet and saxophone together (8 bars)
0:25	Extended saxophone solo in which Parker quotes from another jazz tune, "Cherokee" (64 bars)
1:16	Another saxophone solo (64 bars)
2:07	Drum solo
2:29	First 32 bars repeated

17

The flexibility of jazz and its ability to adapt to trends was evident during the period following World War II. At that time there was a revival of interest in Dixieland and Chicago styles, and a number of swing bands were able to survive and are still active today. Bebop continued as the mainstream of jazz development, evolving in the 1950s into a style known as *hard bop*. Hard bop took the basic feel of bebop and added a more prominent blues influence, simplifying harmonies and putting a greater emphasis on a straightforward, driving beat. Hard bop has continued as part of the "straight-ahead" style of today. Listening to recordings of jazz played by the great musicians of the past is a good way to appreciate jazz, but the improvisation in jazz makes it particularly wonderful to hear live. You can read about what might be expected of you when you attend a live jazz performance in "MusiCurious: Attending a Jazz Concert."

Cool Jazz

Trumpeter **Miles Davis,** who played on the recording "Ko Ko," grew tired of several characteristics of bebop. The format used in "Ko Ko," with front-line instruments playing together at the beginning and the end of the recording and a series of solos in between, had become old. He also felt that the competitive intensity of the solos was taking too much away from the music. In 1947, Davis and arranger Gil Evans (1912–1988) put together a group of nine musicians to experiment with a new style of bebop. Some of the basic characteristics of the new style were playing with a minimal amount of vibrato; concentrating on playing softer and lower, thus avoiding the loud, high solos common in bebop; and putting less emphasis on individual solos and more emphasis on an ensemble sound. The overall mood of this new music was subdued and introspective. At first, the group worked privately to establish the new style, but after Capitol Records released a few single records that impressed jazz critics, they put the group's recordings on the album *Birth of the Cool* (1949). The new style was called **cool jazz.**

The cool jazz sound was further developed by musicians who combined jazz with some characteristics of classical music. Two new groups, the Modern Jazz Quartet and

Trumpeter Miles Davis

 **MusiCurious**

ATTENDING A JAZZ CONCERT

What should I expect at a jazz concert?

You don't know. Jazz concerts can vary greatly, depending on the venue. Jazz is often played in any number of places, including small clubs and restaurants where drinks and possibly food are served. Obviously, the expectations of the listeners in such places differ from those at formal concerts. In jazz concert settings, you will find some similarities to classical concerts, including the fact that you will receive a printed program when you enter the hall.

Will the program list major works with movement titles indented under them so we know when to clap?

Not likely. Some jazz musicians compose music much the way classical composers do, but they do so in a jazz style. Those works might even have movements. On the other hand, jazz groups often play their own versions of standard jazz songs, so the program might just have a list of song titles. In any event, clapping is less of an issue in jazz than it is in classical music. In fact, a lot of clapping is encouraged and expected.

Why is a lot of clapping expected?

There are several reasons. Much of jazz is improvised, and the improvised solos are really the spontaneous invention of the players, so audiences usually applaud those improvised solos. The music continues to play and a new solo might even be beginning, but you are expected to clap after each one.

Sometimes, jazz band leaders turn to the audience and clap to the beat, encouraging everyone to join in. Other times, singers will hold the microphone out to the audience for their response to what has just been sung to create a kind of "call and response" communication with the audience. Much of that is from the African roots of jazz in which the participation of everyone present is an important part of the performance.

What do jazz concert tickets cost?

Ticket prices vary greatly depending on the fame of the performers. A ticket to see a major artist and his or her band might be as expensive as that for a large classical orchestra, but tickets for jazz concerts usually cost less than those for operas. On the other hand, many high schools, colleges, and universities have fine jazz bands, and the tickets for their concerts can cost very little. As with other types of concerts, discounted tickets are often available for those who arrive within an hour or two before the concert, or for those with student identification cards.

How should I dress for a jazz concert?

You should wear clothing that is comfortable and casual, for the most part. Sometimes people will dress up to hear a major performer at a large concert hall, but as with other concerts, you will fit in if you are neat, clean, and polite.

---

the Dave Brubeck Quartet, began to structure their music by using rondo or fugue forms. They sometimes played actual classical compositions with a jazz flavor. Pianist Dave Brubeck had studied classical composition before making jazz his career, and he had his group experiment with odd meters such as five-beat bars, though the standard was four (quadruple meter). Composer Gunther Schuller called his classically influenced jazz *third stream* music. His thinking was that the first stream of music was classical, the second jazz, and the combination of the two was, therefore, the third stream.

By the end of the 1950s, jazz musicians began to look for more ways to structure and create their music. Miles Davis was again at the forefront of a new movement when he recorded his *Kind of Blue* (1959) album, in which he had the musicians play using different scale structures, called *modes,* from the standard major or minor scales that had been the basis of jazz. This idea was then employed by several other musicians and led to the development of a new style, **free jazz.**

New Styles in the 1960s

Free Jazz (1960) was the name of a record by the Ornette Coleman Double Quartet. The album's title gave a name to the style it introduced. The album features a half hour of collective improvisation with no set organization. The music has many complex rhythms and abrasive dissonances. The impetus for this style stemmed primarily from the civil rights movement, with several African American jazz musicians seeking to reaffirm their African roots and abandon any "Europeanisms" in their music. The free jazz movement soon lost much of its momentum because the music was difficult for most jazz enthusiasts to listen to for very long.

By the late 1960s, rock music had gained enough popularity that it was a logical style to combine with jazz. Rock bands such as Electric Flag, Chicago, and Blood, Sweat, and Tears hired horn players to play jazz-styled front-line instruments, along with rock rhythm sections made up of electric guitar, electric bass guitar, and drums. Called *jazz rock,* the music was popular for some years as a rock style and served to introduce many rock fans to elements of jazz.

Fusion

Another successful attempt to combine rock with jazz was by Miles Davis in the 1969 album *Bitches Brew.* The music was more jazz than rock, but because it did "fuse" elements of both styles, it came to be called **fusion.** The rock elements in fusion lie in the basic beat pattern, instruments, and a few other characteristics of rock that are not common in jazz. The beat pattern of fusion uses even beat subdivisions. Most jazz is played using uneven beat subdivisions, as is rock music that developed out of blues or other jazz-related music. Much rock music has roots in country traditions, however, and country is played with even beat subdivisions (a steady "one and two and three and four and" with the numbered beats and the "ands" taking equal amounts of time). Fusion played by Davis in the late 1960s, and all fusion that developed as a result of his work, is played with even beat subdivisions. Rock instruments used in fusion are solid-body electric guitars, electric bass guitars, electric pianos, and other amplified instruments. Before fusion, jazz bands still used hollow-body electric guitars, large stand-up string basses, and acoustic pianos. Other rock characteristics in fusion include short riff (continuously repeating melody) patterns, often no longer than one bar. Before fusion, jazz riff patterns tended to be much longer.

"Miles Runs the Voodoo Down" is taken from the *Bitches Brew* album. The album was popular enough to have made number 35 on *Billboard*'s pop charts in 1970.

CD 3: Track 18

"Miles Runs the Voodoo Down" (beginning) MILES DAVIS

Date: 1969

Genre: Fusion

Tempo: Fairly slow, but it varies with the intensity of the music

Form: There are no repeated sections, but the electric bass plays a four-beat (one bar) riff pattern that repeats throughout the recording with some minimal changes on the repetitions.

Texture: Thick, with dense polyrhythms in the rhythm section

Instruments: One trumpet, one soprano saxophone, one bass clarinet, electric guitar, two electric pianos, electric bass guitar, string bass, three set drummers, and other percussion instruments (some African)

Meter: Quadruple with even beat subdivisions

Duration: We are discussing only the beginning three minutes of a fourteen-minute recording, but the musical characteristics we have discussed are established in those first three minutes.

Context: Electric instruments and even beat subdivisions are the main rock influences on the jazz style called fusion.

	Timing	What to listen for
18	0:00	Subtle opening played by the rhythm section with occasional notes by the bass clarinet
	0:34	Davis begins his trumpet solo that includes clipped notes, long tones, slides up to and the bending of certain pitches, interspersed with silences.
	3:05	Recording fades out.

Many of the musicians who played with Davis on *Bitches Brew* excelled in fusion and started their own groups. Saxophonist Wayne Shorter, who played soprano sax on "Miles Runs the Voodoo Down," and keyboardist Joseph Zawinul formed Weather Report, a group that brought collective improvisation to a new level with selections such as "Heavy Weather" and "Birdland." Guitarist John McLaughlin, who also played on "Miles Runs the Voodoo Down," fused jazz, rock, and Indian music in his recordings with the Mahavishnu Orchestra.

"Hearing the Difference: Parker's 'Ko Ko' and Davis's 'Miles Runs the Voodoo Down'" compares these two pieces.

 **Hearing the Difference**

PARKER'S "KO KO" AND DAVIS'S "MILES RUNS THE VOODOO DOWN"

These works represent different jazz styles: bebop and fusion (see Featured Listening on page 301 and Listening Guide on page 304). Answer the following questions as you listen from one work to the other:

- Both of these pieces are in quadruple meter. Try to count the four beats in each bar or measure. You will be counting much slower in Davis's recording. As you count the beats, which piece has even subdivisions between the beats and which piece has uneven ones?

- Which recording sounds more structured, with sections of equal lengths and sections that repeat?

Does the other recording seem to have anything close to that kind of structure?

- Does either recording sound like the musicians might be competing with one another? If so, which one?

- What instruments do you hear in each recording? Which has the smaller group?

- Do either of the recordings include electric instruments? Which one? Or do they both have electric instruments?

Summary

At the height of the swing era, a small group of musicians rebelled against the commercialism of the big bands and sought to expand the music they played. Their highly innovative experiments resulted in a small ensemble style called bebop, which brought the focus of jazz back to the soloist.

The 1950s and 1960s saw many experiments stemming from the bebop lead. Cool jazz, a reaction to the frenzied quality of bop, brought a more detached emotional quality to jazz. Some musicians looked to classical music to further change their jazz styles, while others dropped all evidences of European classical music. By the late 1960s, some musicians added rock elements to create a music that came to be called fusion, a style often heard in jazz festivals all over the world, continuing into the new century. Of all the styles to develop during that time, fusion was the most enduringly popular.

New People and Concepts

bebop, 300

Charlie Parker, 300

cool jazz, 302

Dizzy Gillespie, 300

free jazz, 304

fusion, 304

Miles Davis, 302

Finale
CD 3: Track 17

Listen again to "Ko Ko" by Parker and compare your impression now with your notes from your First Hearing. Consider the following questions:

- What is the mood of this piece?
- What instruments play most of the solos? What instruments are in the rhythm section?
- Which rhythm section instrument plays a solo, and when does that happen?
- What part of the music repeats, and when does that happen?
- What is the tempo?
- What is the meter?
- If you were going to describe this music to a friend, what would you say?

Further Listening

Jazz: A Film by Ken Burns. This is a nineteen-hour history of the development of jazz in America. It concentrates on the early eras, particularly swing bands, and falls short of covering later jazz styles from the 1960s and beyond. That said, the series does help students understand the roots of jazz. The episodes include: (1) *Gumbo—Beginnings to 1917,* (2) *The Gift 1917–1924,* (3) *Our Language 1924–1928,* (4) *The True Welcome 1929–1935,* (5) *Swing—Pure Pleasure 1935–1937,* (6) *Swing—The Velocity of Celebration 1937–1939,* (7) *Dedicated to Chaos 1940–1945,* (8) *Risk 1945–1956,* (9) *The Adventure 1956–1961,* and (10) *A Masterpiece by Midnight 1961–2001.*

Dizzy Gillespie, *Jazz Signatures—Night in Tunisia: The Very Best of.* Essential recordings of early bebop-styled jazz.

Charlie Parker, *The Best of Charlie Parker: 20th Century Masters—The Millennium Collection.* Essential recordings of early bebop-styled jazz.

Miles Davis, *Birth of the Cool* and *Bitches Brew.* Recordings through which Davis developed the styles of cool jazz and fusion.

Dave Brubeck Quartet, *Time Out.* "West Coast" version of cool jazz, includes their famous "Take Five."

Ornette Coleman, *The Shape of Jazz to Come.* Free improvisations that represented avant-garde jazz of 1959.

American Classical Music Influenced by Early Jazz

> True music . . . must repeat the thought and inspirations of people and the time. My people are Americans. My time is today.
>
> —COMPOSER GEORGE GERSHWIN
> [1898–1937]

 ))) **First Hearing**

 CONNECT   CD 3: Tracks 19–25

Listen to the recording of *Afro-American Symphony*, first movement, by Still and take notes on what you hear. Even if you are working with other students in a paired or group listening session, keep your own notes. Give some attention to the following:

● This work, titled *Afro-American Symphony*, was composed by an African American. Describe what you hear in the music that comes from African American musical traditions such as blues or jazz.

● What instruments do you hear playing the early melodies? Does it sound like only one woodwind or brass instrument is featured, or are there several instruments taking turns?

● There is a harp in the orchestra. Do you ever hear it featured? If so, when?

● Do you hear any melodies repeat? If so, when? Try to guess what the form might be.

● What would you guess is the tempo? Is the tempo steady, or does it vary?

● What might the meter be?

Keep your notes from this First Hearing to compare with your impressions about the piece after you study the information in this chapter.

33

By the early 1920s, jazz had spread from New Orleans to many parts of the country. The 1920s are sometimes called the Jazz Age for that reason. The jazz of this period was played by small groups composed of three or four front-line instruments and rhythm sections involving piano, bass, drums, and sometimes guitar and/or banjo. Collective improvisation was the front line, creating music that was lively, energetic, and complex. Another jazz-related music that had been popular since the late nineteenth century was ragtime. The ragged rhythms of ragtime bands remained popular into the 1920s.

As jazz was gaining popularity, many dance bands and orchestras were also playing rather sedate and rhythmically uninteresting pop-oriented commercial music in dance halls, nightclubs, and ballrooms. This music was easy to dance to, with none of the rhythmic or melodic complexity of jazz. These groups usually included violins and other string instruments, along with wind and rhythm instruments. Their style of dance music was sneeringly referred to, by jazz musicians, as "businessman's bounce."

As jazz became more popular, young people began to demand that it be played at their dances. Some of the dance halls or ballrooms were large enough to accommodate a thousand or more dancers, which meant that a smaller jazz group could not be heard, particularly before electronic amplification came into common use. Adding musicians to the jazz group would not work as long as the front-line instruments used collective improvisation, because from six to ten people all improvising a different melody at the same time would sound overly cluttered. The solution came with the development of the big band swing style of jazz, in which the three or four instruments of the front line were replaced by sections of several trumpets, trombones, clarinets, and/or saxophones. The large horn section played with a rhythm section of piano, bass, and drums. Collective improvisation was no longer used, and arrangers wrote for the horn section in a block style, with most of the players keeping together and playing in similar rhythm patterns. They were still playing jazz in that they used ragged or syncopated rhythms and melodic lines with slides and blue notes, but the only improvisation was in individual solos. Fletcher Henderson was one of the first band leaders to organize a big band. His early band featured Louis Armstrong in the trumpet section.

George Gershwin

The swing jazz bands gained enough attention that some of the commercial dance orchestras began to move in their direction. Paul Whiteman was among the first to add jazz styles and rhythms to his orchestral dance arrangements. He commissioned **George Gershwin** (1898–1937) to write *Rhapsody in Blue* (1924) for his orchestra to play on one of its first U.S. tours. The idea of adding jazz influences to what was otherwise symphonic music was new enough that Whiteman called the program "An Experiment in Modern Music." *Rhapsody in Blue* is essentially a piano concerto, and the composer, George Gershwin, played the piano for the first performance.

George Gershwin was born in New York, the son of Russian Jewish immigrants. Neither of his parents was a musician, but when a piano was purchased for the household, 12-year-old George took to it immediately. By the time he was 15 he had dropped out of school and begun working as a pianist for Jerome H. Remick & Co., a music publishing company. He also cut piano rolls to be used by player pianos, which were popular at the time. The process of cutting piano rolls involves playing music on a keyboard that puts a spot of ink on a long, moving roll of very strong paper each time a note is played. Someone else then cuts holes in the paper roll at the ink spots. When the roll is put into a player piano, the holes in the paper signal the mechanical player what notes to play when. Gershwin had cut more than a hundred piano rolls by the time he was 28.

Gershwin's background as a pianist had included the study of classical music, but most of his work experience was in popular genres. As a songwriter, he worked with his older brother Ira, who wrote lyrics. A number of their songs were published and featured in musicals. When Paul Whiteman hired Gershwin to write and play *Rhapsody in Blue*, most classical musicians and critics, even those in the commercial dance bands such as Whiteman's, thought of jazz as a sloppy kind of music played by bad musicians. The way jazz musicians tended to slide from one note to another, to play blue notes that were out of tune with the traditional scale, and to play rhythms very freely went against classical traditions.

Jazz horn players also tended to vary the timbre of their instruments in distinctive ways; for example, they would start to play a note while holding a mute in the bell and then gradually move the mute away. This created a "wah-wah" kind of sound that is very different from the classical horn style. Gershwin's goal was to compose a piece that was long enough to be included on a concert program and that used jazz rhythms and phrasing while being fully composed and having no places for players to improvise. His efforts were successful. Audiences and critics alike loved *Rhapsody in Blue*, and Gershwin became known as the man who brought jazz into the concert hall. George Gershwin died when he was only 38 years old, after surgery to remove a brain tumor.

GEORGE GERSHWIN
(1898–1937)

- Born in Brooklyn, New York; died at age 38 in Hollywood, California.

- Best known for *Rhapsody in Blue* for piano and orchestra, the opera *Porgy and Bess*, the musical *Of Thee I Sing*, and *George Gershwin's Song Book*.

 **Listening Guide**

 CONNECT   **CD 6: Tracks 7–12**

Rhapsody in Blue GEORGE GERSHWIN

Date: 1924 (this version for larger orchestra, 1942)

Genre: Music for piano and orchestra

Tempo: Varies from section to section and varies within individual sections

Form: Irregular sectional form

Instruments: One clarinet (playing several sizes of clarinet, including bass), one soprano saxophone, one alto saxophone, one tenor saxophone, one baritone saxophone, two French horns, two trombones, one tuba, eight violins, double bass, timpani, banjo, celesta, and piano

Meter: Quadruple

Duration: 16:12

Context: The introductory glissando played by the clarinet sets the jazzy mood for the entire piece. No classical player would slide from note to note that way without having been influenced by jazz.

	Timing		What to listen for
7	0:00	Introduction	Clarinet trill, glissando to bluesy theme; reaches climax on high note, held; repeated-note theme, muted horns; clarinet trill, glissando
8	0:00	A section	Bluesy theme, muted trumpet; piano, five-note motive extended; bluesy theme, orchestra; five-note motive developed; pianistic display ends in upward scale
	1:04		Bluesy theme and five-note motive alternate, ending in pianistic display
	2:21		Bluesy theme and five-note motive, faster tempo, orchestra
	2:57	Bridge	Short, exuberant melody ends in brief arpeggios in piano, directly into:
9	0:00	B section	Repeated-note theme (from introduction), clarinet, against sustained chords
	0:17		Assertive version of repeated-note theme, with motive from bluesy theme (A); sudden slowing at new idea in clarinet, muted trumpet, muted trombone; loud chords
10	0:00	C section	Exciting, jazzy theme, low instruments; developed at length, builds in tension
	1:00	B section	Piano enters on low note, rising passage to extended development of repeated-note theme; motion slows, meditative development of end of theme, pause
	1:56	A/C sections	Bluesy theme, piano, woodwinds with piano running notes; piano solo, trills and runs, arpeggio plunging downward
	3:40		Piano develops jazzy theme (C) at length, mounting excitement and brilliance; short cadenza with soft, rising conclusion; pause
11	0:00	D section	Warm, sensuous melody, orchestra, includes three-note circular motive; solo violin; orchestra, fuller instrumentation; transition, soft fragment of theme in bells
	1:43		Piano, develops circular motive; sensuous melody with added flourishes from piano; fragments developed

(continued)

	Timing		What to listen for
12	0:00	Piano cadenza	Rapid-fire repeated notes; short pause, five-note motive (A); rapid-fire notes, upward glissando
	0:48	D section	Orchestra returns with sensuous theme now in faster, exciting rhythm, piano figurations; builds to dissonant chord
	1:20	A section	Agitated development of five-note motive; emphatic rising chords
	1:42	B section	Exuberant statement of repeated-note theme
	2:13	A section	Full orchestra, bluesy theme, Hollywood style; piano, five-note motive; climactic ending

The Piano Lesson (Homage to Mary Lou Williams), by Romare Bearden (1914–1988).

By the early decades of the twentieth century, quite a few African American composers were writing music in the classical tradition. Certainly even Scott Joplin, who was best known for his ragtime piano pieces, also composed classically oriented concert works, including two operas, songs with piano accompaniment, and other works for piano solo. Other composers included Henry T. Burleigh (1866–1949), Florence B. Price (1888–1953), and William Dawson (1899–1990). Price was the first African American woman to write a symphonic work and have it performed by a major symphony orchestra, the Chicago Symphony Orchestra (1933). Although these composers adhered to the European traditions in which they had been trained, they were also acutely aware of the music in their culture. Spiritual and minstrel melodies were influential on their works. Dawson, in particular, arranged many spirituals that are still performed today. Sometimes those melodies were quoted directly. The man who came to be known as the Dean of Afro-American Composers was William Grant Still.

William Grant Still

William Grant Still (1885–1978) was born into a musical family in Woodville, Mississippi. His father was the town bandmaster. As a young man he intended to go to medical school but was drawn to music. He excelled in composition while a student at Oberlin College Conservatory, but his schooling was interrupted by his military service in World War I. After graduation he moved to New York, where he continued to work as a composer while also playing oboe and other instruments in different performing groups.

Throughout a long career, Still proved to be versatile and resilient. He played in theaters, orchestras, and dance bands; wrote arrangements for radio shows; composed for films (*Lost Horizon*, 1935; *Pennies from Heaven*, 1936; *Stormy Weather*, 1943) and television (*Gunsmoke* and *Perry Mason*); and wrote a large number and wide variety of concert works, among them operas, music for ballets, chamber music, and vocal and choral music, along with many art songs and symphonic works. Among his many awards are prizes from the CBS television network, the New York World's Fair (1939), and the League of Composers. His opera *A Bayou Legend* (1941) was produced and broadcast on public television in 1981. Still died in 1978 at age 83.

Still is perhaps best known for his first symphony, *Afro-American Symphony* (1930). It was the first symphonic work by an African American composer to be performed by a major symphony orchestra, the Rochester Philharmonic in 1931. In it, Still fully employed African American musical ingredients, including spirituals, blues, work songs, ragtime, and jazz, within a general style that is often described as neoromantic. He was also the first composer to introduce the tenor banjo into the ranks of a symphony orchestra. It is featured in the third movement.

The *Afro-American Symphony* (which Still revised in 1969) is laid out in four movements and is scored for a large symphony orchestra. After the piece was finished, Still chose selected parts of poems by the African American poet Paul Laurence Dunbar (1872–1906) to reflect the spirit of each movement, giving the piece a kind of programmatic flavor. Dunbar, the son of a slave, became known for his writing in an African American dialect. The poem Still chose for the first movement of the symphony follows:

> All my life long twell de night has pas'
> Let de wo'k come ez it will,
> So dat I fin' you, my honey, at las',
> Some whaih des ovah de hill.

WILLIAM GRANT STILL
(1895–1978)

- Born in Woodville, Mississippi; died at age 83 in Los Angeles, California.
- Best known for his *Afro-American Symphony*, film music for *Lost Horizon* and *Pennies from Heaven*, television music for *Gunsmoke* and *Perry Mason*, and the opera *A Bayou Legend*.

 ))) **Featured Listening**   CONNECT   **CD 3: Tracks 19–25**

Afro-American Symphony, first movement   WILLIAM GRANT STILL

Date: 1930

Genre: Symphony

Tempo: Moderato assai (very moderately), but the tempo varies

Form: Sonata

Instruments: Three flutes (one with piccolo), two oboes, one English horn, two clarinets, one bass clarinet, two bassoons, four horns, three trumpets, three trombones, one tuba, first violins, second violins, violas, cellos, double basses, harp, and a large percussion section including vibraphone, celesta (the tenor banjo is used only in the third movement)

Meter: Quadruple

Duration: 7:20

Context: Like Gershwin's *Rhapsody in Blue*, this symphony was influenced by the early jazz styles of blues and swing jazz.

Timing		What to listen for
Exposition		
0:00	Introductory theme	Slow, bluesy melody in English horn, begins monophonically; closes with accompaniment interjections

(continued)

	Timing		What to listen for
20	0:00	Theme 1	Muted trumpet states theme 1 in three short phrases, syncopated responses between phrases
	0:40		Clarinet repeats theme 1, over rhythmic string accompaniment with clicking sound, syncopated woodwind responses between phrases
	1:13	Bridge	Transitional fragments circle through woodwinds, ending with bassoon.
	1:25		Strings develop three-note pattern over long timpani roll, tempo accelerates; changes to two-note motive, tempo retards to cadence.
21	0:00	Theme 2	Tender, singing theme in oboe, accompanied by harp arpeggio, responses from woodwinds, muted brass, solo violin; second half of theme sung in violins; variant of first part of theme in flute to close
	0:34		Cellos sing first half of theme; harp plays variant of second half of theme.

Development

	Timing		What to listen for
22	0:00		Two-note motive accelerates to allegro, rhythmic accompaniment pattern; violins alternate fragments of theme 2 with other sections of orchestra.
	0:10		Violin fragments crescendo to full orchestra playing fragments of theme 2, forte.
	0:54		Fragments move to English horn, softer dynamic; bass clarinet alternates with celesta as tempo slows.

Recapitulation

	Timing		What to listen for
23	0:00	Theme 2	Tender, singing theme in shortened form, violins
	0:29	Bridge	Slow transition in woodwinds, trill in low strings
24	0:00	Theme 1	Two-note motive against strong rhythm accompaniment in pizzicato strings; muted trumpets play first theme (three phrases) in swing rhythm, interjected responses from other sections of orchestra
	0:47		Harp solo, slowing tempo provide transition
25	0:00	Introductory theme	Yearning strings introduce slow, bluesy theme, bass clarinet; quiet concluding chords

Although *Rhapsody in Blue* remains the most famous classical work that makes use of jazz stylings, at least from the Jazz Age of the 1920s, and *Afro-American Symphony* is a close second, there were other works that combined jazz and classical music, including Darius Milhaud's *La creation du monde* (1923) and Cole Porter's *Within the Quota* (1923). Gershwin continued to write jazz-influenced music, including his piano concerto of 1925 and his opera *Porgy and Bess* (1935). Meanwhile, some jazz band leaders moved in the direction of classical music. Duke Ellington's *Creole Rhapsody* (1931) and *Reminiscing in Tempo* (1935) are among the best-known jazz-influenced classical pieces. Jazz was an important influence on Aaron Copland, whose music we will hear in the next chapter.

Summary

The widespread popularity of jazz in the Jazz Age of the 1920s caused many dance band leaders and even classically trained composers to put jazz stylings into their music. They did this in several ways.

They increased the size of jazz bands, making the front line a whole section of instruments that had to play arrangements instead of the old jazz style of collective improvisation. Collective improvisation involved each player improvising his own part, which would produce a cluttered sound if more than three players played at the same time. Larger bands marked the beginning of the swing style of jazz.

Commercial dance bands began to add jazz-styled solos to their arrangements. Jazz styling gave players more freedom with the rhythms they played, allowing them to slide between notes at times, to use mutes to give horns a wah-wah tone quality, and to play blue notes that sound out of tune with the standard scale. George Gershwin's *Rhapsody in Blue* is an example of this style.

African American composers added the spirituals and blues of their culture to their otherwise classical, even neoromantic, concert music. William Grant Still's *Afro-American Symphony* (1930) is one of the most famous works in this category.

Other classical composers also began to add jazz to their music, as we will see in the music of Aaron Copland in the next chapter.

New People

George Gershwin, 308   William Grant Still, 310

))) Finale

CD 3: Tracks 19–25

CONNECT

Listen again to the recording of *Afro-American Symphony*, first movement, by Still and compare your impression now with your notes from your First Hearing. Consider the following questions:

- What blues or jazz elements do you hear in this symphony?
- What woodwind and brass instruments are featured?
- Where is the harp featured as an accompaniment and as a solo instrument?
- What is the form? When the two principal themes repeat in the recapitulation, are they in the same order as they were in the exposition, or are they reversed?
- What is the tempo, and does it vary?
- What is the meter?
- If you were going to describe this music to a friend, what would you say?

Further Listening

William Grant Still, *Afro-American Symphony*. We heard only the first movement in this chapter, which features elements of the blues. Other African American styles, such as spirituals and ragtime, influence later movements, making the entire symphony a classical elevation of all of those styles. A tenor banjo is used in the third movement. The movements are (1) Moderato assai, (2) Adagio, (3) Animato, and (4) Lento, con risoluzione.

George Gershwin, *Porgy and Bess*. This "American folk opera" is set in an African American slum in South Caro-

lina called Catfish Row. The characters include a crippled beggar named Porgy, who loves Bess, a troubled woman who already has a possessive lover, Crown. Another character is Sportin' Life, a drug dealer. Porgy eventually kills Crown and must hide to keep from getting arrested. Bess ends up going off with Sportin' Life. Songs such as "Summertime," "It Ain't Necessarily So," and "Bess, You Is My Woman Now" have helped sustain the folk opera's popularity over the decades since its first performance in 1935.

Twentieth-Century American Classical Styles

))) **First Hearing** CONNECT · CD 3: Track 26

Listen to the recording of "Fanfare for the Common Man" by Copland and take notes on what you hear. Even if you are working with other students in a paired or group listening session, keep your own notes. Give some attention to the following:

- This piece is composed for only two families of instruments commonly found in an orchestra. What two families are they? What specific instruments can you identify in this piece?

- What is the mood at the beginning of the piece? Does the mood change, and, if so, in what way?

- Do you hear any melodies that repeat? How many do you hear? When does/do the melody/melodies repeat?

- What is the tempo? Is it steady throughout the piece, or does it vary?

- Can you guess at the meter?

Keep your notes from this First Hearing to compare with your impressions about the piece after you study the information in this chapter.

34

During the first two decades of the twentieth century the German romantic tradition continued to influence the work of American composers. Eventually, however, French impressionism by such composers as Claude Debussy and Maurice Ravel, as well as the music of Igor Stravinsky, made some inroads in American music.

Charles Ives

There were a few American musical pioneers, however, who began to experiment with new musical ideas of their own. One of those was **Charles Ives** (1874–1954). Not only did Ives use advanced techniques such as atonality, free dissonance, and extreme rhythmic complexity, but he also made effective use of homegrown musical and personal experience. Popular American songs and marches, hymn tunes, and quotations from famous European classics all made their way into his music. In a statement reflecting his open-minded approach, Ives said, "There can be nothing *'exclusive'* about a substantial art. It comes directly out of the heart of experience of life and thinking about life and living life."

Charles Ives was raised in the small town of Danbury, Connecticut, where his father was town bandleader, church organist, music teacher, and composer. His father had an unusual interest in musical experimentation and a fascination with unconventional sounds, which he transmitted to his son. This was undoubtedly one of the most important musical influences in Ives's life.

The young Ives studied music at Yale and then launched a successful career in life insurance. He deliberately chose to earn his living in an enterprise separate from his composing, on the theory that both efforts would be better for it, and he never regretted the decision. He composed furiously during evenings and weekends, storing his manuscripts in his barn. Ives's music was totally unknown until he published his *Concord Sonata,* a volume of songs, and a collection of essays in the early 1920s. His works were not readily accepted until after World War II, when they finally received significant recognition. They were then performed, published, and recorded. As his works became better known, Ives's influence increased, and successive generations of composers still draw inspiration from various aspects of his wide-ranging compositional techniques. The one hundredth anniversary of his birth was widely celebrated in 1974.

The musical isolation in which Ives worked led to the development of an unusual philosophy of music. Ives idealized the strength and simple virtue of ordinary people. He had little regard for technical skill, either in composition or in performance, but placed high value on the spirit and earnestness with which amateurs sang and played their popular hymns and songs. The freedom that Ives permitted himself in the choice of musical materials he also extended to performers of his works. Undismayed by an enthusiastic but inaccurate performance of his *Three Places in New England* (1903–1914), Ives remarked approvingly, "Just like a town meeting—every man for himself. Wonderful how it came out!"

Remembering that Ives saw music as a representation of life, it is interesting to see ways in which he re-created live listening experiences in his music. *Three Places in New England,* for example, contains a famous musical representation of two marching bands playing in the same parade. Anyone who has seen a live parade that includes bands might have experienced the effect in which one band has already passed the listener and the other band is approaching. If the bands are both still close enough to the listener, there is a point at which both can be heard at the same time. Usually, listeners tune out the band that has already passed and concentrate on listening to the approaching one. Ives, however, forced the awareness of actually hearing both bands at once. To do that he set up a mood of a Fourth of July parade in which both bands are clearly heard at the same time as if they were marching back to back or even passing each other. Each band is playing in a different rhythm and key, as if they cannot hear each other. This creates the sound we call **polytonality** because we hear more than one tonality at the same time. The piece also contains bits of the melodies of his day, "Rally Round the Flag," "Yankee Doodle," and "The British Grenadiers."

American nationalism, at least in terms of the use of quotes of patriotic or popular American themes, is common in Ives's music. His piano sonata, *The Concord Sonata,* also credited several great American writers. The names of its four movements are "Emerson," "Hawthorne," "The Alcotts," and "Thoreau." Ralph Waldo Emerson and Henry David Thoreau were both nineteenth-century transcendentalist philosophers and writers who, among other things, emphasized the strength people can gain from communing with nature. Hawthorne is best known for his book *The Scarlet Letter,* and Louisa May Alcott for *Little Women.* The third movement, "The Alcotts," also

CHARLES IVES
(1874–1954)

- Born in Danbury, Connecticut; died at age 79 in New York.

- Best known for a piano sonata, *The Concord Sonata;* the orchestral works *Three Places in New England, The Unanswered Question,* and Symphonies no. 1 and 2; and *Variations on "America"* for organ.

credits Louisa May Alcott's father Bronson Alcott, who was a writer and philosopher. Charles Ives died at age 79, having influenced many composers to follow him.

We will listen to one of Ives's most popular orchestral works, *The Unanswered Question*. It was composed in 1906 for string quartet, woodwind quartet, and trumpet, but the version we will hear is one he recomposed for chamber orchestra in the early 1930s.

The strings play a constant, very soft progression of long-held chords throughout the work. Their part is in a G major tonality, and they represent, as Ives said, "the silences of the Druids—who know, see, and hear nothing." (Druids were Celtic priests and sorcerers who advised the Celtic leaders and arbitrated disputes among the ancient Celtic peoples.) Seven times during the work, the solo trumpet plays a five-note motive that is atonal and dissonant to what the strings are playing. This trumpet motive (short theme) represents what Ives called "the perennial question of existence."

Following each of the trumpet motives except the last one is a dissonant group of woodwinds playing responses that begin as short and tentative and gradually become louder, longer, and more active and dissonant. According to Ives, the woodwinds represent the human quest to answer the question of existence. The later woodwind responses mock the question in their frustration with it. Finally, the question is asked again, but there is no answer—just the continuing, soft sounds of the strings that eventually fade into silence.

Also, the three levels of sound—the strings, trumpet, and woodwinds—are not notated exactly as they are to be performed and are not set to any steady beat or tempo. The work requires two conductors—one to direct the strings and another the woodwinds. The trumpet plays independently of both groups, keeping the order of the questions and responses as Ives directs them.

 **Listening Guide**

 CD 6: Track 13

The Unanswered Question CHARLES IVES

Date: 1906, recomposed 1930s

Genre: Chamber orchestra

Tempo: Utterly quiet, serene, and solemn

Form: Not structured except that the trumpet's repeating motive provides a sense of unity

Instruments: Flute, oboe, clarinet, bassoon, trumpet, first violins, second violins, violas, cellos, double basses

Meter: None

Duration: 7:09

Context: Each performance of this work will be different from other performances because the exact relationship among the groups of strings, woodwinds, and the solo trumpet is left to chance. No one counts any steady beat to know exactly when to come in. Two conductors are needed to direct the string and woodwind groups in relation to the trumpet solos.

	Timing	What to listen for
13	0:00	The strings begin a very soft, gentle background of long-held chords that continues throughout the work.

Timing	What to listen for
1:38	The trumpet plays a five-note motive that represents the question.
2:13	Woodwinds play a short tentative response to the question; strings continue to hold chords.
2:36	The trumpet repeats the question motive.
3:00	Woodwinds play another short response; strings continue to hold chords.
3:34	The trumpet repeats the question motive.
3:54	Woodwinds play another short response; strings continue to hold chords.
4:30	The trumpet repeats the question motive.
4:48	The woodwinds' response is louder and longer; strings continue to hold chords.
5:17	The trumpet repeats the question motive.
5:32	The woodwinds' response consist of more confused sounds and begins to mock the question; strings continue to hold chords.
5:54	The trumpet repeats the question motive.
6:04	Woodwinds' response still confused; strings continue to hold chords.
6:46	The final repeat of the trumpet's question; strings continue to hold chords, then fade into silence.

Aaron Copland

Another important American nationalist was **Aaron Copland** (1900–1990). Copland was born in Brooklyn, New York, the fifth child of Harris and Sarah Copland, both of Russian Jewish heritage. He was drawn to music at an early age and first took piano lessons from his sister and then from a series of professional piano teachers. At age 20 he went to Paris to study at an American conservatory, where he met and studied composition with Nadia Boulanger, one of the most important composition teachers of the early twentieth century. While he was based in Paris, Copland also traveled to England, Belgium, Italy, and Germany. In those places he was able to meet and hear music by most of the major composers of the era. The thing that impressed him the most was the fact that music by French composers sounded French, music by German composers sounded German, and music by Russians sounded Russian. He decided that his goal was to write music that would sound American. He was familiar with Charles Ives's music, but he wanted to capture the American spirit in ways other than the quoting of popular melodies (although he also did that).

When he returned to Brooklyn in 1924, he composed *Music for the Theater,* in which he included jazz rhythms and melodies with blue notes as sounds that were, at that time, exclusively American. At this point in his career, Copland began taking private composition students. He joined the League of Composers, founded music festivals, and started the Arrow Music Press, which specialized in the publication of contemporary music. His composition *Piano Variations* (1930) was widely acknowledged as a masterwork, but its use of dissonances and syncopated rhythms kept it from becoming popular with nonmusicians. Copland became dissatisfied with what he saw as the growing distance between the concertgoing public and the contemporary composer. "I felt that it was worth the effort to see if I couldn't say what I had to say in the simplest terms possible,"

AARON COPLAND
(1900–1990)

- Born in Brooklyn, New York; died at age 90 in North Tarrytown (now Sleepy Hollow), New York.

- Best known for "Fanfare for the Common Man"; *Piano Variations* for solo piano; the orchestral work *Music for the Theater*; ballet music for *Billy the Kid, Rodeo,* and *Appalachian Spring*; and film music for *Of Mice and Men, Our Town, The Red Pony,* and *The Heiress.*

Copland wrote. Increasingly thereafter, he drew on themes of regional America. Some of his best-known scores are three ballets: *Billy the Kid* (1938) and *Rodeo* (1942) are based on frontier stories and use melodies from actual cowboy songs, whereas *Appalachian Spring* (1944) depicts life in rural Pennsylvania and is among the most beautiful and enduring representatives of Americana in our musical heritage. The Shaker hymn "Simple Gifts" is the centerpiece of *Appalachian Spring*.

Copland also wrote film scores during this period, including scores for *Of Mice and Men* (1939), *Our Town* (1940), *The Red Pony* (1948), and *The Heiress* (1948). He won an Academy Award for his score to *The Heiress*. Other major awards he received include the Pulitzer Prize (1945), the New York Music Critics' Circle Award (1945), the Presidential Medal of Freedom (1964), and honorary degrees from Princeton University, Oberlin College, and Harvard University. When Spike Lee was looking for music to put to his film *He Got Game* (1998), he chose music by Copland for the soundtrack, saying, "When I listen to Copland's music, I hear America, and basketball is America. It's like he wrote the score for this film."

Two compositions from 1942, "Fanfare for the Common Man" and "Lincoln Portrait," display Copland's American patriotism as well as any compositions can. Both works were inspired by the entry of the United States into World War II. "Fanfare for the Common Man" is a piece for brass and percussion instruments, as fanfares usually are. Fanfares have traditionally been works intended to introduce royal or state leaders. Copland's decision to write such a work dedicated to the common man, or, one could say, the average American citizen, displayed a democratic attitude that includes respect for every citizen. "Lincoln Portrait" features an introduction composed of popular melodies from Lincoln's lifetime followed by a spoken text derived from President Lincoln's speeches and letters. We will listen to "Fanfare for the Common Man" here.

)))) **Featured Listening**  **CD 3: Track 26**

CONNECT

"Fanfare for the Common Man" AARON COPLAND

Date: 1942

Genre: Brass and percussion fanfare

Tempo: Very deliberately (52 beats per minute)

Form: One main theme is repeated with some variation

Instruments: Three trumpets, four horns, three trombones, one tuba, timpani, bass drum, and gong

Meter: Quadruple

Duration: 3:16

Context: Notice how the trumpets and horns are often used together as a single unit; the trombones and tuba are a separate unit; and the timpani, bass drum, and gong another unit. Those three units sometimes imitate or otherwise respond to one another, and sometimes they all play together.

	Timing	What to listen for
26	0:00	Bass drum, timpani, and gong play together on a somber rhythm.
	0:22	Fanfare melody played by all three trumpets in **unison** (all playing the same notes at the same time).
	0:53	French horns join the trumpets on the fanfare theme.

Timing	What to listen for
1:14	The percussion unit repeats its introductory rhythm.
1:37	Trombones and tuba begin the theme with imitative responses by the timpani; trumpets and horns join trombones on the theme.
2:18	Trombones and tuba begin the theme again, answered by the trumpets and horns; all play together with much force and power.
2:43	Trombones and trumpets play a slower and very deliberate version of the theme; the fanfare finishes with a loud crescendo accompanied by a drum roll.

Like Stravinsky and many other composers of the period, Copland turned to serial composition after 1950. His *Connotations for Orchestra* (1962) adapts the twelve-tone system to his special musical style. He did not use that technique for long, having a lifelong concern for bridging the gap between the concertgoing public, which generally rejected serialism, and the modern composer. During the last several decades of his life, Copland spent much of his time conducting concerts of his music all over the world. Copland died in 1990 at age 90.

Ellen Taaffe Zwilich

Ellen Taaffe Zwilich (b. 1939) became one of the most accomplished and recognized American composers in the second half of the twentieth century. She was born and raised in Miami, Florida, and studied piano and violin as a child. Composition always interested her, and she composed music for her high school band while she was a student playing in it. After high school she went to the Juilliard School in New York to study music and concentrate more on composition. In 1975, she was the first woman to receive the Doctor of Musical Arts degree from that prestigious institution. Her Symphony no. 1, *Three Movements for Orchestra* (1983), won the Pulitzer Prize in music. She was the first woman to be so honored. We will listen to the first movement of that symphony as an example of modern orchestral music. "Hearing the Difference: Mozart's Symphony no. 40, first movement, and Zwilich's Symphony no. 1, first movement" contrasts the first movements from very different musical eras.

ELLEN TAAFFE ZWILICH
(b. 1939)

- Born in Miami, Florida.
- Best known for *String Quartet* and the orchestral works *Concerto Grosso 1985*, *Concerto for Trombone*, and Symphonies no. 1 and 2.

 **Listening Guide**

 **CONNECT** CD 3: Tracks 27–29

Symphony no. 1, first movement ELLEN TAAFFE ZWILICH

Date: 1983

Genre: Symphony

Tempo: The introductory section is contemplative, the second allegro, and the coda again contemplative.

Form: Continuous development of motives through three sections

(continued)

Instruments: One piccolo, two flutes, one oboe, one English horn, one clarinet, one bass clarinet, one bassoon, one contrabassoon, four horns, two trumpets, two trombones, one tuba, piano, harp, first violins, second violins, violas, cellos, string basses, timpani, cymbals, tambourine, two bass drums, orchestral bells, vibraphone, tubular bells, snare drum, and suspended cymbals

Meter: Mostly duple with some interpolations of triple meter

Duration: 6:58

Context: Because this movement constantly varies and develops the introductory motive, *or motto,* it is necessary to remember the sound of that motive the first few times it is played to recognize when it repeats in varied versions.

	Timing	What to listen for
	Introductory section	
27	0:00	Motto (germ motive stated three times) played piano (soft), continued with varied echo
	0:28	Motto begins in winds, covered by energetic violin theme climbing to high pitch, continues into intensely yearning melody that falls abruptly
	0:50	Motto in violins echoed in basses; horns state a melody beginning with repeated notes; violins take over and climb to high pitch; trumpets proclaim repeated-note melody (varied)
	1:11	Motto in violins, high pitch, jumpy motive in flutes and piano, trumpet plays repeated notes; fast six-note idea tossed through orchestra in ascending, then descending pattern; repeated-note idea in bass instruments
	1:31	Strings state motto against gradually ascending line, jumpy motive in flutes and piano
	1:44	Trumpets open motto with dissonant chord, development of germ motive
	2:00	Motto in flutes, dissonant chord held in horns, sustained descending line in strings overlaps into:
	2:04	Expansion of motto in brass recalling opening bars, now faster; interjections from woodwinds and strings
	2:17	Brass continues, motto in trumpets, intensity builds; sudden pause
	2:22	Brass begins motto, others join as tension builds further; emphatic descent to short break
	Central section (allegro)	
28	0:00	Pizzicato strings accompany broad melody in horns, fast repeated notes also accompany; trumpet states broad melody; texture becomes fragmented
	0:23	Four-note scale fragment rises and falls, echoed through the orchestra, while suspended cymbal tapping continues repeated-note accompaniment; three-note upward thrust in trumpet, plus repeated notes, abrupt descent
	0:33	Powerful chords hammered, downward-tumbling scale appears; vigorous development of minor third in various instruments; repeated-note tapping on suspended cymbal
	0:46	Extended development of minor-third motives combined with downward-tumbling scale and repeated-note motive in snare drum; cymbal crash and snare drum statement alone twice, with pauses
	1:04	Minor thirds and downward scales continue; rising and falling four-note scale fragment and suspended cymbal take over; repeated-note accompaniment moves to bass drum, downward scales return with hammered chords
	1:28	Three-note upward thrust from basses, repeated bass drum notes; vigorous development of minor thirds in low strings; suspended cymbal returns; upward thrust in trombones continues into broad melody, repeated notes in brass and strings; hammered chords, downward scales, vigorous minor thirds in trombones, fragments into:

Timing	What to listen for
2:00	Faster rhythms in strings, winds, and suspended cymbal; hammered chords crescendo to climax, upward thrust from trombones
2:10	Single chime and sustained chord dissipate energy; double third motive repeated, linked with new two-note motive rocking back and forth; chord dies away, chime strikes three times
Coda	
0:00	Chord dies away as two-note motive continues rocking movement; quiet chord in trombones
0:20	Germ motive gently in oboe; motto (both ascending and descending) in bass instruments; warm, sustained melody in cellos
0:53	Rocking motive alternates with quiet final statement of motto, peaceful close

(29)

Hearing the Difference

**MOZART'S SYMPHONY NO. 40, FIRST MOVEMENT,
AND ZWILICH'S SYMPHONY NO. 1, FIRST MOVEMENT**

Both of these works are first movements from symphonies. (see Listening Guides on page 121 and page 319). Mozart's symphony is from the classical period and is based on the sonata form, which has often been used as the basis of first movements. Zwilich's symphony is from the late twentieth century and is structured much differently from traditional symphony form. Answer the following questions as you listen from one work to the other:

- Which work keeps a constant tempo throughout, and which contains sections with different tempos?

- Which work has more of a sense of symmetrical balance with themes presented at the beginning and

repeated again at the end, and which work is held together by a gradually developing motive without a repeat of the beginning at the end?

- Can you relate the general thinking of the era to which each work belongs with the type of structure it has? You might want to look back at the Preludes to remind yourself about the characteristics of these eras.

- How do the instruments in the orchestra compare? What instruments do you hear in Zwilich's symphony that are not present in Mozart's?

- Which work maintains a duple meter, and which one is duple with some interpolations of triple meter?

Summary

Early twentieth-century composers began to invent their own kinds of new music. Charles Ives was one of the most extraordinary and original composers that America produced in that era. His music contains elements drawn from a variety of American and European traditions. He used advanced techniques such as atonality, free dissonance, polytonality, and extreme rhythmic complexity, along with traditional procedures, in a fresh and free manner. At the same time, Ives included popular and patriotic American melodies in his music, giving it a tremendous appeal to listeners who might otherwise have been put

off by its contemporary compositional techniques. Ives's works have had a profound influence on later composers.

Another important American patriot whose music has affected many composers was Aaron Copland. Copland experimented with contemporary techniques such as free and syncopated rhythms and even serialism, but his basic belief was that the gap between contemporary composers and the general concertgoing audience needed to be closed. Much of his music does that by being quite listenable while still having a contemporary feel. He expressed his nationalistic feelings by including jazz rhythms and melodies with blue notes in some works, by using cowboy and Shaker melodies in his ballet music, and by composing such works as "Fanfare for the Common Man" and "Lincoln Portrait" to help the war effort when the United States entered World War II in 1942. Copland also composed movie scores and received countless awards and honorary degrees from prestigious institutions. His music and his influence will live long beyond his lifetime.

Ellen Taaffe Zwilich represents an American composer of the late-twentieth and early twenty-first centuries who composes in a modern musical language without being overly dissonant or difficult to hear. She writes in a style that she developed out of classical traditions, but she develops ideas in complex ways, not relying on traditional formulas. The first movement of her first symphony, for example, uses a germ motive that she varies and develops in a variety of ways without fitting it into a classical sonata form. She has not completely thrown out the traditional sense of balance, however, because she begins and ends the movement in a contemplative mood and inserts a powerful allegro section in the middle.

New People and Concepts

Aaron Copland, 317

Charles Ives, 314

Ellen Taaffe Zwilich, 319

polytonality, 315

unison, 318

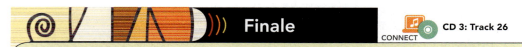

Finale

CONNECT   CD 3: Track 26

Listen again to the recording of "Fanfare for the Common Man" by Copland and compare your impression now with your notes from your First Hearing. Consider the following questions:

- What two families of musical instruments do you hear in this piece? What specific instruments are featured?
- What is the mood of the piece, and in what way does it change?
- Do any themes repeat? When do they repeat?
- What is the tempo? Is it steady?
- What is the meter?
- If you were going to describe this music to a friend, what would you say?

Further Listening

Charles Ives, *Three Places in New England*. This piece is a wonderful illustration of Ives's patriotism and his father's experience as a band director. The first movement refers to a Civil War monument to the 54th Massachusetts Volunteer Infantry (also featured in the 1989 film *Glory*), which was the first "colored" regiment in the Union Army. The second movement is set at a Fourth of July parade with bands playing in contrast with one another, and it quotes the melodies of "Rally Round the Flag," "Yankee Doodle," and "The British Grenadiers." The third movement is Ives's reminiscence of a river where he and his wife walked on their honeymoon. The movements are titled (1) The "St. Gaudens" in Boston Common (Col. Shaw and his Colored Regiment), (2) Putnam's Camp, Redding, Connecticut, and (3) The Housatonic at Stockbridge.

Aaron Copland, *Lincoln Portrait*. This is a work for narrator and orchestra. Copland included popular melodies from President Lincoln's time, together with a narrative compiled from speeches and letters by Lincoln. The result is a very patriotic statement that helped earn Copland the title "The Dean of American Music."

Ellen Taaffe Zwilich, Symphony no. 1 (Three Movements for Orchestra). Only the first movement of this symphony was heard in this chapter. The other two movements are equally colorful, conveying the timbres of a vibraphone, solo tuba, and bells. The movements are numbered without further titles as (1) I, (2) II, and (3) III.

> Our attitudes control our lives. Attitudes are a secret power working 24 hours a day, for good or bad. It is of paramount importance that we know how to harness and control this great force.
>
> —COMPOSER-PIANIST IRVING BERLIN
> [1888–1989]

Musical Theater

))) First Hearing

 CONNECT   CD 3: Tracks 30–33

Listen to the recording of "America," from *West Side Story,* by Bernstein and take notes on what you hear. Even if you are working with other students in a paired or group listening session, keep your own notes. Give some attention to the following:

● Listen to the lyrics, which are in English. What is the song about? Do you hear a difference in attitudes about life in America? Which singer, the first or the second, likes America, and which does not?

● What do you think about the use of accents in the rhythm pattern? Do they seem to fit a regular meter with which you are familiar, or do they vary in some way? Can you tell what the meter might be?

● What kind of instrumental group accompanies the singers? Does it sound like a full orchestra or a smaller group of instruments?

● In the story, the singers are from Puerto Rico. Is there anything about the use of instruments that sounds Latin?

● What might the tempo be?

Keep your notes from this First Hearing to compare with your impressions about the piece after you study the information in this chapter.

35

Broadway Musicals

Many types of popular entertainments, such as vaudeville shows, were popular in America in the nineteenth century, but American **musicals** developed most directly out of European operettas, such as Gilbert and Sullivan's *H.M.S. Pinafore* (1878), *The Pirates of Penzance* (1879), and *The Mikado* (1885). American musicals were so often written and produced on or near Broadway in New York that they came to be called *Broadway musicals.* Broadway musicals differed from European **operettas** in that they were usually based on everyday stories, the dialogue was spoken in everyday language, and the songs were musically important for their own sake. Such popular songs as "Over There," "I'm a Yankee Doodle Dandy," "(You're a) Grand Old Flag," and "Give My Regards to Broadway" all came from musicals written between 1901 and 1912 by **George M. Cohan** (1878–1942). Cohan's life was the subject of the Academy Award–winning movie *Yankee Doodle Dandy* (1943), which popularized his songs once again for the World War II generation.

Most Broadway musicals of the 1920s and 1930s were based on the light "boy meets girl and they fall in love" genre of stories. An important exception was *Show Boat* (1927), with music by Jerome Kern (1885–1945) and lyrics by Oscar Hammerstein II (1895–1960). *Show Boat* was based on a novel by Edna Ferber that described the lives of a family who ran a showboat on the Mississippi River. The musical had a more serious tone than was common in musicals of the time. It even included an interracial married couple, which was a very controversial subject when the musical was first performed. Many lastingly popular songs came from *Show Boat,* including "Ol' Man River," "Make Believe," and "Why Do I Love You?" With the success of *Show Boat,* musical writers and composers understood that audiences were ready to accept more serious themes as long as the songs were accessible.

Generally, musicals differ from operas in that they include memorable and easily singable songs. Operas often include brilliant arias, but performing them requires quite a bit of vocal training. Operas also tend to concentrate on the drama of their plots and may continue for a long time before offering an unforgettable melody. Musicals, on the other hand, use one song after another to help relate the story. The program for an opera includes a synopsis of the plot, while the program for a musical merely lists the songs in the order you will hear them; it is assumed that the audience can follow the plot as it is presented.

Of course, some musicals are also quite operatic. When George Gershwin's *Porgy and Bess* opened in 1935 it was called a *folk opera,* and it is still performed by both opera companies and musical companies. *Porgy and Bess* is set in an African American community in South Carolina. The characters are poor and the plot involves a crippled man, Porgy, who commits murder to gain the woman he loves, Bess. While he is in prison, another man takes Bess off to New York, promising her a better life. When Porgy is freed from prison, he heads to New York to win Bess back. George Gershwin had been working with jazz melodies and rhythms in combination with classical music for some time. *Rhapsody in Blue* (1924) was one of his greatest accomplishments before *Porgy and Bess.* He again used jazz, as well as African American spirituals, in the opera, combining popular and classical styles of music. The song "Summertime," from *Porgy and Bess,* became a jazz standard.

By the middle of the 1940s, a number of musicals in New York had topped a thousand performances, and many musicals began touring the country with great success. Some of the most memorable musicals from that era include *Oklahoma* (1943), *South Pacific* (1949), and *The Sound of Music* (1959). All three of those musicals were written by Richard Rodgers and Oscar Hammerstein, popularly known as **Rodgers and Hammerstein.**

Leonard Bernstein

Leonard Bernstein (1918–1990) composed the music for *West Side Story* (1957), which was based on the plot of Shakespeare's play *Romeo and Juliet.* Bernstein was as interested and successful in the world of serious concert music as he was in the world of pop-

LEONARD BERNSTEIN
(1918–1990)

- Born in Lawrence, Massachusetts; died at age 72 in New York City.

- Best known for his televised Young People's Concerts, the musicals *On the Town* and *West Side Story* (which were also filmed), music for the operetta *Candide,* and the choral work *Chichester Psalms.*

ular musicals. Born in Massachusetts, he graduated from Harvard and worked as assistant conductor of the New York Philharmonic Orchestra. He became famous overnight when he filled in for a conductor who had fallen sick, and he led the orchestra through a concert that was broadcast nationwide. At age 40, Bernstein was the first American-born conductor to be hired as director of the New York Philharmonic. He composed many orchestral, choral, chamber, and operatic works, and gained fame for the much more pop-oriented musical *West Side Story,* which was made into an Academy Award–winning film in 1967. The plot of *Romeo and Juliet* was discussed in Chapter 20 when we listened to Tchaikovsky's *Romeo and Juliet* Overture. For the musical, the feuding families were transformed into two New York street gangs, the Jets and the Sharks. Romeo's counterpart is Tony of the Jets, and Juliet's is Maria of the Sharks. Because the Sharks are Puerto Rican immigrants, Bernstein composed some wonderful jazzy, Latin-influenced music to set the atmosphere. We will listen to "America," which is full of complex and exciting rhythms. It is sung by the Sharks. Notice ways in which the lyrics refer to unfair treatment experienced by the Puerto Rican immigrants and the split between Rosalia, who dislikes America, and Anita, who is happy being in her new country.

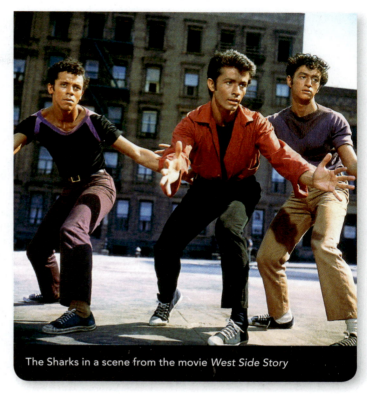
The Sharks in a scene from the movie *West Side Story*

 ))) **Featured Listening**   **CD 3: Tracks 30–33**

"America" from *West Side Story* LEONARD BERNSTEIN

Date: 1957

Genre: American musical

Tempo: Beginning, moderato; sextuple section, fast

Form: Introduction, introduction repeated with extension, ABABA–Dance–BA–Dance–B

Voices and Instruments: Members of the Sharks: Rosalia, Anita, and other Shark girls; instrumentation: three flutes/piccolos, one bass clarinet, one bassoon, two French horns, three trumpets, two trombones, violins, cellos, contrabass, Spanish guitar, and percussion, including timpani, celesta, and the Latin sounds of claves (solid wood cylinders that hit one another), güiro (a notched hollow gourd that is scraped with a stick), and maracas (rattles made of a gourd or wood with seeds or other small items inside that rattle when the instrument is shaken)

Language: English

Meter: Introduction: Duple with many triplet patterns inside the two beats;
A sections: Alternating 6/8 and 3/4 measures. This can be counted within the sextuple beats by accenting **1** 2 3 **4** 5 6 followed by **1** 2 **3** 4 **5** 6.
B sections: Sextuple
Dance sections; use both 6/8 and 3/4 meters

Duration: 4:32

(continued)

Context: Occasional responses from the group add to the solo texts given here to create a party atmosphere.

	Timing		Text	Form
30	0:00	Instrumental introduction		
	0:17	ROSALIA	Puerto Rico, you lovely island, Island of tropical breezes. Always the pineapples growing Always the coffee blossoms blowing.	Introduction
	0:37	ANITA	Puerto Rico, you ugly island Island of tropic diseases. Always the hurricanes blowing, Always the population growing, And the money owing, And the babies crying And the bullets flying. I like the island Manhattan! Smoke on your pipe and put that in!	Introduction repeats with extension
31	0:00	OTHERS	I like to be in America! O.K. by me in America! Ev'rything free in America. For a small fee in America!	A (alternating sextuple patterns)
32	0:00	ROSALIA	I like the city of San Juan.	B (sextuple meter)
		ANITA	I know a boat you can get on.	
		ROSALIA	Hundreds of flowers in full bloom.	
		ANITA	Hundreds of people in each room.	
	0:12	ALL	Automobile in America, Chromium steel in America, Wire-spoke wheel in America, Very big deal in America!	A
	0:25	ROSALIA	I'll drive a Buick through San Juan.	B
		ANITA	If there's a road you can drive on.	
		ROSALIA	I'll give my cousins a free ride.	
		ANITA	How do you get all of them inside?	
	0:36	ALL	Immigrant goes to America, Many hellos in America; Nobody knows in America Puerto Rico's in America!	A
33	0:00	Dance music		Mixed sextuple and triple meters
	0:36	ROSALIA	I'll bring a TV to San Juan.	B
		ANITA	If there's a current to turn on!	
		ROSALIA	I'll give them a new washing machine.	
		ANITA	What have they got there to keep clean?	

Timing		Text	Form
0:48	**ALL**	I like the shores of America! Comfort is yours in America! Knobs on the doors in America, Wall to wall floors in America!	A
1:01	Dance music		Mixed sextuple and triple meters
1:38	**ROSALIA**	When I will go back to San Juan	B
	ANITA	When you will shut up and get gone?	
	ROSALIA	Ev'ryone there will give big cheer!	
	ANITA	Ev'ryone there will have moved here!	
	Instrumental closing		

This is the original recording, but there are other sets of lyrics in common use today. Those lyrics do more to stress the mistreatment of immigrants and have Shark boys and girls singing back and forth about missing Puerto Rico and wanting to stay in New York, but include references to fights and rejections to their skin color and accents. Some of the same text is used, but the overall effect makes more of a social statement. Other musicals by Leonard Bernstein include *On the Town* (1944), *Wonderful Town* (1953), and *Candide* (1956).

Later Musicals

The lyricist for *West Side Story* was **Stephen Sondheim.** He composed both the music and the lyrics for later musicals including *A Funny Thing Happened on the Way to the Forum* (1961), *A Little Night Music* (1972), and *Sweeney Todd* (1979). The 2007 movie *Sweeney Todd: The Demon Barber of Fleet Street,* starring Johnny Depp and directed by Tim Burton, was based on Sondheim's musical.

The widespread popularity of rock music during the 1960s brought about a number of rock-based or -influenced musicals, including *Hair* (1967), which told the story of hippie rock fans who were societal dropouts. The cast was completely nude by the end of Act One. The British rock band The Who performed *Tommy* (1969) as a musical, calling it a *rock opera.* Film and then fully scored musical versions of *Tommy* have been popular in later years. *Jesus Christ Superstar* (1971) and *Grease* (1972) also contained rock influences.

Jesus Christ Superstar, by the English composer **Andrew Lloyd Webber** (b. 1948), brought a more operatic style to musicals by having the dialogue sung instead of spoken. Webber's father was the director of the London College of Music, and Andrew grew up listening to classical music of all kinds, including opera. Webber met Tim Rice when he was in college, and the two began to write songs together. The first major project they completed was *Joseph and the Amazing Technicolor Dreamcoat* (1968), more of a staged cantata than a full musical. *Jesus Christ Superstar* was their second and much more ambitious rock opera.

Some of Webber's other musicals include *Evita* (1978) and *Cats* (1981). *The Phantom of the Opera* (1986) is his most operatic in its elaborate staging and passionate story about a disfigured man, Eric. Eric lives under the Paris Opera House and tries to win the love of a young soprano by impressing her with his musical ability and by

MusiCurious

MUSICALS AND OPERAS: SIMILAR, BUT DIFFERENT

Is there any real difference between musicals and operas? I know they are both dramas that are sung.

Yes. There are many differences. The primary difference is the type of singing. In musicals, the singers' voices are usually amplified, allowing them to use light, pop-styled, vocal techniques. That kind of singing is much less demanding in terms of vocal training, strength, and range than what is required of opera singers. It is common for a singer in a musical to sing a role six to eight times a week. Opera singers are trained in the vocal style called *bel canto* (beautiful song), which allows them to sing florid and complicated dramatic lines and be heard in a large hall without the use of amplification. They are rarely able to sing an entire opera role two nights in a row because of the great demands made on their voices.

Songs from musicals are sometimes popular on their own. Is that also true of opera arias?

Not usually. Opera arias are generally much too complex and virtuosic for the average listener to remember or to sing or hum along with. The songs in musicals are often very memorable and easy to sing. That is one of the greatest strengths of the musical.

What about the dialogue that keeps the plot going?

Dialogue is usually spoken in musicals, whereas in operas the dialogue is usually sung. The style used for the sung dialogue in opera, called *recitative,* follows the inflections of the voice and is less dramatic than the singing in operatic arias.

Don't both musicals and operas use orchestras?

Well-funded musical productions still use orchestras, although they are often smaller than those used for most operas. However, orchestras are expensive, and some musical productions have cut their budgets by using prerecorded music or a few electronic instruments to accompany the singing and dancing. Opera audiences would not tolerate either prerecorded or synthesized instrumental accompaniments because orchestral accompaniment is so integral to the opera experience.

There are at least some similarities, aren't there?

Yes. Professionally produced musicals often equal operas in their elaborate staging, costuming, and dancing. Plots of musicals can have just as much depth and drama as operas, and they can be just as entertaining. On the other hand, the stories of musicals are usually much easier to understand by listening to the songs than are opera plots, which are often very complicated and sung in a foreign language. The programs given out to audiences reflect this difference by simply listing the songs for a musical but providing an act-by-act synopsis for an opera.

training her to be a star. Webber has also composed music for movies and television. He was knighted by Queen Elizabeth and was later given an honorary life peerage, making him Lord Andrew Lloyd Webber.

The Frenchman Claude-Michel Schonberg added *Les Misérables* (1987) and *Miss Saigon* (1988) to the repertoire of Broadway musicals. *Miss Saigon* is based on the plot of Puccini's opera *Madame Butterfly* (1904). The opera's story of an American serviceman stationed in Japan and his mistreatment of a Japanese lover has been updated to Vietnam in 1975, with an American serviceman who leaves a Vietnamese woman and takes their child, knowing that the woman will die as a result.

The Phantom and Christine in *The Phantom of the Opera.*

As we discussed in Chapter 24, the opera *La Bohéme* (*Bohemian Life,* 1896) served as the model for Jonathan Larson's musical *Rent* (1996) with a similar updating of the story. "MusiCurious: Musicals and Operas: Similar, but Different" discusses some of the differences between these forms.

Summary

Musicals developed out of several earlier theatrical styles. The English ballad operas were first composed in the middle 1700s and became popular in the American colonies. They were different from operas in that they used spoken dialogue instead of recitative and had short popular songs instead of the more elaborate arias of opera. Vaudeville shows and operettas by Gilbert and Sullivan also contributed to the development of the Broadway musical.

At the beginning of the twentieth century, George M. Cohan composed musicals that used everyday language and plots to relate to real life in America, giving him the name "Yankee Doodle Dandy." The success of Kern and Hammerstein's musical *Show Boat* allowed other musical writers and composers to use more serious plots than they had previously thought audiences wanted. Gershwin's *Porgy and Bess* also featured a serious plot, and it added African American and jazz music to the genre.

Rodgers and Hammerstein wrote many popular musicals in the 1940s, and Leonard Bernstein followed with several in the 1950s. Among Bernstein's successes was *West Side Story,* which set Shakespeare's tale of *Romeo and Juliet* in modern-day New York and added Latin instruments and rhythms to the American musical's repertoire.

Rock music influenced a number of musicals in the 1960s and early 1970s. One of those, *Jesus Christ Superstar* by Andrew Lloyd Webber, used sung dialogue, making Webber's musicals more operatic than earlier musicals. Singing styles of musicals and operas differ in a number of ways, particularly in that the songs in musicals are more easily singable and often become popular on their own. Professional productions of both operas and musicals enhance the drama with elaborate sets and costumes.

New People and Concepts

Andrew Lloyd Webber, 327

George M. Cohan, 323

Leonard Bernstein, 324

musicals, 323

operetta, 323

Rodgers and Hammerstein, 324

Stephen Sondheim, 327

Finale

CD 3: Tracks 30–33

Listen again to the recording of "America," from *West Side Story,* by Bernstein and compare your impression now with your notes from your First Hearing. Consider the following questions:

- What is this song about? Who is singing, and what positions do they take on the subject of being in America?
- What is the meter, and how are the beats accented?
- What kind of instrumental group accompanies the singers?
- What Latin instruments are used to support the Puerto Rican identity of the singers?
- What is the tempo?
- If you were going to describe this music to a friend, what would you say?

Further Listening

Broadway—The American Musical (PBS Series), DVD boxed set. This five-DVD set includes 106 songs from popular musicals.

Gilbert and Sullivan, *H.M.S. Pinafore.* Gilbert and Sullivan's most popular operetta is also a marvelous satire on the British class system, with characters that include a lawyer who rises to be "ruler of the Queen's Navy."

Claude-Michel Schonberg, *Miss Saigon.* This musical emerged from the recent memory of the end of the Vietnam War. The plot parallels Puccini's opera *Madame Butterfly,* placing it in Vietnam instead of Japan.

Andrew Lloyd Webber, *The Phantom of the Opera.* Webber's most "operatic" musical is distinguished for its many memorable tunes, the pathos of the Phantom, and its allusions to Mozart's operas.

Jonathan Larson, *Rent.* This musical is based on the story of Puccini's opera *La Bohème,* which we studied in Chapter 24. The story has been updated so that Mimi has AIDS instead of tuberculosis, while Rodolfo is renamed Roger and is an HIV-positive songwriter instead of a poet/playwright.

> . . . in film composing, you're not in full control of it the way you are in concert music—so the risk of compromise, or dilution of idea or structure, is great. In film, it's the director's vision, even of the music, which prevails, whereas in concert composing, it's your own vision.
>
> —COMPOSER–FILM COMPOSER
> JOHN CORIGLIANO [B. 1938]

Film Music

 ))) **First Hearing**

 CD 3: Track 34
CONNECT

Listen to the recording of "Main Theme" from *Star Wars* by Williams and take notes on what you hear. Even if you are working with other students in a paired or group listening session, keep your own notes. Give some attention to the following:

- This music might be familiar to you. If it is and you know the *Star Wars* movies, can you identify the characters or events these opening themes represent? If not, what different moods do you hear in the various sections of this music?

- What instruments can you identify? Write down the names as you hear them come in.

- Do any melodies repeat?

- This opening has sections in different meters. Try to identify which sections are in which meter.

- What is the tempo? Does it vary or remain steady?

Keep your notes from this First Hearing to compare with your impressions about the piece after you study the information in this chapter.

36

By the early twenty-first century, film music had evolved into an independent genre. In the 1980s, when cable television and VCRs first became available, movie executives worried that these new technologies would replace movie theaters. Of course, their worries were misplaced. People still wanted to experience visual effects on a big screen, and they wanted to hear the high-quality sound that only theaters could provide. Film companies found that they could create independent profit centers by releasing films first in theaters and then on VCR, DVD, cable, and satellite. Soundtracks created yet another source of revenue, and for this reason studios began spending a good deal of money to produce music of the highest possible quality. By the 1990s, it was not uncommon to see a movie soundtrack on CD advertised at the end of a film.

The Earliest Film Music

Films offered an entirely new type of entertainment to a few select audiences during the middle to late 1890s. These early films were silent, and the projectors in use at the time were very noisy. Theaters solved this problem by having live music played during the film. This practice began in Paris in 1895, when a solo pianist played light popular tunes throughout a screening. There was no effort to connect the music to the action or moods in the film. The following year in London, a harmonium (a type of reed organ) was used to accompany the showing of a film. By April 1896, some London theaters were using small orchestras to accompany their films.

In 1908, Le Film d'Art company in Paris decided to have music composed specifically for its film *L'Assassinat du Duc de Guise*. The company hired a well-known and respected French composer, **Camille Saint-Saëns** (1835–1921), to compose the score. Saint-Saëns had previously composed incidental music for a ballet and for a number of plays, and he was anxious to attempt a film score. The film company was happy with the result, and Saint-Saëns made further use of his score by rewriting it as his concert work Opus 128 for Strings, Piano, and Harmonium. Live musicians played the score during screenings of the film, and the idea of having music designed to fit the film was generally thought to be a good one. However, there was a problem with this approach in that it not only required the film producers to pay a composer, but it also required each movie theater to rent a particular score and to hire the musicians necessary to play it. This added expense prevented theaters and movie companies from making the film-specific score a regular practice.

In 1909, the Edison film company offered a solution by creating lists of well-known classical works that would fit different moods and dramatic situations. Other publishers produced similar lists. By 1912, an American named Max Winkler was not only suggesting certain music but also designing what he called music **cue sheets.** The cue sheet told the musicians exactly when to start and stop playing the suggested music in order to make sure that it matched the action of the film. He used classical works for his suggestions, fully recognizing that he was taking them out of their intended context: "In desperation we turned to crime. We began to dismember the great masters. We began to murder the works of Beethoven, Mozart, Grieg, J. S. Bach, Verdi, Bizet, Tchaikovsky, and Wagner—everything that wasn't protected by copyright from our pilfering."

Early Sound Films

In 1926, the Warner Brothers Studio produced the **Vitaphone** system, an invention that allowed music recorded on phonograph records to be played simultaneously with the film. The first film to use the system was *Don Juan*. The following year, *The Jazz Singer* (1927) used the Vitaphone to include both the first spoken dialogue and the first song in a movie. The dialogue and singing were synchronized with the actors' mouth movements. The vaudeville entertainer Al Jolson starred in the film, and the score added to his popularity by showcasing his singing. Many future films would use the Vitaphone in this way.

By the early 1930s, films had become very popular with the general public, with some 80 million Americans going to the movies as often as once a week. Because movies offered an inexpensive and much needed escape from the problems of the time, the film industry was one of the few businesses to succeed during the Great Depression. American movie studios produced as many as five hundred films a year, and there was much incentive to improve the movie experience.

One of the first movie composers was **Max Steiner** (1888–1971). Steiner was born into a musical family in Vienna. His godfather was composer Richard Strauss, and he studied conducting with composer-conductor Gustav Mahler, whose first symphony was discussed in Chapter 23. Steiner learned to play instruments of several types, including strings, brass, and keyboards. While he was still a teenager he worked as a conductor in Vienna and then in Britain. He took an opportunity to move to New York at the beginning of World War I, where he composed and conducted music for theatrical productions. In 1929 he moved to Hollywood, where he worked on a num-

ber of films. His first major achievement in film music was the score for *King Kong* (1933), made by the RKO Studio. The film was made under a tight budget, and Steiner was instructed to put together a score from tracks that had already been recorded for earlier films. Of course, this was the studio's first film about a giant ape threatening the population of an American city. Steiner's response to the suggestion that he use existing music was "For God's sake . . . what am I gonna use—music from *Little Women*?" The company gave in, and Steiner composed a score that helped make the movie a tremendous success. Income from the film actually saved the RKO Studio from having to close its doors.

Six years later, Steiner was given a chance to make his mark on the movie industry by composing a full three hours and forty-five minutes of music for *Gone with the Wind* (1939). The piece known as "Tara's Theme," which represented the Southern plantation, became one of the most memorable movie themes ever composed. Steiner wrote many other film scores during the 1940s, including the forever popular *Casablanca* (1942). (He did not write "As Time Goes By"—he took that from a musical called *Everybody's Welcome,* then on Broadway—but the rest of the score was his, and it added much to the romantic tension of the movie.)

Scene from the film *King Kong*

World War II had taken such a toll on many parts of Europe that moviemakers there could hardly keep up with the advancements being made in Hollywood. Europeans continued to produce movies, but the great film masterpieces were coming from the Hollywood studios. That is not to say that people in California were unaffected by the war. Money was tighter than it had been, and the large, lush orchestras were reduced to smaller ensembles. One of the great movie classics from the early 1940s was Orson Welles's *Citizen Kane* (1941). American composer **Bernard Herrmann** (1911–1975) added to the dark character of the movie by using more dissonance than had been common in past movie scores. His work on *Citizen Kane* was so effective that horror filmmaker Alfred Hitchcock chose him to compose scores for his films *The Man Who Knew Too Much* (1934—the 1956 remake also used Herrmann's music)*, The Trouble with Harry* (1955)*, The Wrong Man* (1956)*, Vertigo* (1958)*, North by Northwest* (1959)*, Psycho* (1960)*,* and *Marnie* (1964).

American composer Aaron Copland was already well known for his classical compositions (Chapter 34) when he began writing for the movies in 1939. Copland won an Academy Award for his movie score for *The Heiress* (1948). In one scene, the main character, Catherine, has her bags packed and is sitting with her aunt waiting for her fiancé to pick her up. A carriage is heard, and Catherine says good-bye to her aunt and runs outside with her bags. The carriage, however, is not for her and just passes her by. When her fiancé never arrives, she slinks back into the house feeling depressed and disillusioned. When the movie was first screened in previews, audiences laughed at Catherine's having been rejected. That was not the response the director wanted, so he asked Copland to write music that would give the viewers a sense of the tragedy of the situation. Copland composed dissonant music for muted brass instruments, and both the scene and the movie were saved. As Copland said later, "I am sure that the audience had no idea that music was playing." Such is the effect music can have on movie audiences.

Later Film Scoring Practices

Many movies, from the silent era to the present, have used existing music as part or all of their soundtracks. One famous example is *2001: A Space Odyssey* (1968), directed by Stanley Kubrick. The movie portrays the silence of space by devoting no more than forty minutes of its entire running time to dialogue. The first word is not spoken until almost a half hour into the film. The lengthy score is made up of carefully chosen compositions, including the tone poem *Thus Spake Zarathustra* by Richard Strauss; *The Blue Danube Waltz* by Johann Strauss; *Atmospheres, Lux Aeterna,* and *Requiem for Soprano, Mezzo-Soprano, Two Mixed Choirs and Orchestra,* by György Ligeti; and *Gayane Ballet Suite* by Aram Khatchaturian. The movie was nominated for five Academy Awards and won in the Best Visual Effects category. In many ways the music did more than the story line to give the effects the support they needed to make *2001: A Space Odyssey* one of the most popular science fiction films of all time.

Scene from the film *Star Wars*

It was another science fiction movie, *Star Wars* (1977), that successfully combined brilliant visual effects with the almost constant dramatic support of a large symphony orchestra: the music plays for 88 of the 121 minutes of the movie. Actually, the director of *Star Wars,* George Lucas, had originally intended to use previously composed music in much the same way that Kubrick had for *2001: A Space Odyssey,* but he decided to have composer **John Williams** (b. 1932) write the score, including some of the music that Lucas had chosen. Williams had had tremendous success with various television scores and with the movie *Jaws* (1975). The works Williams incorporated into the *Star Wars* score included music by film composers Eric Korngold and Alessandro Cicognini and music by classical composers Gustav Holst, Peter Ilyich Tchaikovsky, Sir Edward William Elgar, and Carl Orff. The famous heroic theme at the opening to *Star Wars* was a quote from the score to *The Sea Hawk* (1940) by Eric Korngold.

The "Main Theme" from *Star Wars* opens the movie and functions much like an opera overture in that it sets the mood for *Star Wars* by quoting themes that will be heard throughout the movie. Like Richard Wagner (Chapter 25), Williams assigns each character his or her own theme. *Star Wars* begins with a fanfare and a theme that represents the movie's hero, Luke Skywalker. (Because the same theme was used in the later *Star Wars* films to represent a larger heroism, we will call it the *heroic theme*; however, it was specific to Luke in the original movie.) The heroic theme is followed by music that foretells the impending battle between the Empire and the Rebel Alliance, and then Princess Leia is introduced by her theme. Apart from Leia's gentle introduction, the opening music projects the heroic nature of the film and foreshadows the conflicts to come.

))) **Featured Listening**  **CD 3: Track 34**

"Main Theme" from *Star Wars* JOHN WILLIAMS

Date: 1977

Genre: Movie music

Tempo: Moderate, but slows near the end

Instruments: Three flutes (including piccolo), three oboes (including English horn), three clarinets (including bass clarinet), two bassoons, six French horns, five trumpets, three trombones, one tuba, percussion, first violins, second violins, violas, cellos, double basses, and harp

Meter: Mostly quadruple, but the battle music is triple

Duration: 5:47

Context: This is the music that opens the *Star Wars* movie. It includes themes that represent Luke Skywalker (the heroic theme), a battle, and Princess Leia and ends with a march.

	Timing	What to listen for
34	0:00	Fanfare
	0:09	Heroic theme played by brass and percussion then continued by the orchestra
	1:18	Light and soft transition
	1:36	Strings build intensity.
	2:03	Battle music (triple meter), then syncopated punctuations obscure meter
	2:22	Heroic theme returns in quadruple meter.
	3:19	Princess Leia's leitmotif is played by cellos and basses.
	4:07	Heroic theme in high brass
	4:39	Fanfare-like statements in brass with a background of swirling strings
	5:02	Strings slow tempo and intensity drops.
	5:17	March music taken from "The Coronation March" by Elgar, music builds to a dramatic finale

The oversized orchestra used for the soundtrack of *Star Wars* was very expensive. Musicians who played on the film score not only received money for their time in the recording studio but also received continuing residual payments after the film was released for rental, sale, or televised showings, as well as other royalties for soundtrack sales. These payments had been negotiated between movie companies and musicians' unions, and, as a result of such negotiations, the 1970s saw many Hollywood musicians make good incomes by playing for film and television soundtracks. However, there was a new sound maker on the horizon: the synthesizer.

Trends in Movie Music

Robert Moog unveiled his synthesizer in 1964, and it became widely popular through Walter Carlos's album *Switched-On Bach* (1968). By 1970, rock bands and musicians such as Pink Floyd, Kraftwerk, Tangerine Dream, Mike Oldfield, Rick Wakeman (keyboardist for Yes), Jimmy Page (guitarist for Led Zeppelin), and Keith Emerson (keyboardist for Emerson, Lake, and Palmer) were using it on a regular basis. Throughout the 1970s, the Moog synthesizer continued to be improved, and soon other synthesizers and computerized sound makers were developed, including the Jupiter-8, Prophet-5, and the Synclavier II. These instruments could produce sounds that imitated those of orchestral instruments and could generate sound effects ideal for film scores. What did this mean for Hollywood film studios? It meant that a single composer with a synthesizer could produce an entire soundtrack and consequently save the studio a great deal of money on residuals and royalties. This practice, along with the practice of having movie scores recorded in countries that did not come under Hollywood musicians' union agreements, greatly reduced the number of musicians enjoying successful careers in Hollywood. Of course, something similar happened in the 1920s when the first sound films did away with the need for pianists and orchestras in movie theaters.

It did not take long for synthesizer-produced music to gain acceptance among movie fans. The first synthesizer movie score to win an Academy Award was *Midnight Express* (1978), with music by Italian-Swiss producer Giorgio Moroder. (Moroder was also famous for having invented the sound called *eurodisco* through his synthesized productions of hits by Donna Summer, including "Love to Love You Baby" and "Hot Stuff.") In 1981, another synthesized score, this time for *Chariots of Fire*, won an Academy Award for Greek composer-producer Vangelis.

Despite their popularity, not all scores today are synthesized scores. In many cases, film scores have been composed for live orchestras by some of the most successful classical composers of our time. Two of those composers are **John Corigliano** (b. 1938) and **Philip Glass** (whose music we will study in Chapter 39). Corigliano is well known for his concert works, including his opera *The Ghosts of Versailles*, produced by the Metropolitan Opera Company of New York in 1991. His film scores include *Altered States* (1980), for which he received an Academy Award nomination; *Revolution* (1985), which won an award from the British Film Institute; and *The Red Violin* (1999), which won an Academy Award for Best Original Score. Like Saint-Saëns before him, Corigliano used musical themes he had composed for the movie *The Red Violin* for his concert work, *The Red Violin: Chaconne for Violin and Orchestra*.

Philip Glass's first film score to gain widespread public attention was *Koyaanisqatsi* (1983). The film is a collage of images of nature that accumulatively demonstrate the negative effects mankind has had on the world. Although Glass has often composed for live orchestras, he used a synthesizer to produce sound effects for *Koyaanisqa-tsi*. For a later project that ultimately grew into two semi-horror movies, *Candyman* (1992) and its sequel, *Farewell to the Flesh* (1995), Glass made effective use of gothic-influenced organ music. His next film project, *Kundun* (1997), was set in Tibet and related the early life of the Dalai Lama. Glass's later film scores include *The Hours* (2002) and *Undertow* (2004).

One of the most highly respected composers in film music today is **James Horner** (b. 1953). Horner received a PhD in music composition and theory from UCLA and gained experience in film scoring at the American Film Institute. His first commercial film was *Wolfen* (1981). It was followed by *Aliens* (1986), for which he was nominated for an Academy Award. He has also been nominated for *Field of Dreams* (1989), *Braveheart* and *Apollo 13* (both 1995), and *A Beautiful Mind* (2001); in 1997 he won the award for *Titanic* (1997). His other film scores are too numerous to list here. Horner effectively uses both recordings made by live musicians and synthesizer-produced sounds in his film scores. He describes his process as follows:

> I'm a throwback. I know all about the machines. . . . When I work with synths, I don't want what you think of . . . as synthetic sounds. I want very organic sounds that I can manipulate. The orchestral stuff, I write at a desk and orchestrate, and then send it off to the copyist. The synth stuff, I play ideas to myself on the piano, and notate ideas, but most of it happens by coloring in, like painting, at the actual recording session, because I play everything myself on a MIDI keyboard.

Summary

The relationship between music and film has changed a great deal in the past hundred and twenty years. In the silent era, live music was played as much to drown out the sound of the projector as to add to the film experience. The progress from silent films to those with sound took over thirty years, and even then the music was minimal. Today, film extravaganzas filled with visual effects of all kinds are accompanied by music as good as any other composed in the twenty-first century.

By the mid-1920s, the Vitaphone system allowed previously recorded music and dialogue to be played along with films. Soon original scores were being composed and recorded, adding much to the impact of the movie experience. By the late 1930s, the art of film scoring had developed to include the sound of full orchestras recorded to play simultaneously with the film. Tighter wartime budgets reduced the size of those orchestras, but composers adjusted their writing accordingly.

During the late 1960s and through the 1970s, science fiction movies such as *2001: A Space Odyssey* and *Star Wars* expanded the visual effects to represent their space-age themes, and the music used to support those, whether borrowed from previously composed classical scores or newly composed, further popularized the effects music can have on a film.

Synthesizers began to be used to produce film scores during the 1970s, and since then film composers have used them, used live orchestras, or combined the two for many very successful and popular soundtracks. Many of the major classical composers today write for films, and many composers who concentrate on film music write at the same level of quality as do composers of other art music of our time.

New People and Concepts

Listen again to the recording of "Main Theme" from *Star Wars* by Williams and compare your impression now with your notes from your First Hearing. Consider the following questions:

- What characters or events from the *Star Wars* movie are represented by the themes in this opening?
- What instruments are used to represent Luke Skywalker, and what instruments represent Princess Leia? Does the contrasting sound of the instruments fit the contrasting characters?
- The theme of which character repeats two times after it is first played?
- Which section is in triple meter, when the rest of the music is in quadruple?
- What is the tempo, and how does it vary?
- If you were going to describe this music to a friend, what would you say?

Further Listening

Paramount Pictures 90th Anniversary Memorable Scores. A two-disc set that includes memorable clips from the scores of 43 Paramount films from the 1940s through the 2000s.

Best Film Classics 100. This six-CD set includes classical compositions that have been used in films. Each CD has themes for the types of films used as sources, including (1) The Great Blockbusters, (2) The Classic Movies, (3) The Favorite Movies, (4) The Piano at the Cinema, (5) Opera at the Cinema, and (6) Baroque Goes to the Cinema. The music is not original for films, but the collection does show how often classical works have been used in films.

CHARACTERISTICS OF MUSIC IN AMERICA

Texture	Monophonic melodies composed to be sung as polyphonic fuging tunes; homophonic songs with simple piano accompaniment; works with a variety of textures in the European tradition; complex textures in bebop jazz
Tonality	Major-minor system retained; modes used in some jazz or jazz-influenced works; atonality in some works
Rhythm	Standard meters following European traditions; swing beat (uneven beat subdivisions) in jazz and blues-based rock; free rhythms in free jazz and much electronic music
Harmony	Traditional European harmonies in song accompaniments; chord extensions common in advanced jazz styles
Tone color	Some jazz instruments use mutes to create wah-wah timbres; guitars amplified for use in jazz and rock; rock music uses solid-body electric guitars, electric bass guitars, and electric pianos to create a loud and full sound from few instruments; electronic sounds manipulated on tape add to the tone color of electronic and other works; singers' voices are amplified in musicals
Musical instruments	In addition to the widespread use of amplified instruments, electronic instruments become capable of both producing unnatural sounds and imitating acoustic sounds
Form	Twelve-bar blues form used in the blues, some jazz styles, and blues-based rock; free forms in free jazz and electronic music; traditional forms also used

Prelude

New Ideas and Styles from Twentieth-Century Internationalism

The first Prelude on the twentieth century made the point that a World Exposition in Paris in 1889 introduced European artists and musicians to music, costumes, and dances from Asia, the Middle East, and Africa. By the time Debussy composed his prelude to "The Afternoon of a Faun" in 1894, the sense of rhythmic freedom heard in some world musics had become part of Debussy's style and added much to the beauty and interest of the work. Influences of music from outside of Europe continued to affect European and American composers through the twentieth century.

By the 1970s, the United States had been involved in two world wars and a series of smaller wars in such places as Korea, Vietnam, and Cambodia. In the 1990s, Iraq was added to the list. The American forces who served in those wars returned to the United States with some experience and understanding of those cultures. Through contact with veterans, as well as through reports in the media, Americans learned about the people and cultures of those places.

World Music Influences on Early Rock (1960s–1970s)

Improvements in transportation, particularly the development and widespread use of jet planes, allowed many Americans and Europeans to travel to regions all over the globe. Included among those travelers were musicians who not only visited and experienced music from distant places but also took advantage of opportunities to study music during their visits. One of the most famous examples occurred in 1965 when the Beatles' guitarist George Harrison became interested in the Indian religion of Hinduism. He bought an Indian sitar and played it on Beatles recordings such as "Norwegian Wood" and "Within You Without You." In 1968, Harrison and other members of the Beatles, the Beach Boys, and other musicians took a trip to India to study the Hindu religion and its related meditation and music.

Harrison studied the sitar with Indian virtuoso Ravi Shankar, and the two became close friends. The Beatles' popularity gave Shankar fame outside of India, allowing him to be featured in such important rock events as the 1967 Monterey Music Festival in San Francisco. Shankar was a serious and talented classical musician in India, something quite different from the many rock musicians who also played at Monterey. Shankar also played at the famous Woodstock Festival in 1969. Harrison's friendship with Ravi Shankar and his relationship with Indian culture continued throughout his career and life. In 1971 Harrison organized a charity concert, called the "Concert for Bangladesh," to raise money to feed starving people in Bangladesh.

World Music Influences on Folk and Popular Rock (1980s–Present)

By the 1980s, many other popular musicians were listening to music from all over the world and adding performers from faraway places like Africa to their recordings. American folk-rock musician Paul Simon added the South Af-

George Harrison with Ravi Shankar

rican vocal group Ladysmith Black Mambazo to his Grammy Award–winning *Graceland* album in 1986. He then went on to produce two albums of Ladysmith Black Mambazo's music for world-wide sale. Through Simon's work, many music fans heard the gentle vocal style of Ladysmith Black Mambazo for the first time, and this ended up influencing the styles of many male vocal groups the world over. Simon went on to record *The Rhythm of the Saints* (1990), with musicians from West Africa and Brazil, further popularizing world music and rhythms.

British singer-songwriter Peter Gabriel added Senegalese singer-percussionist Youssou N'Dour to his *So* album in 1986, helping to popularize N'Dour's West African vocal style. N'Dour has continued to be popular with rock fans through his work for Amnesty International. Gabriel and N'Dour have often performed at Amnesty International fund-raising events and concerts, sharing bills with Bruce Springsteen, Sting, and Tracy Chapman.

Also in the realm of rock music, Talking Heads' former singer David Byrne moved in the direction of world music after he began his solo career. He included African poly-

rhythms in the *My Life in the Bush of Ghosts* (1981) album and added musicians from Brazil, Cuba, and Asia to his *Rei Momo* (1989) album and tour. He also has a record label, called Luaka Bop, that produces music from all over the world, though primarily from Latin America. Former Led Zeppelin members Robert Plant and Jimmy Page included Egyptian musicians and instruments on their *No Quarter* (1994) album, and Tracy Chapman sometimes plays an Australian aboriginal wind instrument called the didjeridoo in her performances.

World Music Influences on Classical Music

The trend toward world music has also manifested itself in classical music. Since the beginning of the twentieth century, classical composers have continually been looking for new sounds and ideas in a series of efforts to move music beyond the traditions of the nineteenth century. Schoenberg's development of the twelve-tone compositional technique was very much a part of that urge to be new and different. The Kronos Quartet, a string quartet from San Francisco, has concentrated on broadening the string quartet repertoire beyond its traditional European base. The quartet has commissioned works from many contemporary composers and has reached out to composers in a variety of non-Western cultures. It played works by African composers on its *Pieces of Africa* (1992) album; works influenced by music from Portugal, Hungary, Turkey, Romania, Lebanon, Iran, and India on its *Caravan* (2000) album; and Latin music on its Grammy Award–winning *Nuevo* (2002). On other albums the Kronos Quartet has recorded works by a great variety of modern composers whose music is also rooted in world music, including Terry Riley, John Cage, Steve Reich, Philip Glass, and George Crumb.

Cross-Cultural Impact of Music

The music in this last set of chapters represents the interaction and communication among people from many different cultural backgrounds. Anyone who has traveled to a variety of distant places knows that Western music has greatly affected other cultures. Certainly rock, jazz, and other music popular in the United States and Europe have received almost universal acceptance. Interest in the popular music recorded in the United States and Europe extends to musicians in non-Western countries who play their versions of rock, jazz, or other popular music. One can walk the streets of Tokyo, Japan, on a Sunday afternoon and hear a fabulous jazz group that sounds straight out of New Orleans or Chicago, only to get closer and see that the musicians are all Japanese. Whether people from various parts of the world play each other's music or add influences of it to their own, the European and American traditions that have been the subject of this text to this point have been, and continue to be, greatly enriched by such cross-culturalization.

> When you learn something from people, or from a culture, you accept it as a gift, and it is your lifelong commitment to preserve it and build on it.
>
> —CELLIST YO-YO MA (B. 1955)

World Musics

Listen to the recording of "Srepegan (slendro nim)" by a gamelan ensemble and take notes on what you hear. Even if you are working with other students in a paired or group listening session, keep your own notes. Give some attention to the following:

- Do you hear any instruments you have heard before? If so, which ones? How would you describe most of the instrumental sounds you hear?

- This chapter is called "World Musics," so it is easy to assume that "Srepegan (slendro nim)" is a work from a culture outside of Europe or America. Which region of the world might this music come from?

- Listen for repeated sections. Is the music a constant repetition of one theme, or are there any contrasting themes?

- What do you think the tempo might be?

- What do you think the meter might be?

Keep your notes from this First Hearing to compare with your impressions about the piece after you study the information in this chapter.

37

The concert music of Western Europe, the United States, and Canada is based on a tradition of written notation through which the artistic expression of individual composers is carefully preserved. This written music is usually re-created in performance by highly trained musicians at scheduled concerts and recitals. While the performer may take some liberties, such as the use of rubato (slowing down or speeding up the music as a display of expressiveness), the final role of performance is to re-create sounds as intended by individual composers.

European and American traditions also include folk music that was learned and performed for centuries without the use of written notation. Folk music is music of average people who might or might not have any formal musical training. Folk music includes casual dances and songs from everyday life such as lullabies, love songs, and ballads.

The musical heritages of many world cultures also include both formal or classical music and folk music, but in many cases the classical music has been transmitted orally. Young musicians have traditionally learned by carefully listening to, observing, and imitating older musicians. The music and the way of playing it are memorized; music notation is not used. This way of learning music is referred to as an *oral tradition*.

By the late twentieth century, recorded music available from all over the world began to interest composers from Europe and the United States. Easier world travel made it possible for international musicians to tour and perform in Western countries, and for Western musicians to study with non-Western musicians. By the late twentieth century, musical styles in the West had been significantly influenced by other cultures. Before we study the resulting music, we will listen to some of the world musics that influenced it.

Musical Elements in Non-Western Musics

Pitch and Scale Systems

The scales employed in many non-Western cultures are often different from those in Western cultures. Octaves frequently have more, or less, than twelve subdivisions. The smallest pitch differences found in non-Western musics are often larger, or smaller, than the Western semi-tone (half step).

One of the most prevalent combinations of pitches is the **pentatonic scale,** a series of five notes. Pentatonic scales are found in the musics of North and South American Indians and in African and many Asian cultures. One type of pentatonic scale is made up of the notes C-D-E-G-A-(C). That is the same scale structure as that produced by playing only the five black keys of the piano.

African cultures south of the Sahara use, in addition to pentatonic scales, a variety of *tritonic* (three-note) and *heptatonic* (seven-note) scales, including patterns of whole and half steps that are common in Western music. In the classical music of India, sequences of pitches known as *ragas* are employed. The basic notes of a raga are modified by the use of **microtones,** which are intervals smaller than a half step. Microtones cannot be played on the piano, but they can be produced on stringed instruments by bending the strings to tighten them, therefore raising the pitch slightly. Of course, they also can be, and often are, sung.

Harmony

Most cultures use simultaneous sounds. As we have seen, Western music is governed by a long tradition of rules of harmonic organization. Melody generally tends to be more important than harmony in non-Western musics. We use the term *texture* to describe how many melodies are being performed at one time. The music of some world cultures uses **heterophonic texture.** To create that texture, two or more individuals perform the same melody at the same time, and they each add rhythmic or melodic modifications as they play or sing. They also sometimes vary their tone quality and vocal inflections using slides, trills, and vibrato.

Rhythm

Much Western music is based on symmetrical rhythmic patterns and uniform time intervals. However, many cultures use complex, irregular, and free rhythms. Many cultures use primarily vocal forms; in these cultures, rhythms conform to the stress patterns of the words sung. In African music, *polyrhythms*—two or more contrasting and independent rhythms used at the same time—are common; the sophistication of the use of rhythm in Africa is unmatched in any other culture. We heard polyrhythms when we studied some of the African roots of the blues and jazz earlier.

Instruments

Ethnomusicologists, or people who study world musics, generally categorize musical instruments differently from Western instruments. Non-Western cultures have a more diverse selection of percussion instruments and many fewer woodwind or brass instruments. As a result, percussion instruments are put in two categories, and wood-

Gamelan group

winds and brass are put together in one. The categories (listed on page 25) are *chordo-phones* (stringed instruments), *aerophones* (wind instruments), *idiophones* (solid instruments that are hit, struck together, shaken, scraped, or rubbed), and *membrano-phones* (drums that have a vibrating membrane).

Music from Indonesia

Indonesia is in Southeast Asia, just north of Australia, southeast of India and south-west of the Philippine Islands. **Gamelan** ("gah-muh-lahn") is the Indonesian term for a musical ensemble. The instruments in gamelan groups can vary, but idiophones made of metal are often the most prevalent. Xylophones with metal bars are some-times called **metallophones,** although they still fall into the general category of idio-phones. A gamelan will typically have sets of knobbed and hanging gongs of various sizes, in addition to metal xylophones. Membranophones, both plucked and bowed chordophones, and aerophones can also be part of the gamelan. Singers are some-times included. The musical example we will listen to is played by an Indonesian gamelan ensemble.

))) **Featured Listening**   CONNECT ♫ ◉ CD 3: Track 35

"Srepegan (slendro nim)" WAYANG KULIT AND DANCE REPERTOIRE

Genre: Indonesian gamelan music

Tempo: Moderate with some variations to the speed of the beat

Form: No large repeated sections, but much repetition of short rhythmic and melodic patterns

Instruments: Gamelan including a variety of metallophones and knobbed metal idiophones

Meter: Gantra (4 beats)

Duration: 2:53

(continued)

Context: This gamelan is played by musicians from the STSI Conservatory of Surakarta in Central Java.

	Timing	What to listen for
35	0:00	Repeated patterns and some variation in tempo
	1:34	Tempo gets faster.
	1:45	Return of beginning tempo
	2:05	Tempo gets faster.
	2:33	Gradual retard to a slow ending

Music from China

Chinese music and culture have had important influences on European and American art music. From its beginnings, Chinese music was conceived of as a system that would reflect the order of the universe. Musicians and philosophers in ancient China believed in the existence of one true *foundation tone,* or *huang chung,* on which the whole edifice of musical composition should be built. The *huang chung* was thought to have social, cosmological, and mystical significance. For many centuries, the disappearance of a dynasty was attributed to its inability to find the true *huang chung.* Several methods were used to discover the elusive tone. One method prescribed the correct height of the pipe that would produce the true *huang chung:* it would be equal to ninety average-sized grains of millet laid end to end. From this tone the Chinese musical system derived twelve tones, or *lu.* The tones were comparable to the twelve months of the year, so that each month had its own tone.

Because each tone was invested with mystical significance, Chinese music developed as a system in which the perfect performance of individual tones was regarded as the highest art. The philosopher Confucius (ca. 551–479 BCE) played a stone slab on which only one note could be produced. Yet he is said to have played it with such a full heart that its sound was captivating.

The sophistication needed to enjoy subtle colorations and inflections on only one tone was not, of course, a universal gift among the ancient Chinese. Popular discontent with "scholarly music" led to the development of more accessible forms that could be enjoyed by everyone.

Orchestras in ancient China were immense in size and diverse in instrumentation. The orchestra of the Temple of the Ancestors at Beijing included more than 150 players. Some musicologists have come to believe that the Chinese used a variety of instrumental timbres to give the music a dense texture. The existence of this variety of instruments also encouraged programmatic styles, in which the instruments were used to create realistic sound effects, such as animal cries or roaring gales.

Our Chinese listening example is played by a much smaller group, which allows each instrument to be heard fairly clearly. The instruments are an *erhu,* a bowed string instrument with two steel strings; a *pi-p'a,* a plucked string instrument with a mandolin-like tone; and a *hsaio,* a flutelike instrument with a somewhat nasal tone quality. The melody comes from the T'ang Dynasty (the seventh to the tenth centuries CE). There was no music notation during that era, but melodies were written down with words representing each note and other signs indicating the length of time each note was to be held.

As is common in much Chinese music, the scale used is *pentatonic.* The texture is *heterophonic,* which means that the music is based on a single melody being played at any one time, with the instrumentalists adding their own variations to the melody as they play it.

 Listening Guide

"Moonlight on the Ching Yang River" YO SU-NAN

Date: Tang Dynasty

Genre: Traditional Chinese music

Tempo: Moderate with fluctuations

Form: A melody repeats with variations

Texture: Heterophonic

Instruments: *Pi-p'a, hsaio, erhu*

Scale: Pentatonic

Meter: Duple

Duration: 5:54

Context: This music is from the oral traditions of China. It might have been put into notation today, but it was transmitted from one generation to another by memorization. This piece of programmatic music is intended to portray the moonlight on the river, as indicated by the title.

Timing	What to listen for
14 0:00	Introduction by *pi-p'a*
0:12	*Hsaio* joins the *pi-p'a*.
0:24	*Erhu* joins other instruments to begin playing the melody, each playing its own variations.
0:58	The melody repeats, again with all three instruments playing variations.
1:38	The melody repeats, with variations.
2:26	The melody continues to repeat with variations.

Indian musical instruments include the tabla and the sitar.

Music from India

The cultural heritage of India is divided between two basic traditions: the Muslim culture of the north and the Hindu tradition of the south. Indian music, too, reflects this cultural split; for example, the two systems use different instruments and different naming systems. Yet they also hold many things in common, including the philosophic premise that music is intimately connected with the spiritual world.

The basic motive force of Indian music has remained constant: music must reflect the inherent order and majesty of the universe and contribute to a performer's spiritual development. This deep and sustaining motivation, which anchors Indian music to its mystical, philosophic framework, is reflected in the ordering of the melodic modes known as **ragas.** Each raga is related to a certain time of day or night. Indian historians tell of a musician at the court of the sixteenth-century emperor Akbar who sang a night raga at midday with such power and beauty that "darkness fell on the place where he stood." Each raga is associated also with a definite mood, a color, a festival, a deity, and certain specific natural events. Sexual differentiation of the ragas into male *ragas* and female *raginis* completes the unification of Indian music with the total surrounding cosmology.

A teacher of Indian music is considered a true guru, responsible not only for his students' musical progress but also for their spiritual development. The guru receives no money for his services. The knowledge and wisdom he imparts are thought to be priceless and far beyond any conceivable financial remuneration. Often, a student binds himself to one guru for a period of ten years or more. During that time he will be expected to memorize more than sixty ragas and rhythmic cycles called **talas.** The memorization is demanded not to ensure perfect reproduction of the ragas as such but to promote the complete familiarity and understanding needed to master the pinnacle of Indian musical art—the art of improvisation.

When playing a raga, the players are free to explore and improvise on their own rhythms, competing with each other in a contest of rhythmic skill. The rhythmic tension is increased only by the requirement that all players reach the *saman,* or first beat of the cycle, exactly together. As the players attempt more and more daring cross-rhythms and yet still manage to come out together on the *saman,* the audience begins to assist the performers by clapping out the beat of the tala.

The example of Indian music we will listen to is from North India. It is folk music based on a particular type of pentatonic scale that has some notes lowered in its descending form. The *sitar* (a plucked string instrument with *sympathetic* strings that vibrate to create the sound of a drone) uses much pitch variation because the strings can be pushed toward the finger board by the player to tighten them, creating a constant variety of microtones. There is a certain amount of pitch variation in the *tabla* (a pair of drums) too because the player sometimes pushes the palm of his hand on the drum head to tighten it and raise the pitch.

Folk Melody Based on Raga Des   BALUJI SHRIVASTAV

Date: Unknown

Genre: Folk music from India

Tempo: Moderate

Form: Constant repetition of a short melody, but with much improvised variation on each repetition

Instruments: Sitar and tabla

Scale: Pentatonic

Meter: Kaherva tala (4 + 4 beat patterns)

Duration: 7:10

Context: This is an example of folk music from North India that is often sung at weddings, births, and the first month of the Indian New Year.

	Timing	What to listen for
15	0:00	Introduction played by the sitar
	0:14	The tabla joins the introduction.
	0:19	The eight-beat melody begins and continues to repeat with variation.
	7:05	Recording ends with the sitar.

Music from Africa

Nowhere in the world is music more a part of the very process of everyday living than in Africa. Almost all communal activities are accompanied by singing, dancing, and drumming. These three activities are rarely separated; they are interdependent. As a whole, the music is characterized by sophisticated and complex rhythmic structures, a wide range of indigenous instruments, a strong oral tradition of songs, and a vast store of dances to accompany and celebrate all aspects of life.

Most African cultures greatly respect the spoken word, which is believed to be the life force and called *nommo* in the Bantu languages. The languages are inflective, and common speech assumes musiclike qualities. The musical sounds produced most often are percussive, and players use bodily gestures to enhance a performance.

Much African music is meant to be heard by the deity. The Dogon people of Mali believe that music, specifically that played on drums, is the vehicle through which the sacred word is brought to human beings. More commonly, music is used to lift up prayers to a divinity. To ensure the delivery of a healthy baby, special songs are sung during the hours of childbirth. After birth, the gratitude of the family finds expression

African drum ensemble with dancers

in chants and dancing. The naming of the baby, the loss of a first tooth, and other incidents in the life of the child from infancy through puberty are celebrated with music.

In addition to marking the stages of life, music deepens and defines African existence. Through songs and dances young men and women are taught the language of the tribe, the traditions of family living, and the obligations they will be expected to fulfill. Communal holidays and festivals are celebrated through seasonal musical offerings. In some West African cultures, political music is considered so important to the general welfare that singers (the griots, or tribal historians, whose connection with blues singers we discussed in Chapter 31) specialize in songs of governmental and social information.

Ewe Drum Ensembles

In our chapter on early jazz, we discussed music from northwestern Africa, because jazz is so clearly rooted in that music. In this chapter we concentrate on Ewe ("ay'-way") drumming from Ghana. This particular type of drumming has influenced several contemporary composers, particularly Steve Reich, who studied it in Ghana. We will discuss his music in Chapter 39. His music manifests the general characteristics of African music that we discussed earlier: call and response, polyrhythms, and the repetition of individual rhythmic patterns.

For ceremonial occasions it is often customary to bring together large ensembles. Traditional festivals may extend over several days, with different programs of music planned for each day. A festival drum orchestra of the Ewe, who inhabit southeastern Ghana, usually consists of a drum section led by the master drummer, a percussion section (for timekeeping), singers, dancers, and a master of ceremonies. The drum section consists of three to seven drums of various sizes and tones. The percussion section consists of *gankogui* (two bells that are tapered and joined together to form a handle) and an *axatse* (rattle with a husklike shape, made from a dried gourd covered with nets of beads). These instruments usually act as timekeepers and, in almost every case, play a standard, regular pattern, such as tap-rest-tap-rest, while other members of the orchestra play contrasting rhythmic parts.

The vocal section of the orchestra consists of a trained chorus, headed by one or two cantors, which claps as it sings. The drum orchestra is completed by a group of costumed dancers, male and female. The master of ceremonies maintains decorum among the dancers and encourages the singers. All of these sections perform in a semicircle facing an open space reserved for dancing. Our listening example was recorded at one of these ceremonies but is played by a slightly smaller ensemble.

 **Listening Guide**

 **CD 6: Track 16**
CONNECT

"Gadzo" ("Kayiboe, the Child Is Not Matured") EWE OF GHANA

Date: Unknown

Genre: African music

Tempo: Moderate

Form: No particular pattern of returning or contrasting sections

Voices and Instruments: Many voices singing in a call-and-response pattern; some voices are part of the ensemble, and others are from people who are dancing with the music; the instruments are *dundun* (drum), *kagann* (congolike drum), five or six *axatses* (rattles)

Language: Ewe, one of many tribal languages in Ghana

Meter: Polyrhythmic

Duration: 2:58

Context: This is based on a dance for young men, originally a war dance but now a general social dance.

	Timing	What to listen for
16	0:00	Call-and-response vocals
	0:08	Drum ensemble enters.

Summary

We have taken a brief look at the musics of four non-Western cultures: Indonesian, Chinese, Indian, and African. From these few examples we can draw three generalizations. First, musical traditions in each culture are based on ancient practices that have been learned through memorization and training in improvisation according to traditional styles of playing or singing. Second, music from these cultures is very much a part of daily life.

It is not reserved for the concert stage or prerecorded listening. Third, in these cultures, melody and a great variety of rhythms, even contrasting rhythms happening simultaneously, are more important than harmony.

In the next two chapters, we will hear more music from the tradition of Western classical music, much of which has been greatly influenced by the non-Western musics we have just heard.

New Concepts

ethnomusicology, 344

gamelan, 345

heterophonic texture, 344

metallophones, 345

microtones, 344

pentatonic scale, 344

raga, 348

tala, 348

Finale

CD 3: Track 35

Listen again to the recording of "Srepegan (slendro nim)" by a gamelan ensemble and compare your impression now with your notes from your First Hearing. Consider the following questions:

- What types of instruments do you hear?
- What area of the world does this music come from?
- What type of form (patterns of repetition and contrast) does this music follow?
- What is the tempo?
- What is the meter?
- If you were going to describe this music to a friend, what would you say?

Further Listening

Java: Court Gamelan (original recording remastered). The original recording was released in 1971 and includes gamelan made up of mostly metallophones and other bronze idiophones.

Phases of the Moon: Traditional Chinese Music. This CD includes music from many areas of China, played on traditional Chinese instruments.

The Ravi Shankar Collection: Three Ragas. This recording was made in 1956, but it has been digitally remastered.

The ragas range from eleven to over twenty-eight minutes, which allows the listener to appreciate the development and complexity of the music more fully than would be possible with shorter examples.

Ewe Drumming from Ghana. This is a collection of music by the Ewe people of Ghana and its eastern neighbor, Togo.

I can't understand why people are frightened of new ideas. I'm frightened of the old ones.

—COMPOSER JOHN CAGE (1912–1992)

Post–World War II Innovations

))) First Hearing

CD 3: Track 36

CONNECT

Listen to the recording of "The Banshee" by Cowell and take notes on what you hear. Even if you are working with other students in a paired or group listening session, keep your own notes. Give some attention to the following:

- Among other things, this piece represents a new way of playing an old and familiar musical instrument. What is that instrument? What would you guess the musician is doing to make it sound the way it does?

- Does this piece have a mood? If so, how would you describe the mood?

- As nontraditional as this piece might sound, it is notated using notes on a staff with both tempo and meter markings. Can you hear any regular beat at all?

- The notated musical score has indications to speed up and slow down the tempo. Can you tell when it speeds up or slows down?

- Do the dynamics remain pretty much the same all the way through, or do you hear sections that are quite soft and other sections that are quite loud?

Keep your notes from this First Hearing to compare with your impressions about the piece after you study the information in this chapter.

38

In the early twentieth century, composers took many new approaches to composition, including, as we have seen, Stravinsky's jarring ever-changing rhythms, Schoenberg's atonal twelve-tone writing, and Ives's three different tempos and rhythms at the same time. Composers of the late twentieth century continued searching for new ideas in their compositions. In many cases, the types of non-Western music we heard in Chapter 37 were influential in the development of those new approaches to composition.

The first composer we will study in this chapter, **Henry Cowell** (1897–1965), did his most important work before World War II, but he is included here because his ideas were extremely influential on the work of some prominent composers who followed him. One of those composers was his student John Cage, whose work we will also study in this chapter.

Henry Cowell

Cowell was born and raised just outside of San Francisco. His Irish father taught him to love music from Ireland, but he also exposed him to Appalachian, Chinese, Japanese, and Tahitian music, all of which were part of his musical experience by the time he began composing. In 1914 Cowell attended the University of California at Berkeley,

HENRY COWELL
(1897–1965)

- Born in Menlo Park, California; died at age 68 in Shady, New York.

- Best known for solo piano works including "The Banshee," "Tiger," and "Aeolian Harp"; "Gaelic," Symphony no. 3; and *Persian Set* for orchestra.

where he was able to study with Charles Seeger (the father of the famous folk banjo player and singer Pete Seeger) who was well known for his work in musicology, including ethnomusicology (the study of non-Western and folk music). By the late 1920s Cowell had moved to New York and was teaching courses in world musics by invitation. He won a Guggenheim Foundation grant to study in Berlin, where he focused on gamelan music with Raden Mas Jodjhana of Java.

In writing music for dancers, Cowell began to think that music should not dominate dance but that dancers should, instead, have freedom with the music to which they were dancing. He suggested that segments of his music be played in any order the dancers chose, an idea that ran counter to the European concept of composers being in complete control of the organization of their work. We will see how this idea led to other, later, composers, such as Cowell's student John Cage, giving much more freedom to performers than ever before. By the 1960s and 1970s this freedom had been taken to the point at which composers actually wrote into a musical score that performers could play or sing the music at any time they chose or even play or sing anything they wanted to for a given amount of time. The use of such randomness creates what is called **aleatory, indeterminacy,** or **chance music.**

Cowell's compositions reflect many characteristics of the international music he had studied throughout his life. He is best known for a very percussive technique of smashing down a large group of adjacent notes on the piano to create a dense and dissonant sound. Although that sound is not exactly like the sound of a gamelan, the percussive influences are certainly there. He called this sound a **tone cluster.** His early piano works, including "Advertisement" (1914) and "Tiger" (1928), popularized the tone cluster. It is said that the Hungarian composer Béla Bartók wrote to Cowell asking permission to use his American colleague's invention in one of his own works.

An accomplished pianist, Cowell did much experimentation to coax new sounds out of the piano. In "Aeolian Harp" (1923), he asked the player to use one hand to silently depress keys so that the strings for those keys would be free to ring. The player then had to reach over the keyboard with the other hand and strum the strings. The light strumming created a quiet and beautiful sound that had not been heard on the piano before. The sound was reminiscent of a real Aeolian harp, which is a sound box with strings that are set to vibrate when wind blows across the box. Aeolian harps were popular in nineteenth-century Ireland. Cowell's Irish heritage also manifested itself in his piece "The Banshee" (1925), in which the player must strum and even scrape the piano's strings while an assistant holds down the damper pedal so that the strings are all free to ring. In Irish mythology, banshees are ghosts that scream to announce an impending death. Some of the scraping on the strings in Cowell's piece sounds like such screams.

))) **Featured Listening**

 CD 3: Track 36

"The Banshee" HENRY COWELL

Date: 1925

Genre: Solo piano music

Tempo: Rubato

Form: No regular repeating sections, although the plucked melody gives the piece a sense of unity

Instrument: One acoustic grand piano with the lid removed

Meter: Duple

Duration: 2:35

Context: Two people are needed to play this piece. One person can play the entire piece by sweeping his or her fingers across, or up and down, the strings, and a second person is needed to sit at the keyboard and hold down the damper pedal so that the strings can continue to vibrate after they are played. The places where the player is directed to pluck specific strings to play a three- or four-note melody are indicated.

	Timing	What to listen for
36	0:00	The player sweeps across strings and along an individual string, with the fingers.
	0:42	A three-note melody is plucked, then a series of three-note chords are strummed.
	1:10	The three-note melody is plucked again, but a new note is added at the end, followed by strummed chords.
	1:42	The three-note melody is plucked again and followed by the strumming of three-note chords.

Cowell also wrote music for instruments other than piano. His *Persian Set* (1957) for orchestra was composed after he returned from long visits to Iran, India, and Japan. The music of Iran was of particular interest to him because he had not heard it before. About *Persian Set* he wrote,

> This is a simple record of musical contagion, written at the end of a three-month stay in Iran, during which I listened for several hours nearly every day to the traditional classical music and folk music of the country. . . . Of course I made no attempt to shed my years of Western symphonic experience; nor have I used actual Iranian melodies or rhythms, nor have I imitated them exactly. Instead I have tried to develop some of the kinds of musical behavior that the two cultures have in common.

We will hear music by other twentieth-century composers who have been influenced by non-Western musics without making any attempt to imitate it.

John Cage

A student of Henry Cowell, **John Cage** (1912–1992), used many of Cowell's innovative ideas. Like Cowell, Cage was also greatly influenced by non-Western musics, particularly that from China.

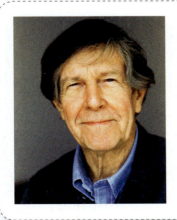

JOHN CAGE
(1912–1992)

- Born in Los Angeles, California; died at age 79 in New York City.
- Best known for his *Sonatas and Interludes for Prepared Piano, 4'33"*, and *Music of Changes*.

The inside of a piano that has been prepared for the performance of a work by John Cage

John Cage was born in Los Angeles. In 1930 he left college to travel in Europe for eighteen months. Composition was part of his concentration, but he was also looking for new ideas about visual images that connected with music. He said, "In Sevilla on a street corner I noticed the multiplicity of simultaneous visual and audible events all going together in one's experience and producing enjoyment. It was the beginning for me of theater and circus."

When he returned to California he applied to study with Arnold Schoenberg, the famous Austrian composer who had developed the twelve-tone system of composition. When the two discussed the cost of lessons, Schoenberg made it clear that he wanted much more than money from Cage. Schoenberg required that Cage promise to devote his entire life to music. Cage agreed to the bargain. The lessons were free. Cage also studied with Henry Cowell, who encouraged him to experiment with what the piano could do.

Cage was hired to provide music for a dance production in 1940. There was no room for instruments other than the piano that was already on the stage, but Cage wanted to come up with something full and percussive to fit the African character of the dance. He replicated that full and percussive sound by placing bolts, screws, bamboo, and pieces of weather stripping on and between the piano's strings so that they would rattle and make other sounds when he played the keyboard. The result was so successful that he continued to write for such a **prepared piano** much of the rest of his life. The music to his prepared piano works has a drawing of the strings showing where all the objects were to be placed to obtain the sounds the piece required. Cage even composed a concerto for prepared piano and orchestra.

Listening Guide

CONNECT   CD 6: Tracks 17–18

Sonata V from *Sonatas and Interludes for Prepared Piano* JOHN CAGE

Date: 1948

Genre: Solo piano music

Tempo: 92 beats per minute

Form: Binary

Instruments: Prepared piano

Meter: Duple

Duration: 1:21

Context: Notice how effective it is when the repetitive accompaniment figures stop and then resume. The upper melody also changes from being fairly active to holding longer notes and then picks up the activity again. The percussive sound of the preparation materials on the piano's strings gives the sonata an almost gamelan-like timbre.

	Timing		What to listen for
17	0:00	A	10¾ bars of an active upper melody, then 8¼ bars in which the melody changes from one long-held note to another
	0:18	A	Repeat of section
18	0:00	B	9 bars of long-held notes in the upper melody followed by 8¼ bars of a new active melody that uses grace notes (fast ornamental notes) in a few places, then a ¾ bar rest and sustained notes; one extra beat is added in the last bar
	0:24	B	Repeat of section

In the mid-1940s Cage discovered Zen Buddhism, an Asian belief system that emphasizes meditation as the means to reach an enlightened state. He also studied with an Indian singer and tabla player, further interesting him in the sounds of Asia. His *Sonatas and Interludes for Prepared Piano* (1946–1948) is a set of sixteen sonatas that are broken up with other pieces, called interludes. Percussive sounds that come from the piano's extensive preparation show clear Asian, including gamelan, influences. We will listen to Sonata V of the work.

In addition to studying Zen Buddhism, Cage became interested in other aspects of Chinese culture, including the *I Ching (Book of Changes),* an ancient text that is meant to provide guidance for its reader. The reader determines what parts of the text he or she should read by throwing coins or yarrow stalks. The idea of making choices in what should be read by such a random method interested Cage. His composition *Music of Changes* (1951) used the tossing of coins to determine the order in which the sections of music should be performed.

In 1952 Cage went into an *anechoic,* or isolation, chamber at Harvard University. The experience of being completely cut off from sounds of the world around him provided him not with silence but with the sounds of his body. As he described it, he heard "the unintended operation of my nervous system and the circulation of my blood." His most famous composition, *4'33″,* resulted from that experience. The piece instructs the performer to walk on stage and sit at the piano. The performer then holds his or her hands over the keys as if to play but never touches a key. When four minutes and thirty-three seconds have elapsed, the performer bows and leaves the stage. The "music" results from members of the audience moving in their seats and whatever other sounds occur during the period of silence. It has been suggested by many historians that the choice of exactly that amount of time was done randomly, but it is also possible that it was chosen because it represents a different kind of silence. Four minutes and thirty-three seconds is equal to 273 seconds. Scientists use the Kelvin scale to measure temperatures, and zero on that scale is equal to negative 273 on the Celsius scale. The temperature at zero or negative 273 is the coldest possible temperature, one at which there can be no motion and therefore no life. The silence of the piece relates to this lack of motion, as well as to the music of one's surroundings.

In later years Cage composed theatrical works and used electronics mixed with live sounds. The idea of randomness continued to interest him in that it made performances of his works *happenings* that would never be repeated in exactly the same way.

A map of the heavens supplied the note heads for Cage's *Atlas Eclipticalis* (1961–1962). This work consisted of eighty-six instrumental parts "to be played in whole or part, any duration, in any ensemble, chamber or orchestral." The effect is as if a traveler with no particular place to go wanders the earth. John Cage is perhaps the best-known composer of chance music, but the idea became popular enough that many other composers used it as well. "Hearing the Difference: Wayang kulit Gamelan Ensemble's

WAYANG KULIT GAMELAN ENSEMBLE'S "SREPEGAN (SLENDRO NIM)" AND CAGE'S SONATA V

These works are very different from each other (see Featured Listening on page 345 and Listening Guide on page 356). "Srepegan (slendro nim)" is an example of Indonesian gamelan music, whereas John Cage's Sonata V is the work of a twentieth-century American composer. The instruments on which the works are played are also quite different. Then again, when you listen to the two works in succession, you might well notice some similarities. Answer the following questions as you listen to the two works:

- The piano is an instrument that has strings, but those strings are played by hammers that strike them, making the piano a kind of percussion instrument. The addition of bolts, nails, and other things placed *on* the strings of the piano adds to the percussive effect. How does that effect compare to the metal metallophones and knobbed metal idiophones in the gamelan? Which is more percussive?

- Both works have at least some repetition. Which work has long repeated sections and which is based more on short repeated patterns?

- Both works are based on a duple or quadruple meter. Which work also includes polyrhythms?

- Compare Cage's Sonata V to Beethoven's "Moonlight" Sonata. Is Cage's work more like the Sonata, or more like "Srepegan (slendro nim)"? What does your answer say about how Cage was influenced?

'Srepegan (slendro nim)' and Cage's Sonata V" contrasts two twentieth-century compositions that come from very different cultures but have some surprising similarities.

Electronic Music

The development of advanced electronic technology in the 1950s and 1960s made possible radical changes in the way music could be composed and performed. Magnetic tape, synthesizers, and computers allowed the composer to control every aspect of music and made possible accurate rendition of the music without relying on live performers. The tape recording became both the music *and* its performance.

One kind of this **electronic music** is **musique concrète,** French for "concrete music." Any kind of sound may be used in *musique concrète,* such as street noise, sounds from nature, human singing and speech, and usual or unusual sounds from traditional musical instruments, all of which can be manipulated and recombined on tape. After prerecording the chosen sounds, the composer can manipulate them in a variety of ways. They can be sped up, slowed down, edited, and combined with other sounds. The tape itself can be cut so that the order of the sounds is changed. By cutting the tape, the composer can cut out or reverse sections of it and then splice it back together in any order he or she chooses. After the sound alteration, cutting, and splicing are finished, the piece has been both composed and performed by the composer in a permanently accurate version.

Synthesizers and computers can create sounds by imitating acoustic musical instruments or other natural sounds or by producing unique sounds that the composer can manipulate with few restrictions. With no performers to play the music too fast or too slow, or to make other mistakes, the composer has complete control. He or she does not even have to notate the music because it exists only as a recording that is unlikely to be produced in the same way a second time. Even when the composer chooses to imitate the sound of natural, acoustic instruments, electronics allow him or her much freedom to compose any note or combination of notes because the electronic instrument is not limited by the number of fingers on the musician's hands or technical difficulties of playing acoustic instruments. For example, certain notes or note combinations can be difficult to play on some musical instruments: a guitarist's or other string player's left hand cannot be both very high and very low on the fingerboard at the same time, and a pianist playing with hands spread far apart cannot also play a note in the middle of the keyboard. The electronic instrument can overcome these limitations, in addition to being able to play higher, lower, louder, and softer sounds than is possible on acoustic instruments. All of these considerations have prompted many movie or television composers to stop writing for live orchestras and produce their soundtracks on their computers.

The practice of radio, television, and movie scores being composed and recorded by synthesizers or computers has devastated musical communities in such places as New York and Hollywood. In those cities and other places that produce recorded music, many composers and musicians have for years depended on work in recording studios for their livelihood. Once electronic instruments advanced to the point of sounding almost live, it became possible for a studio to hire a single composer with a computer and sound equipment to produce a complete orchestral score. Of course, the sound is not really that of a live orchestra, but for a recorded movie score it does not have to be. In the 1990s, many musicians feared that the industry would completely dissolve. Though their fears have not been fully realized, the number of musicians making a good living doing such work has diminished greatly.

In most major cities in the United States, musicians who have been regularly hired to play live music to accompany a musical or other theatrical productions have also found themselves replaced by synthesizers. The result is not only that musicians are not getting work but also that audiences are not hearing the same sound quality they did when the music was played live.

Edgard Varèse

The piece of electronic music we are going to listen to is "Poème électronique" by **Edgard Varèse.** Varèse (1883–1965), one of the most innovative and influential composers of the twentieth century, was born in Paris but moved to New York in 1915. He challenged musical traditions by defining music as "organized sound." He meant *all* sound, including some sounds previously classified as nonmusical noises. Many of Varèse's compositions employ unusual combinations of instruments, which often play at the extremes of their abilities. The sound of the music sometimes tends to recall the noises of mechanized society. His *Ionisation* (1933) was written for percussion ensemble, employing a huge battery of standard orchestral percussion and exotic instruments as well. Included was a lion's-roar (a primitive kind of friction drum that sounds like a roar) and three sirens.

Once he began to use electronically produced sounds, Varèse overcame the problem of combining them with live performances in his work *Déserts* (1954) by not having the

EDGARD VARÈSE
(1883–1965)

- Born in Paris, France; died at age 81 in New York City.
- Best known for the electronic tape-recorded work "Poème électronique," the percussion work "Ionisation," and the solo flute composition "Density 21-5."

Le Corbusier Building at the Brussels World's Fair, 1958

live and recorded sections play together. "Poème électronique" (1958) is made up of both electronically produced sounds and *musique concrète*. It was recorded to be played from 425 speakers spread around the inside of an oddly shaped building featured at the Brussels World's Fair in 1958. The building was designed by a Swiss architect named Le Corbusier. Visitors heard the music as they walked through the building viewing lights, images, and writing that were projected on the angled walls in a variety of shapes. The entire recording is eight minutes long, but there is no real beginning or ending because it was constantly replayed so that the piece was to begin for each listener when he or she entered the building and end when he or she exited the building.

The types of electronic sounds we hear in "Poème électronique" seemed quite modern in 1958 and continued to be used to represent modern times in the early 1960s. One can still hear such sounds in reruns of the television show *The Twilight Zone*, particularly in those episodes that dealt with outer space or the future. Ironically, these sounds seem dated to us today.

 **Listening Guide**

 CD 6: Track 19
CONNECT

"Poème électronique" ("Electronic Poem") EDGARD VARÈSE

Date: 1958

Genre: Recorded electronic work

Form: Some returning sounds, but no structured repeating or contrasting sections

Voices and Instruments: Electronic generators, church bells, organs, human voices, and sirens

Meter: None

Duration: 2:50

Context: The short section we will listen to does not include all of the sound makers listed here. The organs and human voices are clear, although distorted, later in the recording.

	Timing	What to listen for
19	0:00	A large, low bell rings, chirping sounds, sirens, other electronic sounds, including fast tapping and sustained fuzzy tones
	0:43	Dripping sounds, noises, short squawks
	0:56	A pattern of three notes sliding from one to the other plays and then repeats two more times.
	1:10	Low, sustained sounds with rattling, then a siren

Timing	What to listen for
1:30	Short squawks and chirps, three-note group plays again, more squawks and chirps at different pitches
1:46	Squeaking sounds
2:03	A variety of percussion sounds, siren, tapping
2:35	Recording fades during low bell rings.

Terry Riley

Terry Riley was born in 1935 in northern California. He attended San Francisco State College and then transferred to the University of California at Berkeley, where he received a master's degree in composition in 1961. Tape recorders were relatively new in the late 1950s and early 1960s, and they provided musicians with a wealth of new possibilities in the creation and manipulation of sound. Along with other members of the San Francisco Tape Music Center, Riley experimented with tape loops and the multitracking of sounds. To get the effects he wanted, Riley invented some rather unconventional techniques. He described his use of tape loops as follows: "I would take tapes and run them into my yard and around a wine bottle back into my room and I would get a really long loop and then I would cut the tape into all different sizes and I would just run them out into the yard and I would record onto one machine just sound on sound. I would build up this kind of unintelligible layer." In the end, however, he opted for live musicians. "Out of doing all that experimentation with sound I decided I wanted to do it with live musicians. To take repetition, take music fragments and make it live." Riley's most famous piece, *In C,* resulted from that experiment.

In C (1964) was first called "The Global Villages for Symphonic Pieces." The piece is an early example of *minimalism,* a style in which a minimal amount of musical material is repeated many times, often with gradual changes occurring during the repetitions. It is also an example of aleatoric, or chance, music. It consists of fifty-three short bits of melody all based on a C-major scale. A pianist begins the work by repeatedly playing the top two C notes on the piano (an octave) to create a regular beat called the *pulse*. Other musicians play all fifty-three of the melodic patterns in order and in rhythm to the pulse. The aleatoric aspect of the work is that the musicians can play on any instrument they choose as long as it can play the written notes. Each musician can begin playing any time he or she wants, can repeat each pattern as many times as desired, and then moves on to the next pattern. The piece can be as short as ten or fifteen minutes (if the players choose not to repeat the patterns very many times), or it can last for hours.

TERRY RILEY
(b.1935)

- Born in Colfax, California.
- Best known for *In C* and "A Rainbow in Curved Air"

Listening Guide

CD 6: Track 20
CONNECT

In C TERRY RILEY

Date: 1965

Genre: Aleatory

(continued)

Tempo: Moderate

Form: Much repetition of each individual cell, or motive, but no repeats of cells heard earlier in the composition

Instruments: Any instruments the musicians choose that can play a C-major scale

Meter: Varies, but the pulse maintains a steady beat

Duration: 3:07

Context: There is a contradiction here. To record an aleatoric piece runs counter to the idea that aleatoric music differs with every performance.

Timing	What to listen for
20 0:00	A steady beat and the gradual changing of often-repeated melodic patterns

PERFORMING AN ALEATORIC WORK

Why would composers want performers to make up some of the music themselves? Don't composers know what their music should sound like and want it played that way?

Not always. Most composers do want their music played as they have conceived and notated it, but during the late twentieth century, many composers wanted to challenge traditions and try new things. They were excited at the prospect of creating a situation for a musical "happening," in which there was an element of spontaneous creation that made every performance of the work different from any other. That kind of performance event was being done in the visual arts as well as in music.

How could visual art, like paintings and sculptures, be different from one viewing to another?

Easy, and there were many ways that it was done. For example, some artists created "room sculptures" in which the shapes moved around as people walked through the room so that each person's experience was unique. There were "smoke sculptures" that had a constant stream of smoke that took different shapes depending on the number, placement, and movements of people in the room. Other artists created rooms that looked completely empty except for microphones hanging from the ceiling to pick up sounds. Different sounds picked up by the microphones would cause lights to come on and show the artworks behind wall screens or create an elaborate light show. The look would vary with the number, placement, and sounds made by the viewers in the room. Some artists would randomly drop bits of paper, string, or whatever onto a canvas, and then glue each piece as it fell.

How can those kinds of things be done in music?

There are many ways to make aleatoric music. Some composers asked performers to throw individual pages or smaller sections of music notation around and randomly pick them up and play them in the order in which they stacked them. Other composers went so far as to tell performers to play "anything they want to" for a particular amount of time, although that invited any number of sounds that the composer might not have had in mind, including a performer deciding to play some familiar tune that would not fit the character of what others were playing.

In Terry Riley's *In C*, the short sections of music were notated and the players instructed to play whatever instruments they wanted to that could play a C scale, and they could start whenever they wanted and repeat each section of music as often as they wanted. This process guaranteed that different choices made by the performers would create a new sound with each performance, even though the basic bits of melody and the steady tempo would be the same each time.

John Cage included sounds played on radios in a few of his pieces. Since the radio would play very different sounds, depending on the station it was tuned to and whatever happened to be on at the time, the use of a radio in a work guaranteed new sounds in each performance.

It should be clear by now that each performance of a work that includes aleatoric music, or choices made for a single performance, is different from every other performance of the same work. Aleatoric pieces have been recorded—certainly *In C* has been several times—but recording the piece undermines the purpose of aleatory.

Riley went to India to study with Pandit Pran Nath, a master vocalist. In the 1970s he taught both composition and courses in Indian music at Mills College in Oakland, California. Riley's compositions were greatly influenced by his studies of Indian music. He tuned electric pianos and organs to Indian scales for his composition "Shri Camel" (1978), and "Songs for the 10 Voices of the Two Prophets" (1980) was composed using Hindu vocals accompanied by improvisations on synthesizer. While in Oakland, Riley met members of the Kronos Quartet, who specialized (and continue to specialize) in performing and recording music that expands the string quartet literature. During the early 1980s he worked with them and had them perform with the Indian sitar player Krishna Bhatt. He then went on to compose nine string quartets, along with a keyboard quintet (piano and string quartet), and a concerto for string quartet and orchestra. He still returns to India and performs as both a vocalist and a *tambura* (an Indian drone instrument) player with his former teacher. Clearly, music for Riley is an expression of Indian spirituality. In one interview Riley said,

> This morning I was practicing raga, and at one point I was singing a long tone and I became very peaceful and still. I thought this is really the highest point of music for me is to become in a place where there is no desire, no craving, wanting to do anything else, just to be in a state of being to the highest point. Then you get a little meditated, you get to a place that is really still and it is the best place you have ever been and yet there is nothing there. For me, that is what music is. It is a spiritual art.

"MusiCurious: Performing an Aleatoric Work" describes this unique musical event.

Summary

This chapter has concentrated on several new ideas of the latter half of the twentieth century, including the use of traditional instruments in nontraditional ways, tone clusters, aleatoric music, and electronic sound. In many cases, non-Western musics influenced the development of these ideas. Henry Cowell and his student John Cage pioneered the use of aleatory in music, which inspired other composers as well, including Terry Riley. Cowell and Cage each studied the use of percussion instruments in music, such as Indonesian gamelan. They both used those percussive ideas to challenge traditional concepts of what a piano should sound like—by banging dissonant notes to create tone clusters and by placing bolts, screws, and other items on and between the strings of the piano to change the piano's tone quality.

After World War II and the development of magnetic tape recorders and electronic instruments, Edgard Varèse and others created music from tape-recorded sounds, taking the concept of the performer out of the music-making process and allowing the composer full control of the sound of his or her compositions.

New People and Concepts

aleatoric music, 354

chance music, 354

Edgard Varèse, 359

electronic music, 358

Henry Cowell, 353

indeterminacy music, 354

John Cage, 355

musique concrète, 358

prepared piano, 356

Terry Riley, 361

tone cluster, 354

Listen again to the recording of "The Banshee" by Cowell and compare your impression now with your notes from your First Hearing. Consider the following questions:

- What instrument is used to play this work, and how is it played?
- What does the title "Banshee" suggest, and how does the music fit the mood banshee stories create?
- How would you describe the tempo and meter of this work?
- Do the variations of the tempo fit the mood created by the visit of a banshee?
- Describe the use of dynamics in this piece, and tell how they affect the overall mood.
- If you were going to describe this music to a friend, what would you say?

Further Listening

Henry Cowell, "Tiger" and "Aeolian Harp." These solo piano works feature techniques not used in "The Banshee," which we heard in this chapter. "Tiger" uses tone clusters for which Cowell was famous, and "Aeolian Harp" imitates the light sounds of real Aeolian harps that are played by the blowing of wind across strings.

John Cage, "Sonatas and Interludes for Prepared Piano." We heard only one sonata from this set of sixteen sonatas that have four interludes placed among them. These are among Cage's most well known and often performed works.

John Cage, "Imaginary Landscape No. 4." This is one of several pieces that Cage composed to include the playing of a radio—in this case, twelve radios.

Edgard Varèse, "Poème électronique." We heard less than three minutes of this eight-minute work. Other sections include the sounds of human voices and an organ that have been manipulated on the tape that recorded them. That technique is called *musique concrète.*

Edgard Varèse, *Ionisation.* This work includes sounds made by a number of things, including sirens, that are not considered "musical instruments." It opened up the idea for "music" to be defined as "organized sound" in a nontraditional way.

Terry Riley, *In C.* We heard just over three minutes of the beginning of one recording of this work that has no predetermined length. It can be quite interesting to listen to at least one recording of the entire work because of the gradual changes that happen within what seems like constant repetition.

I'm interested in all kinds of music, and sooner or later most of those musics find their way into my own compositions.

—COMPOSER PHILIP GLASS (B. 1937)

Minimalism

))) First Hearing

CONNECT   CD 3: Tracks 37–38

Listen to the recording of *Company*, second movement, by Philip Glass and take notes on what you hear. Even if you are working with other students in a paired or group listening session, keep your own notes. Give some attention to the following:

- What instruments do you hear?

- Do you hear any repetition? Do you hear any sections that contrast with the opening?

- Is the music played to a steady beat? Can you tell what the meter might be?

- How would you describe the texture (monophonic, homophonic, polyphonic, or heterophonic)?

- This is a movement from a programmatic work about an old, dying man who keeps hearing voices from his past. Does anything about the music seem to fit that story? If so, what parts might represent the dying man and what parts the voices?

Keep your notes from this First Hearing to compare with your impressions about the piece after you study the information in this chapter.

39

In Chapter 38, we listened to Terry Riley's composition *In C*. We discussed it as an aleatoric work because the performers make many decisions about their playing that allow each performance to be unique. It is also an example of another late-twentieth-century style of music called **minimalism**. Minimalism is a style in art as well as music. As the name of the style suggests, minimalistic works strip subject matter down to minimal amounts of material, or just basic fundamentals of shape, color, and sound. They use constant repetition and subtle variation to make up the work. A minimal artwork could have many reproductions of the same shape, all the same size and color, spread evenly around a space, perhaps with just slight changes in their rotation. Similarly, in minimal music, one usually hears short bits of melody or other sounds repeated over and over with slight variations that occur so gradually that one must listen very carefully to notice the variation.

Minimalistic music usually has a very steady beat, while not necessarily maintaining a constant metric pattern, and it is typically tonal, without dissonance. Sometimes drones (long-held notes) are also used. Another term for minimalism is *systematic music* because the ideas presented at the beginning of the work set up a system for the rest of the work. Minimalist composers often cite the influence of Indian ragas, which generally include drones and variation, and African tribal drumming, which tends to use constant repetition of a variety of rhythm patterns.

PHILIP GLASS
(b. 1937)

- Born in Baltimore, Maryland.
- Best known for the opera *Einstein on the Beach*, the string orchestral work *Company*, his work with rock musicians on *Songs from Liquid Days*, and many film scores including *Koyaanisqatsi*.

***Empress of India* by Frank Stella.** This artwork shows the kind of repetition with subtle changes that we hear in minimalist music.

Philip Glass

Another composer whose minimalist works have been inspired by Indian music is **Philip Glass** (b. 1937). Glass was born in Baltimore, where his father owned a record store. He grew up hearing music of all kinds, because his father brought home the records that did not sell, and young Philip would listen to them himself. Glass became acquainted with many styles of modern music and jazz through this listening. He also learned to play both the violin and the flute. He studied Arnold Schoenberg's twelve-tone composition techniques at the University of Chicago, where he graduated with degrees in mathematics and philosophy. From there he studied composition at Juilliard. He changed composition teachers often in an effort to find what he described as his "own voice." In 1960 he went to Paris and studied with Nadia Boulanger, the French composer who taught Aaron Copland and other important twentieth-century composers. It was in Paris that Glass became involved with Indian music, which led him to discover the voice he had been looking for in his music.

Glass was introduced to Indian music when a filmmaker hired him to put music by sitarist Ravi Shankar into a notational system that French musicians could read and play. Energized by this initial experience with music from India, Glass went on to study music from North Africa as well. When he returned to composing, he felt a new sense of freedom from traditional European rhythm patterns. He began to let little cells of sound repeat to form hypnotic sound cycles. It is those hypnotic repeating patterns that characterize Glass's work to this day.

Theater had always been an interest of Glass's, and his new style fit well for avant-garde works by Samuel Beckett, Bertold Brecht, and others. After composing many works for theatrical or dance productions, Glass produced his masterpiece, the opera *Einstein on the Beach* (1976). The opera has no plot or storyline. Instead, it musically portrays or describes Albert Einstein (1879–1955), the physicist who is famous for his theory of relativity. It came to be seen as a portrait of Einstein and was lauded by critics. It was followed by a commission from the Netherlands Opera Company to compose a similar portrait of Gandhi, called *Satyagraha* (1982). Mahatma Gandhi (1869–1948) was a Hindu who used *satyagraha* (passive resistance) to free India from the British. Then, Glass was commissioned by the Stuttgart Opera Company to compose a third operatic portrait, that of the famous Egyptian pharaoh, *Akhnaten* (1984). Akhnaten was an eighteenth-dynasty Egyptian pharaoh who rejected the polytheistic beliefs of his people's past in order to worship a single god, Aten. He was the only pharaoh to have held such beliefs.

The work by Glass that we will listen to was originally composed for a theater piece called *Company* by Samuel Beckett, although it is also effective as a concert piece. The drama focuses on an old man at the end of his life who hears voices from his past as he prepares himself for death. We will hear the second movement, which is rather fast. The first and third movements are slow, and the fourth is again fast. The influence of Indian music can be heard in Glass's use of changes between duple and triple meters. Many Indian talas are made up of such patterns. This is often called **additive meter** because a pattern of ten beats, for example, might be made up of two beats + three beats + two beats + three beats.

Featured Listening

CD 3: Tracks 37–38

Company, second movement   PHILIP GLASS

Date: 1983

Genre: String orchestra music

Tempo: 160 beats per minute

Form: Two sections alternate. The first one, A, is a homophonic pounding at a steady beat. The second, B, is made up of short ascending arpeggios that repeat and then sometimes extend or reverse direction, creating an almost swirling motion over a steady pulse in the bass. The A sections are all five seconds long, but the B sections vary in length.

Texture: Homophonic

Instruments: String orchestra made up of first violins, second violins, violas, cellos, and basses (the work can also be played by a string quartet, because the bass part duplicates the cello part and thus can be done without).

Meter: Changes often between duple and triple

Duration: 1:55

Context: One can see how this movement would fit the story of a person contemplating his life during the swirling arpeggios and then being interrupted by voices from the past when the pounding A sections return.

	Timing		What to listen for
37	0:00	A	Homophonic pounding at a steady beat, forte dynamic level
38	0:00	B	Short ascending arpeggios repeat and change by being extended or reversing direction on some repetitions; dynamics change abruptly from mezzo forte to piano and back.
	0:23	A	
	0:27	B	
	0:32	A	
	0:37	B	Arpeggios repeated and extended with same variation
	1:18	A	
	1:23	B	
	1:27	A	
	1:32	A	Louder with more intensity
	1:37	B	Fades at end

Hearing the Difference

HAYDN'S STRING QUARTET, FOURTH MOVEMENT, AND GLASS'S *COMPANY*, SECOND MOVEMENT

These works were composed about two hundred years apart—Haydn's in the classical period (late eighteenth century) and Glass's in the late twentieth century (see Featured Listening on pages 136 and 367). Music in the classical period tended to be based on a balanced formal structure. Classical music often had repeating and contrasting sections with a return of the beginning music at the end of the movement. In the romantic period, which occurred between these two musical periods, composers tended to put the expression of emotion or storytelling before formal structure. Many twentieth-century composers returned to the idea of structure and repetition as an important element of music, and that brought many classical forms back into use. In the case of Philip Glass, the additive meter of Indian music influenced him to change from duple to triple meters. He also used the repetition of short melodic motives as well. We will compare the similar concentration on form in Haydn's work and Glass's. Answer the following questions as you listen from one work to the other:

- Both of these works were composed so that they could be played by a string quartet, but our recording of Glass's work is played by a string orchestra, giving it a fuller sound than Haydn's. What instruments are playing in Haydn's quartet? Try to imagine what Haydn's quartet would sound like if it were played by a string orchestra. Would it be as effective as it is in this recording?

- What would you guess the tempo of each movement to be? Are they close to the same, or is one faster? If they are not the same tempo, which is faster?

- Haydn's movement is in sonata rondo form (AB-Development-AB-Development-A). Where do you hear repeating and contrasting sections in Glass's movement? Haydn's movement ended with the same music it had at the beginning. Does Glass's end like the beginning or like a contrasting section?

- What meter do you hear in each movement? Does either vary from one meter to another? Which movement stresses variation in place of repetition of short patterns?

- Both of these movements are programmatic in that they are composed with a story or the portrayal of something nonmusical in mind. Which represents the sound of birds? How does it do that?

Earlier, we listened to a movement of a string quartet by Haydn. "Hearing the Difference: Haydn's String Quartet, fourth movement, and Glass's *Company*, second movement," compares the two works.

As Glass describes his style, it is "music with repetitive structures," which goes beyond the repetition and slight variation of most minimalism. Glass's music has been an important influence on a number of art-rock groups, including King Crimson, Pink Floyd, and Talking Heads. His *Songs from Liquid Days* (1986) features music that he co-wrote with Paul Simon, Suzanne Vega, David Byrne (of Talking Heads), and Laurie Anderson. Linda Ronstadt, the Roches, and many other singers and instrumentalists from the world of rock and pop music perform on the CD. Glass's *Heroes Symphony* (1997) was based on the music of David Bowie and the composer, producer, and rock musician Brian Eno.

Glass has been an effective film score composer as well, having composed twenty-one scores ranging from *North Star* (1977) to *The Baroness and the Pig* (2002). His soundtracks for *Kundun* (1997) and *The Hours* (2002) were both nominated for Academy Awards, and both won Golden Globes. *The Truman Show* (1999) won him a Golden Globe as well. In 2003, Glass composed the score for the Academy Award–winning documentary feature "The Fog of War: Eleven Lessons from the Life of Rob-

ert S. McNamara." (McNamara was the U.S. Secretary of Defense during
much of the Vietnam War.)

Steve Reich

In Chapter 37 we mentioned composer **Steve Reich** (b. 1936) as having
studied Ewe drumming in Ghana. Reich was born and raised in New
York. He studied philosophy at Cornell University and later attended
Juilliard to pursue a career as a composer. He moved to northern California and completed his master's degree at Mills College in 1963. He
was attracted to Mills College by its faculty, which included two major
composers with whom he wanted to study, Darius Milhaud and Luciano
Berio. Reich played the piano, but his primary skills and interests were in
percussion. When he studied world musics at Mills College, he was particularly taken by the music from Indonesia and from Africa. As he said
in a 2002 interview, "a number of people became aware that non-Western
music was a way of getting to something that we wanted to get to in our
own music."

STEVE REICH
(b. 1936)

- Born in New York City.

- Best known for his combination of
  voices and instruments, including non-
  Western percussion metallophones,
  called *Music for Eighteen Musicians*,
  voices and orchestra in *Tehillim*,
  amplified ensemble and tape *City Life*,
  and *Electric Counterpoint*.

Reich was awarded a grant from the Institute for International Education that allowed him to go to Africa to study drumming at the University
of Ghana in 1970. His composition *Drumming* (1971) resulted from that
study, and much of his music that followed also was affected by African
drumming styles. He pursued his interest in Indonesian gamelan music
by attending the American Society for Eastern Arts back in Berkeley, California, where he concentrated on Balinese gamelan music. In discussing his *Music for
Eighteen Musicians* (1976), he said, "The piece was written so that a conductor would
not be necessary. . . . The conducting responsibilities were delegated to the vibraphone
player who, every time he played, it was a cue to, 'Get ready, here we (gong) go,' and
everybody changes. That was an idea I took directly from Balinese and African music,
where the drummers . . . will make the (call)." The Listening Guide that follows describes the third movement of Reich's 1987 work, *Electric Counterpoint*.

 **Listening Guide**

 CD 6: Track 21

Electric Counterpoint, **third movement** STEVE REICH

Date: 1987

Genre: Guitar ensemble

Tempo: Fast

Form: Continuous repeated patterns with a thinner texture at the beginning and end
and more instruments playing in the middle section

Instruments: Amplified solo guitar, ensemble of twelve classical guitars, and two electric bass guitars (there is another version of the work for solo electric guitar and tape)

Meter: Mostly triple

Duration: 4:27

Context: The music specifies that the players sit so that the audience will hear call-
and-response effects from one side of the stage to the other.

(continued)

	Timing	What to listen for
21	0:00	Two guitars begin, then the soloist and other guitars enter one or two at a time playing a steady, repetitious background pattern.
	0:43	Electric bass guitars enter.
	1:05	Two guitars are featured with one playing echo-like responses to the other.
	3:31	Bass guitars and soloist drop out; ensemble continues the same patterns they played from the beginning.

Reich has composed several pieces for the Kronos Quartet, including one that is performed with a tape recording, *Different Trains* (1988). That composition won him a Grammy Award for Best Contemporary Composition in 1990. His theater piece, *The Cave* (1993), composed in collaboration with Beryl Korot, includes the playing of videos on five screens, along with music played by his eighteen-musician ensemble. The story of *The Cave* is based on the story of Abraham, as told in Genesis 22:1–19 in the Bible. In an often-told part of the story, God tests Abraham's loyalty by commanding him to sacrifice his son Isaac. Just as Abraham is about to kill his son, God steps in and allows the boy to live.

When we talked about electronic music in Chapter 38, we defined the term *musique concrète* as sounds that have been tape recorded and then manipulated in a variety of ways. Reich used that technique very effectively in his 1995 composition, *City Life*. He used samples of a great variety of sounds he recorded around New York, including voices, car horns, door slams, air brakes, subway chimes, car alarms, boat horns, and fire and police sirens. The fire and police sirens were recorded on February 25, 1993, during the commotion after a car bomb exploded under the World Trade Center.

Reich continues to compose music that is touched by minimalistic techniques and influenced by world musics in a variety of ways. In his words, "I studied Balinese and African music because I love them and also because I believe that non-Western music is presently the single most important source of new ideas for Western composers and musicians."

John Adams

JOHN ADAMS
(b. 1947)

- Born in Worcester, Massachusetts.
- Best known for the operas *Nixon in China* and *The Death of Klinghoffer*, the orchestral works *Short Ride in a Fast Machine* and *Harmonium*, and the choral and orchestra work, *On the Transmigration of Souls*.

John Adams (b. 1947) is a composer who, although his music is rooted in minimalism, says that he is bored with that. His music, indeed, uses the kind of constant, fast, repeated motives that are the basis of most minimalism, but he also varies textures and instrumentation to create his unique style. Born and raised in New England, Adams displayed talent in music from an early age. Both of his parents were musicians, and his father taught him to play the clarinet. Encouraged to pursue music as a career, Adams was composing music when he was only 10 years old. He earned his bachelor's and master's degrees in music from Harvard University and then moved to California to teach at the San Francisco Conservatory of Music and compose for the San Francisco Symphony Orchestra.

In the 1980s, Adams composed the music for two operas that were based on real-life events, *Nixon in China* and *The Death of Klinghoffer*. President Nixon's visit to China was a historic event because it opened up a new relationship between the United States and China after more than twenty years of no contact. The opera's libretto used the texts of actual news reports of conversations between President Nixon and China's Chairman Mao. Even the wives of the two leaders were characters in the opera. *The Death of Klinghoffer* was about the much-publicized murder of Leon Klinghoffer, a Jewish American passenger on a hijacked cruise ship, the *Achille Lauro*, in 1985.

Not every composition project by Adams makes a political statement, but he has been lauded for the effective way he portrays such stories. He was awarded the 2003 Pulitzer Prize for Music for his 2002 work *On the Transmigration of Souls.* That piece—a large-scale work for chorus, children's choir, orchestra, and prerecorded sounds—was composed to commemorate the victims of the September 11, 2001, terrorist attack. Much of the text was taken from real missing persons posters, telephone messages, and other attempts to contact possible victims of the attack.

Adams has won numerous awards and continues to compose and tour all over the United States and England; he has conducted major symphony orchestras performing both his works and those by many other composers. He is currently an Artist in Association with the BBC Symphony Orchestra, and he regularly conducts their concerts.

Listening Guide

CONNECT   **CD 6: Track 22**

"Short Ride in a Fast Machine" JOHN ADAMS

Date: 1986

Genre: Minimalism for orchestra

Tempo: Delirando (frenzied)

Form: The beginning sounds repeat at the end, but otherwise the form is not sectional.

Instruments: Large orchestra and two synthesizers

Meter: Quadruple

Duration: 4:05

Context: When John Adams was asked about the title for this work, his response was "You know how it is when someone asks you to ride in a terrific sports car, and then you wish you hadn't?"

	Timing	Musical events
22	0:00	Woodblock begins with a regular, pounding beat, and is then joined by faster patterns played by woodwinds and synthesizers, then four trumpets join in.
	0:27	More brass instruments, side drum, and glockenspiel are added.
	1:04	Bass drum and French horns play syncopated rhythms.
	1:40	Even note patterns, repeating bass pattern, dissonance and intensity grows
	2:54	Brass syncopated fanfare-like patterns
	3:51	Repeat of beginning music

Summary

Minimalism was a popular style in art music of the late twentieth century and continues to be composed and performed in the twenty-first century. Minimalism developed out of the work of Philip Glass, Steve Reich, and others, all of whom studied and were influenced by Indian classical music and by the repeating patterns played by African drummers. It is a style in which a minimal amount of musical material is repeated many times with gradual changes occurring during the repetitions. In art, minimalism also displays repeating and slowly varying patterns.

John Adams is an important minimalist composer, known for breaking away from the early traditions of the style by using large numbers of instruments and a great variety of textures.

New People and Concepts

additive meter, 367

John Adams, 370

minimalism, 365

Philip Glass, 366

Steve Reich, 369

))) **Finale**

CONNECT CD 3: Tracks 37–38

Listen again to the recording of *Company*, second movement, by Glass and compare your impression now with your notes from your First Hearing. Consider the following questions:

- What instruments are playing?
- What is the pattern of repeated and contrasting sections?
- How steady is the beat, and what is the meter?
- What term best describes the texture?
- What is the story behind this work, and how does the music fit, or not fit, that story?
- If you were going to describe this music to a friend, what would you say?

Further Listening

Philip Glass, *Company*. We heard only the second movement of this work, which is Glass's second string quartet. It was originally composed as incidental music for a Samuel Beckett play about a dying old man, but the music stands alone as a concert work. The four movements are numbered without further identification.

Philip Glass, *Glassworks*. This is a six-movement work for chamber ensemble, which Glass intended for the enjoyment of general audiences who do not necessarily already like his larger, more complex works. The instrumentation varies from one movement to the next, beginning with solo piano and then adding horns and other instruments. The movements are (1) Opening, (2) Floe, (3) Island, (4) Rubric, (5) Facades, and (6) Closing.

Steve Reich, *Electric Counterpoint*. We heard only the third of three movements of this work for solo electric guitar, classical guitar ensemble, and two electric bass guitars. Another version of the work replaces the electric bass guitars and the guitar ensemble with pre-recorded music. The movements are (1) Fast, (2) Slow, and (3) Fast.

Steve Reich, *Drumming*. This work was inspired by Reich's study of drum techniques in Ghana. The four movements are numbered without descriptive titles.

John Adams, *Nixon in China*. This opera about President Nixon's visit to China is taken from actual news reports of conversations that took place with China's Chairman Mao and others.

CHARACTERISTICS OF NON-WESTERN-INFLUENCED MUSIC

Texture	Both homophonic and polyphonic textures employed; variety of textures within a single composition; some uses of heterophonic (a single melody improvised on by two or more parts at the same time) texture
Tonality	Major-minor system employed in minimalism; atonality or a constantly changing tonality used by some composers; pentatonic and other non-Western scales commonly used; microtones used in non-Western and non-Western-influenced music
Rhythm	Very complex rhythms used in some music; repetitious rhythm patterns set to a steady beat in minimalism
Form	Some works with repeating and contrasting sections, others with no clear-cut sections but with gradual, continuously evolving structures
Tone color	Non-Western instruments provide new sounds for use by Western composers; percussive sounds on prepared pianos; pianos and other traditional musical instruments played in nontraditional ways to create new sounds
Musical instruments	Non-Western instruments from many cultures used by Western composers; electronic instruments and manipulated tapes are used as musical instruments by themselves or in ensembles with other instruments

Glossary

absolute music Music that is entirely free of extra-musical references or ideas.

a cappella Choral music without instrumental accompaniment.

accent A stress on a particular beat, note, or chord.

act A large section of a play or an opera. An act can be complete in itself, or it might be composed of several scenes.

adagio A leisurely tempo, literally, "at ease."

additive meter Metric patterns that are created by several smaller beat groupings, all added together. For example, a 10-beat meter that is accented as 3 + 3 + 2 + 2.

aerophones A general term for wind instruments in world music.

aleatoric music Music in which some aspect is decided by performers or someone else other than the composer, guaranteeing that every performance of the work will be different from any other performance. See also *chance music* and *indeterminacy music*.

allegretto A moderately fast tempo.

allegro A fast tempo, faster than allegretto.

allegro con brio Fast, with vigor and spirit.

allegro moderato Moderately fast.

alto A low, female voice (also called *contralto*), or an instrument that is lower than a soprano instrument and higher than a tenor instrument.

andante A moderately slow tempo: literally, at a "walking" pace.

andante con moto A tempo that is a walking pace, with a sense of motion (*con moto*).

aria A composition for solo voice and instrumental accompaniment.

arioso A vocal style midway between recitative and aria. Its meter is less flexible than that of recitative, but its form is much simpler and more flexible than that of an aria.

arpeggio A "broken" chord in which the tones are played one after another in rapid succession rather than simultaneously.

articulation The type of attack and release or decay of the sound of an individual note or chord.

art song A musical setting of a poem for solo voice and piano. The German words for song and songs, *lied* and *lieder* (plural), became the standard terms for this type of song.

atonal Lacking a recognizable tonal center or tonic.

avant-garde Very current, modern, and experimental.

baritone A male voice or a musical instrument with a range below the tenor and above the bass.

bass The lowest male voice, or musical instruments that are low in pitch.

bass clarinet A large and low-sounding clarinet.

bass drum A large, low drum that produces an indefinite pitch.

basso continuo Continuous bass. A bass part performed by (1) a chordal instrument such as a keyboard instrument or a lute, and (2) a bass instrument such as a cello, viola da gamba, or bassoon that reinforces the bass line.

bassoon A low-sounding woodwind instrument that uses a mouthpiece with a double reed.

beat Regularly occurring pulsations that create the basic units of musical time.

bebop A jazz style that emphasizes small ensembles playing very active and complex music. Also called *bop*.

bel canto "Beautiful song." A vocal technique emphasizing beauty and purity of tone and agility in executing various ornamental details.

binary form A basic musical form consisting of two contrasting sections (AB), both sections often being repeated (AABB).

blue notes In blues and jazz, any of the notes produced by flatting the third, fifth, or seventh notes of a major scale.

blues A lamenting, melancholy song characterized by a three-line lyrical pattern in AAB form, a twelve-bar harmonic progression, and the frequent use of blue notes.

bongos A pair of attached small drums that produce indefinite pitches.

bridge (1) In a musical composition, a section that connects two themes. (2) In popular music, the bridge is a section between repetitions of the main melody (AABA form, the B is the bridge).

cadence A point of rest at the end of a passage, section, or complete work that gives the music a sense of convincing conclusion. Also, a melodic or harmonic progression that gives the feeling of conclusion.

cadenza A section of music, usually in a concerto, played in an improvisatory style by a solo performer without orchestral accompaniment.

call and response A song style (found in many West African cultures and African American folk music) in which phrases sung by a leader alternate with responding phrases sung by a chorus.

canon A contrapuntal technique in which a melody in one part is strictly imitated by another voice or voices.

cantata A choral work, usually on a sacred subject and frequently built on a chorale tune, combining aria, recitative, chorus, and instrumental accompaniment.

castrato A male singer who was castrated before puberty so that his voice would remain high. Castratos often sang hero roles in baroque operas and were hired by the Catholic Church, which did not want women to sing in the church services.

celesta A keyboard percussion instrument that strikes tuned steel bars and looks something like a small upright piano.

cello A large and fairly low-sounding member of the family of bowed string instruments. Because of its size, it rests on an end pin that sits on the floor. The instrument is held upright between the player's knees. Also called *violoncello*.

chamber music Music written for a small group of instruments, with one player to a part.

chance music Music in which the composer sets out to remove the decision-making process from his or her control. See also *aleatoric music* and *indeterminacy music*.

character pieces Works portraying a single mood, emotion, or idea.

chimes A set of tuned metal tubes suspended vertically in a frame, and played by being hit with mallets. Their sound resembles that of church bells. Also called *tubular bells*.

choir A vocal ensemble consisting of several voice parts with four or five or more singers in each section. Also, a section of the orchestra comprising certain types of instruments, such as a *brass choir*.

chorale A German hymn, often used as a unifying theme for a cantata.

chord Three or more pitches sounded together.

chordophones A general term for stringed instruments in world music.

chord progression A particularly distinctive series of harmonies, or chords.

chorus, choir A vocal ensemble consisting of several voice parts with four or five or more singers in each section. Also, a section of the orchestra comprising certain types of instruments, such as a *brass choir*.

chromatic scale The scale containing all twelve tones within the interval of an octave.

clarinet A high-sounding woodwind instrument that uses a mouthpiece with a single reed.

clavichord A stringed keyboard instrument in common use during the Renaissance and baroque periods. It is softer than a harpsichord because its strings are hit with a tangent to sound instead of being plucked.

clavier A generic term for a keyboard instrument.

coda The concluding section of a musical work or individual movement, often lead-ing to a final climax and coupled with an increase in tempo.

coloratura A high female soprano voice capable of singing fast, florid ornaments.

concerto A work for one or more solo instruments and orchestra.

concerto grosso A multimovement work for instruments in which a solo group called the *concertino* and a full ensemble called the *ripieno* are pitted against each other.

concert overture A one-movement self-contained orchestral concert piece, often in sonata form.

conductor A person who directs a musical ensemble and who is responsible for all aspects of the performance of the ensemble.

congas Long, single-headed Afro-Cuban drums that produce indefinite pitches.

consonance A quality of an interval, chord, or harmony that imparts a sense of stability, repose, or finality.

consort A small group of Renaissance instruments. For example, a recorder consort is made up of recorders of various sizes, and a viol consort is made up of viols of various sizes. A mixed consort includes instruments of more than one instrumental type or family.

continuo See *basso continuo*.

contrabassoon A very low-sounding woodwind instrument that uses a mouthpiece with a double reed.

contrast Something different from what came before.

cool jazz A restrained, controlled jazz style that developed during the late 1940s.

Council of Trent A series of meetings of leaders of the Roman Catholic Church (1545–1563) to discuss church reforms following the Reformation. The decisions generated the Counter-Reformation (Catholic-Reformation).

counterpoint A musical texture consisting of two or more equal and independent melodic lines sounding simultaneously. See also *polyphony*.

Counter-Reformation See *Council of Trent*.

countersubject (of a fugue) In a fugue, new melodic material stated in counterpoint with the subject.

counter tenor A male singer who develops his high vocal range (falsetto range) to be able to sing parts otherwise appropriate for a castrato or a woman.

crescendo Music gradually gets louder.

cue sheet Musical directions used by early film directors to tell musicians when to play what music in order to fit music to the actions in the film.

cyclic form A unifying technique of long musical works in which the same thematic material recurs in succeeding movements.

cymbals Circular metal plates that can be hit together or can be suspended and hit with a beater. They produce an indefinite pitch.

decrescendo Gradually softer (same as *diminuendo*).

development In a general sense, the elaboration of musical material through various procedures. Also, the second section of a movement in sonata form.

"Dies irae" "Day of Wrath." A chant melody from the Middle Ages that represents death in music.

diminuendo Gradually softer (same as *decrescendo*).

dissonance A quality of an interval, chord, or harmony that gives a sense of tension and movement.

Dixieland A jazz style based on the original hot jazz from New Orleans.

double bass The largest and lowest-voiced member of the bowed string family of instruments. Also called *string bass*. Because of its size, the player sits on a stool or stands.

downbeat The first, and often stressed, beat of a metric pattern of beats.

drone A long-held note or notes over or under which other music is played.

duple meter A meter with two beats in each measure.

dynamics Relative degrees of loudness or softness.

electronic music Music produced by such means as magnetic tape, synthesizer, or computer.

embellishment The practice of decorating musical lines by adding notes or ornaments.

English horn A woodwind instrument with a pitch range between the oboe and the bassoon that uses a mouthpiece with a double reed.

episode In a fugue, a transitional passage based on material derived from the subject or based on new material, leading to a new statement of the subject.

ethnomusicology The study of non-Western, or world, musics.

étude A study piece concentrating on a single technical problem.

exposition The first section in sonata form, containing the statement of the principal themes. Also, the first section in a fugue, in which the principal theme or subject is presented imitatively.

expressionism An artistic school of the early twentieth century that attempted to represent the psychological and emotional experience of modern humanity.

fermata (⌢) A notational symbol indicating that a note is to be sounded longer than its normal time value, the exact length being left to the discretion of the performer.

flute A high-sounding woodwind instrument that is played by blowing across a mouthpiece on the side of the instrument. Modern flutes are usually made of metal, but early flutes were made of wood.

form The aspect of music involving the overall structuring and organization of music.

forte (f) A loud dynamic level.

fortissimo (ff) A very loud dynamic level.

free jazz A post-bebop jazz style that freely changed rhythmic patterns and disposed of repeating melodies in favor of free-flowing, improvised playing.

French horn A medium-ranged, mellow-sounding brass instrument.

front line In jazz bands, the instruments that carry the melodic material.

fuging tunes Psalm or hymn melodies that are sung as canons or written to contain imitation, popular in Britain and the U.S. during the 1700s.

fugue A composition that uses imitative polyphony and is organized around the returns of a theme or subject and a countermelody (countersubject) that often appears with it. Fugues can have more than one subject, but just one is more common.

fusion A style of jazz developed in the late 1960s that has been influenced by rock music through the inclusion of amplified instruments, short riffs (repeating melodies), and even beat subdivisions.

gamelan An Indonesian musical ensemble usually consisting of idiophones, metallophones, and sets of knobbed gongs. Membranophones, chordophones, aerophones, and voices can also be included.

glissando A rapid sliding up or down the scale.

glockenspiel A percussion instrument with two rows of steel bars, each of which produces a definite pitch when struck by a mallet.

gong Large Asian metal percussion instrument that produces an indefinite pitch.

grave A slow and solemn tempo.

Gregorian chant A body of music to which the medieval Roman Catholic liturgy was sung, consisting of monophonic, single-line melodies sung without instrumental accompaniment.

griots African singers who memorized their tribe's history through their songs.

ground bass A bass line that constantly repeats a short melody.

guitar A plucked stringed instrument with a fingerboard that exists in both acoustic and electric versions.

harmony A composite sound made up of two or more notes of different pitch that sound simultaneously.

harp A plucked stringed instrument with strings stretched vertically in a triangular frame.

harpsichord A plucked stringed keyboard instrument in common use during the Renaissance and baroque periods. The sound of plucked strings is much crisper than that of other keyboard instruments that produce their tones by tangents or hammers hitting the strings.

heterophonic texture In music, a single melody by two or more individuals who add their own rhythmic or melodic modifications.

homophony Music in which a single melody predominates, while the other voices or instruments provide harmonic accompaniment.

idée fixe A single, recurring motive; for example, in Berlioz's *Symphony fantastique,* a musical idea representing the hero's beloved that recurs throughout the piece.

idiophones A general term for solid percussion instruments in world musics

that are struck together, shaken, scraped, or rubbed to create their sound.

imitation The repetition, in close succession and usually at a different pitch level, of a melody by another voice or voices within a contrapuntal texture.

impressionism A late nineteenth-century artistic movement that sought to capture the visual impression rather than the literal reality of a subject. Also, in music, a style belonging primarily to Debussy, characterized by an emphasis on mood and atmosphere, sensuous tone colors, elegance, and beauty of sound.

improvisation The practice of making up music and performing it on the spot without first having written it down.

incidental music Music written to accompany a play.

indeterminacy music Music in which the composer sets out to remove the decision-making process from his or her control. Chance operations, such as throwing dice, are employed to obtain a random series of musical events. See also *aleatoric music* and *chance music.*

interval The distance in pitch between any two tones.

jazz Improvisatory music based on African American musical traditions. Jazz developed into many styles through the twentieth century and beyond and has come to be widely popular all over the world.

jongleurs Medieval street musicians who sang, played instruments, and sometimes acted in plays.

key Tonality; the relationship of tones to a central tone, the tonic.

key signature The group of sharps or flats placed at the beginning of each staff to indicate which notes are to be raised or lowered a half step. The particular combination of sharps or flats indicates the key of a composition.

largo A very slow and broad tempo.

legato "Linked, tied," indicating a smooth, even style of performance, with each note connected to the next.

leitmotif "Leading motive." A musical motive representing a particular character, object, idea, or emotional state. Used especially in Wagner's operas.

lento A slow tempo.

libretto The text of an opera or similar extended dramatic musical work.

liturgy The text of the Roman Catholic Mass (reenactment of the Last Supper) service, also used by some Protestant religions.

lute song A song sung with accompaniment played on a lute.

madrigal A polyphonic vocal piece set to a short poem; it originated during the Renaissance.

major scale A scale having a pattern of whole and half steps, with the half steps falling between the third and fourth and between the seventh and eighth notes of the scale.

marimba A percussion instrument with tuned wooden bars that produce a hollow sound when struck by mallets and resonators under each bar.

Mass The most solemn service of the Roman Catholic Church. The parts of the Mass most frequently set to music are the Kyrie, Gloria, Credo, Sanctus, and Agnus Dei.

mazurka In romantic music, a small piano piece based on the Polish dance form. Prominent in the works of Chopin.

measured rhythm Regulated rhythm in which precise time values are related to each other.

measures Units of time organization consisting of a fixed number of beats. Measures are separated from one another by vertical bar lines on the staff.

melisma Several notes sung to a single syllable of text.

melody A basic musical element consisting of a series of pitches of particular duration that sound one after another.

membranophones A general term for drums in world music.

metallophones An idiophone with a row of tuned metal bars that are struck with mallets.

meter The organization of rhythmic pulses or beats into equal, recurring groups.

mezzo forte (mf) A moderately loud dynamic level.

mezzo piano (mp) A moderately soft dynamic level.

mezzo soprano A female voice between the ranges of soprano and alto.

microtones Intervals smaller than a half step.

minimalism A late-twentieth-century movement that seeks to return music to its simplest, most basic elements. It is characterized by a very steady beat and gradually changing repeating figures.

minnesingers Medieval German poet-singers.

minor scale A scale having a pattern of whole and half steps, with the half steps falling between the second and third and between the sixth and seventh tones of the scale.

minstrels Medieval wandering street musicians and entertainers.

minuet and trio A form employed in the third movement of many classical symphonies, cast in a stately triple meter and ternary form (ABA).

moderato A moderate tempo.

modified-strophic form A song structure that varies the regularity of the repeated melodies of strophic form by having some verses sung to a new melody.

modulation Gradual or rapid change from one key to another within a composition.

monophony A musical texture consisting of a single melodic line without accompanying material, as in Gregorian chant.

motet A polyphonic choral work set to a sacred text.

motive A short melodic or rhythmic theme that reappears frequently throughout a work or section of a work as a unifying device.

movement Independent section of a longer composition.

musicals Dramas that are told through a series of songs, usually with spoken dialogue between the songs.

music drama Richard Wagner's term for his operas.

musique concrète "Concrete music." A musical style originating in France about 1948; its technique consists of recording natural or "concrete" sounds, altering the sounds by various electronic means, and then combining them into organized pieces.

mute A device used to soften or change the tone quality of an instrument. Mutes can be clamped to the bridge of bowed string instruments. Mutes for brass instruments are cone shaped and fit into the instrument's bell.

neoclassicism In music of the early twentieth century, the philosophy that musical composition should be approached with objectivity and restraint. Neoclassical composers were attracted to the textures and forms of the baroque and classical periods.

New Orleans jazz The first jazz to be recorded and, therefore, the root of later jazz styles.

nocturne A "night piece" that is gentle and reflective.

note A symbol used to notate a pitch and its duration. *Note* is also used to identify a pitch or a tone.

oboe A high-sounding woodwind instrument that uses a mouthpiece with a double reed.

octave An interval between two pitches in which the higher pitch vibrates at twice the frequency of the lower. When sounded simultaneously, the two pitches sound very much alike.

opera A drama set to music and made up of vocal pieces such as recitatives, arias, duets, trios, and ensembles with orchestral accompaniment, and orchestral overtures and interludes. Scenery, stage action, and costuming are employed.

opera buffa Italian comic opera.

opera seria Italian opera with a serious (i.e., noncomic) subject.

operetta Short, small-scale operatic works popular during the nineteenth century.

opus "Work." The term is usually followed by a number that identifies the particular work in the catalog of music by a composer.

oratorio An extended choral work made up of recitatives, arias, and choruses, *without* costuming, stage action, or scenery.

orchestra An ensemble of instruments consisting mainly of strings, but also usually including woodwinds, brass, and percussion. The size and particular instrumentation of an orchestra depends on the needs of the composition to be performed.

orchestration The arrangement of a musical composition for performance by an orchestra. Also, utilization of orchestral instruments for expressive and structural purposes.

Ordinary (of the Mass) The sections of the Mass that stay the same throughout the church year. They are the Kyrie, Gloria, Credo, Sanctus, and Agnus Dei.

organ Originally a wind instrument in which sets of pipes are controlled by a keyboard that sends air from a blower into the pipes. Electronic organs that can imitate the sound of pipe organs are also common in the twenty-first century.

organum The earliest type of medieval polyphonic music.

overture The orchestral introduction to a musical dramatic work.

Passion A musical setting of the story of the suffering and crucifixion of Jesus Christ.

pentatonic scale A five-tone scale. Various pentatonic scales are commonly employed in non-Western music.

phrase A portion of a melody that can sound complete or incomplete. An incomplete-sounding phrase makes the listener want to hear another phrase that completes the melody.

phrasing Musical units consisting of several measures.

pianissimo (pp) A very soft dynamic level.

piano A stringed instrument played by a keyboard that causes hammers to hit the strings.

piano (p) A soft dynamic level.

pianoforte An eighteenth- or early-nineteenth-century piano.

piano, four hands Two players playing one piano at the same time.

piano quartet Usually, a work for one piano and strings. Can be four pianos, but that is rare.

piano quintet Usually, a work for one piano and strings. Can be for five pianos, but that is rare.

piano trio Usually, a work for one piano with violin and cello. Can be for three pianos, but that is rare.

piccolo A small, high-pitched flute.

pitch The highness or lowness of a musical tone, determined by the frequency of vibration of the sounding body.

pitch range The span from low to high pitches that an instrument or a voice can produce.

pizzicato A performance technique in which stringed instruments, such as the violin, are plucked with the fingers instead of bowed.

polonaise In romantic music, a small piano piece based on the Polish dance form.

polyphony Many voices. A texture combining two or more independent melodies

heard simultaneously; generally synonymous with *counterpoint*.

polyrhythms Two or more contrasting and independent rhythms used at the same time.

polytonality The simultaneous use of two or more keys.

première The first or most eminent performance of a work.

prepared piano A piano with the sound altered by the insertion of items such as bolts, screws, pencils, cloth, and even paper on or between the strings.

prestissimo A tempo that is as fast as possible.

presto A very fast tempo.

primitivism In music, the use of frenzied, irregular rhythms and percussive effects to evoke a feeling of primitive power, as in Stravinsky's *The Rite of Spring*.

program music Instrumental music associated with a nonmusical idea, this idea often being stated in the title or in an explanatory program note.

program symphony A symphony with a story line or other type of program.

Proper (of the Mass) The sections of the Catholic Mass that change with the church year. The Proper is generally not set to music because each text is used so seldom.

Protestantism Religions that "protested" against the Church of Rome (later called the Roman Catholic Church) during the Renaissance and broke away from it in what was called the Reformation.

psalms The sacred poems from the book of Psalms in the Bible.

quadruple meter A meter in which each measure has four beats.

quintuple meter A meter in which each measure has five beats.

raga An ancient melodic pattern still employed in Indian music.

ragtime A composed music of the 1890s, usually for piano.

recapitulation The third section of sonata form, which restates the themes from the exposition.

recitative A form of "singing speech" in which the rhythm is dictated by the natural inflection of the words.

recorders A wooden end-blown flute-type instrument common from the Middle Ages through the baroque.

refrain Text and/or music that is returned to or repeated within a larger piece of music.

repetition Music is played again, or repeated.

rhythm The element of music that encompasses all aspects of musical time.

rhythm section In jazz or rock bands, the instruments that supply the harmonic and rhythmic accompaniment.

ritornello "Return." A characteristic form for the first and sometimes the last movement of the baroque concerto grosso. The thematic material given to the ripieno returns between the passages played by the soloists.

rondo An extended alternating form often employed in the fourth movement of classical symphonies; generally spirited and playful in character.

round A contrapuntal technique in which a melody in one part is strictly imitated by another voice or voices. See also *canon*.

rubato "Robbed." A term indicating that a performer may treat the tempo with a certain amount of freedom, shortening the duration of some beats and correspondingly lengthening others.

SATB chorus A four-part group of singers that include sopranos, altos, tenors, and basses. The chorus can include women on the higher two parts and men on the lower two, or it can be all men or men with boys singing the high parts.

saxophone A woodwind instrument that uses a mouthpiece with a single reed and is made of brass. Saxophones come in many sizes and pitch ranges.

scat singing A jazz vocal style in which the singer uses nonsense syllables in the place of words.

scene A subsection of an act in a play or opera.

scherzo Literally, "joke." A sprightly, humorous instrumental piece, swift in tempo; developed by Beethoven to replace the minuet.

secular Nonreligious.

septuple meter A meter in which each measure has seven beats.

sequence The repetition of a motive or melody at different pitch levels.

serialism See *twelve-tone*.

sextuple meter A meter in which each measure has six beats.

side (snare) drum A drum with two heads, the bottom head having snares or metal wires that can be tightened to rattle against it when the upper head is hit.

sight sing Sing by looking at musical notation instead of having memorized the music in advance.

solo concerto A multimovement baroque work that differs from concerto grosso in that the concertino consists of only one instrument.

sonata An instrumental work consisting of three or four contrasting movements.

sonata form A musical form encompassing one movement of a composition and consisting of three sections—exposition, development, and recapitulation—the last often followed by a coda.

sonata rondo The form of a movement that shares characteristics of both the sonata and the rondo forms. It usually has an A section that returns as it would in a rondo, but it also has a development section such as that found in a movement in sonata form.

song cycle A series of art songs that tell a story.

soprano A high, usually female, voice. Also, the high instrument in an instrumental family.

Sprechstimme Literally, "speech voice." A vocal technique in which a pitch is half sung, half spoken. Developed by Schoenberg.

staccato "Detached." Indicating a style of performance in which each note is played in a short, crisp manner.

staff A graphlike structure consisting of five lines and four spaces. Each line and each space represents a different pitch.

string quartet A chamber ensemble consisting of a first and a second violin, a viola, and a cello; also, the form which is a sonata for these instruments.

strophic Designating a song in which all verses of text are sung to the same music.

subject (of a fugue) In a fugue, the principal theme, introduced first in a single voice and then imitated in other voices, returning frequently during the course of the composition.

suite A series of instrumental movements, each based on a particular dance rhythm.

swing A big-band jazz style particularly popular for dance music during the 1930s through the middle 1940s.

symbolism A subtle French poetic style from the late nineteenth century that stressed the sound and color of the words and suggested rather than clearly outlined the meaning or story behind the text.

symphonic poem See *tone poem.*

symphony A sonata for orchestra.

syncopation A deliberate disturbance of the normal metrical pulse, produced by shifting the accent from a normally strong beat to a weak beat.

synthesizer An electronic instrument that can duplicate almost any sound and can be used to create entirely new sounds.

tala One of the ancient rhythmic patterns still employed in Indian music.

tambourine A single-headed drum with metal discs loosely set in the frame. The instrument is handheld and shaken or struck to produce an indefinite pitch.

tempo The speed at which a piece of music moves.

tenor A high, male voice, or an instrument that is lower than an alto and higher than a bass instrument.

ternary form A musical form that consists of three sections, ABA, in which the final section (A) is a repetition of the first section (A), and the middle section (B) contrasts with A.

texture The relationship between the melodic and harmonic aspects of a piece of music. The principal classifications in most Western music are monophony, homophony, and polyphony.

thematic transformation The practice of varying a single theme or melody through the different sections of a piece; this procedure was used especially in romantic tone poems.

theme A musical idea that serves as a starting point for development of a composition or section of a composition.

theme and variations A form based on a single theme and its subsequent repetition, with each new statement varied in some way from the original.

through-composed form A term applied to songs in which new music is used for each successive verse.

timbre The characteristic tone quality of a musical sound as produced by a specific instrument or voice, or by a combination of instruments or voices.

timpani Tuned drums each of which has a single head stretched across a kettle-like body. The pitch of each drum is controlled by the player. Also called *kettledrums.*

tom-toms Cylindrical-shaped drums, usually found in sets of assorted sizes that produce indefinite pitches.

tonality The relationship of tones to a central tone called the tonic. See also *key.*

tone cluster A chord produced by playing a large group of adjacent notes on the piano with the flat of the hand. The resulting sound is dense and indistinct.

tone poem, also **symphonic poem** A single-movement programmatic work, relatively long and very free in form, usually involving a dramatic plot or literary idea.

tonic The tonal center. The tone that acts as a musical home base, or point of rest and finality, in a piece of music.

transcription An arrangement of a composition for a medium other than that for which it was originally written.

tremolo Fast repeated notes.

triad A three-note chord in which each note is the interval of a third from the next closest note.

triangle A triangular-shaped metal percussion instrument that is struck by a metal bar to produce an indefinite pitch.

trill A musical ornament in which two adjacent notes quickly alternate between one another.

triple meter A meter in which each measure has three beats.

triplet Three notes fitted into the time in which only two of those notes would normally fit.

trombone A brass instrument that is played with a slide and produces a medium- to low-pitch range.

troubadours Medieval poet-singers from southern France. They were often people of noble rank who would not perform in public but would sing to family members and friends.

trouvères Medieval poet-singers from northern France. Like troubadours, they were often people of noble rank who would not perform in public but would sing to family members and friends.

trumpet A brass instrument with a high-pitch range.

tuba A large brass instrument with a low-pitch range.

tutti "All," or the entire ensemble.

twelve tone, also **serialism** A system of composition developed by Schoenberg that consists of arranging the twelve pitches of the chromatic scale in a particular order (known as a tone row, series, or set). Also called *dodecaphony.*

unison Two notes that are the same pitch, or two or more instruments or voices producing the same pitches at the same time.

upbeat One or more unaccented beats that precede the accented downbeat. Also called *pickup.*

variation A modified version of something previously performed in which some elements of the original remain.

verismo "Realism." An Italian operatic point of view favoring realistic subjects taken from everyday, often lower-class, life.

vernacular The everyday spoken language.

vibrato A slight fluctuation in pitch that increases the warmth of a tone.

viola A bowed string instrument slightly larger and lower-sounding than the violin.

violin A high-sounding bowed string instrument, the neck of which is held by the player's left hand, and the tail rests beneath the player's chin.

virtuoso A performer with complete technical control of the playing of his or her musical instrument.

Vitaphone A recording system invented during the mid-1920s to allow previously recorded music to play simultaneously with a film.

vivace A fast and vivacious tempo.

wind ensemble An orchestral type of concert band made up primarily of woodwind, brass, and percussion instruments. Also called *symphonic band* or *concert band.*

word painting Representation of the literal meaning of a text through musical means.

xylophone A pitched percussion instrument with tuned wooden bars that produce a hollow sound when struck by mallets.

Credits

Text

p. 294: "Lost Your Head Blues" by Bessie Smith. © 1925 (Renewed) Frank Music Corp. All Rights Reserved. Reprinted by permission of Hal Leonard Corporation; **p. 297:** "It Don't Mean a Thing (If It Ain't Got That Swing)." Music by Duke Ellington. Words by Irving Mills. © 1932 (Renewed) EMI Mills Music, Inc. and Sony/ATV Music Publishing LLC. All Rights for the World outside of the U.S. Controlled and Administered by EMI Mills Music, Inc. (Print) All Rights Reserved. Used by Permission of Alfred Music Publishing Co., Inc.; "It Don't Mean a Thing (If It Ain't Got That Swing)." © 1932 Sony/ATV Music Publishing LLC, Mills Music Inc. All rights on behalf of Sony/ATV Music Publishing LLC administered by Sony/ATV Music Publishing LLC, 8 Music Square West, Nashville, TN 37203. All rights reserved. Used by Permission; **pp. 326–327:** "America" by Steven Sondheim © 1957, renewed 1991 by Leonard Bernstein Music Publishing Company, LLC administered by Universal-Polygram International Publishing, Inc./ASCAP. Used by permission. International Copyright secured. All Rights Reserved.

Photos

p. 3 (top): Odile Noel/Lebrecht/The Image Works; **p. 3 (bottom):** Design Pics Inc./Alamy; **p. 17:** Chris Pizzello/AP Images; **p. 18, 19 (left):** C Squared Studios/Getty Images; **p. 19 (middle):** © Photodisc Collection/Getty Images; **p. 19 (right):** C Squared Studios/Getty Images; **p. 20 (left), 20 (middle):** © Photo Spin/Getty Images; **p. 20 (right):** C Squared Studios/Getty Images; **p. 21 (left):** Ingram Publishing/SuperStock; **p. 21 (right):** C Squared Studios/Getty Images; **p. 22:** Odile Noel/Lebrecht/The Image Works; **p. 23 (left):** C Squared Studios/Getty Images; **p. 23 (right):** © Ingram Publishing/Alamy; **p. 29 (left):** Poseidon (Zeus). Bronze figure from the Artemisius at Cape Sounion. 460 BCE. H: 1.95m. Inv. 15161. National Archaeological Museum, Athens, Greece. Photo Credit: Erich Lessing/Art Resource, NY; **p. 29 (right):** Apollo Belvedere, 3/4 view. Roman copy after Greek original, c. 350–320 BCE. Museo Pio Clementino, Vatican Museums, Vatican State. Photo Credit: Scala/Art Resource, NY; **p. 30:** Cimabue (1240–1302) Madonna of the Holy Trinity. Uffizi, Florence, Italy. Scala/Art Resource, NY; **p. 32:** Scala/Art Resource; **p. 34:** Erich Lessing/Art Resource; **p. 40:** Heidelberg University Library; **p. 47:** Royalty-free/Corbis; **p. 48:** Madonna del Granduca by Raphael, 1505. Galleria Palatina, Palazzo Pitti, Florence, Italy. Alinari/Art Resource; **p. 50:** Portrait of a Musician, c.1485 (oil on panel); da Vinci, Leonardo (1452–1519); oil on panel; 425 × 600; Ambrosiana, Milan, Italy; possibly Franchino Gafurius (1451–1522) or the composer Josquin des Prez (c.1450–1521). Bridgeman Art Library; **p. 57:** Lebrecht Music Collection; **p. 59:** The Pierpont Morgan Library/Art Resource; **p. 63 (left):** David, Bernini. Marble, 1623–1624. Frontal view. Post-restoration. Galleria Borghese, Rome, Italy. Photo Credit: Scala/Art Resource; **p. 63 (right):** Conversion of St. Paul, Caravaggio. S.Maria del Popolo, Rome, Italy. Photo Credit: Scala/Art Resource; **p. 64:** Le Nain, Louis (1593–1648), Peasant family in an interior. Louvre, Paris, France. Photo Credit: Erich Lessing/Art Resource, NY; **p. 66:** Scala/Art Resource; **p. 68:** Amigoni, Jacopo (1675–1752), The singer Carlo Broschi, called Farinelli (famous castrato). National Museum of Art, Bucarest Romania. Photo Credit: Cameraphoto/Art Resource, NY; **p. 69:** AKG London; **p. 70:** Bridgeman Art Library; **p. 75:** Court Concert at Prince Bishop of Lueltich at Seraing by Paul Joseph Delcloche, Bayerisches National Museum. Photo credit: AKG London; **p. 78:** AKG London; **p. 83:** AKG London; **p. 84:** Stock Montage, Inc.; **p. 91:** Lebrecht Music Collection; **p. 94:** © Eye Ubiquitous/Alamy; **p. 96:** Public Domain; **p. 100:** Didier Zylberyng/Alamy; **p. 104:** Portrait of Vivaldi, Civico Museo Bibliografico Musicale Rossini, Bologna, Italy. Scala/Art Resource; **p. 111:** Gérard Blot/Réunion des Musées Nationaux/Art Resource, NY; **p. 112 (top):** Fragonard, Jean-Honore (1732–1806), The Bathers. Oil on canvas, 64 × 80 cm. Louvre, Paris, France. Photo Credit: Erich Lessing/Art Resource, NY; **p. 112 (bottom):** David, Jacques Louis (1748–1825), The Death of Socrates. 1787. Oil on canvas, 51 × 77-1/4 in. (129.5 × 196.2 cm). Catharine Lorillard Wolfe Collection, Wolfe Fund, 1931 (31.45). The Metropolitan Museum of Art, New York, NY, U.S.A. Photo Credit: Image copyright © The Metropolitan Museum of Art/Art Resource, NY; **p. 113:** Lefevre, Robert (1755–1830), Portrait of Napoleon Bonaparte, Premier Consul. Oil on canvas, 158 × 114 cm. Chateaux de Versailles et deTrianon, Versailles, France. Photo Credit: Gérard Blot/Réunion des Musées Nationaux/Art Resource, NY; **p. 115 (left):** James Davis/Corbis; **p. 115 (right):** Joseph Sohm/Corbis; **p. 119:** Emmanuel Dunand/AFP/Getty Images; **p. 120:** Lebrecht Music Collection; **p. 127:** C. Christodoulou/Lebrecht/The Image Works; **p. 133:** Mary Evans Picture Library/The Image Works; **p. 135 (top):** Lebrecht Music Collection; **p. 135 (bottom):** Vittoriano Rastelli/Corbis; **p. 141:** Dagli Orti/Museum der Stadt, Wien/The Art Archive/The Picture Desk; **p. 144:** ArenaPal/Topham/The Image Works; **p. 150:** Ludwig Von Beethoven, Karl Stieler. Oil on canvas, 1819. Beethoven House, Bonn, Germany. Photo credit: Erich Lessing/Art Resource; **p. 158:** Lebrecht Music Collection; **p. 163:** Turner, Joseph Mallord William (1775–1851), The Fall of an Avalanche in the Grisons. Exhibited 1810. Tate Gallery, London, Great Britain. Photo Credit: Clore Collection, Tate Gallery, London/Art Resource, NY; **p. 164 (top):** Daumier, Honore (1808–1879), The Third-Class

Performance Information for 3-CD Set (Volume I)

Disc 1

1 Léonin: "Viderunt Omnes" ("All Have Seen")
Red Byrd; Cappella Amsterdam
℗ 1997 Hyperion Records Ltd.
Courtesy of Hyperion Records Ltd.

2 Josquin: "Ave Maria" ("Hail, Mary")
La Chapelle Royale; Philippe Herreweghe, director
℗ 1986 harmonia mundi s.a.
Courtesy of harmonia mundi usa

4 Purcell: "Thy Hand Belinda" and "When I am Laid
in Earth" from Act Three of *Dido and Aeneas*
Emily Van Evera, soprano; Taverner Consort;
Andrew Parrott, director
℗ 1994 Sony Music Entertainment

5 Bach: "Wachet auf" ("Sleepers Awake"),
Cantata no. 140, VII
American Bach Soloists; Jeffrey Thomas, director
℗ 1996 Koch International L.P.
Courtesy of The American Bach Soloists

6 Handel: "Ev'ry valley" from *Messiah*
John Aler, tenor; Musica Sacra; Richard Westenburg,
conductor
℗ 1982 Sony Music Entertainment

7 Bach: "The Little Fugue in G Minor"
E. Power Biggs, organ
Originally released 1961. All rights reserved by
Sony Music Entertainment

8 Vivaldi: "La Primavera" ("Spring") from *Le Quattro
Stagione (The Four Seasons),* I
Giuliano Carmignola, violin; Venice Baroque
Orchestra; Andrea Marcon, conductor
℗ 2000 Sony Music Entertainment

13 Mozart: Symphony no. 40 in G Minor, I
Cleveland Orchestra; George Szell, conductor
Originally released 1971. All rights reserved by
Sony Music Entertainment

19 Haydn: "Surprise," Symphony no. 94 in G Major II
Cleveland Orchestra; George Szell, conductor
Originally released 1968. All rights reserved by
Sony Music Entertainment

20 Mozart: Piano Concerto no. 23 in A Major, I
Alicia de Larrocha, piano; English Chamber
Orchestra; Sir Colin Davis, conductor
℗ 1992 Sony Music Entertainment

29 Haydn: String Quartet op. 33, no. 3 ("The Bird"), IV
Tatrai String Quartet
℗ 1979 Hungaroton
Courtesy of Qualiton Imports Ltd.

37 Mozart: "Non più andrai" ("No More Will You")
from *Le Nozze di Figaro (The Marriage of Figaro)*
Michele Pertusi, baritone; Maggio Musicale
Fiorentino; Zubin Mehta, conductor
℗ 1994 Sony Music Entertainment

38 Beethoven: Symphony no. 5 in C Minor, I
Cleveland Orchestra; George Szell, conductor
Originally released 1964. All rights reserved by
Sony Music Entertainment

44 Schubert: "Erlkönig" ("King of the Elves")
Thomas Quasthoff, baritone; Charles Spencer, piano
℗ 1993 Sony Music Entertainment

45 Chopin: Nocturne, op. 9, no. 2
Philippe Entremont, piano
Originally recorded 1966. All rights reserved by
Sony Music Entertainment

Disc 2

1 Berlioz: *Symphonie fantastique,* V, "Dream of a
Witches' Sabbath"
New York Philharmonic; Leonard Bernstein,
conductor
Originally released 1964. All rights reserved by
Sony Music Entertainment

4 Smetana: "The Moldau"
New York Philharmonic; Leonard Bernstein,
conductor
Originally released 1964. All rights reserved by
Sony Music Entertainment

12 Tchaikovsky: *Romeo and Juliet* Overture
New York Philharmonic; Leonard Bernstein,
conductor
Originally released 1963. All rights reserved by
Sony Music Entertainment

19   Mendelssohn: Violin Concerto in E Minor, op. 64, I
     Hilary Hahn, violin; Oslo Philharmonic; Hugh Wolf,
        conductor
     ℗ 2002 Sony Music Entertainment

20   Brahms: *Eine Deutsche Requiem (A German
        Requiem),* op. 45, IV, "How Lovely Is Thy
        Dwelling Place"
     New Philharmonia Chorus and Orchestra;
        Lorin Maazel, conductor
     ℗ 1977 Sony Music Entertainment

21   Dvořák: *From the New World,* Symphony no. 9
        in E Minor, IV
     Chicago Symphony; Fritz Reiner, conductor
     Originally released 1957. All rights reserved by
        Sony Music Entertainment

32   Verdi: "O terra, addio" ("Oh, Earth, Goodbye")
        from *Aida*
     Placido Domingo; Aprile Millo; Metropolitan Opera
        Orchestra; James Levine, conductor
     ℗ 1991 Sony Music Entertainment

33   Puccini: "Sì, mi chiamano Mimì" ("Yes, They Call Me
        Mimi") from *La Bohème*
     Montserrat Caballe, soprano; London Philharmonic;
        Sir Georg Solti, conductor
     ℗ 1974 Sony Music Entertainment

Disc 3

1   Wagner: "Grane, mein Ross!" ("Grane, My Horse!")
        and finale to *Die Götterdämmerung (The Twilight
        of the Gods)* from *Der Ring des Nibelungen The
        Ring of the Nibelung)*
     Jeannine Altmeyer, soprano; Staatskapelle Dresden;
        Marek Janowski, conductor
     ℗ 1985 Sony Music Entertainment

2   Debussy: *Prélude a L'après-midi d'un faune (Prelude
        to The Afternoon of a Faun)*
     Philharmonia Orchestra; Pierre Boulez, conductor
     Originally released 1969. All rights reserved by
        Sony Music Entertainment

7   Stravinsky: *Le Sacre du printemps (The Rite of Spring),*
        Introduction, "Auguries of Spring—Dances of
        the Young Girls," and "The Ritual of Abduction"
     Cleveland Orchestra; Pierre Boulez, conductor
     Originally released 1969. All rights reserved by
        Sony Music Entertainment

9   Bartók: Concerto for Orchestra, IV
     Chicago Symphony: Fritz Reiner, conductor
     Originally released 1955. All rights reserved by
        Sony Music Entertainment

10   Schoenberg: "Der Mondfleck" ("Moonfleck"), no. 18,
        from *Pierrot Lunaire (Moonstruck Pierrot)*
     Yvonne Minton, reciter; Ensemble conducted by
        Pierre Boulez
     ℗ 1978 Sony Music Entertainment

11   Billings: "When Jesus Wept"
     Gregg Smith Singers
     Originally released 1969. All rights reserved by
        Sony Music Entertainment

12   Smith: "Lost Your Head Blues"
     Bessie Smith
     Originally released 1926. All rights reserved by
        Sony Music Entertainment

17   Parker: "Ko Ko"
     Charlie Parker and His Re-Boppers
     Courtesy of Savoy Label Group

18   Davis: "Miles Runs The Voodoo Down"
     Miles Davis
     Originally released 1970. All rights reserved by
        Sony Music Entertainment

19   Still: *Afro-American Symphony,* I
     London Symphony; Paul Freeman, conductor
     ℗ 1974 Sony Music Entertainment

26   Copland: "Fanfare for the Common Man"
     London Symphony Orchestra; Aaron Copland,
        conductor
     Originally released 1971. All rights reserved by
        Sony Music Entertainment

27   Zwilich: Symphony no. 1, I
     Indianapolis Symphony; John Nelson, conductor
     ℗ 1986 Recorded Anthology of American Music, Inc.
     Courtesy of New World Records

30   Bernstein: "America" from *West Side Story*
     Original Broadway Cast
     Originally released 1957. All rights reserved by
        Sony Music Entertainment

34   Williams: "Main Theme" from *Star Wars*
     Skywalker Symphony; John Williams, conductor
     ℗ 1990 Sony Music Entertainment

35   Indonesian: "Srepegan (slendro nim)"
     Javanese gamelan ensemble
     ℗ 2004 ARC Music Productins Int. Ltd.
     Courtesy of ARC Music Productins Int. Ltd.

36   Cowell: "The Banshee"
     Henry Cowell, piano
     Courtesy of Smithsonian Folkways Recordings

37   Glass: *Company,* II
     Ulster Orchestra; Takuo Yuasa, conductor
     ℗ 2000 HNH International Ltd.
     Courtesy of Naxos of America

Index

Page references in *italic* indicate illustrations and page numbers in **bold** indicate Featured Listening and Listening Guides.